Crime and Punishment in the Middle Ages and Early Modern Age

Fundamentals of Medieval and Early Modern Culture

Edited by
Albrecht Classen and Marilyn Sandidge

11

De Gruyter

Crime and Punishment in the Middle Ages and Early Modern Age

Mental-Historical Investigations of Basic Human Problems and Social Responses

Edited by

Albrecht Classen and Connie Scarborough

De Gruyter

MIX
Papier aus verantwortungsvollen Quellen
FSC® C016439

ISBN 978-3-11-029451-4
e-ISBN 978-3-11-029458-3
ISSN 1864-3396

Library of Congress Cataloging-in-Publication Data

A CIP catalog record for this book has been applied for at the Library of Congress.

Bibliographic information published by the Deutsche Nationalbibliothek

The Deutsche Nationalbibliothek lists this publication in the Deutsche Nationalbibliografie; detailed bibliographic data are available in the Internet at http://dnb.dnb.de.

Printing and binding: Hubert & Co. GmbH & Co. KG, Göttingen
∞ Printed on acid-free paper

Printed in Germany

www.degruyter.com

Table of Contents

Introduction

Crime, Transgression, and Deviancy: Behaviors that Defines Us All

Albrecht Classen and Connie Scarborough

When one naively thinks of the concepts of crime and punishment in the Middle Ages and early modern period the first aspects that probably come to mind are arbitrary systems of judges, and harsh and often barbarous corporal punishments. Executions or dismemberment were, as we hear in popular media, the norm during the premodern world, and so cruel judgments, ruthless treatment of even the slightest transgression, and, worst, the absolute power exerted first by the king, and then, often even superseding him, the Church. Romantic, often highly dramatized and emotional perceptions of the past continue to influence the public minds until today, and hence the broad approach to a world in which crime and punishments were, as it seems, simply rampant, crude and cruel, almost beastly. Suffice, of course, to remember this popular opinion, and then to dismiss it quickly since it does not live up to what we really know about crime and punishment in the Middle Ages. After all, crime itself constitutes a highly complex phenomenon representing the norms and their transgression by an individual, a group, or a whole society. Similarly, punishment can be meted out in a vast array of possible degrees and procedures, so both aspects addressed in the present volume alert us to the constant need to revisit the basic assumptions about the premodern or any other world, especially because the concept of what a crime actually means appears to be in constant flux.

Every society lives by its own norms and standards, and cultures have differed from each other profoundly from period to period, from country to country, and from religion to religion. Moreover, we would be well advised to abstain from quick evaluations simply because of differences in approaches and attitudes throughout time as far as fundamental concepts of right and wrong change, if we disregard, for instance, those cases addressed by the Ten Commandments as formulated in the Old Testament (in the Septuagint [or LXX] at Exodus 34:28[3] and Deuteronomy 10:4). The danger could be that in a hasty condemnation of the past world or culture as being below our modern standards with respect to the legal system we might fall into the trap of idealizing our own world as vastly superior to anything that might have existed before. Of course, here we face the Scylla of glorifying the premodern world and the Charybdis of condemning it as the allegedly 'dark age,' neither one of which is truly correct.

Yet, when carefully examined in a comparative method, we would suddenly come across the rather alarming observation that the twentieth century, for instance, has witnessed many more systems of brutal, merciless, and devilish forms of persecutions and punishments for ideological crimes than ever before. Neither the Nazis nor the Communists, not to mention countless other dicatorships in Asia, Africa, and Latin-America, can be credited with having significantly improved human rights and the legal system at large, or with having been successful in suppressing crime in general terms and thus in providing more security to the people. By contrast, their way of dealing with infractions, transgressions, and crimes were often more brutal and torturous than ever before in human history, especially because those systems regularly determined specific forms of behavior (rituals, ceremonies, patterns, practices), ideas, and values, not to mention sexual, racial, or religious identities, as crimes against the leader, the party, or society at large, which we today would reject as absurd, fanatical, and purely ideology driven. Of course, this sobering realization does not force us to portray medieval law and the criminal judgment system, in radical oppositions, as better or preferable, but it should warn us to avoid demonizing the past simply because today we want it to be identified as so much better than the present. Myths continue to enjoy a high popularity, and they live on from generation to generation, without thereby gaining more historical veracity or validity.[1]

Legal history, to put it bluntly, is a tricky business, especially in cultural-historical terms. Generally speaking, there still is very good reason to believe that today, after hundreds of years of intensive work toward the improvement of the legal system in order to comply with the principles of humanism, enlightenment, tolerance, and justice within a democratic framework, crime and punishment are treated and dealt with in a very different manner than in the past, nonewithstanding constant complaints or criticism of severe infractions, disregard, and breaking of even some of the basic norms by which we orient ourselves in the Western world.

---

1 See the contributions to *Misconceptions about the Middle Ages*, ed. Stephen J. Harris and Bryon L. Grigsby. Routledge Studies in Medieval Religion and Culture, 7 (New York: Routledge, 2008); Albrecht Classen, *The Medieval Chastity Belt: A Myth-Making Process*. The New Middle Ages (Houndmills, Basingstoke, Hampshire, and New York: Palgrave macmillan, 2007), 7–16; 147–54.

Each social system believes, of course, in the full validity of its own legal codes and legal practices, otherwise it would convert to another, better one in order to survive. The great success story of Eike von Repgow's famous *Sachsenspiegel* (*The Saxons Mirror*) from ca. 1225–1230, for instance, much adapted, modified, and translated throughout the late Middle Ages, confirms this observation, but many other law books both from the Middle Ages and the early modern time would provided similar evidence. While Eike did not have any written sources, as far as we can tell, his collection of legal stipulations, regulations, explanations, and rules became the foundation for many other law books all over northern Germany, as documented by more than 450 surviving manuscripts—truly a record for the Middle Ages.[2]

While there were certainly cases of unjust sentences and cruel punishments—and when did those not occur in the history of mankind?—the contributions to the present volume show that, in many cases, courts or other judicial officials were genuinely concerned with the letter and spirit of the law. Punishments could be corporal, suspension of rights or privileges, exile, or monetary fines. The epithets 'unjust' and 'cruel' are, however, not easy to determine in the context of their time, and they do not mean much in comparison with our laws today, at least in the western world, since medieval society, for instance, to generalize here deliberately in a perhaps inappropriately gross manner, embraced its own laws and regarded them as appropriate and effective, since they allowed them to function more or less in practical terms. At the same time, we need to consider what the basic purpose of laws had been or would be at any time and in any culture.

Laws are made in order to cope in practical terms with crimes (actual or perceived), hence they reveal much about certain conditions of a given society and its mental-historical framework. For instance, in the US many laws regulate or rather forbid the use of drugs because they have entered this country and threaten the well-being of a growing number of people, and ultimately of society at large. The existence of those laws indicates that the government became aware of that problem and realized that it had to react to stem the flood of drugs once critical mass had been reached. In this regard, drug laws inform us fundamentally about the changing conditions within a society since people are either beginning to take dangerous drugs or they are, after having been regular drug users, suddenly treated as criminals because new laws were instituted to suppress drugs altogether.

---

2 *The Saxon Mirror: A* Sachsenspiegel *of the Fourteenth Century*, trans. Maria Dobozy. The Middle Ages Series (Philadelphia: University of Pennsylvania Press, 1999), 28–33. Dobozy either means the history of reception with the date in her subtitle, or she simply meant 'of the thirteenth century.'

Since judicial practices and sentences varied over time and place, it is indeed difficult to draw any monolithic conclusions about the perceptions or actualities of crimes and punishment in the Middle Ages and early modern period, although the historical investigation of the justice system in the past by now looks back to more than two hundred years at least.[3] Esther Cohen, in fact, warns against approaching the idea of a legal system as a unified whole in the medieval period. She states that "the multiplicity and occasional contradictions of different legal levels was the most real and persistent characteristic of late medieval society."[4]

Just as we cannot impose a single judicial system on law during this period, neither should we impose modern standards about what constitutes "cruel and unusual punishment" as Daniel Baraz points out in his book, *Medieval Cruelty: Changing Perceptions, Late Antiquity to the Early Modern Period*.[5] Cruelty as a construct can be applied both to cases of crime as well as the subsequent punishments inflicted on those found guilty of crimes. Among crimes most frequently cited as "violent" are murder, rape, assault, and robbery even though what constitutes these crimes may vary across cultures as well as the enforcement of laws against them.[6] For the periods we are discussing documentation also becomes problematic and it is difficult to reach any definitive conclusions about which specific acts were viewed as criminal. Did these change with regard to circumstance, social standing of perpetrators, or other mitigating factors? Was punishment always imposed when a crime or other violent act was proven to have been committed? Were certain persons exempt from punishment and would

3 See, for instance, Franz Heinemann, *Der Richter und die Rechtspflege in der deutschen Vergangenheit*. Monographien zur deutschen Kulturgeschichte, 4 ([Leipzig: Diederichs], 1900; Edward Jenks, *Law and Politics in the Middle Ages with a Synoptic Table of Sources* (1898; London : Murray, 1913); Fritz Kern, *Gottesgnadentum und Widerstandsrecht im Früheren Mittelalter: Zur Entwicklungsgeschichte der Monarchie*. Mittelalterliche Studien, I, 2 (Leipzig: K. F. Koehler, 1914); William Seagle, *The History of Law* (New York: Tudor Publishing Co., 1946); R. C. van Caenegem, *Legal History: A European Perspective* (London and Rio Grande, OH: Hambledon Press, 1991). Research has grown in leaps and bounds ever since, both in Europe and in North America; see, for instance, Anthony Musson, *Medieval Law in Context: The Growth of Legal Consciousness from Magna Carta to the Peasants' Revolt*. Manchester Medieval Studies (Manchester, UK: Manchester University Press; New York: Palgrave, 2001); Alan Harding, *Medieval Law and the Foundations of the State* (Oxford and New York: Oxford University Press, 2002); see also the contributions to *Boundaries of the Law: Geography, Gender and Jurisdiction in Medieval and Early Modern Europe*, ed. Anthony Musson (Aldershot, England, and Burlington, VT: Ashgate, 2005); and to *Law and Sovereignty in the Middle Ages and the Renaissance*, ed. Robert S. Sturgess. Arizona Studies in the Middle Ages and the Renaissance, 28 ([Turnhout]: Brepols, 2011).

4 Esther Cohen, *The Crossroads of Justice: Law and Culture in Late Medieval France*, Brill's Studies in Intellectual History, 36 (Leiden, New York, and Cologne: E. J. Brill, 1993), 16.

5 Daniel Baraz, *Medieval Cruelty: Changing Perceptions, Late Antiquity to the Early Modern Period*, Conjunctions of Religion & Power in the Medieval Past (Ithaca and London: Cornell University Press, 2003), 4.

6 Baraz,"*Medieval Cruelty*," 6 (see note 2).

punishment vary according to one's social standing or rank? Were there minority groups signaled out for harshest punishment if a member of a marginalized group was convicted of a crime?

The sources that one may consult to find answers to these complex questions, while scant in comparison to modern statistical data, can be discoverd in countless records of court proceedings, histories, legal codes, and literary texts. Albrecht Classen has addressed the viability of using literary texts for a study of such epistemological concerns as human transgression and retribution. Since the majority of the articles in this collection use literary texts as a basis for their analyses, Classen's explanations that literature is "one of the central media of human consciousness and has offered both descriptive and prescriptive models of human interaction" and that literature reflects society's efforts "to come to terms with its endemic and external problems and crises" seems worth repeating here.[7]

Also, literary texts played a role in shaping as well as reflecting social realities as Robert Mills reminds us.[8] Mills speaks of modern critical views of the Middle Ages in terms of alterity and studies in this volume will hopefully move beyond seeing the concepts of punishment or cruelty merely in terms of constitutive difference with contemporary notions of law-breakers and punitive practices. This critic also points out that by focusing on the abject difference between the modern concept of punishment and medieval and early modern perceptions we actually reinforce the view of our desire to identify with an idea of ourselves which is inherently western, civilized, and progressive.[9]

When addressing the issue of torture, Mills contends that "The critical tendency to condemn, excuse or even celebrate images of torture with references to notions of medieval alterity may ultimately derive less from an understanding of the Middle Ages 'on its own terms' than from false notions of our own moral superiority and ethical progression."[10] The articles in the present volume are mindful of this potential pitfall and seek to avoid sensationalizing either the crimes or the punishments as more inherently violent or cruel than at other moments in history.

For example, recent studies indicate that capital punishment was not the pervasive sentence meted out in medieval systems as many scholars have previously asserted. It was far more common of people convicted of crimes to escape the death penalty either because they were able to escape from their

---

7 Albrecht Classen, "Introduction," *Sexual Violence and Rape in the Middle Ages: A Critical Discourse in Premodern German and European Literature*, Fundamentals of Medieval Culture 7 (Berlin and Boston: Walter de Gruyter, 2011), 2.

8 Robert Mills, *Suspended Animation: Pain, Pleasure and Punishment in Medieval Culture* (London: Reaktion Books, 2005), 10.

9 Mills, *Suspended Animation*, 13 (see note 5).

10 Mills, *Suspended Animation*, 14 (see note 5).

accusers, leave the area under jurisdiction, were pardoned, or died of other causes.[11] As our studies indicate, the imposition of fines, banishment, public humiliation, or imprisonment in almost all areas of the West were more prevalent than public executions. The imposition of a pilgrimage, or of fines in religious terms—fasting, prayers, spending time in a monastic cell, exile, or the seeking of dispensation by a high-ranking church authority, especially the pope—proved to be quite successful strategies and provided people with successful alternatives.

Punishment can be levied on an individual level, taking the form of personal revenge or redress for grievances committed, or on an institutional level, administered by a judge, court, or other legal authority. Punishments may also be exacted by a community or group who determines that one of its members has transgressed commonly agreed-upon norms for acceptable behavior. When a judicial body was charged with determining guilt or innocence and meting out punishment against those found guilty, the judiciary was, in most cases, more concerned with general security than in abstract notions of justice.[12]

Henry Maine, writing in the nineteenth century, stressed that penal law was not originally about crimes but about wrongdoing and concern that the wronged person be properly compensated.[13] This compensation often took the form of a monetary settlement. Fines were based on both the severity and nature of the damage done and also on the social standing or sex of the offended party.[14] Damage consisted of bodily injury (including murder) as well as theft of one's property or any other possession(s).

Rape was much more seriously punished than, perhaps, in some modern societies, especially because the woman's victimization was regarded mostly more as a matter of hurting a father's or a husband's rights than as an attack against the woman all by itself.[15] According to Ives, compensation was extracted not from any

---

11 Mills, *Suspended Animation*, 14 (see note 5).

12 René Girard, *Violence and the Sacred*, trans. Patrick Gregory (Baltimore and London: The Johns Hopkins University Press, 1989), 22,

13 Henry Sumner Maine, *Ancient Law: Its Connection with the Early History of Society, and Its Relation to Modern Ideas* (New York: H. Holt and Company, 1878), 379.

14 George Ives, *A History of Penal Methods: Criminals, Witches, Lunatics*, Patterson Smith Reprint Series in Criminology, Law Enforcement, and Social Problems, 124 (1914; Montclair, NJ: Patterson Smith, 1970), 8.

15 Albrecht Classen, *Sexual Violence* (see note); Jeremy Goldberg, *Communal Discord, Child Abduction, and Rape in the Later Middle Ages*. The New Middle Ages (New York: Palgrave Macmillan, 2008); see also the contributions to Representing Rape in Medieval and Early Modern Literature, ed. Elizabeth Robertson and Christine M. Rose The New Middle Ages (New York: Palgrave Macmillan, 2001); Kathryn Gravdal, *Ravishing Maidens: Writing Rape in Medieval French Literature and Law* (Philadelphia: University of Pennsylvania Press, 1991); siehe auch Hilde Schmölzer, *Die Frau: das gekaufte Geschlecht; Ehe, Liebe und Prostitution im Patriarchat* (Bad Sauerbrunn : Ed. Tau, 1993).

humane objection to physical punishment but rather out of a fear of vendetta on the part of the victim or his/her family.[16] Part of the compensation might also accrue to the crown or other authority as a type of compensation for disturbing the peace.[17] Criminals were kept in prison until their cases were adjudicated but long prison sentences as punishment were not as common a practice as is often assumed.[18]

Persons accused of crimes could be found innocent through various types of ordeals, with the most common being that of the heated iron bar, or ring. After carrying the heated iron for a specified distance, the accused hands were bandaged and if, after three days, they were found clean and not infected he was declared innocent. Ordeals were condemned in 1251 by the Fourth Lateran Council and since the ordeal required the presence of a priest when it was administered, trial by ordeal largely ceased after this date.[19] Trial by battle was another form of ordeal although this practice appears rarely after the thirteenth century. Criminals could also seek sanctuary, and thus freedom from persecution, by seeking asylum within a church or monastery. There is evidence that colonies of fugitives grew up at some of the great seats of worship.

Irrespective of the ban by the Church on the ordeal, duels and similar procedures to determine someone's guilt or honor continued to enjoy considerable popularity far into the nineteenth and even twentieth century. Many scholars have questioned whether we could even characterize such a duel as a form of ordeal, but both methods certainly reflected on the need to appeal to higher powers to determine human guilt or innocence.[20]

Public shaming of criminals was also part of the arsenal of medieval and early modern punishments. The most severe form of shaming was a public flogging but there was also exposure in the stocks or in a neck pillory.[21] Criminals might also be required to wear some sort of badge on their clothing as a sign of their

---

16 Ives, *A History of Penal Methods,* 4 (see note 11).

17 Ives, *A History of Penal Methods,* 8 (see note 11).

18 Jean Dunbabin, *Captivity and Imprisonment in Medieval Europe, 1000–1300* (New York: Palgrave Macmillan, 2002); see also the contributions to Orte der Verwahrung: die innere Organisation von Gefängnissen, Hospitälern und Klöstern seit dem Spätmittelalter, ed. Gerhard Ammerer. Geschlossene Häuser – historische Studien zu Institutionen und Orten der Separierung, Verwahrung und Bestrafung, 1 (Leipzig: Leipziger Universitäts-Verlag, 2010); *Enfermements le cloître et la prison: VIe - XVIIIe siècle; actes du colloque international organisé par le Centre d'Étude et de Recherche en Histoire Culturelle,* ed. Isabelle Heullant-Donat, Julie Claustre, and Lusset Elisabeth. Homme et société (Paris: Publications de la Sorbonne, 2011).

19 John Briggs, Christopher Harrison, Angus McInnes, and David Vincent, *Crime and Punishment in England: An Introductory History* (New York: St Martin's Press, 1996), 10.

20 Sarah Neumann, *Der gerichtliche Zweikampf: Gottesurteil – Wettstreit – Ehrensache.* Mittelalter-Forschungen, 31 (Sigmaringen: Jan Thorbecke Verlag, 2011).

21 Ives, *A History of Penal Methods,* 54-55 (see note11).

malfeasance. One example was the pieces of red cloth in the shape of tongues that a false witness was required to wear on his breast and on his shoulders for the rest of his life.[22] Dishonoring at the pillory sometimes involved the criminal wearing animal masks or wooden yokes that heightened the sense of shame these punishments were meant to convey. Tortures or branding that left permanent marks on the body were also signs of infamy and disgrace.[23]

Trial by jury was instituted in England in 1166 for decisions about land cases and was soon afterward extended for use in criminal cases. An essential difference between medieval jury trails and the modern concept is that medieval jurors based their verdicts on their knowledge about the crime and not on the basis of evidence presented in the course of the trial.[24] Also it is important to keep in mind that criminal law was rather limited and unsophisticated in contrast to civil law. And most civil cases were heard before a magistrate who rendered judgment rather than a jury.[25] Additionally, the Church had its own courts and their jurisdiction extended to clerics and church buildings. These Church tribunals also dealt with sexual offenses and testamentary disputes.[26]

A wonderful and still not sufficiently scoured source for Church law in the late Middle Ages proves to be the Apostolic Penitentiary at the Vatican, which has been more critically examined in recent years especially by Swedish scholars for the Church province of Uppsala from 1410 to 1452. Apart from the usual cases of theft, murder, and even rape, the Penitentiary heard many cases pertaining to marriage, birth rights, blood relationships, then relating to violent behavior, apostacy, religious conflicts (including breaking monastic rules and vows). Violence, manslaughter, and participation in military actions were the most common issues, closely followed by sexual crimes (including rape, as mentioned above, breaking the vow of celibacy, illegal positions in the sexual act, homosexuality, etc.), then disobedience, failing to fast, committing simony, having a concubine, committing adultery, etc.

The range of possible wrongdoings in medieval society was very broad, quite similar to our world, but the impositions by the Church on all people, both cleric and lay, increased the danger of transgressing and becoming guilty of a sin and a crime multifold.[27] As the documents in the Apostolic Penitentiary also often

---

22 Ives, *A History of Penal Methods*, 56 (see note 11).

23 Mitchell B. Merback, *The Thief, the Cross and the Wheel: Pain and the Spectacle of Punishment in Medieval and Renaissance Europe* (Chicago: The University of Chicago Press, 1998), 213.

24 Briggs, et.al, *Crime and Punishment*, 10 (see note 14).

25 Briggs, et.al, *Crime and Punishment*, 11 (see note 14).

26 Briggs, et.al., *Crime and Punishment*, 12 (see note 14).

27 *Auctoritate Papae: The Church Province of Uppsala and the Apostolic Penitentiary 1410–1526*, ed. Sara Risberg, introd. Kirsi Salonen. Diplomatiarium Suecanum Appendix. Acta Pontificum Suecica, II (Stockholm: National Archives of Sweden, 2008).

indicate, many supplicants were simply afraid of potentially having committed a crime or a transgression of church law and tired hard to free themselves from any allegations or accusations, such as of illegitimate birth, of having been passively involved in murder cases, or of other perceived wrong-doings.

Mitchell B. Merback, one of many scholars in the field of crime and punishment in the premodern era, succinctly traces the development of what today we refer to as the legal system.[28] In medieval Europe law was not the professionally controlled and separate sphere of activity as we perceive it now. Customary laws, i.e., practices developed over time and consistently applied, prevailed until well into the eleventh century when Roman law began to play a larger, ultimately dominant, role in secular justice as kings strove to maintain their sovereign and legal controls against the rising authority of the Church. Merback also points out that criminal justice proceedings before the late Middle Ages were accusatorial in nature. The injured parties accused someone of a crime before a judge and the proceedings often took place in public.

However, during the twelfth century, the system changed to an inquisitorial one in which courts conducted their own investigations into the circumstances of the crime, made accusations and arrests, and judicial proceedings were conducted in private. But sentencing and punishment were still conducted in very public settings, serving a distinct performative function. The idea of punishment as spectacle is central to Merback's important 1998 study, *The Thief, the Cross and the Wheel*. He states that "The very idea of punishments enacted as a form of spectacle is predicated on the belief in their educative potential, though 'lessons of the scaffold', as they were later known to the moralists who exploited them, could run the gamut from cautionary tales, through brutalizing threats of violent retribution, to *exempla* of damnation."[29]

Social status of a convicted criminal was an important factor in the type of punishment inflicted. Even in cases of the death penalty some forms of execution were considered disgraceful, such as hanging, breaking on a wheel, and burning at the stake, which was mostly reserved for heretics or apostates, and later, especially in the early modern age, for alleged witches. Decapitation, by contrast was considered an honorable form of execution and usually reserved for members of the aristocracy far into the seventeenth and eighteenth centuries. But executions of any kind were intended to be edifying in the sense that spectators saw the accused confess, show contrition, receive absolution, and endure the pain of death with the promise of redemption in the afterlife.[30] Prior to the fourteenth century many criminals were denied confession before execution but in 1312, Pope

---

28 Merback, *The Thief,* 129-33 (see note 17).

29 Merback, *The Thief,* 135 (see note 17).

30 Merback, *The Thief,* 143 (see note 19).

Clement V forbade this practice and criminals were afterwards, more often than not, given the opportunity to confess, usually in a public forum.[31] According to Merback, "The salvific promise of Christ's self-abasing death on the Cross was nowhere more fully realized than in the redemption of the criminal who confessed, atoned and suffered his pains steadfastly."[32]

Cohen speaks about punitive public rituals as "the most common form of government propaganda."[33] She also asserts that "Like all public ceremonies, public executions were based not only upon a set of shared perceptions, but also upon a set of known symbols, altered only with great difficulty."[34] But this should come as a surprise for us since many aspects of premodern culture were commonly carried out in public, while the private space and private culture emerged only in the late Middle Ages and early modern age, which then had considerable implications for the criminal system especially since the sixteenth century, when the authorities began to develop a more elaborate system of prisons.[35]

The overarching problem of conflict in jurisdictions—lay and religious, royal and seigneurial, local and central—led to confusion about where and by whom an accused should be tried.[36] With regard to lay and ecclesiastical law, Cohen maintains that the two systems "recognized the inherent validity and legality of the other despite constant boundary conflicts."[37] Legal questions about marriage or religious orthodoxy were clearly cases for Church courts but they were also known to excommunicate debtors, even though debt was a civil offense.[38] In the cases of the secular judiciary, the king was the ultimate authority but there were a variety of local courts and, in most cases, their judgments were only overturned on appeal.[39]

By the early modern period there is a shift in legal concerns. Late medieval kings were mostly interested in controlling the wealth, power, and influence of the noble classes but, by the mid-seventeenth century, disorder among common people was seen as a primary obstacle to a peaceful and ordered society. Rises in population growth and increasing levels of poverty contributed to more crimes being committed, especially in urban centers. Vagrants in cities were seen as a real problem and many of them became "professional" criminals who often specialized

---

31 Merback, *The Thief*, 148-49 (see note 19).

32 Merback, *The Thief*, 149 (see note 19).

33 Cohen, *The Crossroads of Justice*, 24 (see note 1).

34 Cohen, *The Crossroads of Justice*, 24 (see note 1).

35 See the contribution to this volume by Patricia Turning.

36 Cohen, *The Crossroads of Justice*, 17 (see note 1)

37 Cohen, *The Crossroads of Justice*, 17 (see note 1).

38 Cohen, *The Crossroads of Justice*, 17 (see note 1).

39 Cohen, *The Crossroads of Justice*, 18 (see note 1).

in certain kinds of crime such as horse theft, con-games, and pick pocketing. In fact, the constantly growing mobility throughout late-medieval Europe, with the roads more and more filled with migrants, students, goliards, pilgrims, merchants, and many others, almost automatically led to the rise of crime as well.[40]

In their book, *Crime and Punishment in England,* Briggs, Harrison, McInnes and Vincent point out that in pre-modern times the rationales for punishment was four-fold. First was that of deterrence. They also refer to the fact that executions were carried out in a public before large crowds and with a good deal of ceremony. The second rationale these critics identify is that of retribution. They assert that punishments were meted out proportionally to the seriousness of the crime committed. Rape or murder were punished by hanging but a crime as serious as high treason warranted that the offender by hanged and then, while still alive, cut down, or quartered, disemboweled, and cut into four pieces. A third rationale was that of ritual cleansing. Good examples are shaming punishments by which the guilty undergo a kind of penance for the offense committed and then are allowed to be reintegrated into society.

By the end of the pre-modern period a fourth rationale begins to emerge—the idea of reforming the wrongdoer within the penal system. This concept developed along with the widespread use of imprisonment as punishment with inmates subject to strict regimes of work and religious instruction to rehabilitate them in both body and spirit.[41]

The articles in this volume deal primarily with literary and historical texts which shed light on medieval and early modern perceptions of what constituted criminal behaviors and how society responded punitively to those found guilty of violating normative patterns of behavior. While recognizing that literary texts of the period reflect, to a certain extent, the expectations and established conventions of style and expression, they present unique portholes into authors' treatment of acts of malfeasance and the meting out of justice or critical attitudes towards the injustice of wrongdoers going unpunished. The volume is roughly arranged in chronological order and, while it is impossible to provide a truly comprehensive view of this multi-faceted topic, the following studies are designed to give insights at specific locales and time frame of medieval and early modern periods based on a variety of texts that deal with criminal behavior and redress against those found guilty of offenses.

---

40 Briggs, et.al, *Crime and Punishment,* 20 (see note 14); see also Ernst Schubert, *Fahrendes Volk im Mittelalter* (Bielefeld: Verlag für Regionalgeschichte, 1995), 264–69.

41 Briggs, et.al, *Crime and Punishment,* 83-85 (see note 14).

As a proviso, however, the purpose of this collection is not to adress, in a classical sense, the broad history of law, the history of crime, and the history of punishment. We do not pursue issues such as those pertaining to the introduction of Roman law in the high Middle Ages, as influential and profound the effect certainly were. The interest also does not rest on comparing, say, Spanish with German, English with French, Swedish with Polish law, etc. The history of lawyers, of the criminal justice system, and, with a small exception, the history of punishment etc. might all be extremely interesting, but the contributors to this volume mostly come from a non-legal based discipline and yet approach the topic of crime and punishment from their specific subject matter.[42]

The critical method generally relies on the principles of the history of mentality which tries to grasp how people in the past perceived their reality by means of a comprehensive analysis of art works, literary expressions, religious comments, and also legal statements, all of which contribute in their own way to the larger picture of how a specific society regulated itself and set up laws and rules to determine the extent to which the individual could operate freely and in accordance with the common agreement. Laws by themselves might not be enough to study the legal consciousness of a society because they are normative, not necessarily descriptive. After all, even within the legal field we easily recognize the degree to which discourse dominates the relationship among all members of a society, a process which has continued until today, without showing any sign of slowing down.[43]

To provide the reader with an overview of what the individual contributions are all about, following we offer brief summaries of each article which will also allow us to reflect on the critical issues brought to the table by each author and hence to develop connections that can establish a larger picture. Bernard Ribémont in "Punier le coupable ou lui pardoner: La question du châtiment dans la chanson de geste" studies Old French *chanson de geste* not, as has often been assumed, purely formulaic treatments of good vs. evil, but rather as nuanced works that examine crime and its punishment in much more complex ways. For example, crimes are evaluated and punishment is conditioned by many factors—both religious and feudal ethical codes, fluctuating and ill-defined laws fluctuating between custom, and individual practice. The *chansons de geste* manifest what Ribémont refers to as a "judicial ethic" that rests as much on literary precedents as historical events.

---

42 For a good survey of the history of law, see Scott L. Taylor, "Law in the Middle Ages," *Handbook of Medieval Studies*, ed. Albrecht Classen. Vol. 1 (Berlin and New York: De Gruyter, 2010), 771–88.

43 Wolfgang Schild, "Recht: Mittelalter," and "Recht: Neuzeit," *Europäische Mentalitätsgeschichte: Hauptthemen in Einzeldarstellungen*, ed. Peter Dinzelbacher. 2nd rev. and expanded ed. Kröners Taschenausgabe, 469 (1993; Stuttgart: Alfred Kröner, 2008), 591–639.

His article challenges the notion that there exists a kind of monolithic perception of "law" in epic poetry by citing examples from works that deal with themes such as homicide, treason, and execution including *Jourdain de Blaye, Girart de Roussillon,* and *Chanson de Roland*. As we can recognize, the heroic world of the *chansons de geste* was not only one in which warriors operate at Charlemagne's court, but a world where personal instincts, desires, fears, and weaknesses also cause severe disruptions and create highly troubling conflicts.

Susanna Niiranen, in "Troubadours—*poètes maudits*?," studies troubadours who were accused of loose morals or other anti-social behaviors. Even though some troubadours were judged harshly by the Church or by their peers, they seemed to have been welcomed into aristocratic circles where their poems were celebrated. Or these poets simply belonged to the highest social classes and yet displayed criminal behavior or performed in a morally dubious manner. Niiranen's study examines the question of whether these poets could be both *fin 'aman* and rascals or scoundrels at the same time. She proposes that, in many ways, the ill-behaved troubadours could be seen as predecessors to the *poètes maudits* of the nineteenth and twentieth century. Since many of the behaviors identified with the *poètes maudits*—abuse of intoxicants, insanity, crime, violence, and social offences in general—were also part of the lifestyle of certain troubadours, the comparison is an apt one. She specifically studies William IX, Duke of Aquitaine who was excommunicated because of bad behaviors, Gaucelm Faidit who was a well-known glutton and drunk addicted to gambling and married to a woman with a dubious past, and Guilhem de Figueira who frequented taverns and consorted with prostitutes. She also includes the legendary figure, Guilhem de Cabestanh, who was killed by the jealous husband of a married woman with whom he was having an affair. The husband then, supposedly, cut out Guilhem's heart and gave it to his faithless wife to eat. Niiranen contrasts these anti-social troubadours with the women troubadours, the *trobairitz*, about whom there is no hint of scandal in the medieval sources.[44] These 'evil' or transgressing poets from the Old Occitan area in the Provence (Languedoc etc.) did not, however, embark on new strategies to test the limits which their society had imposed on them. Instead, as a comparison with the poets of the Latin poets in the *Carmina Burana* would show,

---

44 Here we grasp, of course, the pan-European motif of the eaten heart. See, for instance, Madeleine Jeay, "Consuming Passions: Variations on the Eaten Heart Theme," Violence Against Women in Medieval Texts, ed. Anna Roberts (Gainesville, Tallahassee, et al.: University Press of Florida, 1998), 75–96. See also Mariella Di Maio, *Il cuore mangiato: storia di un tema letterario dal Medioevo all' Ottocento* (Milan: Guerini e Assoc, 1996). Helmut Brall-Tuchel, "Das Motiv des gegessenen Herzens in der mittelalterlichen Novellistik," *La novella europea: origine, sviluppo, teoria; atti del convegno internazionale, Urbino, 30 - 31 maggio 2007*, a cura di Michael Dallapiazza. Aracne, 10, Scienze dell'antichità, filologico-letterarie e storico-artistiche, 443 (Rome: Aracne,2009), 71–89.

here we encounter typically misogynist, bawdy, and macho poets who have made their voices heard throughout the centuries.

Christopher Clason's article, "The Law, Letter and Spirit: Language, Transgression and Justice in Three Medieval German Epic Poems," examines German medieval epics in which the hero must either overcome an imbalance in the configuration of personal virtues or atone for some offense against heavenly or secular law. Clason claims that in many cases the "spirit of the law" governing such offenses is elusive since the actual legal prescriptions are mixed and vague, consisting of secular and ecclesiastical customs, statutes, commandments, or other regulations. He affirms that while the nature of the offenses and the judicial outcomes in many of these poems may appear illogical or arbitrary, to us today they may, in fact, hold keys for a better understanding of medieval social and spiritual attitudes.

Specifically, Clason examines Hartmann von Aue's *Der arme Heinrich* (ca. 1190/1200), Wolfram von Eschenbach's *Parzival* (ca. 1205), and Gottfried von Straßburg's *Tristan und Isolde* (ca. 1210). In all these three works, epistemology and language play significant roles in determining culpability and penalty. In the poems of Hartmann and Wolfram, the protagonists offend the "spirit of the law" and either misinterpret or neglect the "letter of the law." In Hartmann's work the transgression of neglecting God is a spiritual offense, whereas Wolfram's Parzival offends both secular law (stealing a ring and a kiss from the courtly lady Jeschute) and spiritual law (failure to show compassion). In Gottfried, the relationship between God's justice and human investigation and proof is seen in Isolde's trial by hot iron. Her evasive oath fulfills the "letter of the law" and succeeds in fooling members of the court while still satisfying God's will.

In "Crime, Punishment and the Hybrid in Medieval French Romance," Stacey Hahn studies myths about the supernatural origins, whether divine of diabolical, of heroes and historical figures. These hybrid characters, as portrayed in romance, carry immense burdens that potentially wreck havoc and often lead down a path of crime and subsequent punishment. In particular, Hahn examines two medieval French romances, *Robert le Diable* (early thirteenth century) and Jean d'Arras's *Roman de Mélusine* (1393) and their hybrid male protagonists. These protagonists act in remarkably parallel ways—Robert le Diable sets fire to the abbey of Arques, killing all the nuns inside, and Geoffrey Big Tooth commits a similar crime by setting fire to the monastery of Maillezais, killing all the monks within including his own brother Fromont. Both of these characters eventually repent of their actions and redeem themselves by battling against infidels and making a pilgrimage to Rome to receive absolution from the Pope. Geoffrey also seeks to make amends by establishing an abbey, and Robert has an abbey consecrated to him after his death. Neither marries nor bears offspring and humanity is thus spared future potential danger since they do not pass their hybrid nature with its accompanying propensity for criminal violence. Robert's and Geoffrey's acts of evil and contrition are characteristic of a literary sub-genre—the penitential romance. Hahn's detailed study on the crimes and punishment in these two works leads to a better understanding of influence of this distinct sub-category of medieval romance.

Scott Taylor's article, "*Judicium Dei, vulgaris popularisque sensus*: Survival of Customary Justice and Resistance to its Displacement by the 'New' *Ordines iudiciorum* as Evidenced by Francophonic Literature of the High Middle Ages," studies the phenomenon, beginning in the late eleventh and early twelfth centuries, when Romano-canonical judicial procedures based on oral and written evidence began to displace customary procedures for determining guilt and punishment. The latter included trial by ordeal, compurgation, and trial by combat. Taylor reviews the various theories that have been developed to explain why this transformation took place and focuses on the arguments raised against the *iudicium Dei* by both theologians and jurists. He examines popular views of the practitioners of the new legal sciences, and the procedures themselves, often rife with fraud and abuse.

To illustrate instances of ruse and connivery, Taylor uses examples from medieval romances, especially *Le Roman de Tristan* and *Le Chevalier de la charrete,* that some scholars maintain manifest society's recognition of the weaknesses inherent in the customary judicial systems. On the other hand, scholars such as Ronald Gene Koss argue that these romances should be read not as an indictment of customary justice but as a vindication of it, i.e., as manifestations of "swindling justice." Taylor proposes a synthesis which explains the triumph of Romano-canonical procedure based largely on the fact that the new procedures, more often than not, yielded a result that was consistent with local public sentiment.

Albrecht Classen debunks some fantasies about the medieval world of knights, ladies, and clerics all adhering to the ideals of ethics, morality, justice, and fear of God. He treats two texts, Heinrich der Glichezare's late twelfth-century *Reinhard Fuchs*, and Wernher the Gardener's *Helmbrecht*, written about 1260–1270. In these works, violence and crime dominate and the greatest liar receives the greater reward, especially in *Reinhard Fuchs*. Even though some justice is present in *Helmbrecht* the parents of the criminal never experience any consequences for their failures or shortcomings. Classen claims that crime and justice were of special interest to the didactic poets as, for example, Heinrich der Teichner in the fourteenth century.

This study analyzes the dominant critical discourse on criminality and explores the mentality that leads these characters to indulge in criminal behaviors. Literary works seem to feature crimes and criminals with great frequency and the preponderance of nefarious behaviors contrast with the view of law that we find in major law codes such as Eike von Repgow's *Sachsenspiegel*.

John Gough studies the French fifteenth-centurypoet, François Villon. The true identity of the person who signed the name to Villon to his works is still a puzzle for scholars. But Gough claims that the man-author present in his texts allows readers to construct a portrait of an individual either as fictional invention or actual self-portrait of the author. Especially noteworthy in Villon's works are the instances of pain and punishment woven throughout the metaphorical composition of his poems as part of his displays of human emotion and experience.

Pain through punishment is Villon's platform for investigating the nature of man. He views imprisonment as a sort of terrestrial purgatory where a former life and man are shed to reveal a new person who sees as his duty to warn, describe, and bemoan the society of his times. Paradoxically what comes through in Villon's texts, his *Lais* and *Testament*, is an examination of pain and punishment which concludes that pain, in the sense of shared suffering, serves to help mankind to embrace life, and in this process even enhances our mortal existence.

Jean Jost studies a Middle-English verse romance from ca. 1350, the anonymous *Gamelyn*, an example of the "rebel romance." In this work, a knight, on his deathbed, attempts to distribute equitably his lands to his three sons. But a council of elders goes against the father's wishes and decides to deny the youngest son, Gamelyn, any rights of inheritance, a decision that has dire consequences.[45] Gamelyn is deceived by his older brother, John, and finally extracts violent vengeance on John and his household. When Gamelyn is made to answer for his crimes, ironically, he must appear before the local magistrate, his own equally vengeful and violent brother, John. Gamelyn is shut away in the king's prison until a representative of the king's justice arrives to try him. But since John had bribed the jury, Gamelyn declares the proceedings null and void and physically ousts the royal judge from his seat, taking it for himself and declaring himself as the arbiter of justice. At the end of the tale, Gamelyn's rough and ready form of justice prevails and he is exonerated of his crime and is appointed "chief justice of the land." Jost shows how this tale from fourteenth-century England explores issues of law and violence and concludes with the restoration of some kind of justice, as problematic as the entire narrative framework continues to be.

---

45 A similar issue emerges in Wolfram von Eschenbach's *Parzival*(ca. 1205), with Parzival's father Gahmuret being forced to find his good fortune on his own, while his older brother assumes the inheritance and so continues the dynasty.

In the article, "Contra Signum Nostrum: The Symbolism of *Lèse-majesté* under Philip VI Valois," Jolanta Komornicka deals with the changes to the definition of treason in medieval France. After the thirteenth century when crime ceased to be automatically equated with sin, crime began to be defined as an offense against the public interest, not simply against God or against one's lord. The emergence of a new kind of royal court—the Parlement of Paris—and the inquisitional system of the *nova doctrina* brought adjudication of crime, at least in theory, into the public sphere. *Lèse-majesté* was interpreted in various traditions as either an offense against the common good, against royal majesty, or the worst kind of infidelity. The royal court had to negotiate these competing definitions and the evolving understanding of crime itself. Part of what determined whether a crime attained the severity of *lèse-majesté* was the degree of public notoriety it occasioned and the judgment of the Parlement. Also, beginning in the twelfth century, *lèse-majesté* began to designate a broader class of transgressions than only those which harmed the king in either his person, purse, or ability to rule.

The expanded concept included any act that wronged the imperial *regalia*. Also, feudal *lèse-majesté* led to the idea of public crime by suggesting that the territory or the people could suffer the same type of injury as the king. This new brand of treason came to be applied to crimes against the common good, including infractions against the king's officers, making or passing false coinage, armed robbery, and any crime perpetrated on the king's highway. Komornicka addresses three particular questions with regard to the notion of treason in fourteenth-century France: (1) how crimes like armed robbery or kidnapping could be equated with treason and whether the punishments imposed for such crimes demonstrated true equality between these crimes; (2) the relationship of *lèse-majesté* to other high crimes; and (3) what consequences the expanded notion of treason has had for the French government and for social relations in French society.

Connie Scarborough studies how women were treated as both victims and perpetrators of crimes in the Spanish thirteenth-century law code, *Las Siete Partidas*. During his reign (1254–1282) Alfonso X compiled an encyclopedic law code, *Las Siete Partidas.* Each of the seven *partidas,* or divisions, treats a different subject: ecclesiastical regulations, governmental administration, the courts, domestic relationships, business activities, wills and inheritance, and crime and punishment. "Women as Victims and Criminals in *Las Siete Partidas*" focuses on how women are treated in this legal code, especially in Seventh *Partida* which deals with crime and punishment. Scarborough also references other laws in the collection when these are specifically directed at women. It is not surprising that women are mentioned most often in laws concerning sexual relationships and marriage. However, women are also specifically named both as defendants and accusers in a number of other legal matters. Alfonso X and his legal experts recognized women as a special category under the law. Just as men and women are not treated equally in the *Las Siete Partidas*, neither are all women treated equally. Female slaves are considered differently compared to free virgins, for instance. And virgins are treated differently from married women or widows. Female religious formed another category as did women of the Jewish or Muslim faith. To accomplish its goal of inclusivity and comprehensiveness, *Las Siete Partidas* deals with women from all social classes and faiths and, in many cases, differentiates consequences for crimes committed by or against women. An entire Title, Number 27, is set aside for laws dealing with adultery. The striking feature of this set of laws is that a wife cannot accuse her husband of adultery, but a husband may accuse his wife. Husbands also have the option to pardon a wayward wife within the first two years of her confinement. In all, Title 27 contains sixteen individual laws about accusations of adultery, possible defenses, and punishment of the guilty party, almost always the wife.

Cecilia María Ruiz treats another work from medieval Spain, the fourteenth-century collection of moralizing short stories, *El Conde Lucanor* by don Juan Manuel. In "Liars, Criminals, and Victims in *Count Lucanor*," Ruiz studies how Juan Manuel treats sin and crimes as distinct but, at times, overlapping categories of reprehensible behaviors. For example, the greed that motivates Truhana in example VII to fantasize about being rich and envied by her neighbors, whereby she laughs and the pot of honey she is carrying on her head falls to the ground, is different in degree to the greed in example XLV. In this example, a man sells his soul to the devil so that he may steal without being apprehended and punished by the authorities.

Truhana does not commit a crime. Her greediness leads to a miscalculation (distraction) that brings on personal loss. In example XLV, on the other hand, the man's greed motivates him to steal, which is a crime against society. The crime hurts the criminal, society, and God. In this case, sin and crime overlap in another way. The man commits the most heinous crime that one can commit against God—he sells his soul to the devil. In other examples with stories about adultery and murder, Ruiz emphasizes that both sins and crimes are punished in the stories in this collection. No sin or crime goes unpunished and every wrongdoing receives its just consequences. Criminals are apprehended and punished and sinners are punished by God. The greatest punishment, the damnation of one's soul, can only be avoided in these tales when the sinner repents and does good deeds in the service of God. In *Count Lucanor*, good in the end triumphs over evil and God triumphs over the devil.

In "Entrusted with the Key: Jailers and Prison Guards in the Later Middle Ages," Patricia Turning debunks the notion that medieval judicial institutions always punished deviants and criminals in a spectacular and largely physical fashion. Recent scholarship has revealed that by the end of the fourteenth century, municipal, royal, and ecclesiastical courts relied primarily on imprisonment as a means of establishing law and order. As a result, the prison warden and his officials emerged as new and prominent figures in the legal system. For example, in the city of Toulouse, the municipal jailer and his family lived in the town hall and he was entrusted with the keys to the city as well as to the jail. Also, the office appears to have been hereditary, passed down from father to son.

In order to better understand the concepts and realities of the role in the jailer in the later Middle Ages, Turning explores not only the particular responsibilities that prison officers assumed in secular and ecclesiastical jails, but also their portrayal in literature, prescriptive legal documents, and hagiography. She concludes that no single vision of the jailer emerges. For example, some were benevolent and kind, protecting the inmates, while others abused their position of power over others. The jailer served as an important point of contact between criminals (male and female), legal representatives (lawyers, judges, and elected officials), and the outside world (family and friends of the accused). Turning argues that the jailer was a crucial symbol of the growing sophistication of the European legal system in its transition into the modern world.

Birgit Wiedl turns her attention to accusations of desecration of consecrated hosts by Jews in fourteenth-century Austria. In her article, "The Host on the Doorstep: Perpetrators, Victims, and Bystanders in an Alleged Host Desecration in Fourteenth-Century Austria," Wiedl examines the Christian preoccupation with Jews allegedly desecrating the host and, by extension, participating in the crime for which they had been accused for centuries—the killing of Christ. The narrative of host-desecrating Jews can be traced to a tale emerging from Paris in 1290 in which the Jews are punished and the host is rescued. Afterwards, similar tales spread quickly throughout Europe, leading to ever new waves of persecutions, expulsions and murdering of Jews in Ashkenazic and Sephardic areas. By 1305 the story had reached the small Lower Austrian town of Korneuburg. On September 17 of that year, according to monastic reports, a pierced and bloodied host was found on the threshold of a Jew's house. By the end of that same day, the host had been returned to the parish church and the entire Jewish population of the town had been put to death. The rescued host was reported now to have miraculous powers and the Bishop sent a commission of clerics to investigate these claims a few months later. The Bishop also sought to determine whether the wafer had actually been consecrated and whether or not the Jews had been innocent or guilty of the crime.

In the protocol, of the twenty-one citizens questioned by the ecclesiastical commission in Korneuburg, opinion was divided about the Jews' culpability. Some thirty years later the real perpetrator was identified, interestingly enough in the course of a papal investigation into another alleged host desecration. Unfortunately, by then it was too late for the victims, and we face here, maybe, a very similar situation as in the case of Joan of Arc (1412–1431), also falsely accused and then burned at the stake as a pawn in the hands of criminal figures both within the Church and the English government. Justice, as we might have to admit, is a lofty goal, and more often than not an elusive ideal, even though there is justified confidence that we have better courts and a more reliable, even fair, court system in the western world than in the premodern world.

Considering Chaucer's *The Physician's Tale* in his *Canterbury Tales*, hope in justice during the late Middle Ages could easily be crushed, as Daniel F. Pigg examines in his contribution, although at the end the evil judge, the cause of all the tragedy that leads to Virginia's death at her own father's hand in order to protect her from dishonor and shame, is thrown into prison by the people. There he commits suicide, which completes the narrative, as unsatisfactory as that may be for the contemporary and the modern audience. Even though Chaucer mostly adapted the basic narrative material from Livy (59 B.C.–17 C.E.), he also made some significant adaptions, such as moving the killing scene away from the public sphere to Virginius's house, that is, into the private room, with no witnesses.

As Pigg recognizes, the conflict between the lascivious judge Appius and Virginius also hinges on the charge against the latter of being a thief (having stolen the baby girl Virginia) and hence of lacking in true manliness, although the very opposite is the case concerning the father-daughter relationship. Most troublesome proves to be Virginius's quick succumbing to the judge's decision and his subsequent killing of his daughter, instead of fighting for his own innocence and of protecting his daughter from lust-driven monster, Appius, in a reasonable fashion.[46] As much as Chaucer addressed inherent problems in the legal system of his own time, certainly implied by the storytelling itself, the real concern targeted, as Pigg underscores, is the question of Virginius's manliness and control over his own life, since he retires to his own house and kills his daughter there without resorting to any legal means that surely would have been available to him. Moreover, he has failed as a father to protect his daughter properly, which made

46 The same motif reappears several hundred years later in the famous tragedy *Emilia Galotti* (1772) by Gotthold Ephraim Lessing (1729–1781), though there the criticism targets the absolutist prince of Guastalla, who had initiated the plot to have Emilia's fiancé killed on his way to the wedding and the woman 'kidnapped' to his own castle . Eventually her father stabs Emilia to death to protect her honor, but refrains from seeking revenge from the prince out of religious concerns.

it possible for the judge to cast a gaze upon her and to be struck by her beauty in such intensity that now he is willing to commit the crime of rape.

As flawed as Chaucer's *The Physician's Tale* might seem in the eyes of many critics, Pigg's analysis demonstrates that despite its exceptional brevity it carries heavy messages regarding the failure of the public legal system, the collapse of the criminal courts, the downfall of parental supervision, and the exposure of feminized masculinity (Virginius). According to Pigg, the reader/listener could only rely on God's grace and pursue the individual quest via a pilgrimage.

Lia Ross studies the criminal career of the young Breton nobleman and famous comrade of Joan of Arc, Gilles the Rais, in her article "Deviancy in the Late Middle Ages: The Crimes and Punishment of Gilles the Rais." Rais secretly practiced sorcery and serial murder and his crimes are well documented thanks to preservation of records from his double trial. The exhaustive testimony of witnesses and accomplices, with its litany of kidnappings, rapes, murders, and mutilations of children is striking for the similarity between this medieval serial killer and his modern counterparts. While Rais's shocking double life and violent death have inspired numerous modern works (especially fiction), contemporary imagination seems to have been less affected. However, as Ross's studies makes abundantly clear, there is no reason to assume that certain criminal behaviors were typical of the premodern world. In fact, Gilles's contemporaries were as shocked and disgusted when the truth was revealed as modern people are when they learn of a similar crime scene or account. The slaughter of the innocent, as already reported in the New Testament, has always been regarded as a crime against mankind. The true shock resulting from Ross's paper might be that mass murder can happen at any time, at any period, and in any society, since man is always in danger of turning into a berserk, unleashing indiscriminate violence against his fellow-beings. Gilles was certainly motivated by sexual instincts, but ultimately he was a mass murderer, and hence, tragically, one of many all over the world and throughout time.[47]

The reaction of the authorities, in particular, reveals the malaise of a society that was only beginning to return to a rule of law after decades of violence. Despite obvious clues to Rais's criminal activity, investigation of the case was late in coming, his interrogation conducted in an unusually mild manner, and the inevitable death sentence carried out almost reluctantly and mercifully. Even more surprising, comments on the part of the official chronicler Alain Chartier were

---

47 There are so many examples of mass murder in human history, both the countless pogroms against the Jews and the Holocaust including, that Dinah L. Shelton was justified to edit a *Encyclopedia of Genocide and Crimes Against Humanity*. Gale Virtual Reference Library (Detroit: Thomson Gale, 2005).

unexpectedly lenient, given the nature of the crimes. Ross uses the case of Rais to illustrate both the extensiveness and limits of late-medieval tolerance for deviant behavior, even when the perpetrator was noble and enjoyed an otherwise good reputation. This case also calls into question two competing sets of beliefs about that era. On the one hand there is what Ross calls "medieval emotionality," triggered by the culprit's theatrical repentance, and on the other the belief that noblemen cynically disregard the value of the lives of their humble victims.

John Beusterien studies the use of the conical hat and public spectacle as forms of punishment in the early sixteenth-century Spanish masterpiece, *La Celestina*. In his article, "The Spectacle of the Human Head: Punishment in *La Celestina*," Beusterien argues that Fernando de Rojas, through images of the head and the accoutrement of the conical hat, creates a literary world into which justice based on public shaming is no longer operable. The go-between, Celestina, is not punished by the justice system, but rather is stabbed by greedy servants when she does not share her earnings with them. She had earlier reflected on the public shaming of her old friend, Claudina, and had feared that she, too, might be punished in this way, but she meets a more violent end. The servants who murder Celestina flee the justice system by jumping out the window, cracking their skulls when they land on the pavement below. They are almost immediately executed for the murder of Celestina but we only learn of their punishments second hand since none of the main characters witness the executions. The servants' master, Calisto, only worries about damage to his own reputation and does not long reflect either on the crime committed by his men or their punishment.

Rojas uses the execution to criticize a failed justice system since Calisto openly states that the judge's condemnation of the servants is a terrible shock since the judge was a political crony of his family and he was sure that he and his household thus enjoyed immunity from punishment. Calisto himself will shatter his head and literally spill his brains onto the pavement when he later dies, falling from the high garden wall of his lover's house. Beusterien examines how these images of shattered heads and the conical hats are used to comment on a justice system that is dysfunctional. He also studies the complex symbolism of the conical headgear as both power-enabler (for example as a miter) and as a form of social repression that debases its wearer (such as headgear worn by those tried by the Inquisition).

Kathleen Llewellyn treats another important sixteenth-century work, the *Heptaméron,* in her article, "Equal Opportunity Vengeance in the *Heptaméron* of Marguerite de Navarre." Often considered primarily a collection of love stories, Llewellyn considers many of the novellas that make up the *Heptaméron* to be "war" stories in the sense that many deal with time-honored theme of the battle of the sexes. The "crimes" in the work are a series of ill deeds done by women to men and by men to women. Marguerite uses ten storytellers—five men and five women—and one would assume that the punishments meted out by the women would be against the men and vice versa. But this is not the case. Punishments in the *Heptaméron* are generally meted out by men, only rarely by women, reflecting the patriarchal society in which the text was composed. But the reader of the work discovers that the reasons for which women were punished, and even the ways in which they were punished, paradoxically empowered the women in the novellas. For while, historically, women's punishment often differed from men's, in the Heptaméron, Marguerite de Navarre establishes a parallel between men and women, even in their punishment for wrong-doing.

Nicolas Lombart's article concerns crime in the time of civil war, precisely the religious wars taking place in France from 1561-1570. "Crimes et châtiments d'exception en France au temps des Guerres de Religion: La notion de justice expéditive dans les *Commentaires* de Monluc" examines Blaise de Monluc's (ca. 1502-1577) extensive work based on his experiences as a soldier. The *Commentaires* give detailed accounts of war techniques, tactics, and politics but they are also replete with personal reflections. For example, in book six, there is long digression on the need to reform the justice of the realm that Monluc describes as slow, inefficient, and drowning in lawyers' rhetoric. Monluc, in his role as commander of the king, found himself in the position of meting out justice in an expedient manner and rendering sentences on crimes committed by the Huguenots. Accompanied by two executioners, he handed down swift judgments and summary executions, clearly cognizant of his responsibility as the "arm of justice" for the king. In his memoirs, Monluc reflects on these crimes and punishments "of exception" in context of the upheaval of a religious civil war. His comments are strikingly similar to modern evaluations of what we now call "war crimes."

Martha Moffitt Peacock describes the seventeenth-century conditions in the first all-women's prison in the Netherlands, the *Spinhuis*. In her article, "The Amsterdam *Spinhuis* and the 'Art' of Correction," she notes that prisons of the period usually housed both male and female inmates and female prisoners were routinely abused by their male jailers and male prisoners.[48] In contrast, the *Spinhuis* in Amsterdam was created as an all-female prison with both men and women in authority over the inmates who were taught valuable skills in textile production while they were confined. Through a study of the prison, and especially of the portraits of the regents and regentesses who governed the prison,

---

48 The topic of female prisoners is now covered by Gwen Seabourne, *Imprisoning Medieval Women: The Non-Judicial Confinement and Abduction of Women in England, c.1170-1509* (Farnham, Surrey, and Burlington, VT: Ashgate, 2011).

Peacock sees this institution as a unique manifestation of women's power and agency. The *Spinhuis* was created based on the idea that women could be reformed through engaging in honorable and profitable work in the fields of spinning, weaving, sewing and lace-making. Established initially for poor women beggars it had a charitable mission as an institution where women were brought back to God, brought back to honor, and brought back to chastity as they learned to work diligently in a sober and virtuous environment.

Portraits of the regentesses of the *Spinhuis* reveal that these women exercised equal authority with male supervisors and also helped to insure that the women confined there were not abused by men. They formed important oversight for the prison and communicated with magistrates to discuss sentences and punishments for the prisoners. Peacock asserts that the founding of the *Spinhuis* necessitated a cultural circumstance in which women, their skills, and their power, were given voice in the construction of a social institution. As a consequence, when women prisoners walked through the portal of the *Spinhuis* they realized that they were now under female control. And while that discipline was strict, it was certainly more charitable for the long-term benefit of women prisoners than the patriarchal brothel/prisons found in other areas of early modern Europe.

Tom Willard studies cases of deceit and fraud in England during the seventeenth century in "Pimping for the Fairy Queen: Some English Scammers and Their Just Desserts." Using Ben Jonson's great city drama, *The Alchemist* (1610) as a point of departure, Willard catalogs a host of cheating scams associated not only with alchemy, but with millenarian religion, fortune telling, and much more. One scheme includes introducing a gullible person to the Queen of the Fairies and helping to secure her assistance in such matters as winning at cards. Jonson's handling of this ruse not only makes for great stage drama but would also have reminded his original audience of similar cases in recent years.

Six years earlier, for example, one Jane Phillips had been "whipped through the Citie" of London for her part in fleecing a country gentleman who wanted an introduction to the Fairy Queen. And this was not an isolated case, for three years after Jonson's play was performed by Shakespeare's company, a woman, Alice West, was brought to trial with her husband for "the impoverishing of many simple people" of London who had been led to believe that she was the Fairy Queen. The reportage from these trials suggests that the people who flocked to Jonson's play were amused equally by the gullibility of those conned and the outrageousness of the cunning women's artistry. Jonson's prefatory comments on the play show that he did not confine his satire to any one character or social role.

Denis Bjaï studies Montaigne's comments on the punishment of criminals in his article, "En la justice même, tout ce qui est au-delà de la mort simple me semble pure cruauté (*Essais*, II, 11): Réflexions de Montaigne sur le châtiment des criminels." Bjaï points out that Montaigne's reflections about the punishment of criminals were inspired by the juridical, historical, and philosophical works he had read and also by his own personal experience as a magistrate and witness to the tragic errors committed by the justice system of his time. The possibility of punishing an innocent person made him very reticent to condemn.

Montaigne poses many questions in this regard including whether a punishment can be considered just or not. He takes into account the part that emotions (such as anger and vengeance), chance (the good nature, or not, of the judge), and even over-confidence on the part of the judge play in deciding a punishment. He also asks if punishment should be proportional to the severity of the crime committed and concludes that anything beyond simple death constitutes cruelty.

But then Montage goes on to question what constitutes "simple death." He also addresses punishments inflicted on a living being and on a corpse, and he debates the worth of purely symbolic punishments. He next questions whether penal punishment can be useful for a society, i.e., not so much to correct the actions of the criminal but rather that other members of society learn from the criminal's fate. He also asserts that the first punishment suffered by a guilty person is the torment of his own conscience. Montaigne also observed that the worst and most sadistic crimes are those committed during a time of civil war. Bjaï concludes his article with Montaigne's famous observation that we are all guilty, at one time or another in our lives, of some misdeed and, thus, anyone at some point in his life could find himself under the control of the justice system.

Allison P. Coudert investigates the theme of cannibalism in early-modern Europe in her article, "The Ultimate Crime: Cannibalism in Early Modern Minds and Imaginations." She begins by pointing out that accounts and stories of cannibalism have obsessed the western imagination both in fantasy and reality. But with the changes brought about in early modern Europe as a result of the discovery of the "new" world, the religious conflicts generated by the Reformation and Counter-Reformation, and the rise of a proto-capitalist consumer society a new type of cannibal emerged. The new cannibal, on the one hand, represented the primitive "other," a despicable and criminal member of a regressive society that stood in stark opposition to the progressive society of the Europeans. But, on the other hand, the image of the cannibal came to symbolize the very rapaciousness of European colonialism, imperialism, and capitalism as all three literally devoured the peoples and institutions that stood in their way. Christian conflict further complicated the complex meaning of capitalism in the early-modern period. The parallel between Christian communion and cannibal feasts was readily apparent, especially to Protestants, who used it to ridicule Catholic doctrine. Coudert concludes that cannibalism in early-modern Europe was a recurring, multi-faceted theme in public discourse pitting the two sides in the universal religious wars of that time, highlighting the contradictions and conflicts generated by the transition from the pre-modern to the modern world.

Evelyn Luef also addresses issues of early-modern Europe in her article, "Punishment Post Mortem: Suicide in Early Modern Austria and Sweden." Luef examines the question of how to punish someone who is both the perpetrator and victim of a crime, i.e., a suicide. In early-modern Europe, suicide was perceived as a felony, a sinful deed, and a crime against God, nature, and society, and this in close parallel to the perceptions of suicide in the Middle Ages. Both suicide and suicide attempt were criminally prosecuted. Committing suicide not only resulted in legal consequences but it also carried social stigma and implications for the society as a whole. Luef focuses on how the bodies of people who committed suicide were "punished." Using judicial records from the seventeenth and eighteenth centuries in Austria and Sweden she examines issues such as who inspected the bodies of suicides, where these bodies were kept until judgment was rendered, and when the family received the body and when was it handed over to the executioner. From this evidence, Luef contrasts the practical handling of individual suicide cases against normative juridical texts. Her study documents the broad variety of practical reactions toward suicide by authorities, families, and the society at large and investigates decisive criteria for how and by whom the suicide's body was handled.

The articles in this volume find many intersecting points of interest. Classen, Luef, Jost, and Ribémont deal with crimes and punishment in literary texts and how the portrayal of these subjects differs from what we find in proscriptive legal treatises. As these authors note, legal texts do not always reflect or corroborate ways in which criminals are brought to justice or prevailing juridical processes. Furthermore, law codes did not always insure that their precepts were followed in legal practice, i.e., without actual court records or other documentation we cannot be sure that these codes were enforced or, if enforced, whether they were done systematically in all cases or whether there were mitigating factors that allowed some criminal acts to go unpunished. Komornicka, Luef, Ross, and Wiedl directly examine court proceedings and other legal documents with the intent to study issues such treason, suicide, serial murder, and pogroms against Jewish communities. Competing systems of law—customary laws and trials by ordeal or combat and Romano-canonical procedures based on oral and written evidence—are investigated by Taylor through literary texts.

Women, as victims and perpetrators of crimes are the subject of several other articles. Scarborough studies how women were treated in a thirteenth-century legal code, while Llewellyn examines punishments meted out to women in a sixteenth-century collection of novellas. Scarborough notes that female criminals were treated differently and, when a woman was a victim, the punishment meted out to the abusers was often predicated on the woman's social, marital, or racial standing. Pigg, in turn, shows how a flawed justice system can operate and an innocent woman be killed simply because of the feared threat that she might lose her honor through her victimization by a corrupt judge. His analysis underscores that a judicial system can be perverted to the extent that a victim actually suffers the punishment

Llewellyn finds in stories about "the battle of the sexes" that women are more likely to be punished than to mete out punishment to their male counterparts. Beusterien also treats women, especially the act of public shaming, as a punishment for women accused of sorcery or pandering. Peacock reveals a unique all-female prison founded in the late sixteenth-century in Amsterdam—the *Spinhuis*. Women served as operators and overseers of this institution and it was a place of reform for women in sharp contrast to other prisons in early modern Europe in which male and female prisoners were housed together and women were routinely sexually abused or prostituted by male jailers and male inmates alike. Turning also studies jails and jailers and concludes that no single notion emerges about either these institutions or their wardens during the medieval period. Jailers were important players in the judicial system from the end of the fourteenth century.

A pair of articles—those by Bjaï and Gough—approach legal matters from a philosophic viewpoint. Bjaï specifically addresses the fundamental notion of what constitutes cruelty and Gough's piece is concerned with efforts to find a purpose for pain and suffering. In this same vein, Clason and Ruiz treat the ideas of God's justice and sin in contrast to crime as defined by secular or ecclesiastical customs and statutes.

A number of the articles deal with issues that have decidedly contemporary applications and insights. For example, Ross deals with a fifteenth-century serial killer whose behavior is strikingly similar to the modern psychological profiles of this type of criminal. Lombart deals with what actions and under what circumstances can be declared the premodern equivalents of war crimes. Niiranen investigates behavior that we now label as anti-social or deviant. And Willard takes up the idea of con men and con women that prey on the gullible. Hahn and Coudert treat issues that continue to fascinate the Western imagination—creatures of supernatural origins and cannibalism respectively.

This volume explores how different communities, authors, and judicial authorities in the Middle Ages and early modern period dealt with the notion of what constitutes a criminal act and how they choose to punish those found guilty of such behaviors. The articles rely on a wide-range of different sorts of materials—literary works, philosophic texts, memoirs, law codes, court proceedings, other historical documentation, and visual images—to shed light on these key concepts. While no collection on so vast a topic can claim to be exhaustive, the studies included in the present volume provide valuable insights that help us to better understand how medieval and early modern societies perceived and dealt with those who committed reprehensible acts. We hope to have brought together a solid group of relevant studies that create a kaleidoscopic image of what crime and punishment meant in the premodern world. Surprisingly, if not tragically, the differences between criminal behavior in the past and in the present seem to be rather limited, since people have always felt the tendency to transgress, to take what does not belong to them, to overpower others illegally, to abuse the system to their advantage, and to disregard all ethical, moral, and religious norms and ideals. The Ten Commandments have, unfortunately, not lost in relevance, and the comments about the Seven Deadly Sins, preached about throughout the entire Middle Ages and the early modern world, if not until today, have consistently pinpointed the fundamental human frailty, ignorance, greed, hatred, passion, and hence lack of rationality.[49] The masterful allegorical narrative *Piers Plowman* by William Langland (late fourteenth century) provides the perhaps best example in this regard.[50] Considering the virtually uninterrupted history of crime and punishment from the antiquity until today, it makes perfect sense to revisit these issues, to lay the foundation for future research once again, and to allow individual cases from the world of literature, art history, historical and legal documents, etc., to speak up. Crime and punishment are here for good and will be part of all human societies since we do not live in a utopia. Ironically, even the best utopian societies as projected by many different writers throughout time have always known of rules and laws in order to punish those who threaten to transgress or have taken measures that undermine the utopian world. After all, in the medieval world people already had a clear sense of utopias, and the dangers that could destroy them[51]; this also pertaining to the legal system.

---

49 See the contributions to *The Seven Deadly Sins: From Communities to Individuals*, ed. Richard Newhauser. Studies in Medieval and Reformation Traditions, 123 (Leiden and Boston: Brill, 2007).

50 *William Langland's Piers Plowman: A Book of Essays*, ed. Kathleen M. Hewett-Smit (New York: Routledge, 2001); William Langland, *Piers Plowman*, a new annotated edition of the C-text by Derek Pearsall. Exeter Medieval Texts and Studies (1978; Exeter, UK: University of Exeter Press, 2007). See also William Langland, *Piers Plowman: A Parallel-Text Edition of the A, B, C and Z Versions*, ed. A. V. C. Schmidt (vol. 1: London and New York: Longman, 1995; vol. 2: Kalamazoo, MI: Medieval Institute Publications, 2008).

51 Heiko Hartmann, "Utopias/Utopian Thought," *Handbook of Medieval Studies*, ed. Albrecht Classen. Vol. 2 (Berlin and New York: De Gruyter, 2010), 1400–08.

Chapter 1

Bernard Ribémont
(CESFiMA — Université d'Orléans — ANR *Juslittera*)

Le 'crime épique' et sa punition: quelques exemples (XIIe–XIIIe siècles)

La *chanson de geste* offre un terrain particulièrement riche pour qui veut s'intéresser aux relations entre le droit et la littérature. En effet, de nombreuses questions relevant du juridique ou du judiciaire trament les textes épiques du Moyen Âge: distribution de fiefs, héritage, ambassades, légitimité de la guerre, traîtrises et crimes divers sont la base de bien des motifs épiques et, au-delà, structurent en profondeur la plupart de nos chansons.

Partant de ce constat immédiat, il paraît alors légitime de s'interroger sur les relations que l'écriture épique médiévale entretient avec les questions de droit, de justice, de procédure. Deux directions principales de recherche se dégagent alors: selon la première, on proposera une lecture à caractère historiciste, en cherchant à repérer comment nos chansons reflètent une réalité de la justice des XIIe et XIIIe siècle, avec éventuellement un souvenir, plus ou moins nostalgique, plus ou moins fantasmé, des pratiques carolingiennes.[1] La deuxième voie d'investigation est littéraire et s'intéresse à ce qui relève de ce que je nommerai une 'esthétique du juridique/judiciaire' et consiste à mesurer les fonctions littéraires, à analyser les constructions de motifs reposant sur ce qui s'apparente à des problèmes de justice. J'adopterai une démarche qui consiste à croiser ces deux types d'approche, en considérant ici d'une part le motif du crime et certaines de ses déclinaisons dans la *chanson de geste* et d'autre part en tentant de mesurer ce que ce motif doit – ou ne doit pas – au droit et à la procédure du temps. Il conviendra de prendre garde

---

1 C'est dans un cadre plus général, selon surtout une méthodologie de la comparaison, ce que fait R. Howard Bloch dans son ouvrage, *Medieval French Literature and Law* (Berkeley, Los Angeles, and London: University of California Press, 1977).

ici à ne pas tomber dans le piège, tendu aux rares critiques s'intéressant ou s'étant intéressés à ces questions, d'une vision trop naïve ou trop systématique du 'droit féodal'. À y regarder de façon attentive, s'il est probablement légitime de parler de 'pré-droit'[2] et surtout de code d'honneur, il est abusif de faire reposer une analyse sur un droit féodal qui aurait un caractère établi, savant en quelque sorte, et qui n'existe pas en tant que tel; qui, justement, apparaît souvent à travers une fictionnalisation du droit, fictionalisation à laquelle les chansons de geste ne sont pas étrangères.[3] Il est cependant intéressant de mettre en parallèle certains propos des jongleurs avec ce que peuvent dire des coutumiers, en ne perdant pas de vue que ces derniers ont été écrits après la plupart de nos chansons, qu'ils sont influencés par le droit savant et ne correspondent donc pas étroitement à une réalité antérieure essentiellement fluctuante et géographiquement instable.[4] Si la *chanson de geste* est le reflet de certaines pratiques, elle n'en est que le reflet, parfois très déformé. Les textes épiques offrent surtout le témoignage de la place que le juridique et le judiciaire peuvent avoir dans la construction d'un univers de fiction qui se veut, parce qu'épique, la mise en exergue de valeurs essentielles, mais exacerbées, d'une société et surtout d'un groupe social. C'est à la lumière de ces motifs littéraires épiques, dont en termes de représentation, que la *chanson de geste* peut offrir à l'historien d'intéressantes données sur la justice du Moyen Âge central.

Un des moteurs de la *chanson de geste* est bien constitué, selon un schéma de type rupture/réparation, par le manquement d'un personnage ou d'un groupe à un ensemble de règles considérées comme établies, relevant donc de la coutume ou d'un code, principalement code d'honneur, manquement impliquant conflit, puis,

---

2 Voir Philippe Haugeard, "Un baron révolté est-il un hors la loi? Droit et violence dans *Girart de Roussillon*," *Cahiers de Recherches Médiévales* 18 (2009): 279–91.

3 Voir Gérard Giordanengo, "Coutume et droit féodal en France (XIIe–XIVe siècle)," *Féodalités et droits savants dans le Midi Médiéval*. Collected Studies Series, 373 (Aldershot, Hampshire, UK, and Brookfield, VT: Variorum, 1992) chap.XV. Voir également, du même auteur, "Le *Roman de Thèbes*, un roman féodal," *Qui des sept arz set bien entendre… Études sur le* Roman de Thèbes, ed. Bernard Ribémont (Orléans: Paradigme, 2002), 193–99; "Féodalité et droit féodal. Quelques observations", *Histoire et Images médiévales* 15 (Nov./Déc. 2008, Janvier 2009): 4–11. Philippe Haugeard, "Un baron révolté est-il un hors la loi? Droit et violence dans *Girart de Roussillon*," *Cahiers de Recherches Médiévales* 18(2009): 279–91. Bernard Ribémont, "Droit du seigneur, droit du vassal dans la chanson de geste," *Médiévales* 11/12 (2010): 199–210. On rappellera à ce sujet que les *Libri feudorum* sont une compilation lombarde tardive ajoutée au *Corpus juris civilis* et que la rédaction des Coutumes est tardive; par ex. le *Très ancien coutumier* et la *Summa de legibus Normanniae in curia laïcali* datent du milieu du XIIIe s.

4 La rédaction des coutumiers n'est officielle qu'à partir du milieu de XVe siècle; ils sont auparavant rédigés à partir du XIIIe siècle, surtout en France du Nord, à partir d'initiatives privées, comme celles des *Établissements de Saint Louis*, recueil de différentes coutumes, de Philippe de Beaumanoir, bailli de Philippe III, de Jean Bouteiller, lieutenant du bailli de Tournaisis ou de Jacques d'Ableiges, bailli d' Évreux.

par un retour nécessaire à l'équilibre, règlement de ce conflit. Un tel schéma repose sur une structure qui, aux variations et habillages divers près, se décline en cinq étapes: 1) constat, implicite et allant de soi ou bien souligné, d'un ordre; 2) rupture de cet ordre; 3) identification des coupables de la rupture; 4) évaluation/jugement de la culpabilité des coupables; 5) résolution ou tentative de résolution du conflit. Celle-ci peut ne pas se produire ou être sans arrêt remise (geste des Lorrains par exemple); sinon, elle se réalise en général selon deux directions: la première est interne et apparaît comme le résultat d'une procédure judiciaire. La seconde est externe et relève soit de l'intervention divine par le miracle (*Pèlerinage de Charlemagne*) ou par la prise de conscience et l'élévation spirituelle du héros (*Girart de Roussillon*), soit d'un départ en guerre contre les sarrasins (*Charroi de Nîmes*), cette dernière surplombant le conflit et le réduisant à néant; on aura d'ailleurs souvent la conjonction des deux situations (*Chevalerie Ogier*, *Girart de Vienne*).

Je m'intéresserai ici au premier cas, en m'interrogeant sur le traitement du crime dans les chansons de geste du Moyen Âge central. Cette recherche conduit donc à considérer d'une part ce que l'épopée interprète comme crime et d'autre part de quelle façon elle évalue la peine qui s'y rapporte. Le contexte épique favorise la mise en place de situations criminelles particulières, qui ressortissent à l'esthétique de la violence et à la mise en lumière de valeurs guerrières et viriles, ce qui conduit les jongleurs à mettre souvent en scène des homicides. Ces derniers relèvent de deux catégories: selon la première, l'homicide, qui peut avoir de très graves conséquences, est factuel; il est le fruit d'un hasard, d'un funeste concours de circonstances: tel est le cas par exemple lorsque, dans *Jourdain de Blaye*, Lothaire, le fils de Charlemagne, s'en revenant de Saint-Jacques avec son père, et avisant une bataille sous Blaye, se précipite de façon inconsidérée dans la mêlée, ne sachant qui a droit ou tort, et se fait malencontreusement occire par Jourdain. Charlemagne se laissant dominer par le sentiment de la vengeance lignagière, voue sa haine à Jourdain et se rallie ainsi au traître Fromont, sans prendre la peine de juger du cas. Il reviendra sur ses dispositions à la fin, lorsque, sous une forme étonnante qui ressemble quelque peu avant l'heure à une demande officielle de rémission, prié par Rénier, il pardonnera à Jourdain.

Le cas de *Huon de Bordeaux* est proche, tout en étant plus complexe. Huon et son frère Girard, sur la demande de Charles, quittent Bordeaux pour aller faire leur hommage. Mais le traître Amaury monte la tête du jeune Charlot, fils peu malin de Charles, et le convainc de l'accompagner dans un guet-apens tendu aux Bordelais. Charlot se précipite à la rencontre de Huon et de Girard et, sourd aux explications pacificatrices des Bordelais, il blesse Girard; ce qui provoque la colère de Huon, qui tue Charlot en combat. Arrivé à la cour de Charlemagne, Huon l'accuse de trahison; l'empereur, qui ne comprend guère la situation, promet de venger le crime, mais Huon affirme ne pas connaître les agresseurs, ce qui est la vérité absolue. Arrive alors Amaury avec le cadavre de Charlot et il désigne Huon comme meurtrier. Charlemagne entre en rage et veut immédiatement tuer Huon, ce dont l'empêche le sage Naimes. Une procédure judiciaire est alors engagée, sous forme de duel judiciaire. On remarquera au passage le rôle de Naimes, au demeurant traditionnel, qui représente le garant de la justice, celui qui connaît la coutume et tente de la faire toujours appliquer.

Avant le duel, Charlemagne impose une condition particulière, à savoir que le coupable doit avouer. Mais le déroulement du combat, durant lequel Amaury montre encore son caractère de traître, fait que Huon lui coupe la tête avant qu'il ait pu avouer sa forfaiture. Toutes les aventures de Huon sont engendrées par cette clause inhabituelle qui, si elle n'apparaît pas dans la *chanson de geste* en général, témoigne cependant d'une vision plus claire du duel judiciaire; ce dernier en effet, d'après les documents d'archives, arrive rarement à terme et encore plus rarement à la mort d'un des deux champions[5]; l'aveu ou la conciliation étant avant tout le but recherché, souvent atteint dès le serment. On peut également voir ici, le reflet, déformé et réinvesti dans l'économie épique, d'un élément essentiel de la condamnation à mort, tel que le précise par exemple le *Coutumier d'Artois*: "nus le puet iestre mis amort par nul jugement, s'il ne connoist de sa propre volonté, sans contrainte de prison et sans autre force faite."[6]

Ces remarques faites, venons-en à la deuxième catégorie de crime de sang. Celle-ci peut à son tour être décomposée en deux parties. La première ressortit au meurtre ou à l'assassinat[7] et s'inscrit aisément dans un contexte qu'il est fréquent de considérer comme relevant du manichéisme épique. Le second cas est plus complexe et n'implique pas une vision linéaire, voire stéréotypée, car l'homicide est le résultat d'une suite d'événements pouvant le justifier, ou du moins impliquant un débat (*Chanson de Roland*, *Ogier*, *Renaut de Montauban*, *Raoul de Cambrai*).

On peut considérer que la première de ces deux situations est la plus conforme à ce qu'il est courant de considérer comme relevant du manichéisme et de l'hyperbole épiques. Dans ce cas en effet, le meurtrier et le traître se voient dotés d'un portrait souligné au trait noir, leur châtiment ne peut être qu'exemplaire et leur mort inéluctable et infamante.

---

5 Voir, par exemple, Bruno Lemesle, *Conflits et justice au Moyen Âge* (Paris: Presses Universitaires de France, 2008), 186–87 et bibliographie.

6 *Coutumier d'Artois*, éd. Adolphe Tardif (Paris: Picard, 1883), 109.

7 Rappelons que la notion d'assassinat n'existe pas en droit romain ni en droit pénal au Moyen Âge. Il faut attendre la loi du 25 septembre 1791 pour que soit précisé que l'homicide avec préméditation est qualifié d'assassinat.

Remarquons à ce propos que la mise à mort infamante et cruelle – pendaison[8], écartèlement, écorchage – pose quand même problème dans un univers de protagonistes appartenant à la classe chevaleresque et particulièrement fiers de leur position sociale. Il n'est donc pas forcément simple d'appliquer des peines infamantes autrement que sous forme, au demeurant récurrente, de menace.[9] Le jugement d'un seigneur, même traître, n'est pas toujours immédiat, comme le prouve le cas de Ganelon. Les peines infamantes seront donc appliquées le plus aisément du monde aux non-chevaliers, aux brigands en particulier, comme dans le *Moniage Guillaume* où, par deux fois, Guillaume pend à un arbre les corps des brigands qu'il a défaits.[10] Lorsqu'il s'agira d'un *miles*, l'exécution sera partie prenante d'un système de fort contraste, soulignant le caractère particulièrement odieux et surtout un comportement radicalement opposé à celui que l'on attend d'un chevalier. Il faut que le condamné n'ait aux yeux de l'auditeur ou du lecteur aucune excuse à son comportement.

Dans un registre analogue, mais *ex negativo*, la punition infamante – qui ne peut être en ce cas mise en œuvre – est édictée par le ou les traîtres contre un innocent, ce qui souligne leur félonie et prépare en quelque sorte leur propre châtiment à venir. Une telle situation se rencontre dans *Gaydon* où tout le préparatif de la pendaison de Ferraut, ordonnée par le traître Hertaut, est décrit par le jongleur. Mais *in extremis* Gaydon vient sauver Ferraut[11] qui, en toute logique sera pendu sans le moindre procès, Savari indiquant clairement "Ainsiz va d'omme qui mainne traïson" (v. 4684), formule lapidaire qui paraît en écho de certains propos que l'on trouve dans les coutumiers. *Gaydon* offre une autre scène de pendaison ratée riche d'enseignements. Les traîtres qui entourent Charles, décidément aveugle et sourde aux injonctions du héros de la chanson, complotent le meurtre de Gautier, afin de semer le désordre dans le royaume. Ils vont donc organiser un guet-apens pour se saisir de lui. On est donc dans une circonstance, relevée par les coutumiers, d'organisation de meurtre avec préméditation.

Mais, au lieu d'un assassinat pur et simple, les traîtres décident d'une pendaison qui permettrait un maximum de publicité au forfait. Évidemment, le forfait ne réussira pas, les incidents – sans aucun doute voulu par Dieu – se multipliant, de façon même cocasse (l'échelle casse) – et Gautier réussissant à se libérer et à

8 Sur la pendaison dans la *chanson de geste*, je renvoie au bel article de Valérie Naudet, "'Aval le vent la poudre esparse'. La pendaison dans la chanson de geste," *Crimes et châtiments dans la chanson de geste*, ed. Bernard Ribémont. Circare, 2 (Paris: Klincksieck, 2008), 203–33.

9 Tel est le cas, entre autres, dans le *Couronnement de Louis*, envers les prélats qui ont trahi le roi Louis. Guillaume demande à ses barons quelle peine ils doivent encourir et c'est la pendaison qui est prononcée. Mais la peine ne sera pas appliquée, Guillaume se contentant d'arracher les crosses des évêques et de battre ces derniers.

10 *Le Moniage Guillaume*, éd. Nelly Andrieux-Reix (Paris: Champion, 2003), v. 1626–33 et v. 2440–45.

11 *Gaydon*, éd. et trad. Jean Subrenat (Louvain and Paris: Peeters, 2007), 302–05.

assommer ses adversaires. On est ici dans le cadre d'un véritable monde à l'envers où une parodie d'exécution vient souligner la noirceur des traîtres. Des *realia* sont ici à l'œuvre dans le champ épique, l'économie de la narration les détournant de leur fonction: exposition du corps au vu et su de tous mais cette fois-ci non à titre d'exemple, mais de moteur de crise; Providence intervenant par un accident empêchant l'exécution de la peine, incident dirimant au yeux de la justice médiévale.[12]

Quant au meurtrier de nos chansons, il ressortit le plus souvent à la catégorie du traître, ce qui correspond bien à une conception courante du meurtre, si l'on en croit Philippe de Beaumanoir qui explique que "Nus murtres n'est sans traïson."[13] Une telle situation apparaît dans *Jourdain de Blaye*, autour du personnage de Fromont. Celui-ci est un traître patenté: du lignage de Hardré, il est marqué génétiquement, un topos de la *chanson de geste*[14]; sa trahison est surtout motivée par l'envie, la cupidité – le désir de posséder Blaye et de devenir riche et puissant–, qui l'entraînent au meurtre et à la spoliation de Jourdain, héritier légitime de Blaye. Il fait exécuter Girart et sa femme, de nuit, dans leur lit, marque suprême de trahison. Il décapite ensuite lui-même un petit enfant, le fils d'Erembourc et de Renier, croyant qu'il s'agit de Jourdain. Preuve de son absence totale de scrupule et de loyauté, il va jusqu'à faire couper le nez à ses deux plus fidèles complices, sous le seul prétexte qu'il a perdu le sien, tranché par le jeune Jourdain. Le jongleur a donc voulu marquer le personnage de Fromont des attributs les plus sombres; pour ce faire, il entoure le crime du maximum de circonstances aggravantes.

Celles-ci sont de deux ordres: ordre moral, le meurtre étant largement motivé par la cupidité, même si Fromont prétend s'inscrire dans un cycle de *faide*, voulant venger Hardré, tué loyalement par le père de Jourdain dans la chanson *Ami et Amile.*[15] En fait, plus que de vengeance légitime, il s'agit, auréolé d'envie, de haine, de celle que Philippe de Beaumanoir dénonce comme synonyme de trahison: "Traïsons si est quant l'en ne moustre pas semblant de haine et l'en het mortelment si que, par l ahaine, l'en tue ou fet tuer."[16] Il s'agit de haine contenue,

---

12 Voir à ce sujet, Claude Gauvard, *'De grace especial': Crime, État et Société en France à la fin du Moyen Âge*, 2 vol. (Paris: Publications de la Sorbonne, 1991), 179–82; id., *Violence et ordre public au Moyen Âge*. Les médiévistes français, 5 (Paris: Picard, 2005), 68.

13 Philippe de Beaumanoir, *Coutumes du Beauvaisis*, t. 1, éd. Amédée Salmon (Paris: Picard, 1899), 430.

14 Voir, entre autres, les traîtres d'*Aye d'Avignon* ou de *Gaydon*.

15 Au sujet des question juridiques unissant *Ami et Amile* et *Jourdain de Blaye*, voir mon article "Épopée médiévale et questions de droit. Règlement des conflits, résolution des tensions: le cas d'*Ami et Amile* et de *Jourdain de Blaye*," *Romanistische Zeitschrift für Literaturgeschichte* 31 (2007): 249–61.

16 Philippe de Beaumanoir, *Coutumes* (voir note 13), 430.

donc masquée par hypocrisie, ce que le jongleur montre bien en dessinant un Fromont se présentant comme un bon vassal à Girart, avant de l'assassiner. Le personnage apparaît également comme lâche, prétentieux, tyrannique. D'autre part, s'il ressortit à l'hyperbole épique, cet exemple concentre aussi dans la fiction des éléments renvoyant à la conception juridique médiévale du meurtre. Selon la coutume de Touraine et d'Anjou par exemple, la première définition du meurtre repose sur les circonstances: "Murtres si est d'ome ou de fame quant l'en la tue en son lit, ou en aucune meniere por coi ce ne soit en mellée."[17] Est donc coupable de meurtre celui qui tue hors d'un contexte de guerre; la mise en avant de l'homicide perpétré sur une personne en son lit montre que cette circonstance est considérée comme aggravante.

Dans ses *Coutumes du Beauvaisis*, Philippe de Beaumanoir, en donnant lui aussi sa définition du meurtre, abonde dans le même sens, en mentionnant la nuit comme circonstance de l'homicide: "murtres si est quant aucuns tue ou fet tuer autrui en aguet apensé puis soleil esconsant dusques a soleil levant."[18] Dans la *Somme rural*, Jean Bouteiller explique que la procédure extraordinaire peut être appliquée pour les coupables de "grands crimes et enormes [] faits repostement."[19] Fromont a également très bien organisé son crime, avec l'aide de deux complices les "serfs" à ses ordres: la préméditation est donc patente, circonstance aggravante par excellence.[20] Une charte d'Arras datant de 1194 sanctionne ainsi de la peine de mort (*capud pro capite*) tout crime de sang prémédité (*scienter*).[21]

La punition sera donc à la mesure et du crime et de la noirceur du personnage. C'est pourquoi, à la fin de la chanson, la description du procès est réduite à sa plus simple expression et l'accent mis sur la punition, qui s'étend au-delà de la justice humaine, l'âme du meurtrier immédiatement conduite en Enfer:

> Pour le jugement, tous furent assemblés, princes, comtes, seigneurs et vassaux tenant fief. Ils ont suffisamment parlé et délibéré, si bien que tous se sont à la fin mis d'accord pour que le fieffé traître soit écorché vif. Ce qui fut fait sans attendre. Ils ont lié Fromont à un cheval de bât et l'ont traîné parmi la cité, en contrebas. […] Ils tirent Fromont jusqu'à un fossé existant depuis longtemps; ils l'ont écorché comme un bœuf

---

17 *Établissements de Saint Louis*, éd. Paul Viollet, t. 2 (Paris: Renouard, 1881), 37–38.

18 Philippe de Beaumanoir, *Coutumes* (voir note 13), 429. Voir aussi, dans les coutumes de l'Orléanais, la rubrique *De apeler home de murtre te de traïson*, où la circonstance "nuitantre" est soulignée (*Établissements de Saint Louis* (voir note 17), t.2, 358

19 *Somme rural, ou le grand coustumier général de practique civil et canon. Revue, corrigé sur l'exemplaire manuscript, illustré de commentaires & annotations*, l.1, tit.13, éd. Louis Charondas le Caron (Paris: Mace, 1603).

20 Nicole Gonthier, *Le Châtiment du crime au Moyen Âge* (Rennes: Presses Universitaires de Rennes, 1998) 20sq.

21 Nicole Gonthier, *Le Châtiment* (voirs note 20), 94.

> cornu. Il a fini sa vie dans une cruelle souffrance. Les diables, les créatures de l'Enfer ont emporté son âme.[22]

Le narrateur sous-entend que le débat a porté sur la nature châtiment, plus que sur l'évaluation de la faute et de sa punition. Le propos du jongleur implique que la punition est surtout motivée par un sentiment prégnant dans le genre épique, la vengeance qui, *in fine*, occulte l'exemplarité du supplice. Mais celle-ci n'est pas pour autant effacée et elle correspond à certaines pratiques d'infamie mises en œuvre au Moyen Âge. Fromont, avant d'atteindre le lieu de son supplice, est ainsi traîné à travers la cité, ce que préconisent un grand nombre de coutumiers, comme celui d'Artois qui indique qu'"hom atteint de murdre [ ] doit iestre trainés et pendus"[23]; pour Philippe de Beaumanoir, il en va de même: "Quiconque est pris en cas de crime et atains du cas, si comme de murtre, ou de traïson, ou d'homicide, ou de fame esforcier, il doit estre trainés et pendus."[24]

Dans *Jourdain de Blaye*, le condamné est certes traîné, mais nulle mention n'est faite de spectateurs de la cité; Fromont est écorché dans un fossé et rien n'est dit d'une éventuelle exposition de son corps. Le jongleur mentionne seulement que la compagnie de Jourdain a assisté au supplice, ce qui est conforme au droit coutumier qui spécifie qu'aucune pénalité ne doit s'accomplir sans témoin. Ici, les spectateurs sont limités à l'entourage de Jourdain: la vengeance a été accomplie, de façon cruelle, ce qui rétablit l'équilibre selon une justice qui se révèle donc, *in fine*, surtout d'ordre privé et relevant de la *faide*.

Girart de Roussillon offre également une scène de punition infamante, par pendaison. Le traître Richier avait permis la conquête du château de Roussillon par Charles; la reconquête de la place forte va permettre la vengeance. Ici encore, les circonstances de la trahison sont nocturnes: Richier quitte le camp de Roussillon de nuit, va trouver Charles et lui propose de trahir, uniquement pas cupidité: "Queu[s] rendra Rossillon, fera ou gent?/S'il en aura en France nul chasement?" demande le traître dès le seuil de la tente du roi.[25] Lors de la victoire de Girart de Roussillon, Fouque poursuit le traître qui tente de s'échapper et, l'ayant saisi par les cheveux, il le pend aussitôt sur un gibet situé en haut d'une colline, le jongleur précisant que le corps du pendu se balancera là à tout jamais, ce qui correspond à la réalité et à une vision exemplaire du supplice, le corps

---

22 *Jourdain de Blaye*, trad. Bernard Ribémont (Paris: Champion, 2007), 149.

23 *Coutumier d'Artois*, éd. Adolphe Tardif (Paris: Picard, 1883), 111. Dans les images de supplice qu'elle étudie, Christiane Raynaud indique une fréquence de 1/5 de scènes où le condamné est traîné; Christiane Raynaud, *La violence au Moyen Âge* (Paris: Le Léopard d'or, 1990), 45. Voir les exemples donnés par Nicole Gonthier, *Le Châtiment* (voir note 20), 128–29.

24 Philippe de Beaumanoir, *Coutumes* (voir note 13), t. 1, 429. On trouve également de nombreux exemples, pour la fin du Moyen Âge, dans le *Registre criminel du Châtelet*.

25 *Girart de Roussilon*, éd. Micheline De Combarieu, Jean Subrenat (Paris: Librairie Générale de France (Lettres gothiques), 1993), v. 959–60.

exposé devant montrer à ceux qui le voient les risques encourus en cas de crime grave.

Dans une chanson tardive, composé au tournant du XIVe siècle, *Baudoin de Sebourc*, on rencontre une situation-type analogue à celle du *Jourdain de Blaye* du XIIIe siècle. Ici le traître odieux et, tel Fromont, paré de tous les défauts – convoitise, envie, cupidité, lâcheté, déloyauté, orgueil – Gaufroi de Frise – qui a même un cheval significativement nommé Fauvain –, est le sénéchal du roi Ernoul; il s'éprend de Rose, la femme de ce dernier et, à la suite d'une trahison sanctionnée par une alliance lucrative avec les sarrasins (un navire chargée d'or), Gaufroi réussit à éliminer ses concurrents, les chrétiens étant quasiment tous tués lors d'une bataille navale et Ernoul fait prisonnier. Faisant croire à la mort de celui-ci, Gaufroi épouse Rose, puis intrigue à la cour de France, enferme Rose dans une tour et épouse sa propre sœur, empoisonne le roi Philippe et se fait proclamer régent, avec l'espoir de se débarrasser du dauphin.

Mais tout a une fin et Gaufroi, vaincu, finira traîné et pendu,[26] conformément à ce que disent la plupart des coutumiers qui, lorsqu'il s'agit de meurtre et de trahison, préconisent la peine de mort par pendaison, précédée de l'exposition infamante du condamné, traîné sur une claie, ou attaché à un cheval, jusqu'au lieu du supplice. L'auteur de *Baudoin* donne un certain nombre de détails qui soulignent la vengeance contre un traître fieffé: Gaufroi est traîné, puis il est attaché les membres écartelés avec une lourde pierre sur le ventre; on le couronne d'un oignon, on danse autour de lui; les marmitons lui coupent maintes phalanges, puis il est enfin traîné et pendu à Montfaucon. Le jongleur souligne que l'exécution est publique, "Par devant tout le poeple."[27] Mais ici aucune forme de procès n'apparaît pour juger de la nature de la peine: Gaufroi a été vaincu par Baudoin en combat singulier et, au vu de l'ensemble de ses diverses infamies, la punition semble aller de soi: humiliation, torture, pendaison.

Nos chansons cependant ne se cantonnent pas à une criminalité aussi immédiate et, souvent, les cas sont plus complexes et permettent ainsi d'offrir des développements plus sophistiqués sur l'appréciation du crime et de sa punition. Le cas de Ganelon, qui fait date, est à ce titre fort intéressant. Si l'on prend la chronologie des événements à rebours, on part effectivement d'un motif de peine infamante: Ganelon est écartelé, avec quelques détails du supplice, ce qui assez rare dans les premières chansons de geste:

> Quatre destrers funt amener avant,
> Puis si li lient e les piez e les mains.
> Li cheval sunt orgoillus e curant;

---

26 Sur cet épisode, voir Claude Roussel, "Crimes et châtiments dans *Baudoin de Sebourc*," *Crimes et châtiments dans la chanson de geste* (voir note 8), 155–78.

27 *Baudoin de Sebourc*, ed. Larry S. Crist (Paris: Société des Anciens Textes Français, 2001), v. 24070.

Quatre serjanz les acoeillent devant,
Devers un ewe ki est en mi un camp.
Guenes est turnet a perdiciun grant;
Trestuit si nerf mult li sunt estendant
E tuit li membre de sun cors derumpant:
Sur l'erbe verte en espant li clerc sanc.[28]

Cependant, avant d'en arriver là – c'est-à-dire à une vengeance – Charles a dû défendre ce qu'il considérait comme son droit. En effet, la *Chanson de Roland* pose un problème complexe en terme de droit, dans le sens de savoir qui a raison ou qui a tort. La complexité de la question apparaît dès le début de la chanson, lisible à travers un topos, celui du portrait. Contrairement à ceux qui lui succèderont, tels Hardré ou Fromont, Ganelon est doté d'un portrait fort louangé: il est beau, fier, noble, altier. Il est courageux, comme le prouve son attitude première lors de son ambassade auprès de Marsile. Il est significatif que, décrivant le procès, le jongleur fasse une remarque relevant ce caractère complexe du parâtre de Roland: "S'il fust leials, ben resemblast barun" (v.3764). Le nœud de la question est de savoir si Ganelon est véritablement un traître. Car n'avait-il pas, après le débat contre Roland, le droit, peut-être même le devoir d'exercer la *faide?* Roland, en envoyant son parâtre à une mort quasi certaine, trahit un membre de son lignage. Le problème est que, pour exercer sa vengeance, Ganelon s'allie avec les ennemis, militaires et religieux, de son suzerain.

Quant à la "fleur de France" tuée à Roncevaux à cause de Ganelon, faut-il la considérer comme composée des alliés de Roland, contre lesquels Ganelon peut exercer une légitime vengeance, ou bien comme les barons de Charlemagne que Ganelon trahit? Dans un tel contexte, nulle justice expéditive n'est possible et Ganelon ne peut qu'avoir droit à un procès. Il me paraît d'ailleurs très significatif que le jongleur ait jugé nécessaire de préciser, juste à ce moment, que c'est dans l'"anciene geste" (v.3742) qu'il a trouvé que Charlemagne a convoqué ses vassaux. La coutume, sanctionnée par le temps, fait autorité et le procès est bien le résultat de l'application rigoureuse de la procédure. Charlemagne ouvre le plaid en demandant à ses barons de "juger selon le droit" (v. 3751), formule soulignant la nécessité de traiter le cas en terme de justice, avec plaid de l'accusation et de la défense. Charlemagne joue ici le rôle de celui qui prononce devant l'assemblée de justice – composée de ses barons – la *calumpnia,* selon une procédure accusatoire, effectivement en vigueur à la fin du XIe siècle. Il énonce ainsi les crimes de Ganelon (laisse 272). Ce dernier répond vivement, en récusant l'accusation de traîtrise:

---

28 *Chanson de Roland,* édition et traduction Jean Dufournet (Paris: Garnier Flammarion, 1993) v. 3964–72.

Dist Guenelon: "Fel seie se jol ceil!
Rollant me forfist en or et en aveir,
Pur que je quis sa mort e sun destreit;
Mais traïsun nule n'en i otrei." (v. 3757–60)

À ces paroles, les barons répondent qu'ils vont délibérer. Le jongleur, cependant, tient quand même à marquer le caractère négatif de Ganelon: en effet, Roland lui a bien fait tort, mais pas sur le plan matériel de son or et de ses possessions. Le code d'honneur est ici détourné pour faire place à une qualification de cupidité. En fait, ce biais, que l'on peut considérer comme un effet d'annonce par rapport à la mort infamante qui attend Ganelon, ajoute à la complexité de la situation et du personnage.

La laisse suivante en effet développe le plaidoyer de Ganelon qui, ici, relate les événements selon le code d'honneur du lignage: Roland a fait tort à Ganelon qui a le droit de se venger. Et pour parer l'accusation de trahison des barons de Charles, il englobe Olivier et tous les compagnons de Roland. Une fois encore, effet formulaire soulignant bien la complexité du fait de droit, les Francs répondent qu'ils vont délibérer. Dans la laisse suivante est évoquée la pendaison, peine dont parle Pinabel en rassurant Ganelon et que reprend Thierry, lorsqu'il offre ses services à Charles, en considérant que Ganelon est un traître. Mais l'assemblée de justice n'en juge pas ainsi et préfère manifester le désir de règlement du conflit: Roland est mort, rien ne le fera revenir. L'ensemble des Francs considère qu'il faut en rester là, arrêter le procès et demander seulement à Ganelon de servir son empereur avec amour et fidélité. Il s'agit donc de renouer avec l'"amor" ou l'*amicitia,* donc de rétablir le fonctionnement normal de relations féodo-vassaliques. Le duel judiciaire est finalement décidé, ce qui, dans la réalité de la procédure des XIe–XIIIe siècles, période où cette pratique est attestée avec une certaine régularité, correspond à une impasse juridique.[29] Ganelon sera finalement condamné à cause de la victoire de Thierry sur Pinabel et, curieusement, il n'est plus question de pendaison pour Ganelon. En revanche, le duel ayant décidé, tous les Francs sont alors unanimes pour pendre tous les otages, sans que cela semble poser le moindre problème.

Dans un registre analogue, bien qu'assez différent quant aux données, je citerai un deuxième et dernier exemple, fourni par la chanson *Aspremont*. Nous sommes cette fois en domaine sarrasin où va se dérouler à la cour d'Agoulant un fort long

---

29 Paul Ourliac, "Le duel judiciaire dans le sud-ouest," *Études d'histoire du droit médiéval* (Paris: Picard, 1979), 253–58. Jean-Marie Carbasse, "Le duel judiciaire dans les coutumes méridionales", *Annales du Midi* (1975): 385–403. Hélène Couderc-Barraud, "Le duel judiciaire en Gascogne d'après les cartulaires," *Le Règlement des conflits au Moyen Âge,* Actes du XXXIe congrès de la Société des Historiens Médiévistes de l'Enseignement Supérieur, éd. Société des Historiens Médiévistes de l'Enseignement Supérieur (Paris: Presses de la Sorbonne, 2001), 97–115. Bruno Lemesle, *Conflits* (voir note 5).

procès, destiné à juger les rois Maragon et Aprohant, accusés de trahison. Ces derniers étaient aux côtés d'Eaumont, fils d'Agoulant lors d'une bataille contre les Francs. Ces derniers ont réussi à submerger les armées sarrasines – Eaumont sera d'ailleurs tué – et Marangon et Aprohant, jugeant la situation désespérée, mais ignorant le sort d'Eaumont, sont repartis bride abattue pour avertir Agoulant. L'orgueilleux émir, apprenant la défaite de son fils, sans pour autant connaître son sort, considère immédiatement que les deux messagers sont des traîtres et propose de les pendre comme larrons. Cependant, il semble que cette justice personnelle et immédiate ne puisse fonctionner, même en contexte épique, car, justement, les deux accusés ne sont pas des brigands mais des nobles. Agoulant convoque donc tous ses barons, afin de juger ceux qu'il considère comme traîtres et responsables de la mort de ses hommes sur le champ de bataille.

S'en suit un long plaid qui s'étale sur plus de 600 vers, preuve de la complexité de l'affaire. Effectivement, le plaid se prolonge car alternent les interventions de la défense et du soutien à Agoulant; ici, tout est question d'appréciation, car il n'y a aucune preuve de la trahison. La défense repose sur la noblesse des deux hommes, en qui Eaumont avait mis sa confiance: c'est donc un argument de *fama* qui entre en jeu et l'on sait combien celui-ci est important en matière de justice médiévale. La voix de la sagesse se fait entendre par l'entremise du roi Achart qui propose de fait une procédure inquisitoire en demandant que le procès soit remis jusqu'à plus ample information sur ce qui est réellement arrivé à l'avant-garde d'Eaumont. À l'extrême, Sinagon considère que la fuite et l'arrivée de Maragon et Aprohant sains et saufs signe leur trahison, trahison qui a entraîné la mort supposée de ses fils et qu'en conséquence ils doivent être pendus, puis leur corps brûlé et les cendres dispersées. Il précise que ce traitement montrera à toute l'armée la réalisation de leur "vengoisson,"[30] de leur vengeance donc. On voit ici la rencontre entre un châtiment exemplaire, conforme à un jugement de crime odieux et la vengeance privée. L'intervention de Matusalon révèle encore un autre aspect de la question: lui aussi suggère la procédure inquisitoire en rappelant que les faits ne sont pas encore connus et il insiste sur le danger d'infliger une mort honteuse à de puissants nobles entourés d'un important lignage. Ce que Matusalon indique est bien le danger du déclenchement d'une *faide*, ce que, justement, l'exercice de la justice, seigneuriale ou royale, a tenté de juguler.

La conclusion du procès est assez inattendue; en effet, la succession des plaids révèle une impasse qui devrait se conclure par une ordalie ou un duel judiciaire. Mais le jongleur a choisi une autre voie qui allie deux enjeux esthétiques, celui de la violence et celui du judiciaire. Il joue pour ce faire sur ce que l'on peut

---

30 *Chanson d'Aspremont*, présentation, édition et traduction par François Suard d'après le manuscrit 25529 de la BNF. Champion classiques: Série "Moyen Âge", Éditions bilingues, 23 (Paris: Champion, 2008), v. 5798.

considérer comme une amorce de duel, c'est-à-dire sur le succès de l'intimidation, ce qui, comme le prouvent les documents d'archives, intervient assez régulièrement, au seuil d'un duel qui, alors, n'a pas lieu. Dans *Aspremont*, le roi Ulien menace l'assemblée, l'amustant en particulier, d'une double violence. La première émanant de lui, en terme de défi qui évoque le duel judiciaire: quiconque veuille le combattre, qu'il s'arme! La deuxième ressortit à l'exercice d'un pouvoir absolu, voire tyrannique: si l'assemblée décide dans un sens différent des sentiments d'Agoulant, ce dernier les fera tous tuer dans la nuit qui suit. Ces affirmations intimidantes concluent l'affaire de façon radicale, le jongleur notant que ces paroles firent "estuper" les barons, soit, pour reprendre la belle traduction de François Suard, leur a "cloué le bec." Ulien, qui devient le porte-parole de l'assemblée de justice sans autre forme de délibération, s'adresse à Agoulant pour proposer la pire des punitions, que je donne dans la traduction de François Suard:

> Livrez-les au supplice à l'instant,s ans hésiter; faites-les traîner à travers l'armée et à travers la ville devant tout le monde. Faites-en recueillir les restes, sans en perdre aucun, puis jetez-les dans un bourbier puant. Que quatre-vingt ou cents femmes légères, qui vendent leur corps pour de l'argent, soient gratifiées chacune d'un besant: elles viendront toutes avec joie; que chacune fasse à cet égard ce qui convient, et qu'on voie parfaitement ce spectacle; ensuite jetez sur les restes le feu grégeois. Celui qui se venge autrement d'un traître lui fait trop d'honneur s'il le pend au gibet.[31]

C'est effectivement ce supplice qui est retenu; le jongleur précise que l'on recueille chaque lambeau de chair, aussitôt jeté dans un cloaque, devant une large foule, en partie composée de prostituées. L'hyperbole épique est mise au service du soulignement de l'infamie de la peine. Un paroxysme est ici atteint, qui règle définitivement l'affaire, par une forme de terreur en quelque sorte, qui, dans le contexte de la guerre contre les chrétiens, efface toute velléité de vengeance du lignage des suppliciés.

Que conclure (provisoirement) des éléments précédemment évoqués? Il me semble que ces exemples sont révélateurs de la richesse du champ judiciaire dans la *chanson de geste*, qui prend à son compte un ensemble de données ressortissant à la pratique de la justice et au droit coutumier: prise en compte de la *fama*, rejet appuyé de l'homicide associé à la traîtrise – qui montre l'importance du code d'honneur – , applications de peines infamantes selon des procédures proposées dans les coutumiers. Mais ces *realia* s'inscrivent dans un champ littéraire où ils entrent au service d'une esthétique propre à la *chanson de geste*. Si le crime et la trahison offrent un support privilégié à l'exercice de l'hyperbole, s'ils participent d'une esthétique de la violence caractéristique de la *chanson de geste*, ils sont également les vecteurs d'une exploitation complexe de questions juridiques. Entre

---

31 Suard, ed., *Chanson d'Aspremont* (voir note 30), 414–15.

code d'honneur et droit coutumier, la *chanson de geste* pose la question de l'identification de la culpabilité, en rapport à la faute et à la place occupée par le suspect dans la hiérarchie sociale, à la puissance de son lignage.

Elle pose également la question du rapport entre la faute et la peine et donc à la façon de régler un conflit. Les solutions offertes ressortissent dans la majorité des cas au traitement violent, conforme à l'esprit de l'épopée médiévale. En cela, la *chanson de geste* préfigure, dans la fiction, une conception exemplaire, donc cruelle, de la peine, telle qu'on la retrouve chez divers chroniqueurs de la fin du Moyen Âge, tels un Philippe de Vigneulles. Mais, si l'issue se condense sur la violence, le déroulement des plaids, la mise en place de situations aboutissant à une procédure, sont surtout révélateurs d'une conscience du complexe chez les jongleurs. On revient donc ici, plus qu'à une notion de droit, à celle d'un 'pré-droit', notion essentiellement mouvante, faite de coutume et de code d'honneur, à l'aune de la puissance d'une part, de la parole et de l'expérience, d'une forme d'*auctoritas* d'autre part. À l'abri du droit savant qui commence à se répandre, la *chanson de geste* reflète ces fluctuations tout en jouant avec, construisant ainsi une véritable esthétique du juridique/judiciaire.

Chapter 2

Susanna Niiranen
(The University of Jyväskylä, Finland)

"I know how to be a whore and thief" The poet's Reputation: Troubadours—Ancestors of *poètes maudits*?[1]

Since medieval troubadours are best known for their love-songs and invention of courtly love as well as their close connections to the ruling power, they are not easily connected in our mind with the low life (e.g., whores, thieves, drinking, gambling) and with offences viewed as injurious to public morals (e.g., lewdness, adultery, and violence), not to mention with crimes such as murder. However, there are several references to a criminal or at least transgressive way of life both in troubadours' life and works. The question arises how the roles of court poet and love poet could embrace the antisocial behavior and image of certain troubadours or whether there was already an emergent tradition of the culture of *poètes maudits*? And in general, what were the determining characteristics in medieval poet's reputation and remembrance?

In medieval and early modern context, the modern use of the term *poète maudit* ("accursed poet") is restricted to association with the fifteenth century poet François Villon but not used for other medieval poets who seem to have the same characteristics and combination of genial artist, law-breaker, and tragic lover. From Villon, there are only some two hundred years to the poetic flowering of the troubadours and even less to the *trouvères*, whose influence was felt in northern

---

1 This article has been written within the projects *The Philosophical Psychology, Morality and Politics Research Unit*, Finnish Centre of Excellence, and *Medieval States of Welfare*, both funded by the Academy of Finland.

France like that of Villon's. If they share common characteristics with the image that the poet Villon represents, why is Villon (or his legend) the first to manifest the role of the poet at the margins of society? While researching for my doctoral dissertation,[2] I began to think about this aspect: troubadours who came from various social backgrounds and who represent various forms of artistic expression as well as the women troubadours who unanimously represent the aristocratic genre and whose reputation was— in contrast to troubadours— unstained.

The aim of this article is to observe continuities (or discrepancies) in the poet's role and commemoration in medieval and later periods as well as their gendered uses through the modern concept of *poètes maudits*. The term might appear to some as anachronistic but, in the strict sense, the terms and categories such as crime, gender, genre, or *trobairitz*, are conceptions of later generations which should, of course, be redefined each time in relation to their own historical context. However, it has recently been argued that historians have the right to make use of their knowledge of the remote consequences or interpretations of past actions and discuss past activities as ancestral to modern phenomena.[3] Even though the *retrogressive or retrospective* approach is not widely applied in this study, it has brought together new scholarship also in the field of medieval studies.[4]

The French expression *poètes maudits* means literally "accursed poets." The term came into wider usage after Paul Verlaine's series of essays called *Les poètes maudits* published in 1884. In this book, the term was used uniquely for the then little known symbolist poets.[5] Since Verlaine, the term has included the misunderstood genius of the poets as well as the tragedy of their lives, often marked by self-destructive tendencies. Abuse of drugs and alcohol, insanity, crime, violence, and any social offence, often resulting in an early death, are typical

---

2 Susanna Niiranen, "*`Miroir du mérite´: Les valeurs sociales, rôles et image de la femme dans les textes médiévaux des trobairitz*," Jyväskylä Studies in Humanities 115 (Jyväskylä: University of Jyväskylä, 2009). Electronic version at https://jyx.jyu.fi/dspace/handle/123456789/19676 (last accessed on Nov. 1, 2010).

3 Interest in the retrogressive or retrospective approach in history is rooted in the Annales School, see, e.g., Marc Bloch, *Les caractères originaux de l'histoire rurale francaise* (Oslo: H. Aschehoug, 1931); See also, Nick Tosh, "Anachronism and Retrospective Explanation: In Defence of a Present-Centred History of Science," *Studies in History and Philosophy of Science Part A* 34.3 (2003): 647-59.

4 E.g., *The Retrospective Methods Network* (*RMN*) is concerned with strategies and approaches for the diachronic study of cultural phenomena, using later evidence to offer insights into earlier periods. The first conference of the network was on Sept. 13 and 14, 2010 in Bergen, Norway, where the *RMN Newsletter,* a bi-annual electronic publication, was formulated. http://www.uib.no/cms/en/konferanse/2010/04/international-conference-new-focus-on-retrospective-methods (last accessed on Nov. 1, 2010)

5 Tristan Corbière, Arthur Rimbaud, Stéphane Mallarmé, Marceline Desbordes-Valmore (the only female writer included in Verlaine's list), Villiers de l'Isle d'Adam, and Pauvre Lelian, "Poor Lelian," an anagram of Paul Verlaine's own name, Paul Verlaine, *Les Poètes Maudits* (Paris: Léon Vanier, 1888), 1.

elements of the life of a *poète maudit*. In consequence, this group is frequently related to decadence and to the Decadent movement. Its poetic symbolism developed the themes of mysticism and otherworldliness, inevitability of death, and malignity of sexuality.[6]

We are indebted to Théophile Gautier who rediscovered Villon as an ancestor of the *poétes maudits*. With Gautier's interpretation, Villon as a poor and radical youngster, was refashioned into a romantic poet who served as a model for several Parisian poets of the nineteenth century.[7] There were similar tendencies in his image already in the fifteenth century, for in a booklet called "The free meals of Master Villon and his companions," Villon's reputation was determined as that of an errant trickster, vagrant thief, and sympathetic voice of the poor only some fifteen years after his disappearance. This collection of tales from the end of the fifteenth century is crucial in the formation of the image of Villon as we know it today.[8] His assumed way of life and his close relationship to criminal marginality and unhappy love affairs all combine to create a cult-like image of this poetic genius.[9] As for the earlier period, mainly the twelfth and early thirteenth century, we know that Occitan troubadours demonstrated their great concern for their artistic reputation and for the way in which their behavior ennobles them, or makes their reputation fall.[10] This persistence of rhetoric expresses not only limits of self-satisfaction, public praise, or fame but values, behavior, and attitudes considered appropriate in society.

---

6 Poet Albert Samain called sexuality "fruit de mort à l'arbre de la vie" (fruit of death upon the tree of life) and "fin du monde" (end of the world), Albert Samain, "Luxure," *Au jardin de l'infante* (1889; Paris: Mercure, 1920), 179, 188.

7 Théophile Gautier, *Les grotesques* (Paris: Michel Lévy Frères, 1859), 1–39.

8 Jelle Koopmans, "François Villon: Character Within or Without His Own Poetry?,"*The Author as Character: Representing Historical Writers in Western Literature*, ed. Paul Franssen and Ton Hoenselaars (Madison, NJ: Fairleigh Dickinson University Press, and London: Associate University Press, 1999), 68–79; here 71. See also the contribution to this volume by John Gough.

9 See, for instance, Marc Martín, *Villon, ce hongrois, ou, l'édification du culte de François Villon en Hongrie*. Officina Hungarica (Budapest: Nemzetközi Hungarológiai Központ, 1995); Jean Favier, *François Villon* (Paris: Fayard, 1982), especially 143–45, 193–98, and 334–42; see also the contribution to this volume by John Gough, "The Function of Projected Pain: The Poetry of François Villon and the Gift of Self."

10 Nicole M. Schulman, *Where Troubadours were Bishops: The Occitania of Folc of Marseille (1150-1231)*. Studies in Medieval History and Culture (New York, London: Routledge, 2001), 11; Deborah H. Nelson, "Northern France," *A Handbook of the Troubadours*, 255–261; here 257 (see note 10).

Troubadours

As Simon Gaunt and Sarah Kay have beautifully stated, troubadours "are part of the furniture of our cultural knowledge, an unforgettable heirloom in the European heritage."[11] This tradition of poets-composers-performers (460 of whose names we know) flourished in southern parts of France, Occitania and neighboring European courts with their songs, some 2500 of which survive. This considerable amount of texts contains various genres and styles but what posterity knows, apart from some politico-satirical or religious *sirventes*, is their love songs, *cansos*. The most famous troubadours, such as Jaufre Rudel (the motif of faraway love) and Raimbaut d'Aurenga ("archetype of the courtly troubadour"),[12] are also remembered for their legendary lives with an aura of romantic or tragic love. In addition, there is a group of troubadours, who are famous *only* by virtue of their lives and not for their songs. This group consists of such names as Guilhem de Cabestanh (the motif of the eaten heart)[13] and Guilhem de la Tor (extreme passion towards his dead wife). These last examples demonstrate particularly the close relationship of love and death, the model of fatal love and "love's martyrdom" in troubadouresque discourse.[14]

---

11 Simon Gaunt and Sarah Kay, "Introduction," *The Troubadours: An Introduction* (Cambridge: Cambridge University Press, 1999), 1–7; here 1.

12 Leslie Thomas Topsfield, *Troubadours and Love* (Cambridge: Cambridge University Press, 1978), 111.

13 The jealous husband killed the troubadour and gave his heart to the unfaithful wife to eat. When she had eaten it, her husband told her what it was and she threw herself from the window and was killed. The story is known outside the Occitan region in different versions: e.g., a contemporary version by a French trouvère, Châtelain de Coucy, which belongs to the end of the twelfth or to the beginning of the thirteenth century and a later version of Boccaccio's in *Decameron* (tale IV.9.). Questions of intertextuality among these works remain obscure, but Boccaccio cites a "Provencal" source at the story's opening. The source with which Boccaccio was familiar is in all likelihood the medieval biography (*vida*) of Guilhem de Cabestanh, See Susanna Niiranen's paper, "Troubadours, Obsessive Love and the Motif of Eaten Heart," Session 617, The Use of Emotions and Gestures, International Medieval Congress, Leeds, 11 July 2006; a Middle High German poet, Konrad von Würzburg, also wrote a version in one of his verse narratives, "Das Herzmäre," in the second half of the thirteenth century, see, Rüdiger Brandt, *Konrad von Würzburg: Kleinere epische Werke*. Second edition (1999; Berlin: Erich Schmidt, 2009), 79–90; see, also Milad Doueihi, "Cor ne Edito," *Modern Language Notes* 108.4 (1993): 696–709; Jacques Le Goff, "Head or Heart? The Political Use of Body Metaphors in the Middle Ages," *Fragments For a History of the Human Body*, 3 vols, ed. Michel Feher with Ramona Naddaff and Nadia Tazi, trans. Anna Cancogni et al. (New York: Zone, 1989), III, 12–27.

14 About the bond of love and death in troubadour poetry, see, Simon Gaunt, *Love and Death in Medieval French and Occitan Courtly Literature: Martyrs to Love* (Oxford, New York, et al.: Oxford University Press, 2006), 1–72.

However, when we read a *sirventes* of Raimon d'Avinho,[15] in which he says that "E sai far putas e lairons", (I know how to be a whore and thief) or a *vida* of Guilhem Magret,[16] in which it is said that he was a gambler and a tavern-frequenter, it is absolutely a question of the same troubadour culture even though they are not immediately connected with the idea of cultural trappings and traditions in the European heritage. In what way and to what extent then were troubadours *poètes maudits* of their time or associated with the low life and by what criteria was their reputation defined?

As far as we know, very few troubadours broke the law to such a degree that they were taken to court and officially punished. Some of them were imprisoned but such cases (e.g., Bartolomeo Zorzi,[17] Richard Coeur de Lion[18]) were related to warfare. Nonetheless, several of them were accused of having loose morals as well as of behaviors that were considered "deviant" in their society. In the following, I will examine various cases of transgressions and crimes committed by the troubadours and the consequences of those actions in the form of regular punishments, such as excommunication and exile, but particularly the consequences to their reputation as poets. The *vidas* and *razos*, usually referred to together as biographies of the troubadours, are vital in the development and diffusion of fame and ill-fame, first in their initial oral or written form and 50–100 years later in a structurally and stylistically uniform written style. Still today, the reputation of an individual troubadour is commonly based on biographies simply for the reason that they constitute the most abundant surviving source of information about the Old Occitan poets.

---

15 Raimon d'Avinho, *Sirvens sui avutz et arlotz, Chrestomathie Provençale accompagnée d'une grammaire et d'un glossaire*, ed. Karl Bartsch. 5th edition (1866; Berlin: Wiegandt & Schotte 1892), col. 210, line 20.

16 Jean Boutière and Alexander-Herman Schutz, *Biographies des troubadours. Textes Provençaux des XIIIe et XIVe siècles* (Paris: Nizet, 1964), *vida* of Guilhem Magret, 493.

17 Bartolomeo Zorzi was an Italian troubadour and a merchant, who travelled to Constantinople in 1266 and was taken captive in a war with Venice, and was a prisoner in Genoa until 1273. During this time he continued to compose, see the *vida* of Bartolomeo Zorzi, Boutière-Schutz, *Biographies des troubadours*, 576–77 (see note 16). According to Hans-Erich Keller, both *vidas* for Zorzi seem to be reliable, Hans-Erich Keller, "Italian Troubadours," *A Handbook of the Troubadours*, 295–305; here 301 (see note 10).

18 Medieval biographers tell us that *reis Richartz* (Richard Coeur de Lion) wrote a *sirventes* called *Dalfins, jeus voill deraisner*, Boutière-Schutz, *Biographies des troubadours* 1964, *razo* E of Dalfi d'Alvergne, 294–95 (see note 16) and whose relations with the world of the troubadours are well-known, e.g., two troubadours treated in this article, Gaucelm Faidit and Guilhem de Bergueda dedicated their *planhs*, lamentations on his death, to him, *Anthologie des troubadours*, ed. Pierre Bec, Gérard Gonfroy, and Gérard Le Vot. Bibliothèque médiévale (Paris: Union Générale d'Éditions 1979), 227; see, also Bezzola's discussion of "Richard et les troubadours," Reto R. Bezzola, *Les Origines et la formation de la littérature courtoise en Occident (500- 1200)*, 3 vols. (Paris: Champion, 1944-63), III, 220–27.

Guilhem de Bergueda— a Murderer

Guilhem de Bergueda was a Catalan troubadour and viscount of Bergueda whose name appears in various documents between 1138 and 1192. With his thirty surviving poems he is among the most prolific Catalan troubadours of the twelfth century. Most of his songs are *sirventes,* marked by violence and obscenity, from which it has been easy to draw conclusions about his later life as a murderer and as a murder victim.[19] In his *sirventes,* he insulted Raimon Folc, the viscount of Cardona, whom he considered a political rival. On several occasions he participated ardently in feudal struggles in the district. The influential viscount of Cardona sought to ally himself with Alfonso II (another enemy of the troubadour) but in 1175 Guilhem de Bergueda treachrously assassinated Raimon Folc. He was exiled from Catalonia and was not heard of for several years. When his tracks reappear in sources again, it seems that the troubadour and the king were on the road to reconciliation, for in 1185 he figured among Alfonso's supporters at a meeting with Richard Coeur de Lion at the castle of Najac in Rouergue, to confirm their alliance against Raimon VI of Toulouse. The troubadour did not lack enemies but the only information we have about his death is that he was assassinated around 1195 by an ordinary foot- soldier (*peon*).[20]

In his life, Guilhem de Bergueda was associated with his fellow troubadours Pons de Capduelh, Peire Vidal, and Aimeric de Peguilhan but his closest colleague was undoubtedly Bertran de Born, with whom he shared, among other things, a liking for conflict. In their poems they called themselves by *senhals,* certain kind of pseudonyms, like "Tristan," underlining male friendship but they used also the attribute "fraire," brother, in addressing to each other. If Bertran's poems were in praise of war and a warrior's virtues spiced up with the horrors of battle, his fellow Guilhem went much further in his brutality and enmity. His virulence, which has no equal in the troubadour repertoire, appears also in the level of language, for instance in the use of vocabulary.[21] His poetic crudity is addressed in particular towards his adversaries, whom he accuses of multiple murders, rapes, and sodomy.[22] Martín de Riquer, who wrote an exhaustive study of

---

19 Martín de Riquer, "L'ancienne `vida´ provençale du troubadour Guilhem de Berguedan," *Actes de mémoires du 1er Congrès International de langue et littérature du Midi de la France.* (Collection Publications de l'Institut méditerranéen du Palais du Roure - Avignon, Fondation Flandreysy-Espérandiau, 3 (Avignon: Palais du Roure, 1957), 56–67, 64–65.

20 *Anthologie des troubadours,* ed. Pierre Bec et al., 180 (see note 18).

21 Frank M. Chambers, *An Introduction to Old Provençal Versification.* Memoirs, 167 (Philadelphia: American Philosophical Society, 1985), 164; *Anthologie des troubadours,* ed. Pierre Bec et al., 180–81 (see note 18).

22 See, for instance, *Ben ai auzit per cals rasos,* Martín de Riquer, *Guillem de Berguedà,* 2 vols. Scriptorium Populeti, 5 and 6 (Espluga de Francoli, Spain: Abadía de Poblet, 1971), II, 123.

Guilhem de Bergueda's life and work, highlights Guilhem's taste for obscenity stating that "no troubadour is superior to him in that aspect."[23] To some extent, his uninhibited (and male-centered) attitude towards lust and sex resembles that of William IX of Poitiers, as De Riquer points out. Similarly to William of Poitiers's, Guilhem de Bergueda's work did not merely consist of political actualities or obscenities since he also knew perfectly well how to compose graceful love songs in a "conventional" way, such as *Quan vei lo temps*.[24] What William of Aquitaine and Guilhem de Bergueda share more is a reputation as womanizers to such a degree that in the Catalan troubadour's case Boutière and Schutz calls it "donjuanisme."[25]

It would be imprudent to draw sweeping conclusions about his psychology but suffice it to say that he seems to have spent most of life in a male-dominated (homo) social environment marked by a strong warrior ethos to which he himself contributed as best he could. On the basis of documents, such as wills and testaments, and other sources related to him, he did not have a wife or official descendants.[26]

According to his *vida*, Guilhem de Bergueda killed Raimon Folc of Cardona and the incident is supported by other contemporary records,[27] which is one example of many of the events and places *vidas* report which are authentic. The *vida* for Guilhem actually contains a series of verifiable incidents and has proven to be one of the most faithful reconstructions of historical events among all the surviving *vidas*. Similarly, as Elizabeth W. Poe points out, the short synopsis of the Albigensian Crusade at the beginning of one of the *razos* for Raimon de Miraval is reliable in every detail. On the other hand, the end of the same *razo* is far away from the truth, something which an enlightened reader might easily observe. In general, the most accurate area of biographical information is not necessarily related to the deeds or vicissitudes of an individual troubadour or to the historical context, but to the geographical information about his home district and his travels, which are, of course, interconnected. Nevertheless, it is useful to bear in mind that the value of *vidas* and *razos* does not lie with their realistic reporting of the past but more in their own function describing and introducing a poet and his or her work in prose form as an essential part of this lyric-dominated tradition.[28]

---

23 De Riquer, *Guillem de Berguedà*, vol. I, 182 (see note 22).

24 De Riquer, *Guillem de Berguedà*, vol. II, 219 (see note 22).

25 Boutière and Schutz, *Biographies des troubadours*, 529, n. 4 (see note 16).

26 De Riquer, *Guillem de Berguedà*, vol. I, 18 (see note 22).

27 De Riquer, *Guillem de Berguedà*, vol. I, 519 (see note 22).

28 Elizabeth W. Poe, "The *Vidas* and *Razos*," *A Handbook of the Troubadours*, 185–97; here 190 (see note 10).

Clashes with the Church

Already the first known troubadour, William IX, Duke of Aquitaine, transgressed insomuch as he was excommunicated by the Church. This procedure was generally used for actions such as heresy, schism, apostasy, issues of internal governance, murder, and sexual (mis)conduct. From the late eleventh century, the Gregorian reform gave an impetus to this sanction, which became an important expedient for the Church against disobedient lay powers.[29]

There is dispute about the chief cause of the excommunication of the first known troubadour which began in 1114 and lasted until 1117 but, apparently, his extra-marital liaisons (sexual misconduct) caused clashes with the Church together with the ducal and ecclesiastical power struggle for lay and clerical control in the region.[30] Due to William's social position, contemporary Latin writings provide an ample supply of material on these events as well as on the duke's life and personality. These sources include Anglo-Norman chroniclers' accounts of his controversies with the Church and some Latin poems in praise of the bishop who excommunicated William and whom the duke persecuted. As they sketch a portrait of an eminent duke-troubadour and particularly describe contemporary attitudes towards his deviant behavior, I will focus my study mainly on William of Malmesbury's and Orderic Vitalis's chronicles. Bearing in mind that, in most cases, medieval chroniclers reported events and processes with which they had no direct connection, they often provide "a precious store of information on the expectations and fears, emotions in general and prejudices in particular, at a given time and in a given space."[31]

William of Malmesbury, who is the principal source of these incidents, relates in his *History of the English Kings,* that in 1114 first the papal legate Girard, Bishop of Angoulême, and then Peter, Bishop of Poitiers, excommunicated the duke for abandoning his legitimate wife and for refusing to end an adulterous liaison.[32]

---

29 According to the Church, excommunication, in the sense of a formal proceeding, is not a penalty, but rather a formal proclamation of temporary religious and social exclusion. The First Council of Lyons, 1245, stated that "the aim of excommunication is healing and not death, correction and not destruction" (canon 19), Elisabeth Vodola, *Excommunication in the Middle Ages* (Berkeley, Los Angeles, and London: University of California Press, 1986), 7.

30 See, Ruth E. Harvey, "The Wives of the 'First Troubadour,' Duke William IX of Aquitaine," *Journal of Medieval History* 19.4 (1993): 307–25.

31 Sophia Menache, "Chronicles and Historiography: The Interrelationship of Fact and Fiction," *Journal of Medieval History* 32.4 (2006): 333–45; here 345.

32 *William of Malmesbury, Gesta Regum Anglorum: The History of the English Kings I-II,* ed. R. A. B. Mynors, R. M. Thomson and M. Winterbottom. Oxford Medieval Texts (Oxford: Clarendon Press 1998–99), vol. 1, v. 437.2, 782.

Orderic Vitalis in turn tells us that William's wife, "countess of Poitou," herself raised the issue during the proceedings of the Council of Reims telling the Pope and the whole council that she had been deserted by her husband and the woman named Malberge, the wife of the viscount of Châtellerault, had replaced her in his bed.[33] Since William of Malmesbury does not name the duke's concubine, we do not know whether she is the same "Malberge" mentioned by Orderic or possibly another person. Several scholars share the opinion that she can be identified as the same lady.[34] The other name identified with the Viscountess Châtellerault is "Dangeirosa," The Difficult.[35] Another interpretation is that William requested an annulment of his marriage but was not successful. Nevertheless, his second legitimate son, Raimon, with his wife, Philippa, was born ca. 1115 (the exact date is not known) which has led to the conclusion that a brief reconciliation had taken place between the spouses after the first excommunication.[36]

William of Malmesbury presents two accounts of the excommunication of the troubadour-duke. If we are to believe the chronicler, William of Aquitaine replied with jests to the prelates, who exhorted him to change his way of life. In the first account, he is said to have quipped that the bald legate Girard, bishop of Angoulême, would require a comb for his forelock before he would repudiate his vice-countess. In the second one, the duke is said to have threatened Peter, bishop of Poitiers, with a sword, swearing to kill him if he did not pronounce absolution. The bishop calmly offered up his neck and invited William IX to strike but the duke put away his sword. This scene, along with the duke's dramatic and witty words while sheathing his sword: "If you are bound for heaven, expect no help from me" might be a literary contamination of other contemporary accounts. Chroniclers' liking, and especially the taste of the monk of Malmesbury, for entertaining stories is well known. Still, it is more than probable that he would not have applied these anecdotes to just anyone.

First, the use of colorful narration regarding his behavior might be taken as a signal of his ostentatious personality or second, of volatile tensions between ecclesiastical and ducal power in the region. The third possibility is that the combination of his personal characteristics along with his political position invited the use of colorful narration. Yet it is difficult to maintain that all conspicuous accounts related to William IX were the result of pure imagination or literary taste

---

33 *The Ecclesiastical History of Orderic Vitalis*, ed. Marjorie Chibnall, 6 vols. Oxford Medieval Texts (Oxford: Clarendon Press, 1969-1980), vol. 6, 258–60; Harvey scrutinizes the problem of the identification of the assumed wife of the duke whom Orderic Vitalis names "Hildegarde," Harvey, "The Wives of the 'First Troubadour,'" 309–15 (see note 30).

34 Harvey, "The Wives of the `First Troubadour,'" 316 (see note 30).

35 Pierre Bec, *Le comte de Poitiers, premier troubadour: À l'aube d'un verbe et d'une érotique* (Montpellier: Université de Montpellier, 2004), 12.

36 Harvey, "The Wives of the `First Troubadour,'" 321–22 (see note 30).

of the compilers. However, it seems that his extra-marital relationships brought him into open conflict with the Church, but closer investigation shows that his territorial ambitions certainly played a part in the matter. Namely, the duke's prompt reconciliation with his wife Philippa appears to be linked to the Poitevin attempts to assert authority in the Toulousain. Thus, the birth of the second son in Toulouse around the year 1115 can be explained by the project of securing the Poitevin presence in the south, Philippa's county, which finally lead William to war in 1123.[37]

As for his other mentioned characteristics, Orderic Vitalis depicts William IX primarily as a courageous knight and fighter. Incidentally, several chroniclers, both in England and in France (Orderic Vitalis, William of Malmesbury, Etienne de Bourbon), mention his aptitude for foolery and entertainments, which was seen as perfectly appropriate for an aristocratic and a troubadour. In contrast, his proclivity for affairs with women was seen in more pejorative terms, at least in the eyes of churchmen such as Geoffroi de Vigeois, Guibert de Nogent, Geoffroi le Gros, Gérard de Galles, and Hildebert de Lavardin.[38] Particularly, his presumed uncontrolled sexuality, as we have seen, seems to have been the target of resentment.[39] As if to confirm his behavior, some of his surviving poems treat (beyond more conventional love and political themes) adulterous adventures in a very daring way, using vulgar terms which are virtually pornographic, in the modern sense of the word.

The power of the *vidas* and *razos,* commonly referred to as biographies of the troubadours, was crucial in determining a troubadour's reputation. The essential source for the accounts given in *vidas* and *razos* is the troubadour poems. That *vidas* and *razos* draw widely on lyric texts is nothing new.[40] However, the *vida* of William, a short and anonymous biography[41] of the first known troubadour, does not rely on poems as its source of information or, if it does, the compiler does not show his possible resentment of the direct sexual imagery of some of William's poems known by the names *Lo gat ros*[42] (The red cat) or *La lei del con*[43] (The law of

---

37 Harvey, "The Wives of the 'First Troubadour,'" 321–22 (see note 30).

38 Latin references to William IX are collected in the appendix of Gerald A. Bond's edition, Gerald A. Bond, *The Poetry of William VII, Count of Poitiers, IX Duke of Aquitaine* (New York and London: Garland Publishing 1982), and most of them are also cited in Bec's edition *Le comte de Poitiers* (see note 35).

39 See, also Bec, *Le comte de Poitiers*, 18–19 (see note 35).

40 Poe, "The *Vidas* and *Razos,*" 185–90 (see note 28).

41 The shortness of a biography does not correlate with importance of the poet, Pierre Bec, *Chant d'amour des femmes-troubadours.* Moyen Age (Paris: Stock, 1995), 25.

42 *Companho, tan tai agutz d'avols conres*, Bec, *Le comte de Poitiers*, 166 (see note 35).

43 *Farai un vers, pos mi sonelh*, Bec, *Le comte de Poitiers*, 190–95 (see note 35).

the cunt). On the other hand, the biographer does not seem to be interested in his marital affairs or amorous activities more than is the average case in troubadour *vidas*. All known circumstances considered, the *vida* makes only moderate (but apparent) reference to him as a womanizer:

> Lo coms de Peitieus si fo uns dels majors cortes del mon e dels majors trichadors de domnas e bon cavaliers d'armas e larcs de domnejar, e saup ben trobar e cantar. et anet lonc temps per lo mon per enganar las domnas.[44]
>
> [The Count of Poitiers was one of the most courtly men in the world and one of the greatest deceivers of women. He was a fine knight at arms, liberal in his womanizing, and a fine composer and singer. He travelled for a long time through the world, deceiving women.]

The dispassionate attitude of the biographer might also be attributed to the time gap between events related to the first known troubadour at the beginning of the twelfth century and the writing of the *vida* in the first half of the thirteenth century. The time scale of one hundred years is enough to allow individual scandalous episodes to fade in the collective memory of a community. Moreover, the compiler or compilers come from the intermost circle of the troubadours since they are not clerics but troubadours themselves. It has been suggested with good reason that the compilers, at least two known troubadours mentioned by name in the surviving repertory of *vidas* and *razos*, collected the information already in circulation in oral or written form from among their colleagues. They doubtlessly added some of their own material but nevertheless turned *vidas* and *razos* into literature in a more or less systematic way.[45]

If we return to William IX and his remembrance during the troubadour period from the twelfth to thirteenth century, it is good to bear in mind, that his apparent tendency to various kinds of excess described in several sources represents not only his personal character but also his social standing. Early Occitan courts (in the eleventh and twelfth century) actually seek to reinforce their position and demonstrate their superior sophistication through activities which appear to us as arrogant and ostentatiously prodigal but whose fundamental purpose was to display wealth and power, and the aristocratic way of living as distinctive from the other social groups.[46] What makes his case ambiguous is the fact that his work includes songs containing all the conventions of the troubadour lyric in form and

---

44 *Vida* of Guilhem, "Lo coms de Peiteus," Boutière and Schutz, *Biographies des troubadours*, 7 (see note 16).

45 Poe, "The *Vidas* and *Razos*," 188–89 (see note 28).

46 See, Linda M. Paterson, *The World of the Troubadours* (Cambridge: Cambridge University Press, 1995), 100–01.

content as, for example, the descriptions of spring, the beauty of the lady, the desire to be with her, and a longing intensified by various obstacles such as social disparity, physical distance, or guards. As far as a "first known troubadour" is concerned, it has also been claimed that one cause for the clergy's reprehension was his use of the vernacular language in his poetry which may have irritated these teachers of Latin and may have caused tension between the lay and clerical elite.[47]

If William of Aquitaine was at the top of the social scale, troubadour Guilhem Figueira comes from the lower scale; he actually belongs to the lower bourgeoisie, a group which is well represented among the troubadours. He was the son of a tailor and himself a tailor by trade in Toulouse, active in the late period of the troubadours around the 1230's. This period was marked by the Albigensian Crusade— and as we shall see— the war was not without impact on the fate and reputation of the troubadour.

Guilhem possessed a critical mind and his criticism was mainly directed against the papacy as well as the assumed immorality of the clergy. He attacked the crusades, not only the Albigensian Crusade but also the failures of the crusades to the Holy Land, which he saw as manifestations of papal imperialism. Twelve of his poems are extant but his most renowned work, the *sirventes contra Roma,* actually entitled *D'un sirventes far,* was a strong reprimand of the papacy and of the Albigensian Crusade and also of the failure of the fourth and the fifth crusades, imperial policy, and the moral failings of the clergy. The poem was probably written between 1227 and 1229 while Guilhem was still in Toulouse and presumably in a position to witness firsthand circumstances and events in the besieged city. An emblematic passage states:

> Roma als Sarrazis
> faitz vos pauc de dampnatge,
> Mas grecs e latis liuratz a carnalatge.
> Ins el foc d'abis,
> Roma, faitz vostre estatge
> En perdicion.[48]
>
> [Rome, to the Saracens
> you do little damage

---

47 George T. Beech, "Contemporary Views of William, IXth Duke of Aquitaine, 1086–1126," *Medieval Lives and the Historian: Studies in Medieval Prosopography,* ed. Neithard Bulst and Jean-Philippe Genêt (Kalamazoo: Western Michigan University 1986), 73–87; here 83.

48 Katharina Städtler, "The Sirventes by Gormonda de Monpeslier," *The Voice of the Trobairitz: Perspectives on the Women Troubadours,* ed. William D. Paden. Middle Ages Series (Philadelphia: University of Pennsylvania Press, 1989), 129–56; here stanza VI, lines 43–46, 132.

But to the Greeks and Latins massacre and carnage;
In the fire of hell,
Rome you have your seat
In perdition.]

He uses derogatory expressions accusing the Church and the pope of greediness, treachery, simony, and killing the innocent. Consequently, the singing of Figueira's *sirventes* was outlawed by the Inquisition in Toulouse.[49] The troubadour is reported to be living as an exile in Lombardy (as many troubadours did while continuing to employ the Occitan language in poems) where he eventually made his way to Emperor Frederick II's court. Under this eminent protector, he was certainly encouraged to continue his criticism of the papacy. In his *sirventes*, he also promotes peace in Christendom, which did not restrain him from agitating for Fredrick to go on a crusade.

The power of his *sirventes* derives from the subject of a broad political conflict heavily loaded with ideological views and also especially from his literary skill. For example, the first stanza introduces the word "Roma," which later appears once or twice in every stanza of the poem, repeating the message that Rome is the main object of Guilhem's critique and the cause of all the evil things he enumerates in his long poem. He is also a master of alliteration, repeating key sounds in each stanza. Regardless of his easily recognizable poetic technique and power, his medieval biography portrays him as a certain kind of looser poet who frequented wretches, prostitutes, and tavern-keepers and was not welcomed among the nobles.[50] The *vida* makes no reference to the famous *sirventes* but expresses negative attitudes towards Guilhem's harsh criticism of the Church. According to Boutière and Schutz, the biographer was, if not an ecclesiastic, at least a partisan of Rome who feels it his duty to denigrate the reputation of Guilhem in the eyes of posterity.[51]

A woman called Gormonda de Monpeslier wrote a response, *Greu m'es a durar*, to the anti-papal *sirventes* of Guilhem Figueira following Figueira's poem in meter and rhyme for some twenty stanzas. She defends the Church and attacks the heretics. Her style is as ardent as Guilhem's, e.g., she expresses a desire to see Figueira tortured to death. Though nothing is known of Gormonda except for her name recorded in one of the manuscripts that preserves her *sirventes* and what can be deduced from her poem, it seems plausible that she was associated closely with the orthodox clergy, probably with the Dominicans of the region of Montpellier.

---

49 Elaine Graham-Leigh, *The Southern French Nobility and the Albigensian Crusade* (Woodbridge, Suffolk: The Boydell Press, 2005), 36.

50 *Vida* of Guilhem Figueira, Boutière and Schutz, *Biographies des troubadours*, 434 (see note 16).

51 *Vida* of Guilhem Figueira, Boutière and Schutz, *Biographies des troubadours*, 435, n. 3 (see note 16).

Nowadays, she is considered one of the Occitan women troubadours, the *trobairitz*, even if her poem is not of that aristocratic love-poem genre they mainly represent. Actually, Gormonda's poem is a rare example of the genre of *sirventes* attributed to a woman.[52] Since she has no *vida* or *razo* and no other references survive of her, it is a challenging task to make any hypothesis about her reputation. Is it a signal that there is not a single mention of her in any contemporary writings? Was she such a dissident in lay troubadour circles that ordinary troubadour promoters fell silent about her and her work? In modern times, Gormonda like other women troubadours, has been an object of a kind of rehabilitation in which she is credited with writing "the first French political poem by a woman."[53]

Gamblers, Tavern-Goers, and a Fool

In addition to these conflicts with the Church and accusations of loose morals, another group of more or less renowned troubadours were similarly accused of leading immoral lives but without any visible political or other ideological purposes. This group consists of gamblers and tavern-goers. Gaucelm Faidit (ca. 1170–ca. 1202), for example, in his *vida*, was said to be a fat man and a poor singer who only became a musician from necessity when he lost all his property through gambling. In addition, his wife, named Guilhelma Monja, was an ill-reputed *soldadeira*, a female entertainer, sometimes linked with prostitution. According to the *vida*, Guilhelma was also overweight. They had a son of whom we only know that his character was unsympathetic. Despite his bad reputation, Gaucelm Faidit was one of the most prolific troubadours of major importance and whose protectors were the most eminent people of the time (e.g., Richard I of England, Boniface of Monteferrat, and Geoffrey II, Duke of Brittany). About seventy of Gaucelm's songs survive. He dedicated at least thirteen songs to Maria, viscountess of Ventadorn, a woman troubadour herself, a perfectly respectable lady, as are all the Occitan women troubadours depicted in medieval sources.

In Gaucelm Faidit's case, the biographer is in all likelihood making a parody of the genre. The name of the troubadour is already leading the reader or the listener into

52 See Angelica Rieger, Trobairitz: der Beitrag der Frau in der altokzitanischen höfischen Lyrik. *Edition des Gesamtkorpus*. Beihefte zur Zeitschrift für romanische Philologie, 233 (Tübingen: Niemeyer, 1991), 44–45; See also Catherine Léglu, "Did Women Perform Satirical Poetry? Trobairitz and Soldadeiras in Medieval Occitan Poetry," *Forum for Modern Language Studies* 37.1 (2001): 15–25.

53 In her article on Gormonda, Städtler presents the editions of both Gormonda's and Guilhem's songs, Städtler, "The Sirventes by Gormonda de Monpeslier," 129 (see note 48).

the world of deliberate mockery of the usual, sophisticated conventional imagery of *vidas* since the word *faidit* means "outlaw" or "worthless one." The biographer certainly knows that Gaucelm was a nobleman and enjoyed the patronage of many eminent persons whose taste becomes at the same time the object of criticism in the *vida*. Humorous statements, surprising juxtapositions and equations as well as various puns follow one after another. It is legitimate to ask whether the biographer is laughing at troubadours, at rulers, or perhaps at some empty literary conventions he considers corny?[54]

Troubadour Guilhem Magret was also said to be a gambler. According to his *vida* he could not keep the money he earned but frittered it away gambling and frequenting taverns. As a result, he could not afford to buy armor and was ill-equipped as a knight. For a knight, it was shameful and uncourtly to have to beg or borrow pieces of equipment.[55] In a *tenso* with Guilhem Rainol d'At he is despised by his debate partner as a "joglar vielh, nesci, badoc" (an old, silly, stupid *joglar*).[56] It is noteworthy that in this context, he is not called *trobador*, but *joglar*, generally a lower entertainer never associated with aristocratic troubadours. This entertainer is said to be in love with wine, which has caused his thinness and poverty. Despite this, there was nothing wrong with his songs; his biographer notes that he was well-liked and honored and his songs were good.[57]

In this context, it is possible to make a cautious genre identification. The *tenso* between Guilhem Rainol d'At and Guilhem Magret is an exchange of counterparts where "rivals" present one another's vices in an ironical fashion. The themes, language and humoristic tone are reminiscent of some *coblas* produced some decades later among the dispersed troubadours in the courts of Italy and Spain after the Albigensian Crusade. Colloquialism, even obscenity, together with a genuine attempt to entertain are distinctive marks of this genre, which cultivates themes such as prostitution, taverns, gambling and a caricaturized description of the adversary in a poem.[58]

---

54 Poe, "The *Vidas* and *Razos*," 191–92 (see note 28).

55 Paterson, *The World of the Troubadours*, 72 (see the note 46).

56 Guilhem Rainol d'At and Guilhem Magret, *Maigret, pujat m'es el cap*, line 37, Bonaugurio, *Rialto* 7.vi.2003. See at: http://www.rialto.unina.it/GlRain/231.3(Bonaugurio).htm (last accessed on Nov. 1, 2010).

57 *Vida* of Guilhem Magret, Boutière and Schutz, *Biographies des troubadours*, 493 (see note 16).

58 Guilhem Rainol d'At and Guilhem Magret, *Maigret, pujat m'es el cap*, note of the editor. See also Simon Gaunt, *Troubadours and Irony*. Cambridge Studies in Medieval Literature (Cambridge: Cambridge University Press 1989), esp. 5–38; Bonaugurio, *Rialto* 7.vi.2003 (see note 56).

The above-mentioned *sirventes*[59] of Raimon d'Avinho, ca.1230, in which he claims that he knows how to be a whore and a thief, does not belong to the same genre (it is not a *tenso* or an exchange of *coblas* and the style is not caricaturized or obscene even though related to the everyday life) as the "diaspora" poems, which contain a similar humoristic tone and theme. The main focus of the poem is not on taverns or brothels but on professions. The troubadour enumerates a long and humorous list of occupations he claims to have had. In this list, various craftsmen and merchants represent the majority, but also multifarious laborers, a priest, and a physician are mentioned. In my opinion, this variety reflects the professionalism of the troubadours and those manifold skills they were expected to master including the occupation of a thief ("stealing" or borrowing components of songs from other troubadours) and that of a prostitute (entertaining for money). The practice of "borrowing" from other texts was in general not condemned in medieval literature. On the contrary, borrowing lent prestige and authority, indicating both the poet's respect for and knowledge of the tradition in which he or she operates.[60] As for the role of money in the troubadour's occupation, see the footnotes 71 and 72.

The phenomenon of describing gambling, of frequenting taverns and prostitutes in various sources and literary genres is rather interesting from the point of view of personal reputation, which was essential in medieval society. According to Daniel Lord Smail's studies on medieval Marseilles, a wasteful life with money spent on drinks or gambling was considered in the law courts as a marker of a dishonest life and taverns were regarded as vile and dishonorable places. Certain witnesses were challenged on the grounds that they were "men of low status, dice-players, great deniers of God, and frequent tavern-goers."[61] Eating or drinking in a tavern was not necessarily incriminating but drinking in ill-famed "hopeless" (as it was said) taverns was a common attribute of defamed men. Nearly as common were two other accusations, that of fornicating (or pimping) and gambling. These accusations were associated with a man's economic failures implying the idea that he is managing his assets badly because he has been wasting them all on alcohol, prostitutes and gambling. Moral failure was not the excess of consumption but the wasting of one's wealth or associating with low-lives. Other accusations include

---

59 Raimon d'Avinho, *Sirvens sui avutz et arlotz*, Chrestomathie Provençale accompagnée d'une grammaire et d'un glossaire, ed. Karl Bartsch 5th edition (1866; Berlin: Wiegandt & Schotte 1892), "E sai far putas e lairons" (I know how to be a whore and thief), col. 210, line 20.

60 See Paul Zumthor, "Le carrefour des rhétoriqueurs: intertextualité et rhétorique," *Poétique* 7.27 (1976): 317–37; here 320.

61 Daniel Lord Smail, *The Consumption of Justice: Emotions, Publicity, and Legal Culture in Marseille, 1264–1423*. Conjunctions of Religion & Power in the Medieval Past (Ithaca, NY: Cornell University Press, 2003), 124–32.

quarrelsomeness, blasphemy, mendacity and begging, but these characteristics are rarely associated with the troubadours even though some of the troubadours were truly sharp-tongued and blasphemous, as we have seen.[62]

If Guilhem Magret really was a spendthrift and a drunk to such a degree that he could not furnish himself with the equipment of knight as his *vida* states, his only hope lay with compensating for these defects with his songs and his singing. The compensation pattern also suits the case of Peire Vidal because, even if he was neither a gambler nor a tavern-goer, he is the only troubadour described as a "fool." He is continuously called "fol" in his *vidas*, in the texts of his fellow poets and even in his own songs. Of course, there is an interconnectedness between all these three sources but for some reason, the theme of foolishness runs particularly through his biography as a *leitmotif*. His foolishness was often associated with (mis)adventures with women.[63]

In the courtly diction of troubadours, *follia* often signifies transgression because it reduces the lover's capacity for reasoning and makes him forgot the virtue of moderation. In this sense, *follia* is often related to daring behaviour.[64] There might be a correlation between the notion of *follia* and the status of *joglar* or that of *cantaire* (singer) who really do not represent good sense but who know how to blend common sense and folly in their poetry and, especially in their case, during the act of performance.[65] There are similar traits in William of Aquitaine's behavior or what we know of it.

Reputation of the *Trobairitz*

What about the women troubadours? It is not easy to compare an indeterminate but nevertheless small group of women troubadours[66] to the large number of men, but in the *vidas* of female troubadours, there are no mention of low life or

62 *Vida* of Guilhem de Bergueda, for instance, mentions briefly that the troubadour made good *sirventes* in which he spoke bad of some people and good of some others, Boutière and Schutz, *Biographies des troubadours*, 527 (see note 16).

63 Susanna Niiranen, "A Fool and a Troubadour: Folly in the Legend of Peire Vidal," *Behaving like Fools: Voice, Gesture, and Laughter in Texts, Manuscripts, and Early Books 1200–1600*, ed. Lucy Perry and Alexander Schwartz. International Medieval Research, 17 (Turnhout: Brepols, 2011), 47–64.

64 Glynnis M. Cropp, *Le vocabulaire courtois des troubadours de l'époque classique* (Geneva: Librairie Droz, 1975), 133–38.

65 Bec, *Le comte de Poitiers*, 55 (see note 35).

66 By modern scholars, Occitan women troubadours are commonly called *trobairitz* according to the term first used in the thirteenth century text, *Roman de Flamenca*. The word *trobairitz* is used very rarely in Old Occitan texts, as it does not occur in lyrical poetry, grammatical treatises, or in the biographies of the *trobairitz* or troubadours.

dishonest behavior. Women troubadours were never accused of hanging around in taverns, gambling, physical assaults, or associating with low-lives. Nor were they vilified as incapable of managing their assets. This is of course due to their high social standing but social status does not entirely explain the decency, at least as far as men are concerned, as we have seen in the case of William of Poitiers, Gaucelm Faidit, and Guilhem de Bergueda, who were nobles. For a poet's reputation, gender[67] appears to be a more important factor than his/her social group. According to *vidas*, *trobairitz* frequented decent places like castles and abbeys with their peers. In their poems, we meet other *domnas* like the *trobairitz* themselves and *amics*, male friends, as well as some female friends and husbands. Negative characters are represented by collective figures of *lauzengiers, gelos*, and *envejos* and negative emotions by expressions of lacking and frustration. Altogether, the choice of vocabulary (lacking) and syntax (abundant use of negations) has been considered significant and has been precisely interpreted as reflecting women's feelings of frustration. Sexual or political imagery (except for Gormonda's *sirventes*) was not their field and their channel of expression was restricted to the spheres of emotions and morality.[68]

An example of high morality associated with social values is manifested in the terms *pretz* (merit, esteem, reputation) and *onor* (honour, reputation), which correspond widely to the medieval conception of *fama*.[69] None of the *trobairitz* (23 in my corpus) enjoyed *mala fama* until in the seventeenth or possibly eighteenth century when the so-called Béziers manuscript was compiled.[70] It seems that their status was established and esteemed during the twelfth and thirteenth century, the golden period of the troubadours, and that they were distinguished from other female musicians such as *cantairitz* (singers), *joglaressas* (female joglars, plausably musicians), or *soldadeiras*,[71] performers, whose name derives from the word

67 About the problem of *gender* and authorship in the *trobairitz* canon, see Bec, *Le chant d'amour des femmes-troubadours*, 17–29 (see note 41); *Rieger, Trobairitz*, 29–47 (see note 52); Mathilda Tomaryn Bruckner, "The Trobairitz," *A Handbook of the Troubadours*, 214–20 (see note 10); Simon Gaunt, *Gender and Genre in Medieval French Literature*. Cambridge Studies in French, 53 (Cambridge: Cambridge University Press, 1995), 158–65; Niiranen, '*Miroir de mérite*,' 28–38 (see note 2).

68 Niiranen, '*Miroir de mérite*,' 200–05 (see note 2).

69 *Mala fama* is related here more with social infamy (*infamia facti*) born from scandals and idle talk than with legal infamy (*infamia iuris*), originating from Roman law, Winfried Trusen, "Der Inquisitionsprozeß: Seine historischen Grundlagen und frühen Formen," *Zeitschrift der Savigny-Stiftung für Rechtsgeschichte*, Kanonistische Abteilung 74 (1988): 168–230; here 180.

70 In the manuscript of Béziers, some of the *trobairitz* are depicted as cheap entertainers, raising their skirts and showing their legs, Bec, *Chant d'amour des femmes-troubadours*, 60 (see note 41).

71 Singers, jongleuresses, and female entertainers whose functions remain obscure. It has been suggested that *soldadeiras* worked in areas from music to prostitution, cf. Iberian *panaderas, serranas* and *soldadeiras*, Denise K. Filios, *Performing Women in the Middle Ages: Sex, Gender, and the Iberian*

soldada[72] (money), and whose suspicious reputation was inherited from the times of *mimae, scurrae* and *histriones*, condemned by Church moralists. For example, the portrait of the wife of Gaucelm Faidit, a *soldadeira* called Guillelma Monja, is heavily parodied in the *vida*[73] of the troubadour, which leads us to suggest that her position could not have been very highly esteemed or, alternatively, that her profession was related to burlesque and open to humoristic comments. One distinguishing feature in comparing female to male poets is that the *trobairitz* and other high-born *domnas* (and not ordinary *femnas, molhers, cantairitz,* or *soldadeiras*) figuring in *vidas* are never ridiculed, or their irony is far too sophisticated for us to be observed.

Double role of *domna* and Patroness

Strikingly, while the troubadours are parodied and criticized in their own works, where they comment on the works and styles of each other, and in the biographical texts, the *trobairitz* treat themselves and are treated by other troubadours with great esteem. Their social position leads to the double role of *domna* (source of inspiration) and patroness (source of material resources), the latter of which certainly softened the sharp tongues of the troubadours who depended on them. Concerning the information from biographies, it is possible, that after 50–100 years when the "lives" were compiled, the authors of *vidas* and *razos* did not know the *trobairitz* anymore and, without any specific reason to criticize, they chose the positive language register to promote unknown but decent poems of the *trobairitz*. The few manuscripts and abundant *unicas* in them prove that the popularity and diffusion of their works fell far short of that of the most illustrious troubadours, to whom dozens of songs are attributed often with numerous manuscript variations. Nevertheless, the *trobairitzs'* skill in composing is never questioned in contrast to that of many troubadours.

In Occitan law courts, women were most commonly discredited for their inability to governing their mouths, most generally for quarrels and gossiping while "good conversation" was essential in the array of favorable character traits.[74] This appropriation of "good conversation" is also found among the court

Lyric. The New Middle Ages (New York: Palgrave Macmillan, 2005), 179–89.

72 Cf. the word *soldadier* (mercenary soldier), Emil Levy, *Petit dictionnaire Provençal-Français,* (Heidelberg: Carl Winter, 1961), 349–50.

73 As to *vidas* as sources: even if their value lies not in their truthful reconstruction of real events, though occasionally they provide that as well, they can essentially reveal habits, attitudes and modes of conduct and thought attached to the troubadours' world (see notes 28 and 31).

74 Lord Smail, *The Consumption of Justice,* 128 (see note 61).

accomplishments and, for the women troubadours, in the form of "gent parlar," which means lenient, benevolent, and witty parlance. The term also implies that one's voice is neither too loud nor too quiet as well as a moderate speaking speed and was considered part of courtly behavior in which a person had a control over his or her speech and gestures and had agreeable appearance.[75]

Choosing the *pretz* (prestige, which could also be translated as `self-esteem')[76] more or less consciously, *trobairitz* themselves took care of their reputation between the roles of *domnas* (married women whose principal function in the troubadour culture was inspiring and rewarding men other than their husbands) and women-troubadours, evading the bad label of many medieval (female) artists and performers. However, the ideal of *pretz* did not prevent one of the *trobairitz*, Clara d'Anduza, from feeling a "great desire for celebrity."[77] In the same text, she is characterized stereotypically as skilled, agreeable, learned and beautiful. "Strategy of *pretz*" was thus adopted by the biographers, too, even if the trobairitz songs do not seem to have enjoyed great popularity. Similarly, compilers of *chansonniers* (troubadour manuscripts) esteemed the art of women troubadours to the extent that they often grouped them together in their own sections of manuscripts. Moreover, one Italian manuscript contains a remarkable amount of illustrations, miniatures of the *trobairitz*, but none of the troubadours. In this way, original manuscript buyers, copyists, and scribes participated in contributing—consciously or not—to the reputation of the *trobairitz*. The same remark is naturally valid in the terms of the troubadours.

Some Final Remarks

It seems that among the troubadours, any reputation was better than no reputation at all while for the *trobairitz* it was a more delicate question. This study confirms what we know about the gendered ideals and practices in the Middle Ages. Men had greater leeway than women, one indication of which is the physical and material space troubadours occupied on their journeys and at taverns. They also

---

75 Niiranen, '*Miroir de mérite,*' 174–75 (see note 2).

76 See, e.g., the song of Comtessa de Dia, where she lists all of her good qualities (also *pretz*) although her friend has left her: "Valer mi deu mos pretz e mos paratges / e ma beutatz e plus mos fis coratges / per qu'ieu vos mand lai ont es vostr estatges / esta chanson que me sia messatges" (My reputation and lineage should be of help to me, and my beauty and, still more, my true heart; for that I send to you out in your estate this song, which will be my messenger), Comtessa de Dia, *A chantar m'er*, lines 29–32, Bec, *Le chant d'amour des femmes-troubadours*, 102 (see note 41).

77 *Et ac gran volontat de pretz, Razo* of Uc de Saint-Circ, Boutière and Schutz, *Biographies des troubadours*, 244:3 (see note 16).

had a monopoly on various kind of excess in their behavior as well as the presence of humor in their verses.[78] In addition, what unifies these male poets is their anti-clericalism, which reflects the tension between the lay and ecclesiastical political and economical control in the Occitan region from the end of the eleventh until the mid-thirteenth century. Some of them substantiated the spectrum of male fantasies about women whereas *trobairitz* daringly expressed love and longing but more in sensual than in sexual terms. Women troubadours share more common characteristics as a group: they are all aristocrats and treated always with decency and esteem in different sources, Already in the Middle Ages they were treated as a collective and, consequently, their poems and biographies were collected together in manuscripts.

Examination of the construction of the medieval Occitan poet's reputation reveals that it is not question of a subgroup, genre, nor of his socio-economic situation. It is as multifaceted as is the body of Occitan (Limousin, Catalan, Toulousain, etc.) troubadours from the end of the eleventh century until the time of the Albigensian wars in the first decades of the thirteenth century and even beyond. The troubadours came from diverse social groups, from princes to nobles and knights, from merchants and craftsmen to lower classes, and adopted and developed distinctive styles of poetry. Considering this heterogeneity, the troubadours cannot be viewed as a monolith. In their reputation and in their later remembrance, there are some similarities to later *poètes maudits* starting from the abundant consumption of alcohol and amorous misadventures rejecting or accentuating the role of sexuality, and extending to medieval symbolism (use of allusions, metaphors, *senhals*, etc.), and to personal tragedies including premature death.

Their most distinctive feature compared with nineteenth-century poets is that the troubadours were not insecure about their poetic skills; on the contrary, they were extremely conscious of their poetic talent which they promote also in their colleagues, praising their fellows and their sophisticated technique, and encouraging poetic jousts between two or more counterparts, for instance. The compilers of *vidas* and *razos* organically participated in this poetic promotion and their power is undeniable in the process of developing a reputation. A reputation was defined not merely by biographies, but by the troubadours themselves, their patrons, audience, copyists, not forgetting the literary taste of the time. Even if medieval troubadours and their reputation do not entirely fit the category of *poètes maudits*, excluding some individual poetic tales because they were not tragic,

---

78 The exception may prove the rule, see the *tenso, Na Carenza ab bel cors avinen,* between Alaisina Iselda and Carenza which can be interpreted as an ironic parody about traditional love discourse. In the *tenso,* two women are discussing whether it is worthwhile to acquire a husband or a child, Bec, *Le chant d'amour des femmes-troubadours,* 131–35 (see note 41).

mystic or self-destructive enough, their transgressions and foolery were considered a part of their profession as entertainers, and in some sense, as teachers of morals and morality, as they often call themselves. The reversible roles of the "courtly lovers" amused, educated and seemed to appeal to some eternal sympathy for the successful rascal latent in human nature.

One aim of this article has been to show to what extent rascal characters have been used in forming a poet's reputation, and by what kinds of contemporary projections that use was justified. Particular attention has been devoted to the first legendary uses in medieval biographies. If it is evident that legends affect our reading, then one can ask whether a reader can approach the texts of William XI or Guilhem de Bergueda (or Villon or Rimbaud) without knowing their "lives" or "characters," or whether it would be better to open the anthologies without any knowledge of the context.

Moreover, the time scale poses more challenges to modern interpreters. Beyond Villon and known troubadours there is an abundance of anonymous works from the Middle Ages. The tendency to attribute them to well-known poets (as in the case of some supposed women troubadours) proves that the "characters" often formed by "lives" are more easily adopted than authors and texts by contemporary as well as subsequent audiences.[79]

[79] Koopmans, "François Villon: Character Within or Without his Own Poetry?," 77–78 (see note 8).

Chapter 3

Christopher R. Clason
(Oakland University, Rochester, MI)

The Law—Letter and Spirit: Language, Transgression and Justice in Three Medieval German Epic Poems

> "Who also hath made us able ministers of the New Testament; not of the letter, but of the spirit: for the letter killeth, but the spirit giveth life."
>
> (2 Corinthians 3:6)

Often in German medieval epics the hero must either overcome an imbalance in the configuration of personal virtues or (s)he must atone for some offense against heavenly or secular law. Commonly these imbalances or offenses are, at first, unknown or unwittingly committed, and the initial challenge to the hero is to discover the nature of the offenses before she or he can gain knowledge of humane and spiritual values, and finally set out on the path that returns her or him to the good graces of the social *ordo*. The ultimate arbiter of what constitutes offense, what one might term the "spirit of the law," is typically elusive, concealed within, behind or separate from verbal directives that I would like to group together as the "letter of the law": formulations, expressed verbally or in writing, of secular and ecclesiastical customs, statutes, commandments and other regulations.

While the letter-of-the-law is important for the codification of what is required of everyone in the courtly social network, knowledge of the spirit-of-the-law elevates the hero to a higher level of existence. The letter is consistent with an immature, underdeveloped state of consciousness that is bound to the literal word, while the spirit corresponds to mature, sophisticated understanding of what lies behind the written word. The letter may be associated with what is explicit, simple, generally applicable and, in a legal sense, superficial, while the spirit reflects that which is obscure, complex, individual and profound. The former tolerates no interpretation, while the latter demands it. Finally, the letter of the law holds a society together, while the spirit of the law elevates the individual to the highest levels of heroism, altruism and self-fulfillment.[1]

Thus, the question of letter vs. spirit of the law is partly a matter of semantics (in this case, how an expression transmits multiple meanings) and partly of psychology and epistemology (how one develops the ability to perceive and understand the multiple layers of meaning language can contain). Obviously, a thorough treatment of these matters is an immense undertaking, far beyond the scope of this essay. However, there may be some benefits to a judiciously brief and selective discussion of some aspects of this question, which seems to arise in a surprising number and variety of works.

The relationship between knowledge, justice and language comes strikingly into the foreground in three German epic poems of the High Middle Ages: Hartmann von Aue's *Der arme Heinrich,* Wolfram von Eschenbach's *Parzival,* and Gottfried von Straßburg's *Tristan und Isolde.* In all three, epistemology and language play significant roles in determining culpability and penalty, while worldly experiences and struggles provide backdrops and testing grounds for personal development and success (or failure), with profound implications for the characters' spiritual growth and welfare. The letter of the law provides social cohesion. However, the characters in each of the literary works under discussion must move beyond the mere letter to an understanding of the law's spirit—and as a result, they often act in their own self-interest and contrary to the obvious, normative "letter." Hence, the literary works present many ideals that run in opposition to the social structure, and perhaps threaten the social *status quo* with erosion and even disintegration.[2]

---

1 Thus, the relationship between "letter" and "spirit" as I define it incorporates the essential aspects of the traditional semantic/semiotic problem of the relationship between signifier and signified; in this regard, several seminal biblical texts, undoubtedly well-known by medieval authors, present this issue in a similar light, such as, "Woe unto you, scribes and Pharisees, hypocrites! for ye pay tithe of mint and anise and cummin, and have omitted the weightier [matters] of the law, judgment, mercy, and faith: these ought ye to have done, and not to leave the other undone" (*King James Bible* [1769], Matt. 23:23).

2 See, for example, Albrecht Classen's contribution to this volume, "Criminal Minds, Lack of Justice, Perpetration, and Transgression: the Cases of Heinrich der Glichezare's *Reinhard Fuchs* and Wernher the Gardener's *Helmbrecht.*"

The first of the three works, Hartmann's *Der arme Heinrich* (*Poor Henry*),[3] introduces the audience to a social environment in which it seems at first that men and women are leading ethical courtly lives, fulfilling the "letter of the law" and preserving the courtly *ordo*. The opening lines of the poem describe the poet himself, and offer a list of his skills and intellectual capabilities he claims to possess, substantial indeed for a member of the knightly class. In the first three, for example, he establishes his credentials as a capable narrator for this story: "Ein ritter so geleret was, / daz er an den buochen las, / swaz er dar an geschriben vant" (1–3; "There was once a knight so well educated that he was able to read whatever he found written in books").[4] Since he is able to read, he surely possesses the ability to acquire all the information he needs to perform his office in an exemplary manner, and thus Hartmann firmly establishes his claim to authority. But his personal literary abilities pale in comparison to the real-life, knightly attributes of the man he is about to describe. Hartmann immediately commences his hymn of praise to the virtues and abilities possessed by Heinrich, a fictitious Swabian lord, who is the subject of the tale. It would appear that, in regard to the social embellishments highly respected by medieval courtly society, Heinrich has been born with a silver spoon in his mouth, and the narrator finds that,

> . . . an dem enwas vergezzen
> deheiner der tugent
> die ein ritter in siner jugent
> ze vollem lobe haben sol . . .
> sin geburt unwandelbaere
> und wol den vürsten gelich,
> doch was er unnach also rich

---

3 The critical literature on Hartmann's *Der arme Heinrich* is considerable; the older bibliographies by Wapnewski (Peter Wapnewski, *Hartmann von Aue* [Stuttgart: Metzler, 1962; 7th ed. 1979]) and Niehbuhr (Elfriede Niebuhr, *Bibliographie zu Hartmann von Aue.* Bibliographien zur deutschen Literatur des Mittelalters, 6 [Berlin: E. Schmidt, 1977]) can be supplemented by works from Christoph Cormeau and Wilhelm Störmer, *Hartmann von Aue: Epoche, Werk, Wirkung.* Beck'sche Elementarbücher (Munich: Beck, 1985), and Francis G. Gentry, ed. *A Companion to the Works of Hartmann von Aue.* Studies in German Literature, Linguistics and Culture (Rochester, NY: Camden House, 2005), and includes several works that deal with epistemology and punishment; for example, Susan L. Clark (*Hartmann von Aue: Landscapes of Mind* [Houston: Rice University Press, 1989]) examines the text as a process of learning (the lesson is thoroughly religious), not only for Heinrich and his child bride, but also for the reader; and Melitta Weiss Adamson's analysis ("Illness and Cure in Hartmann von Aue's *Der arme Heinrich* and *Iwein*," in Gentry, ed., 125–40).

4 Middle High German text taken from Hartmann von Aue, *Der arme Heinrich: Mittelhochdeutsch / Neuhochdeutsch.* Ed. Ursula Rautenberg, trans. Siegfried Grosse (Stuttgart: Reclam, 2003); English translation text taken from Hartmann von Aue, *Arthurian Romances, Tales and Lyric Poetry: the Complete Works of Hartmann von Aue.* Translated and commentary by Frank Tobin, Kim Vivian and Richard H. Lawson (University Park: Pennsylvania State University, 2001), 217–34; line references to the original are given in parentheses, followed by translation text with page references.

der geburt und des guotes
so der êren und des muotes.[5]

[in [him] no quality had been forgotten that a knight in his prime should have to win full esteem . . . he was still not nearly so endowed in birth and possessions as he was in reputation [*êre*] and noble attitude.[6]]

Hartmann goes on to describe Heinrich's letter-perfect *stæte* (62), *triuwe* (62), *zuht* (63), *erbermde* (65), *milte* (66), *êre* (69), and, in summary, labels him "courtly and wise" (*hövesch unde wîs*, 74).[7] However, what is expressed here as wisdom (*wîs*), in combination with (and following) the adjective that links him to the court (*hövesch*), applies to worldly and social matters, the kinds of things one learns from the words of masters. His mettle has never been tested, since he has never known want, nor apparently has he ever encountered a significant setback. Thus, Hartmann's pronouncement of these virtues echoes a bit hollowly, for if the total of his hero's qualities is merely the sum of all his abundant, but socially typical, "refinements," we have a good bureaucrat, but we don't have what amounts to a hero, or at least not yet.

Heinrich's knowledge of social virtue corresponds to a spiritually juvenile state, in which one acts as one has been told to act, according to a "one-size-fits-all," letter-of-the-law list of *dicta*. Unless the character encounters difficulties and challenges, (s)he will not develop and mature. By experiencing and confronting problems, one discovers and develops the strengths one possesses; in this way the individual gains knowledge of good and evil, and insight into how virtues integrate psychologically into the adult personality. By enduring hardship and prevailing in conflict, the knight moves from obedience to the law's letter to the knowledge and insight required for the fulfillment of its spirit.

For Heinrich, as well as many other medieval literary characters, this becomes an epistemological process—one must perceive, recognize and understand that what one sometimes does is either wrong or that there is a higher purpose toward which one must actively strive. Heinrich is astonished and crushed when he

5 Hartmann von Aue, *Der arme Heinrich*, 32–46 (see note 4).

6 Hartmann von Aue, *Arthurian Romances, Tales and Lyric Poetry*, 217 (see note 4).

7 "Courtly and wise" is my translation. Frank Tobin renders this line as "courtly and had the good sense born of experience," concerning which Tobin explains in a footnote that MHG *wîs* "denotes being intelligent, sensible, reasonable, circumspect, prudent—qualities gained through experience. Rendering it simply as "wise" would be misleading, because wisdom seems to be a virtue of a higher order and, as we shall see through Heinrich's subsequent actions, not a quality he possesses at this point in his life" (218, see note 4). I disagree with Tobin's translation for precisely the reason he gives here: Heinrich's behavior is not the result of wisdom "of a higher order," because it is *not* achieved through experience. The modifier *wîs* might be literally translated here as "able to rule based on the rules one has learned." The higher order of wisdom arrives only after Heinrich has faced enormous difficulty and is able to act compassionately.

contracts leprosy, a disease which to the medieval mind indicates as much an internal, spiritual and moral degeneration as an external, physical corruption.[8] But, as he later is able to admit to the peasant family that generously takes care of him after he has become ill, he becomes convinced that his disease is a punishment for the crime of forgetting about God:

"... wan ich in lützel ane sach,
von des gnaden mir geschach
vil êren unde guotes.
dô des hôchmuotes
den hôhen portenære verdrôz,
die sælden porte er mir beslôz.
dâ kum ich leider niemer in:
daz verworhte mir mîn tumber sin.
got hât durch râche an mich geleit
ein sus gewante siecheit,
die nieman mac erloesen."[9]

["... little did I look to Him from whose favor I had many honors and possessions. When this arrogance angered the exalted Gatekeeper, he shut the gates of happiness in my face. Alas, I'll never get in. My foolishness ruined that for me. As vengeance, God has inflicted on me a sickness from which no one can free me."[10]]

Heinrich has made progress toward a resolution, since he admits his offense; however, he still remains ignorant of the deeper, metaphorical significance of his disease as a challenge and opportunity for growth, and of its spiritual value, keys to his progress beyond the superficiality of courtly social virtues which have thus far constituted the sole focus of his life.

Thus, Heinrich's offense against God is a violation of the spirit of the law (he has forgotten God). And so, when he visits doctors in Monpellier and Salerno to discover how he might be healed, the physicians present him with very bad news:

"dâ von muoz iu diu helfe min
durch alle not sin versaget.
ir müeset haben eine maget,
diu vollen manbære
und des willen wære,

---

8 Peter Wapnewski (see note 3, 95) gives perhaps the best known analysis, linking Heinrich's guilt to *superbia*; Leslie Badanes ("Heinrich's Leprosy: Punishment or Test?" *Modern Language Studies* 10 [1980]: 88–92) considers the disease as a test, similar to the trials of the Old Testament figure, Job; however, the text indicates clearly that Heinrich has already "failed" a test, and my analysis attempts to show that his experiential path points toward inner change through learning, making another test unnecessary until some development has occurred.

9 Hartmann von Aue, *Der arme Heinrich*, 401–11 (see note 4).

10 Hartmann von Aue, *Arthurian Romances, Tales and Lyric Poetry*, 221 (see note 4).

daz sî den tôt durch iuch lite.
nu enist ez niht der liute site,
daz ez ieman gerne tuo.
so enhoert ouch anders niht dar zuo
niuwan der maget herzebluot:
daz wære vür iuwer suht guot."[11]

["And so my help must be denied you throughout all your trials. You would have to have a virgin of clearly marriageable age willing to suffer death for your sake. Now, it's not the usual behavior of people to do this eagerly. Nothing else is required for a cure than the blood from the heart of a virgin. That would be the cure for your disease."[12]]

The formula is expressed in language that, when taken at face value (the "letter of the formula" of the cure), is virtually impossible to satisfy. The idea that someone would actually apply the heart's blood of a virgin girl, extracted while the heart is still beating, to a leper's wounds to effect a cure strikes us as so blatantly barbaric and unjust that one cannot imagine such a procedure being performed in any civilized culture. But only on face value; on the metaphorical level, blood possesses many complex and sophisticated significances that lie at the very core of medieval spiritual life.[13] For example, blood has a strong semantic association with love.[14] As a metaphor, the image of blood, in this instance, draws its significance from the level of the spirit of the law—gaining an understanding of this, an epistemological process, will eventually guide Heinrich to maturity, happiness and salvation.

First things first, however. The daughter of the kind liegeman taking care of the leprous Heinrich offers herself as sacrifice, arguing convincingly that, in so doing, she hopes to achieve quick salvation for her soul. One might object here that her offer, while ostensibly kind, even heroic, lacks a completely proper *intentio,* since self-interest clearly plays a role, but her profound love for Heinrich cannot be denied. The "immature" (with respect to his ability to comprehend the "spirit of the law"), sick nobleman finally acquiesces to her persistent demands, and they

11 Hartmann von Aue, *Der arme Heinrich,* 222–32 (see note 4).

12 Hartmann von Aue, *Arthurian Romances, Tales and Lyric Poetry,* 219 (see note 4).

13 See Caroline Walker Bynum, *Wonderful Blood: Theology and Practice in Late Medieval Northern Germany and Beyond* (Philadelphia: University of Pennsylvania Press, 2007), in which she discusses many of the important medieval connections between blood and theology, as well as medicine, e.g.: "In medical recipes, as in the story of Longinus that circulated in later medieval Europe, blood vivifies and restores; it cures leprosy, blindness, and epilepsy as well as sin" (156).

14 This sense of blood as a metaphor is valid in numerous traditions, from the realm of Christian symbolism, where the blood of Christ was shed for the love of humanity, to interpersonal love, as in *Parzival* where the sight of goose blood on the white snow reminds lonely Parzival of his wife, Condwiramurs, and sends him into a love-trance (see below).

make their way to the Salerno physician who would perform for them this bloody service. However, as she is about to undergo the ordeal, Heinrich views her naked body through a small aperture in the door to the operating room. Suddenly, he feels strongly moved to true compassion and halts the "virgin sacrifice"—he stops the doctor just in time, seconds before he slices into the young girl's thorax. The decisive moment becomes transformative for the sick nobleman. For the first time Heinrich's voice rises to a declaration of his will, unequivocally and with force: "gotes wille muesze an mir geschehen!" (1276; "May God's will with regard to me be done")[15] Like Gretchen at the end of *Faust* Part 1,[16] Heinrich actively removes himself from the plans and designs of others and gives himself over to the judgment of God, emerging from the passivity that has plagued him since the onset of his illness. He becomes a spiritual lover rather than a submissive patient, and carries out a compassionate action, rather than merely receiving the benefit of others' kindness—because what he does involves sacrifice and self-denial purely for the benefit of another human being, it is a true act of love, something he has not yet performed.

His newfound ability to understand what it means to love reflects a psychological and epistemological evolution, signaling a fresh capacity for Heinrich to understand metaphorical language, and his passage to a new appreciation of the spirit of the law. The physician's original recommendation for treatment, "the heart's blood of a maiden" is precisely the correct substance to bathe his dermal lesions, but certainly not as a simple physical liquid that an actual surgeon has in fact cut out of a young, sexually inexperienced girl. Rather, the formula of the treatment must be understood as a figure of speech with a semantic complication, which one must perceive correctly and contemplate with an awareness of its metaphorical quality before one can claim true knowledge of its full meaning.

If blood is a metaphor for love, and this blood-love springs from the heart of someone as pure and as willing as the peasant's magnificent, loving daughter, then certainly the conditions of the cure have been met on the metaphorical level. Thus, on his return home Heinrich discovers that he has been cured, and furthermore that he is deeply in love with the young girl, and she with him. Furthermore, it must be noted that Heinrich is far from his courtly environment when he comes to his realization and is cured. A bothersome question arises that one cannot

15 Hartmann von Aue, *Arthurian Romances, Tales and Lyric Poetry*, 231 (see note 4).

16 See the final scene in Johann Wolfgang von Goethe, *Faust: der Tragödie erster Teil* (*Goethes Werke*, Hamburger Ausgabe, vol. 3, ed. Erich Trunz [Hamburg: Christian Wegner, 1949], 145), where Gretchen, soon to be executed for having murdered her illegitimate baby, responds to Faust's pleadings that she escape with him, exclaiming before her former lover, "Gericht Gottes! dir hab' ich mich übergeben"(4605; "Judgment of God! I deliver myself to you"—my translation).

evade: is it possible to achieve such valuable accomplishments at court? Hartmann seems to be casting a dark shadow of doubt on the value of a courtly education in the virtues of knighthood.

Like Hartmann's Heinrich, Wolfram's Parzival faces a conflict brought on by his early lack of knowledge and understanding: he, too, unwittingly offends the "spirit of the law," while interpreting the "letter of the law" too literally. In the early parts of the epic poem Parzival's immature sensibility cannot penetrate the veneer of external appearances. When experiencing phenomena that require some response on his part, he slavishly applies rules or advice, acquired from his mother or other "masters," that may or may not have relevance to the situation. Whereas in Hartmann's work the transgression of neglecting God is patently spiritual, Wolfram's Parzival manages to offend both secular custom (for example, by stealing a ring and a kiss from Jeschute) and God's will (his great error: failing to show compassion for his uncle, the wounded Fisher King Anfortas). The path back to rectitude brings Parzival through great difficulty and suffering, but his persistence and loyalty atone for his previous wrongdoing.

Because Parzival's mother, Herzeloyde, receives news that her husband, Gahmuret, has died in knightly combat, the disconsolate widow decides to raise her infant son in the remote forests of Soltane, far from the courtly environment that she considers dangerous. While her intention in keeping him ignorant of courtly ways is obviously to protect Parzival from harm, in fact, she does him a great disservice. The boy is destined to become the successor to the Fisher King, the keeper and guardian of the Holy Grail, a position that requires the highest levels of insight, sophistication and good judgment. Most importantly, he needs to feel and express compassion, perhaps the supreme virtue of Christianity and an essential skill for a spiritually enlightened ruler.

However, because young Parzival knows only the natural environment of Soltane, he remains innocent and naive with respect to most aspects of life that an education in courtly surroundings would have taught him. He has little understanding, for example, of cause and effect, so that his hunting instincts compel him to shoot arrows at the forest songbirds he loves, and when they fall dead to his feet he cries bitterly because they no longer sing. His schooling in ethics and proper behavior consists of de-contextualized bits of advice from his mother, such as:

> Ob dich ein grâ wîse man
> zuht wil lêren als er wol kan,
> dem soltu gerne volgen,
> und wis im niht erbolgen.
> sun, lâ dir bevolhen sîn,
> swa du guotes wîbes vingerlîn
> mügest erwerben unt ir gruoz,
> daz nim: ez tuot dir kumbers buoz.

du solt ze ir kusse gâhen
und ir lîp vast umbevâhen:
daz gît gelücke und hôhen muot,
ob si kiusche ist unde guot.[17]

[If a wise, grey-haired man offers to teach you good manners as he would well know how, do as he says with a will, do not fly into a passion. Let me give you this advice, my son. Wherever you can win a lady's ring and greeting, take it—it will rid you of the dumps. Waste no time, but kiss and embrace her. It will bring you good fortune and raise your spirits, granted she be chaste and good.[18]]

Of course, Herzeloyde cannot suppress all traces of courtly sophistication in her discourse—she of course *means* that the boy should take a woman's ring when it is offered, and not rob it from her. But because of his uniquely deficient upbringing, solely in nature, without the benefits of at least some courtly instruction, Parzival cannot interpret the "spirit" informing such wisdom, but rather follows Herzeloyde's counsel naively and without restraint. Thus, the "child of nature's" first significant encounter with the civilized world after leaving the supervision of his mother proves disastrous.[19] For when the young man encounters Jeschute, the beautiful and devoted wife of the great knight Orilus, he recalls the "letter" of his mother's advice and forces himself upon the unwilling woman. He steals from her both a ring and a kiss, and then leaves her shocked, upset and disheveled. As he departs from the scene of his assault, Jeschute's jealous husband spots him. The ensuing chain of events thus set into motion bears a good deal of significance for the letter and the spirit of the law; later we will return to the scene in a more detailed discussion.

Matters grow more serious, however, when Parzival receives instruction in the basics of knighthood from his mentor Gurnemanz.[20] The old, wizened man of experience, Gurnemanz presents Parzival with a list of rules and dicta that a knight ought to follow; nestled among them is a warning against being overly curious: "'irn sult niht vil gevrâgen" (171,17; "'Do not ask many questions'")[21]

---

17 Middle High German text taken from Wolfram von Eschenbach, *Parzival: Mittlehochdeutsch / Neuhochdeutsch*, 2 vols., trans. with an afterword by Wolfgang Spiewok (Stuttgart: Reclam, 1981); here 127,21—128,2.

18 English translation text taken from Wolfram von Eschenbach, *Parzival*, trans. A. T. Hatto (London, New York, et al.: Penguin, 1980).

19 See Otfrid Ehrismann, "Jeschute, or, How to Arrange the Taming of a Hero: The Myth of Parzival from Chrétien to Adolf Muschg, *Studies in Medievalism* 8 (1996): 46–71, who examines this encounter as a function of the antithesis "nature" vs. "civilization."

20 Albrecht Classen finds fault with Gurnemanz for having given a young person so cursory an "education" in what one needs to do to be a knight; see *Verzweiflung und Hoffnung: die Suche nach der kommunikativen Gemeinschaft in der deutschen Literatur des Mittelalters*. Beihefte zur Mediaevistik 1 (Frankfurt a. M. and New York: Peter Lang, 2002), 248.

21 Wolfram von Eschenbach, *Parzival*, (see note 17); trans. Hatto, 96 (see note 18).

—good advice for most social situations, but when Parzival follows the "letter" of this rule and fails to pose the question to the wounded Anfortas, "'oeheim, waz wirret dir?'" (795, 29; "'Dear uncle, what ails you?'"),[22] he throws his entire world into a condition of great sorrow and suffering. Were he to follow his instincts at the Grail Castle and demonstrate the "spirit" of compassion, he would succeed in his adventure; but his naive inclination to follow slavishly the letter of his teacher's rule condemns him to years of atonement and desperate wandering, in search of the Grail Castle and another chance to make amends for his error. Parzival must grow and develop into a mature, compassionate human being before he can take his proper position as Anfortas' heir.

Parzival ultimately succeeds in his endeavor, largely due to the growth he experiences through pain and suffering (especially as a result of the Grail Messenger Cundrie's devastating revelation of his wrongdoing), and later, through the information and instruction he receives from his cousin, Sigune, and the hermit, Trevrizent. However, indications of his development begin to appear already just after he departs from the Grail Castle. A particularly striking sign of growth is revealed when Parzival, riding along a wilderness path covered in snow, discovers a place where a falcon has swooped down upon a flock of geese, injuring one of them, such that three drops of blood have fallen on the ground's white shroud. Spontaneously, Parzival "reads" the image as a metaphor for his beloved wife, Condwiramurs, whom at this point he misses tremendously:

von sînen triuwen daz geschach.
do er die bluotes zäher sach
ûf dem snê (der was al wîz),
dô dâhte er "wer hât sînen vlîz
gewant an dise varwe clâr?
Cundwîer âmûrs, sich mac vür wâr
disiu varwe dir gelîchen . . .
Condwîr âmûrs, hie lît dîn schîn.
sît der snê dem bluote wîze bôt,
und ez den snê sus machet rôt,
Cundwîr âmûrs,
dem glîchet sich dîn bêâ curs:
des enbistu niht erlâzen."[23]

[This came from his loyal attachment. For when he saw the drops of blood on the white, white snow he asked himself, "who has set his hand to these fresh colours? Condwiramurs, these tints may truly be likened to your complexion!. . . Condwiramurs, here lies your bright image! The snow lending its white to the blood,

---

22 Wolfram von Eschenbach, *Parzival*, (see note 17); trans. Hatto, 395 (see note 18).

23 Wolfram von Eschenbach, *Parzival*, 282, 23 –29, 283, 4–9 (see note 17).

the blood reddening snow—Condwiramurs! Your fair person is reflected here, I'll not excuse you the comparison!"[24]]

Like Hartmann's Heinrich, Parzival gradually begins to comprehend the signs he sees in an increasingly complex manner.[25] His ability to perceive and express (albeit inwardly) the metaphorical value of the drops of blood in the snow achieves a much higher level of intellectual accomplishment than the young knight has thus far evinced, and shows that he is indeed on the path leading to fulfillment. Again, as in Heinrich's case, it is love combined with the pain of experience, which stirs complex emotions in the hero and leads him forward to ever greater understanding and knowledge. Eventually, it will be Parzival's love for and loyalty to his wife that will empower him to attain his goal, but only through the insights, skills and knowledge that he gains over the course of the tale will he be able to rule. Thus, he gradually outgrows his reliance on the "letter-of-the-law" and begins to understand and embrace the law's spirit. Given another chance, Parzival will eventually pose the compassionate question, realizing that for one person to inquire about the pain of another is not one question too many, but rather the kind, humane thing to do.

In addition to Parzival's main adventure, Wolfram's epic poem presents another significant situation where the nature of crime, justice and punishment comes into focus. The chain of events that begins with Parzival's abuse of Jeschute (described above), continues with the bitter interrogation she must endure at the hands of her husband Orilus, and subsequently Orilus's unfair judgment and abusive treatment of his innocent wife, results in a somewhat different perspective on the process of falling out of the *ordo*, whether this be a matter of social transgression (crime), religious offense (sin) or personal disloyalty, as in this case. When Orilus returns to his wife's tent, he has already witnessed Parzival leaving the scene and, convinced by his wife's disheveled appearance that she has just enjoyed a tryst with the handsome youth, begins to upbraid her. His inconsiderate accusations arise, to be sure, from emotional turmoil, but nevertheless their vehemence indicates a possible predilection on the part of Orilus for viscerally jumping to conclusions, as he refuses his wife the honor she deserves. Like Parzival in his

---

24 Wolfram von Eschenbach, *Parzival*, trans. Hatto, 148 (see note 18).

25 As Albrecht Classen, "Reading, Writing and Learning in Wolfram von Eschenbach's *Parzival*," *A Companion to Wolfram's Parzival*, ed. Will Hasty. Studies in German Literature, Linguistics, and Culture (Columbia, SC: Camden House, 1999), 189–202, points out, "it is consistent with Wolfram's probable position between orality and literacy that the most important kind of "reading" that takes place in *Parzival* is a metaphorical reading of signs, and not a literal reading of letters" (196); I would only add that, for many authors, "reading" extends beyond the ability merely to know what is written, but also to understand the meaning "between the lines"—perhaps in the sense of Hartmann's claim, that he "an den buochen las, / swaz er dar an geschriben vant " (see above, note 4), including the gist *behind* the written word.

reading of signs, Orilus, too, seems immature, rendering an interpretation that does not take into account possible complexities and extenuating circumstances, even before he has given Jeschute the opportunity to explain. His pride has been wounded, and, in an attempt to reestablish his self-esteem as warrior, he narrates a detailed account of his various deeds and conquests; in his rage, Orilus sinks into the mundane parlance of the knightly resumé.[26] His tirade focuses solely on his own external honor, which he gained through battle by defeating this knight and that, and which he believes his wife's misconduct has besmirched.

This is the honor of appearances, where reputation is affirmed by third-party observers: others look at the knight and his circumstances and give him honor because he appears to be honorable. Orilus's rant regarding his victories and trouncings of this opponent and that, however, is inappropriate for the present situation, perhaps providing him rather with a means of bolstering his ego than a suitable language for communicating with his wife regarding what he thinks is her adultery.[27] The resulting abuse to which he subjects his spouse indicates that Orilus, too, must undergo that inner transformation typical of characters who find themselves under spiritual and psychological duress.

In the meantime Jeschute begins to mount a defense that focuses more appropriately on internal honor, one based on the sense of, and confidence in, personal worthiness rather than deeds of derring-do and the boasting that ensues.[28] Jeschute reprimands Orilus that he not compromise his knightly honor, for he is "getriuwe unde wîs" (136,12; "You are true and discerning.")[29] Again, as in Hartmann's hymn of praise to his character, Heinrich, "wisdom" is connected to one who may be acting in a manner of which courtly bureaucrats would approve, but not as a mature and truly heroic individual.[30] She truthfully declares that she has been faithful and was not the transgressor her husband considers her to be, but rather the victim of another's transgression. Any action that would lower her would not befit a woman of her rank, not merely because others would see it that way but also because she would feel that way. Before she can adequately present her case, however, Orilus silences her, and then humiliates her, depriving

---

26 Wolfram von Eschenbach, *Parzival*, 133, 29–136, 8 (see note 17).

27 See Classen, *Verzweiflung und Hoffnung* (see note 20), 133–35, who discusses this issue in the context of Hartmanns *Erec* as a problem in the social structures and norms for communication between men and women: ". . . die Warnung des Dichters kommt doch deutlich zum Ausdruck, wie leicht das soziale und kommunikative Gewebe der Gesellschaft zerreißen kann, wenn Gewalt die sprachlichen und moralischen Normen zerstört" (134), and further, "offene Rede ist. . . mithin noch nicht möglich, vielmehr muß die Heldin auf die Lüge zurückgreifen, um sich in der männlich dominierten, d.h. tatenorientierten und der Kommunikation abholden Gesellschaft zu behaupten" (135).

28 Wolfram von Eschenbach, *Parzival* 136, 11–22 (see note 17).

29 Wolfram von Eschenbach, *Parzival*, trans. Hatto, 79 (see note 18).

30 See above, note 7.

her of decent clothing, of his companionship and her horse of its saddle, bridle and food. Thus, because his wife apparently breaks the letter of the law, Orilus does not allow for interpretation of the evidence: Jeschute is merely guilty as far as he is concerned, and she must suffer the punishment, which is represented through external signs. Because he can exercise domination over her by wielding brute force, she must submit in silence to his indignities.[31]

Although Orilus denies her the right to speak, Wolfram's description of her inner state indicates that she is thinking with much more spiritual sophistication than her husband, and she expresses a far more profound connection and commitment to their relationship than he does. Hers is the language of selfless love that rises to the level of true compassion, and it evokes noble sentiments from the narrator as well:

al weinde sunder lachen
diu vrouwe jâmers rîche
schiet dannen trûreclîche.
sine müete niht, swaz ir geschach,
wan ir mannes ungemach:
des trûren gap ir grôze nôt,
daz si noch sampfter wære tôt.
nu sult ir si durch triwe clagen:
si beginnt nu hôhen kumber tragen.
wær mir aller wîbe haz bereit,
mich müet doch vroun Jeschûten leit.[32]

[All thought of laughter gone, and in tears, the wretched lady set out dolefully. Whatever she endured she did not mind it, only that her husband suffered so. His unhappiness so distressed her that she would have found death more kind. Her faithful love deserves your pity, since from now on she is to suffer great tribulation. Though I were hated by the whole sex, the wrong done to Lady Jeschute could not fail to anger me.[33]]

Orilus stubbornly adheres to his premature judgment, however, and to break out of this dilemma he requires a significant intervention. Ironically, it turns out that the original source of his emotional anguish provides the solution he needs. Barely maintaining his loving spouse in a pathetic condition as he forces her to ride hungry, lonely and in tatters, atop a starving pony following dejectedly several

31 See Albrecht Classen, *The Power of a Woman's Voice in Medieval and Early Modern Literature: New Approaches to German and European Women Writers and to Violence against Women in Premodern Times.* Fundamentals of Medieval and Early Modern Culture, 1 (Berlin and New York: Walter de Gruyter, 2007), 219–21.

32 Wolfram von Eschenbach, *Parzival*, 137, 20–29 (see note 17).

33 Wolfram von Eschenbach, *Parzival*, trans. Hatto, 80 (see note 18).

hundred meters to his rear, he sets off on a personal mission of vengeance, first to find and then to trounce Parzival. The quest takes a good deal of time, and in the interim Parzival has already visited *Munsalvæsche* for the first time. Having failed to pose the question of compassion to the wounded Fisher King, Anfortas, and now experiencing feelings of guilt and remorse, he is beginning the process of his own transformation from immature innocence to responsible adulthood, from the "letter" to the "spirit."

When Orilus finally overtakes Parzival and challenges him, he finds that he is no match for the young knight. After defeating Orilus, Parzival commands him to reconcile with his wife as one of the conditions for his surrender, and Orilus forgives her most reluctantly. Now, for the first time, Parzival begins to act in a responsible, self-reliant manner. He senses that he must do more than dictate a reconciliation that merely fulfills the letter of the typical demands a conqueror makes of a vanquished opponent, which are not sufficient to facilitate a true transformation of spirit. He still needs to convince this vanquished opponent of Jeschute's innocence, because it is the compassionate thing to do. Therefore, Parzival brings Orilus to a reliquary, whereupon the narrator tells us:

> Parzivâl dô mit triwen vuor:
> er nam daz heiltuom, drûf er swuor.
> sus stabte er selbe sînen eit . . .
> ich hânz dâ vür, die treit got.
> nu müeze ich vlüsteclîchen spot
> ze bêden lîben immer hân
> von sîner kraft, ob missetân
> disiu frouwe habe, dô diz geschach
> daz ich ir vürspan von ir brach.
> ouch vuorte ich mêr goldes dan.
> ich was ein tôre und niht ein man,
> gewahsen niht bî witzen.
> vil weinens, dâ bî switzen
> mit jâmer dolte vil ir lîp.
> si ist benamen ein unschuldic wîp.
> dâne scheide ich ûz niht mêre:
> des sî pfant mîn sælde und êre.
> Ruocht irs, si sol unschuldec sîn.
> seht, gebt ir wider ir vingerlîn.[34]

[Now Parzival did a charitable deed. He took the relics and swore on them, administering his oath to himself . . . "let me be mocked and damned in this life and the next through His power, if this lady did amiss when I chanced to tear her brooch from her, when I also bore off other gold! I was a young fool—no man—not yet grown

34 Wolfram von Eschenbach, *Parzival*, 269,1–3, 269,17–270,2 (see note 17).

to years of discretion. Weeping copiously and bathed in perspiration, she had much to put up with in her wretchedness. I tell you she is an innocent woman. I except nothing from this oath, may my honor and hopes of bliss be pledge for it. By your leave, she shall be innocent! Here, give her back her ring."[35]]

Parzival's honest self-reflection, admission that he was "ein tôre und niht ein man," and unselfish act of kindness are the first indications that the youth is moving from his state of immaturity and crossing the threshold of adulthood, where he must be willing to accept responsibility for his actions. In fact, his admission to foolishness mirrors Orilus's behavior as well, for he, too, has been "gewahsen niht bî witzen" and because of his immature, foolish treatment of Jeschute, "mit jâmer dolte vil ir lîp." But, it would appear that in Wolfram's work, the "spirit" leading to charitable deeds is contagious, and the transformation in Orilus is immediately apparent:

die gâbe enpfienc der degen guot.
dô streich er von dem munde daz bluot
und kuste sînes herzen trût.
ouch wart verdact ir blôziu hût . . .
dô sprach der vürste Orilus
aber ze Parzivâle alsus.
"helt, dîn unbetwungen eit
gît mir grôz liep und crankez leit.
ich hân schumpfentiure gedolt,
diu mir vröude hât erholt.
jâ mac mit êren nu mîn lîp
ergetzen diz werde wîp . . .
nu lôn dir got, si ist valsches vrî.
ich hân unvuoge an ir getân."[36]

[The good knight accepted the gift. Wiping the blood from his lips he kissed the darling of his heart. He also covered her nakedness . . . . Prince Orilus turned to Parzival again. "Knight," he said, "your oath so freely offered gives me much joy and little sorrow. The defeat I have suffered in battle has brought me back my happiness. Now I can make amends to this lady with honor after banishing her from favor . . . she stands cleared of infidelity. It was not as a gentleman that I treated her . . . ."[37]]

Now, Orilus, too, has experienced a period of deep pain and emerges from it a better individual.[38] Finally, he has become capable of showing compassion, and by

---

35 Wolfram von Eschenbach, *Parzival*, trans. Hatto, 141 (see note 18).

36 Wolfram von Eschenbach, *Parzival*, 270,5 – 271,7 (see note 17).

37 Wolfram von Eschenbach, *Parzival*, trans. Hatto, 142 (see note 18).

38 On the topic of pain as a necessary stage of individual development, please see the contribution to this volume by John Gough, "Pain: Suffering, Agony, and Death in the Works of François Villon."

expressing his regret for his foolish and hasty judgment of Jeschute, he can admit his previous "unvuoge" and reestablish a loving relationship with his wife. Although both men treated her horribly, it is clear from her subsequent actions that she is most willing to exonerate her husband. Thus, she becomes one of the most extraordinarily forgiving characters in medieval literature.[39]

The immature state of mind that comprehends only the letter of the law, as I have described it above, is characteristic of many at court, in the opinion of Gottfried von Straßburg, and provides a central thematic problem in his epic poem *Tristan und Isolde*.[40] By contrast, the lovers' relationship reflects the higher qualities of the new *ordo* about which Gottfried writes in his prologue.[41] In the 244 lines comprising Gottfried's complex introduction to his poem, he criticizes his courtly colleagues for their simplistic preoccupation with easy gratification, the many,

> . . . die, von der ich hoere sagen,
> diu keine swære enmüge getragen
> und niwan in vröuden welle sweben.
> die lâze ouch got mit vröuden leben!
> Der werlde und diserne lebene
> enkumt mîn rede niht ebene.
> ir leben und mînez zweient sich.[42]

> [. . . who [as I hear] are unable to endure sorrow and wish only to revel in bliss. (Please God to let them live in their bliss!) What I have to say does not concern that world and such a way of life; their way and mine diverge sharply.[43]]

---

39 Of course, women find themselves in such abusive situations often in medieval literature, and the men who treat them in this manner are rarely accused and even more rarely, if ever, punished appropriately; for example, with reference to a similar case regarding the abuse of Boccaccio's Griselda in his *Decameron* (10, 1).

40 The great body of critical literature on Gottfried's work grows unabatedly, and negotiating its dimensions is a formidable task; fortunately, there are several important bibliographic tools dedicated to Gottfried's work: Gottfried Weber, *Gottfried von Straßburg*, 5th ed., updated by Werner Hoffmann (Stuttgart: Metzler, 1981); Christoph Huber, *Gottfried von Straßburg: Tristan*, Klassiker-Lektüren, 3 (Berlin: Erich Schmidt, 2000); and finally, the journal *Tristania*, which regularly updates current research trends.

41 See Albrecht Schöne, "Zu Gottfrieds 'Tristan'-Prolog," *Deutsche Vierteljahrschrift für Literatur- und Geistesgeschichte* 29 (1955): 447–74; Klaus Speckenbach, *Studien zum Begriff "edelez herze" im Tristan Gottfrieds von Strassburg*. Medium Aevum – Philologische Studien, 6 (Munich: Eidos, 1965); Classen, *Verzweiflung und Hoffnung*, 307–08 (see note 20).

42 Middle High German text taken from Gottfried von Strassburg, *Tristan*, ed. by Friedrich Ranke, re-edited and trans. into New High German by Rüdiger Krohn, 3 vols. (Stuttgart: Reclam, 1980, 1983), with line references (here 51–57).

43 English translation text taken from Gottfried von Strassburg, *Tristan: with the 'Tristan' of Thomas*, trans. by A. T. Hatto (London, New York et al.: Penguin, 1967), with page references given in parentheses (here, 42).

While the courtly retinue seeks merely pleasure and joy, Gottfried envisions a new, revolutionary social order of *edele herzen* ("noble hearts"), whose acceptance of life's difficulty along with its pleasures, and whose embracing of authentic experience, typify an elite group of *cognoscenti*, who have achieved a maturity and wisdom, and can comprehend and appreciate life's complexities, and who do not require the letter of the law to dictate their actions, but rather embrace its spirit.[44] Gottfried writes his poem for this world,

> diu samet in eime herzen treit
> ir süeze sûr, ir liebez leit,
> ir herzeliep, ir senede nôt,
> ir liebez leben, ir leiden tôt,
> ir lieben tôt, ir leidez leben.
> dem lebene sî mîn leben ergeben,
> der werlt wil ich gewerldet wesen,
> mit ir verderben oder genesen.[45]

> [which together in one heart bears its bitter-sweet, its dear sorrow, its heart's joy, its love's pain, its dear life, its sorrowful death, its dear death, its sorrowful life. To this life let my life be given, of this world let me be part, to be damned or saved with it.[46]]

Gottfried's use here of chiasmus and parallel structures, emblematic of a classical education, demonstrates that he is preparing the reader rhetorically for the sophisticated discourse to follow—perhaps announcing to the audience that an understanding of the form of the literary work will be necessary for a thorough appreciation of its content.[47]

Over a large portion of Gottfried's text, the court is obsessed with proving that Tristan and Isolde are carrying on an affair, and the courtiers' repeated attempts to uncover evidence reflects aspects of what we have previously termed letter-of-the-law justice. Even when King Mark himself discovers his wife and his nephew locked in a lovers' embrace, he races back to court in order to fetch witnesses, for it is written that he must do so "also daz lantreht hæte" (18244; "in accordance with the law of the land")[48]—but before he can return with witnesses, Tristan manages to flee. The lovers evade detection and prosecution for a long while, not

---

44 Some critics have elevated this elite group to high levels of sophistication, even mysticism (e.g., Speckenbach, *Studien zum Begriff "edelez herze"*, 105–20 [see note 40].

45 Gottfried von Strassburg, *Tristan*, 59–66 (see note 42).

46 Gottfried von Strassburg, *Tristan*, trans. Hatto, 42 (see note 43).

47 While many critics have found textual evidence of Gottfried's classical education, two works have focused particularly on this theme: C. Stephen Jaeger, *Medieval Humanism in Gottfried von Strassburg's Tristan und Isolde* (Heidelberg: Winter, 1977), and Winfried Christ, *Rhetorik und Roman: Untersuchungen zu Gottfrieds von Strassburg "Tristan und Isold."* Deutsche Studien, 31 (Meisenheim am Glan: Hain, 1977).

48 Gottfried von Strassburg, *Tristan* (see note 42); trans. Hatto, 281 (see note 43).

only as the result of their discretion and astoundingly good fortune, but also because, when it comes to the court and the law, the "letter" can easily be manipulated. Tristan and Isolde develop a mastery of the courtly discourse, the essential, basic form of the courtly *codex*, and employ it to interpret publically the "letter of the law" for the benefit of their less sophisticated courtly colleagues. In the meantime, the lovers cultivate their own form of sophisticated communication, based on metaphor and symbol—the "truth" behind the letter—in order to continue, undetected, their sublime but perilous relationship.[49] Most remarkably, the lovers seem to be able to rely upon the cooperation, if not the collusion, of Divine Providence. If we consider the unsuccessful outcomes of the numerous investigations, traps and surveillances to which the court subjects Tristan and Isolde, we might even suspect that God strongly supports the lovers in their break from sterile courtly traditions. To be sure, Gottfried makes it perfectly clear that, in his opinion, the courtly system of marriage-by-betrothal no longer enjoys God's favor, and that some processes for ascertaining legal proof of guilt or innocence, such as the "ordeal," run contrary to the spirit of the law, by showing the utter futility of such practices.

Let us turn for a moment to the scene of the ordeal, for it provides perhaps the clearest example of the letter-of-the-law's inferiority to the spirit. The formula of the process[50] follows a strict protocol: the accused must make a statement (a

49 While it is clear that Tristan is initially the teacher and Isolde the pupil (on the model of Abelard and Heloise—see Joseph Campbell, *The Masks of God: Creative Mythology* [New York, London, Toronto, etc.: Penguin, 1968], 54; Albrecht Classen, "Abaelards *Historia Calamitatum*, der Briefwechsel mit Heloise und Gottfrieds von Straßburg *Tristan*: Historisch-biographische und fiktionale Schicksale. Eine Untersuchung zur Intertextualität im zwölften und dreizehnten Jahrhundert," *arcadia* 35.2 (2000): 225–53), in the process of learning this new medium of communication, Isolde soon surpasses her teacher not only in her linguistic abilities, but also as the primary designer and developer of their ruses, while Tristan grows ever less capable of sophisticated understanding and planning—a point I will take up later in this essay; see especially Classen, *Verzweiflung und Hoffnung*, 279–358 (see note 20), who develops a theoretical background for their relationship as a communicative community and demonstrates in detail how Gottfried develops their utopian love, not only as *eros*, but also as language; also see my essay on the shift of power in the lovers' relationship and Isolde's new dominant position, "The Bitterness of Love on the Sea: Isolde's Amorous Discourse Viewed through Gottfried's Crystalline Transparency," *Words of Love and Love of Words in the Middle Ages and the Renaissance*, ed. Albrecht Classen (Tempe, AZ: Arizona Center for Medieval and Renaissance Studies, 2008), 275–89.

50 Isolde's trial and how it measures up to the judicial standards of the time are explored by Vickie L. Ziegler, *Trial by Fire and Battle in Medieval German Literature*, Studies in German Literature, Linguistics and Culture (Rochester, New York: Camden House, 2004), 114–45; she suggests (127) that Gottfried narrates some aspects of the trial in far greater detail than others, while some are not mentioned at all, because he wishes to focus his audience's attention on the queen, or, "as a cleric himself, he was reluctant to give the liturgy a prominent role in a procedure of which he himself seemed to be critical"; see also Ernest C. York, "English Legal Customs in the Medieval

"judicial oath" uttered before a tribunal—in the case of Isolde, its members are King Mark and prominent courtiers, with a bishop presiding) that declares her/his innocence; if the tribunal agrees on the acceptability of the statement, the accused swears her/his innocence and takes into her/his hand an iron object that has been heated in fire to a very high temperature; her/his innocence is proven if the hand remains uninjured, supposedly spared by divine intercession if God has deemed the accused to be innocent. Isolde is able to secure this positive outcome for herself by concocting an evasive oath from a string of half-truths.

The inscrutable relationship between God's justice and human investigation and proof comes to expression especially in Isolde's trial by hot iron: her successful (although evasive) oath fulfilling only the "letter of the law" easily fools the members of the court while still apparently satisfying God's will. Gottfried's subsequent digression on how God's judgment, "wintschaffen alse ein ermel ist" (15736; "pliant as a windblown sleeve" [248]),[51] cannot be forced by human beings, serves as both a warning against the presumptuous attempt to fathom the ways of God[52] as well as a suggestion that God condones the amorous behavior of the lovers.[53]

Although Gottfried's version of the tale breaks off long before Tristan's marriage to Isolde of the White Hands, the French source Gottfried claims for his *Tristan*, Thomas of Brittany,[54] provides an interesting variation on the relationship between language and justice. Tristan's ultimate fate is sealed when he is "punished" by his wife for his transgressions against her, which include a number of lies and refusals to participate fully in the marriage contract—he has never consummated the marriage! Her insistence that the white sails on the boat, announcing that Iseut the Fair is aboard bringing healing to her moribund lover Tristan, are black ("Jols sai pur veir. / Sachez que le sigle est tut neir" (1755–56; "I am entirely sure of

---

Tristan Legend," *Studies in Philology* 68 (1971): 1–9, who accounts for a significant deviation in the order of events in the procedure (that the oath of denial occurs so late, giving Isolde more power to manipulate the wording) as a result of local cultural differences (4–6).

51 Gottfried von Strassburg, *Tristan*, (see note 42); trans. Hatto, 248 (see note 43).

52 See Ziegler (see note 50), where she comments on Gottfried's passage: "intellectual opposition to the ordeal, especially strong in late twelfth-century Paris, centered on its roots in superstition and the attempt to manipulate or tempt God, proving the fundamentally unorthodox character of the ordeal process" (129).

53 See H. B. Willson, "The Old and the New Law in Gottfried's 'Tristan,'" *Modern Language Notes* 60 (1965): 212–24; Willson suggests that the key to understanding God's support is the lovers' demonstration of compassion—however, this thesis becomes complicated when one considers Tristan and Isolde's repeated hoodwinkings of King Mark (although he treats them most magnanimously) and other members of the court, and especially Isolde's near murder of her lady-in-waiting Brangæne (12696–934).

54 Thomas, *Les Fragments du Roman de Tristan: Poème du XII siècle*, ed. Bartina H. Wind (Geneva: Droz, 1960).

it—know that the sail is completely white"—*my translation*),[55] condemns Tristan to death. Thus, through her dissemblance, Iseut of the White Hands acquires the role of judge, jury and executioner for the social order that has suffered great offense at the hands of the lovers.

Intriguingly, she has already demonstrated a high level of linguistic sophistication (e.g., her comment regarding water splashing on her thigh making bolder with her than her husband ever had [250–57]),[56] and here she merely employs the same kind of metaphorical discourse the lovers have relied upon to hide their relationship. While the signified reference of her utterance—the sails—are actually not black, but rather white, on the metaphorical level they may indeed achieve blackness. As far as Iseut of the White Hands is concerned, their color represents the arrival of the person who will surely "blacken" any hope she might have for her husband's affection, while at the same time the situation "blackens" her heart to perform such a hateful deed.

It is important to note that Tristan's mastery of language and his powers of insight wane significantly over the course of the work, especially after his declaration of love. Since the moment he and Isolde returned from Ireland on the wooing expedition, it has been she, and not Tristan, who has functioned as the primary planner of their trysts, plots and deceptions. Furthermore, Tristan's placing of the sword between him and Isolde atop the crystalline bed in the *minnegrotte*, while successfully deceiving Mark into believing the pair was remaining chaste, desecrates the metaphorically "pure" environment and signifies their return to court and the end of their relationship. By placing the symbol of honor (the sword) between them on the symbolic bed of love,[57] Tristan himself asserts the primacy of honor over love. It is perhaps the most important incident in which the reputedly consummate lover demonstrates that he no longer understands the power of metaphors, and this "crime" against the purity of their love on metaphorical level condemns it to end. Thus, at the moment of Tristan's death, Iseut of the White Hands' *double-entendre* catches him defenseless, and he must suffer the ultimate ("capital") punishment, an execution for crimes against love.

In conclusion, the three works we have brought under discussion provide different perspectives on the issue of the letter and spirit of law. Each member of the courtly

---

55 Thomas, *Les Fragments du Roman de Tristan* (see note 54).

56 Thomas, *Les Fragments du Roman de Tristan* (see note 54).

57 See Christopher R. Clason, "Deception in the Boudoir: Gottfried's 'Tristan' and 'Lying' in Bed," *Journal of English and Germanic Philology* 103 (2004): 277–96, where I claim that "the sword . . . represents loyalty to one's lord, the feudal obligation that Tristan owes to Marke as his king . . . Tristan unwittingly brings the symbol of courtly duty onto the very altar of the *minne*-sacrament [and thereby] . . . performs a kind of desecration of the *minnegrotte*" (294).

community is subject to what is commanded by social, political or religious power, whether it comes in an explicit *codex* or it is handed down through oral tradition; adherents to the letter become "normal" and undistinguished. In a society where continuity and predictability are crucial, these qualities are perhaps desirous. However, as the three epic tales demonstrate, in cases where the individual is destined for higher, individual, or heroic achievements, a greater consciousness of the spirit and meaning behind the written word is required. The path from immaturity to adulthood is fraught with difficulty, but if the hero is to succeed (s)he must confront it and evolve—develop, grow, and learn. Heinrich is healed, Parzival becomes Grail King, and Orilus turns into a true partner for his loving wife because they undergo this evolution. Tristan's devolution spells the end of his love and his life. In each of these cases, the character's ability to interpret the spirit of the law behind the letter-of-the-law ultimately decides her or his success or failure.

Chapter 4

Stacey Hahn
(Oakland University, Rochester, MI)

Crime, Punishment and the Hybrid in Medieval French Romance: Robert the Devil and Geoffrey Big Tooth

The widespread tendency to trace one's lineage or character to supernatural origins or influences seems a constant throughout mythology, folklore, religion and history. This phenomenon may be observed regarding Aeneas, the founder of Rome and ancestor of Brutus, the first of the Briton Kings, whose mother was the goddess Venus or the offspring of Mélusine, the fairy mistress and founding mother of the Lusignan family of Poitiers. Other examples include Sir Lancelot with his link to the lineage of the biblical King David through his mother or in modern times Dan Brown and his attempt to connect the legend of the Holy Grail to the supposed relationship between Christ and Mary Magdalene that produced between them a human lineage. Supernatural origins, whether of divine or diabolical nature, bring with them immense burdens that wreak potential havoc or grave responsibilities on those born of them. The burden of diabolical origins manifest in the protagonists of medieval romance often leads these characters on the path to crime and subsequent punishment. Nonetheless, no matter how obscure or murky one's origins, it is always possible to repent and redeem oneself, especially within the parameters of the Christian tradition that circumscribes medieval romance.

A diabolical bloodline or, as in the case of Robert the Devil, a conception engineered by a demon does not necessarily dictate a tragic destiny as long as the hybrid owns up to his evil nature, which may occur as the result of self-reflection, or through the misery and isolation brought about by evil deeds. In as much as the criminal possesses free will and has been baptized, his redemption is always possible, provided he repent and make restitution. The journey toward salvation is a slow and difficult process, usually earned through self-sacrifice by completing difficult tasks that restore the very society or individuals which the malefactor attempted to destroy. In the battle between good and evil the hybrid, because of his link with the supernatural, plays a more formidable role than his human counterparts because his strengths and weaknesses are amplified and therefore have a more devastating effect on the social fabric. When the hybrid channels his energy in a positive way, he can accomplish more than all of his peers, and by the same token, when this energy bursts forth in an angry, vengeful manner, his destruction is virtually unstoppable.[1]

Two medieval French romances, *Robert le Diable* and *Le Roman de Mélusine*, are remarkably similar in their treatment of their hybrid male protagonists, each one of whom acts out the mark of his supernatural origins, incurred through the agency of his mother, by wreaking havoc on hallowed communities. The lives of Robert the Devil and Geoffrey Big Tooth, although largely different in many respects given the separate genres to which they belong, share many parallels that indicate that the Robert the Devil legend may have played a strong role in shaping the *Roman de Mélusine*.[2] The following is a list of episodes that link the two protagonists: Robert the Devil sets fire to the abbey of Arques, incinerating all the nuns inside, while Geoffrey Big Tooth, the male hero of *Le Roman de Mélusine*, commits similar injury by setting fire to the monastery of Maillezais, killing all the monks within, including his brother Fromont.

Both renegades will repent of their actions, redeem themselves by proving their worth on the battlefield and make a pilgrimage for absolution to the pope in Rome. Geoffrey will seek to make amends by establishing an abbey in memory of those he has killed and an abbey will be consecrated to Robert after his death. Neither one will marry or bear offspring, thus safely sparing humanity the danger of their evil seeds.[3] In addition, Robert and Geoffrey are affiliated with important medieval dynasties by virtue of their names and place of origin: Robert is linked

---

1 The same pattern is evident in other medieval works such as the *Lancelot-Grail* Cycle where a privileged bloodline guarantees the success of the hero and destines him to accomplish great deeds as was the case for Lancelot and Galahad who can trace their heritage back to the Biblical King David through Lancelot's mother. For the *Lancelot-Grail* Cycle, see *Lancelot: roman en prose du XIIIe siècle*. ed. Alexandre Micha. 9 vols. (Geneva and Paris: Droz, 1978–1983); *La Queste del Saint Graal: roman du XIIIe siècle*. ed. Albert Pauphilet (Paris: Champion, 1978); and *La Mort le roi Artu: roman du XIIIe siècle*. ed. Jean Frappier (Geneva: Droz, 1996). Another example is the twelfth-century *Roman d'Enéas*, a medieval adaptation of Virgil's *Aeneid*, where the hero is predestined by divine will and his lineage to succeed in founding a new Troy in Italy. *Le Roman d'Enéas*. ed. Aimé Petit (Paris: Librairie Générale Française, 1997).

2 Although both works are romances, *Robert le diable* has stronger hagiographical overtones while the *Roman de Mélusine* focuses more strongly on dynastic issues.

3 In later versions of the legend, for example, the *Dit de Robert le Diable* (early fourteenth century), Robert marries the emperor's daughter and becomes a father rather than live out the rest of his life as a hermit.

to the dukes of Normandy, a dynasty located in Northern France while Geoffrey descends from the Lusignan family of Poitiers in Southwestern France.

Because there exists so many similarities between the Robert the Devil legend and later romances both in English and in French, which appear to have been directly or indirectly inspired by Robert the Devil, critics such as Andrea Hopkins and Jane Gilbert have identified these works as belonging to a distinctive literary sub genre, the penitential romance. These romances, which deal with "unnatural mothers and their monstrous offspring" have many commonalities such as hybrid sons, secrecy regarding the identity of a father figure and a quest on the part of the son to seek the nature of his paternal origins.[4]

In addition, the monstrous children commit heinous crimes such as murder and the desecration of monasteries or convents, yet despite their evil deeds, they manage to redeem themselves through acts of penance, which might involve battle against the infidel as proof of a Christian conversion, the construction of religious sites, or a pilgrimage to seek absolution from the pope in Rome. Many of the curious anomalies in Jean d'Arras's *Roman de Mélusine* make sense when viewed in light of this genre. In her study of Middle English penitential romances Andrea Hopkins states in her preface that these romances (*Guy of Warwick, Sir Ysumbras, Sir Gowther*, and *Roberd of Cisyle*) "concern themselves with the sin, repentance, and atonement of their heroes. Despite being few in number they form a coherent and distinctive group and have never previously been studied in association with each other. The main point to emerge from the study is that in this closely related group of texts, the kind of penance experienced by the heroes and its treatment by the authors reflects archaic traditions and views at variance with the contemporary teaching and practice of the Church, and that this surprising departure is largely determined by the nature of the kind of literature to which the poem belongs – romance."[5]

The penitential romance, then, combines elements of romance with hagiography such that the protagonist moves from the secular world of tournaments, sex, violence and sin to a rejection of these values through penance and a movement toward a lifestyle grounded on aesthetic principles more in tune with Christian notions of redemption. These notions of redemption, however, do not always reflect contemporary religious practices, but rather function on a level that corresponds more closely to folklore and myth. The generally accepted source for

4 Jane Gilbert, "Unnatural Mothers and Monstrous Children in *The King of Tars* and *Sir Gowther*," *Medieval Women: Texts and Contexts in Late Medieval Britain: Essays for Felicity Riddy*, ed. Jocelyn Wogan-Browne, Rosalynn Voaden, Arlyn Diamond, Ann Hutchison, and Carol Meale (Turnhout, Belgium: Brepols, 2000), 329–44.

5 Andrea Hopkins, *The Sinful Knights: A Study of Middle English Penitential Romance* (Oxford: Clarendon Press, 1990), Preface.

this unique genre that became increasingly popular throughout the course of the Middle Ages and even into the twentieth century is the legend of *Robert le Diable* which exists in two verse manuscripts, one dating from the latter half of the thirteenth century (BN fr. 25516), referred to as manuscript A, and the other from the late fourteenth or early fifteenth century (BN fr. 24405), manuscript B.

The enormously popular legend was translated into several languages and exists in verse and prose romance, *conte, dit, exemplum*, and miracle play.[6] The legend has also been amplified and secularized with the passage of time so that in later versions the figure of Robert ends up marrying and fathering children rather than reject marriage in order to become a saintly hermit. The genre was particularly successful in England where the figure of Robert evolves into English, secularized heroes who take on various names and guises as in the heroes of the romances mentioned above studied by Andrea Hopkins: Guy of Warwick, Sir Ysumbras, Sir Gowther and Roberd of Cisyle. A comparison of the development of these romances in both French and English might be fruitful in that there are many similarities between Geoffrey Big Tooth, Sir Gowther and Guy of Warwick.[7] As might be expected, many themes in the early Robert the Devil tale become amplified, rationalized, and more fully examined in the *Roman de Mélusine*, just as they have in the English romances derived from the legend.

In this paper I will refer to the later edition of the verse *Robert le diable* based on manuscript B and edited by Elisabeth Gaucher. I have chosen the latter manuscript to be the object of my comparison since manuscript B elaborates more fully on the psychology of Robert's evil deeds and contrition.[8] It is also more approximate in

6 For a thorough analysis of the entire *Robert le Diable* corpus, see Elisabeth Gaucher, *Robert le Diable: Histoire d'une légende* (Paris: Champion, 2003). For a detailed analysis of the two verse manuscripts, 21–97. For a comparison of *Robert le Diable* with *le Roman de Mélusine*, 175–77. Andrea Hopkins also compares *Robert le Diable* to the *Roman de Mélusine* in *The Sinful Knights*: 201–02 (see note 5). Lise Andries compares rewritings of Robert the Devil in "La Bibliothèque bleue: Les réécritures de *Robert le Diable*,"*Littérature* 30 (1978): 51-66.

7 For a comparison between Robert and Sir Gowther, see Dorothy S. McCoy, "From Celibacy to Sexuality: An Examination of Some Medieval and Early Renaissance Versions of the Story of Robert the Devil," *Human Sexuality in the Middle Ages and Renaissance*, ed. Douglas Radcliff-Umstead. University of Pittsburgh Publications on the Middle Ages and Renaissance, 4 (Pittsburgh: Center for Medieval & Renaissance Studies, University of Pittsburgh, 1978), 29-39. See also, Shirley Marchalonis, "*Sir Gowther*: The Process of a Romance," *Chaucer Review: A Journal of Medieval Studies and Literary Criticism* 6.1 (1971): 14-29.

8 All references to *Robert le Diable* are from Elisabeth Gaucher's edition based on the later manuscript B. *Robert le Diable*, ed. Elisabeth Gaucher (Paris: Champion, 2006). For manuscript A, see E. Löseth (ed.), *Robert le Diable: Roman d'aventures* (1903; New York: Johnson, 1968). For a comparison of iconographic images in the two manuscripts, see Meredith T. McMunn, "The Iconography of *Robert le Diable* and the Illustration of Medieval Romance," *Romance Languages Annual* 2 (1990): 141-45. See also Corinne Cooper-Deniau, "Le Diable au Moyen-Age, entre peur

date and spirit to the *Roman de Mélusine* which exists in two manuscripts as well, one written in prose by Jean d'Arras (ca 1393) and another in verse by Coudrette (ca 1401). I will focus on Jean d'Arras's *Mélusine* because of its emphasis on the psychology of its protagonists and because elements of its plot are more closely aligned with those in *Robert le Diable*.[9]

Although I use the word hybrid to characterize both Robert and Geoffrey, there are some subtle distinctions to be made with respect to their biological makeup. Geoffrey Big Tooth is a true hybrid in that he is the offspring of his fairy mistress mother Mélusine and her mortal husband Raymondin. Mélusine is herself the hybrid offspring of her human father Elinas of Scotland and her fairy mistress mother Présine. Geoffrey is in essence a hybrid twice removed—a hybrid of a hybrid—in that the origins of his supernatural fairy bloodline derive not solely from his mother but from his grandmother, both of whom married mortal men and who with these men gave birth to human offspring. One may observe a diminution of fairy blood and its potency across the generations as it becomes diluted as a result of interbreeding with humankind. Présine possesses the ability to cast disparate spells on each of her three daughters as punishment for their having enclosed their father within the mountain of Brumbloremlion in Northumberland. As a result of her mother's spell Mélusine's body is forced to shift shape into serpentine form from the waist down on Saturdays. The spell may be lifted if Mélusine marries a mortal who promises never to see her on Saturday. If such a man keeps his promise, Mélusine's body will revert to human form, thus allowing her to die the death of a mortal woman and hence be redeemed. If he fails to keep his word, Mélusine will be banished from human society and forced to take on permanently her serpent form until Judgment Day.[10]

In contrast to her mother, Mélusine's powers seem to be less potent as the fairy portion of the bloodline with its supernatural gifts is diluted through intermarriage with humankind. Mélusine shares with her mother the ability to predict the future and secret knowledge of ancestral origins. Her knowledge of Raymondin's ancestry propels her to urge him to recover lands wrested unlawfully from his father, Hervy. Her fairy nature also endows her with an enhanced capacity for fertility, the ability to construct castles at record speed and miraculously conjure up land from the dimensions of a stag's hide. The remaining vestiges of fairy nature in Mélusine's children reside in the physical tares or

---

et angoisse: Le Motif de 'l'enfant voué au diable' et la légende de Robert le Diable," *Travaux de Littérature* 16 (2003): 27–45.

9 All references to Jean d'Arras's *Le Roman de Mélusine* are based on the following edition: Jean d'Arras, *Mélusine ou la noble histoire de Lusignan*. ed., intro. and trans. Jean-Jacques Vincensini (Paris: Librairie Générale Française, 2003).

10 Cf. Dorothy Yamamoto, *The Boundaries of the Human in Medieval English Literature* (Oxford: Oxford University Press, 2000).

mother marks born on the faces of eight of her ten sons, the latter sons Raymonnet and Thierry being physically normal as Mélusine's fairy nature becomes diluted throughout the course of her marriage.

Unlike Geoffrey, Robert is not technically a hybrid because the devil did not sire him through sexual relations with his mother the Duchess of Normandy, rather Robert's mother made a pact with the devil to facilitate his conception through normal conjugal means with the caveat that her human offspring be consecrated to the devil's evil intent. Whereas Mélusine is fecund, having given birth to ten sons, Robert's mother has been unable to conceive after seventeen years of marriage. Feeling humiliated for her inability to conceive when women of lesser rank bear children, the duchess accuses God, claiming he lacks the power to give her a child. Since fertility was often viewed as an act of divine grace and its opposite, the inability to conceive, a sign of God's displeasure, the duchess commits a grave error in attributing her barrenness to God rather than to her own unworthiness. She then addresses the devil, telling him that she will henceforth direct her prayers to him if he helps her produce an heir. Shortly thereafter, her husband, the Duke of Normandy, lies with her and she conceives a child that will be consecrated to evil. Robert is the scion of the devil in much the same way that Saint Alexis becomes a holy man: a supernatural being facilitates the birth of a child but in return the child will serve in some way the facilitator of its being. In this case the tie between Robert and the devil is contractual rather than biological, although Robert's distinctively tall and physically strong body type implies his affinity with the supernatural. If not genetically the devil's son in body, Robert will certainly play that role in spirit.

As hybrids, in the sense that Robert and Geoffrey exhibit extraordinary physical and behavioral anomalies typically linked with supernatural agents, their bodies are characterized by gigantism, which in medieval romance often signifies demonic origins and negative human failings such as cruelty, savage strength, anger, pride and lust. Robert's behavior is diabolical from birth as he scratches, kicks, wails, and torments his caretakers. He bites the breasts of his nurses so viciously that they must use a horn in order to feed him. He wreaks havoc wherever he goes, striking and killing anyone who gets in his way. Robert grows more in one year than most children grow in seven and at age twenty he stands taller and is stronger than any of his peers. Robert develops a particular hatred for members of the clergy and his violence against the Church becomes so egregious that the pope excommunicates him. Banished from home by his parents Robert joins up with bandits, terrorizing all who come into contact with him. Like Robert, Geoffrey is described as tall and muscular, a man of extraordinary strength, boldness and ferocity in battle. Geoffrey, however, is a tamer image of Robert. He does not use his extraordinary height or strength for evil purposes until rather late in the romance when his violence erupts unexpectedly against family members.

The emblem of Geoffrey's destructive anger lies in his mother mark, the boar's tooth that juts out of his mouth and serves as a reminder of the boar hunt that led to his father's banishment and union with Mélusine.

The fulcrum and turning point of each romance concerns the destruction of an abbey which is consumed by fire along with all of its inhabitants. This event serves as a catalyst that provokes a crisis of conscience, which forces the malefactor to realize the egregious nature of his crime, thus driving him to seek penance. Robert's destruction of the Abbey of Arques stems from an innate, natural hatred for the clergy since as a scion of the devil he is naturally inclined to hate all things relating to God. However, the realization of the negative impact of this crime hits home when he returns to the city of Arques after having destroyed the abbey and finds no one to take his horse. Robert becomes pensive, wondering why everyone runs from him in fear and why his every attempt at doing good always results in evil. In Rutebeuf's *Miracle de Théophile* (ca 1260) a similar sense of alienation, of being separated from humankind due to evil intent, also moves Théophile to seek redemption through the grace of the Virgin Mary. Neither Théophile's riches nor Robert's glee in sheer destruction result in any long lasting sense of self fulfillment since human happiness relies on communion with others and selfish acts always diminish one's relations with others. There is no greater source of terror than that of being entirely alone.

In contrast to Robert, up until the burning of the Abbey of Maillezais, when Geoffrey killed his brother Fromont and all of the monks within, Geoffrey's behavior had been wholly exemplary. He exhibited nothing but love and charity toward his brothers, even going so far as to risk life and limb defending them in various military campaigns. With the exception of this misadventure sibling rivalry seems to be wholly absent from this romance as evidenced by Guy and Urien who are the first of Mélusine's sons to embark on adventure with the express intent of avoiding possible brotherly conflict over inheritance by seeking lands and empire overseas. Thus far, Geoffrey has followed in his father's footsteps by reclaiming ancestral lands in Ireland just as Raymondin, inspired by Mélusine, reclaimed the lands lost to Hervy, his father in Brittany. During this exploit Geoffrey acts compassionately toward the Lady of Valbruiyant, a resourceful and clever mother resembling Mélusine who manages to smooth over her husband's treason which Geoffrey seems to overlook. Geoffrey then travels to the Holy Land in the name of Christendom to defend his brothers Guy and Urien against Saracen attack.

Not only does Geoffrey prove himself to be the most heroic warrior among his brothers, he manages to make peace with one of Christendom's fiercest enemies, the Sultan of Damascus. Geoffrey is also the only Lusignan to battle against supernatural foes, as embodied in the giant Gardon, who pillages and terrorizes his father's subjects and finally against Grimaut, Gardon's uncle. By defeating this giant Geoffrey acts for the collective good, bringing peace, law and order to his father's kingdom. As Rupert Pickens observes "Although Geoffrey is foolhardy and often callous, nothing in his character and nothing in Jean's plot—not any form of antimonasticism, not a hint of hatred for his brother—anticipates such an effusion of cruelty".[11] While it is true that there did exist an historical Geoffrey of Lusignan who set fire to the Abbey of Maillezais in 1323, the sudden intrusion of this act of violence seems utterly gratuitous and out of character given Geoffrey's behavior in the romance thus far, unless it is understood within the context of the penitential romance, where acts of violence are endemic to offspring of supernatural origins and may crop up unexpectedly.

One might understand why Geoffrey attacks his paternal uncle, the Count of Forest, in revenge against his accusations against Mélusine, which led Raymondin to break his pact with her. However, it is difficult to fathom the cause of Geoffrey's attack against Fromont, who was granted permission to become a monk from his parents. The text clearly indicates that Fromont is not at fault: "Mais sachiéz que ce ne fut mie le fait de Fromont, car il fu moult devot et de moult saincte vie . . . ." (676; But know that this was not Fromont's fault, for he was very devout and led a very holy life . . .). One might surmise that Geoffrey's values are too worldly for him to support his brother's choice of career or that he might love this brother too much, thus turning an excess of love into hatred. At first Geoffrey blames his parents for not providing Fromont with land and a wife which would allow him to lead a secular existence. He then accuses the monks of Maillezais of being lecherous and having enchanted his brother into becoming a monk in order to bring prestige to their order.

He refuses to believe that Fromont has decided to become a monk on his own volition despite Fromont's assertions to the contrary: "Mon chier frere, par l'ame que j'ay a Dieu a rendre, il n'a personne ceans qui oncques le me conseillast. Car je l'ay fait de moy propre, sans conseil d'autrui et par droicte devocion" (682; My dear brother, upon the soul that I owe unto God, no one here has ever advised me, for I have done this of my own free will, without advice from anyone and through pure devotion). In his anger Geoffrey disregards this argument, considering it a personal affront to have a brother as a monk as if this vocation were inherently shameful: ". . . ne il me sera ja reprouvé que j'aye moine a frere!" (682; . . .nor will I ever be reproached for having a monk for a brother). Mélusine seems to affirm this thesis later on when she tries to reconcile father and son over the death of Fromont: "Se Gieffroy, vostre filz, a fait son oultraige par son courage merveilleux et fort, sachiéz que de certain c'est pour le pechié des moines, qui estoient de

11 Rupert Pickens, "The Poetics of Paradox in the *Roman de Mélusine*," *Mélusine of Lusignan: Founding Fiction in Late Medieval France*, ed. Donald Maddox and Sara Sturm-Maddox (Athens and London: The University of Georgia Press, 1996), 48–75; here, 60.

mauvaise vie et desordonnee" (692; If your son Geoffrey has committed an outrage through his marvelous and strong courage, know that for certain it is because of the sin of the monks who lead an evil and dissolute life). To what debauchery is Mélusine referring? Could there be an underlying current of homosexuality implied in this vocation?[12] Or is there a rivalry between the two brothers that parallels the dispute between Cain and Abel? Could Geoffrey be jealous of his brother's less worldly vocation just as Cain was upset that his sacrificial offering was less pleasing to God? At one point Raymondin seems to demonstrate a preference for Fromont: "Il n'avoit yssi de toy plus de bien que Fromont" (694; Fromont was the greatest good that has come from you). On the other hand, this excess of anger that goes beyond the bounds of reason parallels that of Mélusine when she wreaked revenge on her father out of a mistaken sense of loyalty to Presine. By taking justice into his own hands against a family member Geoffrey's behavior reflects that of his mother, thus creating a causal link to anger, homicide and his hybrid origins.[13]

Ten knights of Geoffrey's retinue jump to Fromont's defense, affirming his right and indicating that Fromont, through prayers and good actions, could absolve the sins burdening the souls of his fellow monks. Impervious to reason Geoffrey alone sets fire to the abbey since the knights refuse to take part in this senseless killing. It is only after Geoffrey departs and looks at the scene of the crime from a distance that he repents and realizes the full extent of his actions. If not for the intervention of his men, the text implies that Geoffrey would have committed suicide at sword point out of despair. The solace they give Geoffrey reflects the advice Mélusine will later give her husband when he learns of this crime: "Sire, sire, c'est trop tart a repentir quant la folie est faicte. Le doloser n'y vault desormais rien. Mais pensèz de faire en la satisfacion a Dieu et au monde" (684–86; My lord, my lord, it is too late to repent when the deed is done. From now on sorrow serves no useful purpose. Think instead of making restitution to God and to the world). When evil occurs, there is no use in crying over spilled milk, one must carry on and try to make restitution through good works.

In contrast to Geoffrey, Robert's path to redemption follows an added step that is dimly reflected in the *Roman de Mélusine*. This added step concerns his mother in whom he detects the origins of his wayward tendencies. Robert's early relationship with women is troublesome and fraught with violence beginning with

---

12 It would be interesting to conduct further research into this matter to see if such an accusation could be leveled at any particular monastic order at this time or against any of the Lusignans.

13 For an analysis of the theme of anger in the *Roman de Mélusine*, see my article "'Tel cuide vengier sa honte qui l'accroist': Wrath in Jean Arras's *Roman de Mélusine*," *Courtly Arts and the Art of Courtliness: Selected Papers from the Eleventh Triennial Congress of the International Courtly Literature Society*. University of Wisconsin-Madison, 29 July – 4 August 2005. ed. Keith Busby and Christopher Kleinhenz (Cambridge and Rochester, NY: D. S. Brewer, 2006), 419–30.

his long and painful birth that causes his mother great suffering and the nipple he bites off of his most beautiful wet nurse. After having vented his rage on nuns, perhaps a disguised and unconscious form of mother hatred, Robert wonders why he is always driven to commit mayhem. He surmises that his evil deeds must have something to do with the circumstances attending his birth and that the fault lies with his mother.

We know from romances such as the *Lancelot-Grail* Cycle that the circumstances attending one's birth can be a harbinger of later moral deviation, especially since it was believed that original sin passed from generation to generation through the concupiscence that accompanies sexual relations. As sex was associated with original sin, it was believed that original sin was passed down along the generations through the process of reproduction and that sexual deviance could also be passed along from parent to child just as nobility of character was seen as stemming from a noble lineage. Being born of an adulterous or unnatural coupling increased the chances that one might have a proclivity toward sexual excess. This was the case for King Arthur who was born of an adulterous liaison and who acted out his immoral origins by committing an act of incest with his half-sister, resulting in the engendering of Mordred.

In keeping with this pattern Mordred ends up coveting his father's wife and empire, leading to the final battle between father and son on the plain of Salisbury and their mutual extinction. In most of these cases it is the father who failed to abide by the proper code of sexual relations, which resulted in the moral deficiencies in his offspring. Only divine intervention can rectify the sin in an illegitimate act of conception so that harm does not come to the child. Divine intervention and the virginity or virtue of the mother can smooth over an illegitimate birth, as was the case for Galaad, whose mother was the virgin grail maiden, and Merlin, whose mother repented of the anger which allowed the devil to impregnate her. How Robert makes the leap from masculine to feminine misconduct in his engendering is quite interesting. His suspicions are based on his mother's evasiveness regarding the question of paternity:

Pense que celle mescheance
Li soit venue par naissance,
Et que coupes y ait sa mere,
Qui onques ne fu vers luy clere:
Bien set l'ocoison et le teche
Et l'aventure pour quoy [p]esche. (vv. 647–52)

[Robert thought that this wickedness
Came from his birth
And that his mother was somehow to blame
She had never been straightforward with him

She must know the reason and the stain
And the event because of which he sins.]

Robert threatens his mother at sword point to tell him the truth regarding his conception. It is when she tells of her pact with the devil, that Robert undergoes the transformation necessary for his rehabilitation. The knowledge of his true paternal affiliation creates a shock that rattles Robert to his very core. His immediate reaction is anger, followed by suffering, shame, and finally bitter tears. In his analysis of this motif in the *Romance of Sir Gowther*, which follows a similar pattern, Jeffrey Cohen sees in this reaction the imprint of Freud's Oedipus complex and by extension the Lacanian phenomenon of the Name of the Father.[14] According to this interpretation, the symbolic death of the father, the one Robert believed had engendered him, and acceptance of responsibility for that death causes Robert to enter into the symbolic order, which provokes his conversion. In order to restore loss of the biological father, Robert embraces the symbolic father who represents law and order. It is at this moment that Robert sets off on his pilgrimage to Rome to seek absolution for his sins from the pope, the symbolic father of the Catholic Church.

According to Jane Gilbert, normally monstrous children of the penitential romances "... are images of their father's failure to perform the paternal function ..."[15] Robert's father, the Duke of Normandy, lacked the potency to procreate and as a result his mother asked the devil to help her conceive a child. Although Geoffrey's father Raymondin is sexually potent, having engendered ten sons, he is a rather weak figure who bows to Mélusine in matters of running their estate and directing their children's education. He lacks the temerity to inquire into his wife's upbringing when confronted by his relatives about her origins. Even though Mélusine defers to her husband when appropriate, she tends to dominate, making most of the important decisions.

As Stephen Nichols has pointed out "She has, after all, returned her father to the womb and symbolically assumed the male roles of master builder ..., founder of a lineage, and strategist for the conflicts in which her husband engages."[16] In spite of Mélusine's dominant role both within and outside the family, Geoffrey has a positive relationship with women and commits no violent acts against them, unlike Robert who indiscriminately rapes any woman crossing his path before his

---

14 Jeffrey Jerome Cohen. *Of Giants. Sex, Monsters, and the Middle Ages*. Medieval Cultures, 17 (Minneapolis: University of Minnesota Press, 1999). See his chapter entitled "The Body Hybrid: Giants, Dog-men, and Becoming Inhuman," 119–41.

15 Gilbert, "Unnatural Mothers and Monstrous Children," 340 (see note 4).

16 Stephen Nichols, "Mélusine between Myth and History: Profile of a Female Demon," *Mélusine of Lusignan: Founding Fiction in late Medieval France*, ed. Donald Maddox and Sara Sturm-Maddox (Athens and London: The University of Georgia Press, 1996), 137–64; here 154–55.

conversion. The crime of unbound lust, whether through rape, fornication, or adultery, plays no important role for the Lusignan clan in the *Roman de Mélusine*, since all love relationships end in marriage. Four of Mélusine's sons (Guy, Urien, Renaud and Antoine) engage in battle for the sole purpose of protecting vulnerable daughters from being forced into marriages against their will. They then go on to marry these maidens and become landowners abroad. Unbridled lust occurs only among foreign knights and in the Armenian branch of the family at the very end of the romance when a young Armenian king demonstrates incestuous feelings for his aunt Melior during the Adventure at the Sparrowhawk Castle, which brings about the downfall and eventual decline of his family line. This lack of lust, either forbidden or culminating in adultery, distinguishes the *Roman de Mélusine* from prior major prose romances like the *Lancelot-Grail* Cycle and the Prose *Tristan*, where lust leads to the climatic end of chivalric Arthurian society. Violence and anger appear to have replaced lust as the tragic flaw leading to destruction in the penitential romances.

Whereas it is Robert who rages against his mother, the purported cause of his diabolical origins, by threatening her at knifepoint, it is Mélusine's husband Raymondin and not Geoffrey who rages against Mélusine as the possible source of Geoffrey's demonic behavior. Although it is Geoffrey's violent act of fratricide that provokes his father to break his oath to Mélusine by publically decrying her serpent nature, thus banishing her from the human world, this inadvertent matricide, for which Geoffrey is held responsible, is an unwanted consequence of his crime and not its intent. His sense of outrage regarding the loss of his mother will be taken out on the Count of Forest, the uncle who encouraged Raymondin to spy on his wife, thus causing Raymondin to break his oath to her. In a diatribe that has dire consequences for Mélusine Raymondin makes a direct connection between the criminality of his son and Mélusine's mysterious serpent nature:

> Hee, tresfaulse serpente, par Dieu, ne toy ne tes fais ne sont que fantosme ne ja hoir que tu ayes porté ne vendra a bon chief en la fin. Comment raront les vies ceulx qui sont ars en grief misere ne ton filz qui s'estoit renduz au crucefix? Il n'avoit yssi de toy plus de bien que Fromont. Or est destruit par l'art demoniacle, car tous ceulx qui sont forcennéz de yre sont ou commandement des princes d'enfer et par ce fist Gieffroy le grant et horrible et hideux forfait d'ardoir son frere et les moines, qui mort ne avoient point desservie. (692–94)

> [O false serpent, by God, you and your deeds are nothing but phantasms, and no heir that you have ever borne will turn out well in the end. How will those who were burnt with such painful suffering ever regain their lives, including your own son who dedicated his life to Christ? Fromont was the only good thing that ever came from you. Now he's destroyed by demonic arts, for all those maddened with rage do the bidding of the princes of hell; and so it was that Geoffrey committed this great and heinous

> crime of burning his brother and the monks who never for a moment deserved such a death.[17]]

Raymondin then goes on to wish that his son had never been born. This renunciation of paternity culminates in an oedipal moment as Raymondin vows to kill his son with his bare hands. Both Robert and Geoffrey experience danger with respect to their fathers who wish to put them to death as punishment for their heinous crimes. In both instances the mother plays the role of intercessor. In order to save her son, Robert's mother suggests that he be made a knight in the hope that knighthood might channel his violent tendencies toward some better end. Similarly, Mélusine tries to reconcile Raymondin with Geoffrey by downplaying the gravity of his misdeeds and by predicting his future rehabilitation.

In both romances deviant behavior in offspring is associated with maternal defects. According to medieval medical lore a woman's emotions during her time of pregnancy (her *envie de mère*) could leave a physical and moral imprint on her offspring.[18] Any good accruing to a child would come from its father's seed. Mélusine's mother Présine makes this clear to her by stating that her hope for redemption lies in the good that she inherited from her father. The blame for evil behavior is shifted from male agency and free will onto the female element of generation. Laurence de Looze indicates the lack of fairness in this instance:

> It is hubristic for Raymondin to raise himself above the law and claim no participation in sin's transmission. Second is that Raymondin fails to see his boar-son as a sign of his own violent transgression, also represented by a boar. Finally, Raymondin proves himself a slave to the signifier here, for he focuses entirely on Mélusine as serpent-sign and not at all on her intentions. Accusing her of being Old Testamant in nature, Raymondin is in fact the one who proves *himself* an Old Testament type of interpreter.[19]

According to De Looze, Raymondin represents the Old Testament literal eye for an eye justice while Mélusine represents the New Testament justice of compassion and mercy that stresses intention over act. As stated earlier, the conduct of the father during the time of a child's conception may have a deleterious impact on his offspring as in the *Lancelot-Grail* cycle, yet a child may be spared by divine intervention if the mother happens to be a virgin or repents of the deed that engendered the child as was the case regarding the births of Galaad and Merlin.

---

17 Stephen Nichols, "Mélusine Between Myth and History," 149 (see note 16).

18 Douglas Kelly, "The Domestication of the Marvelous in the Mélusine Romances," *Mélusine of Lusignan: Founding Fiction in Late Medieval France*, ed. Donald Maddox and Sara Sturm-Maddox (Athens and London: The University of Georgia Press, 1996), 32–47; here, 39–40.

19 Laurence de Looze, "'La fourme du pié toute escripte': Mélusine and the Entrance into History," *Mélusine of Lusignan: Founding Fiction in Late Medieval France*, ed. Donald Maddox and Sara Sturm-Maddox (Athens and London: The University of Georgia Press, 1996), 125–36; here, 132.

There seems to be a conflict regarding whether a genetic predisposition towards evil stems from the maternal or paternal line. Raymondin's shortsightedness on this issue is born out when Geoffrey does manage to redeem himself and make amends for his misconduct near the end of the romance.

Although both Geoffrey and Robert repent of their crimes by seeking absolution from the pope in Rome, Robert's penance is far more developed and severe because his crimes are more weighty and endemic to his personality than Geoffrey's crimes. In fact, Robert's crimes are so egregious that the pope is unable to assign him an appropriate penance and sends him to his confessor, a hallowed hermit living in the forest of Marabonde who is only able to obtain the proper penance through divine intervention during mass. The penance arrives in the form of a letter handed down by a mysterious hand as if God alone has the capacity to intervene in the affairs of Satan, his archenemy.

Robert experiences fully the three stages of penance assigned by Abélard and developed by Pierre the Chanter, namely, "contrition of heart, confession by mouth, and satisfaction of works."[20] The first stage occurred immediately upon Robert's acknowledgment of his sin when he first felt anger, then intense suffering and shame, followed by tears. Having thrown away his sword, he then shaves his head and dresses in rags as a sign of humility. Robert confesses his sins to the pope who writes them down in the letter he directs Robert to give to the hermit. According to divine decree Robert's penance is tripartite: 1) he is commanded to play the role of the fool or madman which will give others license to abuse him 2) he must never speak during the period of his penance and 3) he must eat only what he can wrest from the mouths of dogs. He is also told that if a messenger from God sends him on a mission, he must obey, provided the messenger can name his three divinely ordained penances.

Robert then travels to Rome where he lives the life of a madman at the home of an emperor whose only heir is his mute daughter. Once Robert becomes the town fool, citizens have the right to beat and abuse him. The victimizer becomes the victim of collective hatred and rage, thus Robert's earlier unbridled, senseless violence is repaid in kind. Robert's abasement, which has a cathartic effect, amuses the king and the court. Robert's imposed vow of silence represents the silencing of his ego and demonstrates obedience, one of the basic tenants of civility and courtly decorum, which Robert needs to develop in order to return to the social

20 John W. Baldwin, *Aristocratic Life in Medieval France: The Romances of Jean Renart and Gerbert de Montreuil, 1190–1230* (Baltimore and London: The Johns Hopkins University Press, 2000), 225, gives a detailed analysis of the sacrament of penance in several twelfth and thirteenth century French romances based on church doctrine.

order. Since contrition demands humility, the forsaking of ego and the surrender of self, Robert accomplishes this by eating and living among the dogs.[21]

The three penances described above represent an internal cleansing and abasement that must occur in order for Robert to be integrated into the human order, where he learns to behave much like an obedient dog that gains mastery over its selfish, instinctual urges. This allows Robert to exist in society without posing any risks or harm to the populace. The life of a dog, however, is hardly honorable. Robert needs to complete the final phase of his rehabilitation, "the satisfaction of works," that will allow him to be a contributing member of society, capable of sacrificing his own self interests to that of the greater good. Robert will do this on two levels. First, he will risk life and limb in order to defend the social order, as represented in the emperor and his daughter, who are besieged by an angry seneschal. Second, he will uphold the spiritual order, as represented by the Church, which Robert defends against the infidel Turks who besiege Rome.

Because salvation is dependent upon grace, Robert will need outside help in order to vindicate himself on both the social and spiritual levels. One of the instruments of Robert's rehabilitation on the social level will be the emperor's beautiful daughter, who is herself mute due to some unnamed sin: "Mais ne sai quel desloiauté / Ne quelz pechiés mut la pucielle, / C'ainc ne parla, ains est muielle" (1248–1250; Yet I do not know what unlawful act / nor what sin silenced the maiden / she never speaks / rather she is mute). Although the emperor's daughter is able to understand the speech of others, she can only communicate using sign language. Robert and the emperor's daughter will rely upon each other for mutual support as they strive to redeem themselves.

As in the *Roman de Mélusine* a male and female misfit who bear the weight of their sins (paralleling Raymondin and Mélusine, both of whom committed homicide, one involuntarily and the other voluntarily), come together to work out their mutual salvation. Although the text never explicitly refers to the exact nature of the emperor's daughter's sin, Agata Sobczyk believes that the secret sin for which the young woman suffers is hidden incest, for her father is extremely possessive and does not want to marry her to his seneschal who constantly harasses him for her hand in marriage.[22] In fact, according to Sobczyk, the emperor

---

21 Jeffrey Jerome Cohen devotes an entire article to the significance of the dog in the rehabilitation of Sir Gowther, whose life follows the same trajectory as Robert's. Much of his analysis is based on the image of the dog as an oedipalized being that helps Gowther come to terms with his identity, "Gowther Among the Dogs: Becoming Inhuman C. 1400," *Becoming Male in the Middle Ages,"* ed. Jeffrey Jerome Cohen and Bonnie Wheeler (New York: Garland, 1997), 219–44.

22 Agata Sobczyk, "Encore un inceste occulté: l'épisode de la fille de l'empereur dans *Le Roman de Robert le Diable," Etudes médiévales,* ed. Danielle Buschinger. Collection Médiévales (Amiens: Centre d'Etudes Médiévales, Université de Picardie-Jules Verne, 1999), 221–34. Gaucher also affirms that this is a likely assumption, *Robert le Diable*: *Histoire d'une légende,* 34 (see note 6).

permits her to marry only when a worthy suitor (Robert) is wounded in the thigh, symbolically rendering him impotent and therefore unable to enjoy the sexual relations her father might find threatening.

After a lapse of seven years, Robert's life among the dogs takes a new turn when the Turks attack Rome. During this whole period the emperor's seneschal has been waging war against him, leaving him defenseless in a time of need and likely to lose the war. Alarmed, Robert goes off to pray near a fountain, asking that God grant him the opportunity to fight in the emperor's defense. Although Robert prays in silence, the emperor's daughter observes his gestures and understands his prayer. In answer to his plea an angel appears who presents Robert with arms and a sword and commands him to fight for the sake of Christendom.

The angel, dressed in white arms and riding a white steed, resembles the archangel Michael, the sworn enemy of Satan, who protects humanity against diabolical forces. Under the auspices of the angel, we see that Robert is no longer an adversary against Christendom. Rather than wage war against all things holy, he defends the church with all of his strength. The violence that characterized Robert's youth has now been channeled to a higher end. For three years in a row Robert defeats the Turks fighting *incognito* and after each battle he returns bloody and beaten to the fountain where the angel appears to take away his arms. No one at court knows that the silent man who eats with the dogs is actually the valiant warrior who has spared them from Turkish invasion except for the emperor's daughter who has observed his interactions with the angel and his prowess on the battlefield. Since the emperor's daughter is unable to speak and her attempts at communicating his identity through sign language are rebuffed, Robert's identity remains a mystery until the emperor devises a plan to catch him by ambush as he returns from battle.

Unfortunately, the plan backfires and Robert is accidentally wounded in the thigh with a lance whose tip embeds itself in the wound. The emperor's daughter watches Robert dress his wound and pull out the lance head which he then promptly hides. In a final attempt to learn Robert's identity the emperor promises his daughter in marriage to the man who can show both the wound and lance tip that matches the wound. The seneschal uses this opportunity to lay claim to the emperor's daughter by wounding himself at lance point and passing himself off as Robert. The young maiden seems doomed to an unhappy marriage until, through an act of divine intervention, she is given the gift of speech and relates Robert's story. Later, the hermit of Marabonde arrives at court, giving Robert permission to speak. Having redeemed himself and earned a new identity, Robert can now pronounce his name and recount his life story to the court. Shortly thereafter, Robert learns that his parents have died and he is invited to return home to Normandy in order to become king. He is also invited to marry the emperor's daughter and become the future emperor of Rome. Fearful that his soul is still in peril Robert refuses all worldly goods, preferring to dedicate himself to God by living as a hermit in the company of the hermit who saved his life. Robert ends his days performing miracles and is buried in Rome until a powerful count steals his bones and with them founds the Abbey Saint Robert near Puy.

As commonly occurs in medieval romance, feminine agency brings about the integration of the hero into the public domain. Just as Mélusine made Raymondin's return to civilization possible by endowing her husband with a fief through the miracle of the stag's hide, the emperor's daughter plays a similar role by miraculously breaking her silence in order to let the court know of Robert's heroic exploits. Because Robert has committed violent crimes against women, it is fitting that he should repair the injustice by making restitution to a woman. Just as his mother's pact with the devil led to his downfall, the emperor's daughter makes up for this injury, first through her silence and the punishments she receives trying to uphold his honor, and then through the gift of speech, which allows her to make his valor public. The emperor's daughter's wise speech contrasts with Robert's mother's treasonous oath. Robert preserves the worldly order by defending the interests of the emperor's daughter against the wayward seneschal and the spiritual order by engaging in a holy war and thus proving he is a man of God, not the scion of the devil. His marked preference for the celibate life helps mitigate the horrible rapes he performed as a wayward youth.

In the *Roman de Mélusine* a wider gap exists between the commission of the heinous crime centered on the desecration of a holy space, the full consciousness of the egregiousness nature of the crime, and the pilgrimage to Rome. Geoffrey will make his pilgrimage to Rome after his father makes his pilgrimage first as penance for having betrayed Mélusine. It is a general pattern in the prose romance for Geoffrey to follow in his father's footsteps. Narrative events in *Robert the Devil* are altered to suit new circumstances across the generations in the *Roman de Mélusine*. Although both Geoffrey and his father seek absolution for their crimes by visiting the pope, it is Raymondin who becomes a hermit at the end of the romance and not Geoffrey.

Unlike Robert, Geoffrey does not rehabilitate himself through any kind of humiliation or self-abasement. Robert's penance is far more complete and heartfelt than Geoffrey's. In fact, very little space is devoted to describing Geoffrey's mental anguish apart from his initial desire to kill himself out of despair right after he burned down the abbey. Instead, like the heroes of courtly romance, he redeems himself by accomplishing difficult adventures that bring collective peace and reestablish social harmony to a disturbed social order. Whereas Robert has committed a panoply of sins, ranging from robbery, rape, murder, and the desecration of holy spaces, Geoffrey's sins are limited to three:

> Et lui souvint comment il avoit ars les moynes de Malerés et l'abbé et son frere Fromont, sans raison, et que par ce pechié avoit esté sa mere perdue, puis lui ramembre de son oncle, le conte de Forests, lequel il fist saillir de la grosse tour de Marcelli le Chastel sur la roche et le fist tuer. (736)
>
> [And he remembered how he had burned the monks of Maillezais including the abbot and his brother Fromont, without reason, and that through this sin he had lost his mother, then he remembered his uncle, the Count of Forest, whom he killed when he slipped from the high tower of Marcilly Castle onto the rock below.]

The element all three sins have in common is the death of a family member which is occasioned by Geoffrey's initial outburst of anger against Fromont.

In contrast to Robert a huge gap exists between the moment when Geoffrey commits his most heinous crime and his pilgrimage to Rome to seek absolution. After destroying the abbey of Maillezais, Geoffrey causes another homicide, the death of his paternal uncle. Geoffrey will then discover his family origins through battle and in this he resembles the heroes of both verse and prose romance, among them Lancelot and the Fair Unknown, who uncover the secrets of their name and lineage through chivalry. These knights must prove, through accomplishing difficult exploits, that they are worthy of their bloodlines. Geoffrey must conquer and expiate the giant within himself by defeating the giant Grimaut, thus triumphing over his giant nature before reaching the state of surrender and humility requisite for penance.[23]

According to Jeffrey Cohen, "In identity romance, the moment of Oedipalization usually occurs during the fight against the giant. The young hero defeats his monstrous double, rendering a volatile multiplicity of possibility into a unitary, regularized being."[24] After Geoffrey kills Grimaut in the very mountain where his grandfather was interred, Geoffrey learns from an inscription held in the hands of an alabaster statue of Présine that his maternal grandfather is King Elinas of Scotland. He also learns how Elinas came to be imprisoned in this spot, the three punishments allotted to his mother and her two sisters for this crime and how the giant had been placed there to guard the tomb until a descendant of one of Elinas' daughters would banish him.

This event marks Geoffrey as the predestined, elect member of his lineage to whom the full story of his family's transgressions on his mother's side is made known. Geoffrey learns that the Lusignans descend from an illustrious lineage of which they can be proud, thus mitigating the social onus associated with Mélusine's supernatural origins and serpent body. Geoffrey's plumbing of the secret of his origins mimics Robert's discovery of his devil origins. However, the

---

23 Geoffrey defeats a giant before and after the burning of the Abbey of Maillezais.

24 Cohen, *Of Giants*, 125 (see note 14).

narrator attenuates the fairy, maternal element of his lineage in favor of the human, masculine one. Geoffrey's final adventures will be devoted to sharing this information with his father and the rest of his siblings. It appears that Jean d'Arras is legitimizing Mélusine's bloodlines by stressing its human connections. Once these origins have been made clear, Geoffrey makes his pilgrimage to Rome where the pope declares his penance to be the rebuilding of the Abbey of Maillezais and the restoration of its monastic order. The pilgrimage does not take place right away, however, because, as we have already observed in previous adventures, Geoffrey's life path will retrace, in keeping with the genre of the genealogical romances, those of his father. Raymondin will journey to Rome first in order to atone for his betrayal of Mélusine with Geoffrey following in his footsteps after he learns that his father has become a hermit.

Although Geoffrey seems to be the son who resembles Robert the most, Mélusine's ten sons represent variations of behavior that can occur within the hybrid race. If we perceive the Robert the Devil legend as having loosely inspired the *Roman de Mélusine*, Jean d'Arras takes the story of the demon son and turns it into a family drama, drawing it out synchronically within the immediate family so that each son represents a different shade of hybrid conduct and diachronically across the generations as their hybrid nature dissipates through time. As stated earlier, what distinguishes Mélusine's sons as hybrids are the mother marks or congenital defects that mar the faces of eight of her ten offspring, the latter sons Thierry and Raymonnet being physically normal. In addition, the Lusignan family is subject to an innate tendency to commit homicide, whether of a voluntary or involuntary nature, for it was Mélusine's act of parricide and Raymondin's accidental slaying of his uncle Aimery during a boar hunt that brought the banished couple together. It appears that the marriage between them is a test that will result in mutual redemption if the couple can only manage to reconcile their differences.

Seven of Mélusine's ten sons lead rather normal lives in spite of their hybrid nature by marrying mortal women and raising children. Near the end of the romance we hear accounts of Mélusine's grandsons, all of whom are fully human, and who marry and found families. Douglas Kelly brings attention to Mélusine's three celibate sons Geoffrey, Fromont and Horrible who stand out from their brothers by their singular natures.[25] These sons are the last to bear mother-marks, the physical deformities that identify them as hybrids. The remaining sons, Thierry and Remonnet, are normal, which attests to Mélusine's transformation through marriage from fairy mistress to human female. Each one of the three celibate sons embodies in three persons the tripartite evolution or series of stages attained by

25 Douglas Kelly, "The Domestication of the Marvelous," 34–35 (see note 18).

Robert as he evolves from a demonic monster into a saint. Horrible, the unredeemable Lusignan with three eyes, resembles Robert in his most primitive, brutal state, having first killed two nurses by the age of four by biting their nipples, and later, two servants.

This son is so vicious that Mélusine asks that he be put to death by suffocation so that he will not inflict further injury on her subjects.[26] Here, we see how a personality trait in Robert the Devil is reworked and expanded to become a separate character in the *Roman de Mélusine*. Fromont represents the opposite extreme from Horrible, for his heart's desire is to become a monk, a vocation to which Mélusine and Raymondin give their full consent. As we have seen, rather than do harm to others, Fromont becomes the victim of Geoffrey's murderous rage and thus absorbs and suffers the violence to which his lineage seems destined. Geoffrey's behavior represents the mean between abject cruelty and saintliness as he vacillates between the two extremes represented by Horrible and Fromont. Geoffrey is responsible for the death of Fromont and his uncle the Count of Forest, yet he also performs heroically in battle defending the interests of his brothers and prior to his act of fratricide, he crusaded on behalf of the Church in the Holy Lands.[27]

Although Geoffrey never becomes a saintly hermit like Robert, he does remain celibate and devotes the latter part of his life to ensuring the eternal salvation of his family through the construction of an abbey, chapel and hospital. The person who follows in Robert's path as repentant, saintly hermit is Raymondin, and indeed, his penance seems to be more heartfelt and deeper than Geoffrey's. It appears that the character of Robert the Devil has been broken up into four separate, contrasting persons in the *Roman de Mélusine*. First, there is the trinity of male celibate offspring, two of whom represent extremes that cannot survive in the human world. This trinity of male offspring reflects the trinity of female offspring as represented in Mélusine and her two sisters Melior and Palestine, both of whom receive a penance and are banned from participating in the human world.

---

26 Although one may be astonished at Mélusine's lack of maternal affection for Horrible and cringe at her decision to commit infanticide, Horrible's outrageous deeds warrant some sort of objective punishment and indeed he may have suffered a death sentence or banishment if he had lived to commit the crimes predicted. At the same time Mélusine's lack of familial feeling fits in with the general pattern of manslaughter exhibited by both Mélusine and Geoffrey who deliberately killed family members either out of a sense of outrage or a misguided sense of justice. This final act of homicide on the part of Mélusine could also indicate her willingness to place the common good over and above personal and family interests, thus reinforcing the notion of the paradoxical and inscrutable nature of justice that Jean d'Arras discusses in his prologue.

27 Both Geoffrey and Robert do battle against the infidel; however, Geoffrey wages such a war before the burning of the abbey and Robert does so afterwards.

According to Albrecht Classen, "There is, however, a remarkable difference between Mélusine and her two sisters who never manage to join human society and remain rather nebulous fairies who cannot, despite many efforts, be rescued from the banishment imposed on them by their mother Persina."[28] Similarly, Horrible and Fromont are banished from human society by mother and brother respectively, which leaves Geoffrey, like his mother Mélusine, to cope with the effects of his crime in the human world. Finally, there is Raymondin, who withdraws from the world in order to expiate his sins and pray for the salvation of his beloved wife.

In conclusion, the *Roman de Mélusine* incorporates and develops basic narrative patterns and character traits suggested by the legend of Robert the Devil, producing various shades of behavior as a way of exploring the effects of these behaviors on society across the generations. Neither tale follows the trajectory of twelfth or thirteenth century courtly romance in that love plays no major role as a motivating or subversive force. The relationship between Robert and the emperor's daughter is wholly chaste and all love relationships in the *Roman de Mélusine* end in marriage, with love seeming to play a very minor, almost perfunctory role. The element of forbidden, adulterous love is absent. It does seem that the two romances belong to the sub genre of the penitential romance, as many critics have suggested, because the main thrust of the romances is the exposure and expiation of a secret crime linked to one's family heritage and manifest in one's hybrid nature. The main characters must come to terms with their duality, and in so doing forge a new identity more in keeping with Christian values.

The battle between the forces of good and evil plays a particularly strong role in the lives of the hybrids, who intensify, through their excessive behavior, the gift and curse of their supernatural origins. Demonic origins seem to explain outrageous behavior that might otherwise be hard to attribute to people born of noble descent since goodness, intelligence and beauty were commonly associated with royal bloodlines. Alcuin Blamires believes that the hybrid expresses "profound medieval anxieties about the production of heirs, and particularly violent and ungovernable heirs, without laying these phenomena exclusively at the door of fiends."[29] The contradictions in these romances are purposeful and not meant to be clarified, rather they reflect the perplexing state of the world as it exists, full of enigmas regarding good and evil. These romances, written during

---

28 Albrecht Classen, "Love and Fear of the Foreign: Thüring von Ringoltingen's *Melusine* (1456): A Xenological Analysis," *Daphnis* 33.1–2 (2004): 97–122; here, 118.

29 Alcuin Blamires, "The Twin Demons of Aristocratic Society in *Sir Gowther*," *Pulp Fictions of Medieval England: Essays in Popular Romance*, ed. Nicola McDonald (Manchester and New York: Manchester University Press, 2004), 45–62; here 52.

an era when people believed in the supernatural and were unaware of the science behind reproduction, illustrate the contradictions inherent in attempting to assign good and evil to any particular cause, especially a genetic one. The celibacy of the hybrids and the extinction of their bloodline allow us to view them from a safe distance. In addition, the redemption of the demonic child gives us comfort and hope that the evil in humanity can be mitigated.

Chapter 5

Scott L. Taylor
(Pima Community College, Tucson)

Judicium Dei, vulgaris popularisque sensus: Survival of Customary Justice and Resistance to its Displacement by the "New" *Ordines iudiciorum* as Evidenced by Francophonic Literature of the High Middle Ages

Les Encoupements de la Corone,[1] an anonymous and highly practical Anglo-Norman treatise compiled circa 1274 dealing exclusively with criminal law, tells the story of a thief, indicted by the country and brought before Justice Laurence de Brok. De Brok, advising the man of the accusation, enquired of him how he wished to acquit himself. The accused replied, "By my body, sir," which is to say, by combat. And the justice advised him, "my good man, no man makes suit against you except the king, and the king does not do battle. How do you want to prove that you are good and honest?" But the thief insisted on battle, until the justice decided to ask him, "Are you a good and honest man?" "Yes, indeed," proclaimed the accused, "and I am ready to defend myself by my body against this accusation." And the justice continued, "I say, are you good and honest?" And the thief replied, "Yes, sir, I am." And the justice said "How do you wish to prove it?" And the thief said, "By the country, of course!" And the country came, and said he was a thief and had committed the theft for which he had been indicted, and several others as well; and so he was hanged, and in such a way he was tricked.[2]

---

1 Also known as *La Corone Pledee devant Justices,* or *Placita Corone,* under which latter title it has been edited with introduction, notes and translation by J. M. Kaye. Supplementary Series, 4 (London and Colchester: Selden Society, 1966).

2 *Placita Corone,* 23 (see note 1). The author of the text is discussing how to avoid being hanged by

The legal literature of the period abounds in similar games of wits as litigants stalwartly demand their customary rights and royal functionaries no less determinedly undertake to maneuver them into accepting new procedures during a period of legal transition. Beginning in the late eleventh and early twelfth centuries, in a development that would ultimately transform Western law, Romano-canonical judicial procedures based on oral and written evidence came to displace customary procedures for determining guilt and punishment resting on immanent justice. The widely debated reasons for this transformation fall into two schools of thought. The first attributes the change to sociological factors, including widespread skepticism and the growth of urban centers at the expense of small, isolated communities[3]; the other elitist perspective maintains that the ordeal disappeared largely because, on theological principles, the church withdrew its sanction by canon of Fourth Lateran Council, as well as the rise of an intellectual apparatchiki trained in the *ordines iudiciorum*, trial procedures founded upon the Roman law.[4]

---

insisting on battle, instructing the reader: "Et feta saver ke iamnes pendu ne serra tant cum il donne teu respouns, si il ne seit vencu par bataille, mes en prisoun serra tant cum le Roy seit en vie; et si le Roy moerge si serra ill delivers" ("And be assured that he never will be hanged so long as he gives this response, unless he be defeated in battle, but he will remain in prison so long as the King remain alive, and if the King die, then will he be freed"), 23 (see note 1).

3 The most radical of these is Charles Radding, "Superstition to Science: Nature, Fortune and the Passing of the Medieval Ordeal," *The American Historical Review* 84 (1979): 945–69, advancing the thesis that widespread skepticism of divine immanence generally led to a secular perspective, a thesis advanced further in his *A World Made by Men: Cognition and Society, 400–1200* (Chapel Hill, NC, and London: The University of North Carolina Press, 1985). As noted by Kenneth Pennington, *The Prince and the Law 1200–1600: Sovereignty and Rights in the Western Legal Tradition* (Berkeley and Los Angeles: University of California Press, 1993), 134, note 49, few historians have ascribed to Radding's view. See also John Contreni's review of Radding's tome, *Speculum* 63 (1988): 709–14. Peter Brown, "Society and the Supernatural: A Medieval Change," *Daedalus* 104 (1975): 133–51, reprinted with additional notes in *Society and the Holy in Late Antiquity* (Berkeley and Los Angeles: University of California Press, 1982), 302–32, is more moderate in his assessment of the degree of change, but does argue for an increased skepticism at least vis-à-vis immanent justice per se. Paul R. Hyams, "Trial by Ordeal: The Key to Proof in the Early common Law," *On the Laws and Customs of England: Essays in Honor of Samuel E. Thorne,* ed. Morris S. Arnold, Thomas A. Green, Salley A. Scully, and Stephen D. White. Studies in Legal History (Chapel Hill, NC: The University of North Carolina Press, 1981), 90–126, argues that ordeals were rational only in small communities of the early Middle Ages where there existed a common familiarity.

4 The most prominent adherent of this position is Robert Bartlett, *Trial by Fire and Water: The Medieval Judicial Ordeal* (Oxford: Oxford University Press, 1986). To this view emphasizing the importance of the ecclesiastic elites, Kenneth Pennington, *The Prince and the Law* (see note 3), adds the vital role of trained jurists. On the extensive procedural literature of the period adopting Romano-canonical procedures based on written and testimonial evidence, see Linda Fowler-Magerl, *Ordo iudiciorum vel ordo iudiciarius: Begriff und Literaturgattung*. Repertorien zur Frühzeit der gelehrten Rechte. Jus Commune, Sonderhefte 19 (Frankfurt a. M.: Klostermann, 1984).

From the ninth-century polemics of Agobard of Lyon[5] attacking the premises of ordeals both in theory and praxis, and railing against the Gundobadian law adopting the *judicium Dei* out of the concern of Burgundian rulers over rampant perjury, to the fourteenth-century compilations of Giovanni de Legnano, theologians condemned ordeals based not only on scriptural proscriptions against the temptation of God and the shedding of blood, but on grounds they simply did not work.[6] The equity of the law of nations dictates that offenders be punished, the innocent acquitted.[7] But in *Gottesurteil* the opposite sometimes happens. Hence, in 867, Pope Nicholas I forebade judicial duels[8]; in 886, Pope Stephan V enjoined

---

5 *Liber ejusdem ad praefatum imperatorem, adversus legem Gundobadi, et impia certamina quae per eam geruntur,* in J. P. Migne, ed., *Patrologiae cursus completus,* series Latina (PL) (Paris: Migne, 1844–1855), 104: 113–261; *Liber de divinis sententiis digestus, cum brevissimis adnotationibus, contra damnabilem opinionem putantium, divini iudicii veritatem igne, vel aquis, vel conflict armorum patefieri,* PL 104:249–68.

6 "Qualiter duellam hoc purgatorium inhibitum sit iure divino probatur sic ille actus est inhibitus iure divino per quem sit dei temptatio. Sed hoc duellum est huiusmodi ergo probatur maior per illud preceptum. Non temptabis dominum die tui. Probat minor. Nam tunc temptatur deus cum perquiritur aliquid contra naturam quod non est productibile nisi miraculo divino sic est dicere in hoc duello purgationis. Nam natural est quod fortiori et ingeniosior vincat minus fortem et minus ingeniosum nec econtra fieri potest ordine naturali. Sed aliquam minus fortis et minus ingeniosus fovet iusticiam et per duellum quaerimus ut victoriam obtineat ut ipsius iusticia declaret. Sic ergo deus temptatus miraculum faciat. Confirmatur ille actus est inhibitus iure divino quare est ad in ventus fabricante diabolo. Hoc duellum est huius modi, ergo probatur maior, nam nil commune dei ad diabolam lucis ad tenebras. . ." ("How the duel of purgation is forbidden by divine law is demonstrated as follows. An act is forbidden to the extent it is a temptation of God. But this duel is of such kind; thus, the major premise is proven by the precept: Tempt not the Lord thy God. The minor is proved: For then God is tempted when anything is asked of him contrary to nature which cannot arise except by divine miracle, which follows in the case of this duel. For it is natural for the strongest and most adept to defeat the less strong and less adept; nor does it happen in the natural order of things. But sometimes the less strong and less adept favor justice, and we seek by the duel that he achieves victory and that his justice be declared. So thus God is tempted to perform a miracle. It is confirmed: an act is forbidden by divine law to the extent it is a device of the devil. This duel is of such type, hence the major is proved. Since nothing is common to God and the devil, the light and the darkness . . . .") *Tractatus de bello, de represaliis et de duello domini Johannis de Lignano, cum additionibus Domini Pauli de Lignano,* cap. clxxv.

7 "Nam dictat equitas iure gentium delinquents puniri innocents absolui ac in hoc bello contingit quandoquam econtra ergo inhibitum iure gentium" ("For according to the law of nations, equity demands that the guilty be punished, the innocent acquitted. But in this battle, the opposite sometimes happens. Hence, it is forbidden by the law of nations"). *Tractatus de bello* (see note 6).

8 Monomachian uero in lege non assumimus, quam preceptam fuisse non reperimus, quam, licet iniisse quosdam legamus, sicut sanctum David et Goliam sacra prodit istoria, nusquam tamen ut pro lege teneatur alicubi diuina sanxit auctoritas, cum hoc et huiusmodi sectantes Deum solummodo temptare uideantur" (We do not support, however, judicial battle, which we do not find to have been the rule, though we read that once it was practiced, as appears from the sacred story of David and Goliath. Nevertheless, nowhere did divine authority anywhere ratify that the practice be retained as law, when this and similar procedures only seem to tempt God"), C. 2 q. 5 c. 22.

ordeals of hot iron and water, an injunction reissued by Alexander II.[9] When Gratian composed his *Decretum,* the only authority in favor of ordeals he could find were two canons from the Council of Worms (868) allowing the Eucharistic ordeal,[10] and one from the Synod of Seligenstadt (1023), allowing divine judgment in accusations of adultery.[11]

Only later editors succeeded in locating two ninth-century *paleae, Nobilis homo,*[12] from the Council of Tribur (895), and *Qui presbiterum,*[13] from the Council of Mainz

---

9 Consuluisti de infantibus, qui in uno lecto cum parentibus dorminetes mortui reperiuntur, utrum ferro candente, aut aqua feruente, seu alio quolibet examine parentes se purificare debeant eos non obpressisse. Monendi namque sunt et protestandi parentes, ne tam tenellos secum in uno collocent lecto, ne negligentia qualibet prouenient suffocentur uel opprimantur, unde ipsi homicidii rei inueniantur. Nam ferri candentis uel aquae feuentis examinatione confessionem extorqueri a quolibet sacri non consent canones, et quod sanctorum Patrum documento sancitum non est supersticiosa adinuentione non est presumendum. Spontanea enim confessione uel testium approbatione publicata delicta, habito pre oculis Dei timore, commissa sunt regimini iudicare. Occulta uero et incognita sunt illi relinquenda, qui solus nouit corda filliorum hominum. Hi autem, qui probantur, uel confitentur talis reatus se noxios tua eos castiget moderatio, qui si conceptum in utero qui per aborsum deleuerit, homicida, est, quanto magis, qui unius saltem diei puerulum peremerit, homicidam esse se excusare nequibit" ("We have been asked regarding infants who were found dead in the same bed with their sleeping parents, whether they ought clear themselves by hot iron or boiling water, or by some other test, of crushing them. For the parents had been cited and admonished not to let such tender ones to sleep with them in a single bed, lest by some negligence they cause, they should be suffocated or crushed, whence they are found defendants in this homicide. Now to extort a confession through examination by hot iron or boiling water, whence you please the holy canons do not advise, and there is no established example of the holy fathers that would defend superstitious device. Indeed, crimes made public by voluntary confession or by approbation, always in awe before the eyes of God, are committed to rules to judge. However, those that are hidden and unknown are left to him who knows the hearts of the sons of man. Moreover, those defendants proven or confessed to be guilty it is your duty to chastise with moderation, who having conceived in utero had aborted, is a murderer, much more, anyone who would cut off a little child from even a single day shall be unable to absolve himself of being a murderer"), C. 2 q. 5 c. 20.

10 C. 2 q. 5 c. 23 and c. 26.

11 "Statuit quoque sancta sinodus, ut, si duo de adulterio accusati fuerint, et ambo negauerint, et orant sibi concede, ut alter illorum utrosque diuino purget iudicio, si unus in hoc ceciderit, ambo rei habeantur" ("The holy synod holds that if two are accused of adultery, and both deny the charges and plead, yielding themselves, that should either of them proceed according to divine judgment, if one fails therein, both should be held guilty"), C. 2 q. 5 c. 25.

12 "Nobilis homo uel ingenuus si in sinodo accusatur et negauerit, si eum constiterit fidelem esse, cum duodecim ingenuis se expurget; si antea deprehensus fuerit in furto, aut periurio, aut falso testimonio, ad iuramentum non admittatur, sed (sicut qui ingenuus non est) feruenti aqua uel candenti ferro se expurget" ("A nobleman or one freeborn, if he be accused before the synod and deny the charges, if it find him to be faithful, he may acquit himself with twelve freeborn oath helpers; but if previously he had been detected in theft or perjury or false testimony, he shall not be allowed purgation by oath, but just as though he were not freeborn, he must acquit himself by boiling water or hot iron"), C. 2 q. 5. c. 15.

13 "Qui presbiterum occiderit, duodecim annorum ei penitencia secundum canones inponature; aut

(847), allowing purgation by oath to the freeborn and purgation by hot iron or water to the unfree. These editorial additions are indicative of the lively debate[14]

---

si negauerit, si liber est, cum sepuaginta duobus iuret; si autem seruus, super duodecim uomeres feruentes se expurget. Conuictus uero noxae usque ad ultimum uitae tempus miliciae cingulo careat, et absque spe coniugii maneat" ("Whosoever kills a priest shall be sentenced to twelve years of penance, or if he denies the charge, if free, he shall swear with seventy-two oath helpers, but if servile, he shall acquit himself over twelve hot plowshares. Moreover, convicted of the crime, he shall continuously until the end of his life abstain from military service and remain without hope of marriage"), C. 2 q. 5 c.

14 While the rise of a trained juristic elite commencing in the Italian municipallities, see Johannes Fried, *Die Entstehung des Juristenstandes im 12. Jahrhundert: Zur sozialen Stellung und politischen Bedeutung gelehrter Juristen in Bologna und Modena.* Forschungen zur neueren Privatrechts-geschichte, 21 (Cologne and Vienna: Böhlau, 1974), favored the trend toward procedures emphasizing testimony and documentation, see particularly R. C. van Caenegem, "La preuve dans le droit du moyen age occidental: Rapport de synthese," *La Preuve: Moyen Age et temps moderns.* Recueils de la Société Jean Bodin, 17.2 (Brussels: Éd. De la Librairie encyclopédique, 1965), 691–753; Kenneth Pennington, *The Prince and the Law,* 132–35 (see note 4), some legistes maintained if not the consistency of ordeal and Roman law, at least that the two were not inconsistent. See, e.g., Hermann Nottarp, *Gottesurteilstudien.* Bamberger Abhandlungen und Forschungen, 2 (Munich: Kösel, 1956), 49. While James A. Brundage maintains that Gratian was opposed to ordeals and sought to explain away conciliar canons that prescribed them, so that C. 2 q. 5 c. 24–25 need be read in the context of the dicta accompanying c. 22 and c. 26, *Law, Sex, and Christian Society in Medieval Europe* (Chicago and London: University of Chicago Press, 1987), 253, the dicta accompanying c. 20 casts doubt on the extent of prohibition: "Hoc autem utrum ad omnia genera purgationis, an ad hec duo tantum, que his prohbita uidentur, pertineant, non inmerito dubitatur propter sacrificium zelopipiae, et illud Gregorii: 'Si vir, qui frigidae naturae esse dicitur, per uerum iudicium probare potuerit, uxorem suam numquam se cognovisse, separetur ab ea."("However, whether this pertains to all manner of purgation or only the two remains open to doubt, on account of the sacrifice of jealousy, and the statement of Gregory: 'if a man said to be of cold nature can prove by a suitable trial that he never had intercourse with his wife, he may be separated from her'"). The first of these is expanded in c. 21, reciting the ordeal of Bitter waters contained in the old Testament book of Numbers, although in some manuscripts appearing as *palaea,* is undoubtedly by Gratian himself. See the accompanying *notationes correctorum* by Emil Friedberg, *Corpus Iuris Canonici editio Lipsiensis secunda.* 2 vols. (Leipzig: Tauchnitz, 1879–1881). The second instance relating to allegations of sexual incapacity, see C. 27 q. 2 c. 29, raises the question of "per uerum iudicatum." According to the gloss of the Stowe manuscript, British Library Stowe 378, fol. 167 vb: "Probare mulierem debet quod non posit uir cum ea coire si uelt alium accipere, etiam si uir contradicat. Hic enim probabo per uerum iudicium, scilicet aspect corporis . . ." ("It is proper for a woman to prove that her husband is incapable of intercourse with her should she desire to take another, even if her husband denies it. Of course, I will investigate this through suitable trial, certainly physical examination"). Quoted in Brundage, *Law, Sex and Christian Society,* 322, note 308 (see note 14). Joannes Faventius, in his *Summa,* B.L. Royal 9 E. VII, fol. 136ra: "Scilicet membrum eius inspiciatur a mulieribus, quia fote non est aptum carnali opera" ("Certainly his member may be inspected by women, since perchance it is not suitable for carnal operations"). Quoted in Brundgae, *Law, Sex and Christian Society,* 322 (see note 14). The context suggests, however that Gratian had something more in mind than a simple inspection.In cases of heresy, perhaps a majority of clerics supported ordeal, even by hot iron, as witness cap. 1 of the Council of Rheims (1157), *Sacrorum conciliorum nova et*

among twelfth-century legal analysts as to the nature, purpose, efficacy and permissibility of various types of ordeal, in a time when the ordeal itself seemed to be flourishing throughout the European continent, which flowering is the basis for the claim that the prohibitions of Fourth Lateran were the impetus for the subsequent rapid decline of the ordeal in the thirteenth century, rather than any general social change with an attendant metamorphosis in *mentalité*.

Even proponents of this argument concede, however, that compliance with the prohibitions of the Fourth Lateran Council (1215) which provided as part of a canon prohibiting clerks from shedding blood either through participation in legal administration or through the practice of surgery simply that:

> ". . . nec quisquam purgationi aquae ferventis vel frigidae seu ferri candentis ritum cuislibet benedictionis aut consecrationis impendat, salvis nihilominus prohibitionibus de monomachiis sive duellis antea promulgates."[15]
>
> [". . .nor will anyone bestow any rite whatsoever of blessing or consecration upon purgation by boiling or cold water or hot iron, preserving nevertheless the prohibitions against monomachia or duels previously issued."]

were neither particularly swift nor complete.[16] In the subsequent decade, the papacy continued to bemoan the brow-beating of clergy into participation in ordeals, with Honorius III feeling compelled to reissue the injunctions in 1223 or 1224.[17] Nonetheless, councils were continuing to condemn the practice at Bayeux in 1300,[18] while Gregory XI roundly criticized the ordeal provisions of the *Sachsenspiegel* in 1374.[19]

---

amplissima collectio, 2nd ed, 53 vols. (Paris: Welter, 1901–1927), 21–84, which was followed at Arras in 1172 and Cambrai in 1183, see Dominique Barthélemy, "Diversité des ordalies médiévales," *Revue Historique* 280 (1988): 3–25; here 24, n. 24 and n. 84; and shortly before the prohibition of Fourth Lateran, Innocent rebuked the bishop of Strassburg for employing the ordeal. *Verborum abbreviatum* 78, PL 205:230. See generally, John W. Baldwin, "The Intellectual Preparation for the Canons of 1215 Against Ordeals," *Speculum* 36 (1961): 613–36.

15 Canon 18. The identical language appears in X 3.50.9. The previous promulgations seem to refer to the earlier prohibitions against "nundinas vel ferias" ("jousts or fairs") issued, inter alia at Second Lateran, canon 14, and Third Lateran, canon 20.

16 See Bartlett, *Trial by Fire and Water,* 130–31 (see note 4).

17 X 5.35.3; for the earlier date, see *Chronica Minor Minoritae Erphordensis,* ed. Oswald Holder-Egger. Scriptores Rerum Germanicarum, 42 (Hanover and Leipzig: Hahn, 1899), 602.

18 *Sacroram conciliorum nova et amplissima collection,* ed. G. D. Mansi. 2nd. ed., 53 vols. (Paris and Leipzig: Welter, 1901–1927), 25: 67.

19 *De ordaliis,* ed. Peter Browe, 2 vols. Textus et documenta in usum exercitationum et praeiectionum academicarum/Series theologica 4 (Rome: Pontificia Università Gregoriana, 1932–1933), 1:44.

German sources from Lorsch[20] and Hanover[21] continued to cite ordeals as admissible well into the fifteenth century, while in southwestern France, ordeals continued to receive sanction at least as late as 1309 in Article 9 of *Les coutumes d'Alzen (compte de Foix)*.[22] Trial by battle, condemned by the Church earlier and no less vociferously than autonomic ordeal, continued in both England and France into the fifteenth century, and was only abrogated in England in 1818.[23]

This tenacity was not an indication of royal favor. From the ninth century onwards, rulers, secular and ecclesiastic, had adopted or tolerated ordeals in the name of combating perjury, though recognizing the procedures as undependable and susceptible to manipulation. Eadmer's description in the *Historia Novarum* of William Rufus's outburst against the *iudicium Dei*[24] was not so much a manifestation of the king's religious skepticism, as of frustration with the unpredictability of the ordeal.

Granted, the autonomic ordeal, which in England seems to have been used routinely only in what would subsequently come to be denominated "criminal" cases (since most cases arose on appeal, or what today would be called complaint, of a *tort*, or act contrary to law or justice), had no applicability anywhere in cases where the defendant was taken *in flagrante delicto* or confessed, and was everywhere a vehicle only of last resort. In a fictional trial of Godwin for the murder of Alfred, brother of Edward the Confessor, the poet Gaimar in his *Estoire d'Engleis* portrays the barons debating whether a charge of felony requires *jugement*, i.e., ordeal by iron or water, or judicial duel, or whether as the character Frithugist maintains, such *orp apel*, i.e., an accusation without witnesses, can be refuted by oath, with which contention the fictional Leofric agrees. Hence, the suitors determine, in light of the prestigious position of the decedent but lack of witnesses, to make an *esguard*, or arbitration award.[25] Gaimar's grasp of the procedure seems consistent with those assessments suggesting that, at least in criminal cases, only serious crimes attributed to an accused of no or ill-repute

---

20 Jacob Grimm, *Weisthümer*. 7 vols. (Göttingen: Dieterich, 1840–1878), 1:465–66; cited in Bartlett, *Trial by Fire and Water* 131 (see note 4).

21 Hermann Nottarp, *Gottesurteilstudien*, 204 (see note 14).

22 See Paul Ourliac, "Le Duel iudiciaire dans le sud-ouest," *Revue du Nord* 158 [Melanges Raymond Monier] (1958), rpt.. in *Études d'historie du droit medieval* (Paris: A. et J. Picard, 1979), 251–58; here 254 and note 1.

23 St. 59 Geo. III, c. 46

24 "Ad hoc quoque lapsus est, ut Dei iudicio incredulous fieret iniustitiaeque illud arguens, Deum aut facta hominum ignorare aut aequitatis ea lance nolle pensare astrueret" (He sank also to this, that he doubted it had been the judgment of God, arguing that it was unjust and adding that either God did not know the deeds of men or he was unwilling to weigh them impartially"). *Historia novarum* 2, PL 159:412.

25 Geffrei Gaimar, *Estoire des engleis*, ed. and trans. Ian Short (Oxford: Oxford University Press, 2009), lines 4861–5028.

where a prima facie case could be demonstrated ever were referred to an ordeal. In other cases, litigants not infrequently offered to undergo *jugement* as a strategic ploy, and almost as frequently advanced pretences to demur at the last moment.[26]

Even then, across Europe, from England to Hungary, the conviction rate by such means seems to have been less than fifty percent,[27] perhaps in England as low as one in three.[28] Henry II attempted to compensate for this inefficiency by the Assize of Clarendon of 1166, providing that juries of twelve men of every hundred and four of every township provide the names of anyone accused or suspected of robbery within the twelve preceding years, which suspects were rounded-up, those of ill-repute and found with stolen goods being summarily dispatched, the rest being submitted to trial by cold water, those convicted losing a foot, and after the Assize of Northampton in 1175, their right hand as well, those passing but of ill-repute being abjured to quit the kingdom.[29]

Aside from the obvious cynicism in Henry's use of the ordeal, the Angevin assizes are notable for the use of the presenting jury. Whether founded upon the Danish jury of presentment or the Frankish inquest,[30] the procedure certainly was used from the days of the Conqueror forward, although Bongert argues that Henry II's version was once distilled through the practice common in Anjou.[31] With the jury, denunciation emerged as an alternative to appeal, i.e., accusation, which had been until then the primary method of bringing offenses to bar, accounting to no small degree for the want of distinction between civil and criminal pleas. Well before the innovations of Innocent III, it was mentioned in the *ordo, Hactenus magister,* written circa 1167 in Cologne by the canon Renerus, most likely under the influence of Gerard Pucelle.[32] Such *ordines* may explain the treatise written in

---

26 On the strategic use of the ordeal in the Occitan, see Stephen D. White, "Proposing the Ordeal and Avoiding It: Strategy and Power in Western French Litigation, 1050–1110," *Cultures of Power: Lordship, Status and Process in Twelfth-Century Europe,* ed. Thomas N. Bison. Middle Ages Series (Philadelphia: University of Pennsylavania Press, 1995), 89–123.

27 See, e.g., R. Darest, *Études d'histoire du droit* (Paris: L. Larose et Forcel, 1889) I: 259–64, discussing the *Regestrum de Varad,* printed by S. L. Endlicher, *Rerum Hungaricum Monumenta Arpadiana* (1849; rpt.., Leipzig: Hiersemann, 1931), 640–742.

28 See Robert Bartlett, *England Under the Norman and Angevin Kings 1075–1225* (Oxford: Clarendon Press, 2000), 183–84.

29 See W. L. Warren, *Henry II* (Berkeley and Los Angeles: University of California Press, 1973), 355. As Warren points out, the *Dialogus de Scaccario,* attributed to Richard fitzNigel, himself an insider in Henry's court, referred to it as the most severe assize appointed to repress crime.

30 On the issue, see Frank M. Stenton, *Anglo-Saxon England,* 3rd. ed. Oxford History of England, 2 (1943; Oxford: Clarendon, 1971), 651–52.

31 Yvonne Bongert, *Recherches sur les cours laïques du Xe au XIII siècle* (Paris: Picard, 1949). In all likelihood, Henry's innovations borrowed as well from canon law procedures of the period. See R. H. Helmholz, "The Early History of the Grand Jury and the Canon Law," *University of Chicago Law Review* 50 (1983): 613–27.

32 See Linda Fowler-Magerl, *Ordines iudiciarii and Libellis de ordine iudiciorum (From the Middle of the*

Henry's day, commonly known as *Glanvill,* which divides pleas into criminal and civil, reserving the most serious as pleas of the crown, a taxonomy thitherto unknown in English law.

Although the use of jurors in the inquest was known on both sides of the channel, from the mid- to late-twelfth century they began to diverge in practice; certainly by the 1194 establishment of the *custodies placitorum coronae,* when the Angevin system moved toward a double presentment involving multiple juries of *vicini* who acted somewhere between witnesses and fact-finders, with no prescribed rules of evidence, and whose verdicts were in some sense an evidence rather than a judgment.[33] In France, where and when jurors tried cases rather than the bailli or seneschal, officers who were religiously rotated by the reign of Louis IX, to assure their total fidelity to the crown, the jurors functioned more passively in the role of *enqueteurs,* who heard and presumably weighed evidence including testimony and documents, according to evermore precise hierarchical standards of proofs. By the end of the twelfth century, and before 1215, in either location, the defendant appears to have had a choice of standing on an inquiry or inquest or going to the ordeal; after 1215, the alternative was battle, an alternative limited in inquests, and over time even in appeals. Well before the ban on ordeal, at least in England, the defendant could purchase from the crown the right to put himself on the country, i.e., the multiple juries of the assize, a prerogative gladly extended by the Angevin monarchs who always were happy to grant any privilege that contributed to the treasury. The procedure was risky, the juries trying guilt typically being the same as had made the presentment until it was established in the fourteenth century that indictors were to be excluded from the trial jury.[34]

Exceptiones recognized by Francophonic courts were dilatory or preemptive pleas. Generally, the only defense to felony was complete denial. In the Angevin realms, the writ *De odio et atia,* another contributor to the fisc, was available perhaps as early as 1178 to challenge what today would be called overcharging the offense.[35] In the early thirteenth century, the *ordo, Olim,* by Otto Papiensis became quite popular, particularly in England,[36] and in 1234, the Anglo-Norman canonist

---

Twelfth to the End of the Fifteenth Century). Typologie des sources du moyen âge occidental 63 (Turnhout, Belgium: Brepols, 1994), 63; ed., Fowler-Magerl, *Ordo iudiciorum vel ordo iudiciarius,* 290–93 (see note 4).

33 See Mike McNair, "The Origins of the Jury: Vicinage and the Antecedents of the Jury," *Law and History Review* 17 (1999): 537–99.

34 Year Book 30–3,1 Edward I, 531.

35 On the Writ *De odio et atia,* see particularly Naomi D. Hurnard, *The King's Pardon for Homicide before AD 1307* (Oxford: Clarendon Press, 1969), Appendix I, 339–80.

36 Fowler-Magerl, *Ordines iudiciarii,* 94 (see note 32).

composed the *ordo Scietiam*,[37] dealing extensively with *exceptiones*, but the evolution of the defensive plea was a slow, and often costly, one.

In the interim, Innocent III would offer his own variation on the inquest, to wit, inquisitorial procedure, not only without defining the rights of defendants, but in many cases restricting them under the rubric *rei publicae interest, ne criminal remaneant impunita,* a doctrinal phrase borrowed from a treatise composed circa 1190 by a French canon.[38] At the same time, the ban on clerical participation in ordeals played into the hands of royal functionaries already anxious to eliminate the ordeal. Perhaps the injunction of the Fourth Lateran Council (1215) was intended, as one writer has commented, "to bring home to monarchs and other lay authorities the lesson that their capacity to govern depended upon the cooperation of church authorities."[39] If so, it was a challenge that many monarchs were happy to accept.[40]

Magnates and professional jurists also stood to gain by acts of ecclesiastical self-limitation, particularly in an age witnessing the expanding ubiquity of capital punishment, at least until the curia of Boniface VIII recognized the episcopal possession of purely secular jurisdiction obviating the need for advocates to exercise high justice.[41] But it was kings who could see the opportunities for controlling the administration of justice as well as the power and revenue to be derived from their role as ultimate appellate authority, a function scarce available where judgment was of God. Indeed, not only would they have eliminated unilateral ordeal, but the slow, costly, and almost as unpredictable wager of battle as well, had they a means of compelling defendants to accept trial by jury or inquest, which ultimately they undertook to achieve by jailing noncompliant suspects.[42]

---

37 *Fowler-Magerl, Ordo iudiciorum,*138–41 (see note 4).

38 See Richard M. Fraher, "The Theoretical Justification for the New Criminal Law of the High Middle Ages: *Rei Publicae Interest, Ne Crimina Remaneant Impunita,*" *University of Illinois Law Review* (1984): 577–95.

39 James A. Brundage, *Medieval Canon Law* (London and New York: Longman, 1995), 141.

40 Cf. Marie-Noëlle Grippari, "Le jugement de Dieu ou la mise en jeu du pouvoir," *Revue Historique* 278 (1987): 281–91; here 289.

41 See F. Merzbacher, "Hochgerichtsbarkeit," *Handwörterbuch zur deutschen Rechtsgeschichte: HRG,* ed. Adalbert Erler, Ekkehard Kaufmann, and Wolfgang Friedrich Stammler (Berlin: E. Schmidt, 1971–), 2:174.

42 For Normandy, see L'*Ancienne coutume de Normandie,* ed. William Laurence De Gruchy (Jersey: Ch. Le Feuvre, 1881), c. 68, 167: "per iustitiarium debet arrestari et firmo carcere debet observari usque ad diem et annum cum penuria victus et potus (*à peu de menger et de boire*) nisi interim super hoc patriae inquisitionem se offerat sustinere"("he should be arrested and held in a secure prison by the presiding judge for a year and a day with little food or drink, unless meanwhile he present himself to undergo inquisition by the country on this case"). Quoted in Frederick Pollock and Frederic William Maitland, *The History of English Law Before the Time of Edward I,* 2nd ed., 2 vols. (Cambridge: Cambridge University Press, 1898) 2:651, n. 4. In England, the limit of a year and a

As a consequence, it may be said that the criminal defendant of the thirteenth and early fourteenth centuries was often worse off than he would have been in the day of the ordeal. He was all but presumed guilty, afforded no meaningful examination of witnesses, provided no real procedural protections, and given no means either by wit or divine intervention, to escape with his life and body parts intact. Meanwhile, local lords were less than content with the developing system of royal administration whether through justiciars, judges, seneschals or baillis, those "indefatigable levelers," described by Dupont-Ferrier, who envisioned a day when "there would no longer be anyone between the king and his subjects except the king's officers."[43] Finally, the larger public may have appreciated the option of a jury or inquest, but nonetheless were imbued with the concept of battle as the franchise of the *francus homo.* Likewise, they must have appreciated their communal input into imposition and interpretations of ordeals[44]; and in the last analysis, felt comfortable with their customary justice, the spectacle of an ordeal with the prospect of a good castration and blinding or drawing and quartering being as dear to their hearts as public hangings were in nineteenth-century England. As the cartulary of St. Florent-lès-Saumur reads for an ordeal held in 1066:

> ". . . et pene totius plebs civitatis cujus non parva multitudo ad illud iudicium quasi ad spectaculum confluxit."[45]
>
> [". . . and almost all the people of the city, whose multitude was not small, flowed to the trial as if to a spectacle."]

In Angers, the popular interest in ordeals was described with an entry for 1166, noting:

---

day did not appertain, and the prisoner was often kept in irons, see *Britton* 1.26, or laden with as much iron as he could bear. *Year Book* 30–31, Edward I, 511.

43 Gustave Dupont-Ferrier, *Les Officiers royaux des baillages et sénéchaussées et les institutions monarchiques locales en France à la fin du moyen âge* (Paris: E. Bouillon, 1902), 873 ; quoted in Michael Jones, "The Last Capetians and Early Valois Kings, 1314–1364, " *The New Cambridge Medieval History: C. 1300–c. 1415,* ed. Michael Jones (Cambridge: Cambridge University Press, 2000), 388–421; here 410.

44 This seems to have always been the case. Compare, e.g., the political aspects of the ordeal related by Wulfstan in ninth-century England, *Frithegodi Monachi Breviloquium Vitae Beati Wilredi et Wulfstani Cantoris narratio metrica de S. Swithino,* ed. Alistair Campbell. Thesaurus mundi: bibliotheca scriptorium latinorum mediae et recentionris aetatis 1 (Turici and Zurich: In Aedibus Thesauri Mundi, 1950), 150–54, and discussion in Paul Hyams, "Trial by Ordeal," 93–94 (see note 3) with the ordeal held in Florence in 1068 over simoniacal bishops recited in the *Vita Gualberti* of Andreas, cc 73–75, discussed by Colin Morris, "Judicium Dei: The Sociological and Political Significance of the Ordeal in the Eleventh Century," *Church Society and Politics.* Studies in Church History 12 (Oxford: Blackwell, 1975), 95–111; here 97–98.

45 Bibl.Nat. nouv. Acq. Lat. 1930, fol. 99r –100v, transcribed in Yvonne Bongert, *Recherches sur les cours laïques,* 308–10 (see note 31).

> "Viderunt autem, vel iudicium portari, vel manum tertia die more reguardari, fere universi hominess et mulieres de Doado et plures de moniibus dicti Berlaii.[46]
>
> ["Moreover, nearly all the men and women of Doad and many of the men from the said Berlai, came to witness either the imposition of judgment or, foolishly, the inspection of the hand on the third day."]

For many observers, the new procedures, whether adopted or adapted from the Romano-canonical *ordines* must have seemed just plain "foreign," not the least in their separation of court and community.

This xenophobia would naturally be expected in those areas newly under French domination, such as the Midi where for decades after the capitulation of Raymond VII of Toulouse in the 1229 Treaty of Meaux effectively establishing the suzerainty of Louis IX, the denizens of the *méridienne* regarded both French and clergy as their occupiers.[47] From this southern perspective, Roman law was seen as an instrument of that very "foreign" domination.[48] The problem lay not merely with the law, but with the cadre of learned lawyers who applied it: hence, one town actually prohibited the employment of any *legiste* or *canoniste* as attorney for the city.[49] While the troubadours and jongleurs of the Midi found these university-trained jurists subversive of Occitan culture, they were not alone in their sentiments. To the north, a similar resentment is manifest in the *Bible* of Guiot de Provins. Guiot's commentary is not a condemnation of legal practitioners *per se*, but an indictment of the Italian schools and their emphasis on reason and technique over

46 *Cartulaire noir de la cathédrale d'Angers*, ed. Charles Urseau (Paris: A. Picard, 1908), No. 111, 191.

47 See, for example, Bernart Sicart de Marvejos, "La Domination des clercs et des Français," ed. Alfred Jeanroy, rev. ed. J. Boelcke, *Anthologie des Troubadours XIIme–XIIIme siècles*. Les Classiques d'oc (Paris: A.G. Nizet, 1974), 249–53.

48 Wrote Pierre Cardenal, "Etends-tu, toi qui t'es fait legiste et qui supprime publiquement le droit d'autrui"("Listen, you who make a *legiste* of yourself, and who would publically abolish the law of others"). Quoted in Paul Ourliac, "Glose Juridique sur le Troubadour Pierre Cardenal, " *Études d'histoire*, 268 (see note 22). In some sense, this may seem inconsistent with the reputation of the Midi as the *pays du droit écrit*, and the fame of Montpellier as a center of Roman law and its famous teacher, Placentius. However, written law was not restricted to Roman law but included customary and statutory law, as well as written charters and, initially, Roman law served to supplement these—and notable early thirteenth-century Meridional documents manifest just such eclecticism. See Jean Baumel, *Histoire d'une seigneurie du Midi de la France*, 2 vols. (Montpellier: Causse, 1969), I: 295–98; Linda M. Paterson, *The World of the Troubadours: Medieval Occitan Society, c. 110 – c. 1300* (Cambridge: Cambridge University Press, 1993), 173–74.

49 *Coutumes de Pamiers*, discussed in Ourliac, "Glose Juridique" (see note 22).

fundamental justice.[50] His cynicism shines through when he plays with the word *glose,* which can refer either to a gloss or to a reprimand:

> "Cist chapitres fut faiz sens glose,
> mais il ferait une fort glose
> es lengues fauses desliées
> de ceu que j'oi dire decries."[51]

["These chapters are made like a gloss; indeed, it will be a strong reprimand to the false, loose tongues, that ought be tied in view of that which I intend to say about the decrees."]

It is not the lofty honorable books which one calls the law and decrees which bring lawyers to fraud and deceit; nor do they find there their duplicity and double-dealing. Rather:

> "Es lois apregnent tricherie:
> sor les poins et sor les biaus dis
> que il conoissent [es] escris
> baratent loie siècle et engignent."[52]

["They learn treachery about the law, and by their legal points and their fancy words that they learn in their writings, they deceive and defraud the world"].

What Guiot condemns is not cunning, for craft is a staple of French literature. Consider the well-laid plan of Lienor, heroine of Renart's *Guillaume de Dole,* in entrapping the wicked seneschal who has besmirched her reputation, by discovering she bore on her thigh a rose-shaped birthmark, tricking him as to her identity and claiming he had seduced her. Then, since ". . . s'ele fust as loi . . ."[53] (i.e., "she had studied the law"), she demands justice from the king, by *jugement de Dieu.* The seneschal swears he has never laid eyes upon her, and is of course victorious in his ordeal of cold water, at which point the maiden reveals her birthmark, her chastity being vindicated by the very *jugement* that acquits the

50 Eduard Meynial, "Remarques sur la reaction populaire contre l'invasion du droit romain en France aux XIIe et XIIIe siècles,"*Mélanges Chabaneau: Volume offert à Camille Chabaneau à l' occasion du 75. anniversaire de sa naissance – 4 mars 1906 – par ses élèves, ses amis et ses admirateurs* (Erlangen: F. Junge, 1907; rpt. Geneva: Slatkine, 1973), 557–84. However, he attributed this hostility largely to the competition between Paris and Bologna, and the public sentiment that the Italian schools were "foreign." Our suggestion is that the resistance transcends the parochial to the substantive concern for justice.

51 *La Bible de Guiot, Les œuvres de Guiot de Provins, poète lyrique et satirique,* ed. John Orr. University of Manchester: French Series (Manchester and Paris: University of Manchester Press, 1915), 10–93, lines 2429–33.

52 *La Bible,* lines 2512–15 (see note 51).

53 Jean Renart, *Le Roman de la Rose ou de Guillaume de Dole,* ed. Félix Lecoy. Les Classiques Français du Moyen Age (CFMA) 91 (Paris : Champion, 1979), line 4768.

steward of the seduction. The same plot is used in at least three other *romans* of the first half of the thirteenth century, including the *Roman de la violette* by Gerbert de Montreuil, which portrayed the seneschal as undergoing wager of battle rather than unilateral ordeal,[54] and the anonymous works, *Compte de Poitiers* and the prose *Roi Flore et la belle Jeanne*,[55] and clearly depends for its denouement upon the efficacy of the *jugement de Dieu*, as well as a full measure of cleverness on the part of the heroine.

Cunning-like wisdom is a virtue, perhaps a gift, much lauded in literature. One of the few fabliaux to even mention legal practitioners, and then by snidely comparing St. Thomas's phlegmatic reply with the stolidity of the legistes[56], *Le villain qui Conquest Paradis par Plait* ("The Peasant who Plead his Way into Heaven") recounts the trials of a peasant who departs the world and wanders into the celestial kingdom, only to avoid ejectment by the apostles through his superior wit. Ultimately, God, appreciating a well-founded argument, concedes and admits the peasant's soul to paradise. Moral: "Mels valt engines que ne fait force"[57] ("Cleverness is preferable to courage").

So high is the incidence in French romance of clever victories and escapes, through mistaken identities, equivocal oaths and other devices, that some writers, deeming these machinations as ruse and connivance, argue they indicate society's own recognition of the weaknesses in the customary judicial system.[58] Yseut plots to have Tristam, disguised as a beggar, carry her on his shoulders across a muddy river, so she is able to triumph in ordeal by oath by truthfully swearing that no man but king Marc and the beggar who carried her across the river had ever been between her legs.[59] Similarly, following their illicit union, Lancelot defends Guinevere's honor by dispatching her accuser. And, of course, Ami saves his

---

54 Both versions display cleric participation, though some writers have paid particular attention to the use of monomachia rather than unilateral ordeal. See, e.g., John W. Baldwin, *Aristocratic Life in Medieval France: The Romances of Jean Renart and Gerbert de Montreuil, 1190–1230* (Baltimore and London: Johns Hopkins Press, 2000), 211.

55 See Urban Tigner Holmes, Jr., *A History of Old French Literature from the Origins to 1300* (Chapel Hill, NC: Lenker, 1937); Gaston Paris, "Le Cycle de la gageure," *Romania* 32 (1903): 481–551.

56 "...Tumas, Tumas, plus estes coi / Des responsaus que nus legistes!" ("...Thomas, Thomas, you are slower of response than our legistes!") *Nouveau Recuiel complet des fabliaux* (NRCF), ed. Willem Noomen and Nico Van den Boogard, 10 vols. (Assen: Van Gorcum, 1993–1996), vol. 5, #39, lines 62–63.

57 *Le Villain qui Conquest Paradis*, line 172 (see note 56).

58 Perhaps the most prominent of these critics is R. Howard Bloch, *Medieval French Literature and Law* (Berkeley, Los Angeles, and London: University of California Press, 1977).

59 Béroul, *Le Roman de Tristan, poème du XIIe siècle*, ed. Ernest Muret and L.m. Defourques, 4th ed. Les Classiques Français du Moyen Age 12 (Paris: Champion, 1947), lines 4199–4213.

friend Amiles by surreptitiously taking his place in the battle over the honor of Belissant. One writer has labeled this phenomenon as "swindling justice."[60]

But did the medieval readers or listeners of these romances perceive these instances as defaults of justice? Probably not. Rather, these plots appeal to some innate sense of a higher law, of a more substantive justice. Indeed, the popularity of romances in which heroes or heroines avoid strict application of the law should not be surprising. The Christian message itself is founded upon simultaneous fulfillment of the letter of the law and God's gracious mercy to the believer. The purpose of judicial systems, in the estimation of the public, was not strict application of law but the triumph of good over evil. Therefore, the principle virtue required of a judge, according to Beaumanoir, was not knowledge of the law, but wisdom.[61] It was this quality that was poisoned by the *legistes.*

What Guiot condemns is the disjuncture between Roman law and procedure and fundamental justice. When he says of the *legistes* at bar, that "atant aimment tort comme droit . . ."[62] ("then they love wrong as right"), he is expressing his outrage at their disinterest in substantive outcome:

Molt devroient boin fruit porteir,
Et lor oevre si aaismeir
Qu'ell fust chiere et honoree.
Et boin cuer et bone pensee
Ont il quant il sont escolier;
Molt feroient il a prisier
Se lor sens estoit atorneiz
Selonc lois et selonc decreiz;
C'est clergïe loaul et fine.
Molt sont sil en folle doctrine
Qui puisent malvaise science

60 Ronald Gene Koss, "'Swindling Justice': the *iudicium dei* in Medieval French Literature," *Law in Mediaeval Life and Thought,* ed. Edward B. King and Susan J. Ridyard (Sewanee:, TN: The Press of the University of the South, 1990), 233–43.

61 "Il nous est avis que cil qui veut ester loiaus baillis et droituriers doit avoir en soi .x. vertus, es quells l'une est et doit ester dame et mestresse de toutes les autres, ne sans lui ne pueent ester les autres vertus gouvernees. Et cele vertus est appelee sapience, qui vaut autant comme ester sages. Donques disons nous que cil qui' s'entrement de Baillie garder et de justice fere doit ester ages, ne autrement il ne savoit pas fere ce qui apartient a office de bailiff"("It is our opinion that whoever would be a faithful and just judge must possess ten virtues, one of which is and must be the lady and mistress of all the others, lest without it the others cannot be governed. And that virtue is called wisdom, which would be the same as to be wise. Thus we say that he should be wise when he attends to being a judge and doing justice, lest otherwise he know not what to do pertaining to the judicial office"). Phillipe de Beaumanoir, *Coutumes de Beauvaisis,* ed. Amedée Salmon. Collection de textes pour servir à l'étude et à l'enseignement de l'histoire (Paris: Éditions A. et J. Picard, 1889), ¶12.

62 *La Bible de Guiot,* line 2481 (see note 51).

En fontainne de sapience;
Ne sont mie bien abevrei,
Il boivent ou rusiaul trovlei.[63]

[They ought to bear much good fruit, and their work be so directed that it produces good and honor, and they ought to have good care and thoughts when they are schooled, so their manner be turned according to law and decree for which they would merit much esteem: that would be a pure and fine science. Instead, they engage in foolish studies that make an evil science of the fount of wisdom; and they are not refreshed, for they drink where the waters are murky.]

In short, these legal technicians upon whom the new system depends are more interested in legality than in justice, for which latter objective the ordeal seems uniquely qualified. Indeed, Guiot may have played a significant role in the dissemination of the Lohengrin legend, which depends heavily upon the efficacy of trial by combat, if he is indeed the Guiot (Kyot) whom Wolfram von Eschenbach cites as his *Gewährsmann* for the tale.[64]

This distinction between law founded on reason and justice grounded in charity was evidently on the mind of Jean de Meun, when in the *Roman de la Rose,* he relates Livy's tale of Appius and Virginius. Appius, unable to win Virginia, the daughter of Virginius, by legitimate means, allowed his hireling to bring a suit falsely alleging that Virginia was his slave, and demanding possession of his chattel. Hastily, Appius judged in favor of the plaintiff, ordering Virginia to be delivered up immediately. Thereupon, "par amour sans haîne..."[65] ("through love and without any hatred"), Virginius decapitates his daughter to save her from infamy, and presents her head to the judge in open court. Outraged, the judge orders Virginius's execution, but the people of the town, moved by pity, defend Virginius against the authorities, and instead, seize the judge and throw him into prison, where he kills himself before trial.

Under Roman law, Virginius had committed a capital crime. But the townspeople, and by implication, Jean de Meun, and by still further implication, the lay reader or listener, well understand that Virginius does not merit punishment. Similarly, the maiden of the rose deserves vindication, the evil seneschal warrants humiliation, the peasant really does merit paradise, and while Tristan and Iseult and Lancelot and Guinevere ultimately receive punishment of another sort, they do not really deserve to die, particularly at the instigation of an

---

63 *La Bible de Guiot,* lines 2491–504 (see note 51).

64 Albrecht Classen, "Noch einmal zu Wolframs 'spekulativer' Kyôt -Quelle im Licht jüdischer Kultur und Philosophie des zwölften Jahrhunderts," *Studi Medievali* XLVI (2005): 281–308.

65 Guillaume de Lorris et Jean de Meun, *Le Roman de la Rose,* ed. Felix Lécoy, 3 vols. CFMA 92, 93, and 98 (Paris: Champion, 1973–1983), vol. 1, line 5605. See also the contribution to this volume by Daniel F. Pigg.

accuser whose motives are baser than their desires. Such stories are not an indictment of customary justice, but a vindication.[66]

The impact of these stories turns upon the internal motivations and intent of the characters. But an inquisitorial system, while perhaps superior in eliciting historical facts, is no more designed to penetrate psychological and emotional motivation than is the syllogistic analysis applied to the facts derived through the inquisitorial process. The *jugement de Dieu* was designed not so much as a truth-finding enterprise, as a system allowing God to work his justice since He alone knows the human heart and its hidden recesses. After all, under the rubric of confession, preachers continued to employ *exampla* illustrating God's forgiveness and mercy to the penitent sinner through either escape or mitigation of the natural consequences of ordeals.[67] Ideally, when a matter was heard before king or court, or even appointed bailli, the judge was but a meager stand-in for God, requiring his exercise of wisdom rather than technical knowledge. In truly serious cases concerning loss of life or limb, appeal still lay with that "higher authority."

The continued faith in that higher appeal appears from the public satisfaction with the de Gris case of 1386, the last duel fought by orders of the Parlement de Paris. The defendant, a squire of good repute and pious report, was accused of raping the wife of the knight, Jehan de Carrouges, who was unable even to put a date to the alleged crime. Nonetheless, the defeat and death of the squire was greeted as the manifest judgment of God by all the chroniclers of the period, including Jean Froissart and Jean Juvenal.[68]

---

66 Cf. H(arold) B(ernard) Willson, "The Old and the New Law in Gottfried's *Tristan*," *The Modern Language Review* 60 (1965): 212–24, here 218: "For the most striking characteristic of the New Law is indeed its inherent subtlety, its defiance of logic. By the paradox of its forgiveness of sins and the Redemption of guilty man through the death of One who is perfect it makes nonsense of the rigid logic of the Old Law and its maxim of 'an eye for an eye and a tooth for a tooth.' Christ's outwitting the Pharisees is a means to the end of proving that love is a higher and more subtle law than any other. Likewise, in an analogical sense, *list* in *Tristan* is a means to the end of showing that love has its own law and its own subtlety. The essence of *list* is that it emphasizes the contrast between appearance and reality and . . . although the lovers may be guilty according to the law . . . they are not, in fact, as guilty in the sight of the God of Love as they are in the eyes of their envious fellow-men, who are themselves sinners. The latter are therefore outwitted by the lovers just as the Pharisees are outwitted by Christ—and in this battle of wits they are supported by Christ, who is Himself a practitioner of *list*."

67 See Jacques Berlioz, "Les Ordales dans les *exempla* de la Confession (XIIIe – XIVe siècles), " *L'Aveu: Antiquité et Moyen-âge: Actes de la table ronde organizée par l'École française de Rome avec le concours du CNRS et de l'université de Trieste, Rome 28–30 mais 1984.* Collection de L'École Française de Rome, 88 (Rome: École Française de Rome, 1986), 315–40.

68 Jean Froissart, *Chroniques,* ed. Siméon Luce, Gaston Raynaud and Léon Mirot, 15 vols. (Paris: Vv. J. Renouard [puis H. Champion], 1869–1966), 13:102–07; Jean Juvenal des Ursins, *Histoire de Charles VI, roy de France, . . .,* ed. Joseph-François Michaud and Jean Joseph François Poujoulat. Nouvelle collection des mémoires pour servir à l'histoire de France depuis le XIIIe siècle jusqu'à la fin du XVIIIe. Vol., 2 (Paris and Lyon: Guyot, 1850), 371. As pointed out by Esther Cohen, *The Crossroads*

Similarly, public faith in immanent justice is reflected in the popularity over the *très longue-durée* of the ancient tale of the *chien de Montargis,* dog of a knight murdered by his jealous rival, Macaire. The dog returned to court, showing marked friendliness to all but Macaire, arousing suspicion. The king ordered Macaire to offer food to the dog, which it refused from the knight's hand. Taken as a prima facie case, a *jugement* was ordered, Macaire armed with staff and shield, the dog with a barrel. Naturally, the dog won, and Macaire was forced to confess and was executed. This story went through a number of versions and was even recounted approvingly in the early seventeenth century by the French jurist, Claude Expilly who, as had his predecessors, accepted implicitly the historicity of the tale.[69] By comparison, across the channel, Fortescue was touting the glory of the jury system over the inquisitorial system,[70] and Malory, at least *chez* Caxton, had turned Arthurian romance into a tragedy of failed expectations, corruption, murder and incest.[71]

Is there further evidence for public approbation for customary justice? Strangely, perhaps, it is provided by the Anglo-Norman legal treatises of the thirteenth and early fourteenth centuries themselves. If one reads the *Placita Corone,* with which we opened, or the treatise, *Britton,* one would think that few changes had taken place in the operation of law, and that trial by battle, for example, was commonplace. In reality, by mid-century, *jugement de Dieu* had fallen off in England, not only due to the regularization of presentment, but because chancery

---

of Justice: Law and Culture in Late Medieval France. Brill's Studies in Intellectual History 36 (Leiden and New York: E. J. Brill, 1993), 59–60, the jurist Jean le Coq was among the few to record a jaundiced opinion of both procedure and results. *Questiones Johannis Galli,* ed. Margueritte Boulet. Bibliothéque des écoles françaises d'Athénes et de Rome, 156 (Paris: E. de Boccard, 1944), 95–98, writing inter alia, "Et habeo scrupulum quod fuerit Dei vindicta, et sic pluribus visum fuit qui viderunt dictum duellum." ("I have doubts this was the vengeance of God, and so it seemed to several others who witnessed the said duel"), Qu. 89, 110.

69 See Esther Cohen, *The Crossroads of Justice,* 60–61 (see note 68), discussing the version passed down by Claude Expilly, *Plaidoyez de mre Claude Expilly, conseiller du roy et son advocate general... president au Parlement de Grenoble; ensemble plusieurs arrests & reiglemens notables dudit Parlement,* 5th ed. (Lyon : Impr. De S. Rigaud, 1631), 199–200. While Cohen emphasizes the formulaic nature of these late medieval stories, my argument suggests that their favor generally lay in substance rather than form. Cf. J. Viscardi, *Le Chien de Montargis: Etude de folklore juridique* (Paris: F. Loviton, 1932), 54–61.

70 Sir John Fortescue, *De Laudibus Legum Angliae,* c. 20, c. 22, cc. 29–32.

71 See Thomas C. Rumble, "'The Tale of Tristam': Development by Analogy," *Malory's Originality: A Critical Study of Le Mort Darthur,* ed. R. M. Lumiansky (Baltimore: Johns Hopkins Press, 1964), 146; Ralph J. Hexter, *Equivocal Oaths and Ordeals in Medieval Literature (The LeBaron Russel Briggs Prize Honors Essays in English, 1974)* (Cambridge, MA, and London: Harvard University Press, 1975), 42. For the literary tradition of this tale, now see Albrecht Classen's Introduction to *Rural Space in the Middle Ages and Early Modern Age,* ed. id in collaboration with Christopher R. Clason. Fundamentals of Medieval and Early Modern Culture, 9 (Berlin and New York: De Gruyter, 2012), 102–06.

had devised a new writ in what would come to be known as tort, obviating the need for appeal as a tactic in the recovery of damages.[72]

Meanwhile, justices seldom denied the validity of the old laws and procedures, but rather found exceptions to their application. Hence, *Fleta,* the Latin text roughly contemporaneous with *Britton,* seems to recognize that actual practice had changed, despite the effort of justices, in the words of J. M. Kaye, "to leave the façade of the ancient rules standing, whilst demolishing the structure behind."[73] Indeed, as we have noted, wager of battle was not officially abrogated in England until the nineteenth century, despite being whittled down to an oddity by the 1300's. In France, where Louis attempted to prohibit it in royal courts in 1260, it continued to thrive in the provincial courts, where appellees retained the right to demand battle against not only appellants and witnesses, but even against jurors. Instead of prohibiting *battel* in cases involving women, the infirm, or the elderly, as had English courts, most provincial and seigniorial courts on the continent continued to recognize the use of champions. So popular was the *jugement de Dieu,* that Philip the Fair was compelled to restore the practice to royal courts, perhaps because the alternative touted by the crown's trained *legistes* was inquisitorial procedure which by then had found itself largely dependent on torture, which was apparently more popularly embraced in the Italian communes than by the majority of Frenchmen.[74] Only with the official redactions of custom in the fifteenth and sixteenth centuries was the French crown finally successful in establishing a model of justice dispensed from above, in which an insurmountable gulf existed between the court and the litigants.

Meanwhile, across the channel in an England clinging tenuously to its Norman and Angevin roots through the tenacity of that bastardized dialect known as "law French," the crown had been largely successful in transforming the English legal

72 See Daniel Klerman, "Settlement and the Decline of Private Prosecution in Thirteenth-Century England," *Law and History Review* 19 (2001): 1–65.

73 Introduction to *Placita Corone,* xvii (see note 1).

74 See for example, Bartolus de Saxoferrato, *Commentaria in ius universum civile* (Basel 1562), ad Dig. Just. 18.20 s.v. *Qui sine:* "Ideo dico hic quod quidam iudices stulti qui statim cum habeant indicia contra reum cogunt eum ad confitendum. Certe hoc non debet fieri, quia condemnarent eum ex indiciis et suspitionibus, sed debent adhibere tormenta cum moderamine, et ex istis veritatem investigare. Et ita iam feci pluries fieri, sed si habita tortura non inveniebatur verum, absolvebam eum, et hoc faciebam scribi in actis: 'Habita tortura cum moderamine non reperi eum culpabilem.' Et hoc ne tempore syndicatus possit dici, 'Tu debuisti eum torquere'" ("Thus, I say regarding this, that there are some dull judges who immediately when they have information against a defendant compel him to confess. Surely, this should not be done, because they condemn him based on information and suspicion; rather, they should apply torture with moderation and from this, search out the truth. And so several times I undertook to do, but if the truth was not uncovered by application of torture, I acquitted him, and I caused this to be written in the record: 'With torture administered with moderation, I did not find him guilty,' and this, lest sometime the syndicate is able to say, 'you should have tortured him'").

system through change so incremental and so successful in its cooptation of the public[75] that in the process something of a myth of the jury system was born, wherein trial by jury was the customary right of Englishmen.[76]

In conclusion, I would submit that this brief excursion suggests that the passing of the ordeal was neither the product of widespread skepticism, particularly regarding immanent justice, nor was it the immediate consequence of the withdrawal of Church sanction. In various guises, belief in and appeals to immanent justice survived without the immediate and active participation of the clergy. Rather, the decision of the Fouth Lateran Council largely coincided with the objectives of secular rulers and their *legiste* minions, whose ambitions were delayed by a recalcitrant public mindful of its customary prerogatives, and more trustful of the eternal truths of God, than of the innovations of kings, whose function in the popular imagination remained preservation and application of the

75 As a consequence, the conviction rate, despite the fear of some defendants, was notoriously low. See Thomas Andrew Green, *Verdict According to Conscience* (Chicago: University of Chicago Press, 1985); John G. Bellamy, *Crime and Public Order in England in the Later Middle Ages* (London: Routledge and Kegan Paul, 1973). Various reasons have been advanced for this phenomenon, including over-charging and over-presentment. However, in addition to disapproval of law or punishment, it is also possible that juries chose to express a communal mercy not dissimilar to what might have been expected in the *jugement de Dieu.* See Trisha Olson, "Of Enchantment: The Passing of Ordeals and the Rise of Jury Trial," *Syracuse Law Review* 50 (2000): 109–96; here 173–74. Of course, jury nullification and mercy are hardly mutually exclusive categories for a period in which the defense is largely unknown and unavailable. The independence of English juries was grudgingly accepted until the end of the Middle Ages when its role was reined in by the development of jury instructions. See John H. Langbein, "Historical Foundations of the Law of Evidence: A View from the Ryder Sources," *Columbia Law Review* 96 (1996): 1168–99.

76 One cannot deny or discount the happy coincidence of Magna Carta and the development of the jury which led in the early fourteenth century to the identification of that institution with the defendant's peers. See Year Book 30–31, Edward I, 531, and James Clarke Holt, *Magna Carta,* 2nd ed. (Cambridge: University of Cambridge Press, 1992), 397.

law, not legislation. Until and to the extent Roman civil law concepts fostered a Renaissance pretension to absolutism, it could be—and often was—said, "Vox populi, vox Dei."[77]

[77] On the peculiar history of this expression, see George Boas, *"Vox Populi": Essays in the History of an Idea* (Baltimore: Johns Hopkins Press, 1969); S. A. Gallacher, *"Vox populi, vox Dei," Philological Quarterly* 24 (1945): 12–19; Edward Peters, *"Vox populi, vox dei," Law in Mediaeval Life and Thought,* ed. Edward B. King and Susan J. Rodyard (Sewanee, TN: The Press of the University of the South, 1990), 91–120. Despite the variety of senses in which the maxim was used, I think particularly of its use in Philippe de Commynes, *Mémoires,* ed. Joseph Calmette, 3 vols. Les Classiques de L'Histoire de France au Moyen Age 3, 5, and 6 (Paris: Champion, 1924–1925), 3:82: "Par quoy conclud ce propos, disant, après l'avoir ouy dire à plusieurs bons homes de religion et de saincte vie et à mainte aultre sorte de gens (qui est la voix de Dieu que la voix du peuple), que Nostre Seigneur les vouloit pugnir visiblement, et que chascun le cogneüt, et par eulx donner exemple à tous roys et princes de bien vivre et selon ses commendemens . . ." ("Wherefore, this subject concludes, saying as has been heard said by many good men of religion and holy life, and by many other sorts of people (i.e., the voice of the people is the voice of God), that our Lord wished to punish them manifestly that everyone would know it, and by them to provide an example to all kings and princes to live righteously and according to his commandments"). See discussions of this passage in Boas, 26 (see above); Peters, 116–17 (see above). Clearly, this appeal to the punishment of the wicked as an example to others is related in sentiment to the *jugement de Dieu* and the *vindicatio Dei* as interpretations and justifications for warfare. See also, Scott L. Taylor, "The Conquest of Sodom: Symbiosis of Calumny and Canon in the Jus Belli from Ireland to the Indies," *War and Peace: Critical Issues in European Societies and Literature 800-1800,* ed. Albrecht Classen and Nadia Margolis. Fundamentals of Medieval and Early Modern Culture, 7 (Berlin and New York: Walter de Gruyter, 2011), 81–97.

Chapter 6

Albrecht Classen
(The University of Arizona, Tucson)

Crime and Violence in the Middle Ages: The Cases of Heinrich der Glichezare's *Reinhard Fuchs* and Wernher der Gartenære's *Helmbrecht*[1]

Every cultural-historian is faced by the difficult task of selecting his/her documents, data, images, or objects for the evaluation of specific conditions under investigation. This applies as much to our own world as to the Middle Ages. This could mean, for instance, and very much depending on one's point of view, that the medieval period would have to be identified as the 'dark ages.' But no one would be fully able to identify what they mean thereby in specific and detailed terms, in comparison with any other age. In other words, such evaluations are always in the danger of relying on some obscure criteria and standards, as if history itself were, by necessity, progressive and linear.

Of course, if we listen to one group of arguments, the Middle Ages were filled with violence, criminal behavior, and lawlessness, which would justify us today to characterize them as 'dark.' Vengeance and blood-feuds were quite common aspects, and many people suffered badly from being exposed to criminals, gangs of bandits and murderers, and violent suppression by the soldiers of their own lord's neighbor.[2] Feuding, internecine strife, riots, rebellions, and countless wars

---

1 I would like to express my gratitude to Connie Scarborough, Texas Tech University, for having read my article and providing me with valuable feedback. All remaining mistakes are, of course, my own.

2 For an excellent selection of primary texts, see *Vengeance in Medieval Europe: A Reader*, ed. Daniel Lord Smail and Kelly Gibson (Toronto, ON, Tonawanda, NY, et al.: University of Toronto Press, 2009); see also the contributions to *Vengeance in the Middle Ages: Emotion, Religion and Feud*, ed. Susanna A. Throop and Paul R. Hyams (Farnham, Surrey, and Burlington, VT: Ashgate, 2010).

were part of the common experiences far and wide, and this was certainly true during the early Middle Ages,[3] but in later periods as well.

However, the Peace of God movements, at least since the eleventh century, clearly indicated how much people high and low were concerned with finding ways to channel wide-spread and uncontrolled violence, but obviously had a hard time realizing their goals.[4] But has not the idea of peace always been a dream, evanescent in most cases, and are not decades of peaceful existence, such as in the Western world since the end of the Second World War, just temporal respites?[5] Does not barbarism and sheer violence simply lurk around the corner even today?[6] Certainly, there are laws, courts, the police, and other institutions and instruments available today that specifically aim at the containment of crime, but this does not necessarily make people more peaceful, or law-abiding. Considering these contradictions, we can easily recognize that in the Middle Ages similar conditions existed and then were met by time-specific or time-characteristic measures.[7] Sensational murder cases happened as much in the past as they occur today, and we quickly have to realize that human nature does not seem to improve much over time.

As the thirteenth-century Middle High German didactic poet Hugo von Trimberg emphasized in his chapter on robbers, "Swâ volkes grôziu menige sî, / Dâ sî ouch schade und schande bî" (6775–76; Wherever there is a huge crowd of people, there is also to be found damage and shamefulness).[8] Moreover, those who strive to gain power and profit by way of joining the service of a great lord, tend not to acquire much honor or money (6777–80). Greed rules the world, triggering

---

3 Albrecht Classen, "Early Middle Ages," *The Literary Encyclopedia* (4-23-10; by subscription only: http://www.litencyc.com/php/stopics.php?rec=true&UID=7222) (last accessed on May 1, 2010).

4 See, for instance, Dominique Barthélemy, *L'An mil et la paix de Dieu: La France chrétienne et féodale 980-1060* ([Paris]: Librairie Arthème Fayard, 1999).

5 Peter Dinzelbacher, *Lebenswelten des Mittelalters: 1000–1500*. Bachmanns Basiswissen, 1 (Badenweiler: Wissenschaftlicher Verlag Bachmann, 2010), 239-69.

6 Gertrud Nunner-Winkler, "Gewalt – ein Spezifikum der Moderne?," Rpt. *Max-Planck-Institut für Psychologische Forschung*, 18 (Munich: Max-Planck-Inst. für Psychologische Forschung, 1996), 81–95; *Warrior's Dishonour: Barbarity, Morality and Torture in Modern Warfare*, ed. George Kassimeris (Aldershot, England, Burlington, VT: Ashgate, 2006).

7 For a good historical approach to this topic, see Ernst Schubert, *Räuber, Henker, arme Sünder: Verbrechen und Strafe im Mittelalter*. With an epilogue by Thomas Vogtherr (Darmstadt: Wissenschaftliche Buchgesellschaft, 2007). See also the contributions to *Medieval Crime and Social Control*, ed. Barbara A. Hanawalt and David Wallace. Medieval Cultures, 16 (Minneapolis and London: University of Minneapolis Press, 1999); Trevor Dean, *Crime in Medieval Europe 1200–1550* (London: Pearson Education, 2001).

8 Hugo von Trimberg, *Der Renner*, ed. Gustav Ehrismann. Mit einem Nachwort und Ergänzungen von Günther Schweikle. Deutsche Neudrucke. Reihe: Texte des Mittelalters. Vol. 1 (1908; Berlin: Walter de Gruyter, 1970), 282. See now the contributions to *Scham und Schamlosigkeit: Grenzverletzungen in Literatur und Kultur der Vormoderne*, ed. Katja Gvozdeva and Hans Rudolf Velten. Trends in Medieval Philology, 21 (Berlin and New York: De Gruyter, 2011).

constant waves of criminal behavior and sinfulness (6817–18). Whereas in the time of the Old Testament the Jews burnt sacrifical animals in honor of God (6830–32), and whereas good Christians burn thyme, myrrh, and incense in honor of their God (6833–36), now new fires are lit: "Nu brennet man schiuren und ruozigiu dach / Und manic armer liute gemach, / Die frostic, hungeric unde blôz / Beteln gênt, der leit vil grôz / Ist üm ir kleiniu kindelîn, / Diu arm und ellende müezen sîn" (6837–42; Now they burn barns and rustic roofs, and the houses of many poor people. These have to go begging, freezing, hungry, and naked. They suffer greatly, and their little children must be poor and miserable).

The issue for us, however, would be to analyze the specific conditions that lead to crime and violence and then probe what measures have been taken to combat, or at least to contain them. Moreover, we will always have to keep in mind the phenomenon itself that crime is reported and reflected on, signaling either an awareness of the danger for society at large, or an appeal to the authorities to intervene, if not to purge its own ranks from criminal elements.[9]

For a general approach to our topic, it would be extremely important to recognize that medieval society was not at all as homogenous as we regularly assume, so tensions between majority and minority groups in religious terms could easily erupt violently. Christians hating the Jewish communities—the opposite was certainly also the case—increasingly carried out pogroms, relegated Jews to a ghetto, ridiculed them in public ("Judensau"),[10] maligned them, and often persecuted them with every means available.[11] But this global picture dangerously generalizes and relies heavily on stereotypes and highly simplified observations, disregarding a plethora of evidence that speaks to the very opposite,

---

9 See, for instance, Salima Moyard, *Crime de poison et procès politique à la Cour de Savoie: L'Affair Pierre Gerbais (1379–1382)*. Cahiers lausannois d'histoire médiévale, 44 (Lausanne: Université de Lausanne, 2008); Claude Berguerand, *Le Duel d'Othon de Grandson (1397): Mort d'un chevalier-poète à la fin du Moyen-Age*. Cahiers lausannois d'histoire médiévale, 45 (Lausanne: Université de Lausanne, 2008); for a review, see Marina Montessano, *Studi medievali* LI.1 (2010): 459–61.

10 Birgit Wiedl, "Laughing at the Beast: The *Judensau*: Anti-Jewish Propaganda and Humor from the Middle Ages to the Early Modern Period," *Laughter in the Middle Ages and Early Modern Times: Epistemology of a Fundamental Human Behavior, its Meaning, and Consequences*, ed. Albrecht Classen. Fundamentals of Medieval and Early Modern Culture, 5 (Berlin and New York: Walter de Gruyter, 2010), 325–64.

11 This topic has already been studied by many scholars, for instance, Miri Rubin, *Gentile Tales: The Narrative Assault on Late Medieval Jews*. The Middle Ages Series (1999; Philadelphia: University of Pennsylvania Press, 2004); Robert Chazan, *The Jews of Medieval Western Christendom, 1000-1500*. Cambridge Medieval Textbooks (Cambridge, New York, et al.: Cambridge University Press, 2006). Alexandra Cuffel, *Gendering Disgust in Medieval Religious Polemic* (Notre Dame, IN: University of Notre Dame Press, 2007), provides one of the most insightful analysis of hatred among the representatives of all three monotheistic world religions, regularly predicated on the very same stereotypes and images of the enemy. See also the contribution to the present volume by Birgit Wiedl.

whether we think of courtly literature, mystical texts, Gothic cathedrals, the rise of the universities, or the arts at large.[12] In those contexts the term 'dark' has no meaning at all and easily proves to be absurd. Everything depends on local conditions, individuals, mental structures, social and cultural frameworks, etc., which applies almost more to the medieval world than to modern politics, for which this dictum was originally phrased, but it certainly has a timeless relevance.[13]

To illustrate the central issue here, I will discuss two major narratives from medieval German literature where total violence and a ruthless criminal mind characterize the respective protagonist who terrorizes everyone around him, leading to endless suffering and subjugation of the affected people, foe and friend, high and low, lay and clerical. In the Alsatian Heinrich (der Glichezare)'s fable narrative *Reinhard Fuchs* (ca. 1170–1190) and in Wernher der Gardenære's didactic account of *Helmbrecht* (ca. 1260–1274) the fundamental question is raised in unique and ominous ways about where justice lies and whether there is hope for the legal system to intervene and to prevent violence.

Critical mass, in other words, has finally reached unforeseen dimensions in these texts and threatens to engulf the entire world since the evil character in Heinrich's text at first gains the upper hand and then is brought to justice by the authorities. At first, however, the criminal (young Helmbrecht) goes on a rampage of violence aimed at material gains which is tolerated for far too long by the own family back home and the territorial lord, or the government. Although he is ultimately lynched by his previous victims, the peasants, there remains a strong sense that crime is not eliminated at all, and violence is only suspended for a short time.

But let us first gain some insight into the global discourse on suffering, violence, and crime as it dominated the Middle Ages, before we turn to these two texts so we can set up the necessary framework for our investigation. Examining these issues does not imply, however, that I would want to confirm, once again, the notion of the Middle Ages as a brutal, violence-ridden, primitive, and barbaric world. The critical point can only be to uncover a specific discourse in these literary texts and to probe their messages in ethical, legal, moral, religious, and political terms.

---

12 Elisheva Baumgarten, *Mothers and Children: Jewish Family Life in Medieval Europe*, trans. from the Hebrew. Jews, Christians, and Muslims from the Ancient to the Modern World (Princeton: Princeton University Press, 2004). See also Bernard Lewis, *Cultures in Conflict: Christians, Jews, and Muslims in the Age of Discovery* (New York: Oxford University Press, 1995). Further, see the excellent contributions to *Misconceptions about the Middle Ages*, ed. Stephen J. Harris and Bryon L. Grigsby. Routledge Studies in Medieval Religion and Culture, 7 (New York and London: Routledge, 2008).

13 Paul Hyams, "Was there Really Such a Thing as Feud in the High Middle Ages?," *Vengeance in the Middle Ages*, 151–75; here 174 (see note 2).

People have always displayed a tendency to commit crimes, to be violent, to act unfairly and unjustly. The cynic would probably say that we write history in order to record the innumerable cases of crime and to reflect upon possible reactions to violence, if we apply Newton's third law of motion which suggests that every action is followed by an equal and opposite reaction. Moreover, we study the past because the endless human suffering needs to gain a voice, so analyzing the misery and pain that people have gone through in the past might help us to come to terms with our own daily tribulations, sorrow, grief, and pain, but then on a higher level.[14] Of course, we will never be able to overcome injustice completely, for instance, but we will be in a much more constructive position to comprehend the essence of human existence in face of suffering.[15] As the thirteenth-century Dominican preacher and mystic Henry Suso (Heinrich Seuse) emphasized in his highly influential *Horologium Sapientiae* (ca. 1330/31), human life is deeply burdened by suffering from injustice, filled with pain, vilification and mortification. Nevertheless, Suso does not shrink back from any of those aspects; instead he welcomes all tribulations and identifies them as essential catalysts for man to translate the earthly prison of his flesh into the spirit that is thus readied for the union with the Godhead after a long period of testing:

> Quid namque est, quod aeque cor tumidum et animum elatum ac hominem ambitiosum se ipsum magis faciat cognoscere et *non alta sapere*, sed humiliter in se ipso consistere ac timere, et quod proximo patienti condescendere doceat? Haec est nutrix humilitatis, doctrix patientiae, custos virginitatis, comparatrix aeternae felicitatis. Tribulatio habita es adeo salutifera, ut vix sit, qui ab eius se abscondat bonitatis aspergine, sive sit de incipientium numero vel proficientium seu etiam perfectorum. Rubiginem aufert peccatorum, incrementa praestat virtutum et ubertatem confert gratiarum. Quid hoc thesauro pretiosissimo utilius? Ipsa namque peccata tollit, purgatorium minuit, repellit tentationes, exstinguit carnalitates, spiritum renovat,

---

14 Dinzelbacher, *Lebenswelten*, 239–59 (see note 5), depicts a medieval world where brutality, inhumane treatment of prisoners, hostages, opponents, and simply of the inhabitants of conquered castles and cities, not to speak of the peasants, was rampant and horrifying. He minimizes the attempts, very few far and wide, as he sees it, to establish peace and to display mercy, but here as so often in recent scholarship the selection of sources determines the intended goal of presenting the Middle Ages as horrifying. This is also one of the main points raised by Judith M. Bennett, *History Matters: Patriarchy and the Challenges of Feminism* (Philadelphia: University of Pennsylvania Press, 2006), 43–48.

15 Literature often proves to be the platform for what Sigmund Freud had called "Trauerarbeit" (coming to terms with grief), which finds its perhaps best expression in Johannes von Tepl's *Ackermann* from ca. 1400 in which a widower debates with Death about the reasons why his wife had to die. See André Schnyder, "Trauerarbeit des Witwers: Vorläufiger Versuch, ein altbekanntes Werk neu zu sehen," *Jahrbuch der Oswald von Wolkenstein Gesellschaft*, 4 (1986/1987): 25–39. Cf. also the contributions to *Grief and Gender: 700–1700*, ed. Jennifer C. Vaught, with Lynne Dickson Bruckner (New York and Houndmills, Basingstoke, Hampshire, England: Palgrave Macmillan, 2003).

> spem roborat, vultum exhilarat, conscientiae affert serenitatem, et internorum gaudiorum contiunuam praestat ubertatem.[16]
>
> [For what is it that makes a man of haughty heart and puffed-up mind and ambition learn to know himself better, and "not to mind high things," but to remain humbly within himself and to fear, and to teach others to stoop down to their suffering neighbors? Tribulation is the nurse of humility, the teacher of patience, the guardian of virginity, the bringer of everlasting felicity. Tribulation is considered to bring such well-being that it can hardly be that anyone will hide himself when it sprinkles its goodness around, whether he belong to the beginners or to the proficient or even to the perfect. It takes away the rust of sins, it promotes the growth of virtues, and it confers the fullness of graces. What can be of greater use than this most precious treasure? For it takes away sins, it shortens purgatory, it repels temptations, it extinguishes carnality, it renews the spirit, it strengthens hope, it enlivens the countenance, it brings peace of conscience and it offers the unending fullness of inward joys.[17]

Despite the overly optimistic, if not naive, attempts by modern scholars such as the famous sociologist Norbert Elias (1939) to identify knighthood as the essential institution invented and implemented to control endless violence and to inject cultural values predicated on love, peace, mutual respect, and honor, all subsumed under the mantra of the King Arthur myth with its subsequent process of civilization, any careful examination of medieval sources reveals also the dark sides.[18] However, what society or cultural period did not experience both aspects of human life: happiness and sorrow, violence and peace? As Richard W. Kaeuper confirms, "Chivalry was not simply a code integrating generic individual and society, not simply an ideal for relations between the sexes or a means for knocking off the rough warrior edges in preparation for the European gentleman to come. The bloody-minded side of the code—even if it seems to moderns . . . a shuddering matter—was of the essence of chivalry. The knight was a warrior and not Everyman."[19]

---

16 Heinrich Seuse, *Horologium Sapientiae*. Erste kritische Ausgabe unter Benützung der Vorarbeiten von Dominikus Pflanzer OP. Spicilegium Friburgense. Texte zur Geschichte des kirchlichen Lebens, 23 (Freiburg, CH: Universitätsverlag, 1977), 489–90.

17 Bl. Henry Suso, *Wisdom's Watch Upon the Hours*, trans. Edmund Colledge, O.S.A. The Fathers of the Church: Mediaeval Continuation (Washington, DC: The Catholic University of America Press, 1994), 197.

18 See the contributions to *Gewalt im Mittelalter: Realitäten – Imaginationen*, ed. Manuel Braun and Cornelia Herberichs (Paderborn and Munich: Wilhelm Fink, 2005).

19 Richard W. Kaeuper, *Chivalry and Violence in Medieval Europe* (Oxford and New York: Oxford University Press, 1999), 8. See also the contributions to *Violence in Medieval Courtly Literature: A Casebook*, ed. Albrecht Classen. Routledge Medieval Casebooks (New York and London: Routledge, 2004).

It might be futile to carry out a comparison between medieval and modern violence because the radically changed conditions in both worlds would make this truly impossible, although there are indeed sometimes must puzzling and troubling cases of massive child murder then and today.[20] Control of violence, for instance, has obviously been mostly channeled and transferred to the state with its police force and military since, say, the eighteenth century, which were not quite yet in place during the premodern era. Does this mean, however, that people have become less violent, that suffering at large has diminished over time? Is there less need to probe, as Henry Suso and then Johannes von Tepl (*Ackermann*) did ca. seventy years later in Bohemia, why there is suffering and how we are to cope with it? The purely rhetorical nature of this question then leads us to the central concern of this paper, staying clear of the mythical notion of history being a linear, progressive development, moving away from a dark to a light world.

Despite the appearance of a rather idyllic world at King Arthur's court and elsewhere, medieval poets and artists did not hesitate to criticize, or even rip apart, the veil behind the fictionality of their works and everyday reality. Here I want to discuss two major texts where this issue finds powerful expression, the first a significant fable narrative from the late twelfth century, the second a didactic and moralistic verse narrative from the second half of the thirteenth century In both works we are brutally confronted with the consequences of vile characters, criminal behavior, lack of any morality, and of physical violence. We will have to ask ourselves why their authors chose to address their topics, and then try to correlate their observations to larger social and political issues affecting their time. The fact that these medieval writers approached such issues in the first place and explored the nature and meaning of violence so drastically clearly alerts us to avoid such stereotypical, mostly populist, concepts of a 'dark' age vs. an 'enlightened' age.[21]

As a useful springboard for our discussion, let us first look at a most impressive illuminated manuscript where the miniatures for the individual poets prove to be highly revealing as to the cultural-historical issue at stake here. In the early fourteenth century members of the wealthy Zurich family Manesse and probably a group of like-minded friends commissioned a scribe or a whole scriptorium to collect the best or most popular courtly love poetry from the late twelfth to the early fourteenth century in one manuscript and to add a poet portrait for each one of them. The volume consists of 852 folio pages which record ca. 5,400 stanzas and 36 didactic poems by 140 authors; it must have taken at least a whole decade, if not

---

20 See the contribution to this volume by Lia B. Ross.

21 See Hiram Kümper, "The Term Middle Ages," *Handbook of Medieval Studies*, ed. Albrecht Classen (Berlin and New York: Walter de Gruyter, 2010), vol. 2, 1310–19.

more, to compile this massive tome. There are in total 137 full page miniatures, 118 of which contain a coat of arms to emphasize the respective poets' aristocratic rank, although none of the figures are presented in any realistic fashion and never recognizable in individualistic terms.[22] The artists made great efforts to present the poets in an idyllic fashion, almost always placing them in a characteristic courtly setting, showing them playing chess with a lady (no. 6), hunting with birds of prey (no. 7), holding a scroll as a symbol of their creative art (no. 10), presenting a poem to a lady (no. 17), taking a bath (no. 20), or being involved in a tournament (no. 22). The ladies always appear in a most charming pose, beautifully dressed, young, charming, and beautiful, holding a falcon (no. 29), debating with the lover (no. 30), pulling the lover up to their rooms high up in a tower (no. 31), holding a pet in their arms (no. 34, no. 37), or dancing with the poet-knight (no. 46). One of the most appealing images might be the one for Lord Wachsmut von Mühlhausen, showing a lady sitting on a horse and aiming an arrow of love at the man standing behind her (no. 59).

Until today these images have been used for countless book covers dedicated to the study of the Middle Ages, for modern novels set in that time period, for webpages, and art work, and with good reasons. The *Manesse Songbook* reflects in an overwhelming fashion the beauty and ideals of the courtly world where love and chivalry rule. However, a careful examination also reveals very different scenes, such as the portrait of Lord Reinmar von Brennenberg (no. 61) who is shown as being brutally murdered by a gang of criminals, one of them stabbing him in his head with the sword, the other one striking his side, and others raising their swords about to smite him as well. As far as we can tell, the poet, brother of the Regensburg Canon Bruno von Brennenberg, was indeed murdered in 1275, and in 1276 the Bishop of Regensburg promised Bruno vengeance for this heinous act.[23] The image for the poet Düring (no. 75) shows the siege of a castle; the poet Neidhart (no. 92) is beleaguered by mean-spirited peasants, his arch-enemies, at least within his sarcastic Winter songs. In the miniature for Lord Dietmar der Setzer (no. 111) two knights fight against each other with their swords, and one of

---

22 Gisela Kornrumpf, *Vom Codex Manesse zur Kolmarer Liederhandschrift: Aspekte der Überlieferung, Formtraditionen, Texte*. Münchener Texte und Untersuchungen zur deutschen Literatur des Mittelalters, 133 (Tübingen: Niemeyer, 2008). For an online-version of the digitized manuscript, see http://diglit.ub.uni-heidelberg.de/diglit/cpg848/ (last accessed on August 23, 2010). Wikipedia.de offers a surprisingly well-written article, along with updated research: http://de.wikipedia.org/wiki/Codex_Manesse (last accessed on Aug. 23, 2010). For an easy access in print format, see *Codex Manesse: Die Minitaturen der Großen Heidelberger Liederhandschrift*. Ed. and explained by Ingo F. Walther with Gisela Siebert. 6th ed. (1988; Frankfurt a. M.: Insel, 2001). See also *Codex Manesse: Die Große Heidelberger Liederhandschrift. Faksimile-Ausgabe des Codex Palatinus Germanicus 848 der Universitäts-Bibliothek Heidelberg*. Commentary by Walter Koschorreck and Wilfried Werner (Kassel: Ganymed, 1981).

23 Walter, *Codex Manesse*, 124 (see note 22).

them cuts through his opponent's head, sending him to his death. At times we are also confronted with the bloody reality of war, such as in the miniature for Count Albrecht von Hegerloch (no. 18), with four triumphant knights, the poet presumably among them, completely overwhelming their opponents who are all falling to the ground, dying from their wounds.

Altogether, considering the rather contrastive images in the *Manesse* manuscript, it would be erroneous to assume that the world of the medieval courts constituted a peaceful, crime- and violence-free environment where all concerns and energies were dedicated to the pursuance of love and honor. In fact, Western history has always been determined by violence and war, and it would be highly hypocritical to view the Middle Ages either through rosy glasses or through the lenses of the myth of the 'dark ages,' falling prey to the opposite myth regarding that world as utterly determined by violence, brutality, and primitivism, to recapture our theoretical ruminations at the beginning of this study.[24]

Let's simply face it, human nature is violent, and the history of the so-called 'civilization process' primarily reflects the continuous efforts to come to terms with the 'criminal' and beastly, uncivil character in us. Literature has consistently served the extremely important function of mirroring this violence and engaging the listener/reader in a critical discourse on this devastating phenomenon, perhaps as a way to confront us with some of the most dangerous traits in our lives and to find measures to contain that explosive tendency toward violence.[25] Both the Alsatian poet Heinrich and the Austrian writer Wernher the Gardenære made important contributions to the examination of criminality and violence as they observed them at their time.[26]

---

24 Irenäus Eibl-Eibesfeldt, *Love and Hate: The Natural History of Behavior Patterns,* trans. Geoffrey Strachan (1970; New York: Holt, Rinehart and Winston, 1972); J. D. Carthy and F. J. G. Ebling, eds., *The Natural History of Aggression*. Symposia of the Institute of Biology, 13 (London and New York: Academic Press, 1964); G. F. Jones, "The Treatment of Bloodshed in Medieval and Modern Literature," *Studia Neophilologica* 70 (1998): 83–88; Robert L. O'Connell, *Of Arms and Men: A History of War, Weapons, and Aggression* (New York: Oxford University Press, 1989). František Graus, "Gewalt und Recht im Verständnis des Mittelalters," *Basler Beiträge zur Geschichtswissenschaft* 134 (1974): 5–21; Udo Friedrich, "Die Zähmung des Heros: Der Diskurs der Gewalt und Gewaltregulierung im 12. Jahrhundert," *Mittelalter: Neue Wege durch einen alten Kontinent,* hg. Jan-Dirk Müller und Horst Wenzel (Stuttgart und Leipzig: Hirzel, 1999), 149–79; Valentin Groebner, *Defaced: The Visual Culture of Violence in the Late Middle Ages* (New York: Zone Books, 2004).

25 Albrecht Classen, "Gewaltverbrechen als Thema des spätarturischen Romans. Sozialkritisches in Wirnts von Grafenberg *Wigalois,*" *Etudes Germaniques* 62, 2 (2007): 429–55.

26 Late-medieval literature knows many examples of a critical discourse focused on how to combat violence, see Albrecht Classen, "Die sich selbst verschlingende Gewalt: Grundsätzliche Gedanken zu einem global-menschlichen Phänomen mit mediävistischen Perspektiven auf Wernhers des Gaertenære *Helmbrecht* und Heinrich Wittenwilers *Ring,*" *Futhark: Revista de investigación y cultura* 1 (2006): 11–39.

As is so often the case in medieval literature, not much is known about Heinrich—previously identified with the epithet 'Glîchezære,' which, however, seems to be nothing but an allusion to the cunning skills of the literary figure of the fox—but we assume that he originated from the Alsace, if we can trust his references to specific localities and personalities there.[27] It seems most realistic to place him in the second half of the twelfth century, more concretely between 1170 and 1190 (or 1192), but we cannot say whether he belonged to the nobility or to the group of minstrels. Judging from his many literary allusions and his expert knowledge of how to run a legal process, which makes up a major portion of his text, he must have been a highly learned person with detailed understanding of the judicial system, so he could have been a cleric, an administrator, or even a judge.[28] The text of his fable narrative, *Reinhard Fuchs*, has come down to us in two groups of manuscripts, the older one (especially ms. S) from the early thirteenth century, the more recent one (mss. P and K) from the end of the thirteenth century.

The text draws on the Old French *Roman de Renart*, which consists of many different episodic narratives (branches),[29] but Heinrich was the earliest one to blend them all together and to create a comprehensive and consistent epic, the first of its kind based on this extraordinary protagonist, the evil and cunning fox. Only here do we discover a consistent motivational structure and a cohesive account that takes us from the early stages, with the fox committing sporadic acts of violence, deception, or lying, to the final, triumphant moment when the fox has

---

27 Here I will quote from *Der Reinhart Fuchs des Elsässers Heinrich*, ed. Klaus Düwel. Altdeutsche Textbibliothek, 96 (Tübingen: Niemeyer, 1984). See also Heinrich der Glichezâre, *Reinhart Fuchs: Mittelhochdeutsch und Neuhochdeutsch*. Ed., trans., and explained by Karl-Heinz Göttert (1976; Stuttgart: Reclam, 1980). For facsimiles of the relevant manuscripts, see *Der mittelhochdeutsche Reinhart Fuchs: Abbildungen und Materialien zur handschriftlichen Überlieferung*, ed. Otfried [sic] Ehrismann. Litterae, 72 (Göppingen: Kümmerle, 1980).

28 Sigrid Widmaier, *Das Recht im "Reinhart Fuchs"*. Quellen und Forschungen zur Sprach- und Kulturgeschichte der germanischen Völker, 102 (Berlin and New York: Walter de Gruyter, 1993). A parallel case to Heinrich would be the early fifteenth-century Constance public notary Heinrich Wittenwiler who, when he composed his famous *Ring* at ca. 1400, also included much detailed information about the legal process.

29 The Old French Roman de Renart consists of a cycle of animal fables that experienced a considerable popularity, with fourteen complete and nineteen fragmentary manuscripts still extant today. The twenty-seven individual branches, composed between ca. 1174 and 1250, were written by ca. twenty anonymous authors, probably clerics, only some of them known to us, such as Pierre de Saint-Cloud, Richard de Lison, and the priest of La Croix-en-Brie. The text experienced a considerable reception in the late Middle Ages all over Europe; see John Flinn, *Le Roman de Renart dans la littérature française et dans les littératures etrangères au Moyen Age* (Paris: Presses Universitaires de France, 1963); Hermann Krapoth, "Roman de Renart," *Enzyklopädie des Märchens: Handwörterbuch zur historischen und vergleichenden Erzählforschung*, ed. Rolf Wilhelm Brednich. Vol. 11.2 (Berlin and New York: Walter de Gruyter, 2004), 795–803. For the Middle High and Middle Low German, and Middle English versions, plus the long-term reception process until the present, see Klaus Düwel, *Reinhart Fuchs* (see note 27), 488–502.

gained absolute control over the entire court. Whereas we still can laugh about the smart tricks played by Renart in the Old French and older, Latin versions, Heinrich cast his protagonist as a thoroughly evil character, perhaps as 'evil incarnate' in Hans Robert Jauss's terms.[30]

Something is deeply upsetting and unsettling about this narrative, and yet it appealed to its audiences far and wide, both in southern and northern Germany, in Italy, the Netherlands, and England. The French poet Rutebeuf announced in his *Renart le Bestourné*, for instance, "Renart est mort, Renart vit, et Renart règne!," and in Jaquemart Gielée's *Renart le Nouvel* and in the anonymous *Couronnement de Renart* the evil protagonist has even achieved his devious goal to climb the social ladder to the very top—evil rules the world.[31] It might go too far to identify Renart or Reinhart with the devil himself since the text does not aim for a metaphysical explanation of the massive criminal acts committed by the protagonist, but he certainly stands in for some of the worst character traits in human life. However, following John Flinn, we might identify him as the incarnation of all cunning, ruse, and hypocrisy.[32]

Not surprisingly, he represented, indeed, the deeply troubling sense of fear among all people of being duped, deceived, cheated, abused, fooled, and badly treated by a thief, or any kind of criminal, especially if this generic crime is carried out by a member of the clergy or the secular authorities. Little wonder then that we find almost countless images of this notorious fox in a myriad of medieval artworks, such as in misericords, stone capitals, miniatures, corbels, spandrels, wooden doorframes, tapestry, pew ends, stained glasses, and elsewhere.[33]

Although many scholars have already commented on the entire corpus of this beast fable, and so have observed the incredible extent to which the fox steals, rapes, lies, and rules contrary to all moral and ethical standards,[34] here I will revisit

30 Hans Robert Jauss, *Untersuchungen zur mittelalterlichen Tierdichtung*. Beihefte zur Zeitschrift für romanische Philologie, 100 (Tübingen: Niemeyer, 1959), 295. Around 1050 an anonymous author composed the Latin text *Ecbasis cuiusdam captivi per tropologiam* in the region of Lorraine, followed by another Latin version, *Ysengrimus*, ca. 1150, composed in Gent by a Master Nivardus, who was the first to assign names to the individual animals. For a convenient introduction to the individual narratives, see Thomas W. Best, *Reynard the Fox*. Twayne's Author Series (Boston: Twayne Publishers, 1983).

31 Quoted from Flinn, *Le Roman de Renart*, 690 (see note 29).

32 Flinn, *Le Roman de Renart*, 690–91 (see note 29). Heinrichs *Reinhard Fuchs," Scham und Schamlosigkeit* (see note 8), 97–130, warms against a reductionist reading of the fox as the devil, 122–24.

33 Kenneth Varty, *Reynard, Renart, Reinaert and Other Foxes in Medieval England: the Iconographic Evidence. A Study of the Illustrating of Fox Lore and Reynard the Fox Stories in England During the Middle Ages* (Amsterdam: Amsterdam University Press, 1999). See also the excellent catalog for the exhibition, *Reineke Fuchs: Ein europäisches Epos. Eine Ausstellung des Goethe-Museums Düsseldorf*, ed. Jörn Göres. Catalogue by Horst Klitzing (Düsseldorf: Goethe-Museum Düsseldorf, Anton-und-Katharina-Kippenberg-Stiftung, 1989).

34 For a pan-European summary, see Albrecht Classen, "Roman de Renart," *Encyclopedia of Medieval*

the text by the Alsatian-German author to probe how much there is a sense of the devastating consequences of criminality and how Heinrich viewed the social interactions between his protagonist and all the other animals, that is, the other social estates. Subsequently I will examine what Wernher the Gardener had to say about criminal behavior and what consequences society would have to face if it went unchecked.

The narrator in *Reinhard Fuchs* immediately warns his audience about his protagonist, the evil fox, whom he identifies as a "tiere wilde" (3; wild animal) whose intentions were all directed at committing crimes against everyone by way of deception and trickery (7). Subsequently, he provides an example for Reinhard's cunning and evil nature, though it deals only with the fox's killing a chicken, a very common situation in reality, which many fable authors have discussed throughout time. Intriguingly, however, here we observe how much the fox knows how to utilize the power of rhetoric, drawing from traditional courtly language in order to put the rooster off guard and to puff up his arrogance, which then allows him to catch and kill his victim. Claiming to have been a good friend with the rooster's father Sengelin who used to uphold traditional courtly manners and displayed honorable behavior even toward inferiors, Reinhard succeeds in luring the son, Schantecler, down from the tree, to close his eyes, to flap his wings, and to sing "als ein vrolichez hvn" (125; as a happy chicken, i.e., rooster). The fox would have enjoyed his prey, if the rooster had not engaged him in a conversation, forcing the fox to open his mouth, which allows Schantecler to pull out his neck and to escape.

As hilarious as the entire scene might be, the strategy employed by the fox is predicated on the assumption that courtly values have disappeared in practice and yet still are regarded highly as ideals from the past. By implying that the rooster might not maintain the same degree of civility and politeness as his father, Reinhard knows how to tease the simpleton of a rooster down from his tree and thus to become his victim. Of course, the fox himself betrays these ideals by pretending to be a critic of the decline of public mores, echoing general laments about the disappearance of an old world. But Reinhard proves to be the worst offender and to be the crucial catalyst for bringing down the courtly ideals because he perverts them so badly and ruthlessly.

Having lost his meal because Schantecler has regained his freedom, Reinhard tries to convince a titmouse to give him a kiss, hoping that he might bite and kill it at that very moment. Unfortunately for him, the bird sees through his cunning

Literature, ed. Jay Ruud (New York: Facts on File, 2006), 549–50. Hans Rudolf Velten, "Schamlose Bilder – schamloses Sprechen (see note 8), 97–130, discusses the loss of shame and honor in this text, but also points out the intricate pairing of shame and shamelessness.

and deceives him in turn, and gets away without having been hurt by the fox. As silly as the entire scene might be, the narrator has predicated it on the important political custom in the Middle Ages that members of a family or a social group give kisses to each other as an expression of their loyalty and kinship. Among theologians, the kiss represented peace, community, and agreement; for lawyers the kiss sealed a contract; among the ruling class the kiss served as an expression of subservience and kingship. According to Bernard of Clairvaux the kiss was a sign of peace, and for William of Saint-Thierry kissing allowed those involved to express their spiritual commitment to form a community. Those who kissed signaled their mutual solidarity.[35]

The fox deliberately relies on this set of cultural assumptions, tries to force the titmouse to abide by them, but he is completely ready to betray them for his own advantage, no longer caring about any traditional value systems, which he (ab)uses only for his own advantage. What quickly proves to be the central strategy throughout the entire narrative carrying the didactic message, Heinrich reflects globally and in detail on the wide range of courtly ideals and demonstrates, through Reinhard's behavior, how an individual with a criminal mind can easily undermine them and turn them upside down. Moreover, in the case of the raven, who becomes the fox's next victim, singing is no longer valued as in the past; instead, the raven's attempt to live up to the expectations raised by Reinhard travesties all courtly singing; hence courtly love and culture, as represented in the *Manesse* manuscript.

The fox cleverly plays with the concept of love, especially with pain that regularly results from unrequited love, claiming that the cheese that had fallen from the branch where the raven had wanted to eat it would hurt his wound even further through its strong smell. Reinhard knows only too well how to utilize courtly language, claiming "ich wart hivte vrowe wunt" (260; I became wounded by a lady today). Appealing to the raven to remember the "triwe" (265), or loyalty, which his father would have displayed with no delay in such a case,[36] he can lure him down to the ground, where he almost manages to capture the silly bird and devour it. But then Reinhard has to run away because a hunter with two dogs picks on his trail, which allows the raven to express his disgust and irritation about the fox's mean spirit and deceptive behavior that almost cost him his life. The

---

35 Klaus Schreiner, "'Er küsse mich mit dem Kuß seines Mundes' (*Osculetur me osculo oris sui*, Cant 1, 1): Metaphorik, kommunikative und herrschaftliche Funktionen einer symbolischen Handlung," *Höfische Repräsentation: Das Zeremoniell und die Zeichen*, ed. Hedda Ragotzky and Horst Wenzel (Tübingen: Niemeyer, 1990), 89–132.

36 For a detailed discussion of the essential courtly values and their specific terms in Middle High German, see Otfrid Ehrismann, with Albrecht Classen, Winder McConnell et al., *Ehre und Mut, Âventiure und Minne: Höfische Wortgeschichten aus dem Mittelalter* (Munich: C. H. Beck, 1995). For "triuwe," see 211–16.

terms that he uses to comment on his opponent's treachery are important for their cultural-historical relevance: "er sprach: 'daz ein gebvre dem andern tvt, / Kvmt dicke lon, des hore ich iehen. / neve, also ist vch geschehen" (298–300; he said: "what one peasant does to another, often comes around to him, as I have heard. Cousin, that's what has happened to you).

Although he only intends to mock the fox and to expose his evil character, he resorts to the term 'peasant' to indicate the profound transgression that has affected the entire courtly society, perhaps best expressed in the poems by the contemporary Austrian-Bavarian Neidhart (ca. 1220–ca. 1240). In his Summer songs the peasant women are driven by sheer sexual lust to run after the knight of Reuental, whereas in the Winter songs his chances in matters of love have dimmed because the strong and resourceful peasant lads have cut him out of the competition and ridicule him as an impoverished knight.[37] In our context, the raven refers to the world of peasants because Reinhard's trickery almost had cost him his life, so he has good reason to characterize him as a crude and violent person who deservedly suffers now from the hunter's dogs.

As soon as the fox encounters the cat Diprecht, he draws on another traditional courtly value, loyal service, which the former is only too happy to provide: "'. . . min dienst sol dir sin bereit'" (324; I am ready to serve you). Reinhard does not care, however, about any of those values and brutally and gleefully abuses Diprecht's belief in the validity of those values, leading him to a trap set by a hunter. Yet, in this case, he meets his match because the cat is fully aware of the danger and jumps over the trap and so avoids the danger. Worse even for the fox, the cat later pushes him into the trap, making sure that Reinhard's foot gets caught (355), and then runs away: "Vnde bevalch in Lvcifere" (357; entrusted him to Lucifer). But this is, of course, not Reinhard's end because he deceives the peasant who later arrives to check on his trap, pretending to be dead, and when the peasant hits at him, he moves his head so that the trap is struck, liberating its victim. The complexity of the fable narrative comes to the fore particularly drastically here because the fox's devious actions are intriguingly matched with scoffing remarks about the low intellect of the peasant class—a pervasive attitude throughout the Middle Ages.[38]

---

37 Günther Schweikle, *Neidhart*. Sammlung Metzler, 253 (Stuttgart: Metzler, 1990); *Neidhart-Lieder: Texte und Melodien sämtlicher Handschriften und Drucke*, ed. Ulrich Müller, Ingrid Bennewitz, and Franz Viktor Spechtler. 3 vols. Salzburger Neidhart-Edition, 1–3 (Berlin and New York: Walter de Gruyter, 2007).

38 See, for instance, the contributions to *European Peasants and Their Markets: Essays in Agrarian Economic History*, ed. William Nelson Parker and E. L. Jones (Princeton, NJ: Princeton University Press, 1975); and to *Landlords, Peasants, and Politics in Medieval England*, ed. T. H. Aston (Cambridge and New York: Cambridge University Press, 1987); see also Piero Camporesi, *Bauern, Priester, Possenreisser: Volkskultur und Kultur der Eliten im Mittelalter und in der frühen Neuzeit*, trans. from the Italian by Karl F. Hauber (Frankfurt a. M. and New York: Campus Verlag,1997); Paul H.

Next, the fox meets the wolf Ysengrim to whom he offers his service, that is, his cunning as a political strategy as a perfect complement to the other's physical strength (yet also lack of intelligence!). Together, they would be able to overcome all other animals: "'. . . Ich bin listic, so sit starc ir. / ir mohtet gvten trost han zv mir. / Von iwer kraft vnd von minen listen / konde sich niht gevristen. / Ich konde ein bvrc wol zebrechen'" (397–401; "I am sophisticated, and you are strong. You can well trust me. No one will be able to resist your strength and my cunning. I can easily break a castle).

In conformity with much courtly criticism, voiced more or less contemporaneouosly both by clerics such as Walter Map, Gerald of Wales, and John of Salisbury, and by vernacular poets such as Der arme Hartmann, Heinrich von Melk, Werner von Elmendorf, and The Stricker, and most facetiously by the anonymous French author of the *chantefable Aucassin et Nicolette*,[39] Heinrich signals in unmistakable terms how dangerous this new member of the wolf's court soon turns out to be: "Daz er in ze gevatern nam do, / des wart er sint vil vnvro" (405–06; he became very unhappy later that he accepted him as his cousin/courtier). As soon as Reinhard is alone with Ysengrim's wife Hersante, he tries to seduce her, but he does not succeed at first. Later, however, we learn through an indirect report that the fox had raped her, which causes her husband great pain since he has no way of getting his revenge (586–90). The situation for Ysengrim proves to be particularly hurtful because he loves his wife and sings a song in praise of her just before he is informed about her sexual violation (565–76)

At the same time Ysengrim as the ruler of his court also behaves egoistically and rudely, disregarding his servant Reinhard, not sharing food with him, which the latter avenges in his typical fashion by leading the wolf into a dangerous situation in which he almost loses his life. The narrator's criticism is hence directed both at the rulers and their courtiers, both groups making a sham of all traditional courtly values, ideals, ethical norms, and moral criteria. Jean-Marc Pastré recognizes in this scene and many others clear allusions to the political and military situation in contemporary Germany ruled by the Hohenstaufen family:

Freedman, *The Images of the Medieval Peasant*. Figurae (Stanford, CA: Stanford University Press, 1999). The most important study, however, continues to be Werner Rösener, *Peasants in the Middle Ages*. Translated and with foreword and glossary by Alexander Stützer (1985; Cambridge: Polity, 1992). This topic now finds full consideration in the contributions to the volume *Rural Space in the Middle Ages and Early Modern Time*, ed. Albrecht Classen. Fundamentals of Medieval and Early Modern Culture, 9 (Berlin and New York: De Gruyter, 2012).

39 C. Stephen Jaeger, *The Origins of Courtliness: Civilizing Trends and the Formation of Courtly Ideals 939–1210*. The Middle Ages Series (Philadelphia: University of Pennsylvania Press, 1985), 54–66; Joachim Bumke, *Höfische Kultur: Literatur und Gesellschaft im hohen Mittelalter*. Vol. 2 (Munich: Deutscher Taschenbuch Verlag, 1986), 583–94.

> It is the literary and satirical outlook of the moralist which governs the adventurous career of Reinhart, a cynical little lord, ambitious and unscrupulous who, at the risk of losing his life tries, at first in vain, then with success, to quench an inextinguishable thirst for power, exploiting one after the other family ties, courtliness, religion, medicine, until he reaches his goal. As a courtier, Reinhart could well represent that social group which, in Germany, supplanted the old aristocracy of Germanic conquerors, a caricature of those errant knights in search of goodness and honour, and whose new culture was courtliness. Reinhart would be the satirical mirror-image of a certain German aristocracy whose rise corresponds to the cultural flourishing of the years 1180 to 1200.[40]

However, the foundation of the entire narrative by Heinrich and of the long pan-European literary tradition rests on a most troublesome realization that the public ideals and values are no longer upheld and that criminality and violence dominate all aspects of social life. Neither lords nor their inferiors are to be trusted, and everyone is only on the lookout for his/her own well-being, disregarding any ethical or moral standards.

As the subsequent events make abundantly clear, brute force (Ysengrim) is curiously coupled with amazing ignorance and naivete, if not stupidity. Not surprisingly, the greedy wolf repeatedly becomes the fox's victim and barely escapes alive. The wolf suffers physical pain and loss of limbs as the direct results of the snares set for him by the evil-minded fox who cares little about his victim/s and pursues his strategies mostly simply out of enjoyment in causing hurt, and doing evil to his neighbors. Violence rules, powerfully and skillfully manipulated by Reinhard who constantly devices new strategies to get the wolf into danger, particularly, it seems, because he proves to be a fool and always falls prey to the fox's malicious operations: "Isengrin, der tvmme" (984; Ysengrim, the stupid one). Significantly, whatever Reinhard conceives as promising plans for his 'lord' leads to the wolf suffering terrible physical pain, though we do not really feel any sympathy for him either because of his own social crudeness and intellectual ignorance, and especially his extraordinary selfishness and brutality toward all people under his reign.

Not surprisingly, when the fox convinces him to catch fish in the ice-cold lake with the help of his tail, which he ultimately loses because the water freezes over during the night, trapping the dumb beast who can later save his neck only by tearing the body away from the tail, the narrator comments: "Ysengrin phlac tvmbir sinne" (749; Ysengrim displayed a stupid mind). Not that Reinhard does not fall prey to his own lack of reason at times, driven by his love for his wife

---

40 Jean-Marc Pastré, "Morals, Justice and Geopolitics in the *Reinhart Fuchs* of the Alsatian Heinrich der Glichezaere," *Reynhard the Fox: Social Engagement and Cultural Metamorphoses in the Beast Epic from the Middle Ages to the Present*, ed. Kenneth Varty. Polygons: Cultural Diversities and Intersections, 1 (New York and Oxford: Berghahn Books, 2000), 37–53; here 52.

whom he believes to see at the bottom of a well (848). But he survives, and then can utilize the wolf for his own rescue long before the owners of the well arrive and give Ysengrim a rough, almost deadly, beating. The wolf had foolishly believed the fox's false explanation about his reasons for being deep in that hole and so had placed himself into one of the buckets. His weight drags him down, which allows Reinhard to be elevated to the top again, whereupon he abandons the other to his grim destiny.

This episode is well known and has been reproduced, adapted, and translated in many subsequent versions of this text, and we can easily laugh about it, entertained as by the other scenes with the fox triumphing over the wolf. But the situation here gains additional intensity because of Reinhard's devious play on the basic Christian teachings, referring to Paradise and Hell, luring his victim to the bottom of the well where he would not only meet his beloved wife, but would, above all, enjoy the glories of Heaven where he could find an endless amount of prey to satisfy his hunger (923–26). When the wolf asks what the gleaming lights might be that he observes, the fox pretends that his own eyes represent gems and jewels that shine all by themselves as part of the paradisiacal setting.[41]

Although Reinhard is stuck in his miserable position, barely surviving from drowning, he has maintained all his intellect and knows exceedingly well how to manipulate his listener, pretending that both worlds of Heaven and Hell are situated closely together down at the bottom of the well. Ironically, the well belongs to a monastery, so the fox plays with the religious juxtaposition of a Christian stronghold with the site of his misery to create an illusion for the wolf which proves to be so attractive that he wants to join him in the depth of the well. The author obviously reflects sarcastically on the evil strategies employed by the clergy, as he perceived it, to project apocalyptic images and to present to their audiences simple-minded concepts of good and evil, with the former actually easily accessible in return for a small payment, such as indulgences. This finds its perfect illustration in the wolf's voluntary descent into the depth where the fox then can abandon him and expose him, once the wolf has been pulled up again by the monks, to terrible beating because they try to kill him, of course as an evil animal. The entire world of spirituality and theology is travestied and exposed as a sham. And those who preach about the afterworld are caricatured as evil-minded tricksters who only think of their own well-being and how they can exploit their parishioners for their selfish and egoistical schemes.

Here we face an explicit example of anticlericalism, actually a very early one, and yet already harsh, painful, and aggressive, with the fox ridiculing even the

41 Christel Meier, *Gemma spiritalis: Methode und Gebrauch der Edelsteinallegorese vom frühen Christentum bis ins 18. Jahrhundert*. Münstersche Mittelalter-Schriften, 34.1 (Munich: W. Fink, 1977), provides a detailed analysis of the symbolic meaning of gems in the Middle Ages.

basic tenets of the Church regarding both Paradise and Hell, especially since the fox goes so far as to claim that everyone who wants to enter the former first needs to experience the latter where one loses skin and hair from the heat of the fire (910–14).[42] But the promise of an endless amount of food makes the decisive difference for the wolf who then is ready to jump into the bucket as instructed by the fox, and so ends up in the hellish hole while the ruthless fox sails to the top and is rescued, even though he sarcastically describes the situation in just the opposite way: "'. . . hie zv himelriche / Soltv minen stvl han, / wan ich dirs vil wol gan. / Ich wil vz in daz lant, / dv dem tevfel in die hant'" (948–52; here in the realm of heaven you ought to have my chair, which I happily cede to you. I want to go out to the world that belongs to the devil).

Surprisingly, Heinrich does not directly attack the monks, and only mentions their efforts to kill the wolf whose miserable condition they regard as the result of God's vengeance (973). Moreover, his broad criticism finds expression only when Reinhard assumes the role of a monk as a preacher and thus lures his opponent into the well, almost like the devil who tends to deceive his victims by presenting the foul underworld as more beautiful than Heaven. The author ridicules, in other words, primarily those who use sermons as a catalyst to dupe their parishioners and, of course, also the lay people who allow such abuse to happen. As the narrator explicitly comments at the end of this episode, equating Ysengrim with the ordinary person, "die velt stent noch alsust hie, / Daz manic man mit valscheit / vberwant sin arbeit / Baz danne einer, der der triwen pflac" (992–95; the world is thus that many overcome their challenges by means of deception, better than those who pursued loyalty).

Hardly by coincidence the famous minstrel Walther von der Vogelweide (ca. 1200–1220) formulated very similar criticism, claiming that the essential and good values have lost all chances and cannot prevail anymore because "stîg und wege sint in benomen" (2, 20; people took away their paths and roads). The main reason for this misery, as Walther emphasizes, results from the rule of "untriuwe" (21; disloyalty) that lurks behind the corner of everything. He knows only to lament: "gewalt vert ûf der strâze, / fride und reht sint sêre wunt" (22–23; violent force dominates the road, peace and justice are badly wounded).[43]

42 See the contributions to *Anticlericalism in Late Medieval and Early Modern Europe*, ed. Peter A. Dykema and Heiko A. Oberman. Studies in Medieval and Reformation Thought, LI (Leiden, New York, and Cologne: E. J. Brill, 1993); see also Birgit Beine, *Der Wolf in der Kutte: Geistliche in den Mären des deutschen Mittelalters*. Braunschweiger Beiträge zur deutschen Sprache und Literatur, 2 (Bielefeld: Verlag für Regionalgeschichte, 1999). Only Helmut Brall, "'Wahrlich, die Pfaffen sind schlimmer als der Teufel!': Zur Entstehung der deutschen Schwankdichtung im 13. Jahrhundert," *Euphorion* 94.3 (2000): 319–34, also refers, though just in passing, to the *Reinhard Fuchs* tradition (323).

43 Walther von der Vogelweide, *Leich, Lieder, Sangsprüche*. 14th, completely new ed. of the one by Karl Lachmann, ed. Christoph Cormeau (Berlin and New York: Walter de Gruyter, 1996),

Ironically, however, when Ysengrim subsequently tries to find justice at the court of the lion by legal means, all his efforts and those of his companions, who have similarly suffered from Reinhard's countless evil deeds, ultimately turn to nought. Those who have sued him come to realize in the end that they have only suffered as a result and then have been abused as stepping stones for the fox on his climb up the social ladder. In fact, the biggest criminal turns out to be the most powerful person in the state who even disrespects the ruler. In fact, once Reinhard has defeated all his opponents, having convinced the king that he needs some parts of their bodies for his own healing process, he takes the final step, brews a deadly poison, and thus kills the king who realizes the betrayal too late when he bitterly complains about the downfall of social and ethical mores: "'. . . swer sich an den vngetruwen lat, / Dem wirt iz leit, des mvz ich iehen, / alsam ist ovch nv mir geschehen'" (2238–40; he who trusts those who are disloyal will experience suffering, as I must say, since it has happened to me).

Similarly, the narrator comments on the camel's destiny which confirms this maxim as well, especially because she had served as the fox's advocate at the king's court. Reinhard had subsequently asked the king to appoint her as the abbess of the convent of Erstein, but since the nuns revolted against that decision and killed the camel out of protest, we are given the same comments about the evil nature of rotten characters such as the fox: "Iz ist ovch noch also getan, / swer hilfet einem vngetrevwen man, / Daz er sine not vberwindet, / daz er doch an im vindet / Valschs, des han wir gnvc gesehen, / vnd mvz ovch dicke alsam geschehen" (2157–62; This is the way how it happens until today: whoever provides help to an untrustworthy man to overcome suffering will find in him falseness, as we have observed often enough and as it will also happen many times in the future).[44]

As scholarship has noticed numerous times, the references to that political appointment, similarly to the one of the elephant as the king of Bohemia (2097–2116), both of which resulted in deadly consequences for the new honoree, can be read as allusions to specific historical events in German imperial politics at the end of the twelfth century when chaos and violence undermined all traditional legal and political structures.[45] After all, at the end Reinhard even turns against the

---

"Reichston" no. 2, or L. 8.4, here 11. See also Walther von der Vogelweide, *The Single-Stanza Lyrics*, ed. and trans., with introduction and commentary by Frederick Goldin (New York and London: Routledge, 2003), no. 27, 141. I prefer to use my own translation which stays closer to the original. This is not supposed to be a criticism of Goldin's version, but he pursued a different purpose in his approach, making Walther's texts as understandable and palatable as possible.

44 To avoid errors, here I write out all superscripta that serve as typographical cues for umlauts.

45 Ute Schwab, *Zur Datierung und Interpretation des Reinhart Fuchs*. Mit einem textkritischen Beitrag von Klaus Düwel. Quaderni della sezione linguistica degli Annali V (Napels: Cymba, 1967), 31ff. (see now rpt. with an epilogue and a list of corrigenda, Lorch: Erika Kümmerle, 2010); Klaus Düwel, "Namen und Örtlichkeiten," *Der Reinhart Fuchs*, XXVII–XXIX (see note 27); Widmaier, *Das*

king and poisons him, demonstrating how far traitors are willing to go: "Der artzet was mit valsche da, / den kvnic verriet er sa" (2165–66; The medical doctor proceeded with deception; he betrayed the king). This serves as a general warning against the cataclysmic consequences of criminality and violence if they go unchecked for a long time. The king himself proves to be responsible for the rapid decline of his kingdom because he does not care about justice and peace, considers only his own needs, and displays greed, selfishness, and recklessness. For him the suffering of his people means little, or nothing, although he is still willing to set up court and demands the fox to appear before his judges. But we also recognize how little the legal system seems to be working because the biggest perpetrator finds the best lawyers and can thus turn all the court proceedings totally around by way of playing smartly the roles of a penitent, a medical doctor, and a pilgrim. He appeals to the king's base instincts since he needs help to overcome physical problems and quickly forgets the actual cries for help of his subjects who are in need of protection against the arch villain, the fox Reinhard.

Curiously, however, the true and full criticism is not so much directed against the evil fox, the ruthless criminal. Surely, everyone around him, except for his own family, expresses their deep anger and even fury about his endless misdeeds. For that reason they sought help at the royal court. And for that reason they so diligently pursue legal redress. Ultimately, however, and this proves to be the truly critical point of Heinrich's fable narrative, King Vrevel fails in his obligations both as king and as judge, being concerned only with his own needs and desires, abandoning those who have suffered from Reinhard's maliciousness and cruelty, and then even heaps praise, honor, and wealth upon the trickster, deceiver, and assassin who finally manages to kill the king. Whether it might be justified, as Cora Dietl has recently suggested, that the violence exerted by the king differs from the fox's violence only in the way that it is presented in public, seems to stretch the argument a little, but it is still worthy of further examination:

> Die Opfer und die eigentliche Gewaltanwendung werden bei der Ausübung von *potentia* ausgeblendet. Indem Heinrich diese Technik der absichtlichen Ausblendung geradezu plakativ anwendet, legt er offen, wie sehr die Herrscher von einer entsprechenden Darstellung ihrer Macht abhängig sind.[46]
>
> [The victims and the actual exertion of violence are being occluded when the *potestas* is enacted. By drastically employing the technique of intentional occlusion, he reveals how much rulers depend on the appropriate representation of their power.]

Recht, 214–16 (see note 28).

46 Cora Dietl, "*Violentia* und *potestas*: Ein füchsischer Blick auf ritterliche Tugend und gerechte Herrschaft im 'Reinhart Fuchs'," *Dichtung und Didaxe: Lehrhaftes Sprechen in der deutschen Literatur des Mittelalters*, ed. Henrike Lähnemann and Sandra Linden (Berlin and New York: Walter de Gruyter, 2009), 41–54; here 54.

The fox has transgressed not only the basic norms of his society, he has also disregarded the general call for peace announced by the king (1239–41).[47] The many crimes committed by Reinhard would normally be treated as egregious transgressions, leading to his imprisonment, if not execution. But that is not the case. Instead, we encounter a king who carries, in the first place, a curious name, Vrevel: "Ein lewe, der was Vrevel genant" (1241). The meaning could be quite diverse, implying both criminality, arrogance, and hubris, as well as courage, boldness, and lack of fear. In the French versions the king is identified as "Noble," whereas here in the German narrative Heinrich deliberately played with the duplicity of the king's name, signaling thereby the loss of a universal system of values and ideals because the one central institution, the royal court, has failed to uphold its end of the bargain, which subsequently allows the criminals to take total control.[48]

If we did not know that Heinrich had composed this text at the end of the twelfth century, we could easily imagine it as a modern novel about the pervasive intertwining of the Mafia with the state government, and of corruption permeating every strata of society. This narrative in the fable tradition very much reads like a statement reflecting utter despair because all legal, political, ethical, moral, and religious ideals, values, and standards have broken down, with no hope left for a recovery and the reestablishment of a society determined by laws, legality, a fair and just political system.

Although all animals decry the king's death, a victim of an assassination attack by the fox, but also a victim of his own foolishness, egoism, lack of morality, and disregard of the laws, the fox Reinhard goes scot-free and fears no one and nothing: "Sie dreuweten alle harte / dem gvten Reinharte" (2247–48; They all seriously threatened the good [powerful] Reinhard). If we ever dared to laugh about the foolishness of some of those animals in this fable narrative, this final realization must certainly choke it completely. This Alsatian author obviously harbored most cynical perspectives and did not have any hope for a bright future because evil people ruled unchecked and had gained control over all institutions and personalities dominating their world.

Let us add a discussion of a fairly similar text from ca. 1260–1274 where criminality also constitutes the central theme, at first destroying all hope for justice and

---

47 For a discussion of this peace movement, see Elmar Wadl, *Landfrieden, Strafe, Recht: zwölf Studien zum Mittelalter*. Schriften zur europäischen Rechts- und Verfassungsgeschichte, 37 (Berlin: Duncker & Humblot, 2001); and the contributions to Arno Buschmann, *Landfrieden: Anspruch und Wirklichkeit*. Görres-Gesellschaft zur Pflege der Wissenschaft: Neue Folge, 98 (Paderborn, Munich, et al.: Ferdinand Schöningh, 2002).

48 Klaus Düwel, ed., *Reinhart Fuchs*, 71, note to vers 1241 (see note 27).

protection. However, here at least punishment catches up with the criminal in the end, and the reader can breathe a sigh of relief because, despite the enormity of violence exerted by the protagonist,the authorities step in and reconstitute the laws. Wernher der Gärtner, or Gartenære, is not easily identifiable for us, but he was certainly a minstrel of inferior social rank who seems to have worked as a gardener, hence his epithet.[49] His *Helmbrecht* has survived in only two manuscripts, first and foremost in the manuscript A, *Ambraser Heldenbuch* (Vienna, cod. ser. nova 2663, 225rb–29rb), which was copied between 1504 and 1515 by Hans Ried for Emperor Maximilian I, second in the Berlin manuscript B (mgf 470, 229va–40vb), written in the first quarter of the fifteenth century for the wealthy knight Leonhard Meurl zu Leonbach in Traungau, Upper Austria.[50] The former manuscript seems to be the most reliable one, but the final judgment is still outstanding. The dating of *Helmbrecht* remains vague, and it could have been composed as late as ca. 1273–1278, although the years between 1260 and 1274 seem most likely.[51] Scholarship has dealt with this text in numerous fashions and approached it from a variety of perspectives, using both sociological and political-ethical concepts. We have available today both a trustworthy critical edition,[52] a solid commentary,[53] and many scholarly studies that illuminate virtually every aspect relevant of this text.[54]

---

49 Adolf Stelzl, *Meier Helmbrecht von Wernher dem Gartenaere: Eine Spurensuche* (Ried i. I.: Moserbauer Druck & Verlag, 2001), made an interesting effort to identify the poet as a member of the former Augustinian convent of Ranshofen, first mentioned in 788, in Braunau, Upper Austria, but this is basically nothing but a positivistic approach and has not much scholarly validity. See also http://de.wikipedia.org/wiki/Stift_Ranshofen (last access on Aug. 23, 2010)

50 This important manuscript has been discussed many times in a variety of contexts, see, for instance, *Dietrichs Flucht*. Textgeschichtliche Ausgabe, ed. Elisabeth Lienert and Gertrud Beck. Texte und Studien zur mittelhochdeutschen Heldenepik, 1 (Tübingen: Niemeyer, 2003), XV–XVIII, with an extensive bibliography.

51 Fritz Peter Knapp, "Wernher der Gärtner," *Die deutsche Literatur des Mittelalters: Verfasserlexikon*. 2nd compl. rev. ed. by Burghart Wachinger et al. Vol. 10.3/4 (Berlin and New York: Walter de Gruyter, 1998), 927–36. English readers are well served by Linda B. Parshall's introduction to Wernher der Gartenaere, *Helmbrecht*, intro. and trans. by eadem. German edition by Ulrich Seelbach. Garland Library of Medieval Literature, Series A, 28 (New York and London: Garland, 1987), ix–xlvi; see also Linda B. Parshall, "Wernher der Gartenaere," *German Writers and Works of the High Middle Ages: 1170–1280*, ed. James Hardin and Will Hasty. Dictionary of Literary Biography, 138 (Detroit, Washington, DC, and London: Gale Research, 1994), 170–77.

52 Wernher der Gartenære, *Helmbrecht*, ed. Friedrich Panzer and Kurt Ruh. 10th ed. by Hans-Joachim Ziegeler. Altdeutsche Textbibliothek, 11 (Tübingen: Niemeyer, 1993).

53 Ulrich Seelbach, *Kommentar zum "Helmbrecht" von Wernher dem Gartenære*. Göppinger Arbeiten zur Germanistik, 469 (Göppingen: Kümmerle, 1987).

54 Ulrich Seelbach, *Späthöfische Literatur und ihre Rezeption im späten Mittelalter: Studien zum Publikum des 'Helmbrecht' von Wernher dem Gartenaere*. Philologische Studien und Quellen, 115 (Berlin: Erich Schmidt, 1987); Petra Menke, *Recht und Ordo-Gedanke im Helmbrecht*. Germanistische Arbeiten zu Sprache und Kulturgeschichte, 24 (Frankfurt a. M., Berlin, et al.: Peter Lang, 1993; for the older secondary literature, see Ulrich Seelbach, *Bibliographie zu Wernher der Gartenaere*. Bibliographien

The didactic intentions of Wernher's texts are very easy to recognize, dealing with the young son of a wealthy farmer who intends to rise above his own social class and turns into a robber knight. After having spent a considerable time robbing, pillaging, looting, killing, and stealing freely without anyone intervening, young Helmbrecht is finally apprehended by the authorities and quickly punished, losing both his eyes, his right arm, and his left foot, debilitating him so completely that he can no longer step into a stirrup to ride on a horse or wield a sword. A year later peasants who had formerly suffered from his rampage of violence apprehend him and quickly lynch him, thus ventilating their deep frustration and wrath about their total helplessness in the previous situation.

The family structure proves to be the first victim, with the parents being almost as guilty as their son in helping him to equip himself properly for the life of a robber knight. Much more painful proves to be the collapse of the communicative community that forms the essential bond among people. Although father and son engage in a number of ponderous conversations, the elder Helmbrecht trying to warn his son about the dire consequences of his rebelling against the constraints of feudal society, ultimately his son dismisses all prophecies and admonishments. He continues to enjoy the new-found wealth and seemingly powerful position, yet he is then apprehended by the authorities and receives a nearly deadly punishment,[55] soon followed by his execution at the hands of the irate peasants who are determined to eliminate this most violent element of their society.

Despite the father's desperate attempts to dissuade his son from his dangerous career plans, young Helmbrecht disregards all and every advice, entirely bent on gaining wealth and esteem as quickly as possible. None of his father's suggestions to marry a wealthy bride, for instance, appeal to him any longer (279–98) because he almost seems delirious with the idea of joining courtly society and dismissing all traces of his former peasant existence (299–328). He does not realize, however, and probably never learns that the military service that he will enter constitutes nothing but the basest and dirtiest part of knightly activities, not even worthy of the name of a knight.[56] Nevertheless, he enjoys an incredible rush of adrenalin that turns him into a berserk-like robber knight who does not spare anyone or anything, grabbing everything available to him, and delighting in the total freedom that this violence grants him temporarily.

---

zur deutschen Literatur des Mittelalters, 8 (Berlin: Erich Schmidt, 1981).

55 For a communicative approach to this narrative, see Albrecht Classen, *Verzweiflung und Hoffnung: Die Suche nach der kommunikativen Gemeinschaft in der deutschen Literatur des Mittelalters*. Beihefte zur Mediaevistik, 1 (Frankfurt a. M., Berlin, et al.: Peter Lang, 2002), 359–99.

56 Fritz Peter Knapp, "Standesverräter und Heimatverächter in der bayerisch-österreichischen Literatur des Spätmittelalters," *Wernher der Gärtner: 'Helmbrecht'. Die Beiträge des Helmbrecht-Symposions in Burghausen 2001*, ed. Theodor Nolte and Tobias Schneider (Stuttgart: S. Hirzel, 2001), 9–24; here 11.

As young Helmbrecht reports during his first visit home, new courtly customs have been introduced, replacing the traditional values of wooing for love, singing, and dancing. Nowadays, as he brags, courtly lifestyle has turned into wild 'fraternity parties', as we might say today, with excess of drinking (984–1006), and with lying and deceiving enjoying the highest recognition (1007–12). Traditional tournaments have been replaced by actual hunting of innocent people, cutting off their limbs and killing them, taking hostages, whatever might be possible to gain profits (1023–36). This robber knight has found similarly-minded fellows who prove to be nothing but the worst kinds of criminals, priding themselves on being the best thieves and killers far and wide (1185–1230). He himself brags about the extent of violence with which he has treated his countless victims in the most brutal manner (1235–56).

Peevishly the father tries to warn him about the dire consequences, but the young man only considers this as an insult and tells him that he will from then on no longer protect his own family from his friends' criminal behavior and violence (1265–92). Indeed, that is the case for a while, and the feasts which the robbers celebrate by far outdo those, as the narrator emphasizes, which King Arthur used to enjoy (1478–81). All the food and the valuable goods, however, are no longer legitimately acquired, or freely given, or raised through justified taxation. On the contrary, as the narrator underscores, "manec witewe unde weise / an guote wart geletzet / und riuwec gesetzet" (1464–66; many a widow and orphan lost its goods and cast into sorrow). The basic principles of chivalry and knighthood, in the name of King Arthur, are badly transgressed because criminal minds control the lands. The young men roam freely and loot wherever they can, not caring about any person's conditions, needs, poverty, or ailment.

A veritable nightmare has been unleashed upon the land, and no one seems capable of preventing this wave of crime or of arresting the gang of criminals, whom Helmbrecht proudly counts among his friends. Moreover, he obviously exceeds everyone in brutality, rapaciousness, and violent behavior, not sparing even his previous neighbors and perhaps relatives. He goes even so far as to marry off his sister to one of them, Lemberslind (Devourer of Lambs). Not surprisingly, Wernher has chosen most telling names for some of the robbers who devour their food at the wedding feast like wolves: "Wolvesguome und Wolvesdarm / unde Wolvesdrüzzel / lârten manege schüzzel / und manegen becher wîten / ze den selben hôchzîten" (1552–56; Mouth of a Wolf and Gut of a Wolf, and so Throat of a Wolf, they all emptied many dishes and many large cups at that feast). Obviously, here they all become guilty of one of the seven deadly sins, gluttony, and thus betray themselves as some of the worst sinners, or transgressors, of their society.[57]

---

57 Morton W Bloomfield, *The Seven Deadly Sins: an Introduction to the History of a Religious Concept,*

Truly, some of the seven deadly sins seem to have been personified here, all serving as a severe warning against the ghastly transgression committed by Helmbrecht and his gang of accomplices. They do not know any limits, they care only about themselves, they have lost any sense of social obligation, they loot the entire country, devour all food and drink, although they really take mostly, if not exclusively, from their own kin and never engage in any (!) knightly combat or fight against any nobleman. Helmbrecht had only spared his own intimate family back home for a while, but now, in order to enjoy a feast without any sense of self-containment (*mâze*), he and the others simply take whatever they can grab indiscriminately with no concern for the suffering they create everywhere in the countryside. Not surprisingly, however, the narrator describes this scene as tantamount to the last meal a prisoner on death row might enjoy: "ez was ir jungestez maz, / daz si immer mê gâzen / oder frœlîche gesâzen" (1572–74; it was their last meal that they ever could eat or where they could sit carefree). As so often in the Middle Ages, even the meal carried a deeply symbolic meaning, here reflecting upon the total disregard of all virtues and values.[58] In the next scene suddenly the judge with four of his constables arrives and arrests the entire criminal company, bringing them all to justice, an act which could easily be compared to Christ's Last Judgment (1612–30).[59]

We might be well advised to examine the legal-historical grounding of the entire narrative framework, as Petra Menke has already outlined in great detail.[60] But for us it only matters that Wernher reflects upon the widespread criminality in his society and presents the extreme example of Helmbrecht as a drastic warning. After all, everyone of his accomplices meets his death, whereas the protagonist is spared his life, though he loses his eyes, the right hand, and the left foot. His sister Gotelint is shamed and might well have been raped as a form of punishment, although the text is not all that clear about it: "Gotelint verlôs ir briutegewant; / bî einem zûne man sie vant / in vil swacher küste. / si hêt ir beide brüste / mit handen verdecket: / si was unsanfte erschrecket" (1631–36; Gotelint lost her bridal gown. One could see her standing at a fence in very poor shape. She covered both her breasts with the hands: She was crudely frightened). The narrator subsequently wonders himself whether anything worse might have happened to her, but he

with Special Reference to Medieval English Literature. Michigan State College of Agriculture and Applied Science, East Lansing. Studies in Language and Literature ([East Lansing, MI:] Michigan State College Press, 1952); see now also the contributions to *The Seven Deadly Sins: From Communities to Individuals*, ed. Richard Newhauser. Studies in Medieval and Reformation Traditions, 123 (Leiden and Bosten: Brill, 2007).

58 Trude Ehlert, "Zur Semantisierung von Essen und Trinken in Wernhers des Gartenære 'Helmbrecht'," *Zeitschrift für deutsches Altertum und deutsche Literatur* 138.1 (2009): 1–16.

59 Seelbach, *Kommentar*, 188–89, discusses the entire setting only in legal-historical terms and ignores the moral-theological dimension.

60 Menke, *Recht und Ordo-Gedanke*, 170–74 (see note 54)

refuses to specify it, probably because he wanted to intimate that she had suffered sexual violation (1637–38).

Most importantly, however, Wernher emphasizes that no criminal would ever have a chance against judges, or constables, since these were God's own instruments, who would never tolerate any crime to continue for an extended period, "sô got der râche wil selbe phlegen" (1650; when God wants to carry out his revenge Himself). Helmbrecht's suffering after his release proves to be brutal, being blind, having lost two of his major limbs, and finally he falls into the hands of his former victims who quickly lynch him by hanging. Tragically, in the episode before that, the young criminal tries to find refuge in his father's farm, but the laws of the land prohibit that, as much as the old man's heart threatens to break with deep pain because he has to reject his own son (1776).[61]

The narrative concludes with some final didactic comments regarding the exemplary nature of this account. Wernher clearly formulates his warning to anyone among the young generation who might consider following the same path as the one which Helmbrecht had chosen. Clearly reminiscent of the Fourth Commandment, the closing remarks profile the horrible consequences one more time and signal that there is justice, that punishment will follow suit upon a perpetration. Looking around, Wernher observes that violence and highway robbery have come to an end because the criminal Helmbrecht has been hanged (1919–22). This might well have been intended as a direct response to the profound lament uttered by Walther von der Vogelweide regarding the insecurity everywhere, the rampant violence, and the endless crime that all undermined peace and the love of God. If anyone might consider following Helmbrecht's example, he would surely experience, so Wernher contends, the same destiny and end up on the gallows: "si komen ouch danne an die wide" (1930; they will be lifted up at the willow tree).

Let us conclude with some reflections upon the similarities and differences between both verse narratives, separated by ca. eighty to ninety years, the older one composed in Alsace (then in the western parts of the German Empire), the later one created in the area of Upper Austria (territory of the Hapsburgians, in the southeastern parts). Both are predicated on the realization that violence and criminality have gained the upper hand in their society. Once robbery, murder, and rape have become the norm in everyday life, all other values and ideals are seriously endangered. Violence and crime affect everyone and are, as both authors suggest, to be regarded as a cancer that kills the social body altogether. But there are also significant differences. While Heinrich espoused a most pessimistic

---

61 Werner Schröder, "Zur Tragik des Vaters im 'Helmbrecht' Wernhers des Gärtners," *Jahrbuch für internationale Germanistik* 34.2 (2002): 183–205.

outlook and expressed a cynical opinion regarding the needed help from the king, or any other authority figure, Wernher described the outbreak of violence only as a temporary phenomenon that can be contained and overcome in the end because a legal system is in place with sufficient energy, power, and authority to enforce the laws.

Nevertheless, he also recognized the enormous pain and suffering that affected everyone in the peasant communities where the robber knights ravaged and looted. But in contrast to Heinrich, the Austrian author believes in the authority figures, he trusts in the power of the judges, and is confident that God will come to the help of all His people, especially in such times of suffering.[62] The Alsatian writer expresses no interest in the Church and demonstrates no confidence in the clergy, especially because they prove to be part of the criminal system and are just as corrupt as everyone else.

On the other hand, we have to be careful in our assessment of the literary strategies pursued by both authors. Both clearly opposed violence and criminality, but whereas the one perceived the fox as an indefatigable force because of his absolute ruthlessness and lack of conscience, the other utilized his tale as a didactic instrument to prevent the future generation from getting trapped in that kind of mind-set and behavioral patterns. We could almost characterize *Helmbrecht* as pedagogically motivated, whereas *Reinhard Fuchs* emerges as a piece of political reflection, discounting or questioning any existing authority and venting a deep-seated mistrust in any pretense or illusions by the representatives of the legal system. Despite all the differences, however, we suddenly grasp a major discourse on the effectiveness of the laws, the courts, and the enforcement officers (constables, lawyers, etc.) that raged during the twelfth and thirteenth centuries. For Wernher the feudal *ordo* was still, or rather again, the supreme ideal that had to be protected at all costs, especially because his protagonist even transgressed against the rule of peace and the laws of the land.[63] For the cynic Heinrich criminality has already taken over all controls, has permeated all echelons of society, and even the best courtiers and lawyers have lost all chances to defend justice and peace against those brutal and reckless perpetrators amongst their ranks. In *Reinhard Fuchs* even the king, the last beacon of hope in a sea of violence and corruption, succumbs to the fox's ever changing trickery, cunning, and deception because he displays a weak character and a tendency toward tyranny. In *Helmbrecht*, on the other hand, the judge finally appears, the criminals are apprehended, judgments are meted out, and violence comes to an end, even

62 Cornelia Wilhelm-Graf, "Richter und Gerichte im Helmbrecht," *Recht und Juristen im Bild der Literatur*, ed. Hermann Weber (Berlin: Wissenschaftlicher Verlag, 2005), 1–7.

63 Hannes Kästner, "'Fride und reht' im 'Helmbrecht': Wernhers mære im Kontext zeitgenössischer franziskanischer Gesellschafts- und Ordnungsvorstellungen," *Wernher der Gärtner: 'Helmbrecht'*, 25–43; here 37 (see note 56).

though the peasants ultimately have to resort to vengeance to deal with the young erstwhile robber knight the way he deserves, at least in their opinion.

Contemporary authors such as the Anglo-Norman writer Marie de France and Middle High German The Stricker also voiced their fear of rampant violence, especially if originating from the king himself.[64] Probing the issue further, we would have no difficulties detecting many other literary examples concerning the discourse on criminality. This does not, however, make the world of the twelfth and thirteenth centuries the 'dark ages.' On the contrary, the more individual writers came to terms with these fundamental conflicts and pervasive perpetrations of violence, the more their literary documents served as critical media to reflect on violence and invited the audience to take charge against the criminals and to fend off the breakers of the law.

Despite Heinrich's almost devastating cynicism, leaving no real hope for recovery of justice and the fair distribution of power, his fable narrative *Reinhard Fuchs* also added to that discourse and encouraged the audience to oppose criminal transgressors, to fight against corruption, to secure a better legal system, and to keep a watchful eye on their political, military, and religious leaders. The negative examples provided by Heinrich were terrifying enough to make people spring to action. As polemical as his fable account might be, pursuing a strongly anti-Hohenstaufen agenda, it is determined by global messages about the dangers of the fall-out from uncontrolled violence and abuse of the political system. Although crime here seems to pay off, the text actually expresses hope that people will stand up and defend themselves in time against the downfall of their world. The horror conveyed here was supposed to ring an alarm bell, and the outcome of Heinrich's account certainly proves his point.[65]

64 Albrecht Classen, "The People Rise Up against the Tyrants in the Courtly World: John of Salisbury's *Policraticus*, the *Fables* by Marie de France and the anonymous *Mai und Beaflor*," *Neohelicon* 35.1 (2008): 17–29.

65 Dean, *Crime in Medieval Europe*, 144–59 (see note 7), rightly alerts us to the danger of correlating too closely a literary account about a crime or a criminal with a historical case. Nevertheless, literary examples about criminal behavior resonate with the audience or serve as a mirror of criminal cases, or as warnings about the ominous threats resulting from uncontrolled, brutal violence.

Chapter 7

John P. Gough
(New York University)

The Function of Projected Pain: The Poetry of François Villon and the Gift of Self[1]

In the work of the late fifteenth-century French poet François Villon, pain manifests itself under various guises and forms. To read and draw a thread from one instance of pain to another in the poems is difficult; each instance stands alone while retaining an inherently physical substantive relation to the whole. To what end does Villon include the various instances of pain, punishment and torture? What purpose do they serve in the broader framework of the poems? It will be argued here that Villon uses pain and suffering to elucidate the contrast, transition, and relationship between life and death, to explore the destructive and reconstructive nature of pain, and to transmit a fundamentally inaccessible part of self through acts of pain willed or gifted. To illustrate this argument, the following is an examination of three aspects of Villon's poetry: the *Ballade des pendus*, the prison at Meung, and finally pain as it is further manifest in the *Testament*. This will be prefaced by: a short discussion of Villon and his authorship of the poems, pain and its definition, and a brief portrait of pain, death, and punishment in fifteenth-century Paris.

Before we turn to our principal topic, it is necessary that we clarify some points of scholarly dispute as to the autobiographical nature of the corpus of Villon's work. There is a lengthy and continued debate surrounding Villon pertaining to the actual identity of 'Villon the author' as opposed to 'Villon the character.' Little

1 I would like to express my appreciation to Connie Scarborough, Texas Tech University, and Albrecht Classen, University of Arizona, for having read and edited this article. Also, my thanks to Evelyn Birge Vitz and Nancy Freeman Regalado, New York University, for their invaluable and continued support in the realization of this project. Finally, my gratitude to a loving family and beautiful wife, Tanya.

is known about the man who signs his name François Villon; time and loss of clear historical data have obscured his true identity. Theories range widely and have invested the name 'Villon' with a sense of mystique and to some degree an almost cavalier quality reminiscent of something one might expect from a Robin Hood. The true identity of Villon will not concern us here. What follows will not depend on the accuracy of an autobiographical interpretation, but will rather focus on the poetry itself. What is important to understand before proceeding is that there was an author who called himself Villon who developed this 'Villon' into the character that we encounter through his works. We can be certain that the author was very familiar with the Paris of the fifteenth-century, and that this Paris served as a source of inspiration and as a platform for his poems. Autobiographical or not, the poems are still deliberately constructed and intentionally organized into a narrative, recounting events in the life of this 'Villon.'

The definition of pain as it will be used in this article includes: affliction, agony, anguish, fear, humiliation, hurt, injury, punishment, sorrow, and suffering. Pain is any negative action, emotion, or sensation that is imposed either voluntarily, or involuntary upon any particular individual or group of individuals by forces interior or exterior, which are often beyond the capability of those experiencing them to control. Pain is most frequently something inflicted and which is endured. Granted, this is a broad definition, but a definition nonetheless that will provide us with the necessary latitude to explore the various types and instances of pain in the works of Villon.[2] The inability to control personal pain—pain endured by the individual—will be of particular interest to us as well as the transformation which occurs from a pre- to post-pain state.

When one thinks of pain in the fifteenth-century it is difficult to disassociate the notions of death, disease, and punishment, from the word. Only several decades after the conflict that later came to be known as the Hundred Years War, Villon was writing in a time when manifestations of pain were very real and quite frequently acutely present in everyday life. Having stated that Paris served as a backdrop to the poems, let us explore the Paris of the fifteenth-century by looking at a singular form of punishment known as gibbeting (or hanging) which will then lead us to one of our principle points of interest: the *Ballade des pendus*.

---

2 This is not a definition of pain as it would have been understood in the fifteenth-century, but rather a definition of the word as it will be used in this article. For further scholarship on pain in the Middle Ages, see Scott E. Pincikowski, *Bodies of Pain: Suffering in the Works of Hartmann von Aue*. Studies in Medieval History and Culture (New York and London: Routledge, 2002); cf. also the contributions to *Piacere e dolore: materiali per una storia delle passioni nel Medioevo*, ed. Carla Casagrande and Silvana Vecchio. Micrologus' Library, 29 (Florence: SISMEL, Ed. del Galluzzo, 2009); *Schmerz in der Literatur des Mittelalters und der Frühen Neuzeit*, ed. Hans-Jochen Schiewer, Stefan Seeber, and Markus Stock. Transatlantische Studien zu Mittelalter und Früher Neuzeit, 4 (Göttingen: V & R Unipress, 2010).

The practice of gibbeting was well established in the Paris of the fifteenth-century. This, along with other forms of execution, was designed to deter criminal activity. Death by hanging was a public spectacle and an exceptionally enduring one at that, as the corpses of the malefactors were generally left hanging on display until decomposition had run its course, reducing the bodies to bone. Hanging victims were not the only bodies displayed during this period, in fact most executions were public with the remains of the executed exhibited throughout the city, either at the place of execution, or near the place where the initial criminal act had been carried out. Because of this, the Paris of Villon could have had at any given time any number of corpses at various stages of decomposition publicly placed in the squares and *quartiers* of the city. The enduring nature of public display after execution extended the punishment beyond the initially painful moments of death to the indignity of public decomposition. The dead literally coexisted with the living in an immediate and direct sense. This directness could only have been for the benefit of the living; the dead being beyond feeling.[3] However, the living would be reminded of the painful death act each time they passed the putrid exemplars of the Parisian criminal justice system. This pain was not the pain of direct experience, however, but sympathetic pain as experienced by the spectator. Though the spectator does not feel pain, the imagined and inherent pain as exercised through the body of another could have exerted just as powerful (if not greater) an effect as having experienced the actual death act oneself.

In 1893, Albert Hartshorne published a work entitled *Hanging in Chains*. His text provides an excellent study of the practice and history of gibbeting in Europe. Hartshorne's description of this method of execution in fifteenth-century Paris is riveting and informative, justifying its reproduction here:

> It is certain that there was already at the end of the twelfth century a great monumental gibbet on the eminence of Montfaucon, between the faubourgs of St. Martin and the Temple, in Paris. Sauval gives a remarkable description of it as at that period, and, although he does not give his authorities quite in the way English antiquaries might wish, there can be no doubt, from the documents of the thirteenth century, that the monument was as Sauval describes it. It underwent extensive repairs, if not partial re-building in 1425, when forty-eight old beams were replaced by new ones. It is also recorded that in 1466 "at the Great Justice of Paris were attached and nailed fifty-two iron chains to hang and strangle the malefactors who have been and shall be sent here by order of justice." Eight new ladders were subsequently added, and all these details are corroborated by a representation in an old tapestry at the Hotel de Ville . . . the fourth, or open side, allowed access to the interior by a broad flight of

3 Henrietta Benveniste, "Dead Body, Public Body: Notes on Death by Execution in the Middle Ages," *Law and Critique* 4.1 (1993): 21–42; here 26.

steps leading to a wide platform on what may be called the first floor, running round the sides of the interior. Upon this platform the executioner, with his ladders and assistants, performed his office.

This arrangement enabled the designer of the building to form a vault in the center, lighted by a small loop. It had an entrance, or "eye," in the crown, at the crossing of the ribs, through which were swept from time to time the bones and fragments that fell from above, the ossuarium, or charnel-house, being cleared out, as necessity dictated, through a doorway level with the outside ground on the further or sinister side of the building. It must have been a thing quite unique in the world, somewhat recalling the Towers of Silence of the Parsees.

The mode of operation was as follows:

The executioner, in his rayed and party-colored habit of red and yellow, mounted the ladder, placed opposite a convenient space, backwards, holding in his hand the slack ends of the three cords placed round the culprit's neck; two of the cords, "les totouses," had slip-knots. The wretch under treatment was encouraged to follow "le maistre des haultes oeuvres," driven up after him—no doubt with blows and execrations, according to the Gallic fashion—and drawn forward by means of a third cord, "le jet." Arrived at the proper height, the operator, the mediaeval "Monseiur de Paris," rapidly attached the "tortouses" to the gallows, or chain pendent from it, and, twisting the "jet" firmly round his arm, by means of this, and the action of his knee, threw the culprit off the ladder into mid-air; the knots of the "tortouses" ran home, and the man was strangled. The executioner then gripped the crossbeam, and, placing his feet in the loop formed by the bound hands of the patient, by dint of repeated vigorous shocks terminated his sufferings.

It may not be questioned that death under the circumstances and the complicated conditions above described cannot have been other than a very shocking spectacle, and particularly when it is noticed from the arrangement of the chains that many a malefactor may in his agony have broken loose from his bonds, and clutched and grappled in his last moments with a decaying carcass at his side.

We can gather a further idea of the strange and dismal appearance of the Gibbet of Montfaucon, if we consider that the quantity of bodies attached to it, and ceaselessly renewed, attracted thousands of carrion birds to the spot. But that its hideous aspect of pestilential surroundings prevented not the establishment, in its immediate vicinity, of places of amusement and debauch, one would almost have been slow to believe were it not for the testimony of ancient poetry:

Pour passer temps joyeuesement,
Raconter vueil une repeue
Qui fut faicte subtillement
Près Montfaulcon, c'est chose sceüe,

Tant parlèrent du bas mestier,
Qui fut conclud, par leur façon,
Qu'ils yroyent, ce soir-là, coucher

Près le gibet de Montfaulcon,
Et auroyent pour provision,
Ung pasté de façon subtile,
Et menroyent, en conclusion,
Avec eulx chascun une fille."[4]

[To pass the time merrily,
I wish to tell you of a meal
Which was subtly had
Near Montfaulcon, 'tis well known,

Much bespoke of the low livelihood,
Which was conducted, by their fashion,
They went, that night, to lie
Near the gibbet of Montfaulcon,
And had for provision,
A pastry of subtle fashion,
And brought, in the end,
With them each one a girl.]

Hartshorne continues by attributing the above poem to Villon himself, while modern scholarship has not accepted it as part of the œuvre that can be authenticated as having been truly composed by that poet. Whether this be the case or not, it is clear that Villon would have been familiar with the gibbet at Montfaucon. It is an intriguing prospect to visualize Montfaucon in the mid-fifteenth-century; the dead hanging as watchmen over the places of amusement and debauch; it seems a fitting ambiance for much of what Villon depicts in the *Lais* and again later in the *Testament*.

With this vision of Paris and this form of execution freshly imprinted on our minds, let us now turn our attention to the *Ballade des pendus*. Perhaps the most conventional use of pain is found in this ballad, combining several forms of pain: physical, psychological, and emotional, to create a wrenching entreaty from the dead to the living, illustrating the relationship between life and death in a moving *memento mori*. The central subjects are presumably criminals, strung up as cautionary sentinels to warn the passer by: "Vous nous voiez cy attachés, cinq, six" ("You see us here attached, five, six"). Villon graphically describes the process of decomposition and decay in the corpses of the hanged men by referring to the flesh:

---

4 The entire passage, including the verses, is copied from Albert Hartshorne, *Hanging in Chains* (New York: The Castle Publishing Company, 1893), 32–38. The translations are all my own, but see now also François Villon, *Complete Poems*, ed. with English trans. and commentary by Barbara N. Sargent-Baur. Toronto Medieval Texts and Translations, 9 (Toronto, Buffalo, and London: University of Toronto Press, 1994).

Quant de la chair que trop avons nourrie,
Elle est pieça devoree et pourrie,
Et nous, les os, devenons cendre et pouldre . . . .[5]

[As for the flesh which we over nourished,
It is eaten and rotted,
And we, the bones, have become ashes and dust . . . .]

La pluye nous a debuez et lavez
Et le soleil deceschez et noriciz.
Pies, corbeaux nous ont les yeulx cavez
Et arraché la barbe et les sourcilz . . . .[6]

[The rain has cleaned and washed us
And the sun dried and turned black.
Magpies, ravens have pecked out our eyes
And torn out our beards and eyebrows . . .]

The poem is written in the first person. These are not bodies-inanimate, freed of their conscious selves, but rather inhabited corpses with cognizance and self-awareness, capable of saying *nous* and interacting with those still living. Understanding that these malefactors are yet conscious, it becomes difficult to remove the concept of pain from the decay their bodies are undergoing[7]; it is as if they are experiencing their own decay. The imploration, "Car se pitié de nous povres avez," ("Have pity for us wretches") strikes home with greater force as one comprehends that these corpses are suffering individuals; these are people in pain.

The presence of physical pain in the ballad is accompanied by the underpinnings of emotional pain contained within the text. In the scholarly literature surrounding Villon much has been written about the relationship between the physical suffering portrayed and its relation to the religious models of the late Middle Ages; the words *purgatory* and *hell* surface constantly in the debate as themes of great interest. It is true that this ballad is steeped in religious significance. It is a plea from the dead—whom we can assume find themselves in a state of purgatory—to the living.[8] The term purgatory is fitting because these individuals are in an in-

5 François Villon, *Lais, Testament, Poésies Diverses*, ed. Jean-Claude Mühlethaler (Paris: Champion, 2004), 300. All citations from the *Lais, Testament*, and *Ballade des pendus* are from this edition.

6 Villon, *Lais, Testament, Poésies Diverses*, 300 (see note 5).

7 Beveniste, "Dead Body, Public Body," explains: "It is remarkable that the penal ritual goes beyond the administration of death. The dead body is brought to the gibbet. . .Death, the removal of life, seems to recede into the background. The dead body is foregrounded. The enemy is reduced to his dead body" (32; see note 3) As the enemy is reduced to *his dead body*, his identity, or essence, becomes locked within the corporality of his own dead flesh. Whatever transpires then to the corpse, could be viewed as having transpired against the individual.

8 Benveniste, "Dead Body, Public Body," 29–30 (see note 3).

between state. They are no longer "living" in the conventional sense as their bodies are visibly decayed before the spectator, however, it would seem that they have not yet achieved their final state of existence in that they plead for intercession, implying the possibility of yet another transition. It is a warning against gluttony and avarice, as well as a petition for pity and prayer. Scenes of physical pain, punishment, and degradation are juxtaposed with spiritual hopes and longings.

This is a supplication for the cessation of pain through intercessory prayer: "Mais priez Dieu que tous nous veuille absouldre!" ("But pray to God that we all be absolved!") There is a sense of hope in the ballad, hope of a release from suffering through the imploration and prayers of others. This poem is also distilled into a simple, unadorned admonition. The jester and the satirist disappear, and the reader is introduced to a seemingly contemplative Villon, one who is concerned with the afterlife and its predetermination in this life. Where the references to pain in Villon's work are predominantly concerned with mortality and the transition between life and death, here, pain is detailed as it is experienced beyond death and brought from a future non-corporeal experience and joined to the present corporeal.

Though speaking through the dead is not unique to Villon, the minimalist approach he takes leaves the reader with a sense of immediacy, as if the dead really did suffer in and through their decomposed corpses. It becomes a dual suffering, the suffering of the soul[9] (wherever or whatever that soul may be) and the destruction of the physical remnants left behind; the soul still connected to the body whose dissipation compounds and magnifies the torment, allowing the sufferer a sufficient foothold in mortality to transmit his urgent message. Pain becomes a timeless and universal mode of communication, its elucidation and declaration transcending the seemingly fixed limits of life and death, past and present.[10]

The primary function of pain in this ballad is to motivate. Just as the actual hanging and public display of decomposition was meant by the authorities to motivate a more law abiding citizenry, pain becomes a motivation for the reader; a motivation to abstain from the sins of the flesh, motivation to look to a continued existence beyond the grave, and finally, motivation to pray for those already departed that their pain may be alleviated.

The pain of a spiritual purgatory or captivity as a theme is paralleled in the *Testament* as the author describes a period of physical captivity in prison. The *Testament* begins with an assertion that 'Villon' has suffered:

---

9 See Esther Cohen, "The Animated Body of Pain," *The American Historical Review* 105.1 (2000): 30–68, for a discussion of the relation between body, pain, and soul.

10 Robert Mills, *Suspended Animation* (London: Reaktion Books, 2005), 31.

[E]n l'an de mon trentiesme aage
Que toutes mes hontes j'euz beues,
Ne de tout fol ne du tout saige,
Non obstant maintes peines eues,
Lesquelles j'ay toutes receues
Soubz la main Thibault d'Aucigny . . .[11]

[In my thirtieth year
Having drunken all of my shame,
Neither completely foolish nor completely wise,
Despite having suffered many punishments,
All of which I received
At the hand of Thibault d'Aucigny . . .]

This overture to the *Testament* is striking. It is difficult to dismiss the significance of the proximity between the name Thibault d'Aucigny and this declaration of suffering. Its importance is further underlined by its prominent position at the head of what is to follow. Its introduction at the beginning is an intentional choice. Because the *Testament* takes the form of a legal will and testament, this is where one would naturally expect a declaration of intent or an assertion of identity. The author begins by recounting the character's biography; out of all of the experiences of a lifetime, that which stands out, and that which he chooses to open what is presumably his last will—his last declaration to the world of the living—is a description of his agony in prison. Other than the general statements referring to the agonies and torments suffered under the hand of Thibault d'Aucigny, we find two distinct passages that outline specifics of the prison experience:

Peu m'a d'une petite miche
Et de froide eau(e) tout ung esté:
Large ou estroit, moult me fut chiche—
Tel luy soit Dieu qu'il m'a esté![12]

[With not but a small loaf
And cold water he fed me for a summer:
Large or narrow, he was stingy with me
May God be to him as he has been to me!]

Dieu mercy et Tacque Thibault,
Qui tant d'eaue froide m'a fait boire
En ung bas, non pas en ung hault,

11 Villon, *Lais, Testament, Poésies Diverses*, 84 (see note 5).

12 Villon, *Lais, Testament, Poésies Diverses*, 84 (see note 5).

Mengier d'angoisse mainte poire,
Enferré Quant j'en ay memoire[13]

[God be thanked and Tacque Thibault,
Who made me drink much cold water
In a low place, and not a high one,
To consume with agony many pears,
Shackled such as I remember it]

The first excerpt is what one might expect from a conventional prison stay: bad food, stingy jailors, and a sense of lost time with the passage of the seasons. The second, however, is slightly more sinister. We read that the prisoner was kept in 'a low place'; this means most likely that he was kept in a dungeon and not given the quarters, tower, or privileges of nobler, more important prisoners. There is a sense of interment, of being hidden, or buried, below ground in a deep place. The repetition of the drinking of cold water marks a difference between the water of alimentation and this second water; which seems to have served a more sinister purpose in that it was forced upon in him in large quantities. The forced drinking of water is a method of torture still practiced today. As with the gibbet, to understand Villon fully one must understand the grim details of that which he invokes. Though few accounts of the practice have survived from the fifteenth-century, there is a detailed account dating to the early seventeenth-century. In the 1620's, Scottish traveler and adventurer William Lithgow was captured and detained in Spain where he underwent various tortures including that of water torture. He recounts:

> Then the Tormentor . . . went to an earthen Jarre standing full of water, a little beneath my head: from whence carrying a pot full of water; in the bottome whereof, there was an incised hole, which being stopd by his thumb, till it came to my mouth, hee did power it in my bellie . . . .The first and second services I gladly received, such was the scorching drouth of my tormenting payne, and likewise I had drunke none for three days before. But afterward, at the third charge, perceiving these measures of water to be inflicted upon me as tortures, O strangling tortures! I closed my lips, gaine-standing that eager crudelity. Whereat the Alcalde inraging, set my teeth asunder with a payre of iron cadges, detaining them there, at every severall turne, both mainely and manually; whereupon my hunger-clunged bellie waxing great, grew Drum-like imbolstered: for it being a suffocating payne, in regard of my head hanging downeward, and the water reingorging it selfe in my throat with the struggling force; it strangled and swallowed up my breath from youling and groaning.[14]

---

13 Villon, *Lais, Testament, Poésies Diverses,* 126 (see note 5).

14 William Lithgow, *The Totall Discourse of The Rare Adventures & Painefull Peregrinations of long Nineteene Yeares Travayles from Scotland to the most famous Kingdomes in Europe, Asisa and Africa* (Glasgow: James MacLehouse & Sons, 1906), 403–04.

This torture is also accomplished by forcing the victim to swallow a thin cloth, or wrapping their face in cloth to avoid water escaping, and slowly administering water until it is saturated, forcing the victim to swallow large quantities of liquid over a period of time simulating drowning. For the prisoner—as is made obvious in Lithgow's account—this is a horrific experience. Though we do not have such an explicit account in what we read in the *Testament*, it is clear that this experience with water held no small significance for the sufferer.

A second portion of the description of confinement stands out as one reads "Mengier d'angoisse mainte poire" ("To consume with agony many pears"). This can be understood in two different ways. It can first be understood as a figure of speech. In old French, "to eat an anguish pear" [de bien manger des poires d'angoisse] meant that one was in a miserable state of suffering or captivity.[15] The second, more literal, reference is to an actual *poire d'angoisse* [pear of anguish], which was a medieval torture device. The *poire d'angoisse* is a pear shaped device which functions on a corkscrew action opening gradually like a flower blossom, the edges of which are sharpened, tapering down to a point.[16] This would be inserted into any number of orifices in the victim's body and opened gradually, tearing soft tissue and membrane, until the desired affect had been achieved.[17] This device was generally reserved for witches, women accused of abortion, homosexuals, and individuals of whom a confession was required but no outward signs of compulsion were desired.[18] That is not to infer that Villon is trying to make a statement about the reason for his incarceration (which is never clearly explained) but rather that the prisoner portrayed in the *Testament* suffered quite excruciatingly.

The life Villon portrays as being his prior to the creation of his 'will' (the *Testament*) is thus represented by a captivity; an exclusion from life in a living interment. The repeated references to his tormentor, Thibault d'Aucigny, show on the part of Villon an important and perhaps complex relationship between himself and his captor. During this period of confinement, pain, and torture a 'new' Villon will emerge who—as we have stated—will have gained the necessary knowledge, discernment, and vision to proceed with the rest of the *Testament*. The idea of a

---

15 Antoine Furetiere, *Dictionnaire Universel*, Poire d'Angoisse, Tome III (La Haye: Pierre Husson, 1727). I have relied on the google book digitized version which has no pagination.

16 Philip M. Parker, *Chokes: Webster's Quotations, Facts, and Phrases* (San Diego: ICON Group International, 2008), 123.

17 La Curne de Sainte-Palaye, *Dictionnaire Historique de l'Ancien Langue François*, ed. L. Favre Noirt, Tome X (Paris: H. Champion, 1882), 334.

18 Philip M. Parker, *Anguishing: Webster's Quotations, Facts, and Phrases* (San Diego: ICON Group International, 2008), 115. See also M. A. de Chesnel, *Dictionnaire des Superstitions, Erreurs, Préjugés, et Traditions Populaires* (Paris: M. J.-P. Migne, 1836), 915; Joaquin de la Sierra, *The Pear of Anguish*, http://www.medievality.com/pear-of-anguish.html (last accessed on March 5, 2012).

'new' Villon or the re-birth of the Villon character through imprisonment and pain is an interesting one. We find evidence that Villon thinks in terms of death and rebirth when we read:

Et escript l'an soixante et ung,
Lors que le roy me delivra
De la dure prison de Mehun
Et que vië me recouvra . . .[19]

[Written in the year sixty-and-one,
After the King had me delivered
From the hard prison at Meung
And had returned me to life . . .]

The King frees Villon from prison, which freedom he describes as a return to life. It is not a far stretch to call this 'return to life' a rebirth. The descent to prison is then akin to physical death; the man disappears from the light of the surface and is lost to the darkness of 'a low place.' This 'low place' is a period of transition, a sort of purgatory (if the term may be borrowed for our purposes) in which a transformation is enacted upon the captive through pain before he is again released and reintroduced into the light of society a 'changed' man:[20]

Or est vray qu(e)' aprés plains et pleurs
Et angoisseux gemissemens,
Aprés tristesses et douleurs,
Labours et grief[s] cheminemens,
Travail mes lubres sentemens,
Esguisez comme une pelocte,
M'ouvrist plus que tous les commens
D'Averroÿs sur Arristote.[21]

[It's true that after laments
And tears and groans of anguish
After sadness and sorrows
Hard labor and bitter days on the road
Suffering unlocked my tangled feelings

---

19 Villon, *Lais, Testament, Poésies Diverses*, 88 (see note 5).

20 Guy Geltner, *The Medieval Prison* (Princeton: Princeton University Press, 2008). Geltner writes concerning the prison experience: "Put differently, when Purgatory was imagined in the thirteenth century, the prison was one of its obvious models; but if Purgatory was God's great prison, could the earthly prison become an earthly Purgatory?" (90). Pain is inherent in the notion of Purgatory as the souls of men are chastened and refined; purged from sin. So to, in a way, prison becomes a place of purging, a place of re-creation through suffering. It is unclear if this purging consists of an expiation of sin for the "Augustinian" soul, or rather of a re-creation of personal identity as Foucault will later describe it.

21 Villon, *Lais, Testament, Poésies Diverses*, 88 (see note 5).

About as sharp as a ball of wool
More than all the *Commentaries*
Of Averroës opened Aristotle.][22]

After the anguish, sorrow, pain, labor, and grief of prison, Villon found himself opened, and his understanding sharpened. It is perhaps from this overture that Villon claims the authority to make the assertions and pass the judgments that seem so readily and so eagerly to flow from his pen. Now that he can see, now that his soul has been shaped and defined, now that he has been born into the world through the pain of his own suffering, he can look upon Paris with the discerning eyes of a man "ne de tout fol ne du tout saige" ("neither completely foolish nor completely wise").

From these few verses in the *Testament* we learn much about the Villon character and the role of pain in the formation of his identity. The torture of Meung could be viewed as a transformation of sorts, an initiation from an old life to a new. Freed by the king, Villon's emergence from the prison represents the rebirth of the individual; his reintroduction to civilization with his newly-forged soul. This would explain the emphasis placed on these experiences and their inclusion in the *Testament,* for they in large measure represent Villon's identity.

Passing now from the role of pain in confinement, let us examine the purpose of pain as it is inflicted upon others. Several exceptional instances of pain appear under the guise of objects willed in the *Testament*. An example that is at once humorous and painful is as follows:

Item, a maistre Jehan Laurens,
Qui a les povres yeulx si rouges
Pour le pechié de ses parens
Qui boivent en baris et courges,
Je donne l'envers de mes bouges
Pour tous les matins les torcher.
S'il fu[s]t arcevesque de Bourges,
Du cendail eust, mais il est cher.[23]

[Item, to Master Jehan Laurens,
Whose poor eyes are so red
For the sin of his parents
Who drink from both barrels and gourds
I give the interior of my underpants
For with to wipe them every morning,

---

22 Galway Kinnell, *The Poems of François Villon* (London: University Press of New England, 1977), 31–33.

23 Villon, *Lais, Testament, Poésies Diverses,* 154 (see note 5).

If only he had been archbishop of Bourges,
He would have had silk, but it is too expensive.]

This instance of an object willed is almost comic. The notion of a dying man bequeathing the interior of his underpants as a bandage for red and inflamed eyes has an absurd ring to it. However, there is also a deeply painful and humiliating side to what Villon requests be done here. It is possible that what we are witnessing is a tongue in cheek jab at Jehan as he could have been connected with the interrogation of a robbery in 1458 in which it is believed several of Villon's circle participated, if not Villon himself.[24] If this is the case, then it is quite probable that Villon is taking a comic stand against the interrogator of a fellow conspirator. We cannot, however, verify this relationship, which leaves us little choice but to take the text at face value. What we understand then is that there is a man, who, due to the faults of his parents (be it his actual parents or a veiled reference to Adam, Eve, and mortality through the fall) has a condition of the eye causing redness and presumably inflammation. Villon proposes the interior of his undergarment as a remedy. The image of anyone wiping irritated eyes on the underpants of a dead man is a painful one indeed. Before attempting an explanation of this unique bestowal, let us examine another apparition of pain in the *Testament*.

This instance of pain is found in the *Ballade des langues ennuyeuses* with its graphic descriptions; we read:

En rïagal, en alcenic rocher,
En orpiment, [en] salpestre et chaulx vive,
En plomb boulant, pour mieulx les esmorcher,
En suye et poix destrempee de lessive
Faicte d'estronc et de pissat de Juisve,
En lavailles de jambs a meseaux,
En raclure de piez et vieulx houzeaux,
En sang d'aspic et drocques venimeuses,
En fiel de loups, de regnars, de blereaux,
Soient frictes ces langues ennuyeuses![25]

[In smoke of minerals, in arsenic
In orpiment, saltpeter, and quicklime
In boiling lead they should be parboiled
In soot and pitch marinated in lye
Made from the turds and piss of Jews
In old washwater from lepers' legs
In items scraped off feet and shoe soles

24 Villon, *Lais, Testament, Poésies Diverses*, 452 (see note 5).
25 Villon, *Lais, Testament, Poésies Diverses*, 166 (see note 5).

In blood of asps and poisonous drugs
In wolf, fox, and polecat gall
These evil tongues should be fried.][26]

What a horrific strophe! Often when reading this ballad the tongue is visualized as being separate from the body as it is objectified. However, nowhere in the ballad do we find an explicit acknowledgment that these tongues are severed from the bodies of their proprietors. That being said, one cannot exclude that what Villon suggests in this ballad is not only happening to the tongues of his victims, but is also presumably localized within their mouths. The painfully abhorrent acts described in this ballad seem to be used as a means of retribution for offenses offered by the tongues of those so tortured. However, this ballad and the other instances of gifted pain seem to extend beyond this simple explanation and beg further justification.

It is very difficult to attempt an over-arching assimilation or interpretation of pain within the corpus of Villon. Each occurrence standing alone in its individuality and purpose; however, there is perhaps one characteristic of pain that runs throughout the work that allows us to forge at least a partial interpretation of the existence of this almost indefinable aspect of the human experience. Personal physical pain cannot be shared and thus becomes one of the most intimate aspects of individuality in that it can never be fully communicated or expressed to those other than the sufferer.[27] It becomes one of the most influential shaping agents of identity and possibly one of the most difficult to understand because it cannot be properly shared with others.

The gifting of pain through a will seems, then, to remove it from the 'unsharable' individual instance, and place it within the forged comradery of mutual experience. In a sense, one could say that Villon is bequeathing that which is at once the most innate, as well as the most specifically personal, part of himself in the *Testament*: personal pain being amongst the most essential defining and creative elements of the individual (as seen in the prison experience) and also the most difficult to communicate. In a way reaching out and saying: "I suffered, this is what I became through suffering, this is Villon." Though the causes of pain differ, the essential seems to be that pain is experienced. Even if is true that these instances, as they appear in the *Testament,* may be but retributions for past offences, one cannot ignore the overture of Villon's personal experience and reformation with his own experience in pain. If these are simple acts of revenge, though they be merited—as Villon's imprisonment may well have been—is it not plausible that the pain willed upon these individuals was meant to serve the same

26 Kinnell, *The Poems of François Villon* (see note 19).
27 Elaine Scarry, *The Body in Pain* (New York: Oxford University Press, 1985), 4.

reformative function as experienced by Villon? Thus the perception of the recipient would align with that of the giver through that seemingly noncommunicable part of self—pain. Passing into the realm of shared experience, the individual experience would thus be shared and the self multiplied. It is a surprisingly positive function, the pain 'willed' becoming Villon's gift of self to others.

We have seen that pain serves various functions in Villon's work, from the conventional emotive *memento mor*i of the *Ballade des pendus*, to the destructive and reconstructive effect upon the identity of the individual as described in the prison experience, to the originality of pain gifted in the *Testament* as a profound transmission, indeed gift, of self. Villon uses pain to elucidate the contrast, transition, and relationship between life and death, both the physical, and the fractured internal expirations and re-creations of the sufferer. The poems are an exposition of the destructive and reconstructive nature of pain, leading finally to the extension of interior pain and the renewed perception gained through its experience to others.

Chapter 8

Jean E. Jost
(Bradley University, Peoria, IL)

Retribution in *Gamelyn:* A Case in the Courts

> From the twelfth century onwards, English criminal law and procedure had diverged from continental Europe . . . . The key difference lies in the reception and influence of Roman law: without this as an anchor and inspiration, English law developed its own categories and methods, which vested much more influence in judges and custom, and much less in codified legislation or learned lawyers. (Trevor Dean)[1]

This summary by Trevor Dean reflects one legal basis on which the trial of Sir Gamelyn and his brother Sir Ote was based, but in fact, great violence between local and monarchical authority is evident throughout the latter part of the tale. The fourteenth-century popular epic *Gamelyn,* what Lee C. Ramsey has called one of the rough and ready "rebel romances,"[2] relies on the system of justice commonly enacted at the time. Until the late twelfth and thirteenth centuries in Europe, crimes came to court through private accusation, and contests of prosecution and defense by the adversarial parties were played out as a debate.[3] The court-appointed compurgation or "oath-helpers" swearing to the accused's innocence, or stipulated an ordeal of fire, water, or combat. After that time, three

1 Trevor Dean, *Crime in Medieval Europe 1200–1550* (Harlow, London, New York, et al.: Longman, 2001), 5.

2 Lee C. Ramsey, *Chivalric Romances* (Bloomington: Indiana University Press, 1983), 93.

3 See the introduction of Connie L. Scarborough's article "Women as Victims and Criminals in the *Siete Partidas*" in this volume for a discussion of Alfonso X's development of law in thirteenth-century Spain.

substitutes replaced this method as university-trained lawyers posited "a procedure based on evidence and argument;" secondly, "the growth of royal power led to the emergence of denunciation as a means of prosecuting criminals;" and thirdly, the inquisitorial method of torture and prosecution was included in the judicial armory.[4] England somewhat modified this European system, using juries, as in *Gamelyn*, to denounce serious crime rather than employing the ordeal, inquisitorial methods or compensation payments.[5] Further, "there was an overlapping structure of local, county, and central courts, and an evolving pattern of supervision and intervention in the shires,"[6] also revealed in the romance, as will become evident. In fact, Gamelyn reveals the violence and corruption rampant at every level of judicial government in this most vehement depiction of law and order

The anonymous *Gamelyn* poet situates his fictitious tale on the borderlands belonging to one widowed knight, on an English manor North of London, where Sir John Boundis, on his deathbed, attempts to distribute his lands equitably to his three sons. According to Robert C. Palmer, "Primogeniture was sensible custom before it was a rule of law. But as custom it was not a rule: an unacceptable eldest son would be rejected in favor of another, but acceptable descendent, now heir . . . . The right thus was not in a person designated by abstract law, even though there certainly were customs for preference."[7] Although Sir John Boundis did not follow primogeniture or adhere to what C. W. Dunn notes is the folklore motif of maltreatment of the youngest child or fair unknown,[8] his eldest son is disposed to treat his younger brother poorly. In this case, Sir John Boundis chose his three sons as descendants, not his firstborn.[9] In this endeavor,

> . . . sent he into countré after wise knightes
> To helpe delen his londes and dressed [divided] hem to rightes.[10]

---

4 Dean, *Crime in Medieval Europe*, chapter 1, especially 6 (see note 1).

5 Dean, *Crime in Medieval Europe*, 7 (see note 1).

6 Dean, *Crime in Medieval Europe*, 7 (see note 1).

7 Robert C. Palmer, "The Origins of Property in England," *Law and History Review* 3 (1985): 1–50; here 6, n. 20.

8 C. W. Dunn, "Romances Derived from English Legend," *Manuel of Writings in Middle English, 1050–1500*. Vol. I. *Romances*, ed. J. Burke Severs (New Haven: The Connecticut Academy of Arts and Sciences, 1967), 17–37.

9 Albrecht Classen points to blood-feuds, internecine strife, riots, and rebellion in his article in this volume entitled "Crime and Violence in the Middle Ages: The Cases of Heinrich der Glichezare's *Reinhard Fuchs* and Werner der Gartenære's *Helmbrecht*."

10 Donald B. Sands, ed. *Middle English Verse Romances* (New York, Chicago, et al.: Rinehart and Winston, Inc, 1966), 154–81; here 157.

As though prescient, the widely traveled, worldly wise Sir John anticipates hostilities among his sons and even where these hostilities may lie.[11] Thus he especially requests that his youngest son Gamelyn not be forgotten, for "Selde ye see ony eir helpen his brother" (40). Unfortunately, the old man's premonitions are proven right. In a somewhat lawless society in which violence may overrule right, or confirm it, behavior is often ambiguous. In the matter of the law, the father knows his sons—Sir John the aggressor, "a moche shewe" (6), Sir Ote the compassionate, and the youngest, favored son Sir Gamelyn.

This rollicking, violent Middle English verse romance of ca. 1350 (albeit with a somewhat earlier setting) is neither chivalric nor amatory; rather it disregards social authority, utilizes brutality, criminality, and physical force, thus foreshadowing the historic and literary breakdown of law and order marking the fifteenth century. In a prototypical Robin Hood scenario, Gamelyn sometimes even retreats to the greenwood, living as an outlaw, quite unlike the more traditionally romantic escape of Tristan to the woodland. But Gamelyn's context is not chivalric, for his knighted father does not come from nobility or royalty, but won his lands by purchase, not inheritance. Nor is the character or behavior of the characters remotely chivalric. Although Gamelyn of ca. 1350 is not the prototype of Robin in the later Robin Hood Ballads, since Gamelyn often appears as Robin's equal or rival, avenges Robin's murder in "Robin and Gamelyn," or joins his band as Will Scarlet, similar legal issues appear in both the romance and the ballads.[12]

As Christine Chism indicates, the Robin Hood "outlaw ballads critique the exercise of judicial authority in a variety of ways . . . [particularly] the localization of law enforcement that accompanied the centralization of monarchical authority over the law."[13] In similar fashion, the earlier *Gamelyn* romance presents conflicting sources of authority to resolve its legal conflicts. For example, *Gamelyn* and *A Gest of Robin Hood* both take issue with what Chism calls "the networks that bound the provincial elite and with the forged ties between local officials and royal authority . . . . [including] the local monopoly formed by the abbot, the sheriff, the local lordings, and the king's justice."[14] The legal provisions of inheritance, confusion of the seats of power, and an awareness of the violent times perhaps motivate Sir

---

11 Thomas Willard describes the comparable practice of "cozenage," relating to the deliberate greed-based fraud perpetrated between close relatives prevalent in the late sixteenth and early seventeenth century in his article "Pimping for the Fairy Queen: Some Cozeners in Shakespeare's England" in this volume.

12 Sands, ed. *Middle English Verse Romances*, 155 (see note 10).

13 Christine Chism, "Robin Hood: Thinking Globally, Acting Locally in the Fifteenth-Century Ballads," *The Letter of the Law: Legal Practice and Literary Production in Medieval England*, ed. Emily Steiner and Candace Barrington (Ithaca, NY, and London: Cornell University Press, 2002), 12–39; here 12–13.

14 Chism, "Robin Hood," 13 (see note 13).

John's own desire to ensure the laws of inheritance for his sons. In the romance, behavior is not genteel or refined, but rough and brutish. As Richard W. Kaeuper points out,

> Incidents of violence crowd the lines of the romance and create an atmosphere punctuated by the sound of oaken staves thwacking ribs and cracking bones . . . [Violence in] this tale of repeated beatings, graphically and even gleefully told . . . is peculiar to XIV-century England. It seems to be characteristic of one particular (if broad) stratum . . . the action takes place on foot, [and] the weapon is the humble staff in the late mediaeval English countryside where the country gentry and yeoman are the actors.[15]

But Sir John's awareness and foresight of the situation prove to be in vain as the designated council of elders, rather unchivalric knights, fail to understand his concern. While pitying his imminent demise, they miss his message: "distribute my wealth to each of my sons." Thinking they understood his complaint, and being power-hungry themselves, they are determined to usurp the dying man's power and ignore his last wishes; they are as craven as any "eir." No one respects the law. When these knights went into council to apportion his lands, then,

> For to delen hem alle   to oon , that was her thought.
> And for Gamelyn was the yongest,   he should have nought
> All the lond that ther was   they dalten it in two
> And leeten Gamelyn the yonge   withoute lond go.[16]

The first crime of the romance is thus misapplying Sir John's last-stated will and testament by not equally distributing his property. When the ailing Sir John learns about the impending disposition of his lands, he swears by St. Martin that the land is still his, becoming furious and yelling

> For Godes love neihebours,   stondeth alle stille,
> And I will dele my lond   after my wille.
> . . . I biseke you,   goode men,   that law conne of londe,
> For Gamelynes love   That my quest stonde.[17]

The tale examines the consequences of these false judiciaries' actions, too often the stuff of actual legal practices, and how punishment finally redounds upon the violators.

The wily eldest son John nevertheless beguiles his young brother, keeping him on John's land, letting Gamelyn's property, parks, and woods fall into disarray.

---

15 Richard W. Kaeuper, "An Historian's Reading of *The Tale of Gamelyn*," *Medium Aevum* 52 (1983): 51–62; here 52.

16 Sands, *Middle English Romances*, "Gamelyn," 43–46 (see note 10).

17 Sands, *Middle English Romances*, "Gamelyn," 55–56; 63–64 (see note 10).

His deer, his houses, his steeds are all lost or ruined. The dismayed Gamelyn stands fingering his beard, lamenting his plight, and refusing to cook John's meals. He lists all the abuses he has suffered and curses the brother responsible for his situation, erupting into righteous anger. Perhaps his later disdain for the law occurs because his own rights were consistently trampled on. With no role models who respect the law, is it any wonder the young man disdains legal authority? The quick-tempered John calls Gamelyn names and orders his men to beat the young man senseless. This kind of negative camaraderie reinforces cruel behavior, and ultimately will send Gamelyn to the outliers, the outlaws, those out of the mainstream. But here the young, strong Gamelyn finds a pestle to use as defense and, like a wild lion, leaves the men in a heap. When the fearful John asks Gamelyn to lay down his arms, he reminds his younger brother that he could break Gamelyn's bones. John defends his own illegitimate bullying as merely a test of Gamelyn's strength and accepts Gamelyn's request for his proper inheritance and the brothers appear reconciled. But his acceptance is a sham, for:

> Thus saide the knight to Gamelyn with mouthe
> And thought eek of falsnes as he well couthe.
> The knight thought on tresoun and Gamelyn on noon.[18]

The family dispute ends with a treasonous kiss from John, leading to further violence. The naive Gamelyn does not realize the extent of his brother's malice which later comes as a shock and influences his own behavior and attitudes.

When a wrestling match is announced, the strong-muscled Gamelyn decides to enter the competition but John locks the gate after Gamelyn has ridden away, and prays that his brother will break his neck. But Gamelyn, "the 'male Cinderella' proves his worth in an athletic contest,"[19] as Sands notes, overcomes the wrestling champion, and wins the prize. When he and his companions return home, he finds that John has maliciously barred and locked the gate against him: "thanne was it yshet faste with a pin."[20] With emotional, familial ties sundered, his comrades are the first support system Gamelyn finds. Those companions–"all manner men"—admire his animal strength. In retribution for being locked out, the angry Gamelyn "smote the wiket with his foot and brake away the pin"[21] before killing the porter—

> . . . gert him in the necke that the bon tobrack
> And took him by that oon arm and threw him in a welle—
> Seven fadmen it was deep.[22]

18 Sands, *Middle English Romances*, "Gamelyn," 163–65 (see note 10).
19 Sands, *Middle English Romances*, "Gamelyn," 154 (see note 10).
20 Sands, *Middle English Romances*, "Gamelyn," 292 (see note 10).
21 Sands, *Middle English Romances*, "Gamelyn," 298 (see note 10).
22 Sands, *Middle English Romances*, "Gamelyn," 304–06 (see note 10).

The cold-blooded murder, the second major crime of the romance, complicates the tale and does nothing to stir audience sympathy for the excessively strong hero, despite the injustice done him. Indeed, the mainstream culture is represented by his brother John, as lord of the manor house. In opposition to the outlaws of the forest, John nevertheless recalls the lawless viciousness of forests where bandits and brigands ruthlessly murdered victims. And Gamelyn's personal familial culture has done nothing to nurture or support him. Surely Gamelyn finds greater affinity with the forest outlaws and brigands to whom he rides when he is barred from his home than with those in the supposed norm of society from the manor and town. How do the two cultures, the mainstream in the town, including his brother John, and the marginal in the forest, coexist? What is the social and legal relationship between the two? Those in the mainstream, such as John, and those marginal beggars outside of it, such as Gemelyn? Barbara Hanawalt answers this way:

> Medieval and early modern society was tolerant of those outside the mainstream until they came to the attention of authorities or until the public became frightened of personal violence or began to feel that their space was somehow polluted by the presence of marginals. The local neighborhood beggar was a figure of pity and charity but when the population of Europe began to move around in the fifteenth century, and to flood the cities, urban and royal authorities began to promulgate laws against "sturdy beggars" who were disruptive and unproductive. . . . A traditional tolerance for those living dangerously and outside the normal constraints of society began to change in the later Middle Ages as the power of the central state grew stronger.[23]

Thus, as the central government strengthened, acceptance of that outlaw society improved because those within the margins did not fear the power of the outsiders, having a centralized government upon which to rely for protection. Will the hero, "Gamelyn the yonge," be punished for his brazen and unwarranted cruelty to the porter in this time of social unrest? Is he part of society, as a member of his affluent family, an outsider as a member of the outlaws, or both? Tolerated or punished? Curiously, the metaphor for repeated brutality throughout the poem is ironically that of "play": ". . . Gamelyn the yonge thus hadde plaid his play"[24]—destructive play indeed. In retribution against John for locking him out of the castle, Gamelyn invites all his company to partake of his brother's food and drink. As Kaeuper points out, these characters are from "the amorphous social level of minor landowners, lesser knights and retainers–those who might at most hobnob with the prior of a nearby religious house and know the sheriff, but whose horizons are essentially

23 Barbara Hanawalt, "Introduction," *Living Dangerously: On the Margins in Medieval and Early Modern Europe,* ed. Barbara Hanawalt and Anna Grotans (Notre Dame, IN: Notre Dame University Press, 2007), 2, 3.

24 Sands, *Middle English Romances*, "Gamelyn," 307 (see note 10).

local."[25] Gamelyn's companions are not the social elite or representatives of the ruling elite. Gamelyn challenges John to complain, and curses him when he does. He who grumbles shall join the porter!

A week later, when the sated companions leave the castle, "His brother thought on [Gamelyn] be wreke With his treccherie,"[26] but Gamelyn justifies his actions by noting that the fruits of the feast came from lands his father had bequeathed him—not John. Therefore, his bounty to his friends was not theft. When John duplicitously promises to make Gamelyn his heir, a temporary truce is reached. But soon the guileful John lies to Gamelyn claiming that he previously vowed to bind Gamelyn hand and foot for killing the porter, and wishes not be foresworn.

Respecting his brother's putative vow, Gamelyn foolishly allows himself to be bound. To Gamelyn's shocked amazement, John tells the castle visitors Gamelyn has gone insane and must be confined. Bound to a hall post without food or drink for two days and nights, Gamelyn accuses:

> ". . . thou art a party fals;
> Had I wist that tresoun that thou hast found,
> I wolde have yeve thee strokes Or I had be bounde."[27]

Finally Gamelyn convinces Adam Spencer, his father's and brother's servant, to steal the keys and free him, despite Adam's fear of being accused of treason by John. Here begins a kind of homosocial bonding and second support system wherein Gamelyn and Adam share their actions, their plans, their resistance to authority of the law, and their fear of its consequences. Once freed, Gamelyn's immediate response is vindictive. He vows to cut off John's head, but the wiser Adam restrains him by suggesting a milder, smarter method to effect their plan. Although Adam had unlocked his chains, the young Gamelyn feigns bondage and begs the clergy, "abbotes and priours"[28] for freedom when they come to a banquet. The clergy will either free Gamelyn or be beaten with staffs by Adam and Gamelyn for their failure to do so. Of course the vicious clergy deny Gamelyn help, even claiming "I wold thin heed were off Though thou were my brother;"[29] "It is moche skathe, boy, that thou are on live."[30]

In retribution, Adam and Gamelyn soundly beat them with their staffs, "For they had no rewthe of men of holy cherche / Abbot or priour, monk or

---

25 Kaeuper, "An Historian's Reading," 52 (see note 15).
26 Sands, *Middle English Romances*, "Gamelyn," 346 (see note 10).
27 Sands, *Middle English Verse Romances*, "Gamelyn," 392–94 (see note 10).
28 Sands, *Middle English Verse Romances*, "Gamelyn," 435 (see note 10).
29 Sands, *Middle English Verse Romances*, "Gamelyn," 484 (see note 10).
30 Sands, *Middle English Verse Romances*, "Gamelyn," 488 (see note 10).

chanoun."[31] Why should they be pitied, when they themselves exhibited no such pity or concern for Gamelyn, supposedly mad and in chains. Adam suggests Gamelyn "brek bothe her legges and sithen here armes,"[32] further escalating the level of violence. Thus retributive justice ultimately wins, for the clerics "came there riding jauntily with their servants and were brought back [unconscious] in carts and wagons."[33]

Gamelyn's vengeance against his brother is equally damaging: with his staff he "girt him in the necke that he overthrew (such that he fell down). A litel above the girdel The riggebon tobarst (the backbone broke)."[34] Sitting John in fetters like those in which he was locked "For to colin thy blod, as I did min"[35] the youth avenges his brother's cruelty. But soon twenty-four of the sheriff's hostile deputies arrive to swear vengeance on Gamelyn, having heard of the violent melee at the castle. Although Adam and Gamelyn defeat five foes and the others flee, the sheriff himself, representing the local legal establishment, arrives with a large posse to extract vengeance. The two men are forced to escape into the forest lest they be caught. There they come upon a band of outlaws with whom they make friends and share food. The locus of escape, the persona of the chasing sheriff, and the friendly outlaws whom Gamelyn calls "his merry men"[36]are clearly parallel to those elements in the Robin Hood stories. Eventually Gamelyn is "Made maister outlawe and crouned her king"[37]over those outlaws who have become his third source of comfort–a kind of personal and anti-establishment institution. But John soon supercedes Gamelyn's power:

> The fals knight his brother was sherreve and sire
> And leet his brother endite for hate and for ire. [38]

His cohorts warn him "Now is thy brother sherreve and hath the baillie"[39] (709)—from which office he indicts Gamelyn. Thus formal legal proceedings are initiated and tensions grow between local (John) and monarchical authority. Ironically, the legitimate king, through his local minions, is indicting the king of the outlaws. Hearing of his indictment by this local agent, his brother the sheriff,

---

31 Sands, *Middle English Verse Romances*, "Gamelyn," 509–09 (see note 10).
32 Sands, *Middle English Verse Romances*, "Gamelyn," 524 (see note 10).
33 Sands, *Middle English Verse Romances*, note 527–28 (see note 10).
34 Sands, *Middle English Verse Romances*, "Gamelyn," 536–37 (see note 10).
35 Sands, *Middle English Verse Romances*, "Gamelyn," 540 (see note 10).
36 Sands, *Middle English Verse Romances*, "Gamelyn," 774 (see note 10).
37 Sands, *Middle English Verse Romances*, "Gamelyn," 694 (see note 10).
38 Sands, *Middle English Verse Romances*, "Gamelyn," 697–98 (see note 10).
39 Sands, *Middle English Verse Romances*, "Gamelyn," 709 (see note 10).

"Allas," saide Gamelyn, "that ever I was so slak
That I ne hadde broke his necke Tho his rigge brak!"[40]
[When I broke his back]

Gamelyn's aggressive stance marks the latter segment of the romance, his fraternal experiences generating his evolution from mild-mannered, light-hearted, cooperative brother to vindictive, cold-hearted, controlling machine. Marching boldly into John's assembly hall to which he has been called, Gamelyn curses the indignities heaped upon him by his brother, the local law establishment. He rails against the indictment, as well as John's order setting his life at the value of a wolf, "And all his good reved and his men shent"[41] (his property despoiled and his men poorly treated). First Gamelyn removes his hood as a symbolic gesture of respect to the lords present, except his deceitful brother, greeting them with

"God save you alle, lordings, that now here be,
But brokebak sherreve— evil mot thou thee!"[42]

Gamelyn's anger prompts John to seize him, and Gamelyn at last vengefully "Was cast into prisoun and fettered full fast."[43] The nature and degree of seriousness of John's violently criminal behavior, his conformity to law, or the legitimacy of his vengeance is not always clear. Perhaps Sir Ote represents the best balance between civil disobedience and accommodation with his measured, reasoned manner. Here the good Sir Ote, Gamelyn's appropriately " middle" brother (in age and relationship to the other two), intervenes, saying to John:

We been but three brethren Shull we never be mo—
And thou has yprisoned the best of us alle
Swiche another brother ivil mot him bifalle. [44]
[evil to any brother such as you]

The vindictive John claims

By God for thy wordes, he shall fare the wurs!
To the kinges prisoun anon is he y-nome. [45]

Because of Ote's curse, Gamelyn is summarily taken to the king's prison "till the justice come."[46] The punishment reflects both local and monarchial authority since he is imprisoned on orders of the local sheriff and housed in the king's prison. It

40 Sands, *Middle English Verse Romances*, "Gamelyn," 711–12 (see note 10).
41 Sands, *Middle English Verse Romances*, "Gamelyn," 604 (see note 10).
42 Sands, *Middle English Verse Romances*, "Gamelyn," 719–20 (see note 10).
43 Sands, *Middle English Verse Romances*, "Gamelyn," 726 (see note 10).
44 Sands, *Middle English Verse Romances*, "Gamelyn," 736–38 (see note 10).
45 Sands, *Middle English Verse Romances*, "Gamelyn," 740–41 (see note 10).
46 Sands, *Middle English Verse Romances*, "Gamelyn," 742 (see note 10).

is thus dually instituted. From this point on, the legal dimension of this romance will shape its resolution. A representative of the monarchy possesses the greatest authority and subjugation over Gamelyn, perhaps in conjunction with John, the newly appointed sheriff. As Dean points out, "in the late twelfth and thirteenth centuries, royal judges were sent out from central courts in circuits of groups of counties . . . After this system broke down through overload in the years around 1300, a combination of central and local judges eventually took its place: central judges on circuit and local 'Justices of the Peace' in each county held regular court sessions."[47] This romance appears to draw from the second tradition as central and local authority collude. Waiting for the arrival of a centralized traveling judge would have been a regular occurrence. However, in the meantime Ote demands bail be set for Gamelyn ("mainpris"[48]) with himself as collateral until the next legal hearing, when a traveling justice arrives from the King's retinue. John grants this request, reminding Ote:

> "Brother, in swich a forthward, I take him to thee;
> And by thy fader soule that thee begat and me
> But-if he be redy whan the justice sitte,
> Thou shalt bere the juggement for alle thy grete witte." [49]

Ote fears Gamelyn will not return when he visits his outlaw band, and Ote, his surety, will be punished. When he begs "God shilde thee from shame; / Com whan thou seest time and bring us out of blame,"[50] Gamelyn reassures him of his fidelity and promises his faithful, timely return.

The issue of the green or the forest to which Gamelyn temporarily returns had also become a legal concern of demarcating social classes by now. The forest is a place of potential criminal activity involving those below the noble class, especially regarding hunting regulations. As William Perry Marvin notes:

> Whereas hunting reserves delineated the difference between licit and criminal activity according to real topographical criteria, the game law draws a boundary at points contrived to mark a cleavage in the social hierarchy, demarcating a level of nominal or performative gentility below which a large part of the hunting public was at best to be disenfranchised and at worst criminalized. . . . The game law, in that it revoked the individual right to hunt from persons who did not meet the property qualifications it

47 Dean, *Crime in Medieval Europe*, 7 (see note 1).

48 Sands, *Middle English Verse Romances*, "Gamelyn," 744 (see note 10).

49 Sands, *Middle English Verse Romances*, "Gamelyn," 747–50 (see note 10).

50 Sands, *Middle English Verse Romances*, "Gamelyn," 767–68 (see note 10).

> established, in effect legally closed the common chase to the majority of the population.[51]

Gamelyn and certainly his comrades would have fallen below the level of gentility needed to frequent the green. Nevertheless, Gamelyn retreats to the forest to join his supportive companions, ignoring game laws in effect.

Meanwhile, Sheriff John is busily trying to bribe witnesses:

> For he was fast about bothe day and other
> For to hire the quest to hangen his brother.[52]

This illegal behavior by one of the local officials against his own flesh and blood is highlighted; if the audience did not know already, they would now be fully aware of his ulterior motives.

Gamelyn tells his men they will now return to court, for he has pledged this to his brother Ote, having promised his return to sit in judgment lest Ote be punished. But John, in his capacity of sheriff, would punish Ote if not Gamelyn:

> The fals knight his brother Foryat he nat that
> To huire men the men on his quest to hangen his brother;
> [bribe men on the inquest]
> Though he hadde nought that oon, he wolde have that other.[53]

John will make the brother who stands surety for the bail pay if the other, namely Gamelyn, is not nearby as soon as the justice arrives. As all return to the court with the justice's arrival, Adam enters the hall and scopes out the situation, feeling "as he were agast"[54] at Ote's confinement in fetters–the verdict was given that Ote, Gamelyn's surety, be hanged in Gamelyn's place because Gamelyn has yet to arrive. Gamelyn, discovering his brother Ote "fettered well fast"[55] in the assembly hall, vows revenge: "He shall it abegge that broughte thertoo."[56] Adam suggests vengeance–in fact decapitation—of the entire group, but Gamelyn wisely, and legally, says

> ". . . we wilne nought don so
> We will slee the giltif [the bribed] and let the other go.

---

51 William Perry Marvin, "Slaughter and Romance: Hunting Reserves in Late Medieval England," *Medieval Crime and Social Control,* ed. Barbara A. Hanawalt and David Wallace (Minneapolis and London: University of Minnesota Press, 1999), 224–52; here 229.

52 Sands, *Middle English Verse Romances,* "Gamelyn," 785–86 (see note 10).

53 Sands, *Middle English Verse Romances,* "Gamelyn," 800–02 (see note 10).

54 Sands, *Middle English Verse Romances,* "Gamelyn," 810 (see note 10).

55 Sands, *Middle English Verse Romances,* "Gamelyn," 809 (see note 10).

56 Sands, *Middle English Verse Romances,* "Gamelyn," 816 (see note 10).

I will into the halle   and with the justice speke
On them that been giltif   I will been awreke."[57]   (821–24)

He more moderately concludes "I will be justice this day   domes to deme./ God spede me this day at my newe werk!"[58] In this realm of physical violence, in a court presided over by a vengeful sheriff who stoops to bribery, a kind of rough justice will prevail. Gamelyn enters the assembly hall where the king's justice sits, and unfetters his innocent brother Ote when learning he was scheduled to be hanged. Gamelyn keeps his promise to punish the briber and the bribed:

"This day they shuln been hanged   that been on thy quest [inquest];
And the justice bothe,   that is jugge-man,
And the sherreve bothe—   thurgh him it bigan."[59]

Boldly Gamelyn challenges the monarchical judge for his false decision based on bribery, and says that he will sit as justice in the judge's place:

"Now is thy power ydon;   thou must nedes arise;
Thou has yeven domes   that ben ivel dight;
I wol sitten in thy sete   and dressen hem aright."[60]

Getting no response, Gamelyn violently ousts the judge, "clevede his cheeke boon . . . / threw him over the barre   and his arm tobrak,"[61] frightening everyone else in the room. Then he sits down in the judge's seat and proclaims the punishments: he fetters the king's justice and the local sheriff, his brother John, usurping both kingly and local power. He then inquires about who was on the jury, deliberates long and hard, fetters the jurors as well, and offers judgment on them all. Just such a case of jurors indicting the accused and hanging him is described by Trevor Dean in a similar historic case:

> [I]n London, in January 1417, 'Edmund ate Chapell' of Finsbury was indicted before the sheriffs and coroner of robbing John Stowe of Norwich at the end of December of a white horse, four bolts of cloth, a knife, a fur and other goods. He pleaded not guilty, and opted for jury trial. A jury was summoned and sworn in. They said on oath that Edmund was guilty, so he was sentenced to death by hanging. . . . In England, a jury of local men simply gave a verdict, apparently without much in the way of hearing evidence or witnesses, and the judge issued the sentence.[62]

---

57 Sands, *Middle English Verse Romances*, "Gamelyn," 821–24(see note 10).
58 Sands, *Middle English Verse Romances*, "Gamelyn," 826–27 (see note 10).
59 Sands, *Middle English Verse Romances*, "Gamelyn," 842–44 (see note 10).
60 Sands, *Middle English Verse Romances*, "Gamelyn," 846–48 (see note 10).
61 Sands, *Middle English Verse Romances*, "Gamelyn," 850, 852 (see note 10).
62 Dean, *Crime in Medieval Europe*, 2, 3 (see note 1). Original source is in the *Calendar of Plea and Memoranda Rolls . . . of the City of London AD 1413–1437*, ed. A. H. Thomas (Cambridge: Cambridge

Gamelyn rules that the local sheriff is a rogue, the monarch's justice flawed and that the twelve jurymen had been bribed.

> The justice and sherreve both honged hie
> To waiven with ropes and with the wind drie
> And the twelve sisours— sorrow have that recke!—
> Alle they were hanged fast by the necke.[63]

Gamelyn's conclusion, however, contradicts Sir John Fortescue's reasoning, as summarized by Trevor Dean:

> Jurors can not easily be corrupted . . . because they are local property holders, not greedy paupers. Suspects can object to individual jurors who will then be replaced, thus insuring impartiality. The fact that witnesses have to deliver their statements before a jury of twelve neighbours, who know them and their credibility, ensures that false charges cannot easily be sustained. . . . The use of neighbours, "sound in repute and fair-minded," is thus contrasted to the use of suborned witnesses, "unreliable hirelings, paupers, and vagrants." "Who then in England can die unjustly for a crime, when he can have so many aids in favor of his life, and none save his neighbours can condemn him?"[64]

The likelihood that Ote had the opportunity to reject a peer is slight; that his peers are impartial neighbors, not bribed hirelings is impossible, as the tale tells. After an inquest into John's activities by a jury of men chosen by Gamelyn, about as impartial as the former jury hand-picked by John, retributive justice wins out and

> Thus ended the fals knight with his treccherie
> That ever had y-lad his lif in falsnes and folie.[65]

In the case of bribing jurors and legal corruption, Donald B. Sands affirms that,

> In government records of the thirteenth century in particular, there are instances of corrupt judges and bribed juries being called to account and ultimately suffering for their misdeeds. And the final scene in *Gamelyn* probably arises, not from one particular legal scandal, but from the general impression many such legal crises would have had on any right-thinking onlooker.[66]

A concordance with the king concludes the tale, confirming the harsh justice of the punishment against both local and monarchical representatives which Gamelyn

---

University Press, 1943), 54–55.

63 Sands, *Middle English Verse Romances,* "Gamelyn," 879–82 (see note 10).

64 Dean, *Crime in Medieval Europe,* 4 (see note 1), quoting Sir John Fortescue, *On the Laws and Governance of England,* ed. Shelley Lockwood (Cambridge: Cambridge University Press, 1997), 30–47.

65 Sands, *Middle English Verse Romances,* "Gamelyn," 883–84 (see note 10).

66 Sands, *Middle English Verse Romances,* 155 (see note 10).

the judge meted out to the king's justice, the local justice (his brother John), the peers, and the porter he earlier killed. It exonerates Gamelyn and his cohorts of any other potential crimes such as usurping his brother's meat and drink; it rewards Ote by conferring on him the local position and title of "justice" and Gamelyn the monarchical, national position and title of "chief justice of the land," thus replacing both local and national authorities. Further, it acquits his loyal outlaws of wrongdoing:

> Thus wan Gamelyn his lond and leede [tenants]
> And wrack [avenge] him of his enemies and quit hem of here meede.[67]

The tale of crime and punishment has come full circle, establishing punishment for the guilty and exoneration of the innocent. It recognizes and duly accords the local and kingly judiciary positions of legal authority. Gamelyn and Ote are now meted out restorative justice sufficient to offset the unwarranted punishment they underwent from their brother John, the malevolent local sheriff, and the equally corrupt monarchical chief justice. This pattern, like other correspondences noted above, can likewise be found in certain Robin Hood tales. For example, *Gamelyn*, like *A Gest of Robin Hood*, as Chism notes,

> in effect works simultaneously as an ethical and as an affective condemnation of local and monarchical legal authority, and this suggests that it is precisely the deficiency of the affective that renders authority impotent . . . . [T]his impotence results from the unchivalric need to play things safe, to anchor networks of association with hard cash, rather than to distribute the kind of continually negotiated largesse that animates the economy of the greenwood (where no association is entirely safe but where many prove beyond expectation to be true).[68]

When law and violence collide, history and literature collude in the exploration, and sometimes restoration, here, of some kind of English justice, in this fine tale of crime and punishment. Richard Kaeuper concludes that this poet "portrays violence and revenge on the edges of privileged society . . . [he] expertly conveys the tone of country society and faithfully mirrors contemporary practices and attitudes regarding law and order."[69] In this tale a young unprivileged son achieves victory through persistence, strength and a coterie of supportive colleagues. This rough-and-tumble exposé of justice in late medieval England is poetically conveyed to an audience appreciative of vindictive, punitive retribution in a brutally realistic, yet historic fashion.

---

67 Sands, *Middle English Verse Romances*, "Gamelyn," 895–96.

68 Chism, "Robin Hood," 13 (see note 13).

69 Kaeuper, "An Historian's Reading," 53 (see note 15).

Chapter 9

Jolanta N. Komornicka
(Boston University)

Contra Signum Nostrum: The Symbolism of *Lèse-majesté* under Philip VI Valois

The umbrella term *lèse-majesté* was coming into use in France in the late thirteenth century to designate all crimes that infringed upon the royal majesty. Not a new phrase, it had its origins in three legal sources. First, the Roman law of *crimen laesae majestatis*, codified in the sixth century in the *Digest* and *Code* of the Emperor Justinian and only rediscovered in the twelfth, identified treason as, on the one hand, crimes committed against the common good and, on the other, crimes that harmed the person or *majestas* of the ruler. Second, Carolingian law and that of the Germanic tribes understood treason as infidelity, a breach of the most sacred trust within society. Finally, canon lawyers had reinterpreted the *lèse-majesté* of Roman law in order to advance papal majesty, in the process binding it more closely to the Christian ideas of sacrilege and blasphemy.

The multiplicity of perspectives provided by these three antecedents resulted in *lèse-majesté* developing a unique character in late medieval France, one which addressed a broad spectrum of crimes and victims. The king ceased to be the primary focus of the criminal act. By the time Philip VI assumed the throne in 1328 as the first Valois king, *lèse-majesté* served as a rubric for crimes that can appear to us as remote and disconnected from the interests, not to mention the person, of the monarch. Crimes like kidnapping were considered as serious and injurious to the royal majesty as rebellion. Sometimes, the criminal registers of the Parlement of Paris label these crimes as treason or *lèse-majesté*, but more often they were simply identified in terms of the principal criminal activity.

The twelfth-century jurist Philippe de Beaumanoir states in his compilation of local laws, the *Coutumes de Beauvaisis*, that "as not all crimes are the same, not all punishments are the same."[1] Crimes are unequal not only in the gravity of their offense and attendant punishment, but also in their perpetrators and victims. Beaumanoir's discussion opens his chapter on severe crimes in which he examines treason and other offenses. Beaumanoir examines these crimes from a variety of angles appropriate to his background as a jurist and bailiff of Clermont: the social station of offender and victim, the intention and motive behind the offense, and the designated authority appropriate to handle the case. There is little surprising in these attentions, as Beaumanoir wrote a work of reference for the customary laws of his locale.

Nevertheless, the fact the *Coutumes* were intended as more of a guide than a work of legal theory means that other elements, just as pertinent to understanding crime and criminality, were left out. I begin with Beaumanoir because, although he wrote in the 1280s and what concerns me here is the second quarter of the fourteenth century, his work was one of only a handful used by the Parlement of Paris in makings its judgments. Like these other texts, Beaumanoir pays scant attention to the symbolism that colored a given crime, yet symbolism features heavily in any understanding of *lèse-majesté*. Beaumanoir's chapter on severe crimes encompasses *lèse-majesté*, but a handbook of the law had no room for discourses on theory. The court had to rely upon more than strict definitions of crimes to equate kidnapping with treason.

This paper explores that equivalence in how the crimes were tried and punished. Doing so will show how the analogies created between types of crime strengthened the power of the king and his court[2] in the short term, and how, in the long term, such analogizing sowed the seeds for understanding the crime as more important than the person by or against whom it was committed.

I. The Rubric of *Lèse-Majesté*

Though there existed no universal list of crimes that everyone agreed constituted *lèse-majesté*, we can, however, approximate such a list by compiling those from the various legal texts used most commonly by the Parlement of Paris. Doing so gives us the following offenses: armed robbery, any crime committed on a royal road, betrayal of one's lord, breach of an *assurément*, counterfeiting, forgery, the illicit

---

1 "... car aussi comme li mesfet ne sont pas onni, ne sont pas les venjances onnies." Philippe de Remi Beaumanoir, *Coutumes de Beauvaisis: texte critique publié avec une introduction, un glossaire et une table analytique*, ed. Amédée Salmon. Vol. 1 (Paris: A. Picard et fils, 1899), 428. All citations from this text are from this edition.

2 Unless otherwise noted, all references to the court or the king's court indicate the Parlement of Paris.

bearing of arms, kidnapping, murder of a royal officer, private war,[3] rebellion, treason, and violations against royal officers, royal ordinances, and the royal safeguard. By sorting the crimes into the categories of Feudal and Breach of the Peace, with the sub-headings Violent and Non-Violent, we get the distribution seen in Figure 1 (these groups are artificial and the reality presents us with a great deal of overlap).

By and large, the violent crimes under the heading Feudal[4] require little imagination to understand why the highest court in the land would regard them as dangerous. Treason, being a synonym of *lèse-majesté*, needs little explanation, but it is worth noting that it could be applied to familial settings, reminiscent of treason under the Roman law. Betrayal of one's lord, according to the canonist Alanus Anglicus (ca. 1200), was also equivalent to treason under the Roman law.[5] Rebellion took some time to rise to the level of treason, especially when the uprising was not against the king directly. Over the course of the thirteenth century, it most often appeared as an aggressive form of politics.[6] As the last Capetian kings and Philip VI began to more forcefully assert their position as fully sovereign (*rex franciae est princeps in regno suo*), rebellion ceased to be an acceptable means of renegotiating the distribution of power in France.[7] Once jurists began to gloss rebellion as treason in the fourteenth century, the primary material difference between the two crimes, when both were explicitly directed against the

---

3 Private war in some sources is also glossed as the illicit carrying of arms (*port d'armes*). For the sake of clarity, I have chosen to use the English "private war" for all military actions between two parties of equal or near equal status, whatever the term in the Latin or French. I have reserved "illicit bearing of arms" to refer to those offenses that involved carrying military weapons in an affray or in the commission of a crime. This in turn overlaps with *main armée*, which I have split between "illicit carrying of arms" and "armed robbery." For more on the overlap between these terms, see Ernest Perrot, *Les Cas Royaux: Origine et développement de la théorie aux XIIIe et XIVe siècles* (1910; Geneva: Slatkine-Megariotis Reprints, 1975), 184 n. 2. All citations from this text are from this edition.

4 I have chosen this category name for these offenses because they all hinge on an attack against duly-constituted authority. Some scholars, such as Claude Gauvard, distinguish between the political and non-political manifestations of *lèse-majéste*. Such a division, however, does not accurately reflect the political reality of those offenses designated non-political.

5 In the *Lex Quisquis*, treason against the emperor derived from the same type of offense as an attack against the *pater familias*, though it was of greater severity due to the emperor's being the father of all the people. On the relationship between patricide and treason in Roman law, see Theodor Mommsen, *Römisches Strafrecht* (Leipzig: Dunker and Humbolt, 1899), 527. By extension, treason could arise at all levels of the social and political hierarchy.

6 Jonathan Sumption, *The Hundred Years War: Trial by Battle*. Middle Ages Series (Philadelphia: University of Pennsylvania Press, 1990), 23.

7 Marguerite Boulet-Sautel, "Jean de Blanot et la conception du pouvoir royal au temps de Louis XI," *Septième centenaire de la mort de Saint Louis: actes des colloques de Royaumont et de Paris, 21–27 mai 1970* (Paris: Belles Lettres, 1976), 57–68; here 64.

monarchy,[8] was one of numbers and violent action, with rebellion involving more people and military stratagems. Both were intimately bound to ideas surrounding right authority, but treason emphasized a betrayal of the relationship joining two parties of markedly unequal status, while rebellion existed as a wholesale rejection of that relationship.[9]

In contrast, private war most often involved participants of equivalent rank. Though fielding independent armies and rendering roads and regions unsafe for travel presented real and practical problems, I want to highlight the symbolic issues. The breach of an *assurément* (a truce or peace agreement made between two parties and identified as *lèse-majesté* on the basis of Roman law[10]) often accompanied private war. Its violation of a feudal contract threatened not only the king's peace, but the fabric of social relations. With only a few exceptions, only the king was supposed to be able to unfurl the banner of war.[11] When others did so, even when claiming the traditional grievance of *deni de justice*, they infringed upon the royal sovereignty, suggesting the king was little more than a powerful provincial lord and not the divinely appointed ruler of the entire realm with justice over all disputes. The idea that not all rights were private rights was a new one in fourteenth-century France.[12]

The king's insistence on his enlarged authority at the expense of long-standing custom, especially during the war in Flanders at the beginning of the century and the Hundred Years War only a few years later, created a sore point between the king and his nobles. Yet however disruptive and destructive private war could be, that it had its foundations in customary law and involved the very people the king relied on most for his own military endeavors meant that the matter had to be handled more gingerly, lest the king unnecessarily alienate allies.

This was less true in cases where the king's officers[13] or his ordinances were attacked outright. The king and Parlement viewed these acts as inexcusable defiances of royal authority. Because the source of an ordinance's power, as well as that of an officer, was none other than the king, to violate either meant a direct

8 Even under Philip VI, the majority of cases involving rebellion were against the local lord (secular or ecclesiastic) or royal officers.

9 Claude Gauvard, *De Grace Especial: Crime, état et société en France à la fin du Moyen Âge* (Paris: Publications de la Sorbonne, 1991), 22.

10 Esther Cohen, *The Crossroads of Justice: Law and Culture in Late Medieval France*. Brill's Studies in Intellectual History, 36 (Leiden and Boston: E.J. Brill, 1993), 36.

11 Simon Hirsch Cuttler, *The Law of Treason and Treason Trials in Later Medieval France* (Cambridge: Cambridge University Press, 1981), 31; Perrot, *Les Cas Royaux*, 150 (see note 3).

12 Maurice Hugh Keen, *The Laws of War in the Late Middle Ages*. Studies in Political History (London: Routledge and K. Paul, 1965), 73.

13 For more on the development of the offense against royal officers, see Perrot, *Les Cas Royaux*, 105 (see note 3).

affront to the monarch.[14] Violence against royal officers naturally included such severities as beatings and murder, but also encompassed ill-treatment, like that suffered by the bailiff of Sens and the court commissioners at the hands of the knight Hugues de Monéteau. The officers were subjected to the taunts of hooligans, shitheads, thieves, and tricksters,[15] received death threats, and were besieged for two days in a strong house where they had sought refuge. The Parlement, unamused, quartered soldiers ("eaters") in Hugues' home and sought his arrest. Whether physically attacked or simply mocked, the court took all insults to its personnel and the king's officers seriously.

How the crimes of Breach of the Peace from Figure 1 constituted treason is less readily apparent. They arose from the *cas royaux*, cases which the king reserved for his sole jurisdiction and that of his court. The crimes of *lèse-majesté* that had their origins in *cas royaux* share a common feature: their public nature. The king was the guardian of the common good and the peace of the realm. Therefore, the king retained jurisdiction in any case that threatened the *res publica*.[16] Not all cases of homicide (manslaughter) had a public component, and those without it tended to remain under the purview of the local jurisdiction unless one of the parties sent an appeal to the Parlement.[17] In the twelfth century, however, murder became incorporated into treason, functioning legally as a public crime.[18] Kidnapping, because it involved stealth (*traïson*), not infrequently ransom demands, and the crossing of jurisdictional boundaries also had a public component to it. The purest form of a public crime, however, was any offense committed on a royal road.[19] Travel in the fourteenth century could be an arduous task, and dangerous in trouble-spots like Gascony and Brittany. The main thoroughfares were the arteries of the kingdom—not just for trade, but all manner of social commerce—and fell under the jurisdiction of the king.[20] Beaumanoir believed the Church should never provide sanctuary to highway robbers and justice against them should be swift,

---

14 Perrot, *Les Cas Royaux*, 183–84, 247–48 (see note 3).

15 ". . . ribaldi, stercosi, latrones, ganciones." *Registres Criminel du Parlement de Paris* (Archives Nationales, Paris), X2a5 fol. 186.

16 Adhémar Esmein, *Cours élémentaire d'histoire du droit Français: a l'usage des étudiants de première année*. 3rd ed. (1892; Paris: Libraire de la société du recueil général des lois et des arrêts, 1898), 420–21.

17 In 1341, the Parlement granted the municipal courts jurisdiction over homicide, though it still heard cases on appeal or with outstanding circumstances. Gauvard, *De Grace*, 802–03 (see note 9).

18 Pascal Texier, "Qui parlera pour le mort? Les droits de la patrie offensée dans les actes de grâce pénale (XIIIe–XVe siècles)," *Procéder: Pas d'action, pas de droit ou pas de droit, pas d'action?* ed. by Jacqueline Hoareau-Dodinau, Guillaume Métairie, and Pascal Texier (Limoges: Pulim, 2006), 139–53; here 142; Gauvard, *De Grace*, 803 (see note 9).

19 The royal road denotes the widest of the roads, termed *chemin royal*, but could extend to the smaller cart and animal roads meant for travel between villages, towns, marketplaces, and castles.

20 Perrot, *Les Cas Royaux*, 217, 367 (see note 3).

without the usual procedural delays, so important and valuable was it that travel on the roads be safe.[21]

As jurisdiction over the royal roads fell to the king, no other held high or low justice over offenses perpetrated along the highway and so these cases found their way to the Parlement. An attack right under the king's nose, metaphorically speaking, constituted a violation of that unspoken protection that the sovereign guaranteed to his people as part of the fabric of the late medieval state, which dovetailed with the idea that the king could not, without consultation or provocation, dissolve a contract with his vassals.[22] Any misdeed along the royal roads imperiled the ability of the king to govern. The bureaucracy of the French government grew throughout the century as the kings in Paris sought to bring more and more of the kingdom under their direct control. The diverse travelers—pilgrims, messengers, envoys, merchants of all stripes—would suffer if the roads were poorly maintained or lawless. All crimes, therefore, if committed on a royal road, from petty theft to murder, were of equal magnitude in what they meant for the functioning of the realm. Whether the *rei publica* had its own *majestas* that could be violated, as in the Roman law of the *Lex Julia Majestatis*, or whether the king's majesty, in the king's role as representative of the state, encompassed the *rei publica*, the breach of the peace on the roadways could be understood as nothing other than *lèse-majesté*.

This brings us to counterfeiting. The crime of making or passing false currency both symbolically and materially injured the king. Entire towns could be in on the scheme[23] and a lack of bullion encouraged some enterprising counterfeiters to look for opportunities abroad.[24] False money and adulterated coins circulating in an economy stressed by war, famine, and plague (all of which took their toll on France in the first half of the fourteenth century) presented problems for everyone, from merchants' strongboxes to the king's treasury. Counterfeiting exacerbated these tensions, which were compounded by Philip VI's numerous currency devaluations and the closing of the royal mints in 1335.[25] Philip's actions did little

---

21 Beamanoir, *Coutumes de Beauvaisis*, 161 (see note 1).

22 Thomas Aquinas, *On Kingship to the King of Cyprus*, ed. Ignatius Theodore Eschmann, trans. Gerald B. Phelan. Mediaeval Sources in Translation (Toronto: Pontifical Institute of Medieval Studies, 1982), 3–10. See also Kenneth Pennington, "Politics in Western Jurisprudence," *The Jurist's Philosophy of Law from Rome to the Seventeenth Century*, ed. by Andrea Padovani and Peter G. Stein. A Treatise of Legal Philosophy and General Jurisprudence (Dordrecht: Springer, 2007), 157–211; here 200–02. John of Paris defines kingship as "the rule over a perfect multitude by one man for the sake of the common good." Jean Leclercq, *Jean de Paris et l'ecclésiologie du XIII*[e] *siècle* (Paris: J. Vrin, 1942), 189.

23 *Registres Criminel*, X2a3 fol. 56v (see note 15).

24 *Registres Criminel*, X2a3 fol. 39v (see note 15).

25 Sumption, *The Hundred Years War* (see note 6), 160. For more on devaluations, see Thomas J. Sargent and François R. Velde, *The Big Problem of Small Change*. Princeton Economic History of the

to help matters, as the scarcity of bullion for the nine years between 1328 and 1337 saw almost half the counterfeiting cases (47%) for the twenty-two years of his reign.[26] That 47%, though in actual numbers is only nine out of nineteen recorded cases, represents a dramatic increase in the Parlement's concern with counterfeiting than it had shown under previous kings. From 1226–1332, the court heard five cases of counterfeiting—five cases in 106 years, compared to nineteen in twenty-two.

So why, under Philip VI, was counterfeiting more heavily prosecuted and how did it move from the periphery of judicial concern to being a crime of *lèse-majesté*? A *cas royaux*, counterfeiting, like kidnapping, became part of *lèse-majesté* due in part to its public nature, but also because it had an undeniable impact on the royal domain.[27] Symbolically, however, counterfeiting started off as *lèse-majesté* under Roman law. In the *Lex Cornelia*, acts of fabrication, including counterfeiting, were categorized as part of the *crimen laesae majestatis*. Similarly, in the *Les Julia Majestatis*, it was treasonous to melt down any statues or likenesses of the emperor.[28] The damage done to the emperor's image on a clipped or melted-down coin and the forging of his image on a counterfeit coin was a desecration. To deface the image was to attack the man and the office, neither of which Roman emperors were prepared to tolerate. With the rediscovery of the Roman law and its subsequent adoption in France in the High Middle Ages, this idea came to permeate royal thought on counterfeiting.[29] For Philip VI and his Parlement, the desire to save face, as it were, was all the stronger because of the contested status of his crown, as Edward III in England gradually defied his sovereign lord with growing audacity. Roman law provided the precedent for attaching counterfeiting to *lèse-majesté*. Political and economic realities made it a pressing concern.

Western World (Princeton: Princeton University Press, 2002), 88–89. See also H. R. T. Summerson, "The Structure of Law Enforcement in Thirteenth-Century England," *American Journal of Legal History* 23.4 (1979): 313–27, on counterfeiting and forgery as discussed by Bracton.

26 For other impacts of the shortage, see Sargent, *The Big Problem*, 135–36 (see note 25).

27 Félix Aubert, *Histoire du Parlement de Paris de l'origine à François Ier: 1250–1515*. Rpt. Mégariotis Reprints (1894; Geneva: Mégariotis Reprints, 1978), 266. For more on the idea that offenses against the royal domain or fisc were glossed as *lèse-majesté*, see Jacques Chiffoleau, "Sur le crime de majesté médiéval," *Genèse de l'état moderne en méditerranée: Approches historique et anthropologique des pratiques et des representations*. Actes des tables rondes internationals tenues à Paris les 24, 25 et 26 septembre 1987 et les 18 et 19 mars 1988 (Rome: École Française de Rome, 1993), 183–213; here 187.

28 *Digesta*, ed. by Theodor Mommsen and Paul Krueger, trans. Alan Watson (1893; Philadelphia: University of Pennsylvania Press, 1985), XLVIII 4.6.

29 Alfred Hiatt, *The Making of Medieval Forgeries: False Documents in Fifteenth-Century England* (London: British Library and University of Toronto Press, 2004), 27; Nigel Ramsay, "Forgery and the Rise of the London Scrivener's Company," *Fakes and Frauds: Varieties of Deception in Print and Manuscript*, ed. by Robin Myers and Michael Harris (Winchester: St. Paul's Bibliographies, 1989), 99–108; here 100.

I have left until last two offenses: violation of the royal safeguard and forgery. They represent the height of symbolic crimes and it is with them that the remainder of the discussion of the symbolism of crime is concerned.

II. The Royal Safeguard

Violation of the royal safeguard was by far the most common crime, with 138 cases of it during the reign of Philip VI. To put this number in perspective, the criminal registers of the Parlement of Paris, when a crime is specified,[30] record 126 cases of theft and fifty-eight cases of treason. In large part, this is because violation of the royal safeguard almost never appears in the registers as a stand-alone crime, and when it does the context always suggests that another crime accompanied it. The royal safeguard placed particular individuals, religious houses, towns, and others under the king's protection.[31] It gave people freedom to travel without harassment by the local lords or bailiffs, offered protection against a rival litigant in court, and informed would-be trespassers that a given property sat under the eye of the king—royal reprisal for infringement was inevitable.

A breach of the royal safeguard in the commission of a crime made the offense committed more severe.[32] To attack an officer as he was carrying out his duties, while he was under the royal safeguard, was more than either infraction on its own. It was true disobedience, even rebellion, and therefore indisputably an attack on the king and a crime of lèse-majesté.[33] But the accompanying offense did not have to be a serious crime in itself for safegaurd to magnify the iniquity. Theft provides the clearest example of this phenomenon.

The handful of cases of theft that are not joined to any other crime, including the royal safeguard, always have a mitigating circumstance that explains why the Parlement took the time to hear what was otherwise not a capital crime (except in how it was punished). For instance, theft appeared in the court on its own when there was a dispute over jurisdiction,[34] an appeal of a local court's sentence was

30 Due to the day-book nature of these registers, not all cases have crimes attached to them, or if they do, the type of crime has been left unspecified by the scribe. In addition, many such entries are not clearly associated with any other cases, thus providing information only on more procedural aspects of the court and not on criminality.

31 The safeguard could be awarded to whomever the king desired, but particular groups of people frequently were habitually under the safeguard unless it was revoked: the king's army, anyone going to or from a fair, orphans, monestaries, universities, the counselors of the Parlement, and litigants before the Parlement.

32 Perrot, *Les Cas Royaux*, 261–62 (see note 3).

33 Perrot, *Les Cas Royaux*, 139–40 (see note 3).

34 *Registres Criminel*, X2a4 fol. 122 (see note 15).

made by either party,[35] or the theft was committed by an officer of the court.[36] All other cases of theft were part of other crimes, most often violations of the royal safeguard. In the few cases where there are no other crimes but these two, the registry entries make it clear that the theft has become graver due to the attendant violation. One young nobleman was exiled for stealing a horse from a man protected by the safeguard.[37] He was only permitted re-entry and a pardon after the king's consideration of the young man's wartime service.

In another case, from 1349, the Parlement marshaled local officers to respond to the claim of a local prosecutor, who was attacked, while under safeguard, because he refused to surrender his horse to a thief.[38] Simple cases of theft or attempted robbery, which would otherwise have stayed in the hands of the local lord, became matters for the Parlement of Paris when the safeguard was breached, though the crimes be as far away as Cotentin in Normandy,[39] Marmoutiers in Burgundy,[40] and Poitiers in Poitou.[41] While travel for judicial purposes was not rare in the fourteenth century, a journey of nearly 250 miles (Poitiers to Paris) is a lengthy one over the matter of a horse-thief. Nor was it only the culprit who made the journey. Court officials, witnesses, and the victim could all find themselves traveling to and from Paris over a few missing animals.

Unlike in the preceding cases, where the victim's possession of a safeguard was incidental to the crime, in some cases the violation was a specific, violent, and intentional part of the offense. Those under the care of the royal safeguard bore a sign of that special status—individuals carried letters of safeguard while places under the king's protection had placards with the fleur-de-lys posted. On the one hand, this meant that a criminal had little chance of claiming he was unaware of his victim's status (in fact, I have come across no mention in any of the registers of a criminal maintaining his ignorance on the matter). On the other, these signs of the king's favor could themselves become the target, compounding the offense. In 1350, an orderly for the Viscount of Carlat occupied a priory and, throwing the placard proclaiming the royal safeguard to the ground, broke it in two and trampled it beneath his feet.[42] The orderly, Arnaud Vigier, did this (and more besides) as an act of revenge against the prior, who had brought suit against him in the Parlement for an earlier matter. The breach of the safeguard was thus much

35 *Registres Criminel*, X2a5 fol. 132 (see note 15).

36 *Registres Criminel*, X2a5 fol. 150v (see note 15).

37 *Registres du Trésor de Chartes* (Archives Nationales, Paris), JJ72 fol. 280v.

38 *Registres Criminel*, X2a5 fol. 164v (see note 15).

39 *Registres Criminel*, X2a5 fol. 62 (see note 15).

40 *Registres Criminel*, X2a5 fol. 158v (see note 15).

41 *Registres Criminel*, X2a5 fol. 164 (see note 15).

42 ". . . .siguum dicte salue gardie patenter existentes admonerant et ad terram pro reterant ut dilaminantum et pedibus conculcarant." *Registres Criminel*, X2a5 fol. 205 (see note 15).

more than the brigandage to which Arnaud subjected the priory and its inhabitants. Arnaud rejected the authority of the Parlement to arbitrate the on-going dispute, demonstrated both by his breaking the placard and his chasing out the household from the priory and installing therein a garrison comprised of exiled criminals and Englishmen.[43] His deliberate defiance of the king's protection of the priory challenged the king to make good on the promise the safeguard implied.

More common than acts that directly targeted the safeguard were cases concerning various crimes in which its violation appeared as a modifier for the other offenses. Frequently, after a list of transgressions of varying severity, the court scribe appended a phrase to the effect of "committed in spite of the royal safeguard."[44] In a case from the 1340s, the phrase follows an indictment of illicit assembly, conspiracy, monopoly, and general offenses committed against the Hospital of St. John of Jerusalem in Aquitaine, and which resulted in the mortal wounding of one of the brothers.[45] Though this particular entry opens with the affirmation that the house was under the protection of the royal safeguard, less than ten lines later the scribe reinforces the message by affirming that the attacks on the Hospital broke (*frangendo*) that protection. On other occasions, however, the record makes no mention as to the holding of the safeguard, simply appending its violation to the end of a laundry-list of crimes. Therefore, in 1349, the court recorded that the knight Sarrasin d'Angle and his accomplices perpetrated insults, burglary, depredations, incarceration in a private prison, hostilities, and excessive injuries, all of which violated the royal safeguard.[46] Throughout the criminal registers, violation of the safeguard is the one act most likely to be reiterated, both within a single entry and across multiple installments of a case. The position of the term in the text gives the safeguard an extra emphasis. Thus, while it acted as an adverb toward the other offenses, it could dominate the registry entry.

Why did the Parlement focus so heavily on the safeguard? Though granting safeguards was not a new practice under Philip VI, concern over its violation was. In the registers of the *Olim*—which contain the sentences rendered by the king's court[47] in the reigns of Saint Louis, Philip the Bold, Philip the Fair, Louis X, and Philip V (1226–1322)—there appear only two cases involving the safeguard. One,

---

43 For a similar case, see *Registres Criminel*, X2a5 fol. 74 (see note 15).

44 ". . . .dictam gardiam nostram [nostra gardia superiali] frangendo in dicte gardie." *Registres Criminel*, X2a5 fol. 74 (see note 15).

45 *Registres Criminel*, X2a5 fol. 74 (see note 15).

46 ". . . .plura maleficia. Insultus, domorum fractores, depredaciones, carceres privatos, hostilitates. Iniurias excessus. Alios et ceteria saluam gardiam nostram frangendo." *Registres Criminel*, X2a5 fol. 162 (see note 15).

47 This court, the forerunner of the Parlement of Paris, did not meet independently, being more closely bound to the personal justice of the king.

from 1309, involved an attack on a prior, the other the kidnapping of a knight.[48] The emphasis on safeguard in the registers may thus be a feature of a new focus on the violation. When we examine the safeguard in light of the large number of people to whom it was awarded and that those groups—even if not the individuals themselves—held a symbolic relationship with the king outside of the safeguard, the interest in it becomes less that of a novelty and more a concern over an item of value. The crime that most embodied the idea of the king's enlarged authority over the entire realm, with every attack on royal officers and any others under his protection interpreted as an attack on the king himself, naturally garnered increased scrutiny.

The repetition of the safeguard's importance can also be read as the men of the Parlement asserting their authority over a given affair, for no other court, save the king himself, had the power to try such cases. This had to do in large part with the allegorical reading of safeguard that made any slight against its bearer a personal affront against the king. It was also grounded in what the king's protection meant; absent an armed retinue, the safeguard offered defense by placing its bearer under royal jurisdiction. All justice in the kingdom, theoretically, flowed from the king.[49] At any time the king could intercede in any affair, save those wholly belonging to the Church. The reality was not always so neat.

The granting of a safeguard circumvented the need for the king or the Parlement to claim cognizance in a particular case, as it was theirs automatically. In this way, the royal safeguard was a profoundly judicial matter. To disregard it was to flout the royal justice itself, an inalienable part of sovereignty in the fourteenth century.[50] The villainy of Jourdain de l'Isle, the lord of Cassaubon, illustrates the point well, though the record dates from the beginning of Charles IV's reign. Since 1314, Jourdain appeared in the registers of the Parlement as a scourge on the land. A murderer, thief, rapist, and all-around brigand,[51] he was accused of rebellion by the king's men.[52]

Not until 1323, soon after Charles IV assumed the throne, did the Parlement condemn him as harming the king's justice. Jourdain had kidnapped two men who had appealed to the king against the ravages of their troublesome lord. The king, by granting them both safeguards, removed them from Jourdain's jurisdiction and

48 Arthur Auguste Beugnot, ed., *Les Olim, ou registres des arrêts rendus par la Cour du Roi sous les règnes de Saint Louis, de Philippe le Hardi, de Philippe le Bel, de Louis de Hutin, et de Philippe le Long*. Vol. 3 (Paris: Imprimerie Royale, 1844), 281–82, 479–80.

49 ". . . .et en a li rois la connaissance, car toute la laie juridicion du roiaume est tenue du roi en fief ou en arriere fief." Beaumanoir, *Coutumes de Beauvaisis*, 158 (see note 1).

50 Joseph Hugh Shennan, *The Parlement of Paris* (Ithaca, NY: Cornell University Press, 1968), 151.

51 *Registres Criminel*, X2a1 fol. 58v, X2a2 fol. 18 (see note 15).

52 *Registres Criminel*, X2a2 fol. 28 (see note 15).

placed them under his own.[53] Jourdain's subsequent kidnapping occurred despite the king, his jurisdiction, his sovereignty, and his protection.[54] The Parlement's record of the trial encourages the reader to see the safeguard as the extension of the king's majesty. To violate it was none other than *lèse-majesté*.

Given the abundance of people under the royal safeguard and the high number of infractions, it may be tempting to suppose that the king and his court would be happy to see any officer of the law or local judge handle the case and punish the malefactor. In fact, the king jealously guarded his right, and that of the Parlement, to be the sole arbiter in cases involving breach of the safeguard. Multiple times the criminal registers make it clear that only the king and his court had jurisdiction in such cases.[55] In 1346–1347, the court heard a case on the homicide of Jean Boquet, *massier* of the bishop of Noyon, royal sergeant and peer of France, who had been attacked by three men. These men then proceeded to break Jean Boquet's symbol of office and threaten the bishop, his mayor, servants and officers. By the time the bailiff of Amiens received orders from the Parlement to look into the matter, two of the malefactors were being held in ecclesiastical prison: one in the prison of the monks of Saint-Eloi in Noyon, one in the prison of the bishop of Therouanne.

The men stood accused, among other things, of breaching the royal safeguard, over which the king alone had cognizance.[56] The court forbade the monks and bishop from either freeing or condemning the prisoners; judgment was to be made only by the king's representatives.[57] Nor was this kind of injunction seen only in cases involving a peer of the realm or other individuals of high status, which would suggest more of a concern with the victim than the crime. In 1335, the court sent a reminder that knowledge of the cases of breach of the safeguard belonged to the king. Because the local court had begun procedures against Ulfard de Ghistelles and his wife over the homicide of the attorney for the cathedral chapter of Tournai, who held a royal safeguard, the Parlement authorized the bailiff of Lille to revoke all actions and decisions by the lower court, which had been done in prejudice to the justice and rights of the king.[58]

Though the Parlement felt it necessary on occasion to remind people who owned the rights to high justice in these cases, the records leave little room for doubt that

---

53 The two men appealed to the king and "par vertu de ladite appellacion, estoient exempt du tout de sa juridiction et en l'especial garde du roy." *Registres Criminel* (see ntoe 15), X2a4 fol. 177v.

54 ". . . .il les avoit fait trayner et pendre en grant despit du roy et de sa juridiction et de sa souveraineté et de sa garde." *Registres Criminel*, X2a4 fol. 177v (see note 15).

55 *Registres Criminel*, X2a3 fol. 23v, X2a4 fol. 170, X2a5 fols. 3, 62v, 179v (see note 15).

56 "... de fracture dicte garde nostre cognoscere et punie pertineat." *Registres Criminel*, X2a5 fol. 62v (see note 15).

57 *Registres Criminel*, X2a5 fol. 62v (see note 15).

58 "Et cum Gardie nostre fractorus armorumque portantonis cognitio et punito ad nos et non ad alium pertinent." *Registres Criminel*, X2a3 fol. 23v (see note 15).

it was well-known. Apart from instances such as the vandalizing of the safeguard notices, criminals would at times attempt to circumvent the king's justice in a bid to secure a more favorable outcome. So in a case from 1350, after having invited the abbot of Eaucourt-l'Abbaye to Arras under false pretenses and there attacking him in spite of the royal safeguard, André de Monchy[59] forced his victim to promise that he would not accuse André before a lay tribunal, which reported to the Parlement and king. Rather, the abbot was forced to promise under duress that he would only bring suit before the official of Arras, an ecclesiastic, in breach of the royal justice, which, the scribe reminds the reader, had sole competence in matters of the violation of the safeguard.[60] The abbot, however, once free from Arras and André de Monchy, swiftly accused his assailant before the Parlement of Paris. The court annulled the procedures and judgments of the official of Arras, in the process seizing the temporal justice of the official and his bishop, thereby preventing either from having cognizance over secular matters.

Although violations of the safeguard were relatively common, holding a safeguard was a net benefit. Even if it failed in the first instance—protecting the bearer from harm—it guaranteed that the king would take a keen interest in seeing that the attackers were punished. While we cannot know how many crimes the safeguard prevented, the number of people requesting its protection suggests that they they believed it to be effective or otherwise beneficial. Hence in 1334, the knight Gui Grimaut, imprisoned in Paris, requested a safegaurd from the court. Gui had in 1328 participated in a two-part conspiracy: one, to capture the Count of Flanders, Louis de Nevers, and two, to turn Charles of Valois, the Count of Alençon and king's brother, from the cause of the French and convince him to ally with England. Only the first part succeeded. Gui was held in the Chatelet while his trial stalled, as many of the witnesses against him were in Flanders and could not come to Paris.

The Parlement invited Gui to send an attorney north to gather the testimony, but upon his lawyer's counsel, he refused. When the court offered to permit him to travel to Flanders himself for this purpose, Gui agreed upon the condition that he be granted a safeguard for the journey.[61] The court permitted him an escort, which satisfied the prisoner.[62] In the context of the uprisings in Flanders against the French Crown and the count, who spent much of his time in exile at the court of Philip VI, Gui's desire to be under the king's undisputed jurisdiction is surprising unless we assume that the safeguard had a real power as a deterrent.

59 Possibly the former *receveur général* of Artois.

60 *Registres Criminel*, X2a5 fol. 179v (see note 15).

61 *Registres Criminel*, X2a3 fol. 218 (see note 15).

62 *Registres Criminel*, X2a4 fol. 201 (see note 15).

The bearers of the royal safeguard were not the only ones to view its bestowal as advantageous. With the breadth of people who routinely held a safeguard, a greater number of individuals came under the king's direct jurisdiction. Moreover, the inclusion of religious houses meant that the king gained a claim over religious affairs. As the *rex christianissimus*, anointed with the holy chrism at Saint-Denis, the safeguard bolstered the king's contention that he was the defender of Christianity (even if reality might prove to be more complicated).

In contrast to Philip's Capetian predecessors (excepting perhaps Charles IV) and the Parlement's fitful start as an *ad hoc* judicial assembly, the use to which the safeguard was put under the first Valois king suggests an increased desire to ensure that the most vulnerable segments of society and the most important for its government received a special status. But the increased awareness, if not use, indicates that the Parlement was growing more and more interested in preserving and extending the king's authority, all the while centralizing it under a single judicial body. The safeguard extended the zone of crimes answerable to the king,[63] along with the people who were both victim and criminal. The symbolism inherent in the safeguard legitimized the Parlement's increase of its own authority over other jurisdictions, as well as the king's power. The king's ability to dispense justice and protect the realm lay at the heart of his *majestas*.

With the extension of the safeguard and the court's greater focus on preserving it, a by-product was that more crimes rose to the level of *lèse-majesté*, simply because in the process of committing the crime one was also violating the royal safeguard. Acts of theft became more serious. Breaching the safeguard often appeared as a vital modifier for the other crimes at the center of a case. At times, the royal safeguard's violation emerged from the realm of implication and metaphor to explicitly equal *lèse-majesté*. In 1348–1350, the Parlement of Paris heard the case against Gui d'Apremont. Gui and his men committed a series of attacks, including homicide, rape, theft, torture, and arson, against the priory of Moutiers-les-Mauxfaits.

Terrible as these crimes were, what earned the full condemnation of the court was the marauders' setting fire to the post on which the royal safeguard was displayed. In no uncertain terms, the Parlement branded that specific act a crime against the royal majesty.[64] But as with the case of Jourdain de l'Isle kidnapping the two appellants of the king, spurning the royal majesty need not be as direct as burning the fleur-de-lys. In the affair of Pierre de Turlande against the lord of Pierrefort, the court recorded a host of crimes committed against Pierre by the lord of Pierrefort and his men while the two were in litigation in the Parlement: the homicide of a sergeant of Pierre de Turlande; the attempted murder of Pierre's

---

63 Gauvard, *De Grace*, 180–81 (see note 9).

64 "In frangendo nostramque maestatem Regiam." *Registres Criminel*, X2a5 fol. 156 (see note 15).

nephew; acts of brigandage committed on lands Pierre held in fief from the king as well as on others; the armed assault upon and capture of the castle of Turlande, done in order to kill Pierre, his children, and members of his household, which resulted in the mortal wounding of one of the latter; and finally the presence among the men of the lord of Pierrefort of exiled criminals and known murderers. The record denounces this entire list as having been done at the expense of the public good and of the royal sovereignty.[65] Before the scribe comes to the injuries done to the king and public, he caps the list with mention of the royal safeguard. The formulation of this list therefore encourages a reading that it was not these acts alone that amounted to an offense against the royal majesty, but their taking place in contravention of a royal safeguard held by Pierre de Turlande.

Violation of the royal safeguard, like treason, was another way of expressing *lèse-majesté*—only the means are different, not the result. But unlike treason or rebellion, safeguard was almost entirely a symbolic crime. The theft of Raymond Bernard's horse was a concrete, tangible act, but not one demanding the time of anyone but the local bailiff or seneschal; it was Raymond's holding letters of safeguard that brought it to the attention of the highest court in the land—no matter Raymond's rank as a cleric or the value of his horse.[66] Though the piece of paper or placard had no innate power to protect, succumbing to fire and other vandalisms, it remained a sought-after commodity.[67] The safeguard's effective power lay not only in the reprisals that followed upon its infringement, but depended upon an agreement between the king and his subjects that those proclaimed inviolable would, in fact, remain inviolate.

III. Forgery

In 1339, Gaston II, Count of Foix, Viscount of Béarn and of Marsan, found occasion to write to the men of the Parlement of Paris. Sometime earlier, this powerful court had imprisoned in Paris two of Gaston's men under the suspicion that they had forged and otherwise falsified the seal of the count. Gaston assured the Parlement that in fact he had sent these men to Paris to perform sundry tasks, not the least of which was obtaining a new seal of his arms. The count not only requested that the court rectify the matter and free his men, but that they do so without harassing or in any other manner mistreating them.[68]

65 *Registres Criminel*, X2a5 fol. 65 (see note 15).

66 *Registers du Trésor*, JJ72 fol. 280v (see note 37).

67 For example, the criminal registers relate the forging of letters of safeguard and their theft. *Registres Criminel*, X2a4 fol. 181v, X2a5 fol. 174 (see note 15).

68 *Registres Criminel*, X2a2 fol. 7v (see note 15).

The Parlement's sensitivity to forgery, to the degree that it would arrest individuals carrying out the legitimate orders of their lord, follows from forgery's being, along with the violation of the safeguard, the quintessential crime of *lèse-majesté*. While most of the crimes under the rubric of *lèse-majesté* (see Figure 1) were treasonous through analogy, forgery was a crime *of* analogy and impacted much of society the way that only king and Church were meant to. It caused the king to speak by pretending to be his own words and wishes, interfered with the administration of the realm and in the workings of the court, and bred distrust. In this way, forgery, though not originally a high crime, sat at the heart of *lèse-majesté*, threatening the expression of the royal will and the performance of majesty, to say nothing of the ability of people to recognize those performances as authentic. Dependent upon physical objects and their conventions of use—specifically the seal and the letter—forgery was a concrete crime that manipulated these objects as symbols of royal authority.

First, there is the symbolism of the document itself. In the fourteenth century, the "ceremonial role of the document continue[d] to be paramount" as it could enact and re-enact the events described and embodied in itself.[69] Forgery usurped this performativity for the forger's own ends. The forger simultaneously deceived the audience and became a puppeteer controlling those enactments. It was precisely this combination of deceiver and puppeteer that made forgery so representative of *lèse-majesté*. Yet, while the Parlement of Paris treated forgery as one of these highest of high crimes, written law said nothing about it. The customary laws used by the Parlement make no mention of the offense; only by extrapolating from the laws against counterfeiting in the Roman law did forgery rise to one of the *crimen laesae majestatis*: the defacement of the emperor's (or king's) image on a coin being analogous to the defacement of the royal seal, and from there to the document to which the seal was attached.

Lèse-majesté as a theory of crime and criminality is all about symbolism. The offenses that amounted to the violation of majesty in the fourteenth century did so primarily through metaphor and analogy. Forgery was not simply a crime within this system of analogy, it was, as I said earlier, a crime of analogy. It took the markers of kingship and right governance and perverted their meaning, thereby putting at risk the structure on which the monarchy and its administration depended.

Forgeries injured the royal justice, as disputants proffered false documents in court in an attempt to deceive the judges and win their cases[70] or to change the jurisdiction of their trial.[71] Forgeries like these did not so much cause the king or

69 Hiatt, *The Making of Medieval Forgeries*, 12 (see note 29).

70 *Registres Criminel*, X2a3 fol. 56, X2a4 fol. 50 (see note 15).

71 *Registres Criminel*, X2a4 fol. 219 (see note 15).

his court to speak, but set up obstacles in the path of justice. They made life harder for the court and risked elevating the level of distrust in legal battles. Harmful as these effects were, other forgers took the injury to the heart of majesty. In 1328, Henri de Mareuil, a clerk in the *Palais de la Cité*, confessed to forging a letter of safeguard for a client and falsely signing it.[72] In light of the importance of the royal safeguard, a promise of the king's protection, to forge one meant no less than to unjustly bind the king to an agreement he never made and give illegitimate instructions to royal and local officers alike. Forging letters of commission had a similar effect. The Parlement regarded stealing a letter of commission as an offense against *lèse-majesté*.[73] Forging one was just as bad, if not worse. In the process of the forgery, one not only wrote for the king, but copied his great seal to append to the document.

The instances of forged commissions were without exception treated as extremely grave, even within the context of the overall severity to which cases of forgery in general were subjected (see Section IV below). Torture was a common feature of the proceedings. Such forgeries not only assumed the right to issue orders in place of the king and parcel out his justice without cause or authority, they could also sow confusion and distrust of the bureaucracy by leveraging the power of clerks' offices. Pierre Samadet, believing himself to be sergeant general in the seneschally of Perigord and Quercy, fell victim to a forger in 1333. He bore a letter of his appointment to the office, sealed with the great seal of the king. The trouble, he learned upon being arrested and imprisoned, was that the letter was a fake. Under oath, Pierre swore he knew nothing of the forgery; he had bought the commission[74] from one Aymard Johannin of Cahors. Aymard had supplied a forged letter, pocketed the sixty-two *soldi*, and left Pierre holding the bag when the Parlement got wind of the deceit.[75]

The trick of forgery, like that of counterfeiting, is to disguise either the substance or the provenance: "A counterfeit coin belies either its content or its origin. With false content, the counterfeiter cheats the recipient of the coin, who receives less than he thought. With false origin, the counterfeiter cheats the monetary authority of its seigniorage."[76] So too with forgery, and one could never be sure that either one was genuine.

Forgery is fundamentally about deception. Since at least the twelfth century, and earlier depending on locale, written culture had gained a growing foothold in European society. Not only were documents becoming more common, slowly

---

72 *Registres Criminel*, X2a4 fol. 181v (see note 15).

73 *Registres Criminel*, X2a5 fol. 159 (see note 15).

74 This was not an uncommon practice and one which passed without comment in the criminal register.

75 *Registres Criminel*, X2a4 fol. 199v, 200v (see note 15).

76 Sargent, *The Big Problem*, 64 (see note 25).

permeating more levels of society, medieval society writ large had begun to give the written word greater weight, particularly as compared to memory.[77] Karl F. Werner has argued that the "number of forgeries in France [in the twelfth and thirteenth centuries] reflected . . . a new confidence not only in written documents, especially royal charters, but also in the monarchy itself."[78]

For forgery to be profitable there had to be a market for these royal letters already in place. At the same time, an over-reliance on this confidence in the monarchy held the seeds of forgery's own destruction, as too many fake royal letters would result in the collapse of the documents' symbolic value. For the deception to work, it had to rely on the symbolic weight of the thing forged. This was particularly true for the forgeries tried by the Parlement. In contrast to texts such as the Donation of Constantine or the constructed histories of monastic houses, these documents were predicated on the idea that their audience was *not* complicit in the deceit, as Pierre Samadet discovered to his dismay. Unlike the more famous medieval forgeries that have come down to us, those the Parlement handled did not possess a natural "rightness" in their presentation of events. There was no inherent, even if previously unwritten, truth to Pierre Samadet's claim that he was the sergeant general of Perigord and Quercy. Thus, the fake letter of commission he bore had to supply a level of authenticity and validity through its physical presentation: the great seal of Philip VI.[79]

In the twelfth century, John of Salisbury contemplated forgery and came to the following conclusion: "the falsification of [the papal] seal is a peril to the universal Church, since by the marks of a single impress the mouths of all the pontiffs may be opened or closed."[80] Though John was specifically concerned with the evils of clerical forgery, his expression of the danger inherent in permitting forgers to operate unchecked is apt and his worries were also those of the Parlement in regard to the king. Consider the case of Jacques Galian. While the record gives no indication of the motive, the facts of the case are that Jacques had forged sealed letters in the name of the king of Aragon, which he addressed to king Philip of France. He was apprehended by the court after having engaged the help of a Parisian seal-maker to forge the great seal of the French king. In his confession, Jacques admitted that he did so because he was planning to forge a letter by Philip to be addressed to the king of Aragon.[81]

---

77 Giles Constable, "Forgery and Plagiarism in the Middle Ages," *Archiv für Diplomatik, Schriftgeschichte, Siegel- und Wappenkunde* 29 (1983): 1–41; here 22–23.

78 Constable, "Forgery and Plagiarism", 12–13 (see note 77).

79 *Registres Criminel*, X2a4 fol. 200v (see note 15).

80 *The Letters of John of Salisbury*. Vol. 1, ed. by William J. Millor and Harold E. Butler. Medieval Texts (London, Edinburgh, and Paris: T. Nelson, 1955), 95.

81 *Registres Criminel*, X2a4 fol. 211v–212 (see note 15).

Jacques's misappropriation of right authority through the seal and the letter meant that he could make the king say anything at all. Unfortunately, I have been unable to find any record of what Jacques's letters contained, though given the period and the fact that his master was the archdeacon of Lérida, one may assume that it concerned the Hundred Years War. The possibility that Jacques could, in the words of John of Salisbury, open or close the king's mouth, thereby not only desecrating the royal majesty but throwing the entire realm into perdition, threatened the monarchy and all it hoped to represent.

Not all threats to the king's majesty were as obvious as penning a letter in the king's name during a time of war. Some more generally concerned the administration of the realm. In the 1330s, the lords of Fiennes and Dossemer were feuding with each other over land and revenue rights. In 1331, several men belonging to the lord of Dossemer, led by Robert Amplumus, were out collecting the wages of the soldiers of the lord of Fiennes, to be used by Dossemer, as they had been authorized to do by a royal letter. Guillemet Baillés and three others of the lord of Fiennes came upon them and, claiming to possess a letter repealing Dossemer's, demanded that Robert show his letter.

Unfortunately for Guillemet, Robert's was the more recent and final, as proved by the date. The royal letter Robert carried was dated the 26th of April, 1331, while Guillemet's was for the 17th. Spotting the problem, Guillemet proposed to his own party that he would put the matter right (as one of his party confessed, Guillemet "respondi que il l'i mettroit bien"[82]). Turning his back so the others could not see, Guillemet inserted an extra Roman numeral X into his own letter, thereby changing the primacy of the two directives. This act did more than open and close the king's mouth, for changing the order of the issuance of the letters worked much like taking a sentence out of context, distorting the meaning and the intent. It changed into whose hands the soldiers' wages fell, a matter of particular concern for the king's war effort both generally and in the contentious region of Flanders.

Yet these kinds of forgeries did not cause trouble only for the king in his attempts to govern the realm. The court itself found its job made harder by the presence of forgeries. The modifications made by Guillemet were used by his party to advance the suit of the lord of Fiennes against that of the lord of Dossemer. To make the Parlement's task all the more difficult, prior to appearing in court with the letter, Guillemet received coaching on how to make the addition less messy and conspicuous. More generally, the court's troubles with forgery were made worse by the engagement of court officers in the crime. Whenever an accusation to this end was made, the Parlement pursued it. In the case of a clerk suspected of falsifying a deposition record, he was tortured in order to learn the truth, and

82 *Registres Criminel*, X2a4 fol. 209 (see note 15).

ultimately exonerated.[83] The knight Adam d'Hordain, in charge of an inquest, was not so lucky. Charged with conducting irregular procedures, corruption, and the production of many forgeries and falsifications in the case he had been investigating, he was hanged by the Parlement.[84]

In part, we can read the Parlement's response to forgeries in its own domain as a combination of a concern for the integrity of the court[85] and simply a continuation of its normal pursuit of the offense. Yet the production of forgeries that traded on the trust people gave to the symbols of state power had the by-product of engendering distrust of those same symbols. While the criminal registers are sparing in terms of the motives and thoughts of the people who plead before the court, one case from 1346 betrays distrust toward these markers of power. Three men brought a suit before the Parlement alleging that two royal sergeants had been making use of a counterfeit royal seal; they therefore deemed their orders and actions suspect, if not illicit.[86]

Regrettably, the registers having nothing more to say on the matter and so we cannot know if the allegation was true or what personal quarrel might have prompted it. However, the fact that on various occasions litigants felt the need to call into question the validity of official documents[87] suggests that the confidence in the monarchy, buoyed by the document culture, was suffering from the advantage forgers had taken of it. Within a society in which many offices were commonly bought and sold, forgers had created a niche for themselves, setting up dispensaries that produced letters of commission and debt relief for a fee. Some were multi-member operations, with an inside man at the king's court bringing the forgers letters, who would then copy them and affix new seals.[88]

Others were conducted by a lone opportunist, such as the clerk in the chancellery who, over the course of six years, produced more than a hundred forgeries.[89] These dispensaries not only marred the image and reputation of the royal offices, they often caught up the innocent, as not a few individuals turn up in the records completely unaware that the letter they held had been forged and was worthless.

Even the Parlement grew more cautious in the fourteenth century about the provenance of its correspondence. Sometime around 1345, the court adopted a new policy with regard to the inquiries made on a given case. Whereas in the past the Parlement had been content to order the local official to send back information

---

83 *Registres Criminel*, X2a5 fol. 146 (see note 15).
84 *Registres Criminel*, X2a4 fol. 288v (see note 15).
85 Shennan, *The Parlement of Paris*, 28 (see note 50).
86 *Registres Criminel*, X2a5 fol. 4 (see note 15).
87 *Registres Criminel*, X2a5 fol. 200v (see note 15).
88 *Registres Criminel*, X2a4 fol. 223 (see note 15).
89 *Registres Criminel*, X2a4 fol. 181 (see note 15).

to the court once it had been gathered, now the official was expressly to send it sealed with his own seal (*sub suo sigillo*). This worry over falsifications within the bureaucratic system was not entirely anecdotal. Under the reign of Philip VI, 24% of cases of forgery concerned misdeeds by royal officers, 14% concerned court or trial documents, and 10% involved false letters of commission granting the bearer a government office. Nor was the Parlement solely animated by false letters potentially winding their way up from below; the court also began to expressly state that it reviewed the royal letters that came down to it prior to granting approval.

This evaluation of the king's commands gives us a fascinating glimpse at how the Parlement perceived itself to be the defender of royal authority; there were numerous times when the court rejected the king's letters of pardon on the basis that they had been forged or gained through trickery.[90] To have permitted the words and justice of the king to be bought and sold on slips of paper would have been to undermine the monarchy and the realm itself. Forgery could be nothing less than *lèse-majesté*.

IV. Punishment

Just as crimes were symbolic, so too were their punishments. While the law codes are fairly unimaginative in their corporal punishments, prescribing death by hanging for capital crimes (including theft) and a fine for everything else, with the occasional branding, chopping off of the hand, or being thrown into boiling water added in, the Parlement's actual sentencing was more robust (see Figure 2). The fourteenth century was a time of increasing harshness in the penalties awarded, a development coupled to a rising concern over the public good.[91] Criminals saw their fair share of the pillory, branding, mutilation, and exile. Indeed, these additional punishments were not infrequently joined to an execution or a fine. The public display that accompanied the punishment served to instruct and warn the local population, sometimes even supplying a cathartic moment for the community,[92] and to humiliate the offender. Beaumanoir recommended that judges take a firm hand with miscreants, punishing them according to their misdeeds and so strictly that others would view them as an example and would

90 *Registres Criminel*, X2a3 fol. 65v, X2a5 fol. 50 (see note 15).

91 Edward Peters, "'Crimen exceptum': The History of an Idea," *Proceedings of the Tenth International Congress of Medieval Canon Law*, ed. Kenneth Pennington, Stanley Chodorow, Keith H. Kendall. Monumenta Iuris Canonici, Series C, 11 (Vatican: Biblioteca apostolica vaticana, 2001), 137–94; here 186–87.

92 Mitchell B. Merback, *The Thief, the Cross and the Wheel: Pain and the Spectacle of Punishment in Medieval and Renaissance Europe* (Chicago: University of Chicago Press, 1998), 145–46.

themselves not offend.[93] Yet, however much the judicial system may have wished to catch and make an example of an offender, this was not always possible. In those instances when the accused had yet to be caught, but his or her guilt was known (either through the trial process or the implied confession of one who fled justice), a medieval court would order that the malefactor, if caught, should be punished in the normal way.[94] For crimes of *lèse-majesté*, the Parlement of Paris would instruct the bailiff of seneschal to punish the contumacious in an exemplary manner.[95] Such exemplary punishments included public execution, branding, the pillory, and the dunce cap. Sometimes, the punishment reflected an aspect of the crime, as when thieves would have a hand cut off[96] or when counterfeiters, in imitation of the process of preparing bullion for minting, would be boiled alive prior to hanging.[97]

Both the criminal registers and the chronicles tell us that a hanging could stir the sentiment of the crowd, even if it was not always in the desired direction. Renaud de Pressigny, lord of Marans, hanged the provost Nicholas Arnaud on the basis that Nicholas had abused his authority and stolen from the people of the area. Renaud, after a farcical trial, had Nicholas dragged to the gallows and hanged, without even permitting him a final farewell to his wife and children. However, as Nicholas had been beloved by the people and had taken on the duties of provost when the lord had abandoned Marans (which sat uncomfortably close to the border with the king's enemies), the demonstration did little to warn the onlookers away from the life led by the provost—other than to caution them against incurring the wrath of their lord. Rather, they mourned the loss of this "saintly man"[98] who had cared for the poor, the sick and injured, and orphans out of his own pocket.

The execution of Guillaume de Decken garnered a different response. At the beginning of the fourteenth century, the people of Flanders unceasingly revolted against the nobility, who often found support in the count of Flanders and the king of France. A peace was signed in 1305 between Flanders and France, with the former paying a considerable fine, provoking considerable unrest in the local population. In 1322, when Louis de Nevers became count, the fines still had not

---

93 "Bonne chose est que l'en queure au devant des maufeteurs et qu'il soient si radement puni et justicié selonc les mesfes que, pour la doute de la justice, li autres en prengnent essample si qu'il se gardent de mesfere." Beaumanoir, *Coutumes de Beauvaisis*, 446 (see note 1).

94 Adhémar Esmein, *A History of Continenal Criminal Procedure: With Special Reference to France*, trans. John Simpson. The Continental Legal History Series (New York: Augustus M. Kelly Publishers, 1968), 75–76.

95 ". . . cedit in exemplum," *Registres Criminel*, X2a2 fol. 7v, X2a3 fol. 115 (see note 15).

96 *Registres Criminel*, X2a3 fol. 25v (see note 15).

97 *Registres Criminel*, X2a4 fol. 228 (see note 15).

98 "Sanctum," *Registres Criminel*, X2a6 fol. 132 (see note 15).

been paid and his favorable attitude toward France only further riled the Flemings. Guillaume de Decken, bourgmestre of Bruges, led a violent uprising against France and the count. In 1328, the resistance was soundly defeated by the French and Guillaume de Decken was arrested for his crimes of rebellion, murder, and treason. Unlike in the case of Nicholas Arnaud, who had committed no real crime and was hanged on trumped-up charges,[99] none questioned Guillaume's guilt. Nevertheless, contemporaries describe his execution as shameful[100] and the cruelty of his death resonated with the chroniclers, as many of them take the unusual step of detailing how he had both his hands chopped off before being sent to the pillory for a day, then being drawn and hanged from the gibbet in Paris.[101] The Parisian crowd reacted strongly to the message, though how the rebels in Flanders felt we do not know.

Even the non-corporal and non-public punishments could involve a symbolic component. While prison closed the condemned away from society, proclamations of a person's guilt often included their sentence, which, even if it did not include a visual display, could still serve an admonitory purpose. Moreover, the proclamation of banishment meant that while the convict would not be seen by his or her community, the community was expected to report to the local bailiff should the exile return. The larger population thus came to play a part in the ostracizing and shaming of the individual, in a manner not entirely dissimilar to that of the pillory. However closely tied to the body, physical punishments did not have to involve physical suffering. Étienne Montanier defamed the first president of the Parlement, Simon de Bucy. He claimed that Simon had wrongly decided a case against him and loudly denounced and slandered him in the streets. The Parlement sentenced Étienne to ask pardon of Simon on his knees, his hands clasped in supplication. In addition, he was to promise to obey the sentence already issued in his case. Only upon doing so would Étienne be freed from prison, though should he fail to keep his word and return to speaking ill of the president, the subsequent reprisal would be not merely incarceration, but corporal punishment as well.[102] Such public acts of contrition relied on an interior

---

99 The Parlement later tried and executed the lord of Marans for his handling of the Nicholas Arnaud affair, among other crimes.

100 ". . . moult honteusement condamné." Paulin Paris, ed., *Le premier volume des grandes chroniques de France: selon que elles sont conservées en l'église de Saint-Denis en France* (Paris: Techener, 1836), 1290.

101 *Registres Criminel*, X2a4 fol. 180v (see note 15). For contemporary descriptions, in addition to the *Grandes chroniques* (see note 100), see Guillaume de Nangis, *Chronique latine de Guillaume de Nangis*. Vol. 2. Société de l'histoire de France (Paris: Renouard, 1843), 103; Auguste and Émile Molinier, eds., *Chronique normande du XIVe siècle*. Société de l'Histoire de France (Paris: Renouard, 1882), 33–34.

102 *Registres Criminel*, X2a5 fol. 188v (see note 15).

penitential spirit that signified the criminal's turning away from iniquity and resultant positive participation in the peace of the realm.[103]

Punishment, however much it could serve to educate and warn the general populace, ultimately comes back to the criminal and crime committed. Punishments possessed a corrective function for the criminal as much as for the viewing audience. Suffering was a desirable component,[104] part of the medieval ethos. Pain was justice[105] and a criminal could expect it as part of his sentence, but it was a pain meant equally to serve the needs of vengeance as to help the condemned find redemption.[106] By the opening decades of the fourteenth century, this vengeance could no longer be administered by the aggrieved party. Justice belonged to the state. Reprisals not sanctioned by the state were inherently unjust, uninstructive, and a threat to the realm.[107] Nicholas Arnaud, innocent to all except his cruel lord, suffered a Christ-like death and was praised for it. Renaud de Pressigny, for his part, lost his life for the impropriety of the punishment. Guillaume de Decken, innocent in the eyes of no one, underwent excruciating torment, seen as harsh by his contemporaries, but not unjust or cruel.[108]

In modern society, we like to think that the punishment should fit the crime. Such an idea was not foreign to late medieval France. Beaumanoir takes his time specifying the various penalties associated with the offenses he enumerates, providing harsher ones as the crime increases in severity. The penalty for a beating was five *deniers* when no blood had been shed, unless it occurred on a market day when the fine rose to sixty *sous*. If blood had been spilled, the assailant was to be arrested until it could be ascertained that the victim would not die of his wounds. If the victim recovered, the fine was sixty *sous* (more on market days), and if he died the assailant was drawn and hanged as a homicide and all his goods were confiscated.[109]

According to the *Établissements de Saint-Louis*, regarding minor thefts that did not initially warrant hanging, the culprit should lose his ear for the first offense, upon the second his foot; he should be hanged only after three infractions, "because one

---

103 Claude Gauvard, "L'Honneur du roi: Peines et rituels judiciaires au Parlement de Paris à la fin du Moyen Âge," *Les rites de la justice: Gestes et rituels judiciaires au Moyen Âge*, ed. Claude Gauvard and Robert Jacob (Paris: Le Léopard d'Or, 1999), 99–123; here 111.

104 Thomas Aquinas, *Summa Theologica*, 2a2ae, q. 43, a. 7, ad 1; q. 66, a. 6, ad. 2.

105 Esther Cohen, "The Animated Pain of the Body," *The American Historical Review* 105 (2000): 36–48; here 47; Cohen, *The Crossroads*, 151 (see note 10).

106 Gauvard, "L'Honneur du roi," 123 (see note 103); Merback, *The Thief*, 20 (see note 92); Richard M. Fraher, "Conviction According to Conscience: The Medieval Jurists' Debate Concerning Judicial Discretion and the Law of Proof," *Law and History Review* 7 (1989): 23–88, here 588.

107 Merback, *The Thief*, 134 (see note 92).

108 On the medieval idea of cruelty, see Daniel Baraz, "Seneca, Ethics, and the Body: The Treatment of Cruelty in Medieval Thought," *Journal of the History of Ideas* 59 (1998): 195–215; here 199–202.

109 Beaumanoir, *Coutumes de Beauvasis*, 432–33 (see note 1).

should not go from the large limb to the small, but from the small to the large."[110] When we compare those crimes of *lèse-majesté* tried by the Parlement against cases the court heard that did not involve such offenses, this general principle holds (see Figure 3). Cases that had no *lèse-majesté* associated with them make up only 21% of the instances of banishment and less than 6% of the offenders suffered capital punishment. These same cases see a significant number of fines (a monetary penalty) and fees (damages and expenses paid to the opposing party): 30% and 34% respectively. Overall, these minor offenses favor sentences focused on monetary and generally less long-term punishments. The harsher and more permanent penalties tend to be reserved for serious crimes. Aside from one instance of mutilation and one of whipping, both in cases of theft, there are no brandings, boilings, or drawings prior to hanging. As less serious infractions, they garner less serious penalties.

Thus far, the criminal registers provide nothing surprising about fourteenth-century punishments. However, when the data for crimes of *lèse-majesté* is examined in itself, we find disparities in sentencing severity, and in surprising ways (see Figure 4). While we might expect instances of treason to earn strict and permanent sentences, they account for only 23% of the executions, the same amount as forgery. In terms of the exemplary punishments meant for public consumption, treason cases make up 26% of the total,[111] compared to forgery's 42%.[112] The distribution of punishments suggests that not all crimes of *lèse-majesté* are created equal. Forgery, as one of the most highly symbolic crimes of *lèse-majesté*, provides a telling case study.

Let us return to the Count of Foix, Gaston II, and his concern that his two men, apprehended by the Parlement, would be mistreated, even though they had committed no forgeries and had acted on his orders. In light of the Parlement's track record in handling forgers, his concern would appear to be well-placed. Unlike treason, which favors exile, confiscation of property, and prison terms, forgery prompts more branding, pillorying, dunce capping, and executing.[113] Compared with treason, twice as many cases of forgery resulted in the Parlement torturing the accused to elicit a confession.

---

110 Paul Viollet, ed., *Les Établissements de Saint Louis: accompagnés des textes primitifs et de textes dérivés, avec une introduction et des notes*. Société de l'histoire de France (Paris: Renouard, 1881), 14.

111 This percent derives from all crimes that were considered treason: conspiracy, lèse-majesté, machinations, and treason—hence the disparity with Figure 4.

112 These percents result from several individual crimes being grouped together as exemplary punishment, such as the pillory, the dunce cap, and public hanging.

113 These values do not change significantly when we control for commoners vs nobles as perpetrators.

The penalties for forgery are weighted in favor of more permanent and shameful public displays. Consider my personal favorite, the dunce cap. Most commonly it was worn when a person was being pilloried, though in one case the cap was placed on the head of a hanging victim.[114] It is described in the registers as a hat or crown made of parchment and for most cases the crimes are to be written in big red letters upon it.[115] In cases of forgery, the red-lettering was usually replaced by the cap being made out of the forged letters themselves. The crime itself, and not just the criminal, was punished and exposed to public ridicule.[116] In a unique instance, the cap is absent, but a transcript of the forgery was placed on the criminal's forehead during his stint in the pillory.[117]

The symbolic way that the Parlement punished not just forgers, but the very crime of forgery is further demonstrated by looking at the distribution of the various penalties across types of forgery (Figure 5). I have divided forgery into four categories. Royal letters and seals include letters of the king, his son the duke of Normandy, and all forged letters of commission. Next are the forgeries of concern to the court. Non-court and non-royal forgeries, labeled Other, concern all other kinds of forgery.[118] The final category denotes the penalties given to royal officers who committed forgeries of any kind. What is notable when looking at the graph is that the royal forgeries dominate all punishments. This distribution, keeping in mind the very small sample size, implies that those cases that infringe most on the monarchy and royal authority are the most severely punished, reinforcing the idea that forgery is about right authority and its commission is an act of *lèse-majesté*, especially when the criminal attempts to speak with the mouth of the king.

Forgery is an attack against the Crown, which is to say that it injures the entirety of what the king and the monarchy represent: the public good, justice, the people, the kingdom. Therefore, forgers receive particularly heavy sentences, especially when what they forge has direct bearing on the Crown. The gradation of punishment spoken of in the *Établissements* and the *Coutumes de Beauvaisis* holds. But these law books contain a further element of gradation: distinction between commoners and nobles. The penalty for striking and beating another man was five *deniers* for a commoner, but for a nobleman ten *sous*. When the assailant in a crime

---

114 *Registres Criminel*, X2a4 fol. 223 (see note 15).

115 *Registres Criminel*, X2a4 fol. 222v (see note 15).

116 *Registres Criminel*, X2a4 fol. 146 (see note 15). For medieval punishment more generally, "neither the criminal nor the deed was regarded as a mutually exclusive target." Merback, *The Thief*, 135 (see note 92).

117 *Regsitres Criminel*, X2a4 fol. 50 (see note 15).

118 None of the penalties are counted double. If a criminal forged letters of the king and of a count, then I have counted the penalty under royal letters. The precedence for these three categories is Royal, Court, Other.

was a commoner and his victim a nobleman, his treatment was to be markedly worse than in the opposite instance. While this fits the common view of the Middle Ages, the registers again present a different picture.

Of the cases for which the criminal registers record a punishment, nobles and commoners perpetrated crimes against each other a similar number of times. On nineteen occasions nobles committed an offense against a commoner, versus fifteen the other way. Commoners suffered twenty-six punishments for these attacks, nobles twenty-tree. While nobles paid more fines and damages to their victims, commoners suffered more humiliating punishments: drawing, mutilation, the pillory. Nevertheless, nobles were executed slightly more often for crimes against commoners. Put in the larger context of the punishments suffered overall, 40% of the executions of nobles came in cases where the injured party was a commoner. For commoners, only 8% of executions happened when their victim was noble.

The registers do not reveal an egalitarian or classless society—far from it. Nobles were awarded more absolutions and pardons for their crimes than commoners. The developing administrative structure of the monarchy, however, and the role of the Parlement of Paris as royal court and the final place of appeal created a space where all litigants were on more equal footing. Claude Gauvard has argued that the crime is not interesting in itself: "the heart of the debate is the criminal."[119] Yet the inclusion of crimes like forgery, safeguard, and any offense committed on a royal road not only extended the reach of the royal government and pulled disparate corners of the realm toward a central point, it made the primary concern the crime and not the status of the criminal or victim.

Although medieval forms of punishment sought to purge the evil from the criminal and return him, humbled and supplicating, to God, we should be wary of understanding medievals as distinguishing between the person and his station in society. The two were largely inseparable. For the heart of the debate to be the criminal, we must place status in the ring as well. Nevertheless, the actions of the Parlement of Paris show that criminal and status had to give way to the crime itself. The decisions of the court under Philip VI set in motion a slow and fitful process, one that never had the abridgement of status as its goal. Yet to achieve a strong central monarchy and an effective judicial bureaucracy, a side-effect was a less deferential attitude toward *privilegium*. What the Parlement recorded was a judicial culture slowly beginning to emphasize crimes over perpetrators.

---

119 Gauvard's argument is more appropriate for understanding royal pardons, which are her main concern. Gauvard, *De Grace*, 235 (see note 9).

Breach of the Peace		
		Any Crime on the Royal Road
	Violent	Armed Robbery
		Homicide
		Kidnapping
		Murder
	Non-Violent	Counterfeiting
		Forgery
Feudal		
	Violent	Private War
		Rebellion
		Treason
		Violence vs Royal Officers
	Non-violent	Betrayal of One's Lord
		Breach of *Assurément*
		Violation of Royal Ordinances
		Violation of the Royal Safeguard

Figure 1: Crimes of *Lèse-majesté*.

Punishment Type	Punishment		No. of Cases	Percent of Cases
Monetary				
	Confiscation		38	21
	Fee		19	11
	Fine		39	22
	Paying for Masses		1	1
		Total Monetary	97	55%
Non-Lethal				
	Banishment		35	20
	Branding		5	3
	Confiscation of Seals		1	1
	Corporal Punishment		2	1
	Drawing/Dragging*		5	3
	Dunce Cap		5	3
	Honor-Fine		3	2
	Ladder		1	1
	Loss of Office		12	7
	Military Service		1	1
	Mutilation		5	3
	Pillory		17	10
	Prison**		52	29
	Restraining Order		1	1
	Torture		1	1
	Whipping		1	1
		Total Non-Lethal	147	87%
Capital				
	Boiling		1	1
	Decapitation		2	1
	Drowning		1	1
	Execution		7	4
	Hanging		24	14
		Total Capital	35	21%

Unknown				
	Exemplary Punishment		12	7
	Unspecified Punishment		10_	6__
		Total Unknown	22	13%

Figure 2: Distribution of punishments as a percent across all cases bearing a recorded sentence of the Parlement.

*Although drawing and dragging are categorized here and in the following figures as non-lethal, they were always followed by a sentence of hanging.

**I have here and in the following figures only counted instances of imprisonment that clearly denote a post-sentencing incarceration. Prison was used at various stages of the judicial process (e.g., to ensure presence at trial, to coerce a confession) and could be of varying severity and duration. I have limited the prison tally to reflect only the punitive detention of the judicially guilty.

Punishment Type	Punishment	Non *Lèse-Majesté*		*Lèse-Majesté*	
		No.	%	No.	%
Monetary					
	Confiscation	10	9	106	91
	Fee	19	34	37	66
	Fine	28	30	64	70
	Paying for Masses	—	—	1	100
Non-Lethal					
	Banishment	16	21	59	79
	Branding	—	—	17	100
	Confiscation of Seals	—	—	6	100
	Corporal Punishment	—	—	2	100
	Drawing/Dragging	—	—	20	100
	Dunce Cap	—	—	12	100
	Honor-Fine	1	16	6	84
	Ladder	—	—	1	100
	Loss of Office	13	59	9	41
	Mutilation	1	6	16	94
	Pillory	8	26	22	71
	Prison	19	14	116	86
	Restraining Order	—	—	1	100
	Whipping	1	100	—	—
Capital					
	Boiling	—	—	1	100
	Decapitation	—	—	13	100
	Drowning	—	—	11	100
	Execution	1	4	25	96
	Hanging	6	8	74	92

Unknown					
	Exemplary Punishment	2	5	36	95
	Unspecified Punishment	5	21	19	79

Figure 3: Instances of punishments as a percent between crimes of lèse-majesté and not, derived from sentencing data of the Parlement. This and the following figures are derived from tabulating the number of instances of a particular punishment against a particular crime, as opposed to the earlier values, which represent the percent of punishments awarded across cases. The difference is that, when looking at how particular crimes were punished, while a case may involve two individuals and crimes of treason and theft, one person could be hanged for the theft while the other was banished for the treason. In order to be able to accurately show the relationship, therefore, the following data is broken down by punishments of crimes awarded by, not by cases tried before, the Parlement.

	Armed Robbery	Counterfeiting	Forgery	Illicit Carrying of Arms	Kidnapping	*Lèse-majesté*	Private War	Rebellion	Royal Road	Viol. of Royal Ordinances	Violation of Royal Safeguard	Violence vs Royal Officers
Monetary												
Confiscation	17	—	7	24	21	29	33	19	—	20	18	20
Fee	17%	—	2%	6%	4%	4	33	6	8	—	9	—
Fine	17	33	—	24	4	17	33	19	—	13	21	13
Paying for Masses	—	—	—	—	—	—	—	—	—	—	—	—
Non-Lethal												
Banishment	—	—	2	—	13	21	—	13	—	13	7	13
Branding	—	—	7	—	—	4	—	—	8	—	—	—
Confiscation of Seals	—	—	—	—	—	4	—	6	—	7	—	7
Drawing/ Dragging	—	—	5	—	—	—	—	6	8	—	—	—
Dunce Cap	—	—	9	—	4	4	—	6	8	—	—	—
Honor-Fine	—	—	—	—	—	—	—	—	—	—	4	—
Ladder	—	—	—	—	4	4	—	6	—	—	—	—
Loss of Office	—	—	7	—	—	—	—	—	—	—	—	—
Mutilation	—	—	5	6	—	4	—	6	15	—	—	—
Pillory	—	—	11	6	4	21	—	13	8	—	2	—
Prison	33	—	9	18	29	25	—	19	—	20	28	20

	Armed Robbery	Counterfeiting	Forgery	Illicit Carrying of Arms	Kidnapping	*Lèse-majesté*	Private War	Rebellion	Royal Road	Viol. of Royal Ordinances	Violation of Royal Safeguard	Violence vs Royal Officers
Capital												
Boiling	—	33	—	—	—	—	--	—	—	—	—	—
Decapitation	—	—	—	—	—	8	—	—	8	—	—	—
Drowning	—	—	—	—	4	—	—	—	8	—	—	—
Execution	—	—	—	—	—	4	—	—	—	7	2	7
Hanging	—	33	18	—	4	21	—	6	31	—	—	—
Unknown												
Exemplary Punishment	—	—	—	12	17	8	—	—	—	13	5	13
Unspecified Punishment	17	—	—	6	8	—	—	—	—	7	5	7

Figure 4: Showing what percent of a given crime of *lèse-majesté* received a particular punishment.

Breach of *assurément*, Homicide, and Murder have been omitted as the data for them is less certain.

	Royal	Court	Other	Officers
Confiscation	50%	50%	—	100%
Dunce Cap	25%	25%	50%	—
Execution	50%	25%	25%	13%
Exile	100%	—	—	100%
Loss of Office	33%	66%	—	66%
Pillory	40%	60%	—	20

Figure 5: Distribution of penalties as percents in crimes of forgery across the categories Forgeries of Royal Letters and Letters of Commission, Forgeries of Court Documents, All Other Forgeries, and Forgeries Committed by Royal Officers.

Chapter 10

Connie L. Scarborough
(Texas Tech University, Lubbock)

Women as Victims and Criminals in the *Siete Partidas*

According to Armin Wolf, the legislative endeavors of Alfonso X in Spain were part of a trend throughout Europe to codify laws during the thirteenth century. During the relatively brief period between 1231 and 1281 major law codes were compiled from Sicily to Iceland.[1] Alfonso, like other rulers of the time, made a significant break with previous legal traditions. Laws, before the reign of Alfonso, were by and large a hodgepodge collection of local customary laws, municipal ordinances (some quite extensive), and local privileges.[2] Alfonso X was not only seeking uniformity of laws across his kingdoms but also wanted to use his authority as legislator to strengthen royal power in general and provide subsequent rulers with tools to confront legal issues that might arise in the future.[3] As many critics have pointed out, it is no coincidence that Alfonso began his greatest legislative project, the *Siete Partidas*, in 1256—the year in which he was first approached as a candidate for the post of Holy Roman Emperor. We may safely conjecture that Alfonso was thinking of his own and his nation's future as a leader in Europe. Spain would need a thorough law code which would potentially serve as a model for all legislative treatises throughout an empire in which Spain would occupy a leadership role.[4]

During the thirty-two years of Alfonso's reign his judicial project evolved in various stages. The first general law code enacted by Alfonso was the *Fuero Real*.

1 Armin Wolf, "El movimiento de legislación y de codificación en Europa en tiempos de Alfonso El Sabio," *Alfonso X el Sabio, vida, obra y época I*, ed. Juan Carlos de Miguel Rodríguez, et. al. (Madrid; Sociedad Española de Estudios Medievales, 1989), 31–37; here 31.

2 Juan Manuel Pérez-Prendes, "Las leyes de Alfonso el Sabio," *Revista de Occidente* 43 (1984): 67–84; here 67.

3 Pérez-Prendes, "Las leyes de Alfonso el Sabio," 68 (see note 2).

4 Pérez-Prendes, "Las leyes de Alfonso el Sabio," 83 (see note 2).

The first manifestation of this treatise in 1255 contained 550 laws. Its main author was probably Jacobo de las Leyes, the most important jurist residing in Alfonso's court.[5] The fourth section of the *Fuero Real* is a penal code which deals with crimes ranging from theft to illegal sexual activities to practicing medicine without a license. It also lays out the corresponding punishments and criminal proceedings for these and other offenses. At the same time that Alfonso and his jurists were compiling the *Fuero Real,* the court was working on a set of judicial norms for judges with legal justifications for the precepts outlined.

The first version of this project was the *Espéculo*. This work did not limit itself to legal precepts as had the *Fuero Real*. The *Espéculo* also contained philosophical and didactic commentary, explanations of legal terminology and institutions, and moral considerations.[6] But the culminating and most complete of the Alfonsine law codes was, without doubt, the *Siete Partidas*. The seven divisions of this treatise deal with (1) the Catholic faith and Canonical Law, (2) the organization of an Empire, especially the duties and proper behavior of the king and his family, (3) lawyers, the courts, and the legal system in general, (4) family law, (5) civil and mercantile obligations and contracts, (6) wills and the rights of inheritance, and (7) penal law for crimes and corresponding punishments and the proper manners for rendering justice.[7]

According to Theresa Vann, Alfonso's *Siete Partidas* "developed the concept of a peaceful kingdom whose law-abiding members co-operated in the defense of the realm under the direction of its head."[8] To develop a law-abiding citizenry meant a clear enumeration of what acts were deemed criminal and how offenders would be prosecuted. This paper will deal primarily with laws from the *Seventh Partida* or *Part* since it deals specifically with crimes and punishments but I will also make some references to laws in the other *Partidas*. Within the wide scope of crimes enumerated in the *Siete Partidas* I want to confine my remarks to those in which women are the perpetrators or victims of crimes. I will also cite examples from literature of the period which depict women involved in legal matters or as victims or accused criminals.

Women are not considered a homogenous group with regard to crimes or the administration of justice. It is not surprising that women are mentioned most often

---

5 Antonio Pérez Martín, "Hacia un Derecho Común Europeo: la obra jurídica de Alfonso X," *Alfonso X: Aprotaciones de un rey castellano a la construcción de Europa*, ed. Carlos Estepa Díez, et al. (Murcia: Región de Murcia, Consejaría de Cultura y Educación, 1997), 109–34; here 120.

6 Pérez Martín, "Hacia un Derecho Común Europeo," 121 (see note 5).

7 Pérez Martín, "Hacia un Derecho Común Eurpeo," 122–24 (see note 5).

8 Theresa M. Vann, "Criminal Settlement in Medieval Castilian Towns," *The Final Argument: The Imprint of Violence on Society and in Medieval and Early Modern Europe*, ed. Donald J. Kagay and L. J. Andrew Villalon (Woodbridge, Suffolk, and Rochester, NY: The Boydell Press, 1998), 83–94; here 87.

in laws concerning sexual relationships and marriage. However, women are also specifically named both as defendants and accusers in a number of other legal matters. Alfonso X and his legal experts recognized women as a special category under the law even though most punishments specifically name men as the guilty party.[9] Just as men and women are not always treated equally in the *Siete Partidas*, neither are all women treated equally. Female slaves are considered differently from free virgins. And virgins are treated differently from married women or widows. Female religious formed another category as did women of the Jewish or Muslim faith.

To accomplish its goal of inclusivity and comprehensiveness, the *Siete Partidas* deals with women from all social classes and faiths and, in many cases, differentiates consequences for crimes committed by or against women. For example, no punishment was inflicted on a pregnant woman until after the birth of the child because an unborn child should not be punished for an offense for which the mother is guilty.[10] And, in the same law, we learn that if anyone knowingly executes a pregnant woman, he will suffer the same penalty as one who wrongfully commits murder. These protections for pregnant women were also part of Canon Law. But, according to Richard Sims, "In the medieval world. . ..expectancy would do nothing more than delay the inevitable and, as a result, few women would have feigned pregnancy."[11]

Particularly pertinent to our discussion of women and Alfonsine laws are the strict provisions against abortion. Pregnant women who successfully induce themselves to abort either by taking drugs or by striking the abdomen are condemned to death.[12] A husband who strikes his pregnant wife causing her to abort the child suffers the same penalty.[13] This criminalization of abortion in the Alfonsine laws, interestingly, does not extend to include acts of infanticide. But,

---

9 Asenjo González, in studying the Fuero de Soria, explains that since men are most often named in regard to specific punishments we should assume that there was no difference for penalties levied on women, except in the special cases of crimes dealing with sexual matters in which the woman is most often the victim of the crime. See María Asenjo González, "La mujer y su medio social en el Fuero de Soria," *Las mujeres medievales y su ámbito jurídico: Actas de las Segundas Jornadas de Investigación Interdisciplinaria*, (Madrid: Seminario de Estudios de la Mujer, Universidad Autónoma de Madrid, 1983), 45–57; here 48.

10 This and all subsequent citations from the *Siete Partidas* are from the five-volume edition by Burns of Samuel Parsons Scott's English translation. I first cite volume and page number followed by the Partida, Title and Law referenced. Robert I Burns, S.J., *Las Siete Partidas*, trans. Samuel Parsons Scott. 5 vols. The Middle Ages Series (Philadelphia: University of Pennsylvania Press, 2001); here V: 1468, Partida VII, Title 31, Law 11.

11 Richard J. Sims, "Secondary Offenders? English Women and Crime *c.* 1220–1348," *Victims and Viragos?*, ed. Christine Meek and Catherine Lawless. Studies on Medieval and Early Modern Women, 4 (Dublin: Four Courts Press, 2005), 69–88; here 71.

12 V: 1346–47, Partida VII, Title 8, Law 8.

13 V: 1347, Partida VII, Title 8, Law 8.

canonical decrees from the same period impose "severe penalties for infanticide, for accidental suffocation of infants by parents, and even for the possibility of negligence when a child dies and the parents may not have done everything possible to prevent it."[14]

In the twelfth century, three papal rulings were issued on the issue of infanticide.[15] However, as Boswell notes, "In the law of the Frisians, promulgated under Charlemagne in the ninth century (but reflecting older customs) specifically exempted mothers who killed their newborn children from the normal fines for murder . . . . ."[16] And Sims asserts that "Infanticide has long been perceived as being almost exclusively in the female domain."[17] But Hanawalt, in her studies of Medieval England, concludes that infanticide was extremely rare[18] and Boswell asserts that Hanawalt's findings are probably applicable to continental Europe as well.[19] Sims, on the other hand, disputes both Hanawalt's methodology and conclusions. He claims that, when considering the death of children, we must take into account the deaths of older children in addition to those of infants. He states that "Although [children] were more likely than adults genuinely to encounter accidental death, through folly or curiosity, this also meant that their killings were potentially easier to disguise. If women had a greater ability to conceal crimes, as many have suggested, then infanticide was an ideal opportunity for them to exercise this gift."[20]

An example of infanticide is found in the fifteenth-century *Castigos e documentos del rey don Sancho*. Chapter 82 of this work contains the story of a woman who, after she is widowed, has sexual relations with her deceased husband' s brother. She has three children by him and she kills each one shortly after birth so as to conceal her ongoing relationship with her brother-in-law. She is so distraught by her actions that she eats a poisonous spider in order to kill herself. When she begins to suffer the painful effects of the spider's poison, she calls out to the Virgin to forgive her. Holy Mary reaches out, touches the woman and cleans the poison from her body. She thereafter lives a live of penance and service to the Virgin.[21]

Partida 7, Title 8, Law 12 does not refer to women killing their children, but does address the murder of any family member by another. It prescribes the

---

14 John Boswell, *The Kindness of Strangers: The Abandonment of Children in Western Europe from Late Antiquity to the Renaissance* (New York: Pantheon Books, 1988), 222.

15 Boswell, *The Kindness of Strangers*, 279–80 (see note 14).

16 Boswell, *The Kindness of Strangers*, 211 (see note 14).

17 Sims, "Secondary Offenders?," 72 (see note 11).

18 Barbara A. Hanawalt, *"Of Good and Ill Repute": Gender and Social Control in Medieval England* (New York and Oxford: Oxford University Press, 1998), 168.

19 Boswell, *The Kindness of Strangers*, 411 (see note 14).

20 Sims, "Secondary Ofenders?," 73 (see note 11).

21 This same story appears as no. 201 in the *Cantigas de Santa Maria.*

punishment (accredited to "the emperors and the learned men of the ancients") that the guilty party "should be publicly scourged in the presence of all, and besides should be enclosed in a leather sack, along with a dog, a cock, a serpent, and an ape; and after he had been placed in it with these four animals the mouth of the sack should be sewed up, and they should all be thrown into the sea or into the river nearest to the place where this occurred."[22] Radin claims that this form of execution, known as the *poena cullei,* is ancient in origins. It appears in the *Lex Pompeia de Parricidiis* which extended this specific punishment, earlier exclusively levied for the crime of partricide, to the killing of any other members of one's family. But, as Radin notes, the *Lex Pompeia* incorporated parts of Constantine's constitution and he claims that the introduction of the four specific animals to the punishment is actually Constantine's.[23]

The punishment itself as spelled out in the *Lex Cornelia de Sicarriss* (passed in B.C.E. 82) states that the guilty party was "whipped till he bled, sewn up in a sack with a dog, cock, viper, and ape, and thrown into the sea, if the sea was at hand, and if not, by a constitution of Hadrian, he was exposed to wild beasts, or, in the time of Paulus, to be burnt."[24] By the time of Constantine this law was obsolete and it appears that its revival could have been part of Constantine's efforts to denigrate animals that had been associated with pagan cults or had ritual significance as instruments for carrying off the societal pollution associated with murder.[25] Even though various theories have been postulated regarding the animals used in the *poena cullei,* Radin concludes that their symbolic and ritual meanings are the most probable.[26]

Whether the original punishment stipulated in the *Lex Cornelia de Sicarris* and repeated in the *Siete Partidas* was ever carried out in Spain, we have no records one way or the other. But this extreme form of execution is gruesome enough to substantiate a claim that the *Siete Partidas* considered any murder within one's own

22 V: 1349, Partida 7, Title 8, Law 12.

23 Max Radin, "The Lex Pompeia and the Poena Cullei," *The Journal of Roman Studies* 10 (1920): 119–30; here 126.

24 http://penelope.uchicago.edu/Thayer/E/Roman/Texts/secondary/SMIGRA*/Leges_Corneliae.html#de_Sicariis. My thanks to my colleague, Dr. Jason Banta for this reference (last accessed on May 23, 2010).

25 Radin, "The Lex pompeia," 129 (see note 23). Radin further explains: "This abhorred thing, this *prodigium,* by way of abundant caution, is to have its evil forces still further neutralised by having them first transferred, to certain living animals capable of becoming vehicles of such forces, and then by having these animals promptly killed" (130).

26 Radin discounts other claims for the selection of these creatures for the punishment as mere guesses or fanciful speculation. See especially 121–23 of his article (see note 23). This critic sees a progression in this punishment from the mere tying up in a sack and the introduction of the animals: "if we assume that the sack and its ritual were ancient, that the *Lex Pompeia* introduced the viper, Claudius the ape, and Constantine the dog and the cock" (126).

family as a most grievous crime. Murder of a family member is also one of the very few instances when a woman can bring an accusation of death against the alleged murderer.[27] Slaves or servants are also obliged to go to the help of anyone in the household if he/she is being attacked by another member of the family. If they fail to try to protect the victim, either intervening by force or seeking the intervention of the authorities, the servants or slaves may be put to death[28]

Another matter of serious concern for Alfonsine legislation is prostitution. Interesting, many of the laws in the *Siete Partidas* which deal with prostitution are aimed at the men (procurers) who force women into prostitution. Procurers are divided into five categories. The first are pimps who set up women in brothels and keep part of their earnings for themselves. The second are brokers who, for a price, provide clients with women who prostitute themselves in their (the women's) home. The third kind of procurer keeps captives or other girls in his home for the purpose of prostituting them and keeping the wages. The fourth is one who is a procurer for his own wife and the fifth is one who consents to a married, or otherwise honorable, woman having sexual relationships in his house in return for some gift. The laws state that all these procurers bring dishonor upon the women whom they prostitute and these men are also responsible for the fights and quarrels that break out among the women's clients.[29]

If a procurer is convicted, he is driven out of town along with the women who had been his prostitutes. Anyone who knowingly rents out his house to a woman to serve as a brothel, loses his property which is forfeited to the royal treasury. He also must pay a fine of ten pounds of gold. If a man forces his female slave to prostitute herself for his financial benefit, the women shall be set free. But, if a man forces a free woman into prostitution, he must provide her with a dowry and arrange a good marriage for her. If he fails to do so, after being found guilty of procurement, he is sentenced to death. Any man found guilty of prostituting his wife is put to death. Death is also imposed on anyone who acts is a procurer for any married women, virgin, nun or widow of good reputation.[30] The very last sentence of this Title states that women who serve as procuresses are subject to the same laws and punishments as established for male procurers.

---

27 V: 1350,Partida 7, Title 8, Law 14. Also, Patricia Orr, "*Non Potest Appellum Facere:* Criminal Charges Women could not—but did—bring in Thirteenth-Century English Royal Courts of Justice," *The Final Argument*, 141-60; here 142 (see note 8). Orr has found that, although women in Medieval England by law could only make criminal charges for the death of a husband or injury to herself, this restriction was routinely ignored by the courts and women's charges were most often heard and adjudicated.

28 V: 1350, Partida 7, Title 8, Law 16.

29 V: 1429, Partida 7, Title 22, Law 1.

30 V: 1429, Partida 7, Title 22, Law 2.

An entire Title, number 17, is set aside for laws dealing with adultery. This Title contains sixteen individual laws about accusations of adultery, possible defenses, and punishment of the guilty party, almost always the wife. Adultery is defined as "an offense which a man knowingly commits by lying with a married woman, or one betrothed to another."[31] In the same law where we find this definition we are informed that women, of course, may also commit adultery and, by so doing, they dishonor their husbands. But the husband who has sex with another woman is said to do no dishonor to his wife.

The law argues that a woman who commits adultery potentially could give birth to a child who would inherit equally with her and her husband's legitimate offspring. For this reason, among others, the law states that "the husband should have the . . . power to accuse his wife of adultery if she commits it, and that she should not have the right to accuse him."[32] A woman accused of adultery is acquitted without the need to put up a defense if it is discovered that she committed adultery with the consent of her husband or if he had acted as a procurer for his wife.[33] In this instance, the husband suffers the punishment usually leveled on the adulterous wife, i.e. public scourging and confinement in a monastery. If a man suspects his wife is having an adulterous affair he should send a written statement to the man in question, forbidding him to enter his house, be alone with his wife in any other house, or to speak to her. He is required to warn the suspected adulterer three times in writing. If the man does not heed the warning and stay away from the wife, the husband may kill the man without penalty if he later finds him alone with his wife.[34]

A husband can kill with immunity any man he finds with his wife in the act of committing intercourse, whether the husband had given him previous warning or not. But, in this case, the husband cannot kill his wife, but must turn her over to a judge to pass sentence on her.[35] Alfonsine legislation on this point differs from the older customary laws, or *fueros*, in Spain. For example in the *Fuero de Cuenca* and the *Fuero de Sepúlveda*, "the offended husband has the right to kill without penalty both his wife and the man if discovered in *flagrante delicto*."[36] And this right is extended to any of the woman's kinsmen in the *Fuero de Sepúlveda*.[37]

31 V: 1411, Partida 7, Title 17, Law 1.

32 V: 1411, Partida 7, Title 17, Law 1.

33 V: 1414, Partida VII, Title 17, Law 7.

34 V: 1416, Partida VII, Title 17, Law 12.

35 V: 1417, Partida 7, Title 17, Law 13.

36 Heath Dillard, "Women in Reconquest Castile: The Fueros of Sepúlveda and Cuenca," *Women in Medieval Society*, ed. Susan Mosher Stuard. The Middle Ages Series (Philadelphia: University of Pennsylvania Press, 1976), 71–94; here 81.

37 Dillard, "Women in Reconquest Castille," 81 (see note 36). According to Dillard: "neither *fuero* permits killing the man and not the wife, that is, forgiving her after the fact. It is the dishonor

However, when a father finds his married daughter in *flagrante delicto*, he has the right to kill her and the man. Furthermore, the law stipulates that he should not kill one and leave the other alive.

The reason given for this dictate is that a father may want to spare his daughter but, if he does so, this would leave his son-in-law to suffer dishonor.[38] When a man is found guilty of having committed adultery with another man's wife, he must be put to death. But if the woman is convicted she is punished by being publically scourged and shut up in a convent. She also loses her dowry and her marriage gifts and these are forfeited to her husband. Husbands also have the option to pardon a wayward wife within the first two years of her confinement.[39] In one aspect punishments for men and women in Title 17 are the same. If a man or a woman knowingly marries while his first wife or her first husband is still alive, they are equally guilty of adultery and both are banished to an island for a period of five years. They also lose all their property, with half going to any children or grandchildren they may have and the other half to the royal treasury.[40] Punishment differs, however, if a married woman is convicted of having committed adultery with her slave. In this case, both the slave and the woman are sentenced to death by burning.[41]

An example of this situation is found in the *Cantigas de Santa Maria,* also compiled at Alfonso's court.[42] In *Cantiga 186* a mother-in-law plans the death of her daughter-in-law by ordering a Moorish servant to lie down next to her daughter-in-law while she is sleeping. She summons her son to see that his wife is in bed with the Moor. The husband wants to kill his wife on the spot, but his mother persuades him to accuse her before a magistrate. Both the innocent wife and the Moor are sentenced to be burned in the town square but the woman cries out to Holy Mary to save her from an unjust sentence of death. When the fire is lit, the Moor perishes but the falsely-accused wife is miraculously protected from the flames. In the *Libro de los exenlos por a.b.c.,* the punishment assigned for adultery is gouging out of the perpetrators' eyes and, in the case cited in *exenplo* 224, the son of a king is sentenced to this punishment.[43]

---

brought on the woman's husband and kinsmen which makes the crimes, and both offenders, must be punished."

38 V: 1418, Partida 7, Title 17, Law 14.

39 V: 1418, Partida 7, Title 17, Law 15.

40 V: 1419–20, Partida 7, Title 17, Law 16.

41 V: 1418, Partida 7, Title 17, Law 15.

42 Alfonso X el Sabio, *Cantigas de Santa Maria,* ed. Walter Mettmann. 3 vols. Clásicos Castalia, 134, 172, 178 (Madrid: Castalia, 1986–1989). All quotes from the *Cantigas de Santa Maria* are from this edition.

43 Clemente Sánchez de Vercial, *Libro de los exenplos por a.b.c.,* ed John E. Keller and Connie L. Scarborough. Ediciones Académicas, Serie I. Vol. 1 (Madrid: Ars Libri, 2000), 191. All references to the *Libro de exenplos por a.b.c.* are to this edition.

In chapter 77 of the *Castigos e documentos del Rey Don Sancho* adultery is condemned as antithetical to natural inclinations, even in animals. It cites such examples of monogamy as the turtledove. As punishment for adultery, it cites the case of the female swan who committed adultery and when her mate discovered the truth, he and all the other swans pecked her to death. In another case, a female swan has an adulterous relationship with a crow. When she lays eggs in her husband's nest and he realizes that the eggs are not his, he throws them out of the nest and he and the other swans peck the guilty wife to death. This same chapter of the *Castigos e documentos* likens adultery by either the husband or the wife to robbery since, in matrimony, the couple has exclusive rights to each other's body. If the body is given to another, it robs the offended partner of his "property."[44]

In the *Libro de los exenplos por a.b.c.*, number 63, a Roman kills his wife for merely looking out the window, evidence to him that she has not been faithful. Don Juan Manuel, in the *Crónica abreviada,* recounts the tale of a count from France who, while on pilgrimage in Spain, falls in love with a Spanish noblewoman, doña Argentina, whom he takes back with him to France. Doña Argentina's husband, Count Garci Fernandes, enlists the aid of the French count's daughter to locate his wife and her lover. When Garci Fernandes finds the couple he beheads them both.[45]

The next title in Partida 7, number 18, concerns the punishments for those who have intercourse with their female relatives or with women connected to them by affinity, specifically within the fourth degree. Anyone can bring an accusation against a man for engaging in incestuous relationships. If a man is convicted, he suffers the same punishment as that for adultery.

Likewise any woman who knowingly commits the same offence suffers the same penalty she would have incurred for being an adultress.[46] The punishments differ, however, according to rank. Although this Title makes no mention of how punishment is adjusted for women according to social rank, it does specify that a man of "high position" who is convicted of incest loses his rank and any office he holds and is banished to an island. If he has no legitimate children, all his properties are forfeited to the royal treasury. If the man convicted is of low social stature, he is publically scourged (as would be a woman) and is banished for life. Incest meets with different punishments in literature. In the *Libro de Apolonio*, for

---

44 *Castigos é Documentos del Rey Don Sancho*, ed. Pascual de Gayangos y Arce. Biblioteca de Autores Españoles, Escritores en prosa anteriores al siglo XV. Vol. 51 (Madrid: M. Rivadeneyra, 1860): 79–228, here 208: ". . .la mujer ha poderío sobre el cuerpo de su marido, segund que dice el Apóstol, é el marido sobre el cuerpo de la mujer, é cualquier que toma lo ajeno é lo da á otro comete furto é es ladron . . . ."

45 Don Juan Manuel, *Obras completas*, ed. José Manuel Blecua. 2 vols. Biblioteca Románica Hispánica IV, Textos, 15 (Madrid: Gredos, 1983), 2:279.

46 V: 1421, Partida 7, Title 8, Law 3.

example, a man and his daughter who engage in an incestuous relationship are both killed by a bolt of lightning.[47]

A story in the *Cantigas de Santa Maria* and in the *Libro de los exenplos por a.b.c.* recounts how a grieving widow has an incestuous relationship with her son. She becomes pregnant by her son and, even though, she kills the infant, Holy Mary forgives her both the sin of infanticide and of incest.[48] A most unusual incident involving a rumor of incest is found in the *Cantigas de Santa Maria,* number *255.* In this tale, there are rumors that a woman is having an illicit relationship with her son-in-law. Despite the fact that the rumors are untrue, the woman has her son-in-law murdered to put an end to the gossip. When accused, the mother-in-law claims that she had been driven to such a violent act because of her son-in-law's aggressive pursuit of her. Although this is a fabrication, when the accused woman is being lead through the town, clothed only in a shift, to the outskirts where she will burned, she stops and prays for deliverance before a statue of Holy Mary. The Virgin miraculously preserves her from being burned even though her executioners light the flames twice. This story also appears in chapter 272 of the *Libro de los exenplos por a.b.c.* In this version, the woman pays her neighbors to drown her son-in-law because of the rumors of her relationship with him. She confesses her sin to a priest but the priest betrays the secrecy of the confessional and denounces her to the judge. The young man's relatives demand that she be burned to death. Again, no matter how much wood they add to the fire the woman escapes unharmed because she had pleaded that Holy Mary deliver her.

Another type of incestuous relationship is related in chapter 404 of the *Libro de los exenplos por a.b.c.* In this tale a priest has a sexual relationship with his goddaughter. He thinks he has gotten away with this sin since he suffers no punishment for it. But after seven days he suddenly dies and, when he is buried, smoke and fire completely consume the grave and the priest's corpse.

In *Enxemplo 36* of *El Conde Lucanor,* a merchant goes on a journey, leaving his pregnant wife behind. He spends twenty years away from home, and, when he returns to his house clandestinely, peeks through the window, and sees his wife with a young man. The wife is still pining away for her husband but she takes great comfort in her son with whom she eats and sleeps (chastely). When the husband sees the pair in bed together, his first impulse is to kill them both. But he wisely refrains and soon hears his wife telling the young man to go down to the port the next day and see if her husband, the boy's father, is on the ship that had just arrived. The merchant then realizes that the young man is his own son, born

---

47 *Libro de Apolonio*, ed. Pablo Cabañas, 3rd ed. Odres Nuevos (Madrid: Editorial Castalia, 1969), 76.

48 *Cantiga 17* and *Libro de los exenplos por a.b.c. chapter 274.* In the latter version, no mention is made of the birth of a child to the incestuous pair.

after his departure, and rejoices that he had not given in to his anger and killed his wife and her companion.

Women as victims fall into a number of different categories in the *Siete Partidas* with punishments meted out according to the class and station of the victim. Punishments also differed according to the status of the perpetrator of the crime. For example, if a man of high social status seduces a virgin, widow or female member of a religious order, he loses half of his property which is forfeited to the royal treasury.[49] If the perpetrator of the seduction of these groups of women is of a lower caste, he is publically scourged and banished to an island for five years. And, if the guilty man is a slave or household servant he is burned for the offense.[50]

A complete title of Partida Seven (Title 20) is devoted to the crime of rape. This title covers acts of abduction (*raptus*) as well as cases of forced sexual intercourse. For an act of aggression to be considered rape this title stipulates that it must be perpetrated against a virgin, a married woman, a woman who belongs to a religious order or a widow living honorably. It was extremely difficult for a woman of bad reputation or a prostitute to file a charge of rape. Williams and Echols state that "Municipalities were especially unwilling to pursue complaints against men who raped ladies of the evening, since most people believed that only chaste women could be raped."[51]

Kim Phillips has pointed out some of the difficulties in studying rape in the medieval period. In her studies of English law from the twelfth to the fifteenth centuries, she notes that rape was not defined, as in modern times, by unconsenting will but rather in terms of the woman's assaulted body.[52] Visible injuries, such as bleeding wounds or torn clothing, were prerequisites to an accusation of rape. While such signs seem to imply resistance on the victim's part, it is interesting that loss of virginity or even the sexual act itself is not mentioned in English common law.[53] In contrast, the Alfonsine statue clearly mentions having sexual intercourse with a woman by force in Law 3 of Title 20. Rape of honorable women is called "an act of wickedness" because "great dishonor is inflicted upon the relatives of the woman who is violated, and great insolence is displayed

49 V: 1423, Partida 7, Title 19, Law 2.

50 V: 1423–24, Partida 7, Title 19, Law 2.

51 Marty Williams and Anne Echols, *Between Pit and Pedestal: Women in the Middle Ages* (Princeton, NJ: Markus Wiener Publishers, 1994), 95.

52 Kim M. Phllips, "Written on the Body: Reading Rape from the Twelfth to Fifteenth Centuries," *Medieval Women and the Law*, ed. Noël James Menuge (Woodbridge, Suffolk, UK: The Boydell Press, 2000), 125–44; here 125.

53 Phillips, "Written on the Body," 129 (see note 52).

against her lord by violating her in contempt of the ruler of the land where this is done."[54]

Since a woman's relatives are especially wronged in the case of rape, any of the victim's relatives can bring an accusation. If the relatives are unwilling to make the accusation anyone can denounce the attacker before the judge of the district where the rape occurred or before any magistrate who has authority over the accused.[55] Notably, the victim of the rape is not named among those who can make the accusation. This was also true in medieval England, as Hanawalt has shown. Hanawalt states that a rape victim either "told the crime to a group of neighborhood men who brought the indictment against the suspect in the king's name or her father's voice may be that reporting his despoiled property in the loss of his daughter's virginity."[56]

Hanawalt found in England that many times males involved in the justice system were reluctant to impose the death sentence on a man convicted of rape. Furthermore, the low rate of conviction for rape implies that male jurors did not perceive the damages done to a woman, even if it involved loss of virginity, were great enough to impose the ultimate penalty.[57] Also studying rape in medieval England, Sims concludes that the legal apparatus treated cases of rape with "apparent indifference."[58] He cites the reluctance of juries to convict, the number of appeals withdrawn and out-of-court settlements made as evidence of this indifference. He also adds that "A further impediment to justice was created by the medieval orthodoxy of the time, especially the idea that if a child was conceived, the woman must have consented to the intercourse."[59]

Gravdal examines records from the *Registre de l'Officialité de Cerisy* beginning in 1314, the oldest extant document recording rape trials in France. During a period of 85 years, twelve cases of rape or reported rape are found in the court records. Gravdal states that "The figure is low, partly because in the Middle Ages, as at present, many rapes went unreported and also because only virgins or high-status rape victims actually had their day in court."[60] Interestingly, in ten of these twelve

---

54 V: 1425, Partida 7, Title 20, Law 1.

55 V: 1425, Partida 7, Title 20, Law 1.

56 Hanawalt, "*Of Good and Ill Repute*," 124 (see note 18).

57 Hanawalt, "*Of Good and Ill Repute*," 135–36 (see note 18).

58 Sims, "Secondary Offenders?," 81 (see note 11).

59 Sims, "Secondary Offenders?," 81 (see note 11). William of Conches (d. ca. 1154) had written that even if rape was initially displeasing, female flesh was so libidinousness that she would ultimately give into the pleasure of the act and become pregnant. See Dyan Elliott, *Fallen Bodies: Pollution, Sexuality, and Demonology in the Middle Ages*. The Middle Ages Series (Philadelphia: University of Pennsylvania Press, 1999), 37.

60 Kathryn Gravdal, *Ravishing Maidens: Writing Rape in Medieval French Literature and Law* (Philadelphia: University of Philadelphia Press, 1991), 125. For a study of rape as reflected in Middle High German, Latin, and other literatures, see Albrecht Classen, *Sexual Violence and Rape*

cases identified by Gravdal the accused rapists were churchmen and, in all these cases, the fathers of the accused paid the fines levied on their sons. These facts lead Gravdal to conclude that "these collective rapes may have been a sexual rite of passage, fairly well accepted in the community."[61]

Williams and Echols argue that in some areas, communities forced priests to wed to protect women from unmarried clerics. They conclude that such measures were warranted, citing the case of the vicar of Brent, Eleigh, who raped Margaret Webbe. This clergyman was obviously not a first-time offender because the judge who heard the case called him a "common ravisher of wives and virgins."[62] The *Registre Criminel de la Justice de Saint-Martin-des Champs à Paris*[63] (1332–1357) is more complete than the Cerisy register but it contains only six rape cases in over 25 years of litigation.[64] Among these six accusations of rape, one resulted in imposition of the death penalty, two of the accused disappeared, and three were absolved.[65] The death penalty was imposed for the rape of two twelve-year-old girls both of whom were apprentices to a tailor who was accused of their rape. This punishment seems to have been imposed because the girls were considered "property" placed in the care of the rapist's family.[66]

Rape victims were often required to produce witnesses in court and to demonstrate that they had forcibly resisted the attack. If there were no witnesses, the normal practice was for the accused to be absolved of any guilt.[67] In customary law in Spain, the *Fuero de Sepúlveda*, for example, states that if a woman is raped, "she must walk around the walls of the town and call out her complaints and the name of the rapist as she makes her way up to the gate of the castle, there summoning forth the town's elected officials to hear her grievances. The following Sunday she issues a complaint against the man with two kinsmen and two other

in the Middle Ages: A Critical Discourse in Premodern German and European Literature. Fundamentals of Medieval and Early Modern Culture, 7 (Berlin and New York: De Gruyter, 2011).

61 Gravdal, *Ravishing Maidens*, 125 (see note 60) asserts that "Since the medieval Church was more clement than the state in its dealings with rapists, it is not surprising to discover the leniency with which Church courts treated their own clergymen in rape cases."

62 Williams and Echols, *Between Pit and Pedestral*, 86 (see note 51).

63 Gravdal, *Ravishing Maidens*, 124 (see note 60): This *Registre* contains "the court *acta* of a wealthy seignorial courts, independent of the jurisdiction of the provost of Paris at Châtelet. Saint-Martin was a Benedictine community that derived enormous wealth from its property and rents in the neighborhood. . . . The community hired secular judges, called *maires* (mayors) to man its court and administer justice in its jurisdiction. The secular judges applied criminal law."

64 Gravdal, *Ravishing Maidens*, 128 (see note 60).

65 Gravdal, *Ravishing Maidens*, 128 (see note 60).

66 Gravdal, *Ravishing Maidens*, 129 (see note 60).

67 Gravdal, *Ravishing Maidens*129–30 (see note 60). Gravdal also states that "if any slur could be made on [he rape victim's] character, or if she failed to follow correct legal procedure at any point, the case would be dismissed" (130).

citizens; the man can prove his innocence with twelve witnesses."[68] The *Fuero of Cuenca* gave a woman three days to make a complaint of rape. She had to show her injuries to the town officials and the accused could be absolved if he produced twelve witnesses to support his innocence.[69]

By the thirteenth century, punishments for rape in both civil and canonical law were severe.[70] Ecclesiastical courts could impose fines or order the offender to be flogged, providing the whipping did not draw blood.[71] Secular courts could impose a variety of penalties, ranging from death, mutilation (but the *Siete Partidas* strictly forbid castration, which was allowed in other parts of Europe),[72] exile, loss of property, fines, compensation for the victim or her family, imprisonment, and flogging.[73] In Law 3 of Title 20 of the *Siete Partida* a man convicted of raping a widow of good reputation, a virgin, a married woman, or one belonging to a religious order is sentenced to death and all his property goes to the woman whom he violated.[74]

But, as Brundage and others have observed, rape was very rarely punished with the severity allowed by civic or canon statutes.[75] The most common sentences were fines, imprisonment for a short time or some combination of the two.[76] In the *Fuero Real,* another Alfonsine law code, the fines for rape depended on the marital status on the victim. Rape of widows was penalized at 200 *sueldos,* the rape of a virgin at 100 *sueldos,* and the violation of a married woman at 300 *sueldos.*[77] Brundage

---

68 Dillard, "Women in Reconquest Castile," 80–81 (see note 36).

69 Dillard, "Women in Reconquest Castile," 81 (see note 36).

70 For an interesting discussion of how the royal and legal concerns about rape changed over time from that of imposing royal authority to that of protection of men's "property" rights vis-à-vis profitable marriages (based on the daughters' virginity), see Phillips, "Written on the Body," 138–42 (see note 52).

71 James A. Brundage, *Law, Sex, and Christian Society in Medieval Europe* (Chicago: The University of Chicago Press, 1987), 471.

72 Partida VII, Title 8, Law 8 states in part: "If any one. . .castrates a freeman or directs him to be castrated, we order that punishment shall be inflicted for this not only upon the party who committed the act, but also upon him who ordered it to be committed. . .. If the castrated person is a slave, and his master caused this to be done, he shall lose him, but shall receive no other punishment, and the slave shall become the property of the royal treasury. The physician or surgeon who castrates any one shall suffer the penalty for homicide, except where he performed the operation to cure the person of some disease which he had, or which he feared that he would contract" (V: 1349).

73 Brundage, *Law, Sex, and Christian Society,* 471 (see note 71).

74 V: 1425.

75 Brundage, *Law, Sex, and Christian Society,* 472 (see note 71).

76 Brundage, *Law, Sex, and Christian Society,* 530 (see note 71).

77 Asenjo Gonazález, "La mujer y su medio social," 56 attributes the larger fines imposed for the rape of a widow as opposed to a virgin to dignify the social position of the widow and potentially deter physical aggression towards her since she did not enjoy the protection of a husband (see note 9).

observes that "When compared with the savage mutilations and death sentences routinely handed down for robbery and other kinds of assault, these were very mild punishments indeed."[78] However, Phillips found that in medieval England, a man convicted of the rape of a virgin could be sentenced to the loss of eyes and testicles. On the other hand, this critic observes that if the victim is a married woman, widow, nun, matron, concubine, or prostitute the perpetrator was punished with much less severity.[79]

In some cases the woman chose, or her family forced her, to marry her abductor or rapist. According to the *Siete Partidas,* if she married the accused, the man's property reverts to the father or the mother of the woman who was ravished if they did not consent to the violation or the marriage. If it is proved that the parents consented to their daughter's rape or abduction, all the man's property is forfeited to the royal treasury. If the woman who was abducted or raped is a member of a religious order, all the guilty man's property shall belong to the woman's convent. Brundage notes that in many municipal statutes, rape prosecutions were avoided altogether "if both parties were unmarried and were willing to marry each other, provided that the woman's parents approved the match."[80]

The legal punishments that could be inflicted upon men guilty of abduction or rape are also valid for those who knowingly assist them. But if a man, with or without accomplices, abducts or rapes a woman who is not a virgin, a married woman, a member of a religious order, or an honorable widow, according to the *Siete Partidas,* he suffers only banishment.[81] Gravdal found that in medieval Normandy, women were often harshly punished for being the victims of rape. For example, in 1391, Bertin Quenet was fined five sous for breaking into the house of Alicia, a widow, and raping her. Despite the fact that the court recognized the fact that Quenet had used violence to break into Alicia house, the widow was fined fifteen sous for allowing herself to be raped.[82] In another case from the *Registre Criminel de la Justice de Saint-Martin-des Champs à Paris* Jacqueline la Cyrière was accused of luring a ten-year-old girl into her home where she helped a Lombard soldier to rape the child. Jacqueline is sentenced to be burned at the stake but there is no mention made of the Lombard soldier, who possibly had escaped.[83]

Rape, in literary texts from Spain, is treated quite seriously. For example, in the *Libro de los exenplos por a.b.c.,* we find the story of the rape of the noble Roman woman, Lucrecia, by the son of the emperor.[84] He sneaks into her chamber when

78 Brundage, *Law, Sex, and Christian Society,* 530 (see note 71).
79 Phillips, "Written on the Body," 132 (see note 52).
80 Brundage, *Law, Sex, and Christian Society,* 531 (see note 71).
81 V: 1439, Partida 7, Title 25, Law 3.
82 Gravdal, *Ravishing Maidens,* 127 (see note 60).
83 Gravdal, *Ravishing Maidens,* 128 (see note 60).
84 Clemente Sánchez de Vercial, *Libro de los exenplos por a.b.c,* 73–75 (see note 44).

her husband is at war and puts a knife to her throat. After he rapes her, Lucrecia sends letters to her father, brothers, and husband, denouncing the crime, and telling them that, although she was forced, she cannot live with the dishonor. Lucrecia kills herself. Her male relatives vow revenge and drive the emperor and his guilty son out of Rome. They capture the son and slit his throat, just as he had threatened Lucrecia before the rape. Another story of rape, or attempted rape, is recounted in the *Cantiga de Santa Maria 5*. In this miracle narrative, the emperor of Rome goes off on a crusade, leaving his beloved wife behind. In the emperor's absence, his brother tries to seduce the empress who refuses him and locks him in prison. When the emperor is about to return home, she releases the brother who goes immediately to tell the emperor that his wife had him locked away because he refused to have sex with her. Without waiting to find out the validity of his brother's claim, the emperor condemns his wife to death. He orders two hunters to take her into the woods and kill her. Before they do so, however, they vow to rape her. But, upon calling on the Virgin for help, she is rescued by a count who takes her to his home to serve as a nanny to his son. However, the count's brother soon tries to seduce the poor empress and, when she rejects him, he cuts the child's throat and plants the murder weapon on the empress. When the child's body is discovered, the court demands her death and some advocate burning her and others beheading her. However, she is sentenced to be handed over to a sailor who is to take her to sea and drown her. Not surprisingly, the sailor tries to have his way with her but the woman again cries out to Holy Mary to rescue her.

The sailor leaves off trying to rape her and decides to abandon her on a deserted, barren island. From there, she is miraculously rescued by a group of pilgrims on their way to Rome. When she arrives in Rome, the empress possesses the power to cure lepers. Among those she cures is the brother of the emperor who had falsely accused her. She agrees to cure his illness on the condition that he first confesses his sins. When the emperor learns that he had wrongly accused his wife, he begs her to take him back. But she refuses, preferring to enter a life of dedication to the Virgin.

In *Cantiga 291*, a student in Salamanca rapes a woman and tries to avoid justice by fleeing to the city of Toro. But the woman's parents and an officer of the law track him down and throw him into prison. He fears death in the prison and beseeches the Virgin to save him. He composes a beautiful song for Holy Mary who frees him from his cell, reminding him to live always in service to Her. In this tale, a life of dedication to the Virgin is seen as divine compensation for having committed the crime of rape. In *Cantiga 317*, a man tries to force a woman to have sex with him but she breaks free from him and seeks sanctuary inside a nearby church. She cries out and people come to her defense, shutting the doors of the church to protect her from the would-be rapist who was pursuing her. In his fury and frustration, the man tries to break down the doors of the church but breaks his leg in the process. He faints from the pain and, as a result of his sin, he is struck mute. The poem concludes, "maimed and crazy, he lived a long time and begged from door to door."[85] This is the punishment divinely-determined for trying to rape a woman.

Cantiga 355 is the tale of man saved from hanging after being falsely accused of rape. The punishment of hanging for rape is in keeping with the proscription in the *Siete Partidas* that a man found guilty of the rape of "a widow of good reputation, a virgin, a married woman, or one belonging to a religious order"[86] would be executed. In this *cantiga,* the woman is actually the aggressor. A young woman is madly in love with a youth, who rejects her. When he sets out on pilgrimage, she follows him and insists on accompanying him despite his efforts to dissuade her. He continues on the pilgrimage with the sulking girl in tow. On the return journey, just as they arrive at their hometown, the young woman begins to cry out loudly and scratches her face. She claims that the young pilgrim had raped her on the road and her relatives immediately denounce him to the authorities. Without being allowed to mount a defense, the young man is hanged. However, he prays to Holy Mary who knows that he is innocent. She places a stone under his feet so that he does not die from the hanging. There is no mention made of the fate that befell the woman who had falsely accused him.

Another example of false accusation is found in the *Libro de los exenplos por a.b.c.* In tale no. 172, a young man refuses to sleep with his mother and the mother seeks revenge by claiming before a judge that her son had tried to rape her. The young man does not want to defame his mother in public by refuting the accusation and telling the truth. Since the son refuses to defend himself against his mother's charges, the judge orders him sealed with pitch into a sack and thrown in the river.[87] Even though no less prestigious an advocate than Saint Andrew defends the boy, the judge does not believe him and orders the saint thrown in jail. Imprisoned, Saint Andrew prays and a lightning bolt strikes dead the mother who had falsely accused her son.

Rape is also the subject of chapter 246 of the *Libro de enxienplos por a.b.c.* When her city is besieged by a handsome king, the duchess offers to give up the city and marry him, despite having sons and daughters she should be protecting. When the king's men enter the city, they begin to ravage both men and women alike. The

85 "E des en / tolleit' e sen sen / viveu gran temp' e per portas pidia" (Alfonso X el Sabio, *Cantigas de Santa Maria*, III, 137; see note 42). English translations are from Kathleen Kulp-Hill, trans., *Songs of Holy Mary of Alfonso X, the Wise. A Translation of the* Cantigas de Santa Maria, Medieval and Renaissance Texts and Studies, 173 (Tempe, AZ: Arizona Center for Medieval and Renaissance Studies, 2000), 385.

86 V: 1425, Partida 7, Title 20, Law 1.

87 This is a variation on the *poena cullei* previously discussed as a punishment for killing members of one's family.

duchess's daughters escape rape by affixing rotten chicken meat to their breasts so that the stench drives away their would-be attackers. The king marries the duchess (or at least has one conjugal night with her), but the next day he hands her over to twelve of his men to enjoy her as they please. On the third day, he impales her with a lance through her vagina up to her throat.[88] The moral is that a licentious woman deserves such a punishment.

Separate laws were applied to sexual misconduct which was inter-racial or inter-ethnic, i.e., between a Christian and a Jew or a Moor. Any Jew or Moor who has intercourse with a Christian woman is condemned to death.[89] The death penalty is imposed regardless of the status of the woman. Even if the Christian woman is a prostitute, a Jew who engages in intercourse with her is put to death. The Christian woman who engages in sexual relations with a Jew suffers the same punishment as one who has intercourse with a Moor. If the Christian woman is a virgin or a widow, for the first offense, she forfeits half her property to her parents or grandparents or, if she has no relations, half her property belongs to the king. For a second offense, the Christian woman loses all her property to her relatives or the king, and she is condemned to death.

If a Moor has sexual intercourse with a married Christian woman, he is sentenced to death by stoning and the woman is turned over to her husband who may burn her to death or release her or do whatever he pleases with her.[90] If a Moor has sex with a Christian prostitute or dishonorable woman, for the first offense, the man and woman are scourged together and, for the second offense, both are put to death.[91]

Despite these harsh laws regarding interreligious sexual contact, Louise Mirrer points out that, in literature, the beautiful Jewess is a popular figure and she at times is portrayed as coupling with a Christian male.[92] According to Mirrer, the image of the beautiful Jewish woman was used "to reiterate the weakness of Jewish men, making public the sexual initiatives taken by their women."[93] An example of a Jewess being punished for a crime, probably sexual in nature, is found in song no. 107 of the *Cantigas de Santa Maria*. The poem states that the

---

88 Clemente Sánchez de Vercial, *Libro de los exenplos por a.b.c.*, 208: "fizole poner un palo por la natura fasta la garganta" (see note 44).

89 Partida 7, Title 25, Law 10 specifies that the penalty for a Moor will be death by stoning. In Partida, 7, Title, 24, Law 9 the method of execution for a Jew is not specified.

90 V: 1442, Partida 7, Title 25, Law 10.

91 V: 1442, Partida 7, Title 25, Law 10.

92 Louise Mirrer, *Women, Jews, and Muslims in the Texts of Reconquest Castile*. Studies in Medieval and Early Modern Civilizations (Ann Arbor: The University of Michigan Press, 1996), 31–32.

93 Mirrer, *Women, Jews, and Muslims*, 31–32 (see note 92).

Jewess "was caught in a crime and arrested and taken to be hurled from a high and rugged cliff."[94]

Other versions of this story clearly allude to the sexual nature of her crime and to the fact that the Jewess was accused of having extramarital relations with a Christian man.[95] The text specifies that it is the Jews who condemn and attempt to execute her. Also, as stipulated in the poem, she is dressed only in a shift. This detail is accurately portrayed in the miniatures accompanying the song. Mirrer finds this fact particularly significant since "male Jews would never have really undressed their women in front of Christians—or, for that matter, in front of Jews either. . . . Her stereotypical depiction as a beautiful, sexually attractive Jewess placed on display by male Jews symbolizes, in a variety of ways, male Jewish weakness vis-à-vis the Christian community."[96]

The accused woman, dubbed Marisaltos, calls on Holy Mary to save her after the Jews push her over the cliff. She promises the Virgin that she will convert to Christianity if she saves her. Of course, the Virgin delivers her unharmed to the rocky ground below. Marisaltos goes immediately to a church and is baptized. The Jewish men who had attempted to kill her for sexual misconduct outside the Jewish community are unsuccessful. A peculiar aspect of the Alfonsine version of this tale is that the Jewess is sentenced to death by her coreligionists but, as Benaim de Lasry has pointed out, the death sentence could not be handed out by rabbinical courts in the Middle Ages.[97]

Benaim de Lasry asserts that "A Spanish court . . . might have sentenced a married Jewess to death for committing adultery, whether her paramour was a Jew or a Christian, married or unmarried."[98] Since the *cantiga* does not specify whether Marisaltos was single or married, the fact that the Jews sentence her to execution is strange since, again according to Benaim de Lasry, "no Jewish court ever sentenced an unmarried Jewess to death for what Jewish law calls 'harlotry,' i.e., having sexual relations with a married or unmarried Jew or Gentile."[99] Mirrer

94 Alfonso el Sabio, *Cantigas de Santa Maria*, II, 28: "achada / que foi en err' e fillada / e a esfalfar levada / dũa pena qu' i está" (see note 44).

95 Mirrer, *Women, Jews, and Muslims*, 33 (see note 92).

96 Mirrer, *Women, Jews, and Muslims*, 39 (see note 92).

97 Anita Benaim de Lasry, "Marisaltos: Artificial Purification in Alfonso el Sabio's *Cantiga* 107," *Studies on the* Cantigas de Santa Maria: *Art, Music, and Poetry, Proceedings of the International Symposium on the* Cantigas de Santa Maria *of Alfonso X, el Sabio (1221–1284) in Commemoration of Its 700th Anniversary Year—1981 (New York, November 19–21)*, ed. Israel J. Katz and John E. Keller (Madison, WI: Hispanic Seminary of Medieval Studies, 1987), 299–311; here 301.

98 Benaim de Lasry, "Marisaltos," 302 (see note 97).

99 Benaim de Lasry, "Marisaltos," 301 (see note 97). Benaim de Lasry relates one example of a severe punishment handed down by a rabbinical tribunal on an unmarried Jewess who confessed to having sexual relations with a married Christian man: "When she became pregnant, she confessed her illicit relationship. After the birth of her children (twins), she was sentenced to have her nose

concludes that Alfonso's version of Marisaltos's story has political implications because a guilty Jewish woman who turns to Christianity is portrayed as immune to Jewish justice.[100]

As we have seen, the death penalty is imposed for a variety of crimes committed by men or women. Louis Gernet maintains that "The Death Penalty is a means of eliminating pollution . . . . It purifies the affected group, who are often partly or wholly absolved of responsibility for the newly spilt blood."[101] If we accept this theory, then women criminals were considered an especially grievous form of societal pollution. Gravdal's examination of court records in fourteenth-century France reveals that, although women were much less frequently accused of crimes than men, women's cases resulted in the death penalty being imposed three times more frequently than in cases involving men.[102] Also, in France, the methods of execution differed for men and women. Since hanging was ruled offensive to women's modesty, women sentenced to death were killed by burial alive for lesser offenses and by burning at the stake for serious offenses.[103] This observation about the severity of punishment for female offenders is reflected in the equally harsh punishments meted out in the *Siete Partidas* for crimes committed by Moors and Jews against Christians. Even though Alfonso X is often commended for the equable treatment of his subjects from these minority groups, his laws are quick to punish those Jewish or Moorish citizens who have inappropriate contact with Christians or who lead Christians astray.

Although imprisonment for a set number of years or months is not a punishment often specified in the *Siete Partidas*, the need to hold accused persons in custody until they are tried and convicted, or while they await a sentence to be carried out, is regulated by the laws in Partida 7, Title 29.[104] Among the seven kinds of punishment listed in Partida 7, Title 31, Law 31, the only mention of imprisonment is that which can be imposed on a slave. The Law emphatically states that no freeman shall suffer imprisonment as a form of punishment because "a prison is not for the purpose of punishing offenses, but only to secure persons until they are tried."[105] Law 5 of Title 31 deals exclusively with women prisoners.

---

cut off, so that the beauty of her face which she adorned for her adulterous wooer be disfigured, and that she be made to pay a fine to the lords of the city" (302).

100 Mirrer, *Women, Jews, and Muslims*, 44 (see note 92).

101 Quoted in René Girard, *Violence and the Sacred*, trans. Patrick Gregory (Baltimore and London: The Johns Hopkins University Press, 1977), 298.

102 Gravdal, *Ravishing Maidens*, 130 (see note 60).

103 Gravdal, *Ravishing Maidens*, 130 (see note 60).

104 Although a penal system, as such, did not exist in thirteenth-century Spain, there were circumstances where imprisonment was imposed. For example, see Michel Foucault, *The Foucault Reader*, ed. Paul Pabinow (New York: Pantheon Books, 1984), 214: "The prison predates its systematic use in the penal system."

105 V: 1465, Partida 7, Title 31, Law 4.

Female prisoners should not be put in prisons with men but rather confined to a convent. They are to be guarded by "good women until the judge makes such disposition of her as the laws direct."[106]

Torture is considered under Title 30 of the seventh Partida. No pregnant woman can be tortured until she gives birth.[107] Wives cannot be subjected to compulsion or torture in order to testify against their husbands nor can a husband be tortured to testify against his wife.[108]

Richard Sims claims that, among the general defenses available for a woman accused of a felony was that of marital coercion.[109] He states that "it was not necessary to take part in wrongdoing to prove [marital] obedience but the law was sympathetic to women who did take their loyalty to felonious ends."[110] While he is dealing specifically with law in medieval England, it seems likely that this was the case in Spain as well since the institution of marriage and control of women throughout Europe put a very high value on wifely obedience.[111] In order to protect innocent women from sharing in their husbands' guilt, Partida 7, Title 31, Law 9 specifies that a wife or child could not be punished because of any crime committed by her husband or the child's father.[112] Even if a wife stole from her husband, she cannot be charged with theft before the courts.[113] However, if it is determined that the wife had the assistance or advice of another in stealing from her husband, this third party can be sued for the stolen property.[114]

Foucault argues that we must view systems of punishment as "social phenomena that cannot be accounted for by the juridical structure of society alone, nor by its fundamental ethical choices."[115] He attributes the high rates of corporeal punishments during the feudal period to the fact that the body was in many cases the only property accessible to the judicial system.[116] While there are a number of corporeal penalties in the *Siete Partidas* and in the literary pieces we have examined, it is significant that monetary compensation in terms of retribution, fines, or loss of properties were also common means of punishment. Alfonso X was concerned about the future of his kingdom, how power would be exercised

---

106 V: 1453, Partida 7, Title 29, Law 5.

107 V: 1458, Partida 7, Title 30, Law 2.

108 V: 1461, Partida 7, Title 30, Law 9. This prohibition against torture to obtain testimony also applies to the father-in-law, mother-in-law, stepfather, stepmother, stepchildren, and emancipated slaves or their children of the accused (V: 1461, Partida 7, Title 30, Law 9).

109 Sims, "Secondary Offenders?," 71 (see note 11).

110 Sims, "Secondary Offenders?," 71 (see note 11).

111 Sims, "Secondary Offenders?," 71 (see note 11).

112 V: 1467, Partida 7, Title 31, Law 9.

113 V: 1380, Partida 7, Title 14, Law 4.

114 V: 1380, Partida 7, Title 14, Law 4.

115 Foucault, *The Foucault Reader*, 171 (see note 104).

116 Foucault, *The Foucault Reader*, 172 (see note 104).

and how kingly authority and justice would be wielded. He seems to have been fully aware of and in agreement with Foucault's analysis of punitive methods as not merely consequences of legislation but "as techniques possessing their own specificity in the more general field of other ways of exercising power."[117]

Alfonso X and his legal experts recognized women as a special category under the law. Just as men and women are not treated equally in the *Siete Partidas*, neither are all women treated equally, as we have seen. Honorable women such as virgins, married women, or widows were considered a category apart from women of bad repute or prostitutes. Female slaves are considered differently from free women. Female religious formed another category as did women of the Jewish or Muslim faith. Women as victims of crimes were also considered under various categories and the severity of punishment for the perpetrator of a crime varies when the victim is a virgin, a married woman, a widow, a religious, or a prostitute. Distinctions for women as victims are also made between free women and slaves, and Jewish, Christian, or Muslim women. To accomplish its goal of inclusivity and comprehensiveness, the *Siete Partidas* deals with women from different social classes, faiths/ethnicities, and marital status. Not only in the law codes but in literature, a wide variety of women are seen both as criminals and as victims. While literary texts do not always follow the letter of the law spelled out in the law code, there are significant examples of women involved in crimes, punishments, reprieves, and pardons in the texts we have seen.

117 Foucault, *The Foucault Reader*, 170 (see note 104). Similarly, but in a different context, Girard, *Violence and the Sacred*, 23, states that a judicial system "can only exist in conjunction with a firmly established political power" (see note 101).

Chapter 11

Maria Cecilia Ruiz
(University of San Diego)

Theft in Juan Manuel's *El Conde Lucanor*

Theft takes place in a number of stories in Juan Manuel's *El Conde Lucanor* (1335).[1] What is interesting about these stories, looked at together, is their variety: some focus on the thief or thieves, others focus on the targets and/or victims, depending on the didactic intent. There is invariably a possession or possessions that the thief or would be thief desires and that is owned by the victim or target. Objects of theft are, beside something material or wealth of some kind, the body, love, honor or even identity, reputation, credit and opportunities. The thieves carry out different strategies for carrying out their thefts. It is up to the targets (potential victims) to identify these strategies for what they are (see through the deceit) in order to not fall victim.[2] Some characters are successful and some are not. Whatever the result, Juan Manuel's unwavering stance is that there is no victim of theft who is completely without responsibility for falling victim (except the sick and the dead, as we shall see).

---

1 For the prevalence of theft in Spanish folk narratives in general, see Harriet Goldberg's *Motif-index of Medieval Spanish Folk Narratives* (Tempe, AZ: Medieval & Renaissance Texts & Studies, 1998). Pertaining to the stories' souces, see Reynaldo Ayerbe-Chaux, *El Conde Lucanor. Materia tradicional y originalidad creadora* (Madrid: José Porrúa Turanzas, S.A.,1975).

2 Marta Ana Diz's book, *Count Lucanor y Patronio: la lectura inteligente en "el tiempo que es turbio"* (Potomac, MD: Scripta Humanística, 1984) explains how the stories in the collection are about losing (negative examples) and not losing (positive examples) possessions, be they materialistic, temporal (like honor and fame), and/or spiritual (connection with God, the salvation of the soul, etc.). These possessions are organized by Catholic belief (or by common sense) in a hierarchy of importance, the salvation of the soul being the most important. Indeed, giving too much importance to one type of possession over another of less importance, for example, material wealth over one's own life, leads to loss of everything: wealth, life and soul. See also Marta Ana Diz, "Cambio, especulación e impostura en los relates de Patronio," *Homenaje a Ana María Barrenechea*, eds. Isaías and Lia Schwartz de Lerner (Madrid: Castalia, 1984), 229–34.

The stories that depict theft are varied also with respect to their sources and their varying degrees of Catholic content. For example, the only Catholic content that Juan Manuel put in the Aesopic tale of the fox who steals the cheese from the crow ("De lo que contesçio a vn raposo con vn cueruo que tenie un pedaço de queso en el pico," "What happened to the fox with the crow that had a piece of cheese in his beak"), is that the fox mentions God to the crow.[3] The moral, to see through flattery, is the same in both versions. On the opposite end, the Catholic content is paramount and theft is associated with sin and the devil, as in the tale of the thief who befriended the devil ("De lo que contesçio a vn omne que se fizo amigo et vasallo del diablo," "What happened to a man who made friends with the devil"). Catholic content is not developed in "De lo que contesçio a vn rey con vn omne quel dixo quel faria alquimia" (XX; "What happened to a king with a man who said he could do alchemy"), and "De lo que contesçio a vn rey con los burladores que fizieron vn panno" (XXXII; "What happened to a king with three tricksters who made him clothes"). However, both tales depict greedy kings. Though greed is not framed as a sin in either (example XXXII is of Arabic origin), the depiction of greed nevertheless indirectly reinforces the Catholic frame of the collection in which Patronio and Lucanor are Catholic and discuss what it means to be Catholic.

Two other tales that portray thieves and their victims are of Arabic origin; one of them ("De lo que contesçio a Saladin con vna buena duenna muger de vn su vasallo"; "What happened to Saladin with a good woman who was the wife of a vassal of his") has Catholic content, while the other ("De lo que contesçio a vn moro con vna su hermana que daua a entender que era muy medrosa"; "What happened to a Moor with his sister who acted very fearful") does not.[4] This latter tale, as I will show, contrasts remarkably with the very Catholic tale of the thief who befriends the devil. I link the two examples to the topic of poverty.

Both main characters are poor and resort to stealing in order to get out of poverty. In the Catholic example the thief's greed leads to his final punishment. The Arabic tale, on the other hand, does not portray theft as a sin. In other words, Juan Manuel's treatment of theft in this tale is worked so as to focus on something else, hypocrisy. As to the tale of Saladin (L), it is also about theft, the intended theft of a woman's loyalty to her husband (Saladin's vassal), and/or the intended theft of the vassal's woman. As has been discussed by many critics, this example has a Catholic message that binds and reinforces the Catholic content of all the stories. This example is closely related to another example about theft and the devil, XLVII, "De lo que contesçio a una falsa beguina"; "What happened to a false

---

3 All translations are mine.

4 See Ian MacPherson, "Dios y el mundo: the Didacticism of *El Conde Lucanor*," *Romance Philology* 29 (1970): 26–38.

beguine"). In this tale a beguine does the devil's work of planting distrust between a married couple. She steals love and trust from the couple.

Both tales in the collection that have the devil as a character, XLII and XLV, are about the devil stealing souls from God. Yet, Juan Manuel is very careful to show that the victims are to blame, either for a sinful nature, for a character weakness or for lack of knowledge and preparation. I also discuss identity theft in example LI, "Lo que contesçio a vn rey christiano que era muy poderoso et muy soberbioso" ("What happened to a Christian king who was very powerful and arrogant"). In this story an angel, obeying God's instructions, steals the identity of a too proud and arrogant king. The agents of the theft are God and an angel. Obviously, the Catholic content in Juan Manuel is intense whenever we have supernatural beings of the Catholic faith interceding in human affairs (as in the tale of the thief and the devil).

All three elements receive equal importance: the angel-thief, who acts as God's agent, the victim, the proud king, and the possessions, the identity as king and the soul of the man. Finally, as kinds of theft, I look at character assassination, ingratitude and stolen opportunities in a number of stories. The purpose of this paper is precisely to show the variety with which the topic of theft is developed in the collection, and to show how the three categories, thieves, victims, and possessions, operate together in a dynamic and complex way.

I begin with two stories that do not depict theft per se, but they are what I call "almost theft" tales, and they help us understand the concepts of possessions and victims. These are example VIII, "De lo que contesçio a vn omne que avian de alimpiar el figado" ("What happened to a man who was having his liver cleansed"), and example XXIX, "De lo que contesçio a vn raposo que se echo en la calle et se fizo muerto" ("What happened to a fox who threw himself on the street and played dead").

Body Parts: Possessions and Objects of Desire

Example VIII ("De lo que contesçio a vn omne que avian de alimpiar el figado"), ("What happened to a man who was having his liver cleansed"), does not portray a theft in the proper sense, but because the tale does present the other factors that are in general present in the tales about theft and victimization, I am using it as a point of departure. What the tale has in common with other tales about theft are a possession and the two agents, a would-be victim who is the owner of the possession and another person who desires the other person's possession. The possession in question is a body part, the liver of a man who is being operated on (his liver is being cleansed). The physician has the liver in his hand when a man, upon seeing the liver, asks for it so he could feed it to his cat: "Estando el sufriendo este dolor et teniendo el fisico el figado en la mano, otro omne que estaua y çerca del començo de rogar le quell diesse de aquel figado para vn su gato"[5] ("Suffering from his pain and while the phsysician had his liver in his hand, another man who was close by started asking for the liver so he could feed it too his cat").

The man who desires to have and to take the liver of another man is not a thief in the proper sense, as we have said; he sees the liver, he desires it and he asks for it. Yet his interpretation of the circumstance reveals his potential to be a thief; he sees only how the liver can be useful to him and disregards the consequences for the would-be victim if his liver were taken away. Samuel G. Armistead believes that Juan Manuel's source for the story is a Spanish-Jewish proverb ("Dame tus tripas para mi gato" / "Give me your intestines for my cat") that indeed depicts this type of selfishness.

In a footnote Armistead quotes two almost exact interpretations of the proverb: 1) "Denota el egoísmo de quien, para su propia satisfacción o provecho, pide a otro lo que a éste no es menos útil e indispensable." 2) "S'applique aux égocentriques qui ne se feraient aucun scrupule de vous demander le meilleur de vous-meme."[6] The man who asks for the liver for his cat has no scruples and is, in effect, a quasi-thief; his propensity is to take selfishly.

On the other hand, the liver in the physician's hands is in a sense in a no man's land, not in the body of its original owner; it's in transit. That the sick man is incapable of protecting his possession of his own liver underscores his vulnerability and his helplessness. He is one of two victims in the collection (the other one is a cadaver) who has no responsibility for his situation, who can't react to the danger he is in. His life is out of his control and in the hands of the physician. That the man asks for the liver for his cat is the comic element (based on the comic proverb) in the tale that connects to the moral of the story, which is not to give away what you need to someone who does not need it. (In the story it is the physician who has this power, not the sick man.) In addition, the situation between the sick man and the healthy one with a cat demonstrates that there is

---

5 Juan Manuel, *El Conde Lucanor, Obras completas,* volume II, ed. Jose Manuel Blecua, (Madrid: Gredos, 1982–1983), 19–503; here 86:26–29.

6 Samuel G. Armistead, "Un *congère* para el ejemplum VII de *El Conde Lucanor,*" *Dicenda. Cuadernos de Filología Hispánica* 6 (1987):67–69; here 68, n. 5. Armistead adds in this article that he did not find the saying in any collection of sayings or proverbs. José Mohedamo Barceló, citing Armistead, points out that the saying is Andalusian (which does not mean it could not have a Jewish origin) and is in Ibn Asim al-Garnati's collection of sayings. The Spanish translation that Mohedano Barceló provides is "Uno con las tripas en el brazo, y el otro le dice: 'Dame pitrafilla para el gato,'" "Paremiología y material literaria: el refranero andalusí en *El Conde Lucanor,*" *Anaquel de estudios árabes* X (1999): 49–77; here 72. On the question of this saying (proverb), Armistead is also cited by Harriet Goldberg in "The Judeo-Spanish Proverb in its Narrative Context," *PMLA* 108.1 (1993): 106–20; here 108.

always the danger of someone else seeing what you have (the exposed liver in the hands of the physician) and wanting it for whatever use it may be.

Story VIII allows us to identify two other elements that are present in the stories about theft and victims of theft, appreciation and protection. The owner of a possession needs to appreciate its value and have the desire, the resources and the skills to protect it. Patronio scolds the Count Lucanor in the frame of the story for even entertaining the idea of giving money away that he needs: "Et vos, sennor conde Lucanor, si queredes fazer muy grand vuestro danno por auer dineros et dar los do se deuen escudar, digo vos que lo podiedes fazer por vuestra voluntad, mas nunca la faredes por el mi conseio"[7] ("And you, my lord Count Lucanor, if you want to do yourself harm by giving money away to people who don't need it, do so if you want to, but don't do it saying I advised you"). In other words, the Count Lucanor (and the reader) needs to appreciate and protect what he has. If not, he has only himself to blame for the harm that his carelessness could bring: "Se non sabedes que deuedes dar, / a grand danno se vos podria tornar"[8] ("If you don't know what is right to give, a lot of harm can come to you"). The lack of responsibility (appreciation and protection) on the part of an owner toward a possession, as we shall see further along in the discussion, is an invitation for theft to take place successfully.

Story XXIX, "De lo que contesçio a vn raposo que se echo en la calle et se fizo muerto" ("What happened to a fox who threw himself on the street and pretended to be dead") develops the subject of responsibility, appreciation and protection of a possession, in this case, again, body parts, and life itself.[9] A fox spends the night in a chicken's coop and is surprised by daylight and people coming out to walk the streets. The only way to hide is to lie on the street and pretend to be dead. For different medicinal purposes, one by one villagers tear off body parts: hair from the front, hair from the back, the index finger, and a tooth, and throughout the painful ordeal the fox does not move. When a villager is about to take out his heart with a knife, the fox realizes he will not survive this assault, so he risks all and runs away, successfully. Patronio tells the story in order to advise the Count Lucanor to put up with and ignore minor disturbances from a powerful relative.

---

7 *El Conde Lucanor*, 86: 30–34 (see note 4).

8 *El Conde Lucanor*, 86: 39–40 (see note 4).

9 According to Harriet Goldberg in *Motif-Index of Medieval Spanish Folk Narratives* (see note 1), the tale of the fox who plays dead and has his bodies parts removed by passersby also appears in *Libro de Buen Amor* (lines 1412–21) and in a sermon compiled by Frederic Tubach in *Index Exemplorum: A Handbook of Medieval Religious Tales*, (Helsinki: Suomalainen Tiedeakatemia, 1969): J351.2. Fox, in danger of being caught, plays dead. Allows tail to be cut off, teeth to be pulled, ears to be cut off, but will not permit heart to be removed. *LBA* cc. 1412–21; Lucanor Ex. 29; Tubach 2176," 65. Reynaldo Ayerbe-Chaux discusses thoroughly the sources of the story in *El Conde Lucanor: material tradicional y originalidad creadora* (see note 1), 66–69.

If the relative strives to seriously hurt him, however, he should defend and protect his rights, risking his life:

> E por ende, a las cosas passaderas, pues non se pueden estrannar commo deuen, es mejor de les dar passada, mas si llegare el fecho a alguna cosa que sea grand danno o grand mengua, entonçe se aventure et non le sufra, ca mejor es la perdida o la muerte, defendiendo omne su derecho et su onra et su estado, que bevir passando en estas cosas mal et desonrada mente.[10]
>
> [That being said, about things that happen out of our control and that will eventually pass, it is best to put up with them; however if anything causes great damage or hurt, it is best to risk everything, even greater loss or death, defending a man's rights, honor and station in life than to live subjected to dishonor and bad situations.]

There is no theft here in the proper sense either, but this story, like story VIII, also has elements in common with the stories about theft that I discuss later, mainly a possession, the body (live) and its parts, an owner and people who see the supposedly dead body of the fox and who desire and take different parts of his body for different medicinal uses. The anonymous passers-by are takers and opportunists (in the positive sense) who find a traditional medicinal use for most everything, in this case, the fox's body parts.[11] The story illustrates the responsibility of the would-be victim, the fox, to save himself. His first strategy, playing dead, works only up to a certain point; he loses his fur, his teeth and his index finger. His second strategy, to save his life, is to stop the pretense and run away.

Stories VIII and XXIX both illustrate three facts about theft and victimhood that are implicit in *El Conde Lucanor*: 1) possessions can be reduced to the body, yet even the body and its parts can and often do become someone else's objects of desire for intended appropriation; 2) would be victims are in varying degrees of vulnerability; 3) thieves (or, in these two stories, takers) are everywhere, if the right occasion presents itself, if there is a ready justification or desire at hand (to feed a cat or for medicine for a sick son), and if there is no fear of sin and God (this is the case in the more fully developed stories that have more Catholic content). In effect, the stories on theft in *El Conde Lucanor* transmit the message that because there are always possessions in the world there are always thieves (or potential thieves) and victims (or potential victims) of theft. In addition, we see in the two stories, in different ways, how the roles are reversed or could be reversed. The thief can become the victim, as in the case of the fox who at the start of the story

---

10 *El Conde Lucanor*, 253: 58–64 (see note 4).

11 See Hans-Jörg Uther, "The Fox in World Literature: Reflections on a "Fictional Animal," *Asian Folklore Studies* 65.2 (2006): 133–60. "The intestines of the fox (especially the lung and liver) were accorded great significance as medicine for a variety of diseases;" here 135.

is stealing chickens in the chicken coop and who himself later almost gets quartered by the villagers. If the healthy man with the cat were the sick one on the operating table, he would also be vulnerable to the potential insensitivity of anybody healthy, for the message of the Andalusian proverb on which the story is likely based is that personal misfortune is often met with opportunism.

Gullible Victims: Vanity, Stupidity, and Greed

The fox in story V ("De lo que contesçio a vn raposo con vn cueruo que tenie un pedaço de queso en el pico"), ("What happened to the fox with the crow that had a piece of cheese in his beak"), the false alchemist in story XX ("De lo que contesçio a vn rey con vn omne quell dixo que faría alquimia"), ("What happened to a king with a man who said he could do alchemy"), and the tricksters ("burladores") in story XXXII ("De lo que contesçio a vn rey con los burladores que fizieron vn panno"), ("What happened to a king with three tricksters who made a him clothes") are thieves who lie to their targets in order to carry out their thefts. They want something material, the fox, the cheese the crow has in his beak, the false alchemist, the king's money, and the three tricksters, the kings' gold, silver and silk (the material for the phantom clothes, which they run away with). The thieves are not punished in either one of the three stories, because the focus is on the gullibility of the victims. Behind their gullibility are their character flaws or their sinful nature. The crow is vain; the king in story XX is greedy, and the king in story XXXII is both stupid and greedy.

Juan Manuel's adaptation of the well-known fable of the fox and the crow is perhaps the most simple, straightforward and traditional representation of a thief and his victim in *El Conde Lucanor*.[12] Wanting the piece of cheese that the crow has in his beak, the fox lies to the crow by telling him that all his body parts are beautiful because they are black, contrary to popular opinion. He also says that he believes that God made him also a good singer and that he would like to hear him sing. The crow opens his mouth to sing and lets fall the piece of cheese, which the fox runs away with. The responsibility for the theft is placed not on the fox (after all, a fox will be a fox, cunning) but on the crow who let vanity blind him to the truth, that he is not beautiful nor a good singer and that the fox wanted to steal something from him.[13] The moral of the story is: "Qui te alaba con lo que non es

---

12 According to Harriett Goldberg, the fable is found in four other Spanish medieval texts: Juan Ruiz's *Libro de buen amor* (lines 1437–43), *Esopete*, *Libro de los exenplos por a.b.c.*, and in a religious tale used for sermons (Frederick Tubach, *Index Exemplorum: A Handbook of Medieval Religious Tales* (see note 6); cf. *Motif-Index of Spanish Medieval Narratives* (see note 1), 95.

13 See Carmen Hernández Valcárcel, *El cuento medieval español: Revisión crítica y antología* (Murcia:

en ti, sabe que quiere leuar lo que as de ti" ("The person who praises you falsely only wants to take advantage of you and steal something from you").

One of the main objectives of *El Conde Lucanor* is to educate the receptor about the evil ways of the world. The dictums are: be good but not stupid; be trustworthy but distrustful; take time to investigate the truth, which many times is hiding behind appearances; tread carefully, don't fall victim. The crow is stupid and vain. He falls victim to the fox's lies and theft not only because he can't see the fox's true nature and intentions, but also because he has not come to terms with his own nature, that he is ugly and not too smart. He has not measured his attributes and deficiencies correctly. He does not know himself. For Juan Manuel, developing knowledge of oneself is one of the primary goals of education, and one of the main dictums of the collection of stories. It is needed in order to make up for one's weaknesses and to capitalize on one's strengths and gifts. It is necessary so as to combat the evil within, in oneself, and without, in the world, so as to not fall victim of either. Without knowledge of oneself, evil will have the upper hand in the battle between good and evil. If the crow knew himself, he would recognize the lies of the fox for what they are.[14]

Universidad de Murcia, 1997), 68. Hernández Valcárcel echoes Menéndez Pidal's comparison of Juan Manuel's version of the fable with Juan Ruiz's in the *Libro de buen amor*, concluding that Juan Manuel's fox lies in a more cerebral fashion, manipulating truth in order to deceive the crow, whereas the fox in Juan Ruiz's version uses blatant lies to appeal to the crow's emotions, his vanity. Nevertheless, it is still the crow's vanity that Juan Manuel's fox, though more cerebral his method, appeals to. For a thorough comparison of the fable in *Libro de buen amor* with its source, see Margherita Morreale's article, '"Enxiemplo de la raposa e del cuervo' o 'La zorra y la corneja' en *Libro del Arcipestre de Hita* (1437–43)," *Revista de Literatura Medieval* 2 (1990): 49–83. Morreale's article also explains why the two versions, the version in *Libro de Buen Amor* and the version in *El Conde Lucanor*, are different: the sources used are different. Juan Manuel used the *LBG* (London, Brussels, Göttingen) of the *R* (*Romuli*) and Juan Ruiz used the *GI* (*Gualterio el Inglés*) of the *Romuli*. There are more amplifications in Juan Manuel's version, mainly emphasis on the premeditation of the theft, the elaboration of the lie, and the thought process of the crow. See also Reynaldo Ayerbe-Chaux, *El Conde Lucanor, Materia tradicional y originalidad creadora* (see note 1), 56–59.

14 Likewise, it is the ability to be an independent thinker that is required in order not to fall victim. Obviously, the crow is not an independent thinker. In the second example of the collection of stories, "De lo que contesçio a vn omne bueno con su fijo," (What happened to a good man with his son"), a father teaches his son that he cannot please everybody, for everybody will have a different opinion as to how to proceed. He must use his own judgment. Without the ability to make independent value judgments and decisions—they need to have a foundation in Christian education—it is easy to be led astray. Without independent thinking there is no defense against lies, and falling victim to them is a guarantee. As is well known, this value of independent thinking based on experience and intelligence provides a marked contrast with the submissiveness of the character donna Vascunnana in example XXVII, "De lo que contesçio a un enperador et a don Aluar Hannez Minaya con sus mugeres." ("What happened to an emperor and to Alvar Hannez Minaya with their wives.)" She gives up one good, to express her own opinion based on her own experience, in favor of what for her is a higher good, to show her loyalty to her husband, Alvar Hannez. We could easily expand on this with reference to countless other didactic

This is the case of the king in example XXXII, "De lo que contesçio a vn rey con los burladores que fizieron un panno," who instead of believing his own perception of reality, that he is naked in public, chooses to believe what his deceivers and their duped followers want him to believe—that he is wearing the most lavish and beautiful clothing ever made.[15] It is not that the king really believes that he is dressed in clothing. He can see that he is naked. He believes the story of the deceivers, that if he can't see the clothing, it is because he is illegitimate. This is why the people in the crowd, fearing their own illegitimacy, don't want to tell the truth either. It is an orphan boy in the crowd who has the courage to tell the truth, because he already knows he is illegitimate. He says to the king, "Sennor, a mi non me enpeçe que me tengades por fijo de aquel padre que yo digo, nin de otro, et por ende, digo vos que so çiego, o vos desnudo ydes."[16] ("Lord, I do not care if you believe who I say my father is, whether this man or that man, and so I am telling you, either I am blind or you are naked.") By the time the king and the rest of the people understand the deception, the thieves have made off with the money that the king has paid them for the clothing. The thieves escape apprehension and punishment.

Thieves do get away with their crimes. These thieves in example XXXII escape punishment from the system of human justice for a reason we can easily understand. Juan Manuel wants to keep the focus on the punishment that the king deserves, for his lack of courage, his fear of illegitimacy, and his gullibility. Could he have fallen in a more embarrassing situation, stupid and naked in public among his subjects? The one thing a king needs is the ability to discriminate between what is true and what is a lie, in order to govern with justice. The thieves are "burladores" ("burlar," to deceive). They have no fear themselves. On the other hand, they use their victim's fears, the king's, to commit their crime. The story also illustrates that everybody, no matter what position they occupy in society, is a potential victim. The king's position does not protect him. Only his capacity to discriminate and the integrity of his own moral character could, and both are lacking.

---

texts from the Middle Ages encouraging the readers/listeners to think for themselves and to avoid lies. See, for instance, the contributions to *What Nature Does not Teach: Didactic Literature in the Medieval and Early Modern Periods*, ed. Juanita Feros Ruys. Disputatio, 15 (Turnhout: Brepols, 2008).

15 According to Archer Taylor in "The Emperor's New Clothes," *Modern Philology*, 25.1 (1927): 17–27, the story of a weaver (or weavers) who deceives a king has its origin in an Arabic story that is also the source of the story in the Turkish collection, *The Forty Vezirs*. Of Juan Manuel's originality, Archer Taylor writes, "The merit of Juan Manuel's invention lies in the drastic utilization of the King's credulity to bring about the catastrophe; only in Juan Manuel and in the literary tradition dependent on him is this so cleverly brought about;" here 24. Please see also Please see also Reynaldo Ayerbe-Chaux, *El Conde Lucanor, Materia tradicional y originalidad creadora* , 140–49 (see note 1).

16 *El Conde Lucanor*, 269:109–11 (see note 4).

The king in story XX, "De lo que contesçio a vn rey con vn omne quel dixo quel faria alquimia," ("What happened to a king with a man who said he could do alchemy") is likewise gullible and greedy.[17] Indeed, the "golfín" choses his target, the king, because of his two well-known character flaws, that he is not too bright and that he is obsessed with alchemy: "Et aquel omne sopo que vn rey que non era de muy buen recado se trabaiaua de fazer alquimia"[18] ("And that man found out about a king who was not too bright and wanted to do alchemy"). In other words, the king's obsession with the fantasy of getting rich via alchemy reveals his gullible and greedy nature. The "golfín" uses his knowledge of the king's character weaknesses to deceive him and get rich off of him.[19]

The ploy is detailed, elaborate, and very well planned out: the counterfeit coins, the disguise as an alchemist, the "ingredient" ("tabardie") he sells to the grocer that he says is required to practice alchemy, the secretive conversation with the king, the demonstration of alchemy (after buying the key scarce ingredient), the king's own experience making gold coins with the secret ingredient, and finally the crisis (the secret ingredient runs out) and the success of the theft, the alchemist runs off with the great amount of money that the king has given him to buy more of the precious secret ingredient: "E desque el golfin lo touo en su poder, fuesse su carrera et nunca se torno al rey. Et assi finco el rey engannado por su mal

17 In "Tres nuevos análogos españoles para un cuento inglés," Jesús L. Serrano Reyes explains that the topic of alchemy in a story format is found in four medieval texts, and in chronological order they are: *Llibre des merevalles* by Ramon Lull, *Libro del caballero Zifar, El Conde Lucanor* and Chaucer's *The Canterbury Tales*. He explains that Lida de Malkiel, Marín and Ayerbe-Chaux believe that the Spanish versions most probably had a common Arab source. Ayerbe-Chaux believes in addition that Ramón Lull's text is the direct source for *El caballero Zifar* and Juan Manuel's *El Conde Lucanor. Didactismo y Moralismo en Geoffrey Chaucer y Don Juan Manuel: Un estudio comparativo textual* (Córdoba: Servicio de Publicaciones de la Universidad de Córdoba, 1996), 252–73. Reproduced in http://www.ucm.es/info/especulo/numero9/canon1.html (last accessed on Dec. 29, 2011).

18 *El Conde Lucanor*, 151:18–20 (see note 4).

19 John Burke in "Juan Manuel's *Tabardie* and *Golfín*," *Hispanic Review* 44 (1976): 171–78, presents a thorough study of the words "tabardíe" and "golfín," which are, according to him, of Arabic origin. "Tabardíe" comes from "barada" in Arabic, which Burke explains, has double meaning, "to file" (the coins are filed) and "to become cold." The coldness refers to the king's stupidity: "'Barada,' meaning 'to file,' is a linguistic double of a much more common Arabic verb which means 'to be or become cold.' From this basic idea in Arabic of 'coldness' there derives a secondary meaning of slowness, silliness and stupidity. Blanchere interprets the tenth form of barada as 'to think someone tiresome, gross, stupid'" (here 173). The "tabardíe" would reflect the king's stupidity. "*Golfín*," writes Burke, might derive from the Arabic verb "ghalafa," which "means to cover or envelop" (here 175). Burke comes to these conclusions about the meaning of the word "*golfín*": "The translation which is normally given for *golfín*, "maleante, malhechor," parallels one sense of the word *burlador*, "he who does evil by deceit or trickery." The possibility, then, exists that semantically *golfín* is a kind of back-formation from a stem, which basically means "to conceal." He who conceals very often does it in order to commit evil" (here 176).

recabdo"[20] ("And as soon as the scoundrel had it in his power, he skipped town and he never returned to the king. And that is how the king was deceived because of his lack of common sense").

In effect, the blame for the success of the theft is placed on the king's gullibility, his "mal recabdo." The thief rubs it in by leaving the king a written note attesting to both his own audacity and the king's gullibility: "Bien cred que non a en el mundo tabardie; mas abet que vos he engannado, et quando yo vos dizia que vos faria rico, deuierades me dezir que lo feziesse primero a mi et que me creeriedes"[21] ("I want you to know that there is no such thing as 'tabardie' in this world and that I deceived you, and when I said that I could make you a rich man, you should have asked me to make myself rich first").

In stories XXXII and XX the thieves make off with the kings' money. Money (and silver and gold) is the possession they target for theft. However, the kings also lose other valuable possessions in the transaction. The king in story XXXII is humiliated before his people and the king in story XX is made fun of by his people. They lose respect and credibility. This loss of respect and credibility is especially developed in story XX with Juan Manuel's characteristic humor. The king finds out that two men have made lists of the smart men, the rich men and the stupid men in the kingdom, and that they have put him first on the list of stupid men. He summons the men and asks them why they have placed him on this list, and their candid answer is because he gave a lot of his money to a stranger he had no references for. It is humorous that the king confirms his gullibility when he responds that if the thief returns he will no longer be a stupid man.

The two men, with tongue in cheek, reply that when the thief returns they will take the king off first place on the list of stupid people and put instead the thief first on the list:[22] "Et ellos le dixieron que ellos non perdian nada de su cuenta, ca si el otro viniesse, que sacarian al rey del escripto et que pornian a el"[23] ("And they told him that they did not care one way or another, but if the thief returned they will take the king off the list and they will put him on it").

These are stories that provide negative examples of conduct (the characters fall victims of theft). At the end of the stories Patronio gives advice to Lucanor on how

20 *El Conde Lucanor*, 153: 85–87 (see note 4).

21 *El Conde Lucanor*, 153: 91–93 (see note 4).

22 Graciela Cándano studies what makes the two kings in these two stories comical in her article "Personajes cómicos en la *Disciplina clericales* y *El Conde Lucanor*," *Acta Poética* 30.1 (2009): 29–59. As to the king in story XXXII, it is his nakedness that makes him an "hazmerreir," a laughing stock for his people (here 55). As to the king in example XX, he is comical because he is made fun of by the false alchemist in the note he leaves in the trunk and by the two men who put him on the list of stupid people (here 52). http://www.revistas.unam.mx/index.php/rap/article/view/23130 (last accessed on Dec. 29, 2011).

23 *El Conde Lucanor*, 154: 107–09 (see note 4).

to not fall in the traps that the characters fall in. As we know, these elaborations are reinforced by the moral in the two verses that the author says (referring to himself in third person) he has added to summarize the lesson. In story V (the fox and the crow) Patronio advises Lucanor to beware of flattery, for the intention of the flatterer is to deceive. As mentioned above, the two verses that summarize the moral ("Qui te alaba con lo que non es en it, / sabe que quiere leuar lo que as de ti"; "The person who praises you falsely only wants to take advantage of you and steal something from you") clarify that the flatterer wants to deceive in order to steal something from you. Patronio's advice in story XX (the fake alchemist) focuses on Lucanor's responsibility to be smart enough to protect his own property and wealth from swindlers who promise big returns on his money.

The two verses at the end of the story echo what the "golfín" wrote in his note to the king: see if the person who promises you a good return on your money is wealthy himself, if not, don't believe him: "Non aventurades mucho de tu riqueza,/ por consejo del que a grand pobreza."[24] ("Don't risk a lot of your wealth on the advice of someone who is poor"). In story XXXII (the "burladores") Patronio advises Lucanor to beware of strangers who ask him to keep a profitable negotiation secret from his friends, for their intention is to take advantage of him. They would not ask for secrecy if they were honest: "Et vos, sennor conde Lucanor, pues aquel omne vos dize que non sepa ninguno de los en que vos fiades nada de lo que el vos dize, çierto seed que vos cuyda engannar, . . ."[25] ("And you, my lord Count Lucanor, beware that that man who tells you that no one else should know about the deal between the two of you is trying to deceive you").

The two verses at the end of the story, capturing the moral with humor, also emphasize that imposed secrecy is a sign of danger: "Quien te conseia encobrir de tus amigos, / sabe que mas te quiere engannar que dos figos."[26] The three stories illustrate that it is up to the targets of the thieves to see the warning signals (the red flags) in order to protect themselves and not fall victim: flattery, a discrepancy (like a lack of proof), and sworn secrecy, are all warning signals that the agent is a thief and you are his target.

---

24 *El Conde Lucanor*, 154: 118–19 (see note 4).

25 *El Conde Lucano*, 269: 121–23 (see note 4).

26 Laurence de Looze explains that "dos figos" (two figs) only appears in one manuscript. In other manuscripts it is "dos fijos" (two sons) or "dos enemigos" (two enemies), or "dos testigos" (two witnesses). *Manuscript Diversity, Meaning, and Variance in Juan Manuel's El Conde Lucanor* (Toronto and Buffalo: University of Toronto Press, 2006), 18–21. As is evident, the verse is only humorous with the two figs.

Stealing To Get Out of Poverty

Five stories in *El Conde Lucanor* present characters that are poor who want to find a way to get out of their poverty.[27] In two of these stories, story X, "De lo que contesçio a vn omne que por pobreza et mengua de otra vianda comia atramuzes" ("What happened to a man who because he was so poor and in need had nothing to eat but lupin beans") and story XVII, "De lo que contesçio a vn homne que avia muy grant fanbre quell comidaron muy floxa mente a comer" ("What happened to a man who was very hungry and who got a half-hearted invitation to eat"), the characters change their attitude from negative to positive, from hopelessness to faith in God and industry.

These stories are presented as positive examples: the right way to overcome poverty. Story VII, "De lo que contesçio a vna muger quell dizan donna Truana" ("What happened to a woman who was known as donna Truana"), is a negative example. Even though the character (donna Truana) has a positive attitude and is industrious (she wants to sell her honey in the market), she lets herself be carried away by fantasy (unrealistic expectations) and thereby loses the little wealth (the

---

27 That I am aware of there is no study on the topic of poverty in Juan Manuel like there is for Gonzalo de Berceo, "Pobres y pobreza en la obra de Gonzalo de Berceo," by Carmen López Alonso, *Cuadernos hispanoamericanos* 320–21 (1977): 360–82. (There is a study on the topic of money, which is related. Please see note 18.) In truth, if we wanted to learn about the poor in Castile in the first half of the fourteenth century, we would not think of turning to Juan Manuel. He was not very concerned with the poor as a social class, judging from his books overall. As we know, the majority of the population in the first half of the fourteenth century in Castilla was poor. The author belonged to the aristocratic minority. He himself was among the wealthiest of the nobles of his time. As expected, in *El Conde Lucanor* poverty is not understood as a social problem but rather as an individual problem. The characters in the five stories, rather than representatives of a social class, are individuals who are responsible for their situation. They have the power to overcome their poverty without resorting to stealing; they need only have the right attitude and put their faith in God. Poor for Juan Manuel (in the *Counde Lucanor*) means not having money for sustaining one's station in life. This means that a nobleman can be poor. Poverty in this sense is a topic of personal interest to the aristocrat. "Labradores" (workers) can be well off or poor, depending on their attitude and honest hard work. The author does not support upward mobility, "labradores," for example, working their way up to a higher social rank. He advocates industry in order to maintain the standard of living permitted for each class. Nor does the author believe that the aristocratic class should feel guilty for their privileged position in society. Each individual is born in the social class that God chose for him/ her. Indeed, in Juan Manuel's world-view being rich and powerful is not an obstacle to the salvation of the soul. In fact, God wants each person to save his soul in the estate in which he was born. The rich and powerful should not believe that they have a better chance at saving their soul if they renounce their riches and dedicate themselves to a life of prayer and repentance. This is illustrated in the third story of *El Conde Lucanor*, "Del salto que fizo el rey Richalte de Ingla terra en la mar contra los moros" ("The jump that the king Richard of England performed at sea while fighting against the Moors").

pot of honey) she has. On the other hand, in the two stories I discuss below, the characters resort to stealing in order to overcome their poverty. In the Catholic story the thief receives punishment from both human and divine justice, yet in the story of Arabic origin the thieves, a sister and a brother, are not punished. The story rather contrasts the characters of the sister and brother as revealed by their different styles of stealing.

In story XLV, "De lo que contesçio a vn omne que se fizo amigo et vasallo del diablo" ("What happened to a man who made friends with the devil"), the devil promises an impoverished man that he can help him become a successful thief in order to become rich again.[28] The man agrees. The devil instructs him that if and when he is apprehended to call out to him for help with these exact words, "Acorred me, don Martin" ("Rescue me, don Martin"). He will save him, he promises, from any danger he is in. Following the directives of the devil, the man robs establishments and houses, becoming rich. His greed motivates him to rob even more, and becoming fearless and careless, he gets caught by the authorities. He calls out to the devil to come rescue him, and the devil does.

The thief becomes more reckless with every robbery and every rescue. At the same time the devil takes more time each time to rescue him. At one time the thief has already been sentenced to die by the time the devil appears. The next time the devil does not come to his rescue until he is about to be hanged. It turns out, however, that he has not come to rescue him, but to provide the noose to hang him that could not be found. The devil, the master deceiver, lied to him and broke his promise to rescue him from every danger. Patronio explains that the man lost his life and his soul, because he trusted in the devil, believing his lies: "Et asi perdio

---

28 Thirteenth century (second half) Spanish versions of the story (featuring Teophilus and the Virgin) are Milagro XIV in Berceo's *Milagros de Nuestra Señora* and Cantiga III in Alfonso X's *Cantigas de la Virgen María*. Versions (without Teophilus and the Virgin) from the first half of the Fourteenth century are Juan Manuel's in *El Conde Lucanor* and Juan Ruiz's in *Libro de buen amor*, "Enxiemplo del ladrón que fizo carta al Diablo." Both of these versions feature thieves who abuse their connection with the devil and who are hanged. According to Joaquim Ventura, in "La tradición del pacto diabólico en el *Libro de buen amor*: el "enxienplo del ladrón que fizo carta al Diablo," there is no known source for Ruiz's version (and therefore Juan Manuel's version): "No hay fuente conocida para este ejemplo, por lo cual cabe deducir que el Arcipreste de Hita habría tomado la figura del pacto con el demonio más por el trato con éste que por el documento y la abjuración de Dios (que no se la exige.)" Paper delivered in Alcala de Henares, May 9–11, 2002, at the First International Conference on the *Libro de buen amor*. Reproduced by Cervantes Virtual, http://cvc.cervantes.es/literatura/arcipreste_hita/01/ventura.htm (last accessed on Dec. 29, 2011). There might not be only one known source for the versions such as they appear in Juan Ruiz and Juan Manuel; on the other hand in Harriet Goldberg's *Motif Index of Medieval Spanish Folk Narratives* we can identify a version in the *Espéculo de los legos* (n. 185) with common motifs: the man is poor, the devil promises to make him rich, the devil visits him three times, the devil exacts payment of his soul. (The devil, interestingly, is disguised as a poor man.) Missing are the theft and the hanging. *Motif Index*, 118 (see note 1).

aquel omne el cuerpo et el alma, creyendo al diablo et fiando del"[29] ("And that is how the man lost his body and his soul, believing and trusting him").

The story illustrates what don Juan Manuel believes as a Catholic, that the devil is indeed responsible for the crimes in this world. Without his intervention, there would be no criminals and no crimes. Here in this example the devil makes a criminal out of a man who had not been one before. The thief commits a string of robberies. Nevertheless, the man is never forced into a life of crime by the devil. He makes the choice to accept the devil's offer and terms. The devil waits to make his move when the man is at his weakest and most likely to be tempted by his offer: "Et bien cred que el Diablo sienpre cata tienpo para engannar a los omnes. Quando vee que estan en alguna quexa, o de mengua, o de miedo, o de querer conplir su talante, entonçe libra con ellos todo lo que quiere" (And believe that the Devil always finds the right time to deceive people. When he sees that they are in distress or in need or fearful or bent on getting their way, then he gets from them everything that he wants to").[30] The man is distressed because he has just lost his money and is now impoverished. He has no moral strength, or love for God, to resist the devil's offer. He only wants to be rich again.[31]

Once rich again after a string of successful robberies, his sin of avarice prompts him to commit more robberies: "Et el mal andante, non se teniendo por pagado de commo era fuera de lazeria, començo a furtar avn mas"[32] ("The unfortunate soul, not understanding that he was lucky enough already for getting away, started to rob even more"). He does not stop robbing once having met his initial goal, but instead he chooses to continue, abusing his connection with the devil. The devil does not punish him for being a thief, though the human system of justice does. The devil punishes him for abusing his connection with him, for his arrogance. About to be hanged, the thief calls out to don Martin, the devil, to rescue him. The devil answers that when his friends get to this place where he is at now, about to be hanged, he does not rescue them.

The message is that the devil tempts people to become criminals, but he is not responsible for their sinful nature, which is the primary motivating force behind their criminal behavior. The devil does not put the thief at the scaffold. The arrogant thief who believes he could escape justice forever because of his connections puts himself there. The man falls victim to the devil's influence

---

29 *El Conde Lucanor*, 371: 111–12 (see note 4).

30 *El Conde Lucanor*, 369: 41–44 (se note 4).

31 John England's article, "El omne con bondad…acreçenta las riquezas: Juan Manuel and money," *The Place of Argument: Essays in Honour of Nicholas G. Round*, eds. Rhian Davies and Anny Brooksbank Jones (London: Tamesis Books, 2007, 43–56), provides a thorough discussion on the topic of money as it is developed in Juan Manuel, that is, in association with greed, good deeds, productivity, class, salvation, etc. Poverty is also discussed.

32 *El Conde Lucanor* (see note 4), 370: 61–62.

because he does not do his moral homework. He does not make the necessary preparations for when the devil crosses his path and tempts him. He does not educate himself about his sinful nature and how to overcome it. He becomes a victim of the devil because of his own nature and actions. He has no moral fortitude and no conscience.

In example XLVII, "De lo que contesçio a vn moro con vna su hermana que daua a entender que era muy medrosa" ("What happened to a Moor with his sister who acted very fearful"), two criminals rob graves. They are a brother and sister team. The victims, cadavers, are obviously completely powerless to protect themselves. As I mentioned above, these cadavers in story XLVII and the sick man in story VIII, ("De lo que contesçio a vn omne que avian de alimpiar el figado") ("What happened to a man who was having his liver cleansed") are the only victims of theft who are not held responsible for falling victim. (The sick man and the cadavers are powerless but everybody else is not). Indeed, the focus of the story is another victim, the brother, whose sister is a hypocrite. Like her brother, the sister has no problem stealing, yet she is even more fearless than her brother. In order to not destroy the valuable clothing of a man's cadaver, she does not hesitate to twist his neck off without pity: "fue tomar con las manos, muy sin duelo et sin piedat de la cabeça del muerto et descoiuntolo todo" ("without feeling and pity, she took his head in her hands and she twisted it off").

Back at home, the sister, "muy medrosa" ("very scaredy-cat"), reverts to her normal behavior of taking fright at the smallest things. When her cup shakes making a sound, her brother in his native Arabic, which don Juan Manuel translates, says, "Aha, hermana, despantades vos del sueno de la tarrazuela que faze boc boc, et non vo espantauades del desconjuntamiento del pescueço"[33] ("Ah, Sister, you take fright at the sound of a cup shaking but you are not scared to twist off the head of a dead man").[34]

Patronio tells the story precisely in order to illustrate hypocrisy. When the sister wants something bad enough, she easily overcomes her nervous nature to get it. What is her true nature? Is she the timid and fearful woman or is she the greedy and heartless grave robber? Is one of them an act? Is it that people's true natures are revealed completely only when they are placed in extreme circumstances, when they are put to the test? The brother's words not only scold his sister for her

---

33 *El Conde Lucanor*, 390: 62–64 (see note 4).

34 In 1942 Alois Richard Nykil wrote, "Thus far I could not find an Arabic counterpart of the story, nor could I locate a proverb closely resembling the Arabic phrase," "Arabic Phrases in *El Conde Lucanor*," *Hispanic Review* 10.1 (1942), 12–17; here 16. In 1983 Richard Hitchcock wrote, "I have nothing to add to Nykil's pithy conclusion," "Don Juan Manuel's Knowledge of Arabic," *The Modern Language Review* 80.3 (1985): 594–603. Richard Hitchcock's article summarizes the history of criticism on the subject of the degree of Juan Manuel's knowledge of Arabic while it also provides valuable new information and insights.

hypocrisy; they express his discomfort. His sister's actions, and the character that they revealed, are a surprise to him. He did not know her or that part of her until that night.

The story also weighs the factors that make a thief: circumstances, influence from peers and family, moral character and opportunity. At the beginning of the story the brother is the thief, not the sister. One night he needs her help and that is why she goes along and becomes a thief herself, at least for that night. As we have seen, she turns out to be more natural a criminal than her brother. Opportunity and her brother's influence on her are not stronger factors in her criminal behavior than the factor of her own moral deficiency. She is greedy and heartless. She has no conscience. Juan Manuel makes a point of contrasting the brother and the sister from the very beginning of the story. It seems he even excuses the young man's criminal life. He is very poor and, needing to provide for his family, he resorted to robbing graves.

Don Juan Manuel's tone is sympathetic: "Et aquel su hermano era muy buen mancebo, mas era muy pobre, et por que la grant pobreza faz a omne fazer lo que non querria, non podia escusar aquel mançebo de buscar la vida muy vergonçosa mente"[35] ("And her brother was good young man, but he was very poor, and because extreme poverty makes man often do things that he does not want to, the young man had no other option but to make a livng in a shameful way"). The young man, otherwise having good character, resorts to stealing because of poverty. Though the author does not recommend stealing as a way to get out of poverty, this story frames poverty as a circumstance that can make good people resort to thievery.

Theft and Power Struggles

As we mentioned above, any possession can become an object of desire and theft. In example XLII: "De lo que contesçio a una falsa beguina" ("What happened to a false beguine"), a beguine steals a couple's trust and love for each other, and in example L, "De lo que contesçio a Saladin con vna duenna, muger de vn su vasallo" ("What happened to Saladin with a woman, wife of a vassal of his"), Saladin wants to have sex with his vassal's wife. He wants to steal what belongs to another man (a wife's body) and he wants to steal what belongs to her (her modesty and her loyalty to her husband). Whereas the couple is not successful in protecting their shared immaterial possessions, trust and love for each other, falling victim to the beguine, the woman in example L artfully protects her and her

---

35 *El Conde Lucanor*, 390: 32–35 (see note 4).

husband's possessions from the would be thief/ adulterer, Saladin, by putting on a good act. Both stories depict power struggles, example XLII, not only between the beguine and the couple, and between the husband and the wife, but also between the devil and the beguine; and example L develops a power struggle between the powerful leader and his vassal's wife.

The devil is the master deceiver and the master thief. What does he actually steal in example XLII? It is interesting that the devil is represented only three times in *El Conde Lucanor*, in examples XLII, XLV, and L. Juan Manuel does not go to the extreme in painting the supernatural; in fact, he is somewhat constrained in this respect. In example XLII the devil hates all good things, and he wants to destroy them and put evil in their place. The devil's project is to destroy the happiness and love between a husband and his wife. Their love for each other and the happiness derived from their love are heavily emphasized at the beginning of the story as their most prized possessions. The devil has been trying for a long time to plant evil between them, and has had no success, for which he is actually sad and disheartened: "Et por que el Diablo se despaga sienpre de las buenas cosas, ovo desto muy grand pesar, et pero que andido muy grand tienpo por meter mal entre ellos, nunca lo pudo quisar"[36] ("And because the Devil hates all that is good, he was angry; he had been plotting against the couple for a long time, but he had been till then unsuccessful at separating them").

If we look more closely at this statement, we can see that the devil always ("sienpre") hates good where it exists; and therefore the particular (this love and this happiness between this man and this woman) represents the universal (all happiness and all love, wherever it is found in this world). We can see that the devil is working on this particular project, yet we infer that the devil is doing his dirty work everywhere there is good. In other words, all couples are stalked by the devil, who waits for his opportunity to destroy their bond.

The encounter between the devil and the beguine at the beginning of the story reveals that she wants to help the devil in his task for her own selfish reasons. She wants him to serve her and not the other way around. She wants power over him, as can be understood by the details in the story.[37] The devil and the beguine cross paths when he is returning from an unsuccessful attempt at destroying the couple's bond. He is sad. The devil is in a human body that expresses this sadness. She also recognizes him as the devil: "Et desque se conoscieron, preguntol que por

---

36 *El Conde Lucanor*, 331: 23–25 (see note 4).

37 An essential study on this story is Mike Hammer's article, "A Marginal Woman on the Loose: Revisiting Don Juan Manuel's Beguine," *eHumanista* 11 (2008): 171–82 (http://www.ehumanista.ucsb.edu/volumes/volume_11/Articles/8%20Hammer.pdf (last accessed on Dec. 29, 2011).

que vinia triste"[38] ("And after introducing themselves, she asked him why he was sad"). Juan Manuel does not describe the appearance of the devil or of the beguine.) He explains to her why he is sad and she puts him down by rubbing it in that he, being so knowledgeable, has failed. She tells him if he does what she wants him to do, she will do the job for him.

The transaction between the beguine and the devil is the reverse from the transaction between the devil and the man in story XLV. In story XLV, the devil offers to help the impoverished man get out of his poverty if he promises to do everything he asks. Here the beguine offers to help the devil if he promises to do everything she asks him to do. She wants to show him that she can succeed where he has failed, that she is better at his job than he is. The dynamic is that the devil desires to destroy good and spread evil, and the beguine wants the devil to do her bidding. It is never clear what this bidding entails exactly, but it is clear that she demands from the devil favors in exchange for the favor that she will do for him.[39] The trust and love between the couple that she destroys are not her objects of desire. What she desires is to demonstrate her superior powers to the devil and to have him under her thumb: "Et ella dixol que se marabillaua, pues tanto sabia, commo non lo podia fazer, mas que si fiziesse lo que ella querie, que ella le pornia recabdo en esto"[40] ("And she told him that it amazed her that he knowing so much could not do it, but that if he did what she wanted she would do the job for him").

The beguine's ploy is to become, though virtually a stranger, more familiar, pretending to have a previous connection to the young woman. She introduces herself as a former servant of her mother, and expresses her desire to serve the couple in their household. The beguine then proceeds to make time her weapon, taking a lot of it to gain the trust first of the woman and then of the husband: "Et desque ella ovo morado muy grand tienpo et era priuada de entramos . . ."[41] ("And

38 *El Conde Lucanor*, 331: 28–29 (see note 4).

39 In "Una aproximación al diablo en la literatura medieval española: desde Dominus a Dummteufel" Anthony Cárdenas-Rotunno writes that the topic of a powerful old woman vis a vis an impotent devil is very ancient. He refers to what Blecua has written on the subject, that both Juan Manuel's version and the version in the *Esopete Ystoriado* (1488) have a common Latin source from the ninth century: "Ofrecen dos versiones del mismo cuento que, según las notas de Jose Manuel Blecua, editor del *Conde Lucanor*, encuentran su origen en el siglo nueve en un cuento, 'Devetula que fecit quod dyabolus non poterat facere'," *Hispania* 82 (1999): 202–12; here 204. Mike Hammer, on the topic of the old woman and the devil in other versions, writes, "In its general form this tale resembles several parallel versions that antedate, co-exist with or post date the *Conde Lucanor*. These include, among others, the *Libro de las delicias*, by Joseph Ben Meir Ibn Sabara (Chapter 11), Etienne de Bourbon (no. 245), the *Speculum Laicorum* (no. 463), the 'Poema de Adolfo,' and the *Scala Coeli* (no. 610). In each of these versions, the protagonist is a repugnant old woman who not only consorts with but bests the Devil at his own game" (*A Marginal Woman*, 175, see note 20).

40 *El Conde Lucanor*, 332: 36–38 (see note 4).

41 *El Conde Lucanor*, 332: 49–50 (see note 4).

after she had lived a long time with them and was trusted by both . . ."). When she has their full confidence, and manages their household ("et fiaua della toda su fazienda"; "and she trusted her with her all her affairs"), she carefully goes back and forth between the wife and the husband with false information about the disloyalty of the other, that ultimately creates extreme tension and distrust. She convinces the husband that his wife wants to kill him, and arranges it so that the wife does appear to want to kill him, even though all she is doing is cutting off a lock of his hair while she thinks he is asleep. He reacts and kills her. Then the townspeople seek justice and kill him. His relatives kill her relatives, and her relatives kill his relatives, so that after the turmoil very few people are left alive in the village.

Patronio wants the Count Lucanor to understand that the worst people in the world are the hypocrites that the beguine represents, people who look and act like good Christians but whose true intentions are to hurt others:

> Et vos, sennor conde Lucanor, si queredes saber qual es el pior omne del mundo et de que mas mal puede venir a las gentes, sabet que es el que se muestra por bien christiano et por omne bueno et leal, et la su entençion es falsa, et anda asacando falsedades et mentiras por meter mal entre las gentes.[42]

> [And you, lord Count Lucanor, if you really want to know who is the worst kind of person in the world and who can do the most harm to innocent people, know that it is the person who pretends to be a good Christian and a good and loyal man, and his real intention is false, and he goes around spreading falsehoods and lies in order to alienate people from one another.]

This very Catholic story illustrates at the end that evil (the devil and the beguine) does not triumph. After the first encounter with the beguine, the devil has disappeared from the story. The beguine acts without help from the devil. After succeeding where the devil has failed, the beguine is punished by God. Patronio emphasizes here that God never allows evil deeds to go unmasked and unpunished. God wills that the false beguine be punished for her evil, says Patronio, by making it known to the villagers that she is responsible for the blood bath and destruction, for which the villagers deal her a cruel death:

> Et todo esto vino por las falsas palabras que sopo dezir aquella falsa beguina. Pero por que Dios nunca quiere que el mal fecho faze finque sin pena, nin avn, que el mal fecho sea encubierto, guiso que fuesse sabido que todo aquel mal viniera por aquella falsa beguina, et fizieron della muchas malas iusticias, et dieron le muy mala muerte et muy cruel.[43]

---

42 *El Conde Lucanor*, 334: 139–43 (see note 4).

43 *El Conde Lucanor*, 334: 133–38 (see note 4).

> [And all this happened because of the false words that the false beguine knew how to say. But God never wants a bad deed to go unpunished, nor that a bad deed remain in the dark, so he arranged it so that it would be known that all that evil was caused by that false beguine. The people avenged themselves by torturing her and meting out to her a very bad an cruel death.]

Though Patronio's story zeroes in on the evil nature and deeds of the beguine, the husband and wife nevertheless have only themselves to blame for falling victims to her. The story is indeed another illustration of gullibility and moral weakness. The gullibility involves a series of mistakes that leave them vulnerable to a stranger's evil designs: 1) not checking the veracity of the connection with which the beguine introduces herself; 2) confiding private information to her; 3) giving her too much power in the management of the household; 4) giving credence, though reluctantly at the start, to her destructive gossip.

The couple's moral weakness consists in giving room to doubt about each other's love. In other words, they are little prepared to protect their most valuable possession against the evil in the world, which it is in their power to do. Lack of suspicion allows the beguine to come into their lives, but it is doubt of their love for each other that is the thief that steals their love. Once doubt enters their hearts suspicion and destruction take over. They change their reality despite themselves: they are no longer the loving and supportive couple. The story illustrates that good communication between a married couple is necessary in order to be able to defend its survival against the evil forces (the devil and all who serve him) in the world that seek to destroy it. This Catholic story presents the devil as the thief of good in the world, and evil people in the world who have dealings with him are the thieves of good also. Good people fall victim to evil people because they have not put up strong enough fortifications, letting their guards down when they should keep them up.

As we have seen in a number of the stories, a lack of conscience is a strong factor in the making of a thief. Story L, "De lo que contesçio a Saladin con vna duenna, muger de vn su vasallo" ("What happened to Saladin with a woman, wife of a vassal of his"), is about conscience, shame ("vergüença"), which, according to Juan Manuel is the most important virtue to have, because it is what stops humans from doing evil. Saladin covets his vassal's wife. He sends his vassal off to fight, leaving him free to make his advances. The woman promises to do what he bids if he finds the answer to her question. This sends him on a long trip in search of the answer, at the end of which a hermit gives it to him: "verguença." When Saladin returns to his vassal's wife with the answer, hoping to have now won the right to have sex with her, she patiently demonstrates to him that he now has the answer to his proposal, that it is shameful.[44]

As in the other stories about theft, we have a proprietor, a husband, a possession or object of desire, the wife, and a would-be thief of the possession of another, Saladin. When Saladin first sees his vassal's wife he desires her for himself. In the story it is made clear that it is the devil who put the temptation in him; he is the one who is always at work at influencing people to do evil: "Et el Diablo, que sienpre se trabaja en que faga el omne lo mas desaguisado, puso en el talante de Saladin que olbidasse todo lo que deuia guardar et que amasse aquella duenna non commo deuia"[45] ("And the Devil, who is always at work trying to tempt man to do bad deeds, placed in Saladin's will to forget his principles and to love that woman in the manner he should not"). "Non commo deuia" are the key words: Saladin loves her not as he should, because she is another man's wife.

A bad adviser tells Saladin how to go about getting what he wants—send off the husband, who is a knight, to work far away. Saladin believes he now has no obstacles, yet the wife turns out to be the formidable obstacle, as she uses her wit to protect her honor and her loyalty to her husband. Indeed, what is at stake (the prized possession) is the honor of both the husband and the wife. A power struggle between Saladin and the woman ensues, in which she, using her acting abilities, gains the upper hand. This is primarily because she has both moral fortitude and enough craftiness (she is not too innocent) to know how to manipulate a powerful man. The woman not only understands the situation and resolves to remain faithful to her husband, but she also has very good acting abilities, which save her.[46]

---

44 Harriett Goldberg identifies the woman in the story as a riddler, a traditional function of women in the folktale. She writes, "Despite this handful of masculine riddlers, it seems that women appear with greater frequency as the posers or solvers of riddles, perhaps because of the sexual tension generated by their dramatic confrontation with power." "Women Riddlers in Hispanic Folklore and Literature," *Hispanic Review* 59 (1991): 57–75; here 62. This is indeed the case of this woman in *El Conde Lucanor*; she responds to Saladin's power and sexual advances by stalling him with a riddle. Harriett Goldberg explains, "In *El Conde Lucanor*, for example, Saladin is sent on a riddle quest to find the answer to 'qual es la mejor cosa que ome puede aver en si.' He rejects several answers proffered him until he finally comes upon 'verguenza,' which he accepts as the best possible answer. As it happens, conscience is just the answer his inquisitor had expected"; here 59.

45 *El Conde Lucanor*, 415: 71–74 (see note 4).

46 Mariana Ortiz de la Rosa analyzes both stories (XXV and L) in which Saladin appears in the collection, in "El personaje de Saladino en la literatura hispánica: Los ejemplos XXV y L de *El Conde Lucanor* de don Juan Manuel," *Ensayos: Revista de la educación de Albacete*. http://www.uclm.es/ab/educacion/ensayos/pdf/revista13/13_9.pdf (last accessed on Dec. 29, 2011). Unfortunately, the number of the journal is not provided on the website. In "La vergüenza como constante social y narrativa en don Juan Manuel: el ejemplo L de *El Conde Lucanor*," Antonio Carreño explains the importance of the Catholic concept "vergüença" in Juan Manuel's writing

She pretends first that she does not really understand what he wants from her: "Pero dio a entender que non entendia aquella razon et dixol quel diesse Dios buena vida . . ."[47] ("But she pretended that she did not understand what he was saying and she told him she wished God would bless him with a good life ...") When he insists, she resorts to more acting. She pretends that she is not intelligent, "commo quier que yo so assaz muger de pequenna guisa . . ." ("understand that I am a woman with little intelligence"), but she is devising her plan of action, which involves more acting. She acts as if she is willing to comply with his wishes. She promises to do whatever he asks, only if he first promises to do what she asks of him. This is necessary, she says, because men, especially powerful men like him, make many promises to get what they want, but once they get it they don't keep their promises. She asks him to tell her which virtue is the mother of them all. She acts as if she does not know the answer when she does. He does not know the answer, so in order to keep his promise he is obligated to go in search of it. (Why can't she tell him herself?). She knows the answer, of course. The answer, shame, will make Saladin feel shame for proposing to commit adultery.

Why could the woman not tell Saladin the answer from the beginning, with something like, "¿No tienes verguenza?" ("Aren't you ashamed"?). Of course, there would have been no story, as we know. On the other hand, there are other factors we can consider: because she is a woman, she does not have sufficient authority to say the truth. She not only has to put on an act of ignorance, she has to send her would be aggressor on a trip to obtain the answer elsewhere. This person who does provide the answer to Saladin is indeed an authority to be believed, a wise old knight:

> Et el escudero casara poco tienpo avia, et abia vn padre muy viejo que fuera el mejor cauallero que oviera en toda aquella tierra. Et por la grant vejez, non veya et non podia salir de su casa, pero avia el entendimiento tan bueno et tan conplido, que non le menguaua ninguna cosa por la vejez.[48]
>
> [And the squire had recently gotten married, and he had an old father who was the best knight in that country. Because of his old age, he was blind and he did not leave his house, but he still had a very good and sound mind, and he was not in any way hindered by his old age.]

At opposite ends, then, we have two people who know the answer to the question, a young woman, on one end, and an old knight, on the other, but only one of them can be direct and forthright with the truth. The woman is forced into acting in order to save herself.

---

and he also provides and analysis of story L, *Thesaurus* 23.1 (1977): 54–74.

47 *El Conde Lucanor*, 415–16: 97–98 (see note 4).

48 *El Conde Lucanor*, 417: 168–72 (see note 4).

What is interesting is that Saladin, even though he has the answer, does not give the woman the respect that she deserves immediately upon his return. First she has to recognize his supreme authority as a king and stroke his masculine ego by asking him if he is not the greatest man in the whole world: "Et pido vos por merçed que me digades, assi commo rey deue dezir verdat, si cuydades que ha en el mundo mejor omne que vos"[49] ("And I ask from you as a favor that you tell me as the king that you are who must speak the truth, if you do not agree that there is no better man n the world than you"). Saladin does not hesitate to recognize that to be the truth. It's almost funny that he says that he is ashamed to admit it." "Et Saladín le dixo que commo quier que se le fazia vergüença de dezir, pero pues la avia a dezir verdat commo rey, quell dizia que mas cuydaua que era mejor que los otros, que non que avia otro meior que el"[50] ("And Saladin told her that even though it was embarrassing to say so, he had to say the truth becasue he was the king, and, yes, he did believe that he was better than other men, and that there was no better man than he").

We don't know if the woman's glorification of Saladin is a continuation of her acting or not. When he admits that she is telling the truth about his superiority, she falls on her knees to the floor crying. Her behavior is emotional and submissive. Is this part of the act also? Or is she being herself? In other words, where does the acting end? In any event, she has had to put together two truths, that shame is the highest virtue and that Saladin is the greatest man on earth and therefore should be the most virtuous man, in order to escape from harm. Her cunning and her good acting abilities save three people's honor: her husband's, her own and Saladin's.

Identity Theft, Character Assassination, Ingratitude and Stolen Opportunities

There is a humorous case of identity theft in *El Conde Lucanor*, in story LI, "Lo que contesçio a vn rey christano que era muy poderoso et muy soberbioso" ("What happened to a Christian king who was very powerful and arrogant").[51] (In this story, God sends an angel to steal the identity of a proud and arrogant king,

---

49 *El Conde Lucanor*, 420: 266–69 (see note 4).

50 *El Conde Lucanor*, 420: 270–73 (see note 4).

51 This story is problematic on two fronts, its location in the collection, whether or not it was intended to be part of the collection. José Manuel Blecua positions it not after story L but in an appendix at the end of *El Conde Lucanor*, that is, after parts II, III, IV, and V, and thus puts its authorship in question. Alberto Blecua addresses the problem of the story in *La transmisión textual de El Conde Lucanor* (Barcelona: Universidad Autónoma de Barcelona, 1982), 113–20.

precisely as punishment for his arrogance. The angel lives in the king's body for many years, while the king is forced to live as a pauper. The identity theft is a form of divine punishment in order to bring about a transformation, a soul's salvation. We have a king who has a possession, his position of power on which he places inappropriately too much value. There are, in effect, two possessions, the eternal, which he neglects, and the temporal, which he abuses. Indeed, he places more importance on his position as king than on the salvation of his soul. The king's arrogance is illustrated with a humorous anecdote; he does not agree with the message in a couple of verses in a Canticle to the Virgin. The canticle is "*Maginificat anima mea dominum.*"

The verse the king does not like is "*Nuestro sennor Dios tiro et abaxolos poderosos soberuios del su poderio et ensalço los omildosos*"[52] ("Our lord God toppled the powerful and arrogant from their positions and raised the position of the humble people"). He replaces it with a verse that states the contrary, that God will elevate the powerful and knock down the humble people. The identity theft that God arranges has a positive and successful outcome. The angel stays on earth for many years acting as the king while the king's misfortune and suffering as a pauper open the way for sincere repentance. When the angel restores the throne to the repentant king, the angel acts as a messenger of God's forgiveness.

The angel talks to the repentant king at length about God's will that all sinners repent for their sins sincerely from the heart. The angel tells the king that he is indeed an angel: "et nuestro sennor Dios tiro vos lo por estas razones mismas que vos dezides, et envio a mi, que so su angel, que tomasse vuestra figura et estudiesse en vuestro lugar"[53] ("And our lord God took you out of your position for the reasons that you now understand, and he sent me, his angel, to occupy your body and take your place"). The angel also reveals that he is an angel to the king's people, so they may also be witnesses to the miracle: "Et desque todos fueron ayuntados, el rey predico et conto todo el pleito commo passara. Et el angel, por voluntad de Dios, paresçio a todos manifiesta mente et contoles esso mismo"[54] ("And when all the people were convened, the king made a speech and told them what had happened. And the angel, doing God's will, appeared to all and also told them that that is indeed what happened"). The now humbled king lives many years serving his kingdom and God and when he dies he gains entrance into heaven ("meresçio auer la Gloria del Parayso").

We may think of character assassination as a form of theft, insofar that a good reputation (the possession) is taken from one person by another person. The thief may seek to destroy the good reputation of the victim in order to thereby have

---

52 *El Conde Lucanor*, 495: 26–27 (see note 4).
53 *El Conde Lucanor*, 501: 224–26 (see note 4).
54 *El Conde Lucanor*, 502: 248–50 (see note 4).

access to his position and wealth, which the victim has lost as a consequence of losing his good reputation. A third possession is often on the line, the trust and esteem of a third party. We see all these elements in the first story of the collection, "De lo que contesçio a vn rey con vn su priuado" ("What happened to a king with his trusted courtier"). A king's favorite courtier is envied by the less favorite courtiers. They envy the esteem and the material benefits that the king lavishes on his favorite. Patronio explains that envy is found everywhere there is good fortune:

> Et por que non puede seer que los omnes que alguna buena andança an, que algunos otros non ayan envidia dellos, por la privança et bien andança que aquel su privado avia, otros privados daquel rey avian muy grant envidia et trabaiauan se del buscar mal con el rey, su sennor.[55]

> [And it is just not possible that people who are successful not be envied by others, and because this courtier was benefiting from being the kings favorite, other courtiers of the king were very envious and were plotting to estrange him from the king.]

The envious courtiers work at destroying the favorite's good reputation, all without success, until they hit on the right threat to the king's well-being. They tell the king that his favorite subject is planning on having him murdered whereby he will usurp power and eventually kill the king's young son. Though we are focusing on the character assassination of the courtier, the king himself is by all accounts in danger of being a target of having all that he possesses stolen from him, his life, his kingdom and his son. Though he trusts his favorite, in order to protect himself, he necessarily has to test his favorite's loyalty, for what is at stake is too valuable:

> Et commo quier que fasta entonce non pudieran poner en ninguna dubda al rey contra aquel su priuado, de que esto lo dixieron, non lo pudo sofrir el coraçon que non tomase del reçelo. Ca en las cosas en que tan grant mal ha, que se non pueden cobrar si se fazen, ningun omne cuerdo non deue esperar ende la prueua.[56]

> [And even though uo to the potters had not been able to make the king doubt his favorite's loyalty, when they told him this, his heart could not be but anxious and distrustful. Nobody who is smart and has common sense should wait for more proof in situations that can bring us great harm.]

The king tests his favorite's loyalty by dressing as a hermit and confiding to him that because he is tired of this life he wants to retire as a hermit. He is entrusting his kingdom, his wife and his son to his care until his return. For the most part the subject's heart is loyal; on the other hand, he secretly rejoices at the thought of

---

55 *El Conde Lucanor*, 33: 24–27 (see note 4).
56 *El Conde Lucanor*, 34: 36–41 (see note 4).

having all the power: "plogol mucho en su coraçon, entendiendo que pues todo fincaua en su poder, que podria obrar en ello commo quisiese"[57] ("This pleases him in his heart a lot, thinking that now that he would have the power, he could do whatever he desired"). As we know, it is a servant-advisor that the courtier has in his own house who saves him from falling in the trap of the test, by reading into the intentions of the king, and thereby the courtier is able to respond with an act of his own (he wants to accompany the king into exile) that restores the king's trust in him. In this story, the theft is not successful.[58] The would-be victim of character assassination, though not able himself to read the situation correctly, has his advisor read it for him, whereby he is able to counteract in time and keep his good reputation.[59]

Character assassination also takes place in the story of the beguine, story XLII, that we discussed above. The beguine destroys the character of the wife and the husband in each other's eyes, dividing and conquering them. A very similar scenario develops in story XX, "De lo que contesçio al leon et al toro" ("What happened to the lion and the bull"), in which the other animals, especially the trusted advisors, the bear and the horse, are successful at destroying the strong alliance between the lion and the bull who rule over them. They do this with character assassination, telling each one lies about the other that results in distrust that eventually breaks their friendship. The possessions that they lose are their friendship and their power over the other animals. Patronio points out that the lion and the bull are at fault for not valuing and protecting their friendship.

> Et assi, por que el leon et el toro non entendieron que por el amor et la ayuda que el uno tomaua del otro, eran ellos onrados et apoderados de todas las otras animalias, et non guardaron el amor aprouechoso que avian entre ssi, et non se sopieron guardar de los malos consejos que les dieron para sallir de su premia et apremiara ellos, fincaron el leon et el toro tan mal de aquel pleito, que assi commo ellos eran ante apoderados de todos, asi fueron despues todos apoderados dellos.[60]
>
> [And that is why, because the lion and the bull did not understand that it was their friendship and the help that they gave one another that gave them respect and power

57 *El Conde Lucanor*, 35: 102–03 (see note 4).

58 A very useful and insightful discussion of this story is provided by James A. Grabowska in *The Challenge to Spanish Nobility in the Fourteenth Century: the Struggle for Power in Don Juan Manuel's Conde Lucanor, 1335*, (Lewiston: The Edwin Mellen Press, 2006), in chapter 4, "The moral of the story: politics and morality in exemplary tales," 106–16.

59 Jonathan Burgoyne discusses the ethical ambiguity of this story (that the advisor advises the courtier to lie to the king and Patronio advises Lucanor to lie also) and other stories in the collection in chapter 1, "Ethical ambiguity in El Conde Lucanor," id., *Reading the Exemplum Right: Fixing the Meaning of El Conde Lucanor*, North Carolina Studies in the Romance Languages and Literatures, 289 (Chapel Hill: University of North Carolina Press, 2007).

60 *El Conde Lucanor*, 169: 81–88 (see note 4).

> over the other animals, and because they did not value and care for their beneficial friendship, and because they did not know how to protect themselves from the bad advice from the other animals that sought to divide them, they lost all the power they once hadand now other animals had power over them.]

Ingratitude is a topic that is developed in a number of stories in *El Conde Lucanor*, and it can also be viewed as a type of theft whereby a person accepts a gift or a favor but does not give the giver credit for the favor or the gift. We saw ingratitude in story LI. The king does not give God the credit deserved for the position of power that he enjoys in the temporal world. The king is withholding a good that belongs to another. By not giving it to the person to whom it belongs it is a stolen good. Once the king repents for his pride and arrogance, he places credit for his position in life where it belongs. He now values more the salvation of his soul than any wealth or power on earth: "ca todo esto preçiaua el nada, et non cobdiçiaua otra cosa sinon auer perdon de sus pecados et poder saluar el alma"[61] (" None of this did he value anymore, and he did not desire anything but to be pardoned for his sins and to save his soul").

When the angel restores his position as king, the first thing he does is make amends to God by inscribing in gold all over his kingdom the original verse in the canticle to the Virgin that he had disrespectfully butchered, giving the Virgin now her due credit: "Entonçe el rey fizo quantas emiendas pudo a nuestro sennor Dios; et entre las cosas, mando que, por remembrança desto, que en todo su regno para siempre fuesse escripto aquel viesso que el reuesara con letras de oro"[62] ("Then the king did as many reparations as he could to our lord God, and among them he ordered this, that throughout his kingdom the verse that he desecrated be shown in gold letters").

A humorous treatment of ingratitude is found in story IIII, "De lo que dixo vn genoves a su alma quando se ovo de morir" ("What a Genoese said to his soul when he was dying"). A dying rich man from Genoa scolds his soul for being ungrateful for leaving all the pleasures and possessions that he could still enjoy in this temporal world. After a detailed description of his possession that are indeed marvelous he tells his soul to leave him with the wrath of God. According to the dying man, his soul is making a mistake in choosing the unknown over the good life on earth that is peaceful and safe. Patronio uses this story to illustrate for the Count Lucanor that he should not risk what worldly gains he has worked hard for over the years for an unreliable proposition his envious advisors are encouraging him to go after. These envious advisors want to topple his security and have him fall under their control: "ca por aventura estos vuestros consejeros vos lo dizen por que saben que desque en tal fecho vos ovieren metido, que por fuerça abrades a

---

61 *El Conde Lucanor*, 499: 154–56 (see note 4).
62 *El Conde Lucanor*, 502: 251–54 (see note 4).

fazer lo que ellos quisieren et que avredes a seguir su voluntad desque fueredes en el grant mester . . ."[63] ("for it is possible that these advisors tell this to you because if you get in trouble with the king you will ask them for help and be in their power . . .").

What we have in the story that Patronio tells is a doubling, a man and his ungrateful soul. The soul does not give credit to the rich man for all he has accomplished in life. On the other hand, it is a little different in the explanation of the story that Patronio develops. We can see a target of theft (Lucanor) who needs to be grateful for what he already has and not be greedy so as not to avoid falling victim to risky propositions. He needs to give himself credit for what he already has accomplished: "mas, por el mi conseio, en quanto pudierdes auer paz et assossiego a vuestra onra, et sin vuestra mengua, non vos metades en cosa que lo ayades todo aventurar"[64] ("My advice is that, as long as you can enjoy peace and calm in an honorable fashion, and without any harm coming to you for doing so, don't get involved in anything that asks you to risk everything").

Another ungrateful character in the collection is the deacon of Santiago in story XI, "De lo que contesçio a vn dean de Sanctiago con don Yllan, el grand maestro de Toledo" ("What happened to the deacon of Santiago and don Yllan, the magician from Toledo"). The deacon promises the magician that he will not forget the favor that he has done for him by teaching him his secret knowledge of black magic. He does, however. As he rises in fortune and rank in the church (up until he is elected Pope), he continuously pushes aside the magician's entreaties to be remembered, going so far as to threaten to put him in jail for disturbing the peace. The deacon not only refuses to give the magician credit for his success, he also withholds the favor in kind that he owes him, and both are thefts, keeping what does not rightfully belong to him. The reader (or interlocutor) is wonderfully surprised when s/he learns that all along the magician had been applying his black magic, by having the deacon believe he was actually living all those experiences over many years when he all along (for a few hours) he had been in the magician's basement.[65]

The magician suspected that the deacon was not honest and that he would turn ungrateful. When the deacon realizes the trick, he feels embarrassed: "Quando esto dixo don Yllan, fallose el papa en Toledo dean de Sanctiago, commo lo era quando y bino, et tan grand fue la vergüença que ovo, que non sopo quell dexir"[66]

---

63 *El Conde Lucanor*, 68: 48–51 (see note 4).

64 *El Conde Lucanor*, 68: 55–58 (see note 4).

65 See Francisco Miranda, "Un Dean de Sanctiago y Don Illan, el grand maestro de Toledo: nigromancia e historia en *El Conde Lucanor*," *Revista Canadiense de Estudios Hispánicos* 23.2 (1999): 329–40; also David A. Wacks, "Don Yllán and the Egyptian sorcerer: Vernacular commonality and literary diversity in Medieval Castile," *Sefarad* 65 (2005): 413–33.

66 *El Conde Lucanor*, 102: 141–43 (see note 4).

("When don Yllan said this, the Pope found himself again in Toledo as deacon of Santiago as when he had arrived, and he was so embarrassed that he did not know what to say"). With regard to being victimized, the magician is careful not to be; he sets up a situation that will guarantee that he won't be.

It should not be surprising to find that three women characters in the collection are framed as ungrateful, not giving their husbands their due credit and respect by behaving obediently. These characters are the emperor's wife in story XXVII, "De lo que contesçio a vn emperador et a don Alvar Hannez Minaya con sus mugeres" ("What happened to an emperor and don Alvar Hannez Minaya with their women"), and Ramayquia in story XXX, "De lo que contesçio al rey Abenabet de Seuilla con Ramayquia, su mugger" ("What happened to king Abenabet of Sevilla with his wife Ramayquia"), and the newlywed woman in the famous story XXXV, "De lo que contesçio a vn mançebo que caso con vna muger muy fuerte et muy braua" ("What happened to the young man who married a very strong and fierce woman"). Two of the women women are "bravas" ("fierce"). The emperor's wife is "la mas braua et la mas fuerte et la mas rebassada cosa del mundo," ("the strongest and most contrary person in this world.") She never does what her husband the emperor wants her to do. The woman in story XXXV is also described as "fuerte" and "brava." She is even likened to the devil: "et por ende, omne del mundo non queria casar con aquel diablo" ("and therefore, no man in the world wanted to marry that devil").[67]

She is not marriage material because she is too rebellious. In fact, both the emperor's wife and the strong and fierce single woman have rebellious characters. They are not in the least submissive. Ramayquia in story XXX is a crybaby; she cries all the time until she gets her way, and then the cycle repeats itself again. Ramayquia is an excellent example of an ungrateful woman. She never is satisfied and happy with what her husband gives her. He spoils her and yet she never thanks him for his gifts and his dedication. In the story we see him strive to fulfill her whims, for example, planting almond trees so she could feel like it is winter. She is so impressionable that when she sees through her window a poor woman making mud bricks by the river she starts to cry to her husband, because she also wants to make them herself. Her husband then creates for her a fantasy playground of rose water, good smelling spices and sugar-canes to simulate a river, mud and hay.[68]

---

67 *El Conde Lucanor*, 286: 26–27 (see note 4).

68 It is hard to not read more into Ramayquia's situation and just wonder if her unhappiness might stem from being enclosed in the castle and not enjoying freedom, like the poor woman by the river does. After all, the river she is given to play in is fake, as well as the mud and the hay. Her husband did not give her what she asked for, the real thing.

All three women are punished to varying degrees for their character. The punishment is meant to tame the women into submission. The emperor's wife takes a bottle of poison and ingests it, just as her husband thought she would if he told her expressly not to. Yes, she is submissive now, dead, well under control. Ramayquia is scolded with a reprimand. When she starts to cry again, her husband retorts with "¿Et non el día del lodo?" Patronio clarifies that the reprimand consists in her husband asking her if she has even forgotten the day he arranged mud to be provided for her: "Commo diziendo que pues las otras cosas oluidaua, que non deuia oluidar el lodo que fiiziera por le fazer plazer"[69] ("As if telling her that since she has forgotten all the other things he has done for her, she should not forget the mud that he had made to please her").

The reprimand is meant to chastise her and change her. The husband is fed up with her. The young newlywed in story XXXV is not given a chance to be "brava" and disrespectful to her husband. Right away he intimidates and subjugates her (with violence and bloodshed as he kills the animals) into obedience. At the end of the violent ordeal of her honeymoon she indeed goes from being ungrateful to grateful to be alive. The husbands take matters into their own hands. As victims or potential victims of disobedience, disrespect, ingratitude, all forms of theft of masculine honor, they devise ways to get the upper hand in order to live a peaceful, safe and orderly life.

Two of the stories provide reversed situations. In story XXVII the emperor's wife's rebellious character brings on her death by self poisoning, but in the second part of the story Alvar Hannez's wife, doña Vascunnana, is a paragon of the virtues of obedience, gratitude and submissiveness.[70] In story XXXV, the groom's father-in-law wants to subjugate his wife with intimidation, but the wife is not intimidated; she knows it is just an act. Good timing is essential. They have been married too long.[71]

The last category of theft that I discuss in this article is stolen opportunities. The example that first comes to mind is the opportunity to confess that the sons take away from their father in story XIIII, "Del miraglo que fizo sancto Domingo quando predico sobre el logrero" ("The miracle that St. Dominic performed on the greedy man"). Saint Dominic can't come in person to confess a rich Lombard who is on his deathbed, but sends in his place a friar of his order. The sons, greedy for their father's money, fear that he will give it away to the Dominican order. When the friar arrives, the sons send him away. The father dies without confession. St.

---

69 *El Conde Lucanor*, 258: 53–55 (see note 4).

70 See note 10.

71 See Eukene Lacarra Lanz's article, "El peor enemigo es el enemigo en casa: Violencia de género en la literatura medieval," *Clio & Crimen* 5 (2008): 228–66, for a thorough discussion of stories XXVII and XXXV.

Dominic presides at the funeral and cites the bible, "*Ubi sunt teasurus tuus, ubi est cor tuum.*" In the dead man's trunk (the miracle that St. Dominic performs) friends and family find instead the man's heart covered in worms in place of his money. The father was greedy as well.

The message is that greed for money corrupts. To have both a greedy heart and a giving heart is not possible. Greed takes away opportunity to perform good deeds and earn the salvation of the soul. The capital sins, all very well represented in the collection of stories (but greed more extensively than the other six), are thieves of opportunity to live the Christian life. The sacrament of confession can restore the opportunity to be saved, but only if there is true repentance, as is illustrated in story XL, "De las razones por que perdio el alma un siniscal de Carcassona" ("The reasons why a Seneschal from Carcassonne lost his soul").

Two other stories in the collection are especially good examples of stolen opportunities, story XXVI, "De lo que conteçio al aruol de la mentira" ("What happened to the tree of Deceit"), and story XLIII, "De lo que contesçio al bien et al mal et al cuerdo con el loco" ("What happened to Good and Evil and to the sane man and the crazy man"). In story XXVI, truth and deceit are personified. Being companions, they decide to reside in a tree. Deceit deceives Truth who innocently believes what Deceit tells her, that the roots are the best part of the tree. This is where Truth takes up residence.

Deceit occupies the visible part, the branches and leaves, growing strong and beautiful. People gather under the tree to take shade and to learn from its art of deception. What I want to point out here is that Deceit is a taker; she takes all the best of everything, material goods and opportunities. She pushes Truth aside, or rather, underground, just like a taker of opportunities. Deceit basks in the light and in the limelight. She steals all the attention and takes up as much space as possible. Truth, living underneath in the roots of the tree, starving, gnaws at the roots. However, in the Catholic worldview the truth eventually reveals itself and unmasks lies. As God will triumph over the devil at the end of time, the truth eventually will win the war against deceit, despite its armies of followers. In the story the tree of lies falls when it is hit by a strong wind. (Deceit is not so powerful and strong after all.) The people who had taken shade underneath the tree are either injured or killed.

Truth comes out of hiding and sees the evil deeds of deceit. Patronio explains to the Count Lucanor that "la mentira" ("the lie") has many branches and flowers, and many people are charmed and taken in by its many deceitful ways. "La mentira," however, is all shadow ("sonbra" in Spanish is both shade and shadow) and never bears good fruit. Patronio tells the count to not follow the example of the majority who are deceitful, and who are ultimately punished, but rather embrace and follow the truth, which is the road to salvation. The moral attached at the end of the story is: "Seguid verdad, por la mentira foyr, ca su mal cresçe quien vsa de mentir" ("Follow the truth and run away from lies. Whoever lies will be punished").

In example XLIII, "De lo que contesçio al bien et al mal et al cuerdo con el loco" ("What happened to Good and Evil and to the sane man and the crazy man"), Good and Evil are personified. Evil is the taker; he takes the biggest share and the best parts of everything he divides between himself and Good. Evil lays claim to the wool and the milk of the sheep they share while Good is left with the baby lambs. Evil gets greedier with the pigs. He tells Good that this time he can have the hide and the milk of the pigs, and that he will have the piglets. Good is assigned the visible leaves of the turnips that grow in their vegetable garden, while Evil lays claims to the turnips themselves. With the cabbages, Evil gives Good the roots and he takes the leaves, that is, the cabbages. When it is time to share a woman, Evil prefers the lower half of the woman (and gets to be her husband and sleep with her) leaving Good with the upper half. (The two parts of the body of the woman represent two different uses, one sexual and the other domestic: "Et fue assi: que la parte del Bien fazia lo que cunplia en casa, et la parte del Mal era casada con el et avia de dormir con su marido."[72])

Evil, however, does not get away with all his taking and he falls into a trap of his own making. When a son is born to the woman and Evil, Good refuses to give permission to the woman to nurse the newborn, because that part of her body is his. For the favor of allowing the baby to be nursed, Good makes Evil walk in public announcing that Good triumphs over Evil with good deeds. "Amigos, sabet que con bien vençe el Vien al Mal."[73]

There is an important difference between Truth and Good, as they are portrayed in each of these stories. Truth is innocent and gullible to a fault: "non ay en ella muchas maestrias et es cosa de grand fiança et de grand creençia"[74] (" There is not any malice in her and she is trusting and gullible"). That she eventually escapes her bad situation is more due to her hunger rather than to her astuteness, for she has none. She is the perfect victim. It is bad to be that good. In fact, no human being is that good (not even Good) because it is that amount of "maestría" (evil) there is in everybody (even if it be small amount) that allows everybody to protect themselves from evil. As we see in the case of Good in story XLIII, she wises up. She stops being gullible, stops letting Evil take the best, and stops allowing Evil to steal her opportunities. Even though she makes Evil parade in public announcing that she triumphs over her by doing good, letting the newborn nurse, it is the little evil in herself that she resorts to that puts a stop to the abuse. Instead of turning the other cheek and being generous, she says no, that part of the woman belongs

---

72 *El Conde Lucanor*, 345: 59–61 (see note 4).

73 *El Conde Lucanor*, 346: 95 (see note 4).

74 *El Conde Lucanor*, 210: 42 (see note 4).

to me. So she uses what little she has to bargain with, taking advantage of the opportunity that has luckily come her way (not an event forseen by Evil), to manipulate ("maestría") the situation to her advantage.

In conclusion, I have shown how theft in Juan Manuel's *El Conde Lucanor* can run the gamut from being a simple motif in a tale of Aesopic origin, a morally ambivalent situation in a tale of Arabic origin, a dynamic complex topic that reinforces the collection's Catholic identity, to a portrayal of the world where thieves and victims are always busy in power struggles with each other over their possessions and objects of desire. By no means do I consider that I have studied the topic completely, for greed and theft in the collection have as counterparts doing good deeds and charity. Analyzing these (as they are presented in Juan Manuel's other books as well as in *El Conde Lucanor*) could round out the topic of theft.

Chapter 12

Patricia Turning
(Arizona State University, Tempe)

Competition for the Prisoner's Body: Wardens and Jailers in Fourteenth-Century Southern France

For decades, it seemed as though historians of medieval crime and punishment described institutions that looked like a prison and functioned like a prison, but refrained from using the word because of the influence of Michel Foucault's *Discipline and Punish* (1975). Anyone familiar with Foucault's theory held on to the fundamental premise that prisons as a punitive institution only emerged at the end of the eighteenth century, as a product of the Enlightenment's notion that the State could serve a role in reforming the soul of the offender.[1] In broad overviews of medieval justice, scholars were very conscious in their discussions of medieval prisons to explain their existence as simply holding centers for criminals awaiting their trials or if administrators did use them as a location of coercion, it was primarily for delinquent debtors.

In these works there are concessions, however, of undisputed variations of disciplinary incarceration in the Middle Ages, from the isolation and segregation of erroneous monks to royal prisons like the Châtelet in Paris, but, as the title of Edward Peters's chapter in *The Oxford History of the Prison* suggests, this is still seemingly a discourse of the "Prison before the Prison."[2] Foucault's chronological

---

1 Michel Foucault, *Discipline and Punish: The Birth of the Prison*, trans. Alan Sheridan (1975; New York: Vintage Books, 1979).

2 Edward Peters, "Prisons before the Prison: The Ancient and Medieval Worlds," *The Oxford History of the Prison: The Practice of Punishment in Western Society*, ed. Norval Morris (Oxford: Oxford University Press, 1995), 3–47.

and perspective "birth of the prison" helped shape the general understanding (or dismissal) of prisons in the medieval world: namely, that the Middle Ages had no concept of punitive imprisonment.

There have been a handful of regional studies, however, that have maintained that in concept and in reality, prisons did serve an explicit role in the judicial administrations of the later Middle Ages, much like today's counterparts. Although it predates Foucault, in England, this notion extends back to the definitive work of R. B. Pugh's *Imprisonment in Medieval England* (1968), which argued that prisons were very much a part of official practices of chastisement, and were not simply temporary holding cells.[3] England also provides scholars with some of the most famous of the medieval prisons, the notorious Newgate and Fleet, but for some reason, literature on these institutions is rather scarce.[4] On the continent, two of the most recent influential works to seriously challenge Foucault's theory have been James Given's *Inquisition and Medieval Society* and Guy Geltner's *The Medieval Prison*. Given convincingly elucidates the importance of sequestered containment in the inquisition's success in thirteenth-century Southern France, as the prison became a way to isolate a suspected heretic from social or familial ties, and thus expedite a confession of guilt.[5] Some inmates had no idea how long they would be detained, and inquisitors prayed upon this ignorance to intimidate both the suspect and the surrounding community. In his work, Geltner presents Italian municipal prisons as very recognizably modern institutions.[6] Geltner insists that by the end of the fourteenth century, municipal prisons were visible and centrally located buildings, staffed with a complex administration that made the experience of incarceration if not pleasant, certainly not as horrific as one might imagine. His research reveals that time in Italian medieval jail was by no means comfortable, but if an inmate could afford it, it was certainly tolerable.

It is not surprising, though, that Foucault opened *Discipline and Punish* with a dramatic account of the horrific and public execution of an offender as an example of pre-modern justice. Many medieval chronicles also give the impression that criminal punishment was swift, brutal, and always corporal. But in actuality, municipal and royal officials proved to be fairly restrained and very calculated in their punitive sentences. From a statistical perspective, the number of people executed in France during the later Middle Ages was relatively low in relationship

---

3 Ralph Pugh, *Imprisonment in Medieval England* (Cambridge: Cambridge University Press, 1968).

4 Margery Bassett, "Newgate Prison in the Middle Ages," *Speculum* 18 (1943): 233–46; Margery Bassett, "The Fleet Prison in the Middle Ages," *The University of Toronto Law Journal* 5 (1944): 383–402.

5 James Given, *Inquisition and Medieval Society: Power, Discipline and Resistance in Languedoc* (Ithaca, NY: Cornell University Press, 1997).

6 Guy Geltner, *The Medieval Prison: A Social History* (Princeton, NJ: Princeton University Press, 2008).

to the number of people charged with crimes.[7] Between 1387 and 1400, the Parisian Parlement heard more than two hundred cases, of which only four ended in capital punishment.[8] Recent historians have argued that the real importance of executions and physical punishments in the medieval urban milieu resides not in the frequency, but in the ritual nature behind the events. Esther Cohen believes that medieval authorities created a visual trick through their spectacular executions in medieval cities. Even though the death sentences may not have occurred regularly, she argues, the painstaking processions to the gallows and blood-shed of the prisoner left a lasting impression upon spectators, leading them to recall the particularity and individuality of each execution.[9] If we take this into consideration, secular judicial administrators had to be sure that the public regarded prisons as a legitimate and valid means of establishing justice to victims and to their families, and ecclesiastical officials needed to prove the institution was successful in eradicating heresy in a particular region. Careful attention had to be paid, then, to the men assigned the task of serving as prison wardens and their guards, all of whom became the public figures performing justice on a mundane daily basis, rather than through an affiliation with a dramatic corporal punishment.

What I want to propose in this article, is that if we accept prisons as a recognizable punitive institution by the end of the fourteenth century, then we must consider that the wardens and officers held a tremendous amount of responsibility in not only codifying the nature and function of the prison in medieval society, but also in delineating judicial hierarchies at both a local and royal level. In this respect, the warden or the jailer could become the focal point of a jurisdictional dispute and a symbol of corruption. Because, to complicate matters even further, any given city had overlapping jurisdictions. So potentially, royal prisons could compete with municipal prisons, municipal prisons with ecclesiastical prisons, all over the right to hold and punish a particular criminal. And again, the conduct and reputation of the warden and guards of each particular prison became the impetus of many of these jurisdictional conflicts.

In France, for example, the monarchy had little trouble ensuring that royal justice trumped all of the lesser courts in Paris by the thirteenth century. But as

---

7 Jacques Chiffoleau, *Les Justices du pape: délinquance et criminalité dans la région d'Avignon au XIVe siècle*. Histoire ancienne et médiéval, 14 (Paris: Publications de la Sorbonne, 1984), 211–42.

8 Claude Gauvard, *"De grace especial:" crime, état et société en France à la fin du Moyen Âge* (Paris: Publications de la Sorbonne, 1991), 897.

9 Esther Cohen, "'To Die a Criminal for Public Good:' The Execution Ritual in Late Medieval Paris," *Law, Customs, and Social Fabric in Medieval Europe: Essays in Honor of Bryce Lyon*, ed. Bernard Bacharach. Studies in Medieval Culture (Kalamazoo: Western Michigan University, 1990), 280–304.

Capetian ambitions spread to other territories, the king's lawyers and officers encountered some opposition in their efforts to create a centralized judicial system. In cities like Lyon, Nicole Gonthier has found a pronounced tension between the royal prison and that of the archbishop in the fourteenth and fifteenth centuries, as both sides complained about the conditions of their rival jails in jurisdictional arguments.[10] These criticisms about the conduct of jailers or the treatment of inmates could also became a very practical way for surrounding citizens could call upon either royal or papal intervention into local judicial affairs, and to ensure some sense of regulation and standardization of the organization of these various prisons.

This contention over imprisonment is even more pronounced in Southern France in the later Middle Ages, as the city of Toulouse made the transition from a fairly autonomous municipal government run by twelve elected capitols, to part of the Capetian kingdom and the headquarters of the Dominican inquisition. In 1229, the city and the surrounding region of Languedoc surrendered to the Capetian kings, thus ending the decades long and arduously fought Albigensian Crusade against the Cathar heretics. The peace treaty ordered the capitols to destroy the city walls and defensive garrisons, and also stipulated that the citizens would financially support the foundation of a new university, and would protect university scholars so as to ensure that heresy would not return to the region. In addition, the French monarchy established a new judicial hierarchy over the local court system as a means of state building, and sent royal officials to reside and administer in Toulouse.

The once autonomous capitols now answered to and were regulated by a royal vicar and seneschal in all things legal. The papacy sent Dominican inquisitors into the city, where they established their tribunal headquarters for the persecution of the lingering numbers of suspected Cathars in the area. As a result, the Catholic Church intensified its demands for the legal privileges of the clergy and university students, and the local bishop sought to reinforce his political power in the judicial realm. Each authority (royal, municipal, bishopric, and inquisitorial) all had representatives who oversaw their respective prisons in Toulouse and in Languedoc. And not surprisingly, this generated great debates about who had the right to detain who, and what were acceptable conditions of the institutions. As royal representatives became more intrusive in the judicial system and policing of Toulouse, as Dominican inquisitors pursued and imprisoned suspects, and as the university became a better defined institution, the municipal capitols struggled to maintain relevancy in the legal arena. In each of these capacities, the conduct and

---

10 Nicole Gonthier, "Prisons et prisonniers à Lyon aux XIVe et XVe siècles," *Mémoires de la société pour l'histoire du droit et des institutions des anciens pays bourguignons, comtois, et romands* 39 (1982): 15–30.

reputation of the jailer and his guards became pivotal factors in establishing the hierarchy of authority, and in justifying the function or purpose of the various prisons.

From a practical and theoretical perspective, then, the right to imprison criminals by the thirteenth century gave a certain amount of legitimacy to political administrations, from the king to regional counts to city councils.[11] We may assume that this connection between authority and prisons was internalized to some extent by the late medieval population: in the English uprisings of 1381, for example, protestors targeted both royal and privately owned gaols as part of their agenda. Their release of prisoners was a symbolic means of destroying the old world order and creating a new one.[12] I have written elsewhere about how rulers in each capacity aspired to demonstrate their own respective authority and understanding of law and order over the public at large by maintaining control of the punitive spectacles (like the dramatic public executions), and how the capitols of Toulouse fought ardently with the French monarchy in order to secure control over their local judicial practices, believing that this authority to pass judgment over its inhabitants was one of their most valuable privileges.[13]

For this paper, I would like to consider briefly the role the different jailers and their guards played in shaping the judicial atmosphere of late medieval Languedoc, in order to argue that they too were crucial figures in forming and legitimizing notions of justice and sovereignty by their daily actions in the prison. In order to tease out this premise, I have divided the rest of the paper into two parts. The first portion will serve as a synthesis of some of the available scholarship concerning the responsibilities and dangers of a medieval jailer working in a municipal or royal prison. This is an opportunity to consider how both internal and external officials regulated the prisons, and to search for differences or commonalities of these punitive manifestations in France, England and Italy. The second portion of the paper will narrow in on the experiences of the wardens and jailers in Languedoc during the thirteenth and fourteenth centuries. The fundamental purpose of this discussion is to reinforce my previous notion that there was a pronounced competition between different jails, and these jurisdictional disputes (often involving the jailers) codified concepts and realities of the judicial hierarchy and punitive imprisonment in medieval France.

---

11 Jean Dunbabin, *Captivity and Imprisonment in Medieval Europe, 1000–1300.* Medieval Culture and Society (Houndmills, Basingstoke, Hampshire, and New York: Palgrave Macmillan, 2002), 46–47.

12 Anthony Musson, trans. and ed., *Crime, Law and Society in the Later Middle Ages*. Medieval Sources Series (Manchester and New York: Manchester University Press, 2009), 53.

13 Patricia Turning, "The Right to Punish: Jurisdictional Disputes between Royal and Municipal Officials in Medieval Toulouse," *French History* 24 (2010): 1–19.

***

By the very nature of their office, wardens, jailers, and guards were placed in a fairly multi-faceted role: they were the points of contact between the administrators and the inmate, so they had to make sure they complied with the official stipulations and regulations while also protecting themselves in their daily interactions with the prison population; they stood between the public and those incarcerated, and had to present themselves as both disciplinarian and humanitarian. Unlike today's prisons, which are for the most part tucked away in the countryside, away from public view, most secular medieval prisons were at the heart of city squares. The exception to this notion seems to be Germany, where most places of detention were holes dug in the foundations of castles or local fortifications.[14]

But in other parts of Europe, any urban resident, throughout the normal course of their business day, could pass by and assess the state of the local prison. Geltner's work reveals that in the Italian city-states there was a fairly porous flow between the outside world and the world inside the prison. For example, inmates could leave the prison at times to beg for alms, to attend religious services, or to be present at their relevant legal functions. The Fleet prison in London actually had an officer, known as a *baston*, whose major responsibility was to escort inmates who had business to attend to outside of the institution for an extended period of time.[15] And just as inmates could leave the facility, charitable people and relatives donated bread and money to the prisons, and these visits provided the opportunity for local residents to inspect the living conditions of inmates.

Throughout Europe, it was frequently the public that pushed their government to provide a humane prison environment. After several people from the community complained about the conditions of the Newgate prison, London's city council actually stipulated that inspectors visit the prison regularly in order to ensure that the warden was following city codes protecting the inmates.[16] With this open nature of most prisons taken into consideration, we may presume that the legitimacy of the prison as a punitive institution resided to a certain extent on the integrity of those in charge.

In reality, however, most royal or municipal wardens and their officers earned a fairly modest salary. In some circumstances, the prison staff was paid a salary by their respective administrations. For example, Le Stinche prison in Florence was funded directly by communal revenues.[17] The personnel at Le Stinche included the warden, guards, scribes, chamberlains, physicians, and a coroner. But although

---

14 Peters, "The Prison before the Prison," 37 (see note 2).

15 Bassett, "The Fleet Prison," 397 (see note 4); Pugh, *Imprisonment*, 186 (see note 3).

16 Bassett, "Newgate Prison," 242 (see note 4).

17 Geltner, *The Medieval Prison*, 18 (see note 6).

they were guaranteed a municipal salary, this does not mean that they received it regularly, as there were many complaints about having to wait weeks, or even months to get paid.[18] Most prison wardens and their staffs were completely dependant upon a system of fees to make any money. At prisons like the Châtelet in Paris, inmates paid an entrance fee and an exit fee, and they had to pay for their food and their bed. The Châtelet was even divided into fourteen prisons that separated inmates according to their rank, and provided them with the goods that they could afford.[19] Those who could spend six *derniers* slept on a pallet, or bundle of straw, and those who could only afford one *dernier* spent the night in the cold dank dungeon.[20] This process placed the burden of paying for the imprisonment in the hands of the inmate, and as a result, this reduced the cost of running the institution for the crown or city government.

This financial system of payments brought with it critics and complications, as many jailers found ways to exploit their position out of necessity or greed. Guards could establish arbitrary costs for virtually any material goods, or they could institute fines that would render the prisoner impoverished, and thus, by extension, prolong his stay. And it is not surprising that some inmates successfully bribed prison guards to smuggle in comforts like prostitutes or alcohol.[21] Other prisons employed the practice of "ironing," which theoretically meant that chains, fetters, manacles, rings, and collars were to be used to restrain dangerous inmates, or to transfer them securely to another facility. But enterprising wardens and guards accepted "removal" fees, which either liberated the inmate from the irons, or removed the threat of being shackled from the scenario.[22] Jailers could also be tempted to intercept alms and donations for their own purposes, but this action could bring about serious repercussions for the offender.

The jailer of the Châtelet was responsible for negotiating charitable contributions from the Parisians to make sure that the poor inmates had enough available bread. The baker's guilds always made sure that a portion of their goods made it to the Châtelet, and private donors gave financial contributions to benefit the prisoners as well. The jailer had to make careful records of all of these donations, because if any of the money was misused, he could be arrested by the royal government for theft, for which the punishment was hanging.[23] Throughout England in the fourteenth and fifteenth centuries, there was great concern from the crown and

---

18 Geltner, *The Medieval Prison*, 19 (see note 6).

19 Louis Batiffol, "Le Châtelet de Paris vers 1400," *Revue historique* 61–63 (1896–1897): 225–64, 225–35, 242–55, 266–83; here 47–49.

20 Bronislav Geremek, *The Margins of Society in Late Medieval Paris*, trans. Jean Birrell. Past and Present Publications (Cambridge: Cambridge University Press, 1987), 18.

21 Trevor Dean, *Crime in Medieval Europe 1200–1550* (New York: Longman Publications, 2001), 122.

22 Pugh, *Imprisonment*, 179 (see note 3).

23 Batiffol, "Le Châtelet de Paris," 54 (see note 17).

local administrations to ensure that the prison entrance and exit fees be reasonable and fixed.[24] And they also instituted regulations concerning what specifically jailers could sell to their inmates for a "side" salary, including alcohol.[25]

Beyond the suspicions surrounding the financial actions and intentions of the wardens and guards, critics could point to the treatment of the prisoners as another source of contention. Institutions like the Newgate prison housed some of the most hardened and violent criminals in England. Wardens, then, walked a fine line between reprimanding offenders, and actually harming them. The guards needed to make sure that they were visible figures of authority in the jail, so that they could prevent any type of violence or escape. Most wardens were held personally and financially responsible if an inmate escaped: at Newgate, the warden was subject to a fine of 100s. for each prisoner who got away.[26] Prisoners were sometimes placed in the horrible depths of prisons dungeons, and sometimes suffered in horrible conditions. The jailer of York in 1274 was said to have tied a prisoner naked to a post and kept him starving.[27] In 1305, the Bishop of Lyon's chief judge denounced the local jailer's practice of torturing his inmates so severely that they frequently died from the suffering even after their release.[28] By many accounts, jails were riddled with disease, filth and cold (Geltner, however, insists otherwise for his Italian urban prisons). But despite these reports of deplorable treatment, jailers were still all responsible if someone died on their watch due to extraneous circumstances.[29] In principle, then, those in charge of the prisons needed to make sure that conditions would not cause the death of an inmate. French royal prisons, for instance, were expected to be "reasonable and airy."[30] Even though officers needed to comply with these regulations and stipulations, and to be careful about the ways in which they treated inmates in order to make both the administration and the surrounding public content, there were real dangers lurking in medieval prisons.

Guards were susceptible to individual outbursts of inmate's violence, but perhaps more ominous were riots or rebellions. Although Geltner argues that there were relatively few prison uprisings at Florence's Le Stinche prison in the fourteenth century (and attributes it to the outnumbered staff's humane treatment of the inmates), this was not a universal trend. Both Venetian and Bolognese guards tortured inmates, and they could supplement their income by "flogging

---

24 Pugh, *Imprisonment*, 170 (see note 3).

25 Pugh, *Imprisonment*, 188–91 (see note 3).

26 Bassett, "Newgate Prison," 234 (see note 4).

27 Pugh, *Imprisonment*, 180 (see note 3).

28 Dean, *Crime in medieval Europe*, 123 (see note 19).

29 Pugh, *Imprisonment*, 183 (see note 3).

30 Edwards, "Prison before the Prison," 39 (see note 2).

inmates and performing dismemberments and even executions."[31] This fact contributed to the growing vilification of guards and wardens, and rendered them the targets of prison uprisings. We know, for example, that prisoners killed the jailer of Bristol in 1287, and the gatekeeper of Newgate prison in 1325.[32] Again, jailers had to walk the fine line between protecting themselves while on duty by suppressing the actions and movement of the inmates, all while providing a humane environment for the convicted criminals.

To compound these issues of financial corruption and physical exploitation, there was always the delicate but serious question of how to deal with female inmates. Part of Geltner's argument that Italian prisons were modern punitive institutions by the end of the fourteenth century comes from the fact that the prison was divided into wards. Hardened violent criminals were separated from petty criminals, and women were isolated from men. In its complex organization, the Châtelet in Paris had two prisons built to accommodate female prisoners, known as *la Boucherie* and *la Griesche*.[33]

Ideally, female inmates would be overseen by "honest women" as stipulated by the administration of the Châtelet. But in other scenarios, and in many municipal prisons, women resided in the general prison population under the surveillance of male guards. Even though statistically women were always a small percentage of those incarcerated throughout medieval Europe, it still placed an added burden for jailers and guards. From a practical perspective, Susan Broomhall's study of ecclesiastical jail of Saint Germain des Près from 1537 to 1579 suggests that women inmates were more likely to be released from jail sooner than their male counterparts, primarily because the type of women being incarcerated could not afford to pay the prison's many fines.[34] But female felons still needed to be protected from the assaults or exploitation of both male inmates and guards. When Margery Kempe travelled to Leicester in 1417, the Mayor arrested her for her religious beliefs, and ordered the jailer to take her away to prison. When the jailer responded that he had no place to put her besides in the cell with men, Kempe pleaded for compassion and consideration for her chastity. Her fate was determined only by the kindness of the jailer who brought her home and took her into personal custody.[35] Not surprisingly, guards always fell under suspicion of sexually exploiting their female charges, and at the Newgate prison, one warden

---

31 Geltner, *The Medieval Prison*, 71 (see note 6).

32 Pugh, *Imprisonment*, 183 (see note 3).

33 Batiffol, "Le Châtelet de Paris," 48 (see note 17).

34 Susan Broomhall, "Poverty, Gender and Incarceration in Sixteenth-Century Paris," *French History Journal* 18 (2004): 1–24.

35 *The Book of Margery Kempe*, trans. Barry Windeatt (New York: Penguin Books, 1994), 149–50.

was arrested and actually joined the ranks of prisoners there for violating a female inmate.[36]

And then there was always the complication of how to treat pregnant prisoners. Because most courts refused to execute pregnant women, many women in this condition spent time in the often dangerous jails. In one circumstance heard by the Parlement in Paris, two administrators, Coldard de Gisors, vicomte du Crotoy and Barthélemy du Gué, were "mis en arrêt" and imprisoned for having such rigorous conditions in their prison that a pregnant inmate lost her child.[37] There are examples, however, of female felons released, and then re-arrested and imprisoned once they gave birth to their child.[38] Women were not always hapless victims, though. Matilda Hereward of Branndeston in Northhamptonshire was convicted along with her husband for larceny in June 21, 1301. They both were sentenced to be hanged, but she was put in jail because she was pregnant. When they came back to check on her six times over the course of two years and she was pregnant each time.[39] Because she was in a mixed population it is unclear as to whether the prison guard or a fellow inmate prolonged her life. What this case reveals, though, is that gender and physicality also shaped the relationship between the warden and inmate, with the burden and expectation of responsibility always placed on the shoulders of those in charge.

***

Since the eleventh century, the elected capitols of Toulouse had struggled to gain political and judicial autonomy from their local count, and had to renew their efforts after the Capetian king's conquest in 1229. As the count's (later royal) palace, the Château Narbonnais, loomed over the southeastern portion of the city, the capitols began to purchase property in the center of the city in order to erect their town hall. Like many medieval cities, the town hall was situated in a central location in the urban space, where administrators could meet the needs of their constituents in the courtroom. The building also served as a symbol of civic pride and autonomy, and reportedly stored the trebuchet responsible for the fatal stone that killed the city's major foe Simon de Montfort on June 25, 1218, during the

36 Bassett, "Newgate Prison," 241 (see note 4).

37 Annik Porteau-Bitker, "Criminalité et délinquance féminines dans le droit pénal des XIIIe et XIVe siècles," *Revue historique de droit français et étranger* 58 (1980): 13–57; here 55.

38 Broomhall, "Poverty, Gender and Incarceration," 16 (see note 32).

39 Barbara Hanawalt, "The Female Felon in Fourteenth-Century England," *Viator* 5 (1974): 253–68; here 266.

struggles of the Albigensian Crusade.[40] And perhaps most importantly for this paper, the municipal jail was a part of the town hall.

Toulouse's municipal jail seemed to be a fairly porous institution. The intention of the incarceration was not to remove the criminal from the public eye, but instead the urban population passed the prison and could see the inmates during the course of their business day. This is best evidenced in a variation of punitive containment known as the *costellum* employed by the capitols. In this method, a prisoner would stand bound by an iron collar and chains, exposed in a window of the prison for a variable amount of time. The thirteenth-century commentator of the *coutumes* of Toulouse provides one example of this punishment: one evening, night guards arrested a young apprentice baker, named Guillaume Barrau, for sleeping with his master's wife.[41]

The capitols chose to proceed with the trial and sentenced the youth to decapitation, despite warnings from civic lawyers who argued that, because the he was less than twenty-five years old, the father needed to be present. Barrau quickly appealed his case to the vicar, and the capitols conceded to reducing the sentence to a run of the town, and then confinement in the *costellum* for an unspecified amount of time. The capitols employed a very public means of chastising moral and criminal offenders, and on this occasion, the emphasis was upon the symbolism of the town hall and civic jail. By displaying a criminal in a window of the building, the capitols established the notion that punishment was directly under their power and control, centralized within the city, and available for all of the Toulousains to witness.

Criminal records from the early fourteenth century indicate that a man named Raymundus Bonhomme was the municipal jailer of Toulouse. Not only did he oversee the facility, but he actually lived in the building with his family, feeding and monitoring the detainees at all times. There is some indication in the records that the office might have been passed down from father to son, because in 1322, when the capitols passed the responsibilities of the prison to Raymundus Bonhomme, he was identified as the son of the exiting jailor.[42] We have no way of knowing how long the family held the office in Toulouse, but if this was a hereditary office, kept and passed down in one family, it might suggest that a certain amount of civic pride went along with the office. At the Fleet prison in London, the position of warden was kept in a singular family for over five hundred years. Like Toulouse, Fleet was in close proximity to the central

---

40 Henri Gilles, *Les coutumes de Toulouse (1286) et leur premier commentaire (1296)* (Toulouse: Imprimerie Maurice ESPIC, 1969), 163: "qui lapis fuit projectus per machinam cum quo dictus comes Montisfortis fuit percussus. Que machine est adhuc in palatio communi."

41 Gilles, *Les coutumes de Toulouse*, 187–88 (see note 38).

42 Archives municipales de Toulouse – AA3:246. March 5, 1322. Hereafter referenced as AMT.

administration, and the office was one that carried a certain heraldry and status. The Fleet warden was also keeper of Westminster palace, he received a house with a garden, and was a city salaried official. By most accounts, the dignity of the familial office meant that the Fleet warden was more civil and humane than his British counterparts, as was evidenced by a lack of riots or inmate complaints. In part of the ceremony accepting the office, Toulouse's Raymundus Bonhomme received the keys of the prison, as well as those of the town hall and of the capitols' court. Along with being entrusted with access to the entire building, he pledged an oath of fidelity to the city, and vowed to maintain discretion and integrity with regards to the prisoners.

While part of the office required that he monitor the interaction of detainees with their visitors, the capitols of Toulouse also insisted that the municipal jailer feed them satisfactory amounts of bread and water, and maintain the "tradition" that the prisoners eat at a table. As was discussed before, this is a stipulation that is a bit unheard of in other variations of secular prisons. Again, at most locations, the jailer had no responsibility to feed his prisoners. Instead, the food and provisions came through a system of payments (resulting in wealthier inmates experiencing better accommodations), or through a distribution of charitable donations. Although we have no way of knowing whether or not Toulouse's municipal jailer adhered to the stipulation that his wards eat at a table, its inclusion in the job description from the fourteenth century is worth noting. It seems to imply that the office was intended to serve as a central component of the community at large, which maintained a sense of tradition and continuity with the past, not only in the hereditary office of the prison warden, but also in the open and civilized nature of the treatment of the detainees.

The same Raymundus Bonhomme emerged frequently as a pivotal player in the judicial realm from the 1330s. The jailer was in attendance during certain trials and sentencing which took place in the capitols' court.[43] In order to release a prisoner, the jailer had to receive a proper letter with a seal from the vicar or the capitols, which suggests that the office was a part of the institutionalized bureaucracy. In one circumstance he actually was a protective agent for an imprisoned prostitute, Johaneta de Santolo.[44] In the spring of 1332, Johaneta had suffered a series of misfortunes that culminated in her arrest and conviction for prostitution. As Johaneta waited in jail, she did not spend her time in idle reflection. Instead, she apparently befriended Raymundus Bonhomme, who permitted her to receive guests and gifts. More importantly, the jailer seems to have used the privilege of his office to help secure an audience for Johaneta with the city's judicial

43 AMT-FF 57, 18. Raymundus Bonhomme was listed present as the city's "*carcerarius*" at the death sentence of a squire, Aimery Berenger, in 1332.

44 AMT-FF 57, 156–57.

administrators, the capitols, where she launched a massive accusation that a city sergeant had actually served as her pimp and forced her into the life of prostitution. This led to a city-wide investigation into the sergeant's possible corruption, which indicates that the capitols took her charges seriously enough to attempt to uncover any proof to her claim. In this scenario, it seems as though jailer Raymundus Bonhomme played a pivotal role in providing a venue for the defense of the prostitute in this legal predicament.

Royal and church officials began to plant the roots of their authority in Toulouse by the early thirteenth century. The city's monastery, the Jacobins, became the headquarters of the Dominican inquisitors, while the king's agents stationed themselves in the Château Narbonnais. The other jails of the city, the royal jail in the château and the ecclesiastical prisons, had very different methods of holding prisoners in isolation from the general public. Whereas royal officers and clerks could only be held in their respective prisons, the people of Toulouse could be arrested and held in the Château Narbonnais when royal officials saw opportunities to profit financially from the overlapping jurisdiction in the city. If royal officers arrested a citizen of Toulouse caught in the process of a suspicious act, or they simply heard of the suspicions of criminal activity, the sergeants could imprison the citizen in the royal jail.

For example, in 1332, citizen Arnaldus de Santo Martino was arrested by royal sergeants because several bandits, held in the royal prison awaiting punishment, implicated him in their thefts. But he was later remanded to the capitols, transferred to the jail in the town hall so that he could stand trial for the accusations against him.[45] This, however, provided an opportunity for the vicar and his royal jailers to extort money from the prisoners, only releasing them into the custody of the capitols if they paid a certain fine. In 1313, King Philip IV threatened the royal jailer, under the penalty of dismissal from his post, that he could no longer claim fees from prisoners from the moment when the capitols demanded extradition to their court.[46] This issue came up again one year later, causing the seneschal to reprimand the vicar and his men in charge of the prison at the Château Narbonnais. In this instance, the royal jailer demanded that the each prisoner brought into custody pay a sum of twelve *deniers Toulousains*, three *deniers* for simply entering the jail, and nine *deniers* for the duration of imprisonment.[47] These fees, which contradicted agreements of jurisdiction between the capitols and vicar, and the conduct of the jailer in general, alarmed the

---

45 AMT-FF 57, 143.

46 AMT-AA3:152. May 11, 1313.

47 AMT-AA3:158. June 18, 1314. This was a mandate of Jean de Mauquenchy, seneschal of Toulouse and Albi, to the vicar of Toulouse.

seneschal, and suggested the real lenience of the regional vicar in overseeing the conduct of his men at the Château.

These oversights and exploitations resulted in an overhaul of the regulations of the royal prison to ensure that the prisoner only paid the jail's fines if found guilty by the capitols. In 1327, however, Jean Folenfant, vicar of the Château Narbonnais, was caught again demanding financial penalties from prisoners known to be innocent.[48] Among the complaints of the capitols, which prompted the reactions of the king and seneschal, was the concern that the royal jailer did not feed the prisoners adequate amounts of bread and water, and that they did not eat their food at a table with the jailer. We know that jailer Johanni de Barra of the Château Narbonnais in 1322, spent enough money for bread for the imprisoned poor, along with the other necessary "shackles and keys" to run a prison for the year on a budget of roughly 67 *lires*.[49] But the capitols' concern that prisoners were not treated properly by the royal jailer suggests that there was a much different attitude regarding inmates between the two sets of officials. The royal authorities had a detachment from the prisoners in their custody. There seemed to be a rapid turnover in the men who held the office, and the guilt or innocence of the prisoners seemed secondary to the opportunity for profits and fines. Royal jailers did not have the same interest in creating a communal atmosphere for the prisoners.

Ecclesiastical authorities and the Dominican inquisitors eventually learned they achieved greater success in achieving confessions and conversions from suspected heretics through imprisonment, rather than torture. By the fourteenth century, they had several prisons in Toulouse, which served a very distinct purpose of isolating and containing accused heretics and criminal clerks. According to canon law, ecclesiastical judges were forbidden from shedding blood, so they were particularly interested in using incarceration as a punitive function. The Dominican inquisitors had two prisons to house suspected and convicted heretics: one at the basilica of Saint Sernin, and one in the Cathedral Saint-Étienne. But under the direction of the infamous Bernard Gui, suspected heretics could also be held in the *mur* of the Château Narbonnais. Conditions in the *mur* could vary from a relatively lenient environment of general confinement in which the suspected

48 AMT-AA3:256. July 12, 1327.

49 François Maillard, ed. *Comptes royaux (1314–1328)*. Recueil des Historiens de la France, Documents Financiers, 14 (Paris: Imprimerie Nationale, 1961), no. 2005, 142: "Johanni de Barra, jaulerio castri Narbone Tholose, pro pane plurium pauperum incarceratorum pro toto presenti anno in dicto castro detentorum, compedibus, riblonibus, manotis ferries reparadnis clavibus, serraturis neccessariis pro dictis carceribus et ipsis curandis et pluribus aliis pro dictis prisioniariis neccessariis, juxta compotum cum vicario Tholose factum, partes cum partibus retroacapitum presentis compoti: 67 l. 6 s. t."

criminals had space to wander and interact, or it could be a *murum strictum* in which the prisoner was confined and shackled in a private cell.[50]

Most of the prisoners held in the *mur* were supported by the king, because he profited from the confiscation of their property if they were condemned. James Given has shown that during any one week in these prisons there was an average of 171 prisoners, including children, during the period of May 6, 1255 and February 6, 1256.[51] In 1321, the king supported sixty-six men and women in the *mur* of Toulouse, sentenced to imprisonment for twenty-eight days.[52] Most of the Dominican inquisitors preferred to imprison heretics so they could not corrupt others. It also served to isolate suspected heretics from their social networks which provided moral support and connections to go into hiding, and also could provide the opportunity for them to confess their "corrupt thoughts" in a weakened state of food and sleep deprivation.

But there was great protest from the population of Southern France against the actions of the inquisitors. And the officials overseeing the prison of heretics became easy targets for all of the animosity against the persecution and torment of their actions. One of the most dramatic examples took place in the nearby city of Albi, as the citizens launched an all out uprising against the much hated bishop and inquisitor, Bernard de Castanet who oversaw the local prison. The accusers sent appeals to the king and the pope, and charged that Bernard imprisoned citizens in horrific conditions, without adequate food or water, and that he arbitrarily tortured his inmates. They also charged that he ordered the arrest and the imprisonment for certain women he found sexually appealing. He could then summon the females to his palace whenever he desired, and some witnesses claimed when the women did not return to the prison population, he deposed of the bodies in a suspicious manner.[53] In one allegation, Bernard kept an innocent woman named Marquesia in jail for a number of years before being released, to exploit her explicitly as a sex slave. Although there has been historical debate surrounding the validity of these accusations, the fact remains that the citizens of Albi demanded royal intervention into the affairs of the inquisitorial prison, and the conduct of Bernard de Castanet served as the impetus for that call to action. The denunciation was a political tool: a way in which the citizens of Albi sought protection from the inquisitors, and by extension, could establish the hierarchy of justice and order in the local prisons.

---

50 The term *mur* is a common designation of inquisitorial prisons, borrowed from the monastic usage of a punitive confinement in monasteries. Peters, "Prison before the Prison," 28–29.

51 Given, *Inquisition and Medieval Society*, 79 (see note 5).

52 *Comptes royaux*, no. 1340, 84 (see note 47).

53 Megan Cassidy-Welch, "Testimonies from a Fourteenth-Century Prison: Rumor, Evidence and Truth in the Midi," *French History* 16 (2002): 3–27.

Back in Toulouse, the competition surrounding punishment was even more pronounced, and the municipal jailer found himself in the midst of jurisdictional disputes between municipal and royal authority, signifying again, that he was a key player in local politics that could also get wrapped up in national affairs. One example from 1332 involved the jailer in a fight to punish a mother accused of acting as her daughter's pimp. Initially, the capitols believed that Berengaria Vitalis's daughter, Mastaroza, had been kidnapped and raped by a neighbor Johannes de Manso, son of Lord Helio de Manso.[54] But two weeks later, the municipal sergeants arrested and imprisoned Berengaria Vitalis for prostituting her daughter. There are no extant court records which reveal the investigative process into Berengaria's culpability. Instead, we can only assume that the capitols' had secured the necessary evidence to warrant her arrest and punishment. Berengaria was held in the municipal prison awaiting her appeal to the royal vicar. According to royal decree, the capitols needed the vicar's approval before they enacted any specific punishment for a convicted criminal. But this became a national legal affair because it was an occasion where the capitols and their officers publicly undermined the vicar and sentenced Berengaria to a ritual punishment of running the town without the royal official's knowledge of the case.[55] In the seneschal's later inquest into the jurisdictional dispute between the municipal officials and the vicar, three capitols, several of their sergeants, trumpeter Guillelmus Johannis, and for our purposes, most notably, the same municipal jailer, Raymundus Bonhomme all stood accused of conspiring against royal authority.

According to the charges, three capitols, Petrus Rubey, Raymundus de Santo Paulo, and Vitalis Durandi all gathered at the town hall, and convinced the jailer to release the prisoner into their custody.[56] Raymundus Bonhomme, who lived with his family at the town hall in order to survey and feed the prisoners, claimed in his defense testimony that the capitols provided him with the proper documentation necessary to transfer the criminals into their custody for punishment.[57] In other words, either the capitols forged the royal vicar's seal of approval on the letter and duped the jailer, or Raymundus Bonhomme simply knew how to save himself from losing his home and livelihood. Regardless, the capitols and several officers gathered the prisoner and bound her in shackles, and carried out the punitive spectacle of forcing Berengaria to run the streets of the

---

54 AMT-FF 57, 59.

55 For a discussion of the use of the punishment of running the town, especially in Southern France, see Jean-Marie Carbasse, "Currant nudi: Le répression de l'adultère dans le Midi médiéval, XIIe-VXe siècles," *Droit, Histoire et Sexualité*, ed. Jacques Poumarede and Jean-Pierre Royer. Publications de l'Espace juridique (Lille: Achevé d'imprimer, 1987), 83–102.

56 AMT-FF 59, fol. 11r.

57 AMT-FF 59, fol. 50r.

city, with a crown of straw upon her head. The capitols intended the ritual punishment of Berengaria Vitalis to serve as a statement of their power, and autonomy from royal jurisdiction. In the end, the capitols and several of their officers faced the consequences in the royal court for bypassing the authority of the vicar by denying his participation in the execution, or in the appeals process.[58] What we find, though, is that even when the municipal jailer is not simply tending to his wards, he could be embroiled in larger political and legal disputes that ultimately resulted in efforts to further establish the hierarchy of justice.

***

Much like today, there is no monolithic jailer emerging from the end of the Middle Ages. Some wardens ran their prison and staff with the reverence befitting any other administrative office: heeding the regulations set forth by their supervisors, and in turn, providing a hospitable environment for their inmates. Others saw the position as an opportunity to financially exploit their wards or to satisfy some cruel desire to see them suffer in harsh conditions and through torture. But if we think beyond the individual office holder, and consider the office itself, I believe my initial proposal rings true. The jailer, warden, and their officers all played an integral role in the shaping of the judicial system at the local, regional and royal levels, and in the codification of the prison as a punitive institution in the medieval consciousness.

This article has offered an examination of the situation in fourteenth-century Languedoc as just one example of this theory. In Toulouse, both the royal and ecclesiastical prison administrations preferred to punish criminals and defendants through isolation and series of financial amends. These methods served their intentions to secure confessions from suspects, and to increase the profits of their office. The royal and ecclesiastical jailers and guards employed methods which marginalized the punitive process in the daily lives of the inhabitants of the city. This contradicted the practices and tradition of the capitols and the municipal jailer, who maintained a process of imprisonment that was generally very accessible for the Toulousains to observe and to understand that law and order had been restored. Not surprisingly, each prison maintained its privileges and primacy, which resulted in a direct competition concerning who had the right to incarcerate the Toulousains. It will take further archival inquest beyond that of Southern France to fully develop our understanding of these early formative years of the prison, but perhaps the first step is acknowledging that punitive imprisonment did, in fact, exist by the later Middle Ages.

58 AMT-FF 59, fol. 49r.

Chapter 13

Birgit Wiedl
(Institute for Jewish History in Austria, St. Pölten)

The Host on the Doorstep: Perpetrators, Victims, and Bystanders in an Alleged Host Desecration in Fourteenth-Century Austria

"The body of Christ, tormented by the Jews, was found at Korneuburg on the Friday of the quarter before Michaelmas and therefore, all the Jews there were burnt."[1]

In this brief sum-up in a chronicle of the Lower Austrian monastery of Klosterneuburg of what had, allegedly and for real,[2] happened in the town across the river Danube, the roles are clearly defined: the Jews who had lived there had committed a crime, and had therefore been punished.

"This book is not a whodunnit," Jeremy Cohen states at the beginning of the introduction to his book *Christ Killers*.[3] The question, if applicable at all to a historic

---

1 Österreichische Nationalbibliothek (Austrian National Library), Codex 364, fol. 135v (a later addition to a Salzburg chronicle in a manuscript from the monastery of Klosterneuburg, now kept at the Austrian National Library); Eveline Brugger and Birgit Wiedl, *Regesten zur Geschichte der Juden in Österreich im Mittelalter*, vol. 1: *Von den Anfängen bis 1338* (Innsbruck, Vienna, and Bolzano: StudienVerlag, 2005), 123–24, no. 131 (for the internet version, see http://www.injoest.ac.at/upload/Regesten_Text.pdf (last accessed on March 10, 2012). The research was funded by the Austrian Science Fund (FWF): P 21237–G18. I would like to thank Connie Scarborough for her valuable comments and corrections.

2 On the truthfulness of historiography and literature and its relation to historical texts, see the discussion by Peter Johanek, "Die Wahrheit der mittelalterlichen Historiographen," *Historisches und fiktionales Erzählen im Mittelalter*, ed. Fritz Peter Knapp and Manuela Niesner. Schriften zur Literaturwissenschaft, 19 (Berlin: Duncker & Humblot, 2002), 9–26.

3 Jeremy Cohen, *Christ Killers: The Jews and the Passion from the Bible to the Big Screen* (New York and Oxford: Oxford University Press, 2007). In the introduction to her book *Gentile Tales*, Miri Rubin discusses the 'tedious type of prose' that is a result of all the 'disclaimers such as 'it was alleged'',

scenario, has been sufficiently answered. Although motives, triggers, and courses of action remain open to discussion, there is no doubt as to the fatal role (most of) the Christian authorities and/or neighbours played in the persecution and murdering of medieval Jews; while from a medieval Christian perspective, the ideas of Jewish crime,[4] Jewish guilt, and the existence of crimes that Jews were particularly partial to, were hardly questioned.[5] From the seducer of Christians who lures these back to the old, false faith, the fake convert who secretly indulges in their old suspicious rites, and the merciless usurer[6] to the general questionability of Jewish existence in general, Jewish crimes were manifold.[7] Jews

---

Miri Rubin, *Gentile Tales: The Narrative Assault on Late Medieval Jews* (New Haven, CT, and London: Yale University Press, 1999; sec. ed. Philadelphia: University of Pennsylvania Press, 2004, the quotes herein refer to the first edition), 3.

4 For a quite exceptional case study on 'real' Jewish crime, the story of a 'gang' of Jewish thieves, see Jörg Müller, "Eine jüdische Diebesbande im Südwesten des Reiches in der ersten Hälfte des 14. Jahrhunderts," *Beziehungsnetze aschkenasischer Juden während des Mittelalters und der frühen Neuzeit*, ed. idem. Forschungen zur Geschichte der Juden, Abteilung A: Abhandlungen, 20 (Hanover: Verlag Hahnsche Buchhandlung, 2008), 71–116.

5 For a summary of scholarly Christian opinions on Jews and Judaism, see Gavin I. Langmuir, "Faith of Christians and Hostility to Jews," *Christianity and Judaism*, ed. Diana Wood. Studies in Church History, 29 (Oxford and Cambridge, MA: Blackwell Publishers, 1992), 77–92.

6 See, for example, Pope Innocent III to the French king Philipp II August in 1205: *...quod in regno Francorum Judei adeo insolescunt, ut, sub specie usurarie pravitatis, per quam non solum usuras, sed usuras usurarum extorquent, ecclesiarum bona et possessiones Christanorum usurpent.* Solomon Grayzel, *The Church and the Jews in the Thirteenth Century. A Study of Their Relations During the Years 1198–1254, Based on the Papal Letters and the Conciliar Decrees of the Period* (Philadelphia: The Dropsie College for Hebrew and Cognate Learning, 1933) 104–06, no. 14; Langmuir, "Faith of Christians," 88–89 (see note 5), places the emergence of the motif of the Jew as usurer in the mid-twelfth century. See the contribution of Kenneth R. Stow in the same volume, "The Good of the Church, the Good of the State: The Popes and Jewish Money," *Christianity and Judaism*, 237–52 (see note 5), on the identification of Jewish lending with Jewish acts of homicide against Christian society, 241; see also the overview by Robert Chazan, *Medieval Stereotypes and Modern Antisemitism* (Berkeley, Los Angeles, and London: University of California Press, 1997), 19–40, and particularly 35–40, who ties the usurer-image in with antigovernment sentiments. On the idea that Jews had killed Jesus out of greed, see Anna Sapir Abulafia, *Christians and Jews in the Twelfth-Century Renaissance* (London: Routledge, 1992), 121.

7 E.g., the combined accusations Simon de Montfort arose against the Jew Abraham of Berkhamsted in the 1250s: financial misdeeds and the desecration of an icon of the Virgin Mary (by placing it in his lavatory), see Christoph Cluse, "'Fabula ineptissima'. Die Ritualmordlegende um Adam von Bristol nach der Handschrift London, British Library, Harley 957," *Aschkenas. Zeitschrift für Geschichte und Kultur der Juden*, 5.2 (1995), 293–330; here 296; Anthony Bale, *The Jew in the Medieval Book: English Antisemitisms 1350–1500*. Cambridge Studies in Medieval Literature, 60 (Cambridge: Cambridge University Press, 2006), 8, and generally on the phenomenon of anti-Judaism and anti-Semitism in a country from which the Jews were expelled already at the end of the high Middle Ages (1290), see also Cohen, *Christ Killers*, 103 (see note 3).

were regarded capable of, and prone to, committing specific crimes most of which made their way into the stereotypes of anti-Semitism of later centuries.[8]

The ideas of Jewish responsibility and culpability for the crucifixion of Christ and the identification of Jews as historic enemies of Christianity and Christendom already lay, among other factors, at the core of the crusading assaults on the Rhineland Jewry of around 1096,[9] and had evolved into an imagery of Jewish violence against Christians in general. As a result of the growing humanization, and subsequent vulnerability, of Jesus in the course of the twelfth century, the idea of the Jews killing a deity merged with the images of the murder of a real person, or its personification in the Eucharist. The image of a 'real' killing with a palpable victim was much more relatable for the common people.[10] The theoretical-theological image preached during a sermon was transformed into an image that could be brought up whenever needed, adapted to local circumstances, and repeated time and again—the idea that contemporary Jews behaved towards the host just like their forefathers had behaved towards Christ, and thus, their punishment was intended by God.[11]

What had, in more detail than the annals' succinct entry tells us, happened in the small Lower Austrian town of Korneuburg? On September 17, 1305, a host wafer was found either on the doorstep of the house that was occupied (and, presumably, owned) by the Jew Zerkel, or in his possession.[12] Blood was seeping

---

8 From the vast literature on this topic, see in addition to the study of Chazan, *Medieval Stereotypes* (see note 6), the older but still valid overviews by Gavin I. Langmuir, *Toward a Definition of Antisemitism* (Berkeley, Los Angeles, and Oxford: University of California Press, 1990), particularly 301–10, and Stefan Rohrbacher and Michael Schmidt, *Judenbilder: Kulturgeschichte antijüdischer Mythen und antisemitischer Vorurteil*. kulturen&ideen. rowohlts enzyklopädie (Reinbek bei Hamburg: rowohlt, 1991).

9 Chazan, *Medieval Stereotypes*, 59 (see note 6).

10 Cohen, *Christ Killers* (see note 3), addresses the topic in several chapters; see further Sapir Abulafia, *Christians and Jews*, 107–22 (see note 6), mainly on the development of the theological idea; Björn Berghausen, 'Das Lied von Deggendorf,' *Juden in der deutschen Literatur des Mittelalter: Religiöse Konzepte—Feindbilder—Rechtfertigungen*, ed. Ursula Schulz (Tübingen: Max Niemeyer Verlag, 2002), 233–53; here 238–39.

11 František Graus, *Pest, Geissler, Judenmorde: Das 14. Jahrhundert als Krisenzeit*. Sec. ed., Veröffentlichungen des Max-Planck-Instituts für Geschichte, 86 (Göttingen: Vandenhoeck & Ruprecht, 1988), 289–90.

12 The incident(s) at Korneuburg have frequently been subject to academic analysis; see most notably Winfried Stelzer, "Am Beispiel Korneuburg: Der angebliche Hostienfrevel österreichischer Juden von 1305 und seine Quellen," *Österreich im Mittelalter. Bausteine zu einer revidierten Gesamtdarstellung*, ed. Willibald Rosner. Studien und Forschungen aus dem Niederösterreichischen Institut für Landeskunde, 26, Niederösterreichische Schriften, 109, Wissenschaft. (St. Pölten: Niederösterreichisches Institut für Landeskunde, 1999), 309–48, reg. the dating 323–24, with fn. 43; in the same volume, see for a summary of anti-Jewish polemics in fourteenth-century Austria Fritz Peter Knapp, "Nikolaus von Heiligenkreuz und die Judenpolemik in Österreich zu Anfang des 14. Jahrhunderts," 293–322, on Korneuburg 300–03. Further see Rubin, *Gentile Tales*, 57–65 (see

from the wafer, which made it immediately clear to the bystanders that it was a miraculous object, and indeed, it started to work its first miracles right on the spot. Enraged by the obvious crime that had been committed by the Jewish inhabitants, the citizens got hold of the Jewish scholar (*scolasticus*) who was burnt at the stake. After that, they beat Zerkel to death, and then burnt the other Jewish inhabitants of the small town, raising the death toll to ten people altogether.

The events that led to, and ensued after, the extinction of what might have been the entire Jewish population of Korneuburg[13] are exceptionally well documented. While the chronicle entry cited above merely stated the basic facts, an extensive protocol of the interrogation of twenty-one witnesses provides singularly valuable insights into both the course(s) of events and the perception(s) of these.[14] About three months after the incident, in December 1305, a commission of clerics under the leadership of the Cistercian Ambrose of Heiligenkreuz (a monastery about 20 kilometres south-west of Vienna) looked into the merits of the case of Korneuburg's miracle-working host wafer and the larger issues connected with it. In the course of six days, the witnesses, six clerics and fifteen lay persons, were presented with a detailed catalogue of questions, the main focus of which was to ascertain the authenticity (or not) of the host's miraculous character and the quality of the miracles it worked.[15] Therefore, the questions focussed mainly on the

---

note 3); Eveline Brugger, "Korneuburg 1305," *Nicht in einem Bett—Juden und Christen in Mittelalter und Frühneuzeit,* ed. Institute for Jewish History in Austria (Vienna: rema print, 2005), 20–26 (for the internet version, see:
http://www.injoest.ac.at/upload/JudeninME05_2_19–26.pdf, last accessed on March 10, 2012); eadem, "Von der Ansiedlung bis zur Vertreibung—Juden in Österreich im Mittelalter," *Geschichte der Juden in Österreich,* eadem, Martha Keil, Christoph Lind, Albert Lichtblau, and Barbara Staudinger. Österreichische Geschichte, 15, ed. Herwig Wolfram (Vienna: Ueberreuter, 2006), 123–227; here 211–16.

13 Stelzer, "Am Beispiel Korneuburg," 340 (see note 12), argues against this and points out that Ambrose in his treatise that was written about seven years after the incidents referred to the ten killed people *ex iudeis* and thus indicated that more Jews had lived at Korneuburg at that time. It is however possible that, since the number ten referred to the Jews who had been burnt, Zerkel, who had been beaten to death, was not included. There is no notion of any continuous Jewish presence in Korneuburg for the remainder of the century, see *Germania Judaica,* vol. III: *1350–1519,* part 1: *Aach-Lychen,* ed. Arye Maimon and Yacov Guggenheim (Tübingen: J. C. B. Mohr, 1987), 674, lists, albeit relying on rather problematic sources, altogether nine (mainly Viennese) Jews for the timespan from 1350 to 1420 that were named after *Neunburg,* which could either mean Klosterneuburg or Korneuburg.

14 Haus-, Hof- und Staatsarchiv (HHStA, Austrian State Archives), Notariatsinstrument des Notars Otto von Rußbach, AUR 1305 XII 17; full edition by Brugger and Wiedl, *Regesten 1,* 125–42, no. 133 (see note 1).

15 The commission consisted of four of the episcopal chaplains: Gottfried, Dean of Krems, magister albert, canon of Regensburg, the legally trained magister Konrad von Steinheim, and the notary Otto von Rußbach, who wrote (final version of) the protocol (Brugger and Wiedl, *Regesten 1,* 125, no. 133 and 144, no. 135 [see note 1]). On the catalogue of questions, see Stelzer, "Am Beispiel

host wafer, its condition when it was found, and the miracles it worked *after* it had been installed at the parish church; which also meant after the Jews had been killed. The Jews' fate seemed of secondary, if not altogether negligible, importance to the interrogators whose main concern was whether the wafer had been consecrated or not, meaning, whether the Christians who venerated it were venerating an appropriately consecrated host. Ambrose of Heiligenkreuz, generally sceptical of miraculous hosts, had serious doubts about this. With respect to the Jews and their fate, both questions and answers remained ambiguous, and it is remarkable that none of the interrogators probed into these ambiguities and inconsistencies that appeared as the interrogation continued. *I don't know,* or, *I haven't seen it, but I firmly believe it,* soon turned out to be the default replies the witnesses uttered whenever asked whether they had actually *seen* the host wafer work miracles, or the Jews maltreat it, rendering most of the witnesses' testimonies what we understand as the modern concept of hearsay.

Many of the testimonies contained not only inaccuracies but blatantly contradicted each other, without, however, causing the interrogators to inquire any further. There was no consistency among the answers to the question about how many eyewitnesses there had been to the discovery of the host. The first witness, the Vicar of Korneuburg by the name of Friedrich, who, while not having witnessed much of the whole incident himself, knew of 200 people being present when the bloodied host was found (*et alii quasi CCti, quorum nomina nescit*)—which would, if taken literally, quite likely amount to the entire population of the small town. Despite this suspiciously high number, he was only able to give the names of three witnesses, but knew that one of these, the cobbler's wife, prevented the wafer from being blown away by covering it with a cloth.[16]

In many of the (mostly later) tales of Jews allegedly maltreating host wafers, one of the main concerns involves how the Jews managed to acquire the wafer. Since these were kept in a space not readily accessibly to them, getting hold of a consecrated wafer would require a certain amount of scheming on their part. Mere possession of a wafer alone, without any signs of it having been maltreated, was deemed sufficient proof to justify persecution, even if this possession was only suspected, or claimed by others. The process of acquiring however usually required a Christian accomplice, who, often for pecuniary reasons, stole the consecrated wafer from a church or chapel. Quite often a woman or a girl,[17] the

---

Korneuburg," 321–22 (see note 12); Rubin, *Gentile Tales*, 61–62 (see note 3); see also Wolfgang Stefan Koller, *Die Korneuburger Bluthostie. Historische Quellen und Wirkung*. Unpublished master thesis, Vienna 1991, appendix (table of the testimonies).

16 Reg. the questioning of the priest Friedrich, vicar of Korneuburg (first witness): Brugger and Wiedl, *Regesten 1*, 126, no. 133 (see note 1).

17 Wolfgang Treue, "Schlechte und gute Christen: Zur Rolle von Christen in antijüdischen Ritualmord- und Hostienschändungslegenden," *Aschkenas. Zeitschrift für Geschichte und Kultur des*

Christian offender was usually of a low social standing, and the thief's fate was closely linked with the fate of the Jewish perpetrators. Her (or his) offence against the Christian faith is no less grave than the Jews', and thus the punishment meted out often matched that of the Jews,[18] unless divine justice itself intervened.[19]

In the Korneuburg case, however, the question of how the Jews came to posses the host wafer, and for how long the host had been in their hands, seemed of surprisingly secondary importance; and the striking inconsistencies in the witnesses' answers were not investigated any further. The fifth witness, Konrad, the vicar of Leobendorf (a hamlet north of Korneuburg), declared that he knew that three years ago, the Jews had bought the host wafer for ten pounds from a layperson, the identity of whom he would not reveal since that person had told him about this during confession, although the penitent had asked him to inform the population since he felt remorse about his sinful deed. Konrad remains the only one who comes up with this version in detail, the significance of which will be discussed later.[20] Konrad's version is corroborated by other witnesses: the priest Friedrich, who owned to having known about the confession from, as he said, two priests and other people, Konrad an der Hochstrass (de Alta Strata), one of the three whom Friedrich named as having been present when the wafer was found, and Otto an dem Roßmarkt.

Judentums, 2.1 (1995), 95–116; here 97; Rubin, *Gentile Tales*, 31–32 (see note 3); Friedrich Lotter, "Hostienfrevelvorwurf und Blutwunderfälschung bei den Judenverfolgungen von 1298 ("Rintfleisch") und 1336–1338 ("Armleder")," *Fälschungen im Mittelalter*. MGH Schriften, 33/5: *Fingierte Briefe, Frömmigkeit und Fälschung, Realienfälschungen* (Hanover: Hahnsche Buchhandlung, 1988), 533–83; here 542; on the connection of medieval misogyny and anti-Judaism, see Joan Young Gregg, *Devils, Women, and Jews. Reflections of the Other in Medieval Sermon Stories* (Binghamton, NY: State University of New York Press, 1997).

18 Treue, "Schlechte und gute Christen," 107–08 (see note 17).

19 Quite a "model example" is the story told by (allegedly) the Dominican Rudolf von Schlettstadt that combines several anti-Jewish images: After seducing his Christian maidservant, a nefarious Jew offered the fatuous girl lots of gold for a consecrated host which he maltreated; when his misdeeds were uncovered and he was imprisoned, he bribed the local judge (*Schultheiß*) to set him free again. By divine intervention, the town was devastated by biblical plagues, and on the third day, the judge was struck by lightning; see Johannes Grabmayer, "Rudolf von Schlettstadt und das aschkenasische Judentum um 1300," *Aschkenas. Zeitschrift für Geschichte und Kultur der Juden*, 4.2 (1994), 301–36; here 325–26; see also Rubin, *Gentile Tales*, 84–85 (see note 3). The authorship of Rudolf von Schlettstadt has been disproved by Stefan Georges, *Graf Wilhelm Werner von Zimmern als Historiensammler: Die Wundergeschichtensammlung des neuentdeckten, autographen Sigmaringer Codex 64*. MA thesis, Freiburg im Breisgau 1999, particularly 55–57, who is working on an edition of the codex.

20 Questioning of Konrad, vicar of Leobendorf (fifth witness): Brugger and Wiedl, *Regesten 1*, 130, no. 133 (see note 1).

The latter two gave evidence of the scholar's death and his last words[21]: upon being dragged to the stake by the enraged masses, the scholar not only claimed that he was about to die an innocent death but also accused Zerkel of having bought the host three years ago, at Christmas, from a Christian servant for the price of three *solidi* and a tunic, according to Otto's rendition of the scholar's words—a contradiction to the vicar's testimony who spoke of ten pounds. When Zerkel wanted to get rid of the wafer, he offered a Christian by the name of Ribaldus two pounds if the latter threw the wafer into the Danube; yet upon seeing the wafer in the Jew's hands, Ribaldus exclaimed that this was his creator whom he would not touch for a thousand talents (*hoc est creator meus, hunc ego non tangam eciam pro mille talentis*).

These quite detailed versions tie in in some parts with what can be derived from most of the testimonies that were less elaborate. Most of the witnesses who gave any statement as to how the Jews came into possession of the wafer, and as to how that possession was discovered, did not mention a prior purchase but concurred that on the fateful day, they had seen Zerkel run after a Christian, accusing him of having thrown the host into his house only a few moments ago. The Jewish scholar was following them, carrying the bloodied wafer, which he had presumably picked up from the threshold, in his hands, or wrapped in a cloth, and was begging the surrounding Christians to take it from him. Konrad an der Hochstrass and another witness, the carpenter Sidlo, gave what they claimed to be the exact words the scholar yelled at the gaping bystanders: "Take your god," he allegedly had screamed, "whom that servant has brought into our house, he [the servant] who should rather burn than us."[22]

The Christians who observed the scene however refused to take the host, and when the scholar threw it to the ground, Zerkel trod on it repeatedly.[23] The

21 Questioning of Konrad an der Hochstrass (seventh witness) and of Otto an dem Roßmarkt (eigth witness): Brugger and Wiedl, *Regesten 1*, 132, 134, no. 133 (see note 1).

22 Questioning of Konrad an der Hochstrass (seventh witness), and of the carpenter Sidlo (fourtheenth witness): Brugger and Wiedl, *Regesten 1*, 132, 139, no. 133 (see note 1).

23 The image of Jews maltreating a host wafer by treading on it is a rather rare image, but is vividly exemplified in an incident reported by an English Dominican that had supposedly happened during the German 'Armleder' persecutions: A Jew, who had beforehand bought a host wafer from a knight, mocked the worshippers during the Corpus Christi procession by insisting that he "kept Christ under his foot in his shoe." When he was slain immediately by a bystanding knight, the bloodied host was found in the sole of his shoe, leading to a wide-ranging persecution of the Jews "wherever they could be found in the area." See for an extensive discussion of the motif, Christoph Cluse, 'Blut ist im Schuh. Ein Exempel zur Judenverfolgung des "Rex Armleder."' *Liber Amicorum necnon et amicarum. Für Alfred Heit: Beiträge zur mittelalterlichen Geschichte und geschichtlichen Landeskunde*, ed. Friedhelm Burgard, Christoph Cluse, and Alfred Haverkamp. Trierer Historische Forschungen, 28 (Trier: Verlag Trierer Historische Forschungen, 1996), 371–92 (with an edition of the text, 379).

question of why Zerkel, if he had acquired the host wafer three years ago, would have decided to get rid of it now, is never asked; and the question why, in particular, he would take a bloodied host he had owned for years in his hands and run through the streets of Korneuburg is not even touched upon. The detail however that most of the witnesses agree upon, that they witnessed Zerkel and the scholar as they ran after the Christian and shouted that he had planted the wafer at their doorstep, sounds all the more believable. The panicked Jews ran through the streets of the town with the wafer in their hands, hoping against all odds that they would be exculpated when the real perpetrator was caught. Their awareness of the immediate danger when they found the bloodied wafer on their threshold is reflected in Otto's testimony, albeit with a twist: the Jews were, according to the scholar's last words, well aware of their guilt and well deserved their punishment (*nos merimus illam penam in Deo vestro*).

Another version of how the wafer had made its presence known made use of the already well-established topic of heavenly assistance.[24] Sifridus or Sidlinus, a baker at Korneuburg, claimed in his testimony that while he was at work (*in actu pistandi*), he heard a voice that urged him to go to Zerkel's house, and when he hesitated, he was suddenly grasped by a force that all but dragged him 'under the Jew's door,' *sub portam iudei*.[25] Upon arriving there, he saw the wafer lying on the ground, 'sweating beautiful blood and blistering' (*vidit corpus Domini sudare sanguinem pulcherrimum et bullire guttatim*). He stood mesmerized, but when his gaze drifted back to the street (indicating that he had entered the Jew's house?),[26] the wafer suddenly appeared between his thumb and index finger, and he put it down onto the doorstep of the Jews' house while a small dot of blood remained on his finger. In the meantime, two other witnesses had gathered around him, Bertha, the wife of Konrad Reus, and another woman, Shellerin; a blatant contradiction to several other versions of who had (allegedly) been present when the wafer had been found. It seems that a crowd had gathered rather quickly, which might explain some of the inaccuracies, yet even the testimonies of those who claimed that they had been immediate witnesses are at variance.

The three witnesses to the retrieval that were named by the priest Friedrich are not mentioned by others, while these three—the cobbler's wife, Konrad an der Hochstrass, and Sidlo—either were not questioned at all (the cobbler's wife), or did not give any names. The members of the town council, who had been in a meeting, came running to the Jew's house upon hearing the turmoil, which had

---

24 Lotter, "Hostienfrevelvorwurf," with several examples throughout the article (see note 17).

25 Questioning of Sifridus/Sidlin (eleventh witness): Brugger and Wiedl, *Regesten 1*, 137–38, no. 133 (see note 1).

26 Stelzer, "Am Beispiel Korneuburg," 327 (see note 12), suspects this according to Sidlin's wording (*eoque respiciente per portam ad stratam vidit hostiam predictam in duobus digitis*).

also attracted many others, the majority of whom remained unnamed (and un-interrogated). Furthermore, contradictions about who could provide immediate knowledge of the events were not solved. The carpenter Sidlo, who had been named by Friedrich as one of the eyewitnesses to the discovery, himself declared that he had only left his house, where he had been at work, when he had heard the Jew calling out 'catch him.' Upon entering the street he had seen three Jews running along the street, amongst them the scholar, who had been carrying a cloth from which blood was dripping, which he wiped on his chest. He did not witness, according to his own statement, the actual discovery (neither by the heavenly guided baker nor by Zerkel) of the wafer.[27]

The testimony given by the tenth witness, Heinrich Shem, sheds yet another, surprising, light on the scene. Although when facing the commission, Heinrich emphasized his firm belief in the authenticity of the host and his abhorrence of the Jews' crime, his statement nevertheless speaks of a distinct personal acquaintance with the Jews. He was in Zerkel's house at the time the host was discovered (which the interrogators did not comment on) and he saw it lying on the doorstep and bubbling blood-drops "like an egg that sweats when it is cooked." His testimony not only supported the Jews' claim that the wafer had been planted at their doorstep but also showed clearly that the Jews were absolutely, and immediately, aware of the fact that this had been a malicious action aimed at them: *o domine Henrice,* Zerkel called out to him, "this evil man threw the body of your God into my house and slipped away" *(ecce quidam vilis homo proiecit corpus Dei vestri ad domum meam et recessit*).

Upon seeing the bloodied wafer, though, Heinrich immediately blamed the Jews for it (which Zerkel denied), yet he still admitted to having urged Zerkel to flee, but, he added, not without telling the Jew that he would not be able to escape. Two other citizens, both named Marquard, and members of the town council then ushered Zerkel into the house of Konrad Reus and hid him, telling him to remain there. Yet when the populace returned from burning the scholar, who, as they claimed, had in dying named Zerkel as the sole perpetrator, they broke into Reus's house, dragged him out, and beat him to death.

Then the angry masses proceeded to kill the other Jews, both men and women.[28] The significance of Heinrich Shem's testimony is noteworthy in many regards: several of his statements are blatantly at odds with each other, and his answers may reflect a desire to please the commission. Even more surprising is that although the Marquardus who was interrogated as the sixteenth witness can quite likely be identified as one of the two Marquards, his testimony is nevertheless

---

27 Questioning of Sidlo (fourtenth witness): Brugger and Wiedl, *Regesten 1*, 139, no. 133 (see note 1).

28 Questioning of Heinrich Shem (tenth witness): Brugger and Wiedl, *Regesten 1*, 136, no. 133 (see note 1).

reduced to very few basic facts—that he, along with other members of the sworn council alerted by the clamor, arrived at Zerkel's house to see the bloodied wafer at the doorstep, which he firmly believed to be the genuine body of Christ.[29]

Neither the minutes of the interrogation nor any of the later sources hint at him and his namesake being accused of helping the Jew, nor at any repercussions against them and Heinrich Shem. Konrad Reus, who quite likely was not present during the whole incident, was not consulted as a witness,[30] whereas his wife Bertha, who had been present during the discovery of the wafer, was at no point asked about Zerkel having been brought to her house but was presented with the standard catalogue of questions.

While Zerkel hid in Konrad Reus's house, the host worked its second miracle (after bleeding as a consequence of the treatment it allegedly suffered from the Jews' hands) even before it was taken to the parish church. The scholar's hand, that had held the host during his panic-induced chase through the streets, remained unmarred by the fire.[31] Installed then at the parish church by the priest Friedrich (while the Jews met their tragic fate),[32] it continued to work all kinds of miracles that were listed in detail by the majority of the citizens questioned.[33] The series of miracles the host worked at the church seem to have started on the Sunday after the incidents with the spontaneous lighting of six candles, yet more imposing miracles were about to start another week later. According to the vicar Friedrich, Gertrudis, a young woman of about 20 years, was cured of her blindness on Michaelmas (September 29) when the piece of cloth was placed over her eyes

---

29 Questioning of Marquardus, member of the town council (sixteenth witness), Brugger and Wiedl, *Regesten 1*, 140–41, no. 133 (see note 1).

30 It is not clear whether Konrad Reus is still alive at this time. He is mentioned only in 1293 and 1298 (*Urkundenbuch des Stiftes Klosterneuburg bis zum Ende des vierzehnten Jahrhunderts*, vol. 1, ed. Hartmann Zeibig Fontes Rerum Austriacarum - Österreichische Geschichtsquellen. Zweite Abtheilung: Diplomata et Acta, X [Vienna: Kaiserlich-Königliche Staatsdruckerei, 1857], 45, no. 51, 59–60, no. 66), but since Bertha Reusin is referred to as his wife and not widow, it is more likely that he was still alive but not at home.

31 Questioning of Konrad von Leobersdorf (fifth witness): *Item dixit sibi constare ex auditu nobilium et clericorum, quod sanguis distillavit de manu iudei tenentis hostiam in manu et quod cremato predicto iudeo, de cuius manu distillavit dictus sanguis manus eadem dicti iudei, qua hostiam tenuerat, incombusta remansit*; and of Konrad an der Hochstrass (seventh witness): *manus eadem* [the Jewish scholar's], *qua corpus Domini tenu[er]at incombusta remansit.* Brugger and Wiedl, *Regesten 1*, 130 and 132, no. 133 (see note 1).

32 Questioning of Heinrich Plichel (twelfth witness): upon arriving at the scene, Friedrich took the wafer and carried it *ad primum locum*, presumably the parish church. Stelzer, "Am Beispiel Korneuburg," 327 (see note 12), Brugger and Wiedl, *Regesten 1*, 138, no. 133 (see note 1).

33 For a detailed list of the miracles, see Koller, *Korneuburger Bluthostie*, appendix A (candles), B (blind), C (possessed), and D (handicapped) (see note 16), and, with some errors, Franz Zeissl, *Das ehemalige Augustinerkloster in Korneuburg*, Korneuburger Kulturnachrichten 27 (1965, special issue), 4–5.

at the Jews' house (!). Two other witnesses also reported the healing of one or two girls who were shown the cloth at the Jews' house on that day, yet denied any knowledge of their names and gave quite differing statements as to how long the girl(s) had been blind.

Inconsistencies such as these hamper any definite identification of the (allegedly) cured, yet obviously did not bother the commission. Even more spectacular though, and attracting the presence of such noble witnesses as Otto von Zelking and members of the families of Maissau and Wallsee, was the healing of a fourteen-year-old Bohemian girl possessed by three demons who was shown the host at the altar of the church. According to other witnesses, a man from Vienna and a woman who were shown the cloth at the Jews' house (where the cloth seems to have been kept) and thus freed of their demons. Within only a fortnight, the rumor of the existence of a miraculous host wafer had spread, and other miracles ensued, such as the healing of the Viennese tailors Konrad and Ramungus of Stein, as well as Sifridus and Witigo of Bruck, who had all their vision returned after either having been shown the host and/or the cloth, or by the mere presence of the holy object, around Saint Koloman's Day (October 13) and during Advent.

The powers of the miraculous host were not limited to restoring sight, however. The local weaver Pero, crippled for some years, a handicapped boy called Chunzelinus Schoderleh, the local innkeeper Tasco's son Bruno, paralysed since infancy and only able to "crawl like a reptile," the Viennese woman Alheit Hutterin, paralysed for eight years, Ebermannus from Klosterneuburg, with a paralysed foot, were all healed by looking at the host, or the shrine, while the Viennese woman Gertrud, who had been unable to walk for six years, regained her mobility without being in the presence of the host at all. There is no further mention of the cloth being shown at the Jews' house, suggesting that it had been incorporated into the shrine that had obviously been erected for the host in the meantime.

Only some of the witnesses though were able to give these names, and even fewer could include any further details. Most witnesses either assured that they "had heard about it [the respective handicap and/or the healing] for sure," yet again resorting to quoting hearsay, or, for the most part, cited the healing of blind, lame, and paralysed people who remained anonymous. Neither the cured nor any of the non-local witnesses to the lighting and healing miracles were called in for interrogation, which might come as a surprise given how centred the enquiry was on the question of the authenticity of the host and its miraculous work.

The incidents at Korneuburg fall into the category of a spontaneous persecution of Jews.[34] In the course of the late middle ages, host wafer desecration and/or

---

[34] See Graus, *Pest, Geissler, Judenmorde*, 383–89 (see note 11), although a distinct assignation to a specific type of persecution/pogrom is hardly possible (and highly questionable) for many cases.

blood libels served as the most common reasons for violent outbreaks against Jews on local as well as regional scales.[35] In the Austrian territories, alleged host desecration became the most common accusation to trigger a persecution, while the ritual murder accusation, although not unheard of in Austria, was more frequently made use of in other territories in the German-speaking realm.[36] The instigators of these persecutions however vary. The infamous Rintfleisch pogroms, starting off with an alleged host desecration in the small town of Röttingen and wreaking havoc on the Jewish communities mainly in Franconia in 1298, had been carried out not solely, but mainly by members of the lower classes.[37]

Many of the later persecutions were approved of, or even incited, not only by local authorities, such as municipalities or the lord of the town, but also by the rulers of the respective territories. In contrast to this, the persecutions that sprung up in the Austrian regions until the mid-fourteenth century were carried out solely by the local population, the same people that had, in most of the towns and rural areas, lived side by side rather peacefully with their Jewish neighbors. Immediate vicinity of Jews and Christians was inevitable in the close-knit structures of cities, and the contacts and relationships were quite likely even closer in the rural villages where a small Jewish population, consisting of perhaps one or two families, would need to interact with the surrounding Christian population on a daily basis.[38] There is sufficient evidence that indicates peaceful neighborly

---

35 Michael Toch, "Spätmittelalterliche Rahmenbedingungen jüdischer Existenz: Die Verfolgungen," *Hofjuden und Landjuden: Jüdisches Leben in der Frühen Neuzeit*, ed. Sabine Hödl, Peter Rauscher, and Barbara Staudinger (Berlin and Vienna: Philo, 2004), 19–64; here 44.

36 Still basic for the German-speaking area is the article by Lotter, "Hostienfrevelvorwurf," 548 (see note 17); see also Langmuir, *Toward a Definition of Antisemitism*, 120–33 and 263–81 (see note 8); Rainer Erb, "Zur Erforschung der europäischen Ritualmordbeschuldigungen," *Die Legende vom Ritualmord. Zur Geschichte der Blutbeschuldigung gegen Juden,* ed. idem. Dokumente, Texte, Materialien, Zentrum für Antisemitismusforschung der Technischen Universität Berlin, 6 (Berlin: Metropol, 1993), 9–16; and Israel Jacob Yuval, *Two Nations in Your Womb: Perceptions of Jews and Christians in Late Antiquity and the Middle Ages*, trans. from the Hebrew by Barbara Harshav and Jonathan Chipman (2000; Berkeley, Los Angeles, and London: University of California Press, 2006), 170–73.

37 Lotter, "Hostienfrevelvorwurf," 548–59 (see note 17), and "Die Judenverfolgung des „König Rintfleisch" in Franken um 1298. Die endgültige Wende in den christlich-jüdischen Beziehungen im deutschen Reich des Mittelalters," *Zeitschrift für historische Forschung*, 4 (1988), 385–422; Graus, *Pest, Geissler, Judenmorde*, 290–92 (see note 11).

38 For the duchy of Austria, see Eveline Brugger, "Neighbours, Business Partners, Victims: Jewish-Christian interaction in Austrian towns during the persecutions of the fourteenth century," *Intricate Interfaith Networks: Quotidian Jewish-Christian Contacts in the Middle Ages*, ed. Ephraim Shoam-Steiner (Brepols: Turnhout, 2011) [in print]. See also Jonathan Elukin, *Living Together —Living Apart. Rethinking Jewish-Christian Relations in the Middle Ages* (Princeton: Princeton University Press, 2007), 84–85 and the discussion the book caused, for example the reviews by Michael Toch, *The Catholic Historical Review* 95.3 (2009), 604–07, and, aiming at a broader audience, David Nirenberg, "Hope's Mistakes," *The New Republic*, 13 February, 2008 (for the internet

cohabition over a long time period, yet the incidents at Korneuburg clearly show how fragile the relations between Jews and Christians were. Given the right catalyst, such as a bloodstained wafer, once added to the mix, the normalcy of everyday relations could suddenly erupt into violence.[39]

The (re-)killing of Christ as one of, if not the most abominable of all the Jewish crimes, could be executed in various forms in Christian fantasies. Yet whereas the tales of Jewish ritual murder, the horrendous blood libel accusations that quickly spread throughout the Ashkenazic region in mid-twelfth century,[40] merely played with the equation of the killing of a Christian child and the death of Christ himself, the host wafer actually *was* the body of Christ.[41] This was enhanced by the

---

version, see https://webshare.uchicago.edu/users/nirenberg/Public/hopes-mistakes.pdf, last accessed on March 10, 2012).

39 Bale, *Jew in the Medieval Book*, 5, plate 1 (see note 7), gives the example of an anti-Jewish illustration in a business document. See also Johannes Heil, *"Gottesfeinde" – "Menschenfeinde": Die Vorstellung von jüdischer Weltverschwörung (13.–16. Jahrhundert)*. Antisemitismus: Geschichte und Strukturen, 3 (Essen: Klartext-Verlag, 2006), 60–62; with reference to Austria and Korneuburg, see Brugger, "Neighbours, Business Partners, Victims" (see note 38).

40 For an overview of the vast discussion, see Cohen, *Christ Killers* (see note 3), the anthology by Erb, *Legende vom Ritualmord* (see note 36); Ronnie Po-Chia Hsia, *The Myth of Ritual Murder: Jews and Magic in Reformation Germany* (New Haven, CT: Yale University Press, 1988); Gerd Mentgen, "Über den Ursprung der Ritualmordfabel," *Aschkenas. Zeitschrift für Geschichte und Kultur der Juden*, 4 (1994), 1–12; Jeffrey Cohen, "The Flow of the Blood in Norwich," *Speculum*, 79 (2004), S. 26–65; John M. McCullouh, "Jewish Ritual Murder: William of Norwich, Thomas of Monmouth, and the early dissemination of the myth," *Speculum*, 72.2 (1997), 684–740; here 700, argues that the early ritual murder accusations represent "an important stage in the increasingly negative attitudes of the majority toward the minority" in the sense that the myth aided to justify Christian hostility by establishing the concept of a continuance of Jewish enmity toward Christ since their 'first' killing of him; a development that went hand in hand with a decline in the Jews' legal status as well as economic restrictions; a finding that, however, reflects the situation in England while it took another century for a similar development to take place in the German-speaking territories. On the 'origin' of the concept of Jews committing ritual murders and the discussion whether it was 'invented' by Thomas of Monmouth, or, as suggested by Israel Jacob Yuval, 'imported' from the continent, 699–700, and 731–32 on the 1147 case of Theodoric of Würzburg; see also Chazan, *Medieval Stereotypes*, 59–60 (see note 6) (with an English translation of the chronicle entry); On the general situation of the Jews in England at this time, see Joe Hillaby, "Jewish Colonisation in the Twelfth Century," *The Jews in Medieval Britain: Historical, Literary and Archaeological Perspectives*, ed. Patricia Skinner (Woodbridge, Suffolk: The Boydell Press, 2003), 15–40; here 20–25. The first blood libel accusation in the realm of the Holy Roman Empire was raised in Fulda in 1236, see Bernhard Diestelkamp, "Der Vorwurf des Ritualmordes gegen Juden" *Religiöse Devianz. Untersuchungen zu sozialen, rechtlichen und theologischen Reaktionen auf religiöse Abweichung im westlichen und östlichen Mittelalter*, ed. Dieter Simon. Ius Commune, Sonderhefte: Studien zur Europäischen Rechtsgeschichte, 48 (Frankfurt a. M.: Vittorio Klostermann, 1990), 19–40; see also Langmuir's discussion in *Toward a Definition of Antisemitism*, 263–81 (see note 8).

41 Heil, *"Gottesfeinde" – "Menschenfeinde,"* 242–43 (see note 38). In an interesting and telling twist, the accusation against the Jews of the central Rhine area of having murdered the boy Werner of Oberwesel ("Good Werner") around Easter 1287 that had led to the worst pogrom since the First Crusade in this region was remodelled at the beginning of the fourteenth century: the Jews now

development of a popular piety that increasingly focused on objects of veneration and was especially concerned with their vulnerability to desecration. When the consecrated host was mutilated, stabbed, torn to pieces, thrown into the dirt, into a lavatory, or a well, trampled on, and eventually destroyed, this act was perceived as an re-enactment of the killing of Christ.[42] Thus, on a theological scale, host wafer desecrations were considered an even more abhorrent offence than any other Jewish crime. It was, as the Korneuburg incident, and many more to follow, would prove, also the least laborious way to generate an outburst of anti-Jewish violence.[43]

Given how little time had passed between the first accusation of host desecration that had been raised in 1290 in the considerably far away city of Paris,[44] it is remarkable how quickly these tales had reached the small town at the utmost east of the Holy Roman Empire.[45] Yet in 1305, these accusations were already familiar to the Korneuburg inhabitants, both Christians and Jews, perhaps because of a rather close-by incident. Eleven years earlier, in 1294, Jews at Laa an der Thaya, about 45 kilometres north of Korneuburg, had been accused of hiding a host in a stable and mangling it, and had been killed.[46] It is therefore not surprising that both Zerkel and the scholar were instantly aware when they found the host on the doorstep that they were in mortal danger, and they were correct. Even if the legend of the host wafer desecration by Jews had found its first full execution only a mere one and a half decade earlier, the main elements of the narrative had long

---

had captured and tormented Werner to get the host he had received earlier during mass, see Jörg R. Müller, "*Erez geserah*—'Land of Persecution': Pogroms against the Jews in the *regnum Teutonicum* from *c.* 1280 to 1350," *The Jews of Europe in the Middle Ages (Tenth to Fifteenth Centuries*, ed. Christoph Cluse (Turnhout: Brepols, 2004): 245–260, here 249–51.

42 Lotter, "Hostienfrevelvorwurf" (see note 17), see also Graus, *Pest, Geissler, Judenmorde*, 290–92 (see note 11). The tale of the alleged host desecration of Deggendorf (1338) is one of the few examples where the host was also chewed upon by the Jews—with the appearance of the holy child preventing the host from being swallowed (Berghausen, "Lied von Deggendorf," 247 [see note 10]; the text [the Augsburg rendition of 1520] is edited by Ludwig Steub, *Altbayerische Culturbilder* [Leipzig: Ernst Keil Verlag, 1869], part II: *Der Judenmord zu Deggendorf*, 21–150, the text 146–49); that this image was scarcely used is perhaps due to its closeness to the 'appropriate' Christian usage.

43 Graus, *Pest, Geissler, Judenmorde*, 290–91 (see note 11).

44 On the 1290 Paris telling that is considered by many as the first 'full' rendition of the host desecration tale, see Rubin, *Gentile Tales*, 40–48 (see note 3); Lotter, "Hostienfrevelvorwurf," particularly 536–38 (see note 17).

45 Miri Rubin, "Desecration of the Host: the Birth of an Accusation," *Christianity and Judaism*, 169–85; here 175–77 (see note 5); Jeremy Cohen, *The Friars and the Jews. The Evolution of Medieval Anti-Judaism* (1982; Ithaca, NY: Cornell University Press, 1986); for a summary of later, and still ongoing, discussions regarding the role of the mendicant preachers, see Cluse, "Blut ist im Schuh," 371–73 (see note 23).

46 Brugger and Wiedl, *Regesten 1*, 89–90, no. 82 (see note 1). Brugger, "Von der Ansiedlung," 211 (see note 12); Lotter, "Hostienfrevelvorwurf," 549 (see note 17).

existed. The main patterns of the legend were followed through from Paris onward, with only slight deviations in the cast of the *dramatis personae* Miri Rubin has identified as the 'default' participants of the standard narrative.[47]

However unique the source material for Korneuburg might be, the narrative resembles established patterns. Zerkel clearly served as the main perpetrator, the Jew (in most cases male) who gained possession of the host and desecrated it. The subject of his accomplices, the question whether or not some or all of the other Jews had participated in any way in the purchase and/or desecration of the host, was introduced in a quite twisted way at Korneuburg. Those who had quite likely participated in killing the Jewish scholar (without ever admitting to it) were the ones who repeated to the commission what they claimed the scholar had said: that he had named Zerkel as the only perpetrator, the one who had committed the crime by first buying and then desecrating the host.

Even though the misled Christian who sold the host to the Jews was depicted as being deeply repentant of his sin and praying for forgiveness (as the priest Friedrich told the commission), he did not make any further appearance. The unveiling of the miraculous host however follows already established patterns. The host, as an active participant, reveals itself to the faithful, making its presence known through bleeding, as in Korneuburg, sobbing, flying away, or turning into flesh, or even appearing as a little child.[48]

In some versions of the tale, it is assisted by a Christian—the baker Sidlin in the Korneuburg rendition—who responds to its holiness by letting himself (or, rarely, herself) be led to the maltreated host. The "crowd and its violence"[49] are, in the depictions of the ecclesiastical chronicles, the righteous counterpart to the felonious Jews, the rightfully enraged masses who not only make sure that the abuse, mockery, and, eventually, killing of Christ is avenged but also that justice

---

47 Rubin, *Gentile Tales*, 70–92 (see note 3); see also Lotter, "Hostienfrevelvorwurf" (see note 17), and Erb, "Zur Erforschung der europäischen Ritualmordbeschuldigungen," 10 (see note 36), on the general 'skeleton' of the legends on host desecration.

48 See for example the long list of torments the host wafer had to endure in the *Lied von Deggendorf* ('song of Deggendorf'), a late fourteenth-century rendition of the events during and after the alleged host desecration at Deggendorf in 1338 that triggered one of the most wide-ranging persecution of Bavarian Jews: the host was maltreated with hammers, pliers, and anvil, and thus, it started to bleed; it was burnt in the oven but flew away; it was chewed upon, and the child appeared; angels, doves, and/or the virgin appeared; it started to glow; and, eventually, it moaned. Berghausen, "Lied von Deggendorf," 245–46 (see note 10), Rubin, *Gentile Tales*, 179–81 (see note 3). For the relation with blood and the colour red, see the anthropological study by Claudine Fabre-Vassas, *The Singular Beast. Jews, Christians, & the Pig*. Trans. from the French by Carol Volk (1994; New York and Chichester: Columbia University Press, 1997), 129–59 (blood libel and host desecration accusation), 211–12 (Romanian legend of eggs, that are carried by a Jew, turning red when he passes through the market at Easter).

49 Rubin, *Gentile Tale*, 88–89 (title of her chapter on the role of violence within the Christian mob) (see note 3).

is served. The punishment meted out for the Jews of Korneuburg, with the exception of Zerkel, followed the most common means of retribution—burning at the stake, on a pyre piled up within a very short time.

The interviewers, generally not all that interested in the fate of the Jews when not immediately connected with the bleeding host, did not probe any further or ask who had actually been present when the Jews were consumed by the fire. Despite the 21 interviewees, the additional names that were dropped by these during their interrogation, and the detailed knowledge the commission gained in other regards, the executing masses remained anonymous and only years later, after having learned the truth, would Ambrose of Heiligenkreuz, in his treatise on the miraculous host, scold the townspeople of Korneuburg for their rash, precipitant, and eventually unjust actions. In the Korneuburg case, another member has to be added to the cast, one who is not altogether unknown to the narrative: the priest (and village community) who profited from the establishment of a new pilgrim site in the town.[50]

Christian fantasies of Jews mocking and mistreating Christian symbols were not reduced to the host wafer. In Oxford in 1268, a Jew was accused of having snatched a cross and kicked it into the mud,[51] and in Vienna in 1281, a Jew was stoned for having thrown dirt and/or feces at a priest carrying an ostensory.[52] These objects were also part of the anti-Jewish Christian fantasies as was the idea of Jews ritually killing images of Christ that were made of wax.[53] These ideas, that were already established in the Christian mind, eventually converged with the increased importance that was attributed to the Eucharist, the feast of Corpus Christi, and the subsequent increased importance of the host wafer as a ritual object with its inherent miraculous, almost "magical" qualities.[54] The transubstan

---

50 Graus, *Pest, Geissler, Judenmorde,* 293: "the local priests were both initiators and beneficiaries" (see note 11).

51 Christoph Cluse, "Stories of Breaking and Taking the Cross: A Possible Context for the Oxford Incident of 1268," *Revue d'Histoire Ecclésiastique,* 90.3–4 (1995), 396–442; Heil, *"Gottesfeinde"—"Menschenfeinde,"* 237–38 (see note 38).

52 Brugger and Wiedl, *Regesten 1,* 77–78, no. 62 (see note 1); see Lotter, "Hostienfrevelvorwurf," 545 (see note 17).

53 Cluse, "Blut ist im Schuh," 375, fn. 23 (referring to a thirteenth-century anonymous collection of preach instructions from France that casually adds to the catchword "devil" the information that Jews use to crucify wax images of Christ and, sometimes, children) (see note 23); Heil, *"Gottesfeinde"—"Menschenfeinde,"* 238 (see note 38).

54 Graus, *Pest, Geissler, Judenmorde,* 287 (see note 11); see also the story told by Rudolf von Schlettstadt of the converted Jewess who lists all sorts of magical practices her mother had conducted by using a host that clearly reflects Christian, and not Jewish, ideas about magical (mis)use of wafers (Grabmayer, "Rudolf von Schlettstadt," 319 [see note 19]). On the Christian (mis)use of host wafers for magical practices, see Peter Browe, "Die Eucharistie als Zaubermittel im Mittelalter," Archiv für Kulturgeschichte, 20 (1930), 134–54; and Michael David Bailey, *Magic and Superstition in Europe: A Concize History from Antiquity to the Present* (Landham, Boulder, New

tiation, the turning of the bread, i.e., the host wafer, and the wine into the actual body and blood of Christ during the Consecration of the Eucharist, had been elevated to a Church dogma by the Fourth Lateran Council in 1215, which made the host wafer the most powerful device of them all since it was supposed to be a manifestation of Christ himself.

Considering these "killing of Christ" fantasies that the host desecration was based on, it is not surprising that—even if not at Korneuburg—Easter turned out to be a particularly dangerous time for Jews, even more so when it coincided with Passover. This is eerily reflected in many ecclesiastical law codes that advise Jews not to leave their houses during the high feasts of the Christians, particularly during feasts that were celebrated with processions such as those held during Corpus Christi.[55]

Shortly after, or perhaps already in the Paris legend, a significant paradigm shift can be perceived. The perpetrators of the earlier tales, the origins of which can be traced back to late antiquity,[56] could have been Jews, but also Christians who were not firm in their belief. The crucial element was that he (or, rarely, she) was an eye witness to the host's sanctity that manifested itself in its miracles, first by enduring the ill-treatment meted out by the perpetrator unscathed, by making itself known to the public, and then by working miracles. This visualization[57] of its power was what either prompted the Jew to subsequently seek baptism or the doubtful Christian to be reassured in his/her faith.[58] Those Christians who might be wavering in their faith were a significant part of the target audience for these tales

York, Toronto, and Plymouth UK: Rowman & Littlefield Publishers, 2007), 113–14 (on the host desecration accusation against Jews), 124 (on the magical use of hosts by Christians). On the "magical" presentation of said object during the eucharist and the feast of Corpus Christi, and the impact this had on the audience's ideas of Jewish host desecration, see Mitchell Merback, *The Thief, the Cross and the Wheel: Pain and the Spectacle of Punishment in Medieval and Renaissance Europe* (Chicago: The University of Chicago Press, 1998), 193–95; for an anthropological perspective, see Fabre-Vassas, *The Singular Beast*, 149–52 (see note 48).

55 See Markus Wenninger, "Das gefährliche Fest. Ostern als zeitlicher Kristallisationspunkt antijüdischen Verhaltens," *Feste und Feiern im Mittelalter. Paderborner Symposium des Mediävistenverbandes*, ed. Detlef Altenburg, Jörg Jarnut, and Hans-Hugo Steinhoff (Sigmaringen: Jan Thorbecke, 1991), 323–32; Heil, *"Gottesfeinde"—"Menschenfeinde,"* 227–33 (see note 38); Fabre-Vassas, *The Singular Beast*, 149–54 (see note 48); Müller, "Land of Persecution," 247 (see note 41).

56 Lotter, "Hostienfrevelvorwurf," 539–40 (see note 17); Heil, *"Gottesfeinde"—"Menschenfeinde,"* 242 (see note 38).

57 Fabre-Vassas gives evidence that the Paris incident had been turned into a play that was performed on a chariot during processions up until the sixteenth century, making the scenes—the Jew torturing the host, the long streams of blood that spurted from it, the metamorphosis into a small child—all the more impressive (Fabre-Vassas, *The Singular Beast*, 152–53 [see note 48]).

58 Lotter, "Hostienfrevelvorwurf," 539–43 (see note 17); for a specific example, see Cluse, "Blut ist im Schuh," 380 (see note 23): the tale of the Jew keeping a bloodied host wafer in his shoe is listed among other stories of miraculous hosts, and the added rubric sums up the main message that was to convey with the tales: that the presence of Christ at the altar was indeed possible.

which were, at all times, told by Christians for Christians, with the Jews being the projection of all that was not Christian.[59] The earlier concept is still reflected in the Paris version that is considered by many scholars as the first valid host desecration legend,[60] where only the Jew who stole the host and mistreated it was burnt at the stake (after having been put on trial) while his wife and daughter/children and other Jews were so impressed by the miracles that they converted.[61]

The chance for at least some of the Jews to survive and thus to actually see the errors of their ways was crucial. Their desire for conversion, as the result of the wonders they had witnessed, serves as the narrative tool to illustrate the powers of the host wafer to which even the most obdurate gainsayers, the Jews, had to yield. Only those who had actually performed the misdeed, who prolonged their crimes by choosing to disregard the host's salvific powers and remain in their obduracy, received what they deserved. In the early tales, anti-Jewish elements appear less frequently than tales without such elements and the focus of the stories is educational: to convey the idea of the transubstantiation, the real presence of Christ in the sacrament on the altar, the veneration of the sacramental body of Christ in the host.[62]

While, however, tales about Christians mistreating host wafers continued to exist,[63] the number of tales of the misuse of host wafers with Jewish participation grew in the course of the fourteenth century, developing out of this new Eucharistic lore and other, older tales about Jews.[64] The focus of the stories broadened from showing the power of the sacrament to include the malice and obduracy of the Jews, who had transformed from being at least potentially redeemable subjects that could be gathered into the Christian fold into beings that were beyond redemption, even if they were given the chance.[65]

---

59 Bale, *Jew in the Medieval Book*, 2 (see note 7): "Judaism as a faith and 'Jewishness' as a repository of fantasy projections [that] were central to the self-definition of medieval Christianity."

60 See for an extensive discussion of the Paris narrative and its sources Lotter, "Hostienfrevelvorwurf," 537–36 (see note 17); Rubin, "Desecration of the Host," 169–71 (see note 45).

61 For other, similar, examples from England and France, see Cluse, "Fabula ineptissima," 296–97 (see note 7).

62 Miri Rubin, *Corpus Christi. The Eucharist in Late Medieval Culture* (Cambridge: Cambridge University Press, 1991), 108–29; Heil, *"Gottesfeinde"—"Menschenfeinde,"* 243 (see note 38); see also Graus, *Pest, Geissler, Judenmord*, 286–88 (see note 11), with an emphasis of the "magical" qualities of the transubstantiation.

63 Lotter, "Hostienfrevelvorwurf," 548 (see note 17), lists 36 host miracles in the German-speaking area in the first half of the fourteenth century. 31 of these based upon desecrations, and for 24 out of these 31, Jews were blamed.

64 Rubin, "Desecration of the Host," 173 (see note 45).

65 Wolfgang Treue, *Ritualmord und Hostienschändung*, (unpublished MA thesis), quoted after Cluse, "Blut ist im Schuh," 376 (see note 23); Lotter, "Hostienfrevelvorwurf," 538 (see note 17).

To avenge the crime the Jews, as an entity, had committed against the host, Christ, and Christianity as a whole, their death was the only imaginable punishment, which not only became an inevitable element of the narrative but was translated into reality in the form of persecutions of Jews that went farer and farer beyond the local scale. There was no longer any space left for repentant Jews who wished to join the ranks of the true faith, neither in the course of the narrative nor in the real world. Their role as surviving witnesses, as living proof of the sanctity of the host was no longer required. In the words of the third witness of Korneuburg, the dean Jacob, the mere fact that the bloodied host had been found in *their*, in Jewish, hands, was proof enough that it was a genuine, miracle-working host.

The Jews could, even *should*, be disposed of after they had fulfilled their role in the narrative; their killing had become integral to pilgrimage itself.[66] They are the profaners, the perpetrators who force the host into (re-)action by bleeding, crying, turning into a piece of flesh or a child, or flying away,[67] and are removed from the center of the story, killed at the end of the first act of the narrative. Zerkel, the scholar, and the other eight (or nine) Jews at Korneuburg are hardly even given a chance to witness the host's power and holiness. We do not know exactly how much time had elapsed between the moment the host was found on Zerkel's doorstep and the death of the Jews, but apart from its indestructibility, they do not get to see the miracles it works, thus they have no reason to convert.

Was there any room for doubt at all in the minds of the Christians, to question this seemingly fixed role of the Jews? Ambrose of Heiligenkreuz, the one who is most immediately concerned with the aftermath of the Korneuburg murders seems to be the most doubtful.[68] In his treatise on the miraculous host,[69] he elaborated on the somewhat difficult and trying circumstances under which he had to carry out the investigation. Not only the members of the commission seemed to have been at variance with each other, disputing over the catalogue of questions to present to the witnesses as well as the defining features of miracles,

---

66 Merback, *The Thief, the Cross and the Wheel*, 190 (see note 54).

67 Fabre-Vassas, *The Singular Beast*, 151–52 (see note 48). See for a variety of potential 'revealing acts' Heil, *"Gottesfeinde" – "Menschenfeinde,"* 244 (see note 38).

68 About 100 years later, Jan Hus (then still officially orthodox), in his treatise *De Sanguine Christi* (1404), would condemn all bleeding hosts as fabrications of greedy priests (František Graus, "Fälschungen im Gewand der Frömmigkeit," *Fälschungen im Mittelalter 5*, 261–82; here 269–70, fn. 38 [see note 17]).

69 Library of the Monastery of Klosterneuburg, Codex 825, fol. 1v.–15v. For the relevant paragraphs, see Brugger and Wiedl, *Regesten 1*, 144–46, no. 135 (see note 1). The treatise was written about a year after the incidents, while the prologue was added around 1312, see Stelzer, "Am Beispiel Korneuburg," 332–33 (see note 12).

but the citizens of Korneuburg protested vehemently against the continuing work of the commission.

Suspecting that the commission would forestall, or at least defer, the approval of their miracle-working host, an angry throng gathered in front of the house where the interrogations took place and tried to bar the witnesses from entering. Their wrath was primarily directed against Ambrose and Duke Rudolf III whom they accused of taking "the side of the Jews"—an interesting argument, considering that the main purpose of the commission was to find out whether the host had been consecrated and the miracles genuine, so there was no "side of the Jews" (who had been dead for two and a half months at this time) Ambrose and Rudolf could have possibly taken. Did they refer to any potential doubts regarding the guilt of the Jews and the legitimacy of the deaths the duke and the monk might have harbored or, if Ambrose rendered it correctly to begin with, was it a simple image meant to contrast *them*, the townspeople, with those who were not part of their community?

As with the commission, the focus of Ambrose's treatise lay mainly on the question of the authenticity of the host. Tellingly, as Winfried Stelzer has pointed out, Ambrose mostly used the word for the non-consecrated wafer (*oblata*) instead of the consecrated host (*hostia*), or labelled it *hostia mirificata* instead of *hostia mirifica*,[70] yet he did not come to a final conclusion regarding its power to work miracles. Only in an addentum he revoked the advice he had given the Bishop of Passau to contact the pope in the question of how to handle the veneration of a potentially non-consecrated host. Upon reading of other host miracles, he was now convinced that the miracles alone that the host had worked were sufficient evidence to warrant its veneration.[71]

The same vagueness was applied to the question that is central for the topic at hand—whether the Jews had been rightly punished for their crime, whether the legitimacy of the procedure was questionable, or whether they had actually been wrongfully killed. While Ambrose shied away from making an irrevocable judgment, he concluded that the killing, or even the punishment of the Jews, did not seem justified to him. He argues that the citizens had acted precipitately, without closely scrutinizing what had really happened. His treatise not only reflects the idea of Christian mercy, but he also blames the citizens for not allowing the host to work its salvific purpose of showing the Jews the error of their ways. Ambrose is perhaps the one who reports another, otherwise unknown, accusation of host desecration against the Jews of Vienna that gives interesting insight into the role of the second target of civic critique: Duke Rudolf III.[72] Interestingly, in

70 Stelzer, "Am Beispiel Korneuburg," 336 (see note 12).

71 Stelzer, "Am Beispiel Korneuburg," 341 (see note 12).

72 Brugger and Wiedl, *Regesten 1*, 156–57, no. 147 (see note 1). On the question of authorship, see

retelling the events, the author leaves no doubt about the question of the Jews' innocence. A peasant had stolen a host and thrown it into a jug that stood close to a Viennese Jew's house. When the host miraculously started to whimper from within its prison, people were soon gathered around the jug (the source speaks of 100,000 persons, which is obviously a stereotypical exaggeration) and very quickly identified the Jews (who hadn't even appeared in person yet) as the culprits who had to be punished for their (intended) crime. Only the immediate presence of Duke Rudolf III, who with personal effort placated the enraged masses, saved the lives of 'his beloved Jews' (*suos judeos karissimos*), causing the author to add a scathing remark on Rudolf's preferential treatment of the Jews, from whose usury he profited and as whose protector and benefactor he appeared (*defensor* [. . .] *et fautor eorum*).

The focus of the author's critique is clearly the duke. In addition to profiting from the Jews' property and usury (*participare lucris et usuris eorum*), Rudolf demands heavy taxes and dues from them (*tollendo exacciones et munera maxima ab eis*). Not only does this narrative give an interesting introspection into the quite popular and widespread allusion of rulers being bribed by Jewish money in return for protection,[73] but it clearly conveys another message too. For the population, the combined presence of Jews, even if they were not physically present, and a host wafer could only mean one thing—that the Jews were about to commit, or had already committed, a crime.

These harsh words, if noted down by Ambrose or copied later, were not the first directed at Duke Rudolf III and his preferential treatment of the Jews. Since the Jews were his direct subjects and thus belonged to his immediate treasure, any attack on them he considered an attack on himself.[74] At Korneuburg, he merely supported the investigation, pushing (in contrast to the citizens' accusations) for a quick result and even sent the witnesses home when they angered him with their protesting. A year later, when a similar accusation of Jewish host desecration was raised at St. Pölten, a town that belonged to the bishop of Passau,[75] he came down

Stelzer, "Am Beispiel Korneuburg," 329 (see note 12), who argues quite succinctly that the incident had not been noted down by Ambrose but had merely been copied into the manuscript as a further example of a host-related miracle.

73 The allegation that rulers would profit financially from preventing the persecution of Jews, be it through taxing the Jews or because of having been bribed by them, is quite a commonplace in ecclesiastical chronicles, see the examples quoted by Treue, "Schlechte und gute Christen," 110–12 (see note 17), Lotter, "Hostienfrevelvorwurf," 549 (see note 17), further Johannes Grabmayer, *Zwischen Diesseits und Jenseits. Oberrheinische Chroniken als Quellen zur Kulturgeschichte des späten Mittelalters* (Cologne, Weimar, and Vienna: Böhlau, 1999), 28–29, 242–43, 275.

74 For an overview of the legal standing of the Austrian Jewry with regard to the Austrian duke, see Brugger, "Von der Ansiedlung," 134–51 (see note 12).

75 The bishop of Passau was the ecclesiastical overlord over the duchy of Austria that lay within the diocese of Passau, yet as far as the town of St. Pölten herself is concerned, the bishop was also the

heavily on the citizens, fining them with 3500 pounds for the crime of killing his Jews.[76] In the same year, he successfully quelled a persecution of the Jews of Vienna after another accusation of a host desecration had been raised there (see below).

Another crucial detail is revealed in Ambrose's treatise. Prior to the extensive investigation led by Ambrose, another inquiry of the whole incident had been carried out by Bishop Rudger, the abbot of the Scottish abbey in Vienna (Schottenstift), and the provost of the monastery of Klosterneuburg. Unfortunately, it is not possible with absolute certainty to place the two inquiries in chronological order. Ambrose labelled the one that was held upon the duke's instigation as the "first interrogation of witnesses," but based his arguments on facts that he learned later.

During this investigation, which had been commissioned by Duke Rudolf III, Zerkel's immediate neighbors had been interrogated, and their testimonies are more consistent (albeit only rendered in Ambrose's rather short summary) than the later, contradictory statements.[77] Around the first hour of the day in question, three Jews dashed out of Zerkel's house, screaming and running after a Christian whom they accused of having thrown a host wafer into their house. They begged the bystanders to aid them in catching the culprit, who, they shouted, should rather burn than them (*melius esset quod ipse comburetur quam nos*). Since they were not able to catch him, the Jews returned to their house where the Christians, who in the meantime had gathered there, saw part of a bloodied host, covered by a piece of cloth, in the hand of one of the Jews. In these testimonies, stripped of all allusions to a prior purchase, failed attempts to dispose of the wafer, and of heavenly voices and guided feet, we can most likely recognize the bare facts around which the tale was later woven. The basics—the doorstep of the Jews' house, the Jews running through the town, the accusations towards the Christian, the gathering masses who discover the bloodstained wafer—remained the same, yet in the extensive investigation these facts were presented with a plethora of additional details that emphasized the miracle-working character of the host. These details completely altered the initial situation by introducing the postulate that the Jews had already been in possession of the wafer—meaning, had already executed their vile plans—long before the Christians had come to know of it.

The piece of information Ambrose put before his brief rendition of the first inquiry is central, and might have motivated him to re-write several passages of

---

secular lord of the town. This was not an unusual situation in the Middle Ages; see Norman Roth, "Bishops and Jews in the Middle Ages," *The Catholic Historical Review* 80 (1994): 1–17.

76 Brugger and Wiedl, *Regesten 1*, 154–55, no. 145 (see note 1).

77 Ambrose does not give their names and, although it is highly likely that they had been questioned during the second interrogation as well, it is impossible to positively identify them.

his treatise.[78] The bishop of Passau, Wernhard of Prambach, had informed him that a priest had confessed that he had instigated the whole incident at Korneuburg.[79] By taking a simple oblate, dipping it into goat's blood and depositing it in front of the Jew's house to set up a reason for the defamation (*quod accepisset oblatam simplicem et intinxit sanguine hyrcino et immisit causam calu*[m]*pnie ad domum iudei*), he had created the prerequisite of not only the persecution of the Jews but also of what had, presumably, been his goal—to establish a pilgrimage site.

Together with four accomplices (*consociis*), he was willing to attest to this. Although this critical piece of information is put right before the summary of the first investigation, it is doubtful that either Ambrose, the Viennese Abbot, or any of the other members of the commissions had any knowledge of this prior to conducting the inquiries. In neither of the two investigations, regardless of which came first, was there any mention of a fraudulent priest, even if the possibility that the Jews might have been framed was very tentatively hinted at.

The real perpetrators can therefore be identified as follows: a priest and four accomplices who obviously were in cahoots in the scheme. No names are mentioned, but does it seem too speculative a guess to suspect Konrad, the vicar of Leobersdorf, as the main culprit? In his testimony before the commission, Konrad speaks of a 'repentant Christian' whom he had allegedly shriven, and who had confessed to having sold the wafer to the Jews, which had (further) sealed the belief in the Jews' guilt. In the light of the later findings, it is clear that his statement had to be a blatant lie.

The fact that a host had indeed been planted not only lends credibility to some of the testimonies—people *had* actually seen Zerkel and the scholar running through the town with a bloodstained host in their hands—but it also substantiates the statement of the terrified Jews that 'an evil Christian' had thrown the wafer onto their doorstep. It is, however, unlikely that the Jews were the fraudulent priest's primary target. Already the first alleged host wafer desecration in what is today Austrian territory, the events in Laa an der Thaya in 1294, had resulted not

78 Stelzer, "Am Beispiel Korneuburg," 338–39 (see note 12), argues that the first rendition of the treatise was written in late 1306 while the additions were worked into it around 1311, with the prologue being the last piece added in 1312.

79 The forging of "miracle-working" host wafers was not uncommon; the papal letter to bishop Albrecht II of Passau speaks of 'incidents similar to Korneuburg' that had taken place at Weikersdorf, while his letter to Duke Albrecht II of Austria mentions Linz (Brugger and Wiedl, *Regesten 1*, 339–40, nos. 442 and 443 [see note 1]), yet for neither of these two towns, is there any further documentation of a host desecration and an ensuing pogrom. See for German examples Lotter, "Hostienfrevelvorwurf," 574–81 (see note 17) (with Korneuburg as the main example); Graus, "Fälschungen im Gewand der Frömmigkeit," 268–70 (see note 68), again with Korneuburg (which he mistakes for Pulkau) and the forged host wafer of Wilsnack (that does not include accusations against Jews).

only in the Jews being persecuted but also a chapel being erected on the spot where the 'body of the Lord' had been found.[80]

A miraculous host provided the parish where it was kept with prestige and posed a strong attraction for pilgrims. It is therefore quite logical to assume that it was the priest's main goal to establish a pilgrimage site that would increase both the reputation and the revenues of the parish. To achieve this goal it would not have been enough merely to launch a story about a miraculous host; he needed the wafer itself as a tangible element. In putting all the key elements together—a host wafer, blood, and Jews—the fraudulent priest provided a scenario that allowed Christians to indulge fully their fantasies about the mistreatment and murder of Christ by the Jews.

The killing of the Jews might have been a spur-of-the-moment action, ignited by ubiquitous anti-Jewish sentiment and the desire for revenge, yet when they accused Ambrose and Rudolf III of hampering the investigation, they seemed to have been aware of the material benefits they could gain from an established and approved miraculous host. Pilgrimage hotspots, in turn, prolonged and nourished the Christian ideas of Jews maltreating hosts. Those who visited the site no longer only heard a tale but actually saw the maltreated host, the tangible (or at least visible) proof that Jewish host desecration was indeed a reality. Illustrations such as the (later) altar paintings at Korneuburg further helped the pilgrims to visualize the crime of the Jews, and thus they were bound to feel that the guilty Jews deserved their fate.[81]

It must remain pure speculation to include those witnesses who give the most detailed information as being in cahoots with the priest. Even if we identify the unnamed priest as Konrad of Leobendorf, there is no evidence that the four others he named as his accomplices were interrogated at all. Furthermore, with the intervention of Duke Rudolf III, who wanted the investigation brought to a quick end, there is a notable change in the procedure. The interviews became shorter and shorter, and although the witnesses were presented the full catalogue of questions, they were not encouraged to elaborate. These source-related considerations notwithstanding, some of the witnesses stand out with respect to the details they reveal. Konrad an der Hochstrass not only verified the vicar's testimony on the purchase of the host, but heaped additional blame on the Jews by shifting the confession from the vicar's unnamed layperson to the Jewish scholar. More details, such as the name of the Christian the Jews tried to persuade to dispose of the host

---

80 Brugger and Wiedl, *Regesten 1*, 89–90, no. 82 (see note 1). On the general 'restoration of the order,' the transformation of Jewish houses or synagogues into chapels (that usually housed the maltreated host), see Rubin, *Gentile Tales*, 89–91 (see note 3).

81 Merback, *The Thief, the Cross and the Wheel*, 195 (see note 54), also on the visual presentation of the host wafers.

for them, including the exact wording of this Christian's outburst when confronted with the host, were reported by Konrad an der Hochstrass, albeit, as he claimed, only by him rendering the dying scholar's last words.

Equally suspicious are Otto an dem Roßmarkt, who had the scholar say that the Jews fully deserved their fate for their misdeeds, and, the baker Sifridus (Sidlin) and his heavenly-guided feet. The latter also provided the reason why the host was deposited at Zerkel's doorstep: after seeing the host lying on the floor and standing mesmerized, Sifridus himself put it there when he saw the blood oozing from it. It must, as with the other witnesses, remain pure speculation whether Sifridus was in cahoots with the priest, yet there is much evidence that he, in fact, had been the one to whom the priest had assigned the task of planting the host wafer. First and foremost, as Miri Rubin pointed out, he had the crucial requisite at hand—the wafer itself, which is basically nothing but a piece of baked dough.[82]

Furthermore, his spectacular story of heavenly guidance, the picking up of the host at first and then putting it down again might have served as an explanation should he be caught red-handed. Sifridus himself confirmed that his finger had remained bloodied after he had put the host down. It must, again, remain pure speculation as to whether Sidlin's testimony had been agreed upon beforehand, and if so, to what purpose. It is possible that they sought to introduce the element of the heavenly intervention, to which the priest was hoping the theologically (more or less) versed interrogators would find appealing.

All of this, however, suggests not only Sifridus's involvement, but also points towards a scheme that was not a spur-of-the-moment act, but a premeditated plot that required meticulous planning. Only one other witness, Bertha, the wife of Konrad Reus, confirmed that she had seen him with the host but other than that merely stated that she 'concurs with him in regard of how the host was found.' Other witnesses only name Sidlin as being among those present at the retrieval of the host without crediting him with any special task. The Christian whom the Jews accused of having thrown the host into their house—who, according to his testimony, would have been Sidlin himself—remained anonymous in all other versions.

Most of the witnesses remained extremely vague about actual healings. When asked about specific names and time, the priest Friedrich responded *quod solum ex fama hec scit*. The second priest that was interrogated, Hertricus, responded in a quite similar manner: *quod nichil scit de hoc nisi per auditum et famam*. Otto an dem Roßmarkt, eager to share information, gave suspiciously elaborate details on the miraculous work of the host. He gave details about the cures of the

82 Rubin, *Gentile Tales*, 64 (see note 3).

aforementioned Bohemian girl plagued by demons and of the paralyzed Viennese woman. The former had been suffering for thirteen years and the latter for eight years, four of which had been spent in a hospital in Vienna. Yet, despite his in-depth knowledge, he could not specify the precise day or hour of their healing.

The miraculous healing that was brought up the most was that of the local weaver, Pero. Altogether ten witnesses claim that they knew about his healing, although most of them again resorting to hearsay. Only Otto an dem Roßmarkt explicitly admitted to actually having been present when Pero was healed. According to him, Rapoto Tasch (the eleventh witness) and Konrad Klett had been there too, *et pluribus aliis*.[83] Despite the fact that Pero was "known to everyone in the town," as Otto claimed, his fellow citizens were not able to give any precise details on the amount of time he had spent in his paralysed state, which differed between two and five years in the witnesses's statements.

To suspect that Pero might have been in cahoots with the fraudulent priest by faking a 'spiritual healing' might go too far, since he was not the first but only the most known of the lucky ones through whom the host demonstrated its power. It is surprising that he was not among the witnesses despite the fact that he still lived in Korneuburg, particularly since the commission was more concerned with the miracles (and their genuineness) than with the Jews' fate.

Judging by the list of those that had been miraculously cured within the first months of the host's work, the fame of the site had expanded quite quickly, thus allowing us to speculate that the priest's goal was achieved even if there is no mention of a pilgrimage site in the decades following the incident. Only two papal letters from the year 1338 that investigated the Pulkau persecutions in Lower Austria give insight into the continuing veneration of the Korneuburg host. What had happened in the meantime reads like a reflection of the earlier incidents. Since the original wafer had been eaten away by moths and worms but was still being venerated by the faithful masses, a misled priest (*suggestione diabolica persuasus errorem errori accumulans*) had taken a new, non-consecrated wafer, dipped it in blood and supplanted the old one, presumably not to impede the flourishing of the pilgrimage site.[84]

---

83 Due to the increasing brevity of the interviews, many of the witnesses merely respond that they 'concur with what the others stated,' which makes it impossible to decide whether they meant that they were present or had just heard about it both of which had already been stated by others. Rapoto Tasch for example (the nineteenth witness), who was reported by Otto an dem Roßmarkt as having been present, merely declares that he corroborates what the others had said; only the eleventh witness, the alderman Marquard, explicitly states that he had not been present when Pero had been healed.

84 Odericus Raynaldus and Jacobus de Laderchius, *Annales ecclesiastici denuo excusi et ad nostra usque tempora perducti ab Augustino Theiner*, 25: 1334–1355 (Bar-le-Duc: Ludovicus Guerin et socii, 1872), 118–19. To 'support' a host wafer that was being venerated yet had possibly not been consecrated

In the same year 1338, the Dukes Otto II and Albrecht II gave the Augustinian order a plot of land at Korneuburg that had once belonged to their Jews (*aream olim nostrorum judeorum [...] intra muros in Neunburch*)[85] and granted them the right to erect a monastery there—which also meant that the (former) presence of the Jews and their crimes stayed in the collective memory of the Christian community.[86] According to local tradition that was still (again?) alive in the 1960s,[87] this was the spot where Zerkel's house had once stood—a somewhat believable tradition actually, since it is highly likely that Zerkel's house was the only "Jewish" house in Korneuburg.[88]

With the actual culprit being known to the authorities, the question arises whether he had been punished for his offence. Ambrose in his treatise strongly recommended it, and even declared that the priest alone, and not the Jews, should have borne the consequences and the wording of the papal letter suggests that the felonious priest had indeed not emerged unscathed. Yet the sources are too scarce to track down any details on his potential punishment.[89] What can be gathered however are two things: the idea that a priest would misuse the tales of host desecration to his advantage was not unthinkable to either pope, bishop, or duke, and that, in order to make the scheme work, any fraudulent cleric (or layperson) could safely rely on the concept of the default guilt of the Jews which was firmly ingrained in the common mind-set.[90] The host, as the Korneuburg dean Jacob stated, had been found at the Jews' place, and that alone served as sufficient proof for its authenticity.

---

with a consecrated one is however not unusual: when the same problem arose at Pulkau in 1338, where a bloodied host had been found under rather similar circumstances (in front of a Jew's house, on the street, covered with straw) and was being worshipped at the parish church, the Bishop of Passau had a consecrated host put next to it; Chronicle of Francis of Prague (*Chronicon Aulae Regiae*) from the year 1338, see Brugger and Wiedl, *Regesten 1*, 347, no. 453 (see note 1).

85 Haus-, Hof- und Staatsarchiv (Austrian State Archives), Vienna, AUR 1338 XI 19 (Brugger and Wiedl, *Regesten 1*, 343, no. 447 [see note 1]).

86 See Zeissl, *Das ehemalige Augustinerkloster* (see note 33).

87 *Germania Judaica*, vol. II: *Von 1238 bis zur Mitte des 14. Jahrhunderts*, part 1: *Aachen—Luzern*, ed. Zvi Avneri (Tübingen: J.C.B. Mohr, 1968), 450.

88 The medieval synagogue in Korneuburg was erected in the fourteenth century, but the (sometimes quoted) time span of 1305 to 1325 for its construction seems highly unlikely, since there is no mention of a Jewish presence in Korneuburg up until 1378 (*Germania Judaica* II/1, 450 [see note 87]).

89 If we go with the assumption that it was Konrad, the vicar of Leobendorf, the sources remain silent on him: the *Urkundenbuch des Stiftes Klosterneuburg bis zum Ende des vierzehnten Jahrhunderts* (see note 30) does not mention a Konrad, vicar of Leobendorf.

90 Wolfgang Treue gives examples of Christians who, obviously firmly believing in the Jewish need for consecrated host wafers, tried to make money off this by trying to sell them hosts (and, occasionally, children), which the Jews refused (and sometimes sued them for it); Treue, "Schlechte und gute Christen," 104–06 (see note 17).

The fact that a fraudulent priest had staged the host desecration and brought about the consequences suffered by the Jewish population remained known to both secular and ecclesiastical authorities. In August 1338, Pope Benedict XII commanded the bishop of Passau, Albrecht II of Saxony-Wittenberg, to investigate a wave of anti-Jewish riots that had resulted from alleged host desecrations in the Lower Austrian towns of Pulkau and Weikersdorf, and the Upper Austrian town of Linz.[91] The investigation had been requested by the Austrian Duke Albrecht II, the brother and successor of the late Rudolf III, who had urged the Apostolic See to find out whether Jews had been guilty of the crime or had been innocent as had been the case at Korneuburg, phrasing his suspicions of foul play in no uncertain terms.

In fact, the two letters by Benedict XII are, apart from Ambrose's treatise, the only sources that mention the priest's criminal deed and thus provide information on the real course of events at Korneuburg.[92] The alleged host desecration at Pulkau (80 km/50 mi northeast of Vienna) had triggered the first wave of persecution in Austria that went beyond the local scope. Apart from the Jewish population of Pulkau, the Jews of many small towns in the surrounding area fell prey to the frenzied mob.[93] The Nürnberg memorial book lists 31 "blood sites" in

---

91 For Weikersdorf (west of Wiener Neustadt) and Linz, neither an accusation of host desecration nor a persecution of Jews is documented elsewhere; the Nürnberger Memorbuch ("memorial book"), the list of the 'blood sites' (*Blutstädte*), the sites of Jewish persecutions, cites neither Weikersdorf nor Linz; Siegmund Salfeld, *Das Martyrologium des Nürnberger Memorbuches*. Quellen zur Geschichte der Juden in Deutschland, 3 (Berlin: Leonhard Simion Verlag, 1898), 68 (Hebrew) and 420–21 (German); see also Brugger and Wiedl, *Regesten 1*, 348–49, no. 455 (see note 1), on memorial books in general, see Aubrey Pomerance, "'Bekannt in den Toren:' Name und Nachruf in Memorbüchern," *Erinnerung als Gegenwart: Juüdische Gedenkkulturen*, ed. Sabine Hödl and Eleonore Lappin (Berlin and Vienna: Philo, 2000), 33–54. Alfons Žák, "Zur Kirchengeschichte Niederösterreichs," *Monatsblatt des Vereins für Landeskunde und Heimatschutz von Niederösterreich und Wien*, 12.1/1 (1926/27), 6–7 suspects the Lower Austrian town Retz, close to the Bohemian border and listed in the memorial book of Nürnberg, behind the seriously misspelled name of Linz (*Fyncz, Syntz*). To include the Pulkau persecutions into the wave of persecutions that had sprung up around the same time in the Bavarian town of Deggendorf and had spread quickly throughout the southern regions of the Holy Roman Empire is somewhat problematic for the lack of any immediate connection; although some of the mainly ecclesiastical sources either mix up these two events or merely report of 'Jews being killed in the southern parts'.

92 Editions: Shlomo Simonsohn, *The Apostolic See and the Jews*, vol. 1: *Documents 492–1404*. Pontifical Institute of Medieval Studies, Studies and Texts, 94 (Toronto: Pontifical Institute of Medieval Studies/Brepols, 1988), 371–74, nos. 354–55 (full text of the letter to the bishop of Passau, summary of the letter to Duke Albrecht), and Raynaldus and de Laderchius, *Annales ecclesiastici*, 118–19, nos. 20–21 (full text of the letter to Duke Albrecht, summary of the letter to the bishop).

93 Rubin, *Gentile Tales*, 65 and 68 (see note 3), gives the number of '150 Jews of Pulkau' that were killed during the persecutions, which is by far too high a number for a small Lower Austrian town. Her assessment that it was Duke Otto's 'abandonment' of the Austrian duchy in favour of the 'recently annexed' Styria (which was neither 'annexed' nor recently acquired by the Habsburgs) that made the Pulkau persecutions possible ignores the existence of Otto's brother,

Austrian, Moravian, Bohemian, and Bavarian territory.[94] The incident that had started the Pulkau persecutions reads quite similar to what had happened at Korneuburg (and many others in the centuries to come), containing all the key elements of the classical narrative: a blood-stained host was found in front of a Jew's house,[95] and, incited by what the Jews had undoubtedly done to it, the Christian population sought revenge.

Unfortunately, the outcome (if there was any) of bishop Albrecht's investigation is not documented. Duke Albrecht II, however, proceeded to follow the policy of his older brother Rudolf III in prosecuting anti-Jewish outbreaks. During the period of the Black Plague, that saw the violent end of many Jewish communities in the Holy Roman Empire, Albrecht managed to a large extent to maintain the safety of the Austrian Jewry.[96] Albrecht II did not shy away from resorting to drastic measures when the Jews—and thus a part of his treasury—were attacked. The only persecution of Jews during this time in Austria, in the town of Krems that housed the second-largest Jewish community in Lower Austria, was met not only with heavy fines but the leaders of riot, who were among the most important

---

Duke Albrecht II (whom she mistakes for Albrecht II of Saxony, the bishop of Passau).

94 Some of the listed names, such as Passau (Bavaria) are in today's academic literature counted as part of the Deggendorf persecutions (see *Germania Judaica*, vol. II: *Von 1238 bis zur Mitte des 14. Jahrhunderts*, part 2: *Maastricht—Zwolle*, ed. Zvi Avneri [Tübingen: J.C.B. Mohr, 1968], 647–48, fn. 7), whereas for the Carinthian town of Villach, which is geographically the most remote from the centre of the violent outbreaks, a persecution of the Jews is not documented in any other source; Jewish presence in Villach is after 1338 first documented for the year 1346 (Eveline Brugger and Birgit Wiedl, *Regesten zur Geschichte der Juden in Österreich im Mittelalter*, vol. 2: *1339–1365* [Innsbruck, Vienna, and Bolzano: StudienVerlag, 2010], 62–62, no. 570 (for the internet version, see http://www.injoest.ac.at/projekte/laufend/mittelalterliche_judenurkunden/; last accessed on March 10, 2012).

95 A Jew Merchlin at Pulkau is documented for the year 1329, when he purchases a plot of land from a local nobleman (Brugger and Wiedl, *Regesten 1*, 257–58, no. 303 [see note 1]); it is highly likely that he is identical with the *Marquardus iudeus* in front of whose house the host was found in 1338 (on the equation of Merchlin and Marquart, both derivations of Mordechai, see Alexander Beider, *A Dictionary of Ashkenazic Given Names. Their Origins, Structure, Pronunciation, and Migrations* [Bergenfield, NJ: Avotaynu, 2001], 375–76, 382). For an overview over the Pulkau-related sources, see Brugger and Wiedl, *Regesten 1*), 333–35, nos. 434–36, 339–41, nos. 442–43, 343–51, nos. 448–56 (see note 1); for an overview of the events, see Brugger, "Von der Ansiedlung," 216–19 (see note 12); Manfred Anselgruber and Herbert Puschnik, *Dies trug sich zu anno 1338. Pulkau zur Zeit der Glaubenswirren* (Pulkau: Verlag der Gemeinde, 1992); Rubin, *Gentile Tales*, 65–68 (see note 3); Birgit Wiedl, "Die angebliche Hostienschändung in Pulkau 1338 und ihre Rezeption in der christlichen und jüdischen Geschichtsschreibung," *medaon. Magazin für jüdisches Leben in Forschung und Bildung* 6 (2010), internet journal, see http://medaon.de/pdf/A_Wiedl-6-2010.pdf, last accessed on March 10, 2012.

96 It is against the backdrop of the many massacres in the German-speaking area that Joseph haCohen's description of Austria as a 'safe haven' in his *Emek habacha* becomes understandable, Joseph haCohen, *Emek habacha*. Transl. from the Hebrew into German by M. Wiener (Leipzig: Oskar Leiner, 1859), 54.

citizens, were beheaded.[97] These drastic actions, in turn, earned him the title of *fautor iudeorum*, "benefactor of the Jews," from the clerical chroniclers,[98] subjecting him to the same critique as his brother Rudolf III as well as their father, King Albrecht I, and grandfather, King Rudolf I.[99]

There is no documentation in either Laa an der Thaya or in Korneuburg or Pulkau of anti-Jewish outbreaks before the fateful accusations. A tax regulation of 1277 for the town of Laa that incorporated the tax the Jews had to pay into the general city tax (*in unserr burger dinst*) suggests a rather peaceful cohabitation enjoyed by Christians and Jews in these small towns.[100] While the tax regulation of Laa and the Korneuburg persecution were the first traces of Jews dwelling in these town respectively,[101] we have scarce evidence of Jewish life in Pulkau before the 1338 catastrophe, yet for neither of these towns (and most of the other towns that were afflicted by the Pulkau persecution), a continuance, or reestablishment, of Jewish settlement is documented.

Klaus Lohrmann has suggested that after the Pulkau persecutions, Jewish life tended to focus on the major cities, such as Vienna, that housed bigger Jewish communities which could, if need arose, provide better shelter.[102] Although the

---

97 Brugger and Wiedl, *Regesten 2*, 95–98, nos. 645 and 647 (for Plague-related pogroms in Austria, see generally nos. 645–51) (see note 94).

98 *Kalendarium Zwetlense*, see Brugger and Wiedl, *Regesten 2*, 98, no. 647 (see note 94).

99 Ecclesiastical chronicles continually lambasted the early Habsburgs for their King Rudolf I had been criticized heavily for his intervention in the veneration of Werner of Oberwesel in 1288 ("Chronicon Colmariense," *Monumenta Germaniae Historica, Scriptores*, vol. 17, ed. Georg Heinrich Pertz [Hanover: Hahnsche Buchhandlung, 1861], 240–70; here 255) while Albrecht I's favorism of the Jews resulted not only in his son's Rudolf III's untimely death but also his own violent murder at the hands of his nephew ("Continuatio Zwetlensis Tertia ad a. 1294," ed. Wilhelm Wattenbach. *Monumenta Germaniae Historica, Scriptores*, vol. 9, ed. Georg Heinrich Pertz [Hanover: Hahnsche Buchhandlung 1851, rpt. Stuttgart: Anton Hiersemann Verlag, 1983], 654–69; here 663. For the internet version of the MGH volumes, see www.dmgh.de, last accessed on March 10, 2012). See further Eveline Brugger, "'Minem herren dem hertzogen sein juden': Die Beziehung der Habsburger zu 'ihren' Juden im Österreich des 14. Jahrhunderts," *Tagungsbericht des 25. Österreichischen Historikertags, St. Pölten 2008*, ed. Verband Österreichischer Historiker and Niederösterreichisches Landesarchiv (St. Pölten: Verlag des Landes Niederösterreich, 2010), 742–49; here 746–47.

100 Brugger and Wiedl, *Regesten 1*, 74, no. 57 (see note 1).

101 *Germania Judaica* III/1, 674 (Korneuburg) and 697–98 (Laa) (see note 13). In Laa, a Jew Herzlein is mentioned in the year 1378 (HHStA, AUR 1378 V 14).

102 Klaus Lohrmann, *Judenrecht und Judenpolitik im mittelalterlichen Österreich* (Vienna and Cologne: Böhlau, 1990), 155. A similar development can be detected in other parts of the Holy Roman Empire where the Jewish communities of both urban and rural settlements were hit hard by Plague-related pogroms: the re-settlement took place mainly in the urban centres, see Rainer Barzen, "*Benei haKefarim*—die Leute aus den Dörfern. Zur jüdischen Siedlung auf dem Lande in Aschkenas und Zarfat im hohen und späteren Mittelalter," *Campana pulsante convocati. Festschrift anläßlich der Emeritierung von Prof. Dr. Alfred Haverkamp*, eds. Frank G. Hirschmann and Gerd Mentgen (Trier: Kliomedia, 2005), 21–37; here 27. See also Birgit Wiedl, "'Lazarus and Abraham,

number of Jewish rural settlements should not be underestimated, the assumption that bigger communities could provide better protection holds true for Austria, at least during the thirteenth and fourteenth centuries. For example, the accusations of having committed a ritual murder against the Jews of Krems in 1293 that resulted in the execution of two Jews did not hamper the flourishing of the second-largest Jewish community in the duchy;[103] and neither did the Plague-related accusations of well-poisoning levied against the Jews of Krems in 1349 have any distinct impact on the well-established standing of the Jewish community.[104]

However, even the largest and most prosperous of all Austrian communities, the Jewish community of Vienna, was completely defenseless when, at the beginning of the fifteenth century, the ducal protection, that had seriously waned during the last decades of the preceding century, turned into oppression. The catastrophe that befell the Jewish community of Vienna in the years 1420/21, the incarceration, explusion, forced conversions, and, eventually, burning of more than 200 Jews, differed essentially from the earlier persecutions that had erupted spontaneously. The Vienna *Gesera*, the brutal and ruthless annihilation of the Viennese, and, in succession, the Austrian Jewry, had been meticulously planned and carried out by Duke Albrecht V (the later King Albrecht II).[105] Whereas the manifold motives for

---

our Jews of Eggenburg': Jews in the Austrian Countryside in the Fourteenth Century," *Rural Space in the Middle Ages and Early Modern Age: The Spacial Turn in Premodern Studies*, ed. Albrecht Classen, with the collaboration of Christopher R. Clason. Fundamentals of Medieval and Early Modern Culture, 9 (Berlin and New York: De Gruyter, 2012), 639–71; here 659–60.

103 The two chronicles that refer to the incident are quite vague on this—the *Continuatio Vindobonensis* only mention that Jews had killed a Christian, without any further comment on their fate (*Iudei in Crems occiderunt christianum*), while the *Continuatio Zwetlensis Tertia*, albeit clearly implying a ritualistic motiv, mostly utilizes the incident to scold the Austrian Duke Albrecht I for his 'favouring the Jews.' The way of the Jews' execution (broken on the wheel) suggests a formal verdict (Brugger and Wiedl, *Regesten 1*, 87–88, nos. 78–79 [see note 1]; for executions of Jews, see Ernst Schubert, *Räuber, Henker, arme Sünder: Verbrechen und Strafe im Mittelalter* [Darmstadt: Wissenschaftliche Buchgesellschaft, 2007], 61–64).

104 Brugger and Wiedl, *Regesten 2*, 97–99, nos. 646–47, 649 (see note 94). A *iudex iudeorum* (Judenrichter, 'judge for the Jews'), a Christian who was responsible for Jewish-Christian disputes and business transactions, whose existence is usually a signifier for a larger, and considerably important, Jewish community, is documented quite continually; in 1355, the first Jew is mentioned again when the Jewess Czaetel, widow after Mosche of Krems, sells her house in Krems. See idem, 163, no. 790, and generally Hannelore Hruschka, *Die Geschichte der Juden in Krems von den Anfängen bis 1938*. 2 Vols. (Vienna: University of Vienna, unpublished dissertation, 1978).

105 The only extensive publication on the topic is still Samuel Krauss, *Die Wiener Geserah vom Jahre 1421* (Vienna and Leipzig: Wilhelm Braumüller, 1920). An edition of the text of the "Wiener Gesera," the German-Yiddish report of the incident, and Albrecht's two verdicts, by Artur Goldmann, *Das Judenbuch der Scheffstrasse zu Wien (1389–1420)*. (Vienna and Leipzig: Wilhem Braumüller, 1908), 112–33 (appendix); see also the newer discussions by Klaus Lohrmann, *Die Wiener Juden im Mittelalter* (Berlin and Vienna: Philo, 2000), 155–73, *Judenrecht und Judenpolitik*, 298–309 (see note 101); Brugger, "Von der Ansiedlung," 221–54 (see note 12); and Rubin, *Gentile Tales*, 116–19 (see note 3), with a discussion of the Jewish-Hussite connection (or the lack thereof).

this violent destruction of the Austrian Jewry—a suspected collaboration with the Hussites, the ducal lust for the treasures they had allegedly hidden—and the extent to which the university of Vienna and its anti-Jewish preachers exerted their influence are still discussed, one key element ties in with what had happened more than a century earlier in the small town of Korneuburg. When severely reprimanded for his actions by Pope Martin V,[106] Albrecht V excused his actions with what he knew to be a safe bet. In his verdicts, Albrecht declared that a female sacristian (*mesnerin*) of the Upper Austrian town of Enns had sold a consecrated host several years before to the Jews who intended to desecrate it. Furthermore, the Jews had passed the host among themselves throughout the duchy and abroad, thus implicating more Jews in the crime and adding conspiracy to deicide and profanity.

Since Albrecht's declaration was made only after the Jews were killed, we must take this fact into account when discussing it. Despite the popularity of the tale, there had been no rumors of an accusation of Jewish host desecration at Enns before Albrecht V's verdicts, and interestingly, neither was it taken up by the clerical chroniclers who reported the incidents, nor did a pilgrimage site develop out of it. It is highly plausible that Albrecht utilized a prevalent and well-established pattern to explain and legitimate his actions. Albrecht could safely rely on the default crime scenario that provided all the elements that were crucial to establish the Jews' guilt. It had worked a few years earlier in the archbishopric of Salzburg where the Jews had been made to confess to both host desecrations and ritual murder under torture before they were either killed or expulsed,[107] and it would work numerous times in the fifteenth century, in Breslau (1453), in Passau (1477) and Sternberg (1492), to name but a few,[108] and would remain one of the central fantasies Christians indulged in when contemplating Jewish crime, even if they, in the retrospect of later centuries, would either not fully understand the earlier concept and/or add their own ideas.

At Korneuburg, like in many other towns that hosted a church with a miraculous host (often named 'Church of the Holy Blood'), the centuries to follow did not consider the Jews' possible, or proven, innocence, but added new aspects of the Jews' misdeeds that catered to these centuries' own ideas and readings of the story. The image of Jews desecrating a host by throwing it into a well, a motif

---

106 Goldmann, *Judenbuch*, 120–21 (see note 103), the mention of the papal intervention in the text of the *Gesera* 130.

107 Markus Wenninger, "Die Entwicklung der Stadt Salzburg—zur Geschichte der Juden in Salzburg," *Geschichte Salzburgs Stadt und Land*. Vol. 1/2: *Mittelalter*, ed. Heinz Dopsch and Hans Spatzenegger (Salzburg: Pustet, 1983), 747–56.

108 For further examples, see Lotter, "Hostienfrevelvorwurf," 578–81 (see note 17); Rubin, *Gentile Tales*, 119–31, with other examples throughout chapter 6 (including Passau and Sternberg) (see note 3).

that appears frequently in the later host desecration tales, is found at Korneuburg not in the medieval tale but is only introduced in a cycle of eleven (originally twelve) paintings from 1660 (see Figs. 2–12) that rendered not so much the original incident but this century's idea of it.[109] The creation of this cycle of paintings, that was displayed in the monastery's cloister and had been donated by aldermen, the parish priest, and high-ranking citizens of Korneuburg, coincided with the copying of the protocols in the year 1655[110] that was presumably manufactured on the occasion of the (alleged) retrieval of an almost-saintly object—not the host itself, but the piece of cloth that had once covered the miraculous host.[111]

Again, heavenly intervention had guided the steps of a citizen, the alderman Johann Georg Neckinger (also Reckinger), and had assisted him in finding "the cloth which the most holy host had been wrapped in and hidden in the local parish church for innumerable years" (*das tuechl darin die allerheilig hostia eingewikelt und unerdenkliche jahr in der alhieigen pfarr kirchen verborgen war*). Around the same time, a 'book of miracles' (*Mirakelbuch*) was published by the monastery that retold the story of the miraculous host. In its account, the miracle book left no doubt as to who was to be considered the main perpetrator, and, like the cycle of panels, included the motif of the host being thrown into a well. The general revival of the legend of the miraculous host and the pilgrimage site connected with it were in answer to the precarious situation the monastery found itself in in the middle of the seventeenth century. Re-established in 1624, the monastery had suffered damages from several fires and the Swedish siege in 1645/56.

The temporal coincidence of this revival is striking. Only three years earlier, in 1652, new panels had been added to the main altar of the parish church at Pulkau that illustrated the local miracle-working host wafer, and had successfully provided a popular attraction for both locals and pilgrims. The legend had prevailed in Korneuburg over the centuries, but had suffered a decline in importance. An earlier illustration, from around 1470, can be found on a small portable altar (*Klappaltar*) the centrepiece of which had served as a repository for the blood-stained cloth (see Fig. 1). On the two side wings, four paintings show the Jewish scholar (upper right, already with the infamous yellow circle on his cloak) holding the host and the bloodied cloth in his hand, and three of the wonders that

---

109 Graus, *Pest, Geissler, Judenmorde*, 299–340 (see note 11), on the emergence of the myth of Jewish well-poisoning in the fourteenth century; Rohrbacher and Schmidt, *Judenbilder*, 194–202, for an overview of the later development (see note 8).

110 HHStA, Notariatsinstrument des Notars Otto von Rußbach, AUR 1305 XII 17 (enclosed).

111 The original installation of the paintings is not clear: some of the paintings are numbered, but the sequence of the numbers differs from the course of events (e.g., lighting of candles at the parish church carries the number 5).

the host had worked—the healing of two blind (lower left) and two handicapped (lower right), and the lighting of candles (upper left).[112]

Although the painting does not actually show the Jew maltreating the host, the implication is again clear: a Jew holding a host in his hands means desecration. In the centuries to come, the seventeenth-century paintings reflected the peoples' ideas about the course of events and that would influence future perceptions of them, particularly since copper engravings of them were included in the later editions of the miracle book.

The late nineteenth and the mid-twentieth century left no doubt as to who was to be regarded as the culprit(s).[113] An amalgam of the late-medieval events and the early modern additions, the tale bears only slight resemblance to what the witnesses, convinced of the Jews' guilt or not, had testified 600 years ago: after buying the host from a criminal and/or foolish Christian and doing unspeakable things to it, the Jews threw the maltreated host into a well but retrieved it again since it drew attention by shining brightly from within the water. They then bribed a dim-witted Christian servant to get rid of it for them, and when he refused, they ran after him, accusing him of having thrown the host into their house. The Jewish scholar showed the host wafer, from which blood was seeping so that it soaked the cloth it was wrapped in, to the gathering masses, but no one was willing to take it from him. Zerkel, aggravated, threw the wafer onto the floor and trod it into the dirt. Later, a heavenly vision led the baker's son into Zerkel's house, where the remaining third of the maltreated host, still wrapped in the bloodied cloth, suddenly appeared in his hand. Since he considered himself unworthy of holding the body of Christ in his hands, he put the wafer on the threshold which was seen by two women passing by. The news spread quickly and a throng of people gathered at the Jew's house. Soon, they remembered the recent incident—the Jews chasing after the servant—and started to cry out for punishment. The scholar was burnt at the stake immediately, and Zerkel, who had, with the help of some aldermen, been hiding in a house, was beaten to death by the enraged masses. In this rendition that even made it into a collection of folk tales[114] no doubts were raised about the Jews' guilt and that they received their 'divine retribution.'

---

112 The altar is now kept at the Stiftmuseum Klosterneuburg (Museum of the Monastery of Klosterneuburg), where it was brought to after the dissolution of the Korneuburg monastery in 1808. Stelzer, "Am Beispiel Korneuburg," 317–19, with ill. no. 2 (see note 12).

113 Albert Starzer, *Geschichte der landesfürstlichen Stadt Korneuburg* (1899, rpt.; Korneuburg: Museumsverein, 1991); Franz Zeissl, *Geschichte der Stadt Korneuburg*, vol. 1 (Vienna: Touristik-Verlag, 1959), 73–74, and idem, *Das ehemalige Augustinerkloster in Korneuburg*, 3–7 and 28–30 (see note 33).

114 Stelzer, "Am Beispiel Korneuburg," 316, who also points out that since Starzer quotes Pope Benedict's letter, he must have known about the manufactured evidence, yet chose to give this completely uncritical and clearly biased rendition (see note 12).

What can we conclude about the fourteenth-century citizens of Korneuburg? The contradictions that appear in the record of the interrogations, the accusation by the priest, and the statement 'I did not see it' of the witnesses notwithstanding, the contemporaries of the early fourteenth century, be they rural, urban, or courtly, genuinely believed in the Jews' collective guilt. Yet was this belief unanimous? There seems to have been doubt among some of the theologically trained, although their concern rested more with the question of the genuineness of the host and its miracles. But there was also room for doubt among the Jews' neighbors, those with whom they had lived side by side rather peacefully until then. Disagreements occured during the interrogation: the citizens shifted the blame onto the scholar by claiming that he had named Zerkel as the sole culprit. The suggestion that the scholar might have been innocent hangs in the air, yet is heavily qualified by Otto an dem Roßmarkt who reports that even the scholar himself had conceded that they, the Jews, had met their destiny.[115] Nevertheless, the citizens seemed to have been quite hesitant to state that they firmly believed in the Jews' guilt. None of the interviewees admitted to having actively participated in the killing of the Jews; and we may question whether they said what the authorities wanted to hear, whether they were afraid of admitting to the killings, or whether at least some of them actually harbored doubts about the Jews' guilt.

Konrad Reus's wife testified at the interrogation that she had been present when the host wafer had been found, yet she did not mention (and was not asked) anything about Zerkel being at their home. Had the two Christians, the two Marquards, who had ushered Zerkel into Konrad Reus's house, the moment their neighbors returned (and perhaps told them about the Jewish scholar's last words, and his unmarred head), continued to guard Zerkel, or had they reached for a cudgel and joined the murderous mob? We do not know. The phrasing of the testimony of Heinrich Shem, the witness who tells us about the two Marquards who had tried to hide Zerkel, suggests that Zerkel had indeed hoped to find protection there, and that the mob had entered the house by force. Heinrich too claims not to have partaken in Zerkel's killing, yet we can't be sure, of course. What we do know is that blood had indeed been spilt, and it had been the blood of the Jews.

115 This is the comment by Otto an dem Rossmarkt (eighth witness), who also claims that Heinrich von Etzleinsdorf, Heinrich's brother, and Konrad an der Hochstrass were present during the scholar's alleged confession (Brugger and Wiedl, *Regesten 1*, 134, no. 133 [see note 1]).

Fig. 1: Stiftsmuseum Klosterneuburg, Inge Kitlitschka, Klosterneuburg. Portable altar (around 1470) with four paintings (upper left: spontaneous ignition of candles, upper right: the Jew holding the host, bottom left: two blind regain their sight, bottom right: two crippled are cured)

Figs. 2 – 12: Stadtmuseum Korneuburg. Cycle of paintings, oil, 1660, eleven of the originally twelve paintings that were on display in the cloister of the monastery of Korneuburg, now kept at the Municipal Museum
Fig. 2: "1301, the Jew Zerklin made a Christian sell a holy host wafer for money and a coat." Background, left: Zerkel offers a red coat and money to the Christian. [No donation]

Fig. 3: "Here, the Christian sells the host to Zerkel the Jew for money and a coat." Donated by Wenzeslaus Melzer, CRSA [= Canon Regular], parish priest of Korneuburg

Fig. 4: "Here, the Jew Zerkel throws the host into the well in the presence of the Jew Scholasticus." Donated by Blasius Vitalis Seywald, imperial *Salzgegenschreiber* (official at the imperial salt authority)

Fig. 5: "Here, the Jew Scholasticus retrieves the host from the well, and the Jew Zerkel trods on it." On the base of the well: "Johann Georg Rekinger, member of the local inner council who recovered the cloth which the most holy host had been wrapped in and which had been hidden in the local parish church for innumerable years, through divine direction."

Fig. 6: "Here, the Jew Zerkel shows it [= the host] to a Christian so that he should throw the host together with a white cloth into the Danube, but the Christian did not take the host." Donated by [inscription faded] Jacob Sn[. . .]hackner [. . .]

Fig. 7: "Here, the two Jews Zerkel and the Scholasticus cry and falsely complain, as if the Christian had carried the host into their house." Background: One of the Jews appears on the threshold with the host wrapped in cloth. Donated by Paulus Müller, senator of Korneuburg

Fig. 8: "Here, the two Jews Zerkel and Scholasticus again throw the host and the cloth to the floor and tread on it in anger." Donated by Wenzislaus Dyrnwald, notary public and syndic at Korneuburg

Fig. 9: "Here, an angel guides a backer called Luderich [!] from the bakery to the Jew Zerkel's house so that he should pick up the host; but as he was scared, the host miraculously appeared between his fingers [barely readable]." Background: The baker stoops down to pick up the host. [No donation]

Fig. 10: "Here, the baker puts the host with utmost reverence and obeisance on the stony doorstep, whereupon the host sweated blood and was thusly found." Background: Led by the angel, the baker carries the host. Donation: coat of arms and initials CFVS (according to Zeissl, *Das ehemalige Augustinerkloster*, 30 [see note 33], the coat of arms points at the family of Dachsenbeck)

Fig. 11: "Here, 6 (?) wax candles ignite upon being shown the host and the blood-stained cloth." Donated by Johann Nußdorfer, notary public at Korneuburg

Fig. 12: "Here, the blind are healed by being shown the host and by application of the cloth." [The bearded man appears to be handicapped.] Donated by Georgius Eberschwanger

Chapter 14

Daniel F. Pigg
(The University of Tennessee at Martin)

Does the Punishment Fit the Crime?: Chaucer's *Physician's Tale* and the Worlds of Judgment

Of the tales in the *Canterbury Tales*, the *Physician's Tale* is certainly a selection that has been noted for its lack of narrative unity, its rather bizarre logic at the conclusion, and its horrific representation of judgments in court and at home: the father's and the judge's.[1] As Robin Bott has noted, the tale considers "society's concern with the social and political consequences of sexual access to women."[2] In that way, it coheres with a number of the *fabliaux* as well as the religious tales. In this tale, justice is itself on trial, perhaps even the very open construction of the legal system as Chaucer envisions it. The concerns seem larger than gender, but as will be seen, the two concepts of gender and law or judgment are intertwined. When Virginia asks, "Is ther no grace, is there no remedy?" (VI, 235), she is asking the central question of justice in the tale. However, as several critics have noted, Chaucer's additions and changes move the tale away from the most overtly political possibilities found in the original sources. As Liaanna Farber has observed, "In the *Physician's Tale* politics and governance instead become the process of getting people to agree with you; the process of creating consent."[3]

Chaucer provides us with a tale that has no emotional release. There is no real system whereby a corrupt judgment that is given in a Roman or English court of

---

1 All quotations from the text of *The Physician's Tale* are from *The Riverside Chaucer*, 3rd ed., ed. Larry Benson (Boston: Houghton Mifflin, 1987), 190–93.

2 Robin Bott, "'O Keep Me From Their Worse Than Killing Lust': Ideologies of Rape and Mutilation in Chaucer's *Physician's Tale* and Shakespeare's *Titus Andronicus*," *Representing Rape in Medieval and Early Modern Literature*, ed. Elizabeth Robertson and Christina M. Rose. The New Middle Ages (New York and Houndmills, Basingstoke, Hampshire: Palgrave, 2001), 189–211.

3 Lianna Farber, "The Creation of Consent in the *Physician's Tale*," *Chaucer Review* 39 (2004): 151–64.

law can be overturned. Corrupt desire has become its own law. The tale has been deemed unsatisfactory and enigmatic, but that could simply be because of the image that we have of Chaucer, if we assume that he is the witty and urbane person of the Middle Ages.[4] Has Chaucer through the Physician deconstructed the power of the social order, or has he simply shown gaps within the structure? Has Chaucer through the very fiction of his text moved the world from imperial Rome in some way to medieval Europe where charges in the court could become a critique of masculine power? This essay will assert that Chaucer did precisely that through the Physician.

I

Taking the story from Livy and the *Roman de la rose*,[5] Chaucer makes several unique changes to his sources, including the elaboration on the work on Nature, the warning to parents and governesses to be careful of their children's safety, the scene at home between Virginius and Virginia in which he takes her life, the connection of Virginia's and Jephthah's daughter and thus of Virginius and Jephthah, and the moral tag ending that seems bizarre in its connection to the events of the story.[6]

The judgment scene in which Virginius kills his daughter is moved from the court setting to their home. The means by which Virginius is charged with the crime of theft—the alleged taking of the would-be slave who is actually his daughter—remains in Chaucer's version as in his sources. Taken together, the original tale and the Chaucerian additions contribute to one of the most disturbing examinations of crime and punishment in the *Canterbury Tales*. What seems likely is that Chaucer's unique contributions to the story attempt to address issues of agency and responsibility. What results is a complex web which shows the vital force that the commons exert in the understanding of justice, but even here, that is less of a critique of their voice as it was in the *Clerk's Tale* than in the failures built into a system ripe for perverse abuse.

While the majority of this essay will examine the specific Chaucerian additions to the tale's fictive narrative, it is also important to point out a significant issue

---

4 For a survey of criticism on this tale, see Helen Storm Corsa, ed., *The Physician's Tale: A Variorum Edition of the Works of Geoffrey Chaucer*, vol. 11, part 17 (Norman: The University of Oklahoma Press, 1986), 9–41.

5 The consensus now seems to be that Chaucer knew the story through a shorter version found in Guillaume de Lorris's and Jean de Meun's *Roman de la rose*. For a point by point comparison, see Kenneth Bleeth, "*The Physician's Tale,*" *Sources and Analogues of the Canterbury Tales*, vol. 2, ed., Robert M. Correale and Mary Hamel. Chaucer Studies 35 (Cambridge: D. S. Brewer, 2002), 535–63.

6 Bleeth, "The Physician's Tale," 537 (see note 5).

relative to the court scene. While it is certainly clear that Chaucer's setting for the story is the Roman world, it is his knowledge of English law and court systems that seems most dominant. That is also how his original readers or hearers would have judged the legal system. Claudius in the versions by Livy, Jean de Meun, and Chaucer accuses Virginius of stealing Virginia from his house; she is a slave stolen from his house long ago on an evening. Virginius indicates he can prove otherwise in the case of Claudius's story, but the judge, acting in haste, will not allow witnesses to be brought to the court proceedings. Instead Appius orders Virginius to surrender Virginia to him. No future son-in-law is present in the Chaucerian text as in Livy's version. Livy and Jean de Meun have Virginia kill his daughter in the sight of everyone, while Chaucer moves that experience to Virginius's house.

What would have been most interesting to a medieval audience would relate to the charges themselves. Derek G. Neal has demonstrated that "Accusations of thievery attacked a masculine social self by diminishing it, reducing the symbolic space it occupied in a constellation of other social selves."[7] Further, he provides the additional context of accusations related to the community:

> There were different ways of imagining this aspect of social identity. In the text and context of these defamation suits, the relevant medieval word was *fama*. To be de-*famed* was to have one's *fama* damaged. Yet *fama* was not only part or characteristic of an individual. It was inseparable from the spoken word, as implied by the stock legal phrase *vox et fama*, "common voice and fame," on which all witnesses had to comment. In both a lifeline and as a tether on which either side could pull to its own advantage. . . . Masculine *fama* was larger and more variegated than the feminine variety. Defending one's masculine honor meant holding one's place (not being yanked out of it) and preserving the possibility of improving on it.[8]

For the medieval world, the accusation of being a thief as opposed to being a true man meant that the thief was "the most common personification of unmanliness."[9] Finally, the "true man" distinction signals "an uncomplicated honesty: openness, manifest veracity, a surface meaning that is the only meaning."[10] What seems straightforward in theory becomes significantly complex in the manner of presentation in this short tale.

Virginius, being called a thief in the narrative, has doubts cast on his masculinity in the way that a typical medieval charge would have. That his daughter is called "Virginia" only provides an intriguing grammatically gendered difficulty to the process, as Glenn Burger has noted relative to the fixity of desire on the part of

---

7 Derek G, Neal, *The Masculine Self in Late Medieval England* (Chicago and London: The University of Chicago Press, 2008), 36.

8 Neal, *The Masculine Self in Late Medieval England*, 36 (see note 7).

9 Neal, *The Masculine Self in Late Medieval England*, 41 (see note 7).

10 Neal, *The Masculine Self in Late Medieval England*, 43 (see note 7).

Appius.[11] The desire here is clearly to bring Virginius down, to feminize him in the way that a charge of theft presumes. That the system of justice will not allow him to prove otherwise, given that he is unable to call witnesses before Appius reaches a quick decision, underlines that the whole process of law has been misused. The legal system in its structural form has overturned the meaning of false and true men, assuming that the true man is Virginius and the false one is Appius. Viriginius is also caught in a "no grace, no remedy" (VI, 235) situation; none is rendered to him or perhaps even through him, at least to his innocent daughter. The remedy mitigates against his being a simple true man. Hence this conundrum adds to the tale's typical unsatisfactory nature.

In order to understand the complexities of guilt and innocence, of crime and punishment, and of mercy and meaning, we must untangle the various strata of the story and read those against the cultural expectation of law that would be common in medieval England of Chaucer's day, particularly regarding property. Virginia is property as such and in the tale is treated like symbolic capital, but there is no exchange possible here. This is not a simple patriarchal exchange that will enhance the value of males, but instead will undo all concerned.

Seen in this way, this Chaucerian story—one in which justice is denied and the innocent one is punished along with the guilty—becomes one of the most profound commentaries on the nature of law, crime, and punishment in the *Canterbury Tales*. "Does the punishment fit the crime?" is a question that we must ask with respect to all participants in the story: Virginius, Virginia, Appius, Claudius, and the community. In the end, all are judged, and all are found lacking either explicitly or implicitly. In his remarks at the tale's conclusion, Harry Bailly perceives the injustice of Appius and Claudius and all false voices in the justice system, but adds that Virginia's beauty (Nature and Fortune) was the cause of her death. Is the innocent one then guilty? An historicist reading locates a harsher judgment of crime on Virginius, who really does not act as a knight should, at least a medieval knight who has been defamed. Often regarded as a flawed tale, the *Physician's Tale* evokes visceral reactions within the fiction of the tale, within the dramatic frame of story telling on the way to Canterbury, and within modern reading communities. "Is ther no remedye?" is ultimately the question that must be answered in light of the codes of honor, hospitality, and law.

---

11 Glenn Burger, "Doing What Comes Naturally: The *Physician's Tale* and the Pardoner," *Masculinities in Chaucer: Approaches to Maleness in the Canterbury Tales and Troilus and Criseyde*, ed. Peter G. Beidler. Chaucer Studies, 25 (Cambridge: D. S. Brewer, 1998), 117–30.

II

The first Chaucerian addition to the tale of Virginius and Virginia revolves around the nature of Virginia herself, her physical appearance. Lines 9–71 and 105–17 are typically noted as Chaucer's addition to the materials found in Livy and the *Roman de la rose*. Dating at least from the writings of Albertus Magnus (ca. 1209–1290), there was a belief that the fact as to whom the child resembled was an indictor of male strength or weakness in conception. If the daughter resembled her mother, then her "seed" was stronger than the father's sperm, and by definition the male was "inferior."[12] Virginia's mother is never mentioned directly at all. Nowhere in the text do we learn that Virginia looks anything like Virginius—even the naming connection does not do that. The grammatically gendered aspect of naming, however, is an important connection after all. Thus there may be some essentialist based criticism of Virginius here, which is, of course, rather subtle.

In the tale, Nature itself does seem to speak, as Lomparis has noted, but her voice is controlled by the Physician—another level of masculine control and representation in the tale (23–24).[13] Nature, the feminine, is given credit for Virginia's beauty:

> This mayde of age twelve yeer was and tweye,
> In which that Nature hadde suche delit.
> For right as she kan paynte a lilie whit,
> And reed as rose, right with swich peynture
> She peynted hath this noble creature,
> Er she were born, upon hir lymes fre,
> Where as by right swiche colours should be."
>
> (VI, 30–36)

> [The maiden was fourteen years of age
> In which Nature had such delight,
> For just as she can paint a little white
> And red as a rose, just with such painting
> She has painted this noble creature,
> Before she was born, upon her generous limbs
> Where by right such colors should be.]

---

12 Vern L. Bullough, "On Being a Male in the Middle Ages," *Medieval Masculinities: Regarding Men in the Middle Ages*, ed. Clare A. Lees with Thelma Fenster and Ann McNamara. Medieval Cultures, 7 (Minneapolis: University of Minnesota Press, 1994), 31–45. See also Daniel F. Pigg, "Masculinity Studies," *The Handbook of Medieval Studies*, ed., Albrecht Classen (Berlin and New York: Walter de Gruyter, 2010), 829–35.

13 Linda Lomperis, "Unruly Bodies and Ruling Practices: Chaucer's *Physician's Tale* as Socially Symbolic Act," *Feminist Approaches to the Body in Medieval Literature,* ed. eadem and Sarah Stanbury. New Cultural Studies (Philadelphia: University of Pennsylvania Press, 1993), 21–37.

Nature, not her father, shaped her appearance before she was born. Biology may have won out here against our knight, but the Physician notes that Virginia speaks well in words, "sownynge in vertu and in gentillesse" (VI, 54; inclining to virtue and nobility), which are emblems of the logical mind, gendered male.[14] Beauty in the Roman mind, at least as it pertained to women, was seen as a "dangerous gift, one that put virtue at risk."[15] Is it possible that even Nature itself has set up Virginia for a fall and that by extension the passage becomes a reflection on the abuse of nature? In the opening description, however, this fourteen-year-old daughter seems more advanced than her age would suggest in her ability to manage her virtue and to disentangle herself from situations where any impropriety might be possible. But the Physician notes that "For al to soone mau she learne lore / Of booldnesse, whan she woxen is a wyf" (VI, 70–71; For all too soon she must learn the teaching of boldness when she is grown into a wife). Clearly, she has been taught a pattern of behavior from a male authority, her father, to whom she will readily give assent in his no-win suggestion of action.[16] She is schooled to read all situations under her father's "governance." Given the opening of the text showing Virginia's self management, it may seem very strange that the second addition becomes an admonition to parents and governesses about their protection of children.

III

The admonition to parents has attracted a great deal of attention among scholars, particularly its relation to the tale's logic. What seems apparent here, however, is the notion that the rule of the father is important in preserving the children:

> Under a shepherde softe and necligent
> The wolf hath many a sheep and lamb torent.
> Suffiseth oon ensample now as heere,
> For I moot turne again to my matere.
>
> (VI, 101–04)
>
> [Under an easy and negligent shepherd
> The wolf has killed many a sheep and a lamb.

---

14 Joyce Salisbury, "Gendered Sexuality," *Handbook of Medieval Sexuality*, ed. Vern L. Bullough and James A. Brundage. Garland Reference Library of the Humanities, 1696 (New York: Garland, 1996), 81–102.

15 Aline Rousselle, "The Family Under the Roman Empire: Signs and Gestures," *A History of the Family*, ed. André Burguiére, Christine Klapisch-Zuber, Martine Segalen, and Francoise Zonabend. Vol. 1 (Boston: Harvard University Press, 1996), 270–310.

16 Farber, "The Creation of Consent," 151 (see note 3).

> Suffice it one example now to hear
> For I must turn again to my topic.]

The continuing tale of Virginia and Virginius thus turns into an exemplum. John Pitcher contends that the "wolf" becomes Virginius; "the family itself [is exposed] as an institution of violence."[17] It would seem, however, that such a reading applies to the wolf reference more literally than is intended. The wolf of the narrative would clearly be Appius, given that he is the one who desires to destroy the body of Virginia and in this way by extension to strike at Virginius. As the tale continues, the implicit warning is that someone was not watching Virginia—her family—and someone else was—Appius. Notions of virginity are important to the tale and the construction of masculine desire.

Howard Bloch, attempting to solve the conundrum that the *Physician's Tale* represents, notes that the Church Fathers, and particularly Tertullian, were very much concerned about the sexual desire provoked by women seen in public to the point that any virgin who has been seen is no longer a virgin.[18] Appius identifies her beauty as the snare for his desire—the conclusion that Harry Bailly reaches as to the reason for her death after the conclusion of the tale. She has fallen under the male gaze, and it too is one of governance but more one of predatory manipulation.

IV

Since the court scene itself forms an important frame for understanding crime and punishment in this tale, we need to look further at its construction beyond the issue of gender politics noted earlier. In his study on Chaucer's representation on legal process, Joseph Allen Hornsby has noted that in the case of this tale, the situation is not one of felony, but instead relatively minor. We have an example of a personal injury case, what modern law would call "civil law." Such an accusation could begin with a writ or bill, with the bill being the easiest method to proceed. In that tale, the bill is followed to the letter with painstaking detail. Accordingly, "it could be drafted by the plaintiff and presented directly to the court."[19] The judge would have to look at the principle of equity in restitution in the case of crime. Interestingly enough, such cases expected that principles would

---

17 John A. Pitcher, "Chaucer's Wolf: Exemplary Violence in *The Physician's Tale*," *Genre* 36 (2003): 1–28.

18 R. Howard Bloch, "Chaucer's Maiden Head: 'The Physician's Tale' and the Poetics of Virginity," *Representations* 28 (1989): 113–34.

19 Joseph Allen Hornsby, *Chaucer and the Law* (Norman, OK: Pilgrim Books, 1988), 151.

be followed rather than direct stipulations of law. The judge had the right to make a decision, under the concept of equity.

In the petition of Claudius, Virginia is being held against her will by Virginius, and he simply wants her to be returned. All of this, however, is a lie. One wonders how Claudius would have provided witnesses. Appius, however, speeds up the verdict, without Virginius's saying a word or any witnesses being called.

V

The most significant change and addition to the original story of Virginius and Virginia comes during the court scene. In Chaucer's sources, all of this has been presented in court, and Virginius's actions are in public. The entire scene beginning with the manipulation of social justice controlled and denatured by debased masculine desire is also rooted in class conflict. Claudius, a churl, would have no right to any contact with Virginius's daughter, but Virginius must bow to the whim of a larger masculine-based rule of law. Unlike the *Roman* setting, in the *Physician's Tale* the future bridegroom of Virginia is not included and the role of the public is omitted until after Virginia's death. In both Livy's version and the Roman version, Virginius kills his daughter in front of the court—both would thus be a public spectacle. Moving the scene to their home, having Virginius show a countenance "deed as ashen colde" (VI, 209), and establishing a dialogue designed to increase pathos and to gain consent from Virginia make the experience of the tale gruesome, arresting, and the subject of critique of male authority. The statement, "Allas, that evere Apius the say" (VI, 227; Alas that Appius ever saw you), seems to place the blame on her, for it has made Appius render a false judgment against Virginius. She asks for time to mourn as Jephthah allowed for his daughter. The interesting point here, of course, proves to be that she is the one to mention the Jephthah reference in the lines below:

> "Thanne yif me leyser, fader myn," quod she,
> "My deeth for to compleyne a litel space;
> For, parde, Jepte yaf his doghter grace
> For to compleyne, er he hir slow, alas!
> And, God it woot, no thyng was hir trespas,
> But for she ran hir fader first to see,
> To welcome hym with greet solempnitee."
>
> (VI, 238–44)[20]

[20] John Micheal Crafton, "*The Physician's Tale* and Jephtha's Daughter," *American Notes and Queries* 20.1 (2007): 8–16.

["Then give me time, dear father," she said
"To complain for my death a little space;
For certainly Jephthah gave grace to his daughter
To complain before he slew her!
And God knows it that there was no trespass
Except that she ran out first to see her father,
To welcome him with great solemnity."]

Crafton contends that the reference to the space of time that she is to lament her loss of life found its way into medieval preaching manuals to argue against sinful living. He writes that "We are asked to accept that the narrator is sincerely presenting the tale of Virginia for all of its maximum pathos while having her plea to live longer to follow the example of one who represents the opposite of her virtue."[21] Such a reading does have merits, but it makes the victim responsible for the actions.

The parallels between Jephthah and his daughter and Virginius and Virginia deserve further consideration. It is important to remember that in the medieval Christian mind a Jewish male was less of a male than his Christian counterpart, of course, centered around the notion of loss connected with circumcision.[22] To compare Virginius to him is thus a debasement on several levels. Critical opinion ranges from the notion that the biblical reference must be a mistake based on the Physician's lack of biblical knowledge to comparisons that would privilege more the Abraham/Isaac story or the Crucifixion in place of the actual reference as a gloss on the action. Whether the usage accords with medieval understanding is less significant in one sense than might be noted at first viewing. Assuming, however, that the comparison is correct and intended, several noteworthy readings surrounding Virginius's masculine status appear. In the biblical story, the Deuteronomistic historian first has Jephthah promise to kill as a sacrifice of thanksgiving for successfully defeating the Ammonites (Judges 11) the first person who comes out of his house upon his return.

The folly is apparent; it is most likely that anyone coming out of his house would either be a friend, family member, or a servant. Clearly, to be endowed with the spirit of Yahweh does not keep a person from making rash or foolish statements. What may be more significant is that he is born of a prostitute. Biology and destiny are connected in medieval narrative; they are also connected in biblical narrative. Second, Jephthah's daughter, obviously devoted to her father and his success, meets him with tambourines and dances. Third, he rebukes her for the difficulty that she has brought him to. Applied to the Virginius/Virginia story, a pattern

---

21 Crafton, "*The Physician's Tale* and Jephtha's Daughter," 16 (see note 20).

22 Steven F. Kruger, *The Spectral Jew: Conversion and Embodiment in Medieval Europe.* Medieval Cultures, 40 (Minneapolis: University of Minnesota Press, 2005), 1–25.

emerges. As a "worthy knight" (VI, 203), Virginius sees only two ways to proceed: death or shame. Both will have clear consequences, but for the knight, shame would be greater because his daughter would be treated as property to be abused at will. By extension, he himself is exposed to abuse at will. No knight could uphold this action. Unlike some knights in the later Malory's *Le Morte d'Arthur* (1485), Virginius will not offer his daughter to a successful knight in marriage.

As remarked earlier, it is important to note that Virginia makes the Jephthah reference. In the biblical text, his daughter is allowed to mourn because she will die a virgin, thus never having married. In the *Roman*, Virginia was to be married, and that too will not happen. Chaucer never mentions a marriage possibility at all. Virginia, although silent thus far in the tale, has not been particularly passive in her encounters with the world. She makes judgments and goes to various places with her mother as chaperone; she here, too, desires to be an active agent. In this case, however, she accepts or assents to male authority without question once she is told there is "no grace, no remedye" (VI, 236). Has Virginius's "governance" taken on more sinister dimensions? The Jephthah reference calls into question the "why" of the sacrifice with the potential of a direct rebuke of Virginius. He may be successful in one sense, but he is a fool of historical proportions.

In a most persuasive article, Daniel Kline notes that because Virginius does not even allow Virginia time to mourn as Jephthah did permit for his daughter, we see that "Virginius is even less gracious than Jephthah."[23]In an even more striking judgment, Kline observes that the "theology of sacrifice justifies both the structure and violence of the patriarchal family, and, by extension, the late-medieval culture that depends upon a sacrificial imperative."[24] Virginia then dies for a system. Jephthah's daughter merely dies after a period of mourning, based on her father's rash promise of sacrifice. Judges 11:39–40 sets up the idea of a future memorial remembrance in which the "daughters of Israel" will "lament" the loss of Jephthah's daughter for four days each year. Virginia's death is a tragedy without any emotional release or ritual act to sublimate the injustice.

Feminist critiques of this scene have often seen little difference between the actions of Appius and Claudius whose intentions are clearly rape and other abuse and Virginius's murder.[25] Setting aside the possibility of incest being apparent in this scene, as Lomperis and Rose have noted that it may be a rape, I will outline

---

23 Daniel Kline, "Jephthah's Daughter and Chaucer's Virginia: The Critique of Sacrifice in The Physician's Tale," *Journal of English and Germanic Philology* 107.1 (2008): 77–103.

24 Kline, "Jephthah's Daughter and Chaucer's Virginia: The Critique of Sacrifice in the Physician's Tale," 103 (see note 23).

25 Sandra Pierson Prior, "Virginity and Sacrifice in Chaucer's "Physician's Tale," *Constructions of Widowhood and Virginity in the Middle Ages*, ed., Cindy L. Carlson and Angela Jane Weis. The New Middle Ages (New York: St. Martin's Press, 1999) , 165–80; Christine M. Rose, "Reading Chaucer Reading Rape," *Representing Rape in Medieval and Early Modern Literature*, 21–51 (see note 2).

an alternative reading.[26] The charge of *raptus*—a vexing one in Chaucer studies both biographical and literary—takes on an important dimension in defining their action. The crime to be committed against Virginia in the court of law would actually fall on Virginius. On one level, rape would involve a crime of property, but in another sense, too, it is an action directly against Virginius, an extension of himself. It is no accident that Virginia shares a name with a different grammatical ending. She represents all that he holds valuable in the world, and it is a world that must remain static—at least in Chaucer's version of the story—to retain value. The loss is one of property, masculine self, and ideal; yet he must commit the act of murder for a higher good by his definition, however flawed. The masculine world of Virginius is one of management, but in seeking to maintain it, control is lost. The true man of medieval virtue would not get himself caught in such a challenge that threatens to undermine his entire way of being in the world.

VI

Understood in this cumulative way, the proverbial tag at the end rings in a different key: "Heere may men see how synne hath its merite. / Beth ware, for no man woot whom God wol smyte / In no degree, ne in which mannere wyse" (VI, 277–79; Here may people see how sin has its merits,' Beware for no person knows whom God will strike / In no degree, nor in what manner). As one critic has noted, Virginia is removed from the passage.[27] The point is intriguing given that in the *Clerk's Tale*, when the Clerk provides an allegorical ending to the tale, he includes Griselda as a reference point. Here the reason for the allusion seems to relate more to a critique of male action. The warning is clearly a check on Virginius and Appius.

Virginius is seemingly judged as the parent who has not taken proper heed of his child, according to the Physician's admonition. He has violated the masculine requirements of "protecting dependents."[28] He has lost a part of himself that cannot be renewed. Appius has violated his role as keeper and dispenser of masculine justice by contemplating *raptus* and by his suicide, seen in the Middle Ages as a feminizing act.[29] God has acted through his appointed knight and in

---

26 Rose, "Reading Chaucer Reading Rape," 21–51 (see note 23); Lomperis, "Unruly Bodies and Ruling Practices: Chaucer's *Physician's Tale* as Socially Symbolic Act," 21–37 (see note 13).

27 Rose, "Reading Chaucer Reading Rape," 21–51 (see note 23).

28 Bullough, "On Being Male in the Middle Ages," 31–45 (see note 12)

29 Alexander Murray, *Suicide in the Middle Ages* (Oxford and New York: Oxford University Press, 1988), 9–37; Jacqueline Murray, "Hiding Behind the Universal Man: Male Sexuality in the Middle Ages," *Handbook of Medieval Sexuality*, 123–52 (see note 14).

doing so the experience has called into question the highly staged world of masculine desire and power in an earthly realm. Thus the Jephthah reference is even more highly problematic than has been appreciated by earlier critics.

Chaucer's *Physician's Tale* no doubt provokes a number of vehement responses. It is very likely that it may well have been intended to. Virginius responds; the Roman citizens respond. Harry Bailly responds in a visceral way. Masculinity has been anatomized through an exploration of bodies both material and political, and the gaps and fissures have been revealed for all to see. "No grace" and "no remedy" are seen indeed. Thus rather than a flawed tale as has been normative in much of the critical history of *The Physician's Tale*, this tale, one of the shortest in the Canterbury collection, provides an intriguing commentary on the limits of masculine power and authority in the world of crime and punishment.

Knowing who the thief is here, knowing who is the guilty one, knowing how the justice system has been perverted for the desires of some of Chaucer's most lecherous characters, and knowing how the system of knightly virtue cannot always preserve itself leave readers with a sense of uneasiness. That Virginius thwarts the desire of the commons to see the death of Claudius at the end of the tale may be the only presence of grace in the tale. Appius had already committed suicide. The question remains at what price even that element of grace costs in proportion of the loss to Virginius. He is a medievalized Roman knight who will never be the same again and a man whose world can only reflect the sense of loss of a highly structured universe where the punishment does fit the crime and the crime has some discernible punishment.

Assuming that the tale is finished although not properly fitted into the fictive narrative of the Canterbury journey, humans must continue their quest for true grace and remedy that only a religious pilgrimage will provide. That central question of "Is ther no grace, is ther no remedy?" (VI, 235) has a very haunting answer implicit in it that threatens to undermine the social and cosmic structure as understood in the medieval world. The answer at present is "no," but to preserve the order implicit in the medieval world, perhaps it is better to say at least for now there is a "no" answer. The judgment of the gods or the Christian God remains outside the frame of the narrative. The world of no grace and no remedy is a judgment against the male characters. The death of Virginia only underscores the tragedy in that world of male patriarchy.

Chapter 15

Lia B. Ross
(The University of New Mexico, Albuquerque)

Deviancy in the Late Middle Ages: The Crimes and Punishment of Gilles de Rais

The trial of Gilles de Rais that took place in Nantes in 1440 is exceptional both for the perverse nature of his crimes (he sexually abused, killed, and, in some cases, dismembered perhaps over one hundred children) and for his previous good reputation as companion of Joan of Arc in her early exploits. And yet, this disturbing Breton nobleman has been the subject of only few and far-between historical works.[1] The reason for such weak interest may be that the very abundance of documentation on his case renders it less amenable to discussion, leaving historians with few opportunities for making original contributions. Among the significant studies on this figure three stand out because of their distinctive views, even if all three are based on the same set of primary documents, and all three accept as fact Gilles's culpability.[2]

The first true biography, written by Abbé Eugène Bossard in 1884–1885, is a work that spans over three hundred pages and is notable for the meticulous study of documents (including some that have since been lost) and for representing a current that argues for Gilles's exceptionality.[3] The author wonders how this

---

1 This fact was noted by Jacques Heers, *Gilles de Rais*. Vérités et légendes (Paris: Perrin, 1994), 8. Michelet was the first historian to examine the unpublished documents. Abbé Eugène Bossard, *Gilles de Rais – Maréchal de France dit Barbe-Bleue 1404–1440* (1885; Grenoble: Jérôme Millon, 1992), 201.

2 Heers, *Gilles de Rais*, 154–56 (see note 1), observes that the only records of Gilles's last five years of life are his trial documents, and that they have a ring of truth because they represent the testimonies of various people who were questioned separately. He adds (185–86) that none of Gilles's contemporaries, not even his family, contested the verdict.

3 The documents lost in a fire in 1940 referred to Gilles's stay in Orléans (see below). Georges Bataille, *Le procès de Gilles de Rais* (Paris: Jean-Jacques Pauvert, 1972), 106.

gifted, erudite, brave young man, after an honorable career as companion of Joan of Arc, suddenly plunged into a life of crime that led him to a well-deserved execution by the age of thirty-six. He ventures to attribute Gilles's sudden change to his innate curiosity (in itself a good quality) that became diverted toward the morbid and then the horrific.[4] And while the author judges medieval Breton society in general to have been especially harsh against humble people, he nevertheless argues that Gilles's crimes were particularly perverse and were stopped only thanks to the intervention of the Church.[5] Bossard follows the classical tradition of biographies of tyrants: after leading a virtuous life in his youth the subject experiences the sudden loss of a key figure in his life, such as a parent or tutor (in Gilles's case his grandfather). In turn, this loss marks a break with an upright life and initiates a downward spiral of crimes culminating in the inevitable catastrophic end.[6] Bossard's work has two additional distinguishing features that mar somewhat its historical usefulness: it contains a curious survey of late legends loosely inspired by the memory of Gilles's crimes that converged into the mythical figure of Bluebeard; and it avoids any direct reference to the sexual aspect of the crimes, except for a few bashful hints at "orgies" and "secret pleasures."[7]

The second—and in my opinion the most significant—major study dates from 1965, almost a century after the first, and is not the work of a historian. Georges

---

4 Bossard, *Gilles de Rais,* 15–17 (see note 1). He thought that Gilles spoke Latin, was interested in science, and kept a library of classics. The legend of the dual nature of Gilles is reflected also in literature. The fictitious author in J. K. Huysmans's *Là-bas* laments the sudden personality change of this character, once a brave Christian knight and companion of Joan of Arc, who later on became a "sacrilegious sadist and a coward."But he still cannot but admire some aspects of his personality, for example, the fact that he locked himself up in his castle of Tiffauges to become an "erudite Latinist, a brilliant conversationalist, a sure and generous friend." J. K. Huysmans. *Là-bas (down there),* trans. Keene Wallace (1928; New York: Dover Publications, Inc., 1972), 43, 46. Bataille, *Le procès,* 27 (see note 3), debunks the myth and (35) is shocked at Huysmans's naïve acceptance of it. Gilles's reputation for erudition may have come from the fact that he once pawned a richly decorated copy of Ovid's Metamorphoses. Bataille, *Le procès,* 116–17. Heers, *Gilles de Rais,* 109 (see note 1), states that we do not know what he read or what was in his library.

5 Bossard, *Gilles de Rais,* 249–50 (see note 1). A similar thesis of his exceptionality is sustained in more recent studies, p.e. Hannele Klemettilä, *Ritari Siniparta: Gilles de Rais'n tarina* (Jyväskylä: Atena, 2005). I am grateful to Susanna Niiranen (see her contribution "Poet's Reputation. Troubadours – Ancestors of poètes maudits?" in the present volume) for making available her review of this work.

6 Bossard, *Gilles de Rais,* 152, n. 1 (see note 1), himself saw classical precedents, and compared Gilles to Nero (261).

7 For example, Bossard, *Gilles de Rais,* 136 (see note 1), "débauches", "orgie nocturne" (272), "plaisirs secrets" (153), "caprices mouvants de sa passion" (149), "plaisirs sensuels" (150). He mentions that Gilles's confession embarrassed the judges (169–70). The last portion of his biography (293–325) is a discussion of the late legends of Bluebeard, starting with their diffusion with Perrault.

Bataille's *Le procès de Gilles de Rais*, a true biography despite its deceptively limiting title, dismantles the exceptionalist thesis of his predecessor, while recognizing the value of his research. Bataille challenges the sentimental portrait of the learned and valiant knight turned sinner and substitutes it with his own, based on Gilles's "archaisme" and "niaiserie" (stupidity). He was a childish, violent, and stupid man—Bataille argues—who was propped up for his part as military leader and respectable baron by an archaic feudal system based on privilege and brutality against the weak, a system that allowed his crimes to go unpunished for too long, and that acted with leniency even when forced to take action. The considerable merits of this work include a chronological outline of Gilles's moves correlated with reports of the disappearance of children, a critical analysis of the documents related to his trial, and the inclusion of their text in French translation.[8]

The trend toward diminution of this character reached its zenith with the work of Jacques Heers (1975), a biography that bears the terse title of *Gilles de Rais*. Heers, who questions whether Gilles was such a significant figure as to be worthy of a book, justifies his task though the avowed goal of studying him without romantic exaggerations, as an example of an average baron living in precarious times when violence and illegality were the norm. In other words, he reworks Gilles into mainstream contemporary culture by bringing to the fore not so much his deviancy and crimes, but rather his society and milieu (in fact, he only dedicates the last one-third of the book to the murders and trial).[9] Not an exceptional figure, even less a romantic rogue, in Heers's pages Gilles is knocked even further down from his pedestal and reduced to just another fifteenth-century nobleman, one whose life happens to be better documented than others thanks to a criminal inquiry.[10]

The aspect of this figure that has oddly been brushed aside by his biographers is that of the serial killer. And yet Gilles fits perfectly this definition: one who alone or—less frequently—as part of a small team kills multiple victims in a similar way and over a period of time.[11] Not only that, but his trial preserves for the modern

---

8 The acts of the ecclesiastical court were originally in Latin, later translated into French, hence the modern spelling in most of the direct quotes (only a few are reported in the original Old French). The acts of the secular court were in French. Bossard, *Gilles de Rais*, 201–03 (see note 1) and Heers, *Gilles de Rais*, 191 (see note 1). The documents are contained at pp. 189–338, in modern French. In his critical analysis he exonerates Gilles whenever a disappearance does not fit Gilles's moves at the same time. See for example Bataille, *Le procès*, 129, 132, 33, 141 (see note 3).

9 Heers, *Gilles de Rais*, 12, 15 (see note 1).

10 Heers, *Gilles de Rais*, 16–17 (see note 1), reminds the reader that Gilles did not attract much attention until his trial and is barely mentioned in official chronicles as just another captain fighting beside Joan of Arc.

11 The definition is in Joseph C. Fisher, *Killer Among Us: Public Reactions to Serial Murder* (Westport, CT, and London: Praeger Publishers, 1997), 31. He specifies (18–19) that the central elements of serial murder are: repetitive homicide over a span of months or years, mainly one-on-one and

reader probably the best documented case of serial murder in the Middle Ages.[12] As Heers puts it, Gilles may not deserve a book, but it may be appropriate to discuss him as a criminal in a volume dedicated to medieval crime. It is understandable that historians would shy away from anything that might suggest psychohistory. Still, the study of serial killers, their modus operandi both in the selection of victims and killing methods, their reaction to arrest and conviction, and the reaction of the general public to the same, are not strictly confined to the realm of psychiatry, but rather overflow into those of sociology and criminology, fields that should be of interest to historians because they go beyond examining the sick mind per se to delve in how it affects society at large.

There is little disagreement on the chronological data of Gilles's life. He was born in 1404 to the prominent baronial family of Craon-Laval, who counted possessions in Brittany, Maine, and Anjou.[13] Left orphaned of both parents at the age of eleven, together with his younger brother René he became ward of their grandfather Jean de Craon, a powerful, greedy, and violent feudal lord who through this guardianship added the barony of Rais to his titles.[14] He had a childhood that Bataille calls "sauvage et violente" (savage and violent) after his tutors quit his service and he was left to the care of his grandfather, who, by Gilles's own account, raised him with very lax discipline. In 1420, at the age of sixteen, Gilles kidnapped and married in secret a rich heiress and cousin, Catherine de Thouars, by whom he had a daughter about ten years later. Significantly, both wife and daughter disappeared from his life immediately, only to re-emerge after his execution.[15] By the age of twenty he had committed the

---

perpetrated against strangers, with the motivation to kill arising exclusively from within the killer and apparently irrational (not reflecting passion or personal gain). All conditions, as it will become apparent, are satisfied by Gilles's murders. Since statistically serial killers are overwhelmingly men, I will use the masculine when talking about them in general, following the example of criminologists. See for example, Ronald M. Holmes and James E. De Burger, *Serial Murder*. Studies in Crime, Law and Justice, 2 (Newbury Park, CA, Beverly Hills, CA, and London: SAGE Publications, 1988), 21; and Richard Tithecott, *Of Men and Monsters – Jeffrey Dahmer and the Construction of the Serial Killer* (Madison, WI: The University of Wisconsin Press, 1997), 56–57.

12 Bataille, *Le procès*, 181, n. 1 (see note 3), mentions also the late-sixteenth-century Hungarian countess Elizabeth Bathory, who allegedly tortured and killed numerous young girls in her castle. But details of her crimes are sketchy and she was not tried (also, she belongs more properly to early modern history).

13 His father was Guy de Laval of the line of Laval-Montmorency, and his mother Marie de Craon, from the line of Rais. Bataille, *Le procès*, 25, 27 (see note 3). The full list of fiefs belonging to the two family branches are in Heers, *Gilles de Rais*, 29–30 (see note 1). Significantly, all these possessions came through inheritances and dowries, not through conquest, and most were disputed by rivals.

14 Bossard, *Gilles de Rais*, 18 (see note 1), Bataille, *Le procès*, 27 (see note 3), and Heers, *Gilles de Rais*, 24 (see note 1).

15 Bataille, *Le procès*, 31(see note 3).The marriage followed a (perhaps staged) kidnapping, with the consent of Jean de Craon. It was annulled for consanguinity and then officially celebrated in 1422

usual acts of violence that were typical of noblemen of his age: kidnappings, assaults, and illegal seizure of land.[16] Bataille sees in his violent upbringing the making of a person who would later show complete disregard for the lives of others. In fact, the violence connected with feudal life is part of the "archaisme" that he deems one of the two building blocks of Gilles's personality. Heers, for his part, judges him a brigand who early on alienated the favor of the local nobility and who would pay dearly for this at the time of his trial.[17] Between 1420 and 1427 Gilles participated in small local skirmishes under the leadership of Jean de Craon in support of the duke of Brittany, against both local rebels and the English. In 1429 he enjoyed a brief moment in the limelight, fighting for Charles VII against the English and sharing in the early successes of Joan of Arc, in particular at the siege of Orléans. But there is no evidence that he and she were particularly close, despite the conjectures of Bossard, nor is there evidence that his participation in the fight was decisive. On the contrary, according to Heers, he hesitated to continue the campaign to conquer the rest of the fortresses near the liberated city.[18]

Both Bataille and Heers convincingly minimize Gilles's military achievements and demonstrate that he was propped up by his distant relation, Georges de La Trémoille, who was then a favorite of the king. To this powerful relative Gilles owed his promotion to marshal of France around the time of Charles VII's

---

with the consent of both families after the marriage of Jean de Craon to the bride's grandmother Anne de Sillé and, after a complicated matter of inheritance was settled. Bataille, *Le procès*, 83–84 (see note 3) and Heers, *Gilles de Rais*, 25–26 (see note 1). Bossard, *Gilles de Rais*, 155 (see note 1), and Heers, *Gilles de Rais*, 211 (see note 1) state that Gilles's wife resided in her castle of Pouzauges.

16 Gilles and his grandfather kidnapped Gilles's mother-in-law and threatened to drown her unless she renounced her dowry, the castles of Tiffauges and Pouzauges, which Gilles would continue to hold "in his wife's name." The two also assaulted the president of *parlement* who intervened in this matter. The fine imposed on Gilles and his grandfather for this act of brutality was never paid. Bataille, *Le procès*, 28–29, 84–85 (see note 3) and Heers, *Gilles de Rais*, 26–27 (see note 1).

17 Heers, *Gilles de Rais*, 27(see note 1). He adds that in 1443, three years after Gilles's death, the Paris *parlement* condemned his illegal acts of 1424.

18 For his early military actions see Heers, *Gilles de Rais*, 31–35, 42–46 (see note 1). The author remarks that his periods of military service were few, scattered over a period of fifteen years, and requiring few responsibilities as he was always subordinate to others. On his participation in Joan's campaigns in the period 1428–1430 he states (60–65) that Gilles was never singled out in any action. Despite lack of evidence to support one or the other thesis, in the late nineteenth century a controversy arose between Vallet de Viriville, *Histoire de Charles VII, roi de France, et de son époque, 1403–1461*, 3 vols. (Paris: Yve J. Renouard, 1862–1865), 2:II–V, who claimed that Gilles deliberately betrayed Joan and abandoned her during her later campaigns and Bossard, *Gilles de Rais*, 33 (see note 1), who sustained that Gilles was always her "fidèle" supporter. Heers adds his own conclusion (70–71) that Gilles did not have a policy of his own in her regard, but followed that of his mentor de La Trémoille, who was Joan's rival for influence with the king. Bataille, *Le procès*, 29 (see note 3), insists that Gilles's glory was transitory and not based on particular skills and specifies (90–93) that he was with Joan at the retaking of the Tourelles, at the coronation of Charles VII, and at the (unsuccessful) siege of Paris, but always as a protégé of de La Trémoille.

coronation (July 1429), but by 1430 his days of glory were already over.[19] At this point the twenty-six-year-old baron effectively retired from military affairs with the largely honorific title of marshal of France. By 1433, the fall from favor of his patron de La Trémoille relegated him to a largely provincial presence (yet, even there, he was never much in the duke's favor). From that moment onward Gilles only participated in small local raids, occasionally called upon to perform minor military functions on behalf of a marginalized de La Trémoille. But he did not seem to have missed war as a means to express violence: he left to his brother the command of his last two significant military actions, and delegated to his captains local raids against neighbors.[20]

In fact, I suspect that the violence of feudal war not only did not contribute to Gilles's crimes, but was a distraction from his real interests. Bataille talks about his "savage youth" enmeshed in the barbaric warrior rituals of a fierce society unmitigated by chivalric ethics. However, it seems to me that the author is talking of what Arnold Buss calls "instrumental violence," whose real aim is not so much hurting the victim as acceptance by a peer group.[21] This is not the same as the violence that Gilles will later perpetrate in secret and with the awareness that it constituted a transgression against the very social order that had condoned or even encouraged the other.

With the death of his grandfather in 1432 Gilles became the inheritor of a vast wealth in castles and lands, in part fiefs of the duke of Brittany Jean V and in part of King Charles VII.[22] But this did not improve his fortunes, and soon he found

---

19 Bataille, *Le procès*, 33–34 (see note 3) and Heers, *Gilles de Rais*, 66–67, 69 (see note 1).

20 Bataille, *Le procès*, 51, 57 (see note 3). The last tasks on behalf of de La Trémoille were to relieve the besieged Grancey in 1434 (which Gilles turned to his younger brother) and to lead troops to Laon against Jean of Luxembourg in 1435 (which he abandoned due to lack of captains willing to follow him). He continued proxy attacks against neighbors from 1435 to 1440. Bataille, *Le procès*, 104, 109 (see note 3) and Heers, *Gilles de Rais*, 83–84 (see note 1).

21 Bataille, *Le procès*, 37 (see note 3). Arnold Buss, *Social Behavior and Personality* (Hillsdale, NJ: Lawrence Erlbaum Associates Publisher, 1986), 52 and Leonard Berkowitz, "Violence and Rule-Following Behaviour," *Aggression and Violence*, ed. Marsh Peter and Anne Campbell (Oxford: Basil Blackwell, 1982), 100. Albert Bandura, *Aggression: a Social Learning Analysis.* The Prentice-Hall Series in Social Learning Theory (Englewood Cliffs, NJ: Prentice-Hall, 1973), 3, rejects the distinction, arguing that the so-called hostile aggression is equally instrumental, and it is more useful to differentiate aggressive actions in terms of their functional value.

22 Bossard, *Gilles de Rais*, 52 (see note 1), ventures to guess his annual income as being around forty-five-thousand *livres* a year, which included his regular entries and his salary as marshal. Heers, *Gilles de Rais*, 28–30 (see note 1,) observes that there are no precise records on his wealth. His was one of the nine surviving baronies and included several scattered lands and castles: around twelve *seigneuries* south of the Loire, plus lands in Maine, Anjou, and Bretagne from the Craon side of the family. The principal possessions, some rendered famous for being the sites of his crimes, were the fortresses of Tiffauges, Champtocé, Machecoul, and Saint-Étienne-de-Mer-Morte. His brother René obtained other *seigneuries* (the principal being that of La Suze) and the hotel in Nantes. Bataille, *Le procès*, 96 (see note 3), reports that Jean de Craon left his armor and sword to René,

himself short of funds and haunted by defections, which eventually left him with only a handful of close associates, some of whom at one time or another would become accessories to his crimes.[23]

Some of his early accomplices are only names, whose role and fate are not clear from the documents: choir boys of his chapel like André Buchet, Jean Rossignol, Hicquet de Brémont, and Robin Romulart ("Petit Robin").[24] Two active accomplices who procured victims and killed for him were Gilles de Sillé and his cousin Roger de Bricqueville.[25] Roger is the most mysterious of his associates: he was from a noble family of Normandy who had been dispossessed by the English occupation and had taken refuge with Jean de Craon. He had been a youthful companion of Gilles and, apparently, had helped Gilles in his crimes since 1432. There is no precise information on the extent of his participation, however, because he fled before Gilles's arrest, and later was accepted into the service of Gilles's daughter and her husband, who obtained from the king letters of remission on his behalf. Lastly, there were some old women who would locate and procure children, among whom the best known is one Perrine Martin, who apparently was also arrested and tried but died in prison.[26]

Of the five late accomplices mentioned at the trial two, Étienne Corrillaut (called "Poitou") and Henriet Griart, were his valets and bound to him by an oath of

---

which he interprets as sign of disapproval of Gilles(but of what specific actions?). It is possible, I think, that the grandfather wanted to leave a personal token to the younger man.

23 Heers, *Gilles de Rais*, 85–86 (see note 1). While it is assumed that the modern serial killer acts alone, this is not always the case; in fact, ten to twenty percent of serial murders are "group" murders. Tithecott, *Of Men and Monsters*, 37–38 (see note 11). However, none of the cases discussed by either Tithecott or other authors cited in the following pages belongs to the "group" category, and I would not place in that category even Gilles's murders. He took the initiative and the others simply went along because of fear and/or self-interest. It is possible that Bricqueville and Sillé were more active accomplices and may have had sexual contact with some of the victims prior to turning them over to their master, but given the paucity of information all this is highly speculative.

24 Gilles's servants testified that Buchet sent to Gilles at least one victim in 1438 and one in 1440 (and helped in disposing of the body). Bataille, *Le procès*, 125, 153–54 (see note 3). Bossard, *Gilles de Rais*, 277 (see note 1), states that Robin Romulart and Jean Rossignol were dead by the time of the trial.

25 Bataille, *Le procès*, 64, 101, 155 (see note 3). Little is known about Sillé, who was a distant relation and the captain of Gilles's guard, and who probably fled to his own fief. Heers, *Gilles de Rais*, 210 (see note 1).

26 Bossard, *Gilles de Rais*, 157–60, 278 (see note 1), Bataille, *Le procès*, 43, 108,125–26, 176 (see note 3), and Heers, *Gilles de Rais*, 206–07 (see note 1). The royal "lettres de grâce" of 1446 absolved Bricqueville on the grounds that he was very young (twenty-three) and had been forced to obey Gilles, and that he had left his service as early as 1435, as soon as he suspected foul play (which is false). Heers, *Gilles de Rais*, 206 (see note 1), quotes the statement that Bricqueville had been accepted in Gilles's house on condition of being "subgiect et obéissant sans l'oser desdire ni contrarier de sa volonté en nulle manière," a position that—if true—was no different from that of his two valets, who were not spared.

loyalty (and a salary). Neither of them, as far as it is known, had a criminal past, and Poitou had himself been an early victim of Gilles. By his own admission at the trial, in 1437, when he was not quite twenty, he had become Gilles's personal valet. His master had "commerce charnel" (sexual relations) with him and planned to kill him afterwards, but Bricqueville and Sillé convinced Gilles to spare him and use him as a helper in future crimes. Later in the same year Poitou was ordered to introduce to these secret activities Henriet, who had been in his master's service for a few years but had not yet been involved in his crimes. Both were sworn to secrecy, both procured victims and at times killed them, and both were tasked with disposing of the bodies.[27]

Bataille pointedly remarks that nobody of importance ever asked again for Gilles's help after 1432, and Heers mentions that he was already receiving negative publicity at court for his "indiscrétion et prodigalité" (lack of discretion and extravagance).[28] This could be a clue that something was amiss with him personally, because the disgrace of the patron de La Trémoille at the king's court should not necessarily have resulted in avoidance of the protégé on the part of Duke Jean of Brittany. Gilles's biographers postulate that, as if to compensate for his marginalization, he launched into a series of heavy personal expenditures. He set up a magnificent "maison ecclésiastique" (clerical entourage) supplied with chaplains, vicars, masters, even a "so-called bishop," and a choir, for a total of twenty-five or thirty people, all sumptuously dressed and generously paid, and started traveling with this vast and splendid retinue. He also maintained a "maison militaire" (military entourage) of two hundred mounted troops, a herald, and trumpeters.[29] A more egregious display of prodigality occurred during his lengthy stay in Orléans in 1434–1435. There he spent from eighty thousand to a hundred thousand gold *écus* on lodgings for himself and his household, and the staging of a particularly long and extravagant *mystère*, requiring hundreds of actors, to celebrate the liberation of the city from the English siege six years earlier.[30]

---

27 Bossard, *Gilles de Rais*, 153 (see note 1) and Bataille, *Le procès*, 120 (see note 3). Prelati was aged twenty-three, Poitou twenty-two, and Henriet twenty-six at the time of the trial. Bataille, *Le procès*, 261, 273, 281 (see note 3).

28 Bataille, *Le procès*, 149 (see note 3) and Heers, *Gilles de Rais*, 80–83 (see note 1). Heers specifies that, after an attack against the duke of Bedford in 1432 on behalf of the count of Dunois, he was largely ignored by the royal side, where the constable Arthur de Richemont had succeeded in ousting his rival de La Trémoille.

29 Bossard, *Gilles de Rais*, 56–57 (see note 1), Heers, *Gilles de Rais*, 92–93 (see note 1) who adds that Gilles also made himself *chanoine* of the chapter of the cathedral of Saint-Hilaire of Poitiers, a title that before him only the dukes of Aquitaine had received, and Bataille, *Le procès*, 13, 56–58, 112 (see note 3). Bataille labels the squandering of wealth during this period a "potlatch."

30 The extant documents are rather ambiguous on the actual details of Gilles's contributions to the play. Bataille, *Le procès*, 115 (see note 3). Bossard, *Gilles de Rais*, 81, 84 (see note 1) talks of five

The main source for the information on Gilles's supposedly mad expenditures is a document that was available to all his biographers, the *Mémoires des héritiers*, which was written on behalf of Gilles's brother René de La Suze and his cousin André de Laval-Lohéac in 1435, at a time when Gilles needed to raise cash and was forced to alienate properties, which were eagerly acquired by Duke Jean V of Brittany and his stand-ins.[31] Naturally, the family was concerned about the reduction of its patrimony, and Charles VII, to whom the document was addressed, was equally concerned about the aggrandizement of Jean V, an already powerful and independent vassal.

The recurring motif of the *Mémoires* was Gilles's inability to think rationally: it accused him (albeit in vague terms) of keeping a household worthy of a king and a sumptuous table open to all; of paying for elaborate plays and dances; of endowing an extravagant chapel and acquiring for it huge organs, liturgical vessels, and incensories at many times their value. Worse yet, Gilles had stipulated in writing that his daughter and her heirs would have to continue to endow his chapel after his death, if necessary through the cession of the castellany of Champtocé to the duke of Anjou and of one-half of the *seigneuries* of Rais to the duke of Brittany (thus depriving his heirs of much of their possessions).[32]

The result of the family complaint was a royal interdiction forbidding any further purchase of properties from Gilles, an injunction that—predictably—affected only the properties under royal jurisdiction and was ignored by the duke within his own territories. Bataille accepts the *Mémoires* at face value and calls Gilles a "prodigue insensé" (insane spendthrift), but Heers questions this

---

hundred actors and of Gilles paying for the multiple stages and free admission to the play, and Bataille, *Le procès*, 59–60, 113–15 (see note 3) states that Gilles paid for some costumes and the refreshments that went along with the performance, and Heers, *Gilles de Rais*, 101–02 (see note 3). The play includes direct mention of Gilles's participation in Joan's campaign in two scenes. This may have contributed to the short lifespan of the play, which was already banned by 1441 (108). To face the enormous expenses, Gilles was forced to pawn various valuable objects from his chapel. Heers, *Gilles de Rais*, 110 (see note 1). Bossard, *Gilles de Rais*, 63 (see note 1), specifies that to acquire cash at that point he had to sell at a discounted price the revenues from salt mines and rents. Some of the documents related to this period have not survived to be examined by subsequent biographers.

31 Heers, *Gilles de Rais*, 174 (see note 1). In 1435 the duke, who could not buy directly from a vassal, started acquiring Gilles's properties through intermediaries (among whom the same Jean de Malestroit, bishop of Nantes, who would preside over Gilles's ecclesiastical trial). However, documents relative to the acquisitions of lands show that Gilles had sold them at fair price, and not practically given them away as claimed by his relatives. Heers, *Gilles de Rais*, 215–16 (see note 1).

32 Cited in Bataille, *Le procès*, 14 (see note 3). The document states that Gilles "n'avait ni sens ni entendement." See also Bossard, *Gilles de Rais*, 58–59 (see note 1). The rest is in Heers, *Gilles de Rais*, 94 (see note 1). The disposition of the inheritance on behalf of his chapel is in Bataille, *Le procès*, 110–11 (see note 3).

opinion, as he observes that the interests that it represented render the document suspect at best.[33] He defends both Gilles's provisions for the persistence of his chapel and the extravagant expenditures for his court and table as normal for the nobility of the period: others, including the duke of Brittany, had their own chapels and used to pawn vestments and jewels to raise troops. On the one hand, then, stands the opinion of Gilles's family and of the king, who thought his expenditures exaggerate even by lax fifteenth-century standards. And on the other hand stands the opposite one of the duke of Brittany that Gilles's actions were reasonable, cautiously backed by Heers, and equally biased in the opposed direction.[34]

This document also reveals some aspects of Gilles's tastes: while his love for rich clothes, jewels, and precious accessories were not extraordinary for his age and social class, he manifested an unusual love for the theater, at least compared with his peers, who seemed rather fonder of chess, sports, and hunting. Besides having staged various types of plays, Gilles lavished interest on the one that he helped fund during his visit to Orléans, because it was a re-enactment of Joan's liberation of the city from its siege in 1429, an episode in the real life of Gilles himself, in fact, the highlight of his career. Therefore his participation in the staging of the play (for which he apparently supplied costumes and refreshments and loaned his own standard) was a way to take center stage vicariously, precisely at a time when his real fortunes, political and financial, were on the wane.

Another puzzling piece of evidence from this period is a letter dated December 1434 in which Gilles granted his cousin Roger de Bricqueville full powers to represent him in all financial deals, including arranging a marriage of his choosing for Gilles's own young daughter Marie.[35] Given that a favorable marriage arrangement could have represented a reasonable way to hold on to—and perhaps to enhance—his diminishing wealth, it is difficult not to interpret Gilles's bizarre forfeiture of parental privilege as anything but an admission of failure to handle the most mundane acts of personal administration.

The issue of Gilles's economic activities is of interest here only because this behavior could serve as an early warning sign of a deeper problem on his part, a contributing factor to a general picture of his personality, even if not directly

---

33 Bataille, *Le procès*, 61, 116, (he specifies that before the interdiction Gilles had sold all his own properties in Poitou, Maine, and Anjou, with the exception of Champtocé and Ingrandes, and was left only with his Breton possessions), 119 (see note 3). See also Bossard, *Gilles de Rais*, 68–69 (see note 1) and Heers, *Gilles de Rais*, 175–76 (see note 1).

34 Heers, *Gilles de Rais*, 90, 96–97, 111 (see note 1), discounts the arguments of the *Mémoires* as the product of exaggeration and bias. His main argument for a revision of Gilles's history is based in part on the rejection of this document (17).

35 Bataille, *Le procès*, 108 (see note 3) and Bossard, *Gilles de Rais*, 66 (see note 1) where he justifies Gilles's lack of interest in the details of business transactions.

related to his crimes. Certainly, up to this point there is nothing extremely worrisome in Gilles's outward behavior. But while so far no single clue can be construed as critical in itself, taken as a whole all his actions show a tendency on Gilles's part to brush aside responsibilities and resort to make-believe to enhance his self-esteem. On a different level, his spending spree in Orléans could explain why Gilles could be popular with humble people and retain for a long time a reputation for generosity.

However, it came to light later that by this time he had already embarked for at least three years on a career of sorcery and murder, two activities that apparently became ever more central to his life after his return from Orléans. Their late discovery (in 1438) has contributed to distorting the interpretation of Gilles's character: despite Bataille's insistence on his lifelong exposure to violence, there is a tendency to view his life in two separate time frames, a longer, more-or-less conventional beginning and a brief spiral into crime in the last three years, a distortion that is facilitated by the structure of his biographies. However, Gilles's own confession revealed that he had been interested in sorcery and committed (undetermined) criminal acts perhaps even before the death of his grandfather, and possibly since his return from the campaigns against the English, thus making him a criminal for at least one-half of his life.

Unfortunately little is known about his relation to his fiefs or his management of properties after the ruinous stay in Orléans. All we can tell is that his national fortunes never revived, and that he spent his remaining years committing occasional acts of banditry and moving among a few favorite residences, especially Machecoul, Champtocé, Tiffauges, and La Suze.[36] It was in the first two where, late in 1437 and early in 1438, suddenly something sinister emerged. Fearing Gilles's sale of his favorite fortress, his relatives René de la Suze and André de Laval-Lohéac prepared to send troops to occupy Machecoul to prevent it from falling into ducal hands. Before their retainers came to take possession of it, Gilles quickly sent two servants to recover from a tower the skeletons of several children and burn them in a safe place. The job of clearing the tower pit was done in haste and at night, and therefore not properly, so that the captain in charge of the (temporary) takeover asked embarrassing questions about a couple of remaining skeletons. A similar episode was soon repeated in the fortress of Champtocé, which was one of the properties acquired by Duke Jean V surreptitiously through a front, his chancellor Jean de Malestroit bishop of Nantes. From there the skeletons of several children were removed and transported by boat in trunks to be burned at Machecoul ahead of Malestroit. Poitou and Henriet, the two servants tasked with the macabre duty, later testified having counted around forty-five

36 Heers, *Gilles de Rais*, 125–26 (see note 1). He concludes (138) that Gilles's precarious fortunes and position were the norm within contemporary nobility.

skulls and several dismembered body parts in various stages of decomposition, witnesses to a long murderous spree.[37] Therefore, in the future they would burn the clothes and bodies of the victims in a large chimney in the master's room to hide traces of the crimes (a fact that alone renders impossible an accurate count of his victims).[38] At the same time timid but persistent rumors popped up about the disappearance of local children, usually boys aged between eight and sixteen years, many described as "beautiful," and all last seen around Gilles's favorite residences or in the company of his servants.[39]

In May 1439, perhaps due to growing need for money, Gilles committed another imprudent act: he recruited a twenty-two-year-old cleric from Italy, Francesco Prelati, to help with experiments of alchemy and to summon the devil in the hope of acquiring instant wealth through magical practices. Apparently, he soon became smitten with the young, handsome, and well-educated cleric.[40] Bossard defends Gilles's practice of alchemy as quite legitimate, and in fact, it is hardly mentioned in the list of charges against him, and then only because it occurred in conjunction with summoning of demons.[41] But Prelati, like a few who preceded him in this role, had a dual task, of which the summoning of demons became the primary one. Gilles was present at the first few séances and he enlisted his terrified servants to help set up various objects inside the magic circle where Prelati would draw cryptograms and recite arcane formulas from a book.[42] In particular, the

---

37 Bataille, *Le procès*, 121–25, 273–74 (see note 3) (from the confession of the valet Poitou, who estimated the number of skeletons at Champtocé between thirty-six and forty-six), 282–83 (from the confession of the valet Henriet, who confirms the details given by Poitou), and Bossard, *Gilles de Rais*, 164–65 (see note 1) (over eighty skeletons at Machecoul and over forty at Champtocé).

38 Bataille, *Le procès*, 46, 276 (see note 3) (from the confession of Poitou).

39 See, for example, Bossard, *Gilles de Rais*, 140–41 (see note 1), Bataillle, *Le procès*, 130 (see note 3), and Heers, *Gilles de Rais*, 160 (see note 1). In fact, the "acte d'accusation" refers to victims of both sexes, but the various depositions make no reference to the disappearance of specific girls, and it was generally known that Gilles preferred boys. It is possible that he might have accepted girls when boys were not available.

40 Bossard, *Gilles de Rais*, 119–20 (see note 1). He also states (117) that Gilles used to doubt previous magicians and alchemists, but seemed to have lost his skepticism with Prelati. See also Bataille, *Le procès*, 132 (see note 3). In the absence of evidence, he only speculates (24, 67) whether Prelati was his master's lover. Heers, *Gilles de Rais*, 151 (see note 1), aptly states that the handsome Prelati "séduisait le maître et le tenait prisonnier de ses rêves."

41 Bossard, *Gilles de Rais*, 107 (see note 1) and Heers, *Gilles de Rais*, 143–44 (see note 1). But Bataille, *Le procès*, 66 (see note 3), takes literally an edict of King Charles V forbidding the practice, and relates (69, 146) a visit to Tiffauges by the dauphin Louis in 1439 that prompted a panicky Gilles to have the alchemy ovens destroyed, even if apparently the visit was unrelated to these activities.

42 The first such séance took place in the great room of the castle of Tiffauges in the presence of Gilles, Prelati, Sillé, Blanchet, Henriet, and Poitou. A second one took place on the following night in a meadow outside the same fortress, and in the presence of Prelati, Gilles, and Poitou. The trio was chased back into the castle by a downpour, without sighting the demon. Bataille, *Le procès*, 134–35 (see note 3).

impecunious baron went to extremes to lure a demon that Prelati usually called Barron, and even wrote him a "cédule" (certificate of debt) to be delivered by Prelati, in which he offered him anything that he wanted, except his own life and soul. Useless to say, the devil was offended by such miserliness and never appeared when Gilles was present (but he deigned to appear to Prelati as a handsome young man dressed in violet).[43] Soon Prelati concluded that Gilles's presence was not pleasing to the demon, and conveniently continued the practice alone. This arrangement seemed quite acceptable to Gilles, who never wavered in his trust of the young cleric, whose later career revealed him as a professional charlatan and thief.

The accounts that emerged at the trial of the bungled séances contribute a spark of Italian comedy to the otherwise somber Gothic drama, and reveal Gilles's astonishing gullibility and cowardice.[44] For example, one night Prelati locked himself up in a room, from where soon came sounds of blows and his own pitiful screams, but nobody, including the great lord of Rais, dared break in and attempt a rescue. Prelati emerged much later pale and feverish, and claimed that he had a lively meeting with an irritable Barron. Gilles spent the following week personally nursing his dear friend back to health.[45]

Eventually Barron acceded to Prelati's demands that he supply wealth for Gilles and filled a whole room of the castle with gold bars. But when an elated lord rushed to enjoy the sight of his new wealth, Prelati blocked the entry and announced that the devil had placed a large snake to guard the treasure. In this case, however, greed won over cowardice. Gilles returned armed with a crucifix containing a relic, and Prelati could not keep him from entering the room to verify the claim. A disappointed Gilles only found some pieces of brass, but apparently

43 Bataille, *Le procès*, 135–36, 161 (see note 3) and Bossard, *Gilles de Rais*, 114, 121–28 (see note 1). I have not found any other reference to this demon. Carl Goldberg, *Speaking with the Devil–A Dialogue with Evil* (New York:Penguin Books, 1996), 95–96 discusses a mental patient who identified a demonic aspect of his own personality with Belphegor, the devil that represents the sin of sloth, i.e. the denial of one's potential to wallow in "idle, self-indulgent" life style. Since Belphegor is also reputed to induce people to make discoveries with the promise of wealth, perhaps the name used by Prelati is a bastardization of this. Also, apparently Belphegor could be represented as a beautiful young woman (changed into an attractive youth for Gilles's tastes by his clever associate).

44 Heers, *Gilles de Rais*, 148 (see note 1), talks of "véritables bouffonneries."

45 Bataille, *Le procès*, 136–37, 273(see note 3) (from the deposition of Eustache Blanchet) and Heers, *Gilles de Rais*, 152 (see note 1). Apparently, Prelati borrowed the script from another necromancer who had preceded him, Jean de la Rivière. One night Jean went alone into a wood near Pouzauges to meet with a demon, wearing white armor, and returned frightened, claiming that the demon had appeared in the form of a leopard. After obtaining more money from Gilles, Jean disappeared on the following day. Bataille, *Le procès*, 271–72 (see note 3) and Heers, *Gilles de Rais*, 153 (see note 1) (from the deposition of Eustache Blanchet).

not even then did he suspect that Prelati might have duped him.[46] It seems that Gilles craved guidance, and the clever Prelati, his social inferior but intellectual superior, provided it as he continued to exploit his master for over a year and to exert a dark ascendancy over him. For example, it was apparently Prelati who suggested at one point using an eye, hand, blood, and heart of a murdered child as sacrificial offering to the finicky devil.[47]

All three modern biographers discuss Gilles's magic practices apart from his murderous ones, and I have followed their lead. However, these practices (apart from alchemy) were a major issue at the ecclesiastical trial and occupied a large portion of the depositions of witnesses and accused, intermingled with accounts of murders. Perhaps because such accusations would sound ridiculous today the legitimacy of the entire proceeding has been placed in doubt by (admittedly only a handful of) historians in the early twentieth century. This was a time of violent anticlericalism, when the trial of Joan of Arc (which took place in 1431, only nine years before that of Gilles) was denounced as a fraud, a process that eventually brought about her canonization. Heers's secondary purpose in writing his work is precisely to refute the theory of Gilles's innocence and show that the trial was valid and conducted correctly, and that Gilles's guilt—at least of the murders—was amply proven. His three biographers express no doubts on this point, nor did medieval chroniclers in their terse reporting of the events, nor did Gilles's own family.[48]

---

46 Bataille, *Le procès*, 139 (see note 3).

47 Bossard, *Gilles de Rais*, 129–30 (see note 1) and Bataille, *Le procès*, 69, 144–45 (see note 3). Prelati's statements on this topic, as in Bataille, *Le procès*, 264 (see note 3), are rather confusing. He recalled the devil's demand to receive human offerings, having seen a murdered child (apparently an infant) on the floor of a room at Tiffauges, and having witnessed Gilles carry the organs of a child (another?) in a glass to his room. Still, the demon did not appear and later Prelati buried the remains in a nearby chapel. On the other hand, Prelati could also act as Gilles's social conscience: he claimed that Barron had ordered Gilles to offer three banquets to the poor during the feast of All Saints, and since Gilles offered them only one banquet, Barron refused to appear. Bataille, *Le procès*, 142 (see note 3) and Bossard, *Gilles de Rais*, 129 (see note 1).

48 In 1902 Salomon Reinach made a case for Gilles's innocence, likely spurred by the atmosphere of mistrust for state justice caused by the Dreyfus affair and by the fame of the trial of Joan of Arc. Bataille, *Le procès*, 178–79 (see note 3), criticizes Reinach's lack of analysis of the documents, and Heers *Gilles de Rais*, 186–88 (see note 1), affirms that his pamphlet did not make much of an impression at the time, and its thesis was only taken up twice: briefly in 1921, and then in 1961 by E. Clourec-Kerlouane. The "innocence" thesis consists of putting on trial the judges, by claiming incorrectly that his was an inquisitorial trail, with anonymous witnesses and with its implicit aura of intolerance and obscurantism. Bossard, *Gilles de Rais*, 205–07 (see note 1), makes the same points about the trial. Charles VII did make inquiries on some aspects of the procedure in 1443 (three years after Gilles's execution) in response to a complaint by Gilles's daughter Marie de Craon and her husband Prégent de Coëtivy. But the final verdict was not contested. Heers, *Gilles de Rais*, 205 (see note 1). See also Bossard, *Gilles de Rais*, 274–75 (see note 1).

Experimenting with alchemy sounds reasonable enough if one looks at it as a form of chemistry; and it could bolster Bossard's argument that Gilles was gifted with an inquisitive mind. But while the summoning of demons today would not be added to the list of charges, it could be brought up at a trial as a means to complete the psychological portrait of the accused. In fact, Gilles's behavior in this matter goes beyond the common belief in demons and occasional transgression into black magic. For years he had obsessively dedicated time and resources to recruiting sorcerers, finally settling on Prelati. His naïveté is astonishing when one reads that he had his companions invoke the devil "in the name of the Father, the Son, the Holy Ghost, the Virgin Mary and all the saints," and that after over a year of efforts he would not entertain doubts on the efficacy of Prelati's techniques, in fact believed him his good friend to the end and parted from him in prison with a heartfelt farewell.[49] I see in his delusion to harness demons another example of his tendency to live in a make-believe world in which he felt all-powerful.

A final example of his "niaiserie" is the action that brought about his ruin. After selling the castle of Saint-Étienne-de-Mer-Morte to the treasurer of Brittany Geoffrey Le Ferron (or to his brother Guillaume, bishop of Léon), he decided to take it back by force.[50] The new owner had placed the property in the care of a third brother, a cleric named Jean Le Ferron. On May 15 1440, Gilles, armed with a pike and accompanied by his henchmen, burst into the village church where Le Ferron had officiated mass, threatened the cleric with death, and then spirited him to the fortress, which he had, in the meantime, reoccupied. The ducal court responded by fining Gilles fifty thousand gold *écus*; Gilles not only refused to pay, but in retaliation relocated the prisoner to Tiffauges, outside ducal jurisdiction.[51] This blatant violation of clerical immunity also raised the ire of the bishop of Nantes Jean de Malestroit, in whose diocese the property resided. The bishop had already initiated a rapid series of investigations into Gilles's other criminal activities, and, throughout the summer, the depositions of several parents and acquaintances of lost children were collected, while the murders—incredibly—continued. On July 29, with all appearance of acquiescence on the duke's part,

49 ["par le Père, le Fils et le Saint-Esprit, par la Vierge Marie et tous the saints"] Bataille, *Le procès*, 263 (see note 3) (from the deposition of Prelati). Gilles's farewell to Prelati took place after the two were questioned together in Gilles's cell. Bossard, *Gilles de Rais*, 236–37 (see note 1) and Bataille, *Le procès*, 24, 165 (see note 3). The text, in French ("Adieu, François, mon ami! Jamais plus nous ne nous reverrons en ce monde [. . .]") is in Bataille, *Le procès*, 240–41 (see note 3).

50 Bataille, *Le procès*, 151 (see note 3), gives Geoffrey Le Ferron as the buyer; Heers (*Gilles de Rais*, 178) (see note 1) and Bossard, *Gilles de Rais*, 178 (see note 1), state that the buyer was his brother Guillaume Le Ferron, bishop of Léon. Apparently, Gilles wanted to resell the castle to a cousin, but Le Ferron had refused to return it. Bateille, *Le procès*, 71 (see note 3).

51 The "acte d'accusation" says that he entered the church "de manière furibonde et téméraire." Bataille, *Le procès*, 162 (see note 3). The account, except for some minor details, is also in Bossard, *Gilles de Rais*, 178–81 (see note 1).

the bishop published "lettres patentes" (open letters) accusing Gilles of sodomy, murder, and commerce with devils (curiously, no mention was made of the attack on Le Ferron, perhaps to avoid the impression of political motivation).[52]

From this moment onward events moved quickly. On August 25 the constable of France Arthur de Richemont (a brother of the duke) occupied the French fortress of Tiffauges and freed Le Ferron, at which point Gilles's accomplices Sillé and Bricqueville fled, as well as other servants. On September 13 Gilles was summoned to appear in front of the ecclesiastical tribunal of Nantes to answer the charges contained in the bishop's letters. Two days later ducal troops, accompanied by a notary, arrested Gilles at Machecoul (which was a ducal fief), together with Henriet, Poitou, and Prelati. They were taken to Nantes, where Gilles was comfortably housed in an upper room of the castle of the Tour-Neuve, and the rest in common prisons.[53]

The visit by the ducal gendarmes should not have come as a surprise to Gilles, as in December 1439 one of his previous associates, the priest Eustache Blanchet, had sent him dire warnings that rumors of his crimes were spreading, adding a stern admonition that the lord of Rais should mend his ways. Not only did Gilles not heed the admonitions, but he sent one of his employees, the goldsmith Jean Petit, to return the defector forcibly to Tiffauges.[54] Blanchet was arrested separately in September 1440 in the nearby village of Mortagne where he resided.[55] It seems clear at this point that the Le Ferron incident was only a pretext (not unlike the traditional accusation of tax evasion to justify the arrest of notorious gangsters)

---

52 Apparently the last murder took place around August 15, 1440. Bataille, *Le procès*, 154 (see note 3). Bossard, *Gilles de Rais*, 190 (see note 1), dates the bishop's open letter July 30 and does not mention the last murder. The letter, after supplying a list of witnesses, concludes that Gilles "avec certains de ses complices, avait égorgé, tué et massacré de façon odieuse, plusieurs jeunes garçons innocents, qu'il avait pratiqué avec ces enfants la luxure contre nature et le vice de sodomie, souvent fait et fait faire l'horrible évocation des démons, avait sacrifié à ceux-ci et fait des pactes avec eux." The second letter (dated September 13) accuses him of heresy and summons him to appear in court. Bataille, *Le procès*, 190–92 (see note 3). Jean V, who had recently rebelled against the king, wanted to avoid any confrontation, and negotiated an alliance with his brother the constable Arthur de Richemont, promising him a share of the expected spoils from Gilles's last properties. The trial was apparently only a formality. Bataille, *Le procès*, 154–55 (see note 3).

53 Bossard, *Gilles de Rais*, 191–95 (see note 1), Bataille, *Le procès*, 156 (see note 3), and Heers, *Gilles de Rais*, 179 (see note 1).

54 Bataille, *Le procès*, 66, 142, 144 (see note 3). Apparently (147) Petit was thrown into a dungeon when he returned from his failed mission, but Gilles did not give up and sent other servants to retrieve the runaway priest.

55 Blanchet only confessed to having introduced Prelati to his master. He denied having had anything to do with kidnappings and murders, or having participated of his own will to summons of the devil. He claimed having fled Tiffauges in 1439, and when he later heard rumors about the secret activities that were taking place in that castle of his ex-master, he had severely warned him. Heers, *Gilles de Rais*, 207–08 (see note 1). See also Bossard, *Gilles de Rais*, 173–74 (see note 1).

because the charges of heresy, sodomy, and murder took precedence in the "acte d'accusation" (bill of indictment) over those of aggravated assault on Le Ferron, which had occurred a good three months earlier.[56]

Historians have been puzzled by the omission of references to Le Ferron as well as by the sudden interest of Malestroit in a series of murders that had been allowed to go on for so long. While Bossard defends the bishop's honest intentions, Heers is more skeptical, and offers a less flattering portrait of a greedy and political bishop, who might even have envisioned coming into some of Gilles's possessions. He cautions, however, that the inquiry into Gilles's sinister activities had been ongoing for a while by the time the Le Ferron incident occurred. Malestroit himself stated having initiated it in response to popular demands in the course of his pastoral visits, and the arresting officers were alerted to search the castle for clues of murderous activity.[57] On September 28 the ecclesiastical court opened its first session while, in parallel, the ducal court continued its own inquiries and questioning of witnesses. Their depositions collected throughout the trail, together with the confessions of the accused, have allowed modern biographers to reconstruct a record of criminal activity that started since the death of Jean de Craon in 1432, if not earlier, and that has since been the main source of the Breton's posthumous fame.[58]

Gilles chose his victims one at a time, among boys of poor families, and lured them into his castles with promises of alms and jobs.[59] Once the prey was inside,

---

56 This opinion is shared to some degree by all three biographers. See Heers, *Gilles de Rais*, 180 (see note 1), Bataille, *Le procès*, 154 (see note 3), and Bossard, *Gilles de Rais*, 191 (see note 1). No document related to the ducal inquiry survives, but two related to the ecclesiastical inquiry have survived. Heers, *Gilles de Rais*, 180 (see note 1).

57 They found a small bloody shirt in the residence of Prelati and Blanchet. Heers, *Gilles de Rais*, 181–83 (see note 1) and Bossard, *Gilles de Rais*, 194 (see note 1).

58 The onset of Gilles's criminal activities is debatable, given that sources are contradictory. The "acte d'accusation" dates the first demonic séance and murder to 1426. Bataille, *Le procès*, 211, 214, 217 (see note 3). But Gilles's own confession and all extant testimonies of the victims' parents date it 1432. Gilles, however, confessed to committing (undefined) "actes illicites" since childhood and Bataille, *Le procès*, 39–42 (see note 3), postulates that he may have referred to the butcheries of the war years 1427–1429, which to me sounds unconvincing, because he would not have viewed such acts as illicit. He may instead have been referring to a contact in 1426 with a knight who had been accused of heresy and from whom he admitted having learnt principles of necromancy. Bataille, *Le procès*, 62, 161, 224 (see note 3). As for the chronology of the two parallel trials, Heers, *Gilles de Rais*, 191–92 (see note 1), states that the president of Brittany Pierre de l'Hôpital opened his sessions on September 18, while the court clerk Jean de Toucheron continued collecting the depositions of other witnesses: nine on September 18, four on September 24, thirty-two between September 28 and September 30, twenty on October 4, and fifteen on October 10. The majority of these have not survived. In parallel, between September 28 and October 11, nine more witnesses from Nantes and vicinity were questioned in the episcopal chapel (the majority of whom had already been heard in July).

59 Bataille, *Le procès*, 148 (see note 3), and Heers, *Gilles de Rais*, 192 (see note 1), specify that only two

his servants would take him to a room where Gilles staged his deadly play. At first he terrorized and confused the child, for example by partially hanging him; then he would suddenly take him down and soothe him playfully; then just as suddenly he would sexually assault him. Gilles's three biographers have not commented on the details of the sexual assaults (Bossard avoids specific mention of them), but report without comments the unambiguous depositions of his two servants Henriet and Poitou. Gilles used to masturbate and then rub his penis between the child's legs or against his abdomen.[60] Afterwards he would kill the child, or have him killed by his servants, usually by stabbing, decapitation, or cutting his throat. At times the killing would come first, and Gilles would sit on the abdomen of the dying or dead victim, laughing at the sight of his agony, which—in his own words—intensified his pleasure.[61] Afterwards he might dismember the body to admire its inner organs, or stage grotesque beauty pageants featuring the severed head of the victim of the day and of those of the previous days, and reward the winner with kisses.[62]

This pattern of seizure, frightening, verbal interaction, and sexual release to coincide with murder recalls the style of other serial killers, who in modern times have received as much attention as Gilles did in his own days. An apt example is the notorious Jeffrey Dahmer, who raped, killed, and dismembered sixteen boys and young men in Milwaukee (Wisconsin, United States) between 1987 and 1991.[63]

---

of the victims seem to belong to professional families (a mason and a butcher), and the rest came from humble background.

60 Poitou, in his confession, stated that Gilles used to take "sa verge ou son membre viril entre l'une ou l'autre de ses mains, la frottait ou l'érigeait ou la tendait, puis il la posait entre les cuisses ou les jambes desdits garçons et filles [. . .] avec une grande délectation, une ardeur et une concupiscence libidineuse, jusqu'à ce que le sperme s'émit sur leurs ventres." Bataille, *Le procès*, 275 (see note 3). Apparently he used (the rare) female victims in the same way, as, in his own words, it gave him "plus de plaisir, et moins de peine, qu'à jouir d'elles en leur nature." Bataille, *Le procès*, 172 (see note 3). The "acte d'accusation" reports in scandalized tones that Gilles did not treat his female victims differently from the males and avoided their "vase naturel." Bataille, *Le procès*, 160, 211 (see note 3). But this is not apparently an attitude limited to medieval authorities: an FBI officer seemed appreciative of a rapist who would not beat or verbally abused his victims, and "engaged in vaginal assault only." Tithecott, *Of Men and Monsters*, 152 (see note 11).

61 The "acte d'accusation" specifies that the children were "égorgés, tués et [. . .] tormentés honteusement," and that Gilles committed against them the sin of sodomy while they were still living, dying, or already dead. Bataille, *Le procès*, 160, 210–11 (see note 3). See also Bossard, *Gilles de Rais*, 149 (see note 1). The description of the torments, killings, and dismemberment are in Bataille, *Le procès*, 44–46, 275 (from the deposition of Poitou), 282–83 (from the deposition of Henriet) (see note 3).

62 Bataille, *Le procès*, 45–46, 166, 243–44 (from the confession of *Gilles de Rais*), 285 (from the confession of Henriet) (see note 3).

63 Fisher, *Killer Among Us*, 164 (see note 11). I am limiting recent examples to killers who were (are) male and preyed on young males, for the sake of space and to maintain a close parallel with Gilles. But I do not see much difference in the style of the much more numerous ones whose

Like Gilles, he operated in a limited geographical area and preyed on those marginalized by society: mainly African-Americans or Asian-Americans picked up in shopping malls or gay bathhouses and drawn to his apartment by the prospect of money (for example, to pose for pictures).[64] Also, like Gilles, he preferred sexual contact with a debilitated, unconscious, or even dead partner. Apparently, for both predators domination was the key to pleasure, and therefore both deliberately precluded the possibility of consensual sex. Since Dahmer lacked help in subduing the victim, he would render him incapacitated with a drink laced with a tranquilizer, or, in some cases, by hitting him on the head with a rubber mallet. After murdering his prey he would dismember the body and take pictures at various stages of the procedure, and preserve hands, heads, and other body parts in bizarre ways, for example by freezing them or injecting them with acid, in an attempt at prolonging possession of their beauty, an activity that closely resembled Gilles's own. For both killers the victim was a dehumanized, aesthetic object to be collected.[65]

In his study on the interaction of the serial killer with society, Joseph C. Fisher states that three factors stand in the way of apprehending such a criminal: the characteristics of the victims, the behavior of the killer himself, and the structure of the society in which the killer operates.[66] If one wonders how Gilles could go on for years with his outrageous behavior, it is helpful to consider that he shared all three factors with modern counterparts. First, he chose victims from a segment of society who either would carefully avoid police contact or make police work difficult out of fear for their own existence. Likewise, modern serial killers prefer to prey on transients because a disappearance from within their ranks is hardly noticeable, or on people who belong to a marginal group like the homosexual community of Milwaukee in Dahmer's days. The lucky few among them to escape from him with their lives, but drugged and severely injured, never pressed charges, but only shared in whispers among themselves the disturbing information about him.[67]

---

victims were female. Also for the sake of space I will confine most examples to footnotes.

64 Fisher, *Killer Among Us*, 176 (see note 11). Apparently several were aspiring models. Only the first two victims (one outside the "serial" pattern) and the last were White; two were Hispanic and one Native American. Fisher, *Killer Among Us*, 175, Table 7.1 (see note 11).

65 Tithecott, *Of Men and Monsters*, 120, 163 (see note 11). He adds (171) that Dahmer "confused love with possession." He mentions another serial killer (172) who tried to re-create the beauty of Michelangelo sculptures with the body of a victim. Dahmer's drug of choice was Halcion (Triazolam). Fisher, *Killer Among Us*, 181–82 (see note 11). According to a psychiatrist who studied him, "Dahmer preferred soft sex consisting of holding, caressing, and foreplay. He disliked rougher forms of sex and had a particular aversion to anal intercourse." Fisher, *Killer Among Us*, 174 (see note 11).

66 Fisher, *Killer Among Us*, 164 (see note 11).

67 Fisher, *Killer Among Us*, 179–80 (see note 11). See also Tithecott, *Of Men and Monsters*, 78, 81 (see

From various testimonies it appears that Gilles's servants were sent among the community to intimidate the humble potential witnesses, a task facilitated by the ease with which a kidnapping could then be disguised among a multitude of other causes for a child's disappearance. Such events were so frequent that Bataille records that sometimes the reported loss of a child was unlikely to have been caused by Gilles, because he was not in residence at the time of the vanishing. Thus Gilles's servants could convince desperate parents that their son had fled or had been taken hostage by the English, two acceptable excuses in that tormented period when armed raids were the norm.[68]

The second factor, the behavior of the killer, is the most intriguing piece of the puzzle. Unfortunately there is not enough information about Gilles's youthful transgressions, which he confessed having committed as early as 1426. We only know of a previous clash with the Church when he briefly arrested a cleric from Angers who had been his tutor and of his early quarrels with rivals over properties which, according to Heers, prepared the ground for his later debacle.[69] The fact that there were no serious investigations about murderous activities until late should not come as a surprise, however, as this pattern is evident also with modern serial murderers. As Fisher states, there are several early clues as to what type of person the serial killer may become, but none as obvious as to cause an early arrest.

---

note 11). As a comparison, see the fear of reprisal voiced by the victims' relatives and other servants of Gilles. Heers, *Gilles de Rais*, 163 (see note 1).

68 See, for example, Bataille, *Le procès*, 101 (see note 3). Another modern serial killer who shares some significant points of contact with Gilles is John W. Gacy, who was convicted of the rape and murder of thirty-three adolescent boys between 1972 and 1978 in Illinois (United Sates). Twice-married and father of two daughters, he had been briefly imprisoned for molesting a boy, but had escaped trial by successfully intimidating the potential witness. Using his business (remodeling contractor) as façade, he lured boys to his home with promises of jobs. His methods of abducting, terrorizing, assaulting the victims with partial strangulation and drowning were revealed in his confession or related by a few who managed to escape from him or were voluntarily released. Most of his victims were buried in the crawl space under his house. The data on his case reported here derive from the recollections of an attorney involved with his prosecution, Terry Sullivan with Peter T. Maiken, *Killer Clown* (New York: Grosset & Dunlap Publishers, 1983). Among the points of similarity with Gilles are his methods of subduing the victim by choking or partially drowning him, putting on and then removing handcuffs, and of alternating threats with talks of play (222–23); his ready excuses for the disappearance of his young apprentices (188); and the fact that a few of his victims, who had been brutalized but not killed, complained to the police, but Gacy was never formally charged, and started believing in his immunity (219, 224–25, 245).

69 In 1436 he kidnapped and briefly imprisoned Michel de Fontenay, a priest of Angers who had been his tutor and who had collaborated in the royal letters of interdiction. He was forced to release him by the intervention of the bishop and the University of Angers. Bataille, *Le procès*, 118 (see note 3) and Heers, *Gilles de Rais*, 116 (see note 1) where he states that Gilles held the priest for ransom.

An amazing example is once again Dahmer. He had been fascinated by death since childhood and tortured, killed, and dismembered small animals. In high school he was noted for outrageous behavior and overuse of alcohol, which, as for Gilles, throughout his life was to play a role in overcoming inhibitions. His first murder took place in 1978, well ahead of his serial spree, when he strangled a young man who refused to spend the night with him and dismembered the body, a murder that remained unresolved until Dahmer's arrest years later. After being discharged from the Army for his alcoholism, he went to live with his grandmother until she forced him to move out because of his bizarre behavior: contacts with police for indecent exposure, necrophilia (he tried to exhume the body of a boy recently dead), and drinking a blood sample while working in a plasma center.[70]

Still, despite these disturbing signs, Dahmer remained "invisible, below the threshold of attention," hidden "behind a mask of social convention."[71] Twice the police were called to the housing complex where he went to reside: one time for the murder of a man who lived above his apartment (the police found nothing suspicious) and the other time to investigate the overpowering smell from his own apartment (the police burst into the wrong one). By the time of his final arrest Dahmer had at least seven contacts with the law, was arrested three times for minor charges of sexual misconduct, put on probation twice and in prison once. And yet he was ordinary-looking, polite, and always ready with calm excuses for his major crimes that were accepted at face value by the police. He was finally arrested by chance when his eighteenth victim was able to escape and force the police to investigate. Until the very end his lack of a sense of guilt had allowed him to fool authorities by presenting a suave exterior.[72]

The third factor, the composition of the society in which the serial killer lives, also helps in delaying his discovery, and here once again the medieval baron was not alone in taking advantage of the unconscious societal bias that permits a serial killer to continue undetected. In a city increasingly made up of segregated and poor groups Dahmer, the only white tenant in an apartment complex inhabited by minorities, was readily believed by the police, who failed to check on his history of arrests. He did attract the suspicions of his neighbors, but these being poor and marginal, their suspicions did not provoke serious investigation. For example, they complained of the sound of sawing and foul smell that emanated from his apartment, and noticed that "near-frantic cats followed him to the dumpster and

---

70 Fisher, *Killer Among Us*, 172–74 (see note 11). Also Tithecott, *Of Men and Monsters*, 97 (see note 11).

71 Fisher, *Killer Among Us*, 176–77 (see note 11).

72 Fisher, *Killer Among Us*, 182, 188 (see note 11). At the chocolate factory where he worked he kept the skull of one of his victims in the locker. He removed it when he was finally fired for absenteeism, but still nobody suspected (164–66).

swarmed over the trash bags he threw in."[73] The most notorious episode of what Fisher calls "linkage blindness" (that is, overlooking clues that point to a serial pattern) occurred when some of Dahmer's neighbors called the police to report a dazed, bleeding, fourteen-year-old Laotian boy staggering outside his apartment. Dahmer calmly explained that the boy (whose name he seemed to ignore) was his nineteen-year-old roommate, that he had been drinking, and that they had quarreled. The neighbors insisted in vain that the boy was a minor and that he did not live with Dahmer. Nothing suspicious turned up from a cursory search of the apartment and the boy was returned to his captor, only to be killed shortly after the police had left.[74]

Likewise, Gilles and his entourage came close to disaster a couple of times, but society seems to have turned a blind eye: once when Bricqueville allowed two ladies to spy secretly on the removal of the remains from the tower at Champtocé, and another time when Prelati, accompanied by one of Gilles's captains, paid a visit to the mother of two boys who had disappeared at Machecoul on the previous day, to tease her with mock questions about her missing children.[75] Incredible as they seem, these acts of extreme recklessness on the part of the murderous team failed to provoke a reaction at the time, and it seems that the flood of evidence burst out suddenly only after the official inquiry had started and it was clear that the lord had finally lost his social protective wall.

Dahmer's average appearance and demeanor, and his belonging to a dominant group (he came from a middle-class, educated, professional white family) served him well in deflecting reports of shady activities by his low-class neighbors. Gilles's own lofty status and reputation for accessibility and generosity also

---

73 Fisher, *Killer Among Us*, 178–79 (see note 11). He would explain that the foul smell came from a dirty aquarium or spoiled meat.

74 Fisher, *Killer Among Us*, 184–85 (see note 11). The policemen stated later that they did not see any indication of the boy's age in his clothes left in the apartment and that Dahmer produced a seminude photo of the victim to validate his claim of being acquainted with him. They noticed, but did not question, the foul odor in his apartment that came from the decomposing body of a prior victim (186). Tithecott, *Of Men and Monsters*, 70, 76–77 (see note 11), posits that the cynical attitude of the police was illustrative of their prejudice against homosexuals (and produces a revealing recording of their conversation). Fisher instead asserts (22) that this reaction by the police is quite common in cases of serial murders. It is puzzling that in many cases the killer is one of the suspects and even one of the first to be questioned by investigators. Yet, for a myriad of different reasons, he is let go and inadvertently allowed to continue killing. Fisher calls this "linkage blindness" and concludes (24) that like all humans, police "tend to explain events in terms of experiences that they encounter daily."

75 Bataille, *Le procès*, 286 (see note 3) (from the confession of Henriet), 147–48. Bossard, *Gilles de Rais*, 145 (see note 1), also remarks on the extreme carelessness demonstrated by the episode. The person who accompanied Prelati on his mission was Lenano, marquis of Ceva, who is sometimes mentioned as one of Gilles's aides, and who left a brief deposition on the Le Ferron affair. Bataille, *Le procès*, 289–90 (see note 3).

provided him with a respectable façade.[76] Ironically, the very "average" qualities of the baron Gilles de Rais—on which Heers insists—reinforced his ability to hide as a serial killer. And yet, as in Dahmer's case, the term "hiding" should be qualified. Both killers exploited the casual attitude of the group to which they belonged, but members of the group who perceived them as outsiders, such as the tenants of Dahmer's apartment complex or the poor Breton peasants who would risk the safety of their children for alms and a chance at paid service, had no difficulty in recognizing that something suspicious was going on.[77]

Once Gilles's activities were disclosed, he enjoyed another advantage that further delayed his arrest: the practical difficulty of apprehending a powerful baron, surrounded by armed guards, and able to move residence swiftly to escape the justice of either one of his rival feudal lords. Gilles's biographers have understandably been perplexed by the opportunism evidenced by exploiting the Le Ferron incident. Bataille, in particular, remarks that it took a (relatively minor) episode against authority to spur prosecution of much more serious crimes committed during the course of years against helpless people. However, as evidenced by examples of modern serial killers, the pattern of late arrests is not unusual: according to Fisher, most are captured by chance rather than as the result of a coordinated investigation.[78]

Once the tortuous phases of investigation and arrest were over, Gilles's double trial took place with amazing speed and efficiency. First, the ecclesiastical court, presided by Bishop Malestroit flanked by the vice-inquisitor Jean Blouyn and other church members, opened its sessions on September 28 and was attended by the president of Brittany Pierre de l'Hôpital, the supreme magistrate who would

76 This applied, *mutatis mutandi*, also to Dahmer, who was described as "polite" in Fisher, *Killer Among Us*, 164 (see note 11). Gilles could be courteous in public, for example, waiting his turn in church among commoners to receive the Eucharist. Bataille, *Le procès*, 150 (see note 3).

77 An example of the opposite situation, when the killer is protected by being part of the same group as his victims, is that of Wayne Bertram Williams, a young African American man who was convicted of killing (mainly by asphyxiation) twenty-nine African American children in Atlanta (Georgia, United States) between 1979 and 1981. The victims were in great part boys, aged eight to fifteen (only the last six were young adults), who came predominantly from low-income families and who had disappeared while trying to earn pocket change. The police, who described the victims as "hustlers" and "street-wise," demonstrated how easily a non-threatening person could abduct a child in the targeted neighborhood: it had some of its members in plainclothes approach children and found that virtually all accepted to come along with them for money. Authorities started suspecting that the abductor belonged to the same racial group as the victims, but the Atlanta African American community refused to believe it and opposed authorities from the beginning of the investigation. Fisher, *Killer Among Us*, 129, 136, 149–50 (see note 11).

78 Fisher, *Killer Among Us*, 18, 22 (see note 11). He lists (22–23) some of the other inhibitors in finding and arresting a serial killer in the modern United States, some of which (paradoxically) are not too dissimilar from medieval ones: for example, the multiplicity and overlapping of jurisdictions that render difficult the coordination of investigations.

preside over the swift secular procedure.[79] The formal charges comprised forty-nine articles, of which the first fourteen were purely to establish the competence of the ecclesiastical tribunal and the rest dealt with sodomy, heresy, and violation of ecclesiastic immunity.[80]

At first Gilles attempted a bluff by going on the attack against the judges, calling them "simoniaques" and "ribauds" (debauched) and refusing to acknowledge their right to try him. When he saw that these maneuvers left them undeterred, on October 15 he abruptly switched tactics and asked "humblement, dévotement et en larmes" (with humility, devotion, and tears) their forgiveness for his previous "paroles blessantes à leur adresse" (cutting words against them).[81] But he still only confessed to the lesser charge of having practiced alchemy with the help of three Italians, among them Prelati.[82] He still refuted the charges of heresy and demonic invocations and declared himself ready to undergo "l'épreuve du feu" (trial by fire), an obvious bluff, and challenged the prosecutor Guillaume Chapeillon to provide witnesses for the more serious charges. Chapeillon promptly produced six witnesses, who took their oath in Gilles's presence.[83]

Between October 16 and 17 the tribunal collected the depositions of Poitou, Henriet, Prelati, and Blanchet, which effectively sealed Gilles's fate as well as that of the first two. Their separate confessions (explicitly given "spontaneously" and without the aid of torture) agreed quite comfortably with each other.[84] It is impossible to discern from their detailed but unemotional depositions whether they were willing accomplices. It seems, however, that neither servant was found guilty of sodomy or having initiated or participated on their own initiative in the

---

79 Other members of the court were Guillaume de Malestroit bishop of Le Mans, Jean Prégent, bishop of Saint-Brieuc, and Jacques de Pentcoetdic, judge of the ordinary ecclesiastical tribunal of Nantes. Heers, *Gilles de Rais,* 188 (see note 1).

80 Bossard, *Gilles de Rais,* 216–20 (see note 1). Bataille, *Le procès,* 159–60 (see note 3), remarks that the list of crimes is complete but grouped confusedly, and that some dates in it are unreliable. For example, it gives 1426 as the onset of murders, while Gilles's own confession says 1432, and the recent attack on Le Ferron as occurring in 1438. It also gives the number of victims as one hundred forty, a number that is not backed by the depositions of witnesses.

81 Bataille, *Le procès,* 162–63, 223 (see note 3). See also Bossard, *Gilles de Rais,* 229–30 (see note 1).

82 Prelati, in turn recruited as helper the goldsmith Jean Petit from Paris. Gilles mentioned also one Antonio of Palermo and Francesco Lombardo. Heers, *Gilles de Rais,* 145 (see note 1) and Bataille, *Le procès,* 249 (see note 3) (from the confession of Gilles de Rais). An alchemist who preceded Prelati was fired in 1436 because Gilles found him drunk "on the job." Bataille, *Le procès,* 65 (see note 3) and Heers, *Gilles de Rais,* 144 (see note 1).

83 Bataille, *Le procès,* 225–27 (see note 3). Only the depositions of the first four have reached us. Unfortunately, all the depositions of another fifteen witnesses that were introduced at the session of October 19, among them that of a surgeon and a lawyer, are also lost. Bataille, *Le procès,* 231 (see note 3). For the offer to be subjected to the test of fire, see also Bossard, *Gilles de Rais,* 230 (see note 1).

84 Bossard, *Gilles de Rais,* 232 (see note 1) and Heers, *Gilles de Rais,* 192–93 (see note 1).

demonic séances, and both were only tried by the secular court for kidnapping and murder, for which they were sentenced, on October 23, to death by hanging followed by burning. Prelati was treated with leniency, perhaps because he was a cleric and a foreigner. At any rate, his deposition (preserved in its entirety) must have convinced the judges that he did not participate in the actual murders, and so he received a life sentence but later escaped. Blanchet alone was acquitted.[85]

The judges, armed with the confessions of the other accused, warned Gilles that they needed better information from him, and that he would be scheduled to undergo torture. At this point he broke down and confessed everything privately on October 21 to Pierre de l'Hôpital and the bishop Jean Prégent in his room, and again "en jugement" (in open court session) on the following day, in a long statement that confirmed those of his servants. On October 25 the judges passed their sentence on Gilles: he was excommunicated for "perfide apostasie" (perfidious apostasy) and "horrible évocation des démons," (horrible summoning of demons) as well as for "pratique sodomite" (acts of sodomy) on children of both sexes, and immediately turned over to the secular court for the rest of the judgment. The secular court listed its own accusations: kidnapping, sexual abuse, and murder of "perhaps over two hundred" children; having defied the duke by attempting to repossess a sold property; and having attacked Jean Le Ferron and (later) some officers of the duke who had been sent to collect the fine of fifty thousand *écus* for the attack.[86] It then sentenced him to death by hanging and burning, and also to the expropriation of his ducal fiefs, on the very same day.

Once he saw himself lost, Gilles made a good spectacle of his repentance; in fact from that moment onward it was hard to stop his seemingly uninterrupted flow of words.[87] He knelt in tears, accused himself repeatedly, and then regaled the audience with a sermon on avoiding excessive indulgence in rearing their children. He declared that his grandfather had raised him too leniently and without restraints, and pointed to his lax upbringing and taste for refined food and drinks as the prime causes of his criminal life (thus, in a sense, exculpating

---

85 Heers, *Gilles de Rais*, 193, 209 (see note 1). Gilles's biographers do not dwell on the lenient treatment of Prelati and Blanchet. Prelati was later hired by Duke René of Anjou, together with Blanchet, and made captain of La Roche-sur-Yon, where in 1445 he detained Geoffrey Le Ferron. The latter, in turn, had him arrested and hanged for counterfeiting his signature, which Prelati had found on some blank letters ("blanc-seings"). Bataille, *Le procès*, 1772 (see note 3) and Heers, *Gilles de Rais*, 210 (see note 1).

86 Bossard, *Gilles de Rais*, 243–45, 251 (see note 1), Bataille, *Le procès*, 254–59, 296–97 (see note 3), and Heers, *Gilles de Rais*, 193–94 (see note 1). Gilles's confession "en jugement" is in Bataille, *Le procès*, 241–54 (see note 3), his sentence and that of his servants in Bataille, *Le procès*, 333–35 (see note 3).

87 Likewise Fisher, *Killer Among Us*, 89, 124 (see note 11), says that the serial killer David Berkowitz, the "Son of Sam," who shot thirteen people (killing six) in New York, New York (United States) between 1976 and 1977, once in prison became "a compulsive communicator."

himself).[88] He concluded with an admonition for parents to steer their children away from idleness and the attraction of elegant clothes.[89] What impression this advice made among the families of victims who had lived on charity and odd jobs is not recorded.

While the belief in the influence of food on one's personality, common in medieval times, is no longer accepted in medical theory, the assertion that alcohol is at least partly responsible for the unacceptable behavior of the accused is still ubiquitous in criminal trials. As for Gilles's apparently naïve thesis that being raised with indulgence contributed to his later criminal acts, some researchers have indeed postulated that abnormally low "fear conditioning" in childhood may predispose to criminality.[90] As an example, one finds echoes of Gilles's own lenient upbringing in the background of a notorious modern killer, Wayne Bertram Williams, who was found guilty of having kidnapped and murdered twenty-nine children in Atlanta (Georgia, United States) between 1979 and 1981. The indulged only son of older, educated parents, he was considered a child prodigy. He reached early success in his twenties with a radio venture and tried for the rest of his life to "recapture this brief moment in the limelight." Soon he revealed himself a "profligate spender," and when he failed to obtain a college degree he displayed "a penchant to inflate his accomplishments" and to claim "aggrandizing titles." He fancied himself an entertainment promoter (an activity that gave him access to young boys eager to audition, just as Gilles's dazzling chapel would attract choir boys).[91] After his arrest he called a press conference and distributed a résumé among the reporters, and at his trial he alternated displays of amiability with "petulance and belligerence," all of which call to mind Gilles's own performance.

---

88 Gilles claimed that his "avidité insatiable" for fine wines and rich food was a stimulant to commit his crimes. Bataille, *Le procès*, 160, 252 (see note 3) (from the confession of Gilles de Rais) and Heers, *Gilles de Rais*, 193 (see note 1).

89 Bossard, *Gilles de Rais*, 238–40 (see note 1), Bataille, *Le procès*, 166–67, 252 (see note 3) (from the confession of Gilles de Rais), and Heers, *Gilles de Rais*, 193 (see note 1) where he specifies that the audiences were public. This happened at the session of October 22, following Gilles's private confession of the previous day. He asked that his confession be disseminated in French rather than Latin, to reach a wider audience. Bataille, *Le procès*, 242 (see note 3) (from the confession of Gilles de Rais). Likewise Dahmer's confession was sold to magazines. Tithecott, *Of Men and Monsters*, 101 (see note 11). Also Williams (the Atlanta children murderer) at his trial scolded parents for leaving their children unsupervised. Fisher, *Killer Among Us*, 142 (see note 11). Other details on Williams' background are in note no. 77.

90 Philipp Sterzer, "Born to be Criminal? What to Make of Early Biological Risk Factors for Criminal Behavior," *American Journal of Psychiatry* 167.1 (January 2010): 1–3.

91 Heers, *Gilles de Rais*, 98 (see note 1), denies any evidence that Gilles abused this institution to retain a supply of young boys, and argues that maintaining chapels and choirs was common among the aristocracy.

A friend described him with the incisive statement that he "was a promise always about to be fulfilled," a definition that seems quite applicable to Gilles.[92]

Gilles ended his emotional speech by asking forgiveness from God and the families of the children that he had "so cruelly murdered."[93] While his melodramatic and publicly-staged repentance may be expected as a display of "medieval emotionalism," such behavior is actually emblematic of serial killers: Dahmer, for example, made a big show of his remorse and newly-found Christian faith. In fact, police experts confirm that these criminals seem to feel relief at being finally apprehended, and once arrested are over-eager to confess and cooperate in resolving similar cases, and even to help potential victims in avoiding the fate of their own. Psychiatrists explain this bizarre behavior as originating from the serial killer's feeling of inferiority, which he tries to overcome at first through the repeated murders but then (paradoxically) realizes only through the publicity of the trail. Richard Tithecott, in his work on the "mythification" of the serial killer, even posits that this criminal, once "physically imprisoned, is figured by society as a seer, able to transcend physical barriers and look deep into the soul of fellow monsters [. . .] and consequentially perceived [. . .] as a potential defender of society from further violence."[94] However, there may be more than a suggestion of territorial instinct at work in all this, rather than sudden magnanimity, as each serial killer naturally wants to be the last of his kind.

After a second scene of tearful repentance on October 25, the bishop lifted Gilles's excommunication and acceded to two additional requests of the condemned man: that his body would not be burned but rather interred in a church, and that the entire city would stage a procession on the morning of his execution to pray for the salvation of his soul and of that of his two servants. He also asked to be executed ahead of them, so that they would not despair in the belief that their master—the true instigator of the crimes—was to be spared. In other words, he staged his execution on his own terms, like a leading actor choosing his lines. Bataille, who does not hide his amazement at the leniency of the

---

92 Fisher, *Killer Among Us*, 156–58, 160 (see note 11).

93 ["si cruellement massacrés"] Bataille, *Le procès*, 253 (see note 3).

94 Tithecott, *Of Men and Monsters*, 110 (see note 11) (an example of specific help to the police: the child rapist and killer Westley Allan Dodd, who wrote articles from jail giving advice to children on how to escape sexual attacks), 111 (the quote), 139 (the need to be caught), 137 (Dahmer's late repentance). For the serial killers' talkativeness and eagerness to cooperate, see Tithecott, *Of Men and Monsters*, 101 (see note 11), Sullivan, 205 (see note 68), and Fisher, *Killer Among Us*, 83 (see note 11). Fisher also discusses (85) the behavior of John Norman Chapman Collins, the "Coed Killer" who allegedly killed seven young women between 1967 and 1969 in Michigan (United States) and who, after his arrest, displayed cooperativeness and impeccable manners. Like Gilles he refused to testify in his own defense. Bataille, *Le procès*, 254 (see note 3). Fisher, *Killer Among Us*, 26 (see note 11), mentions the publicity freely lavished by the media on serial killers, even before their arrest and trial.

judges, wonders whether such exhibitionism was due to a last-minute hope of reprieve or because Gilles's mind was "en désordre" (deranged).[95] But criminologists have suggested that serial killers are indeed eager for a theatrical execution, and, to this end, they tend to claim sole responsibility for their actions, refusing the easy excuse of insanity.[96]

All three biographers of Gilles affirm that his double trial was impeccably conducted, swift despite the partial redundancy of procedure and based on solid evidence. The "acte d'accusation" was translated into French to allow the accused to refute each point. Further, far from appearing insensitive to Gilles's humble victims, the records of the depositions of witnesses mention their fate and the grief of their families in heartfelt terms.[97] During the course of the proceedings, which were open to the public, the judges tolerated the defendant's childish outbursts and gave him every opportunity to cross-examine witnesses, while resisting his more frivolous requests.[98] It even appears that they treated him with special respect after his shocking confession. One may be tempted to speculate that Gilles received special treatment because of his social status, or that the judges acted with particular caution in his case to prevent the king from finding fault with the proceedings and de-legitimizing any subsequent confiscation of his property on the duke's part.

Heers, however, convincingly minimizes the impact of calculations and self-interest on the judgment against Gilles. In fact, he brings to notice that neither duke nor king profited much from his demise, and that, in definitive, neither of them had initiated the trial; that his family was rather successful in recuperating some of the lost lands; that if greed had been the reason for eliminating Gilles, it would have been much simpler to plan an assassination than a complex trial with scores of witnesses, who would have to be part of a vast conspiracy. And he

95 Bataille, *Le procès*, 75, 256, 335–36 (see note 3). In fact, he was hanged ahead of his two servants and his body only partially burnt. Then "aucune demoiselle de son lignage et des dames e grand état" (perhaps a reference to his daughter and his widow) collected it and buried it in the church of the monastery of the Carmelites in Nantes. Bossard, *Gilles de Rais,* 256–60 (see note 1), Bataille, *Le procès*, 77–78, 168–69, 336–38 (see note 3) (the original documents describing the triple execution) and Heers, *Gilles de Rais*, 194 (see note 1).

96 Tithecott, *Of Men and Monsters,* 139 (see note 11). He also quotes (136) Dahmer's statement in an interview, that "the person to blame is the person sitting across from you. Not parents, not society, not pornography. Those are just excuses." Dahmer was denied a spectacular execution: he was sentenced to serve fifteen consecutive life sentences in prison but then suffered a second-rate exit when a fellow inmate bludgeoned him to death in 1994. Tithecott, *Of Men and Monsters,* 137, 179 (see note 11) and Fisher, *Killer Among Us*, 198 (see note 11). Bossard, *Gilles de Rais*, 272–73 (see note 1), brings attention to the fact that nobody at his trial (witnesses or judges) thought Gilles insane.

97 The families testified "avec de grandes clameurs, douloureusement et dans les larmes" that their children had been "méchamment abusés." Bataille, *Le procès*, 198 (see note 3).

98 Bataille, *Le procès*, 227–31 (see note 3) and Heers, *Gilles de Rais*, 190 (see note 1). Gilles renounced his right to rebuttals and cross-examination of witnesses. Bataille, *Le procès*, 232–34 (see note 3).

concludes that, if Malestroit did have a personal feud with the accused (which is not proven), this does not exclude Gilles's guilt, which was amply revealed by confessions that were obtained separately and agreed in critical details.[99]

It appears, then, that Gilles's case does not stand out as being all too different from others of this kind, both in respect to his personal history and modus operandi and to his relations with authorities before and after the final arrest. A more complex picture, however, emerges from examining the perception of the serial killer within society. In modern days two opposite views of such criminal have surfaced. One is that society is the victim of an all-powerful, super-intelligent being who acts as if above the law.[100] This view is facilitated when the killer's presence is acknowledged, yet the investigation yields no results and the murders continue. At this point the serial killer appears to taunt authorities, and society transfers its belief in the "omniscience and omnipotence" of those pursuing the killer to the killer himself, who starts taking on "larger than life dimension in the public mind."[101] The other view regards the serial killer as a weak, marginalized individual in an all-powerful society that demands conformity, and his murders as a twisted expression of a need to re-establish a sense of self.[102] The dilemma translates into two conceptions of his prosecution: in the first case it becomes a struggle between Good and Evil, universal forces transcending the individual; in the second case it becomes a medical matter, akin to excising a tumor to heal society while maintaining a detached, clinical view of the criminal's mentality, a task that is usually accomplished with the help of psychiatric experts.[103]

---

99 Heers, *Gilles de Rais*, 195–202 (see note 1). In 1448 the new duke of Brittany Francis II ceded Ingrandes and Champtocé to the admiral de Coetivy, husband of Marie de Craon (Gilles's daughter). But a new dispute arose after the death of the admiral in 1450. Most possessions eventually went to Gilles's brother René de La Suze. Heers, *Gilles de Rais*, 213–14 (see note 1). See also Bossard, *Gilles de Rais*, 290–92 (see note 1).

100 Tithecott, *Of Men and Monsters*, 145, 176 (see note 11). He thinks (39) that this theory finds its appeal among the public because evil originates and dies with the criminal. While his examples include only modern American serial killers, he mentions (48) that in nineteenth-century vampire stories the "beast to be destroyed" was an aristocrat (for example, Dracula).

101 Fisher, *Killer Among Us*, 20–21 (see note 1). He calls this collective response "transference," because of its similarity to the known psychological process of unconscious redirection of feelings toward a new object.

102 Tithecott, *Of Men and Monsters*, 176 (see note 1). The theory that marginalization is a cause of crime is defended, for example, in Goldberg, *Speaking with the Devil*, 31, 38–39, 51, 144, 173 (see note 43). He sees in shame and a sense of inadequacy major developmental forces that produce the "malevolent personality." But Tithecott *Of Men and Monsters*, 42–43 (see note 11), argues that too much emphasis has been placed on the "dysfunctional" family background of the serial killer, noting instead that many such criminals come from normal families, in fact (54) successful bourgeois families with a stable income.

103 Fisher, *Killer Among Us*, 17–18 (see note 11). In this respect, Tithecott, *Of Men and Monsters*, 137 (see note 11), suggests that insanity is "a set of influences dispersed socially."

On the surface the first view appears more appropriate to a medieval setting, as it does not exclude that an external, perhaps supernatural, force has taken possession of the perpetrator. And in fact something akin to this view seems to have resonated with the villagers who knew the Breton lord. According to Blanchet, before Gilles's arrest a rumor was circulating that he murdered children in order to write with their blood a demonic book that would have made him all-powerful and able to conquer any fortress. In effect these people were linking in a logical fashion the killings and the demonic practices, and in so doing they were bestowing some grandeur upon Gilles's sins, an image quite removed from the pathetic reality that eventually emerged from the trial.[104] Yet Gilles never said that the demon that he assiduously pursued (and who perversely eluded him) had ever possessed him, and none of the clerical judges suggested this as a possibility. He reputed himself solely responsible for his actions, and in this he conformed to the behavior of most modern serial killers.[105]

Where modern views diverge mostly from medieval ones is in the second, or psychological, interpretation. But once again the break with the past is not all that abrupt, as it is not difficult to find a niche for Gilles in modern criminal taxonomy. For example, he is recognizable in the succinct manual of criminology by Ronald M. Holmes and James De Burger dedicated to serial killers. He fits the demographics of modern-day serial murderers, usually males in the age range of twenty-five to thirty-five, often from a favorable social background, and gifted with positive physical and mental attributes and status (for example, being the oldest son).[106] He even belongs to a precise category within the larger group, what

---

104 Bossard, *Gilles de Rais,* 131 (see note 1), Bataille, *Le procès,* 144, 269 (see note 3) (from the deposition of Eustache Blanchet) and Heers, *Gilles de Rais,* 157, 208 (see note 1). However, Heers (170) disagrees with those who linked Gilles's thirst for gold to the murders, since the killing started well before his financial difficulties. See also the case of Jack the Ripper: among the pseudo-scientific explanations for the motives of this mysterious assassin, one "popular speculation" suggested that he was hired by "an American anatomist" to supply him with organs for a technical manuscript on which he was working (twenty pounds for each specimen). Fisher, *Killer Among Us,* 204 (see note 11).

105 At least a couple of modern serial killers have made (indirect) reference to the Devil. In a rambling note left beside the bodies of two victims, David Berkowitz (the "Son of Sam") calls himself "Beelzebub" and talks of his old, mean father (Sam) who needs to drink the blood of victims to recover his youth. Fisher, *Killer Among Us,* 103–04 (see note 11). Before his trial the judge commented (113) on his claims of having been led to killing by demons. And Gacy wrote in a letter from jail that "the dark shadow of Satan has come over me." Sullivan, *Killer Clown,* 217 (see note 68).

106 Tithecott, *Of Men and Monsters,* 54 (see note 11), Holmes and De Burger, *Serial Murder,* 21, 48–49 (see note 11). The victims whom they describe, however, are usually females. They also identify (65–67) some social causes present in cases of modern American serial murderers that could apply to Gilles's own background: normalization of interpersonal violence and impulsiveness, strong emphasis on comforts, immediate gratification, and thrills, magical thinking, excess of violent role

the two authors call the "lust-oriented hedonistic" type, whose killings "demonstrate a primary and central focus on sexual gratification" that becomes psychologically linked to the "process of the homicide."[107] As the authors explain, the lust killer is usually in touch with reality except in this one area, in which he receives gratification "from the use and abuse of others." Some psychologists explain his motivation to kill as deriving from unconscious motives, others from a multiple personality structure, a "beast" within, "lurking just below the surface." But in any case the motive is psychogenic, intrinsic within the perpetrator and unknown to others, even family members and intimates.[108] This seems to be the case with Gilles, who claimed at one point that his mysterious murderous impulses were forced on him by planetary influences (which determine one's personality).[109]

The authors further subdivide the lust killer into two types, based on other factors. The "disorganized asocial" offender is usually the product of harsh family discipline: he shows disorganization in all aspects of life, may have below-average intelligence, and lacks basic social skills. Therefore he avoids social situations with peers, including sexual intimacy. The "organized nonsocial" type is more difficult to identify because he appears more "normal." He may have an average or above average intelligence and education, has the skills for competent social interaction, including sexual skills, and often has known success in his field. Most interestingly, this type (like Gilles) is often the product of inconsistent discipline

---

models, and extensive spatial mobility. See also Julie B. Wiest, *Creating Cultural Monsters: Serial Murder in America* (Boca Raton, FL: CRC Press, 2011). The research topic is actually endless.

107 Holmes and De Burger, *Serial Murder*, 76 (see note 11). The authors distinguish four types of serial killers (56–59): visionary (usually psychotic: who murder in response to the command of voices or visions), mission-oriented (who have the conscious goal of eliminating particular people), hedonistic (who murder for pleasure or thrill-seeking), and power/control oriented (who derive satisfaction from the feeling of power of life and death over the victim. The Power/Control-Oriented type, whose primal motivation is to exercise "absolute [. . .] dominance over another human being," is often mistaken for the Hedonistic Lust-oriented one. However, with the Power/Control-Oriented type a history of "self-concept problems" is also present, in particular loss of "hero status" (79). While this type could fit Gilles, too, I find it less likely, because he had already used alternate methods (excessive spending, theater, demonic practices) to satisfy his need for hero status. I also do not find him a particularly controlling person, in fact, rather more inclined to letting himself be controlled, first by his grandfather, then by de La Trémoille, then (possibly) by Bricqueville, and finally by Prelati.

108 Holmes and De Burger, *Serial Murder*, 24–25, 50 (see note 11). They add (56) that the psychogenic origin is almost always "a sociopathic personality pattern" that drives him to kill without remorse, and not, for example, extrinsic motives like those of revolutionaries and terrorists. In other words, the rewards of the homicidal act are purely psychological. See also Tithecott, *Of Men and Monsters*, 28 (see note 11), on the "disregard for motive" of serial killers and Fisher, *Killer Among Us*, 15 (see note 11), on how the motives of the serial killer are unknown, and "the unknown is feared most."

109 Heers, *Gilles de Rais*, 166 (see note 1) and Bataille, *Le procès*, 285 (see note 3) (from the deposition of Henriet).

as a child; resorts to murder during situations of stress; and generally uses alcohol to release his inhibitions during the actual crime. In addition, this type is more deliberate in the selection of victims; is more verbal with the victim; may use restraints and prolong the killing process to enjoy this phase; is less likely to commit necrophilia; and leaves a neat crime scene.[110]

Based on the profile, Gilles seems to belong to the second category. Apparently his planning phase was careful, and probably followed a specific pattern. Assuming that his victims totaled around one hundred (a middle number between what Bataille considers the very minimum of thirty- five and a maximum of two hundred) and assuming the starting date of the serial murders to be 1432 (the one on which most writers agree), then this would bring the homicide rate to around one murder a month.[111] During each period his retainers or a paid procuress spotted a likely victim and lured him into the trap, the crime was perpetrated, and the remains destroyed. Then a few days or weeks of interval may go by to let the latest rumor die, and then the activity would resume with the next victim. The actual murder rate was probably less regular: in fact from various depositions it seems that its frequency increased as time went on, a pattern typical for this type of crime. Unfortunately, it is impossible to associate Gilles's murders with precise events of his life that might have precipitated situational stress, except perhaps toward the very end. It is not far-fetched to postulate that the bishop's letters (posted in July) caused him some stress, and this could account for the fact that he continued to kill through the month of August.

According to Holmes and De Burger the lust killer stages his crimes in four phases: fantasizing, searching for victims, murder with accompanying sexual release, and disposal of remains.[112] In Gilles's case one can only hypothesize on the first phase; and because he could count on helpers, the second and fourth phases were performed by others with apparently only minor involvement on his part. For example, at times he would go to personally inspect a potential victim, but usually others did it for him, and after the murder he would fall asleep on his bed,

---

110 Holmes and De Burger, *Serial Murder*, 101–03 (see note 11) (disorganized), 103–05 (organized), 106–08 (additional characteristics). These labels are applied to real cases. For example, a psychiatrist at Dahmer's trial declared him "an organized, nonsocial, lust murderer [. . .] driven by obsessive fantasies of power over others." Cited in Tithecott, *Of Men and Monsters*, 138 (see note 11).

111 Bataille, *Le procès*, 172 (see note 3), estimates a very minimum of thirty five (but believes it too low). The number of two hundred victims appears in the text of the sentence of the secular tribunal, but is given as a guess only. Bossard, *Gilles de Rais*, 135–38 (see note 1) and Bataille, *Le procès*, 296 (see note 3). The total number of victims is impossible to determine from the depositions of witnesses (for example, more than one witness may refer to the same child) and because too many bodies were burnt. Gilles confessed killing an undetermined "grand nombre" of children. Bataille, *Le procès*, 243 (see note 3) (from the confession of Gilles de Rais).

112 Holmes and De Burger, *Serial Murder*, 97–100 (see note 11).

in a drunken stupor, while his servants went about the task of destroying evidence in his room to leave a "neat" crime scene. Since those are the two most laborious and time-consuming phases, this fact alone may explain Gilles's extremely high killing rate, even by serial killer's standards.[113] As to the verbal interaction, it is known that he did talk to his victims both to threaten and to cajole. And his sexual competence was demonstrated by the fact that he produced a daughter and had relations with homosexual partners who were apparently consenting and not destined to be murdered.[114]

Two elements of the profile are puzzling, however, because they do not quite fit the "organized" type. First, the fact that he committed necrophilia (by his own admission and that of his accomplices), and second, as Bataille has persuasively argued, that he lacked intelligence and the ability to plan. The absolute truth cannot be ascertained from the extant documents, but I would venture a hypothesis that could help justify his presence in the "organized" group. In the first place his necrophilia was relative, because he would perform the sexual act on victims who were dying or just dead but still warm. In other terms, he wanted a passive, helpless partner, but one who would have the attributes of a live being.[115] As for his alleged lack of intelligence, it seems to me that the manifestations of what Bataille calls his "niaiserie" could rather be symptomatic of a personality disorder.

In fact, Gilles fits the portrait of the antisocial personality or sociopath.[116] Granted that his personality traits, when taken singly, cannot serve as irrefutable proof of this theory, nevertheless, when taken as a whole, they strongly suggest this type of disorder. Holmes and De Burger identify sociopathic tendencies as the main component of the personality of the serial killer and, to this end they distinguish the sociopath from the psychopath in that the behavior of this criminal is antisocial in nature, deriving from "an aberrant and socially-defective [. . .] psyche," and avoid suggesting that the serial killer is psychotic, or "mentally ill"

---

113 Bataille, *Le procès*, 276 (see note 3) (from the confession of Poitou). For example, one time Gilles accompanied Poitou to take a child from his home and praised his servant for locating a victim "bel comme un ange," Bataille, *Le procès*, 130, 300 (see note 3) (from the deposition of the victim's mother).

114 At least two of the choir boys were his favorites and Blanchet in his deposition claims that a boy named Perrinet was Gilles's "mignon," apart from Poitou, who was already in his twenties. Bataille, *Le procès*, 271 (see note 3). Note that Gacy was also married twice and a father. Sullivan, *Killer Clown*, 255 (see note 68).

115 In his confession Poitou specifies that. Gilles "commettait ses luxures" on a dead body "tant qu'il restait quelque chaleur." Bataille, *Le procès*, 276 (see note 3).

116 Among the three biographers mentioned in this chapter, only Heers, *Gilles de Rais*, 166–67 (see note 1), dedicates two pages to discussing Gilles's possible mental illness. The only true clinical hypothesis was formulated in 1932 by Robert Soucix, who attributed to him only an "obsession sexuelle et sanguinaire."

in the commonly-understood meaning. This subject is asocial and feels no guilt in breaking collective norms or hurting others; is driven by incontrollable desires; is highly impulsive and shows a tendency to avoid responsibility and social restrictions; is aggressive and tends to react to frustration with fury and assaults against others; and has a warped capacity for love, forming at best only fleeting attachments.[117] There are several theories on the origin of this personality: most researchers attribute it to faulty socialization in the developmental years that blocked the progress of what we call "conscience," for example, by withholding parental affection. However, since there is some vagueness as to what childhood years are formative in this case, and no real explanation of why a malfunctioning family could produce both sociopaths and normal children (like, for example, Gilles's brother René), the only remarkable conclusion that the two authors reach on this topic is that such an environment seems unrelated to socio-economic factors and is found in all social classes.[118]

Framed in such general terms, this profile is not at odds with what is known of Gilles, but does not seem uniquely fitting. However, there is more evidence from other sources. Gilles manifested obvious signs of narcissism, a syndrome allegedly found "to some degree in virtually all individuals with personality disorders." Its symptoms can be summarized as: "grandiosity" (sense of superiority, boastful behavior, arrogance, presence of pretentious fantasies, need for attention and admiration) and "shallow vocational commitment" with "a pattern of early success followed by later mediocrity [and] preoccupation with fantasies of unlimited success."[119] While some of these attitudes (arrogance, boastful behavior) characterize many noblemen of Gilles's age, the presence of all of them in him is strongly suggestive, in particular if one recalls his brief early military success followed by oblivion, his obsession with theatrics and tendency to live in a make-

---

117 Holmes and De Burger, *Serial Murder*, 66–68 (see note 11). The codification of the features of this personality derives from a 1964 study on the criminal mind by McCords. As a practical application, see excerpts of the psychiatric report on Gacy: "a psychopathic (antisocial) personality, with sexual deviation [. . .] Unusual degree of self-reference . . . great need to be loved and admired . . . exploitative . . . charming on the surface, cold and ruthless underneath. . . noticeable absence of feelings of remorse and guilt [. . .] loss of ego-control under the influence of alcohol, drugs, extreme fatigue. . ." but sane to stand trial. Sullivan, *Killer Clown*, 232–33 (see note 68). There is also reference to his narcissism, sadism, egocentrism, need to exert full control over victims, and tendency to rationalization (235). Another psychiatric evaluation concluded that he showed normal intelligence, a tendency to be manipulative, and "total denial of responsibility." Sullivan, *Killer Clown*, 249 (see note 68).

118 Holmes and De Burger, *Serial Murder*, 68–69 (see note 11). The authors caution (80) not to confuse correlation with causation: while it is important to examine the background of those who commit homicides, it would be a mistake to assert that the background is the cause for the homicides.

119 Jonathan D. C. Perry and J. Christopher Perry, *Conflicts, Defenses, and the Stability of Narcissistic Personality Features* (*Psychiatry* 64.4, Winter 2004): 310–30; here 311, 320.

believe world of magic, his grandiose but ill-conceived project of harnessing supernatural forces to achieve success, his irresponsible expenditures, and his over-generous gifts to hangers-on and bare acquaintances (for example, excessive remuneration to a choir boy and the boy's parents).[120] Some have suggested that narcissists are unable "to depend on others, although on the surface they may appear to be 'dependent' because of their strong need for tribute and adoration."[121] This, too, fits Gilles, in whom the need for sadistic violence coexisted with an almost infantile dependency on the thinning ranks of those who accompanied him in his journey to disaster, all of whom lived lavishly at his expenses (for example, Prelati and Bricqueville, into whose hands Gilles left the complete management of his affairs).

If one looks at studies outside criminology, the portrait of the sociopath becomes more complex, the signs of aberration more evident, and Gilles's picture more complete. In his classical work *The Mask of Sanity*, based on his vast clinical experience with this personality disorder, Hervey Cleckley lists sixteen traits, of which at least one-half stand out in Gilles's case: superficial charm, childishness, unreliability, hedonism and egocentricity, markedly eccentric behavior under the influence of alcohol, inability to profit from experience, lack of judgment, and sexual life that is trivial, impersonal, and poorly integrated.[122] While the first seven seem such a perfect fit for him that they do not require any further comment (unreliability may be the reason why, despite his lofty official title, he was not called to participate in any actions on behalf of the king or the duke), the last needs some clarification.

---

120 Bataille, *Le procès*, 113 (see note 3) and Heers, *Gilles de Rais*, 93 (see note 1). He assigned a *rente* worth two hundred *livres* to his favorite choir boy Rossignol and gave two hundred *écus* to the boy's parents. See also Sullivan, *Killer Clown*, 189 (see note 68), on how Gacy would try (in part successfully) to ingratiate his neighbors with Christmas gifts and "huge theme parties." He also posed as a professional clown and at times as a policeman, which indicate a need to playact. His childish behavior was noted by those acquainted with him. Sullivan, *Killer Clown*, 242 (see note 68). On the subject of preference for make-believe see Dahmer's statement "I made my fantasy life more powerful than my real one" cited in Tithecott, *Of Men and Monsters*, 122 (see note 11).

121 Perry and Perry, *Conflicts, Defenses* (see note 119): 310–30. Narcissists also have a low level of inhibition and may manifest severe mood swings and overt anger at being thwarted by others. I do not see direct evidence of abnormal mood swings in Gilles, even if Bossard, *Gilles de Rais*, 117 (see note 1), talks about anger at his failures and alternating hope with despair and Bataille, *Le procès*, 35 (see note 3), talks about mood swings during his trial (which I find rather natural, given that his life was on the line).

122 Harvey Cleckley, M.D., *The Mask of Sanity*, 4th ed. (Saint Louis: The C.V. Mosby Company, 1964), 363, 368–400. On the subject of childishness he notes (208) that sociopaths tend to arouse the maternal instinct of women. Note on the fourth edition: he significantly replaced (8) the older term *psychopathic personality* with *sociopathic personality* in 1955, in line with a change in the official psychiatric nomenclature.

Cleckley suggests that sociopaths in general lack a vigorous libidinous drive that could manifest itself in obsessive erotic forms like masochism, sadism, bestiality, and so forth. But he adds that, given the sociopath's propensity for unacceptable behavior (for example, the tendency to seek sexual gratification "in sordid surroundings with persons of low intellectual or social status"), he needs much less stimulation to indulge in deviant sexual practices. Therefore, in the rare cases when a sociopath is also a sadist he is a very dangerous criminal. He concludes with the ominous statement that people of this sort "are often responsible for perverse and murderous attacks on children."[123] It is evident from the trial records that Gilles's sexual practices ranged from the normal (with his wife and with consenting male partners) to the extremely perverse. Additionally, the latter occurred in the presence of paraphilia, what psychiatrists define as the "recurrent, intense, sexually arousing fantasies" involving fetishes (in his case, body part); the need for humiliation (the initial frightening of the victim with staged hanging); the presence of children or other non-consenting partners; frotteurism and exhibitionism (he masturbated in the presence of victims and servants); sadism and voyeurism (he reached the highest excitement in watching the victim's agony and death).[124]

A major trait of the sociopathic personality is the presence of "capricious irresponsibility," disloyalty, absence of remorse, and in general "poverty in major affective reactions." The sociopath may display "spite, quick and labile flashes of quasi-affection, peevish resentment, shallow moods of self-pity, and [. . .] showy poses of indignation," but is incapable of mature anger, of "honest, solid grief, sustaining pride, deep joy, and genuine despair."[125] While the bishop and his court seemed to have taken at face value Gilles's theatrical display of tears and remorse, these were more likely the result of impulsive playacting. After all, Gilles was conscious of his guilt when he tried to bully his way out of the trial by attacking his judges; then, once cornered, when he attempted to skirt the real issue of his crimes and tried to steer the court toward the lesser charge of having abused alchemy (a ploy, incidentally, noted by Bossard); and lastly, once it was clear that the judges had had enough of his games and threatened torture, when he launched into a tearful confession counting on their paternal instincts. All of these changes

---

123 Cleckley, *Mask of Sanity*, 320–21, 394–99 (see note 122).

124 Michael B. First, M.D. and Robert L. Halon, Ph.D., "Use of DSM Paraphilia Diagnoses in Sexually Violent Predator Commitment Cases," *Journal of the American Academy of Psychiatry, Law*, 36.4 (2008): 443–54.

125 Cleckley, *Mask of Sanity*, 281, 380 (see note 122). In fact, sociopaths almost never commit suicide (393). Compare Gilles's overconfident behavior to that of Henriet, who confessed having attempted suicide after his arrest. Bossard, *Gilles de Rais*, 194 (see note 1), Bataille, *Le procès*, 156, 326 (see note 3) (from the confession of Henriet: he specifies having tried to cut his own throat to avoid interrogation) and Heers, *Gilles de Rais*, 179 (see note 1).

occurred in a matter of days, and I doubt that they followed a true strategy. Rather, like a truant child, he went through a series of ad-hoc survival maneuvers.[126]

Cleckley also talks of the sociopath's extreme lack of insight and self-appraisal, to a degree seldom found in psychotic patients, despite his freedom from delusions. When cornered, he uses pretexts and rationalizations, that is, a "mimicry of insight."[127] A dramatic example of this is Gilles's tortuous response to Pierre de l'Hôpital's question of why he had committed his criminal acts. His initial reaction was one of annoyance, and he quipped, "Come on, sir, you torment me and yourself." Only after the other persisted did he respond, "Truly, there are no other reasons than what I already told you, and what I told you is more than enough to execute ten thousand men."[128] This second answer, which in effect amounts to saying that he had acted entirely of his own will and for his own pleasure, seems to be dictated more by a need to move beyond the question than by genuine insight. In fact, he acted as if he had no idea of what the judge wanted to know, because it had never occurred to him that he should have any motives at all. At times he seemed to exhibit a glimmering of perception of the compulsive nature of his acts of violence. For example, he had made occasional statements to his servants to the effect that he planned to make a clean break and undertake an expiatory pilgrimage to Jerusalem (a plan—typically—never materialized). He appears also to have sensed that there was something sick about his behavior, but could not stop himself, and so he breezily explained that his ruling planet made him commit crimes that could not be understood by others.[129]

Almost as if to contradict Bossard, Cleckley warns against trusting sociopaths on the basis of their outward social graces. They can appear attentive in small courtesies and favors, and even behave generously when the cost is not decisive. But they are prone to squandering family wealth with their inability to follow a life

---

126 Bossard, 107, 230 (see note 1). The lack of planning in his defense was also noted by Bataille, *Le procès*, 35 (see note 3).

127 Cleckley, *Mask of Sanity*, 383–84 (see note 122).

128 The actual text, in old French among the original Latin, goes, "Hélas! monseigneur, vous vous tourmentez et moy avecques [. . .] Vrayement il n'y avoit autre cause, fin ne intencion que ce que je vous ay dit: je vous ay dit de plus grans choses que n'est cest cy et assez pour faire mourir dix mille hommes." Bataille, *Le procès*, 239, note no. 1 and 3 (see note 3) (from the confession of Gilles de Rais). Earlier he had admitted committing his crimes "suivant son imagination et sa pensée, sans le conseil de personne, et selon son propre sens, seulement pour son plaisir et sa délectation charnelle, et non pour quelque autre intention ou quelque autre fin." Bataille, *Le procès*, 165 (see note 3).

129 The "acte d'accusation" summarizes thus Gilles's recidivism after vain talks of contrition and pilgrimages: "le chien retourne à son vomi." Bataille, *Le procès*, 218 (see note 3). Astrological influence as determinant for the future serial killer was also claimed in the case of the "Coed Killer." Fisher, *Killer Among Us*, 73 (see note 11).

plan, and display their pathological condition in other aspects of life (for example, in their outlandish behavior while intoxicated, well beyond what is observable in true alcoholics), and eventually may end up failing "with spectacular and bizarre splendor."[130] In a society used to drinking, Gilles's abuse of alcohol was a recurring theme in the testimonies of his accomplices and his own (in fact, he attributed to it, in part, his murderous behavior). And his tendency to waste his fortune has sufficiently been discussed.

Finally, Cleckley pointedly differentiates the sociopath's modus operandi from that of the "ordinary criminal." In the first place, the latter pursues his own ends with his criminal acts, while the sociopath "almost never works consistently in crime or in anything else to achieve a permanent position of power or wealth or security." Second, the criminal's ends, even if the methods are illicit, are understandable to the average person, while the sociopath will "deliberately throw away so much in order to seek what is very trivial [. . .] and very ephemeral." Third, the criminal will try to spare himself risks and harm others, while the sociopath may incidentally cause trouble for others, but usually places himself in a "shameful and most uncomfortable" position. Lastly, the few sociopaths who indulge in serious criminal activity seem to do so without taking into consideration the consequences of their actions.[131] From Cleckley's arguments Jean de Craon could easily be considered an ordinary criminal (as argued by Bataille), while Gilles, in all activities undergone on his own initiative, seems to have squandered what he had rather than acting purposefully to acquire more.[132]

The utter senselessness of his criminal activities speaks to his incredible lack of judgment. For example, had he been an "ordinary criminal" he would have insisted that Prelati show him some results for his investment of time and money; or after kidnapping and abusing children he could have killed them to prevent them from disclosing his treatment of them. But we know that none of this crossed Gilles's sick mind: the invocation of demons seems to have become an end in itself, perhaps even an excuse to keep Prelati close, with the pursuit of wealth a secondary objective, and the killing was—in his own words—the best part of a fleeting excitement. Further, the Le Ferron incident has not been explained by any historian using logical arguments, and can only become understandable within a pathological framework. It would be even more difficult to try to explain in logical terms why Gilles continued his murderous activity after the first accusatory letter of the bishop became public. But the ultimate question that an ordinary criminal would ask of Gilles is: why did he not flee like Bricqueville and Sillé, given that he

130 Cleckley, *Mask of Sanity*, 387, 388, 390–92, 400 (see note 122).

131 Cleckley, *Mask of Sanity*, 276–77 (see note 122).

132 Bataille, *Le procès*, 29 (see note 3). He calls attention to the contrast between the old man's purposeful violence and the young one's childish brutality.

had the same information as they did prior to his arrest, and that he knew himself guilty of murder?

To summarize, in the modern judicial system the ambivalence of perception about the serial killer—super-intelligent, rational criminal or maladjusted deviant—is always present, with cultural currents favoring one or the other view. But even after routine psychiatric evaluation, the accused is usually deemed competent to stand trial, because nothing in the sociopath's behavior points to inability to perceive the reality of murder, and the verdict is usually "guilty." The medieval system resolved somewhat the ambiguity by compartmentalizing the procedure against the accused. Consequently, the moral aspect of Gilles's activities came under the jurisdiction of the ecclesiastical court while his criminal actions came under that of the secular court. But, as it is true of modern serial killers, in both courts he was judged to be solely responsible for his behavior, an interpretation in which he concurred, even if his explanation for his motives was (typically for a sociopath) superficial and childish. It is however evident from the very discrepancy in extant documentation, which is much more abundant for the ecclesiastical trial, that the key judgment that established Gilles's reputation rested with the bishop's court.

Two attitudes of this court, in particular, may surprise modern readers. The first is a (refreshingly) rational position toward the victims and their families. For example, there was no attempt to attribute to the families part of the responsibility for their children's murders, even if most families had willingly allowed their children to come into Gilles's clutches for money. In contrast, some witnesses at Williams's trial in Atlanta openly accused the parents of being participants to the murders of their children for having allowed the latter too much freedom in the streets. And at Dahmer's trial some members of the press and police blamed the victims themselves for having brought about their death with their "risky" lifestyle.[133]

The second stance of the ecclesiastical court that seems most at odd with modern practices is that of consenting to the ritual of mass reconciliation that was staged to coincide with the execution. Bataille, in particular, has raised doubts about the sincerity of this event, which many might have attended against their will or with

133 Tithecott, *Of Men and Monsters*, 70–72 (see note 11), cites a policeman's statement that Dahmer's victims were "criminal facilitating victims" who chose a risky life style. Fisher, *Killer Among Us*, 143 (see note 11), states that a n FBI agent accused the parents of the Atlanta victims of murdering them because they were "nuisances." He observes (16) that among the modern public there is the tendency to blame victims of assaults and murder who have been selected for their lifestyle (prostitutes, drifters, and homosexuals), in an attempt at relieving the public of collective responsibility. In Gilles's society the sight of boys wandering alone or in groups outside the home and taking care of themselves was not perceived in such negative terms. See, for example, Robert Muchembled, *L'invention de l'homme moderne* (Paris: Fayard, 1988), 296–306.

the secret intent of praying for Gilles's damnation. I think that this collective drama, so alien to our society and which leaves Bataille perplexed, was potentially therapeutic, as it offered a symbolic "closure" of the case also for the bereaved families by placing them—so to speak—in control of the culprit's eternal destiny.[134] On the other hand, during and after some of the most spectacular trials of modern serial killers, the community's wounds seem to be almost perversely reopened as the courtroom drama and its aftermaths are kept alive with endless televised sessions, sale of confessions and other memorabilia, television interviews with anyone remotely associated with the culprit's activities, and the inevitable flurry of law suits.[135]

Tithecott suggests that the public has a need to mythify the serial killer, and make him larger than life (for example, by accepting without question the claim that Dahmer was a cannibal or that Jack the Ripper was an important person somehow connected with the royal court).[136] However nothing indicates that Gilles's contemporaries, after the atonement of his crimes, felt the need to mythify this repulsive figure. Too weak to stand the test of collective memory on his own, a fuzzy remembrance of his crimes has survived in the late Breton legend of Bluebeard, the fearsome nobleman who marries a series of young women only to murder them, with its sanitized and conveniently distorted facts to satisfy

---

134 Bataille, *Le procès,* 77 (see note 3), is baffled by the fact that the court and audience seem to have been moved by Gilles's tears and judges them naïve. Bossard, *Gilles de Rais,* 263 (see note 1), reminds the reader that attendance at public executions was an obligation for heads of households, and takes Gilles's repentance (229, 238) and the bishop's grace (199–200) at face value, stating that after passing sentence "le prêtre prend la place du juge." Heers, *Gilles de Rais,* 204 (see note 1), notes that everyone seemed to have taken part in the procession and pray as expected. In contrast, see the comments of Holmes and De Burger, *Serial Murder,* 143–44 (see note 11), on the anger and sense of betrayal experienced by modern survivors of serial killers, who feel that all resources of society (included psychiatric counseling) are devoted to the killer himself and not to them.

135 Fisher, *Killer Among Us,* 195–98 (see note 11), Tithecott, *Of Men and Monsters,* 125–28 (see note 11). Commercial exploitation of serial killers is not a recent phenomenon, however. After the series of murders of prostitutes attributed to Jack the Ripper in 1888 stopped, the residents of Whitechapel set up refreshment stands at the murder sites to cater to the curious. Fisher, *Killer Among Us,* 209 (see note 11).

136 Tithecott, *Of Men and Monsters,* 65–66 (see note 11), states that Dahmer himself mentioned cannibalism (he allegedly fried and ate a biceps from a victim). But, despite the flurry of stories about his cannibalistic activity, the police reported no conclusive evidence that he had ever engaged in it. Tithecott, however, supplies (86) a curious statistic: out of a group of thirty serial killers, seven were found to be involved in the food business. For additional myths on cannibalism see Allison P. Coudert, "The Ultimate Crime: Cannibalism in Early Modern Minds and Imaginations" in the present volume. As for the various hypotheses on the identity of Jack the Ripper (among the suspects was the duke of Clarence) see Fisher, *Killer Among Us,* 214 (see note 11).

Romantic tastes.[137] As for the reaction of his contemporaries, we are only left with the terse comments of chroniclers. For example, Enguerrand de Monstrelet, who is usually concise and noncommittal in his reporting, states in few sentences that the marshal of France had been accused of heresy and confessed killing several children and pregnant women [sic] to write with their blood books of "diabolical formulas," in order to acquire honors and power. Before being executed he had made a "beautiful and devout" confession asking God's forgiveness. Breton nobles were saddened by his end because "before this calamity happened to him [he] had enjoyed a great reputation as a brave knight." And Jacques Chartier, the official French historiographer notorious for his tendency to whitewash scandals, opens with a concise mention of the execution, ordered by the duke of Brittany. He then briefly adds that Gilles had been accused of the murder of several children, and, having succumbed to the devil, performed acts against the faith through the advice of one of his servants (perhaps a reference to Prelati). Before being hanged "it was said that he repented quite well."[138] Both writers represented what we may call the "establishment" (Monstrelet the gentry and Chartier the Church), and predictably enough they cautiously avoided the details of Gilles's murders and trial, which have so captivated modern audiences.[139] They chose instead to freeze in time, with much exaggeration, Gilles's early chivalric exploits, and delve on his face-saving confession.

In conclusion, I would argue that, while it makes sense to use the known facts about Gilles de Rais as valuable tools to reconstruct the life of an average late-

137 Of the three historians only Bossard, *Gilles de Rais*, 293–325 (see note 1), ties explicitly the legend of Bluebeard with the real Gilles. There are two versions of the late legend. The first is contained in a nineteenth-century Breton ballad: the baron de Rais has killed all his wives and terrorizes the local girls, but an old man, who reveals himself as Jean de Malestroit, promises justice. In the second the evil lord Gilles de Laval, after killing his seven wives and burying them under his castle, is host to a count and his beautiful fiancée Blanche. Suddenly he has the count thrown into a dungeon and forces Blanche to the altar to make her his eighth wife. After some resistance she accepts to marry him, but in that instant she turns into a blue demon that changes Gilles's beard from red to blue and announces his eternal damnation under the name of Bluebeard. See also Bataille, *Le procès*, 182–84 (see note 3) (who notices how the legend has incorporated some correct details that emerged from the trial).

138 ["conjurations dyaboliques [. . .] belle et dévotte [. . .] avant que ceste adventure lui advenist, il estoit moult renommé d'estre très vaillant chevalier"] *La Chronique d'Enguerran de Monstrelet*, ed. L. Douët-d'Arcq, 6 vols. (Paris: 1857–1863), 5:425–26. ["et disoit-on qu'il eut bien bonne repentance"] Jean Chartier, *Chroniques de Charles VII, roi de France*, ed. A. Vallet de Viriville, 3 vols. (Paris: P. Jannet Libraire, 1858), 2: 5–6. Bossard, *Gilles de Rais*, 54 (see note 1), suggests that Chartier might have been part of Gilles's court. For Chartier's avoidance of "gossip," see, for example, his almost ridiculous denial of the liaison between Charles VII and his famous mistress Agnès Sorel (Chartier, 2:182–86).

139 This fact was noted by Heers, *Gilles de Rais*, 141 (see note 1).

medieval baron (as Heers did), nevertheless he was not an average person with average responses to the precarious nature of feudal life.[140] Nor was he an exceptionally gifted young man whose curiosity and daring brought him to play with fire (Bossard's thesis), a brave knight who suddenly turned to crime, a fallen angel, or a victim of over-indulgence and alcoholism. I would even deviate—if less strongly—from Bataille's thesis that he was a stupid person with a criminal mind encouraged by a brutal society that glorified aggression, because his particular brand of criminality was universally condemned.[141] He was a murderer for half of his life and his entire adult life, who was able to fit marginally into society (which in his day implied a certain level of violence) just as other serial killers have done by exploiting the tendency of average people to avoid confronting disturbing suspicions. His behavior was not within the accepted limits in his day any more than it is in modern times, and the reaction of authorities, when eventually faced with it, was to hang him like a common criminal.[142] However, given the medieval belief in individual responsibility, horror at his crimes did not trickle down to his family or contaminate his surroundings. Both his widow and daughter soon contracted marriages with powerful men who would (at least for a while) protect their rights, and his castles, even when they had been the theater of murders, were preserved and later acquired (while, for example, the apartment complex where Dahmer had resided was emptied and later razed).[143]

Tithecott suggests that "serial murders have a certain literary quality to them," as they "happen regularly over time and each new one creates an expectation; they

---

140 Bataille, *Le procès*, 26 (see note 3), summarizes his environment in these terms, "un chaos contradictoire de calculs, de violences, de bonne humeur, de désordre sanglant, d'angoisse mortelle et d'absence de souci."

141 Along these lines Bossard, *Gilles de Rais*, 132 (see note 1), affirms that the acts of perversion and cruelty practiced by Gilles and accomplices surpassed those of all other sorcerers in contemporary accounts.

142 This was noted by Bossard, *Gilles de Rais*, 268 (see note 1).

143 To protect her dowry, his widow Catherine de Thouars married in 1441 (a few months after her husband's execution) Jean de Vendôme, *vidame* of Chartres and chamberlain of the duke. On the other hand, to prevent the family's French possessions from being added to the duke's territories, the king took upon himself to arrange the marriage of Gilles's young daughter Marie (the marriage was stipulated in 1442 and took place in 1444). As soon as she turned fourteen she was married to the admiral of France Prégent de Coëtivy, who (perhaps to please the bride) made a half-hearted attempt to obtain the rehabilitation of his deceased father-in-law. After the admiral's death at the siege of Cherbourg, Marie married her cousin André de Laval-Lohéac, one of the authors of the *Mémoires des héritiers*. She died childless in 1457 and the barony of Rais passed to Gilles's brother René de la Suze. Bossard, *Gilles de Rais*, 283–92 (see note 1), Bataille, *Le procès*, 174–75 (see note 3), and Heers, *Gilles de Rais*, 211–13 (see note 1). On the other hand, the entire housing complex of which Dahmer's apartment was part was razed as the site itself assumed "an evil aura." Fisher, *Killer Among Us*, 19, 190 (see note 11). Simon Kemp, *Medieval Psychology* (New York: Greenwood Press, 1990), 159 explains that the importance of individual responsibility in medieval mind was likely related to the concept of individual salvation.

involve plot, a consummate villain and an absolutely pure [. . .] victim."[144] And Fisher observes that although rare, serial murder receives "inordinate attention in the media" and in academic studies, which may be the reason why so much material is available on them.[145] This attitude may have been present also in Gilles's days, with the (lucky) result that enough material has been preserved on his crimes and punishment to build a fairly complete sketch of this individual. In fact, I would suggest that the main difference between his case and similar modern ones rests on the amount and quality of data pertaining to the victims. But the records collected during Gilles's own case compare quite favorably with modern ones as means to shed light into the psyche of the perpetrator. Or, to turn the argument upside-down, we do not necessarily "know" Dahmer or Williams any better as a person than we "know" Gilles.[146] What has contributed to the recent volume of research on serial killers is the fact that sufficient information has been collected from enough cases to be able to trace a pattern of personality, modus operandi, and behavior before and after arrest and during trial to place these criminals in a category of their own. To that end, the extant records on Gilles de Rais do shed enough light on his mentality and criminal methods to reserve for him a place in the annals of criminology as a sociopathic killer. In addition, they permit the modern reader to complete a coherent psychological portrait that incorporates collateral personality traits (such as narcissism, irresponsibility, and inability to manage his affairs) whose significance, if taken singly and in the absence of his murderous activities, could have been overlooked in building his profile.[147]

144 Tithecott, *Of Men and Monsters*, 122–23 (see note 11).

145 *Killer Among Us*, 13, 17 (see note 11). He deems the flurry of academic studies on this topic a "type of collective defense mechanism."

146 The serial killer may contribute information about the mentality of a person like himself in general terms, not necessarily via any personal reference. For example Ted Bundy, a charming Law student who was convicted of killing several women between 1974 and 1978, was ready to concede an informative interview in prison, but during it he always referred to hypothetical serial killers "whom he had known," not to himself, as he claimed his innocence. Yet he was very talkative and insightful. Holmes and De Burger, *Serial Murder*, 134–36 (see note 11).

147 Editor's note: Ben Parsons, "Sympathy for the Devil: Gilles de Rais and His Modern Apologists," *Fifteenth-Century Studies* 37 (2012): 113–37, observes that Gilles's contemporaries paid surprisingly little attention to his massive number of murdering of children, and that instead he was made into a mythical figure associated with evil. "In effect the transformation of Gilles into a wife-killing ogre is another manifestation of medieval indifference to his crimes. The *lais* and pantomimes can afford to dispense with the nature of his actions because it is not significant for them: it is enough that he is regarded as evil in a general sense, and the fact that he targeted childrenis unimportant for these texts and their audiences" (129).

Chapter 16

John Beusterien
(Texas Tech University, Lubbock)

The Celebratory Conical Hat in *La Celestina*

Let's begin by pointing out two apparently unrelated instances of the conical hat: one as headgear of celebration and one as headgear for the Klan. People wear brightly colored conical hats for birthday parties and every year people in Louisiana dress up with large colored conical hats for Courir de Mardi Gras, a traditional Mardi Gras event held in many Cajun communities of south Louisiana on the Tuesday before Ash Wednesday. In contrast to these celebration events, in the early twentieth century the Ku Klux Klan adopted the white conical hat as part of its costume. Early versions of the Klan's use of the conical hat can be first seen in the film *Birth of a Nation.*

The conical hat's early function as sign of humiliation provides an explanation for how it became headgear of the Klan *and* party headwear. Ever since the Middle Ages, wearing a large conical hat was a sign of public shame.[1] The punished and the penitent wore the hat in public, marked as sinner or criminal in a show of public shame. In Spain, it was worn in the parades by brotherhoods (*hermandades*) dressed as hooded penitents during Holy Week (parades that still can be seen today across southern Spain) and, following its function as marker of a brotherhood, the Ku Klux Klan adopted the Spanish hooded penitent costume.[2]

---

1 I should mention that, in contrast to the conical hat, authorities also made punished men go bareheaded (they could not cover their head), another sign of public humiliation in the medieval period. I would like to thank Rosa A. Perez, another contributor to this volume, for this information.

2 For more on the Spanish-Klan connection, see Donald Robert Beagle and Bryan Albin Giemza, *Poet of the Lost Cause: A Life of Father Ryan* (Knoxville: University of Tennessee Press. 2008), 169.

As a response to the penitent that wore the hat in imitation of public shaming during Holy Week, the hat was worn in festivity and celebration to open the Lent season. The world-upside-down celebration of carnival radically altered the conical hat's meaning as punishment and penitence. In carnival, the sign of the sinner transformed into the sign of saved, the sign of the outcast transformed into the sign of inclusion, and the sign of public shame transformed into the sign of a party. Since the conical hat had meaning as a sign of self-inflicted punishment when worn by penitents during the sacred time of Lent—Holy Week and the remembrance of Christ's passion and public humiliation—people turned its value as sign of public shame into that of festive icon in the costume for carnival at the beginning of Lent.

Understanding the history of the conical hat as sign of public shame helps elucidate how it evolved into a festive hat and, alternatively, the headgear of one of the most dreadful groups that blot U.S. history. The following essay first examines how the Spanish use of the conical hat in public punishment was one of the most significant post-medieval instances of the conical hat as a sign of public shame. The Spanish, in fact, kept the practice alive after the medieval period and were directly and indirectly responsible for its more recent permutations as headgear in festivities and for the Klan.

After examining its history in the Spanish context, this essay takes up the conical hat as a sign of public shame in *La Celestina,* a classic late fifteenth-century work from Spain about a woman who procures sex for men and who has a brothel with prostitutes. Essentially I want to argue that the story of the conical hat in *La Celestina* reflects the principal character Celestina's desire to convert the hat into a sign of celebration. Celestina yearns for the hat not to signify punishment, but rather female power. The hat for Celestina reflects her nostalgia for a time in which female friendship, female midwifery, and female authority were not demonized, but practiced in broad daylight.

One late permutation of the conical hat as sign of punishment was the dunce cap. The practice of punishing students with a dunce cap did not begin until the nineteenth century—one of the earliest appearances of the word in English was chapter 24 of Charles Dicken's 1840 novel *The Old Curiousity Shop.*[3] But early manifestations of the dunce cap as sign of public shame, often including ass's ears, formed part of the medieval punishment spectacle across Europe. Medieval canon law often included punishments that consisted of putting people in the pillory with a cone hat that depicted the wearer's crime and scenes of damnation. In early fourteenth-century France, one source records that the punished individual had

3 See Charles Dickens, *The Old Curiosity Shop* (http://dickens.thefreelibrary.com/The-Old-Curiosity-Shop/1-24; last accessed 5 March 2012).

to wear a "parchment crown on which the cause of his condemnation was written in large red letters."[4]

Just as it began dying out in Europe as a form a punishment, the tradition of the cone hat as public punishment spectacle began to flourish in early modern Spain. The hat would form an essential part of the punishment ceremony instituted by the Inquisition. The sambenito was a special uniform that served as part of punishment instituted by the Spanish Inquisition. The sambenito comes from the combined Spanish words *saco bendito* or holy sack. In medieval Christian tradition, the outcast and sinner wore a hair shirt or sack cloth and *saco* in this Spanish context indicates that the heretic wore the sack garment that calls attention to his fallen condition. The *saco benito* uniform was not complete without the large conical hat. The robe often had a black cross painted on it and the hat often had flames, indicating the infernal destination of the heretic. The painted conical hat left the face exposed because public shaming constituted the crux of the punishment. Significantly and in contrast to the conical hat's punishment function, when the conical hat and *saco* were adopted by penitent brotherhood groups, the face was generally covered by a hood, preserving the penitent's anonymity (the same Spanish public penitent uniform of conical hat, covered face, and robes with a cross can be seen in the costume in the Klan figures in *The Birth of the Nation*).

The visual display of the sixteenth-century sambenito costume in Spain was not limited to the moment of sentencing of the accused. Initially, the heretic, forced to wear the long robe traversed by a black cross and a large conical hat, was exposed to scorn and derision and put on display in the town square, but that costume would have a life that outlived its wearer. After its immediate utility had passed, the sambenito was often hung up in the parish church, accompanied by an inscription intended to humiliate the wearer and family. The display of the sambenito hung in churches inspired the practice of hanging a cloth in churches that listed heretical names.

The Inquisition released the names of the people that had been tried and wrote them on a "manta" (a large cloth or "blanket") in a conspicuous place in the church. The sambenito also spawned a social craze as manifest in the dissemination of "green" books that consisted of the names of those tried by the Inquisition read aloud in parishes. In the popular tradition, some of the green books were also known as "Stains and Sambenitos of Noble Lineages."[5] The

---

4 Monique Langlois and Yvonne Lanhers, *Confessions et jugements de criminels au parlement de Paris (1319–1350)* (Paris: S. E. V. E. N., 1971), 156. I would like to thank Jolanta N. Komorrnicka, another contributor to this volume, for this reference.

5 See Francisco de Mendoza y Bobadilla, *El tizón de la nobleza española o máculas y sambenitos de sus linajes* (Barcelona: La Selecta, 1880). For more on the tradition of name slandering, green books,

conical hat began as standard Inquisitional punishment in the sixteenth century and still could be found in early nineteenth century. Goya explores the shaming punishment of the sambenito on two occasions. In his *Inquisitional Tribunal Questioning Heretics* (1812–1819), the accused wear painted hats and one sits on a platform in front of the audience of the court. In another Goya ink and brush piece produced in the same period, the heretic penitent covers his face, the locus of shame, wearing the sambenito gown and conical hat.

Even though the sambenito did not develop into a full-fledged institutional punishment practice that slandered family names linked to unorthodox religious practice until the sixteenth century, sambenito logic already affected and influenced the author of the *La Celestina* in the fifteenth century. Fernando de Rojas had family members tried by the Inquisition. The Inquisition sentenced his father as a Judaizer in 1488, burning him alive at the stake. Rojas indirectly suggests his concern with these events when Celestina recalls the history of Claudina. Celestina's best friend was Claudina and she often remembers her fondly in the work. After describing the conical hat punishment of Claudina, Celestina states "they made her confess to being what she wasn't,"[6] a reference that evokes the forced and coerced religious conversions occurring when Rojas was writing.[7]

Despite the suggested connections between the conical hat in *La Celestina* and the sambenito headgear, my interest in the *La Celestina* is not an attempt to link Rojas to religious heterodoxy. Rather, my primary interest is to perform a close reading of the text in order to examine Celestina's depiction of the conical hat.[8] Women transferred the meaning of the conical hat in the fifteenth century into their own

the "manta," and sambenitos, see John Beusterien, "Blotted Genealogies: A Survey of the *libros verdes*," *Bulletin of Hispanic Studies* (2001): 183–97.

6 Fernando de Rojas, *La Celestina: Comedia o tragicomedia de Calisto y Melibea*, ed. Peter Russell (Madrid: Castalia, 1991), 369: "la hizieron aquella vez confessar lo que no era." English translations are from Peter Bush, trans., Fernando de Rojas, *Celestina*, intro. Juan Goytisolo (New York: Penguin, 2010), 82.

7 Stephen Gilman has interpreted this quote by suggesting that Claudina has been punished by the Inquisition. See *The Spain of Fernando de Rojas* (Princeton: Princeton University Press, 1972). Peter Russel, in turn, points out that Gilman's conclusion may be unfounded since the Inquisition still had not taken over the jurisdiction in such matters. See Peter Russell, *Temas de La Celestina y otros estudios: Del Cid al Quijote* (Barcelona: Ariel, 1978), 367.

8 The interest in the hat itself in this chapter follows on the work of Hispanists of the early modern period that seeks to examine costume history and material culture. For further reading on different approaches to these two critical inquiries, see: Barbara Fuchs, *Exotic Nation: Maurophilia and the Construction of Early Modern Spain* (Philadelphia: University of Pennsylvania Press. 2009); Enrique García Santo-Tomás, *Modernidad bajo sospecha: Salas Barbadillo y la cultura material del siglo XVII* (Madrid: Consejo Superior de Investigaciones Científicas, 2008); and Laura Bass, *The Drama of the Portrait: Theater and Visual Culture in Early Modern Spain* (University Park: Penn State University Press, 2008).

fashion item. This conical hat, known as the henin, also included a hanging veil.[9] In Celestina's case, as the title of this chapter suggests, Celestina does not make the conical hat a sign of fashion, but invests a unique pride in the hat and, I will argue in what follows, she celebrates it as an icon of women's power and her friendship with Claudina.[10]

The conical hat was a shaming punishment reserved for the social outcast, but, in the context of the plot of *La Celestina,* the hat is specifically a punishment for witch practice. Celestina tells the servant Pármeno that

> (t)he first time they accused (Claudina) of being a witch because they'd caught her at night collecting earth by a crossroads by candlelight, and they put her in the stocks to be pilloried in the town square for half a day, with a painted cone on her head.[11]

Rojas wrote at a time when, fueled by publications like the witch-hunting guide *Malleus Malificarum* (1484), religious and political institutions across Europe were stepping up their persecution of witches. In Spain, civil law code demanded that a witch be sentenced to death by fire. Religious law (that is, the canonical law out of which many Inquisition punishments would develop) classified two types of witches. The *bruja* worshipped the devil and was often charged with fornicating with him while the *hechicera* did not worship the devil, but held certain powers over him.[12]

The first scholar to comment on the *La Celestina,* an anonymous sixteenth-century Spanish churchman, notes that the reference to the conical hat in *La Celestina* is an example of a witch punishment as described in canonical law. The anonymous churchman writes that the punishment of Claudina and the conical hat scene in *La Celestina* are an example in which the witch is placed on a platform in public spectacle and is "mitered."[13] Antonio de Nebrija, writing at the time of the publication of *La Celestina,* further glosses the notion of "mitering" by writing

---

9 Hilda Amphlett, *Hats: A History of Fashion in Headwear* (London: Richard Sadler Ltd., 1974), 55–56.

10 This study examines Celestina's personal view of Claudina and not the rhetorical strategies employed in her description of Claudina. Joseph Snow has focused on how Celestina's memory of Claudina forms part of rhetorical strategy that is designed to manipulate and to win over Pármeno's favor. Snow argues that the memory of his mother Claudina only angers Pármeno since the story makes him aware of his ignoble heritage. The Claudina story ultimately backfires on Celestina since Pármeno stabs Celestina out of rage and humiliation. See "Celestina's Claudina," *Hispanic Studies in Honor of Alan D. Deyermond: A North American Tribute,* ed. John S. Miletich (Madison: Hispanic Seminary of Medieval Studies, 1986), 257–77.

11 Fernando de Rojas, *La Celestina,* 367: "Y aun la una le levantaron que era bruxa, porque la hallaron de noche con unas candelillas, cogendo tierra de una encruzijada, y la tovieron medio día en una escalera en la plaça, puesto uno como rocadero pintado en la cabeça." English translation Bush, *Celestina,* 82 (see note 6).

12 See Russell, *Temas de La Celestina,* 330 (see note 7).

13 *Celestina comentada,* ed. Louise Fothergill-Payne, Enrique Fernández Rivera, Peter Fothergill-Payne (Salamanca: Universidad de Salamanca, 2002).

that the conical hat is also called a *mitra sclerata* a terminology that translates as "cursed" or "damning" miter.[14]

Painting infernal images on the damning miter (both in the punishment of witches and other religious heretics such as *conversos*) contrasted with the religious practice of painting holy images on the religious miter. Parishioners began to see their highest religious figures wearing a cone hat with the institutionalization of the miter as headgear in the thirteenth century. In medieval Christianity, while the crown signaled the head of the sovereign ruler, a long, often conical, hat signaled religious authority. The pope or bishop wore a miter, an elaborate headdress often painted with images of sacred scenes.

Headgear that served as emblem of salvation took on more majestic significance in Spain in the fifteenth and sixteenth century. The painted miter, amplifying the human head as a vehicle for the observer to comprehend heaven and make its wearer an exemplary celestial figure, became especially magnificent at the beginning of Spain's tenure as world power. In *The Burial of Count Orgaz* (1586–1588), one of El Greco's most famous works, Saint Augustine has come down from heaven to assist in the burial of Count of Orgaz, wearing an embroidered garment with images and a magnificent gold miter.

The El Greco miter is only a represented image, but many real early Spanish miters still exist, such as the famed sixteenth-century Escorial miter. The Escorial miter contains a Mexican feather mosaic arranged to resemble a stained glass window. Its textile support portrays multiple iconographic images, including: Christ's Redemption of Humanity; episodes of Christ's Passion; the Crucifixion; the Resurrection; the Ascension of Christ; the Last Judgment; the Assumption and Coronation of the Virgin Mary; and the Holy Trinity. Aside from these images, more than two hundred human faces are represented in the multicolored composition on the miter.[15]

The Escorial miter on the head of the sacred authoritative figure and its images served as a vehicle directing the religious observer toward the heavenly realm. In contrast, the painted cursed miter became a sign of its wearer's infernal connection just as the sacred painted miter signaled its wearer's celestial connection. Specifically, in *La Celestina*, the *mitra sclerata* would not have portrayed images of sacred scenes and the road to heaven, but a description of Claudina's sins as witch and images that conjured hell. John Mabbe's 1631 English translation of the

---

14 See the entry "coroza," in Lidio Nieto Jiménez and Manuel Alvar Ezquerra, ed., *Nuevo tesoro lexicográfico del español (s. XIV – 1726)*, vol. 4. (Madrid: Arco Libros, 2007), 2968.

15 Teresa Ortiz Salazar, "The Feather Adarga of Phillip II and the Escorial Miter," *Nuevo mundo, mundos nuevos* (1–25–2006; http://nuevomundo.revues.org/pdf/1468; last accessed on March 5, 2012).

Claudina passage highlights the conical hat's role as head ornament that contains damning text and image. Mabbe describes the cone hat as "a high paper Hat painted full of Divels, whereon her fault was written."[16]

Faulting not only Claudina, but also Celestina, the first sixteenth-century scholar to write about *La Celestina* begins a long moralizing critical tradition that understands *La Celestina* as witch worthy of contempt. Indeed, that scholar argues that her name is a borrowing of *scelus*, the same Latin root word that gives *sclerata*. This paper, however, diverges from the critical tradition that understands Celestina as part of the "bad witch" tradition, that is, that envisions as her morally retrograde.[17] Instead, it conceives *La Celestina* in general and the conical hat specifically within the context of a "good witch" tradition, that is, a tradition in which the word "Celestina" does not point to the Latin word meaning "damned," but rather a Latin word that connects her to the stars or the celestial.

Celestina remembers the time that her beloved friend Claudina had once worn the cone hat with pride. Celestina reminisces about the fact that her friend Claudina wore the hat in broad daylight in front of onlookers and did not feel shame. Celestina, in a posthumous panegyric for Claudina, recalls the Claudina episode:

> She didn't mind . . . . She always got it right, I swear to God and my conscience. Even when she was in that pillory, her looks and gestures showed she couldn't care less about the people looking up at her.[18]

Indeed, Celestina points out that Claudina, subjected to public scorn in the cone hat, in no way should lose her reputation just as Virgil should not either. Celestina concludes:

> I suppose you've heard about that clever Virgil. They put him in a basket and hung him from a tower with all Rome watching. It didn't mean he was no longer respected or that the good name of Virgil was soiled.[19]

---

16 James Mabbe, *Celestina or The Tragicke-Comedy of Calisto and Melibea*, Intro.James Fitzmaurice-Kelley, *The Tudor Translations*, ed. W. E. Henley, vol. 6. (London: David Nutt, 1894), 132.

17 One example of the critical "bad witch" tradition can be found in Jean Dangler's argument that Rojas deprecates Celestina so as to dissuade readers from seeking the service of women. Dangler writes: "Rojas's attack is particularly directed toward women healers, whose legitimate medieval status increasingly eroded in the fifteenth and sixteenth centuries with the professionalization of medicine" (Jean Dangler, *Making Difference in Medieval and Early Modern Iberia* [Notre Dame, IN: University of Notre Dame Press, 2005], 111).

18 Fernando de Rojas, *La Celestina*, 367: "Y mira en qué tan poco lo tuvo con su buen seso ... En todo tenía gracia; que en Dios y en mi conciencia, aun en aquella escalera estava y parecía que a todos los de baxo no tenía en una blanca, según su meneo y presencia." English translation Bush, *Celestina*, 82 (see note 6).

19 Fernando de Rojas, *La Celestina*, 368: "Verás quién fue Virgilio y qué tanto supo; mas ya havrás oýdo cómo estovo en un cesto colgado de una torre, mirándole toda Roma. Pero por eso no dexó

Claudina is Celestina's Virgil. Virgil was not just the premier poetic model (particularly his use of the epic) for the medieval mind, but also one of the period's most important historical authorities. Claudina, can, like the court jester or the clown, wear the hat in an imitation of masculine authority. But she does not only wear the hat in a carnival act that simply mocks authority. Claudina is an authority for Celestina like Virgil is to the male establishment. In Celestina's mind, Claudina wears the crown of a sage authority.

As critics have commented, Rojas was interested in the medieval notion of Lady Fortune when he constructed the plot of *La Celestina*.[20] The two lovers in the story, after being at the "top," quite literally fall to their deaths: Calisto from a wall and Melibea from a tower. The medieval allegory of Fortune is connected with the semiotics of the conical hat. The tip of the hat pointing upward suggests the top of Fortune's wheel and when fallen and pointing downward it suggests the bottom of the wheel. One may think of a jester's hat with the tip pointing downward. Fortune was connected with knowing what is in the stars and the conical hat signaled the one that was able to read the stars. With its circular base and point reaching up to the heavens, the conical hat evokes the mind of the wise sage familiar with the stars.

The meaning of the hat in Celestina's mind is meant to cast aside the sign of shame and to evoke a cone of power, like the conical crown of Egyptian pharaohs that denoted the king's union with the Sky-goddess or the Roman apex that was sometimes described as a conical hat worn by a priesthood of women. Celestina reminisces when she met Claudina at night with other women and formed a circle with a candle in the middle to practice their arts. The early Spanish meaning of the word *cerco* (from Latin *circus*) had a specific meaning in a military context, referring to a group of male soldiers that formed a circular formation in the siege of a city.[21] Rojas uses the character of the Celestina to use the word *cerco*, not to mean a group of men forming a circle of military might, but to refer to a group of women forming a different sort of circle of power.

Celestina's use of the word *cerco* to describe her time in the circle with Claudina is not only one of her fondest memories of Claudina, but also, I would argue, contributes to more fully understanding the logic for the shape of the conical hat

---

de ser honrrado ni perdió el nombre de Virgilio." English translation Bush, *Celestina*, 82 (see note 6).

20 Stephen Gilman makes one of the most extensive analyses of Fortune's Wheel at work in the *Art of* La Celestina (Madison: University of Wisconsin Press, 1956), here 125.

21 See the entry "cerco" in Nieto Jiménez and Alvar Ezquerra, ed., *Nuevo tesoro lexicográfico*, 2382 (see note 14).

as Celestina envisions it on Claudina's head. The shape of the traditional witch *cerco* is a shape in which women form a circle and envision their placement in that circle as part of a larger cone in which the center of their circle does not correspond to the two dimensional center of the circle, but to the top of a cone that reaches into the heavens. Indeed, the imagined cone shape of the female *cerco* connects to the cone shape of the hat as well as the energy from which the witch gathers her energy: the cone of power. Much later, Goya will offer one good visual example of the divergent and converging meanings of the cone. In *Witches in the Air* (1797–1798), a group of witches wear painted cone hats. The women are also arranged in a circle, but have conjured their power in a successful act of levitation: the three cone-headed witches are levitating in the air. The grouped bodies of the witches form the shape of a flying cone.

The Claudina story represents a moment of Celestina´s nostalgia. Her nostalgia enfolds a time in which she and Claudina held special power in their community and were not scorned as "bad witches." Everyone knew both of them and greeted them on the street. When Celestina remembers Claudina, she yearns for a moment of female agency condemned by male authorities. Even as male practitioners increasingly took over the work of childbirth, Claudina practiced midwifery, having helped deliver countless children in the community: "When we were in the street, everyone she bumped into she'd brought into this world."[22] Celestina and Claudina were also *curanderas* since they were familiar with curative herbs and other medicinal practice. They procured sexual partners for the men in the town Finally, they had a close and special friendship. They went out to drink wine together. Celestina says that she and Claudina did everything together and that "in this life I never had a greater friend, companion or comfort in my travails."[23] In a powerful elegy to her friend she states: "Who shared my secrets? Who could I tell my cares to?"[24]

The plot of *La Celestina* ultimately celebrates female sexuality, female community and female justice. Even though Claudina has died, Celestina continues to have close relationships with women. Areúsa is another important female character in the work. She practices prostitution secretly and is thereby in a dangerous social position since she could be denounced by her neighbors and punished. Nonetheless, she is an example of an independent woman and in one scene

---

22 Fernando de Rojas, *La Celestina*, 366: "Si salíamos por la calle, quantos topávamos eran sus ahijados." English translation Bush, *Celestina*, 81 (see note 6).

23 Fernando de Rojas, *La Celestina*, 364: "y tuve yo en este mundo otra tal amiga, otra tal compañera, tal aliviadora de mis trabajos y fatigas." English translation Bush, *Celestina*, 80 (see note 6).

24 Fernando de Rojas, *La Celestina*, 364:"¿quién sabía mis secretos, a quién descobría mi coraçón?" English translation, Peter Bush, *Celestina*, 80 (see note 6).

Celestina and Areúsa overtly flirt and fondle each other.[25] Moreover, the character of Areúsa forms part of a female microsociety that exercises justice in constrast to the examples of a failed male justice system in the work.[26] In *La Celestina,* the justice system's male representatives, the judge and the constable, do not serve their purpose and flounder in failure.

The judge who sentences Pármeno and Sempronio for the death of Celestina is corrupt (he is a personal crony of Calisto's family), the constable arrives too late to save Celestina, and the servants jump from the window thwarting the legal system in acting against their crime (since they are already near dead before the "execution"). Even the punishment of the conical hat, at least for Celestina, fails as an instrument of justice on Claudina's head.

In turn, the women effectively carry out justice, albeit not necessarily as planned. Areúsa has used her influence as prostitute to free her client Centurio, a scoundrel soldier, three times from punishment. Aside from influencing the authorities to release Centurio, Areúsa also takes justice in her own hands by seeking revenge for the deaths of Pármeno and Sempronio. Areúsa employs Centurio to kill Calisto in order to avenge the death of her lover, Pármeno. Although Centurio fails on his mission, he does get Traso to create a scuffle that leads to Calisto's death and, although not carried out as she expected, Areúsa's revenge plot and justice bring about the desired end. Areúsa therefore construes her own version of justice in parallel to Celestina who also construes her own meaning of justice when she rejects the meaning to the conical hat as it serves the needs of the male justice system.

Celestina reconstrues the meaning of the conical hat, converting it from an object of the male justice system that punishes the female into a sign of woman's pride. Like Celestina, who inverts the meaning of the hat as sign of humiliation, the carnival costume can also turn meaning. In a rural community in Galicia, Spain, carnival goers sometimes combine signs of medieval public shame in the same costume. It is not uncommon to find a carnival costume that not only consists of the decorated conical hat, but also feathers. In the medieval and early modern period in Spain, female pimps (*alcahuetas*) were animalized and shamed through the practice of feathering: Celestina supposedly was feathered on three occasions.[27]

---

25 See Sherry M. Velasco, *Lesbians in Early Modern Spain* (Nashville, TN: Vanderbilt University Press, 2011), and Mary S. Gossy, *Empire on the Verge of a Nervous Breakdown* (Liverpool: Liverpool University Press, 2009).

26 For more on the *Celestina's* female microsociety, see Alan Deyermond, "Female Societies in *Celestina,*" *Fernando de Rojas and* Celestina: *Approaching the Fifth Centenary,* ed. Ivy A. Corfis and Joseph T. Snow (Madison, WI: The Hispanic Seminary of Medieval Studies, 1993), 1–32.

27 Fernando de Rojas, *La Celestina,* 274: ". . . y lo que más de ello siento es venir a manos de aquella trotaconventos, después de tres veces emplumada" (see note 6). According to one early source,

The story of the Claudina conical hat, however, is not a mocking of authority by putting on a temporary costume in carnival.

For Celestina, the conical hat on Claudina is an instance of female pride and Celestina's celebration of the conical hat rejects the male-dominated religious and political institutions that marginalized expressions of female power. The conical hat is not a shaming punishment imposed by the emerging male-dominated state apparatus, but a hat with its own power symbolics, including female authority in medical practice, midwifery, non-sanctioned female religious practice, and female sexual agency, including prostitution, lesbian desire and freedom for a woman who procured sex for others.

---

the feathering punishment is reserved for *alcahuetas* and it consisted of stripping the upper half of the woman's body, spreading it with honey and then sticking little feathers to the torso. Sebastián de Covarrubias writes in the *Tesoro de la lengua castellana o española*: "A las alcahuetas acostumbran desnudarlas del medio cuerpo arriba y, untadas con miel, las siebran de plumas menudas, que parecen monstruos, medio aves medio mugeres" (ed. Martín de Riquer [Barcelona: S. A. Horta, 1943], 508).

Chapter 17

Kathleen M. Llewellyn
(Saint Louis University, St. Louis)

Equal Opportunity Vengeance in the *Heptaméron* of Marguerite de Navarre

A cunning husband lusts after his wife's buxom young chambermaid. He suggests to his wife that he punish the chambermaid for her laziness by whipping her out of bed on the Feast of the Innocents, a proposition that his wife accepts. But he "whips" her *in* the bed rather than out of it, the tool he uses is no whip, neither he nor the chambermaid regards the activity as punishment, and the only "innocent" involved in this story is the rather dim-witted wife, who refuses to believe reports of her husband's infidelity. This forty-fifth novella of Marguerite de Navarre's *Heptaméron* asks fundamental questions that we are pondering in this collection of essays: what constitutes a crime and who decides? what is punishment and who dispenses it? who is innocent and who is guilty? Like the *Heptaméron* as a whole, in which there is no dominant voice, no prevailing point of view, no one truth, novella 45 provides no real answers to these questions. The husband in this story is unfaithful, but that was not much of a crime in Renaissance France. It seems that no one was punished, not the unfaithful husband nor the vivacious chambermaid. Nor, according to at least one of the *Heptaméron*'s storytellers, the duped wife. In the discussion that follows this tale, Parlamente, a woman, asserts that "'Cest homme-là . . . estoit merveilleusement mauvays'" ("'The man in the story was an extremely bad character'"),[1] whereupon Hircan, her husband, counters: "'Vous n'avez doncques pas bien entendu le compte . . . pour ce qu'il est dict qu'il les contanta toutes deux en une matinée; que je trouve ung grand acte de vertu'"

1 Marguerite de Navarre, *L'Heptaméron*, ed. Michel François (Paris: Bordas, 1991), 307. Translation of *L'Heptaméron* is from Marguerite de Navarre, *The Heptameron*, ed. and trans. P. A. Chilton (London: Penguin Books, 1984), 404. Unless otherwise indicated, all English translations of *L'Heptaméron* are from this text.

("'You haven't understood the story properly . . . . The point is that the man satisfied them both in one morning! *I* think that he showed great prowess'").[2]

The characters in this novella are utterly conventional: the cheating husband, the foolish wife, the lusty chambermaid (not to mention the lusty neighbor, who wishes she, too, had a husband like that). But if the characters in this tale are stereotypical, they exist in the *Heptaméron* alongside characters from other novellas who are singular and highly nuanced. And similarly, the cavalier attitude toward wrongdoing and its consequences that this novella seems to imply is not representative of the whole of Marguerite de Navarre's treatment of the subject in her *Heptaméron*. In this essay, I argue that the queen of Navarre uses crime and punishment in the *Heptaméron* to comment on right and wrong in early modern France, and to reconsider the role of women as both victims and perpetrators of wrongdoing. The reader of the *Heptaméron* discovers that the reasons for which women were punished, and even the ways in which they were punished, paradoxically empower the women in the novellas. For while historically, women's punishment often differed from men's,[3] in the *Heptaméron*, Marguerite de Navarre establishes a certain equivalency between men and women, even in their punishment for wrongdoing.

Marguerite de Navarre's *Heptaméron*, written in mid-sixteenth century France, is considered by many to be primarily a collection of love stories. Elizabeth C. Zegura describes the *Heptaméron* as "a veritable compendium of variations on the theme of love."[4] Indeed, sixty-four of the seventy-two stories are tales of love, or at least of lust. But many of those tales might be considered "war stories" of a sort, for, as Jules Gelernt observes, Marguerite de Navarre's novellas are "so many skirmishes in the ubiquitous battle of the sexes for which the over-all design of the

---

2 Marguerite de Navarre, *L'Heptaméron*, 307–08; *The Heptaméron*, 404 (see note 1).

3 For example, "Women were often executed in a manner different from men, buried alive or drowned instead of being beheaded, largely because city executioners thought women would faint at the sight of the sword or ax and make their job more difficult," Merry E. Wiesner, *Women and Gender in Early Modern Europe* (Cambridge: Cambridge University Press, 1993), 33. Furthermore, Claude Gauvard has observed that: "il apparaît . . . que des femmes qui ont avoué des crimes graves sous la torture peuvent, plus facilement que les hommes traités dans les mêmes conditions, échapper à la condamnation à mort . . . . Les délibérations des juges montrent aussi leurs hésitations" ("It appears that women who confessed under torture to serious crimes could, more easily than men treated in similar fashion, escape the death penalty . . . . the deliberations of the judges also demonstrate their hesitation"). Claude Gauvard, *De Grace Especial: Crime, état et société en France à la fin du Moyen Age*, vol. 1. Histoire ancienne et médiévale, 24 (Paris: Publications de la Sorbonne, 1991), 303.

4 Elizabeth C. Zegura, "True Stories and Alternative Discourses: The Game of Love in Marguerite de Navarre's *Heptaméron*," *Discourses on Love, Marriage, and Transgression in Medieval and Early Modern Literature*, ed. Albrecht Classen. Medieval and Renaissance Texts and Studies, 278 (Tempe, AZ: Arizona Center for Medieval and Renaissance Studies, 2004), 351–68; here 351.

Heptameron provides the battleground."[5] The "crimes" in the *Heptaméron* are generally perpetrated by one sex against the other; the first day's stories, for example, are delicately described as "des mauvais tours que les femmes ont faicts aux hommes et les hommes aux femmes"[6] ("ill turns that women did to men and men did to women").

The *Heptaméron* is a particularly rich source for the study of fictional crime and punishment during the French Renaissance. The reader of this text has access not only to the narrator's judgment (both implied and stated) regarding "crimes" and their "punishment," and to the judgment of the characters within the novellas, but another set of commentary as well, due to the structure of this text. For Marguerite de Navarre has created a group of storytellers, *devisants*, who not only recount the tales, but discuss them afterward, passing judgment on the characters within the tales (which are claimed by the *devisants* to be true) and sometimes passing judgment on each other.

The characters in Marguerite de Navarre's novellas are punished for a wide variety of transgressions, both real and imagined: murder, infidelity, indiscretion, attempted rape, and threatening the honor of one's own family or that of another. Reflecting French society at the time, both men and women in the *Heptaméron* are punished for their offenses; as Merry E. Weisner points out, during the sixteenth century, "In general, women throughout Europe were responsible for their own criminal actions and could be tortured and executed just like men."[7] One might imagine, given the deliberate balance that the Queen of Navarre establishes among her storytellers—five men and five women—and the carrying out of "ill turns" by both sexes, that in the *Heptaméron* men would punish women and women would punish men. Or perhaps that the opinion of Oisille, the eldest (and wisest) of the storytellers, would be respected, that "'La correction des hommes appartient aux hommes et des femmes aux femmes'" ("'Corporal punishment should be administered to men by men, and to women by women'").[8] However, punishment in Marguerite de Navarre's novellas is generally meted out by men, only rarely by women, no matter what the offense against them might be. From this perspective, treatment of punishment in the *Heptaméron* appears utterly traditional, a product of the patriarchal society in which the text was composed.

The fourth novella in this collection, one of the best known of the *Heptaméron*'s tales, is a typical example of a wronged woman choosing not to punish a guilty man. This is the story of an attempted rape, featuring a despicable villain and an

5 Jules Gelernt, *World of Many Loves: The* Heptameron *of Marguerite de Navarre* (Chapel Hill, NC: University of North Carolina Press, 1966), 68.

6 Marguerite de Navarre, *L'Heptaméron*, 11; my translation (see note 1).

7 Weisner, *Women and Gender in Early Modern Europe*, 33 (see note 3).

8 Marguerite de Navarre, *L'Heptaméron*, 310; *The Heptameron*, 408 (see note 1).

innocent victim. Many scholars believe it is based on a true story, an attack on the queen of Navarre herself.[9] The assailant in this tale is a charming and handsome gentleman who is enamored of a young and vivacious princess. She rebuffs his amorous advances: "sa responce fust telle qu'il appartenoit à une princesse et vraye femme de bien ("her response was the sort of answer that becomes an honest woman and a princess").[10] But because she is a widow, and a lively, young widow at that, he convinces himself that "s'il la povoit trouver en lieu à son avantaige, elle qui estoit vefve, jeune, et en bon poinct, et de fort bonne complexion, prandroit peult-estre pitié de luy et d'elle ensemble" ("[i]f he could find the right time and place, then [she might] relent and indulge him a little, and indulge herself at the same time").[11] He sneaks into her bed one night and tries to take her by force.

The princess manages to fight him off and call for help; afraid that he might be caught, her attacker escapes. The princess, triumphant, declares: "'sa teste sera tesmoing de ma chasteté'" ("'I'll have the man's head as proof of my chastity!'").[12] But her lady-in-waiting convinces her not to seek revenge, for doing so would make the attack public, and would ruin the princess' reputation. She warns: "'si courra le bruict partout qu'il aura faict de vous à sa volunté'" ("'people will say that he *must* have had his way with you'"),[13] and furthermore, they will blame the princess for having encouraged the man. The lady-in-waiting advises: "'laissez faire à l'amour et à la honte, qui le sçauront mieulx tormenter que vous'" ("'You should leave him to his passion and his humiliation – he'll torture himself much more than you could'").[14] So it was a man, the guilty party himself, who ends up punishing the attacker.[15] His victim does not permit herself to punish him, and indeed keeps the assault a secret, in order to protect her own reputation.

---

9 "Novella 4, a story of attempted rape, is believed to be based on what happened to the writer in her own bed." Patricia Francis Cholakian, *Rape and Writing in the* Heptaméron *of Marguerite de Navarre* (Carbondale and Edwardsville, IL: Southern Illinois University Press, 1991), 7.

10 Marguerite de Navarre, *L'Heptaméron*, 28; *The Heptameron*, 90 (see note 1).

11 Marguerite de Navarre, *L'Heptaméron*, 28; *The Heptameron*, 90–91 (see note 1).

12 Marguerite de Navarre, *L'Heptaméron*, 31; *The Heptameron*, 93 (see note 1).

13 Marguerite de Navarre, *L'Heptaméron*, 32; *The Heptameron*, 94 (see note 1).

14 Marguerite de Navarre, *L'Heptaméron*, 31; *The Heptameron*, 94 (see note 1).

15 Although the princess in novella 4 does injure her attacker, it is with the intention of fighting him off, not punishing him. "elle ... se desfit de ses mains, ... se meit à le fraper, mordre et esgratiner" ("Struggling out of his clutches, she ... proceeded to lash out, scratching and biting for all she was worth"), Marguerite de Navarre, *L'Heptaméron*, 30; *The Heptameron*, 92 (see note 1). A similar situation occurs in Novella 46, when a woman kicks her pursuer down the stairs. He is injured; the narrator tells us that "il oblia le mal qu'il s'estoit faict à cheoir, et s'enfouyt le plus tost qu'il peut hors de la ville ... " ("he did not even stop to lick his wounds, but fled from the town as fast as he could . . ."), Marguerite de Navarre, *L'Heptaméron*, 309; *The Heptameron*, 406 (see note 1). However, the woman's goal is to protect herself, not to punish the offending friar.

Men, though, are allowed to punish those who offend them, and certain very righteous and honorable men in the *Heptaméron* punish men who harm women, or even threaten to harm them. Novella 12 tells the story of a Duke of the house of Medici, and a gentleman in his service. The Duke lusts after the gentleman's sister, a thoroughly virtuous woman. He tearfully explains to the gentleman that "si par son moyen n'en avoit la joissance, il ne voyoit pas qu'il peust vivre longuement" ("if his friend did not make it possible for him to enjoy her favours, then he could not see how he could go on living").[16] The narrator of this tale, Dagoucin, makes it abundantly clear that the gentleman is motivated by the desire, indeed the obligation, to protect the honor of his family. He tells us: "Le frere . . . aymoit sa seur et l'honneur de sa maison plus que le pliasir du duc" ("the brother had more concern for his sister's honour, and for that of his family name, than for the Duke's pleasures").[17] So the gentleman protests, he implores the Duke not to take advantage of him, of their relationship, by forcing him "de pourchasser le deshonneur de son sang" ("to bring dishonour upon his own lineage").[18] This response to the Duke's appeal not only emphasizes the gentleman's motivation for the benefit of the tale's audience (both internal and external to the text), but also makes it clear that both noblemen in this story, the gentleman himself and the Duke, would understand the importance of protecting family honor. The narrator tells us: "que son sang, son cueur ne son honneur ne se povoient accorder à luy faire ce service" ("His honour, his heart, the very blood that flowed in his veins prevented him from lending himself to such a service").[19] Indeed, protecting family honor is so significant, and such a compelling reason *not* to grant the Duke his sister's favors, that it is the only argument that the gentleman makes against arranging such a tryst.

The Duke is not to be reasoned with, though, and issues a veiled threat: "'Si vous aymez ma vie, aussi feray-je la vostre'" ("'Take care for my life, and I will do the same for you'")[20] which the gentleman understands to mean that he will be killed if he does not comply with the Duke's demand. The gentleman wrestles with this dilemma for a day or two. He owes the Duke greatly for honors and material benefits. But, and again the narrator reminds us, the gentleman is keenly aware of the danger to "l'honneur de sa maison, l'honnesteté et chasteté de sa seur" ("the honour of his family name, the chastity of his sister").[21] Even if she were tricked into an assignation with the Duke, or raped by him, "à jamays luy et les siens en

---

16 Marguerite de Navarre, *L'Heptaméron*, 91; *The Heptameron*, 159 (see note 1).
17 Marguerite de Navarre, *L'Heptaméron*, 91; *The Heptameron*, 159 (see note 1).
18 Marguerite de Navarre, *L'Heptaméron*, 91; *The Heptameron*, 159 (see note 1).
19 Marguerite de Navarre, *L'Heptaméron*, 91; *The Heptameron*, 159 (see note 1).
20 Marguerite de Navarre, *L'Heptaméron*, 91; *The Heptameron*, 159 (see note 1).
21 Marguerite de Navarre, *L'Heptaméron*, 91; *The Heptameron*, 159 (see note 1).

seroient diffamez" ("it would bring down infamy on himself and his whole family for the rest of time").[22] Finally, despite all that he owes the Duke, despite his initial internal conflict, the gentleman decides to kill the Duke, as he puts it: "'venger du plus grand ennemy qu j'aye en ce monde'" ("'to avenge myself of the greatest enemy I have in this world'").[23] In one of the goriest scenes in the *Heptaméron*, he and his own manservant slay the Duke with their daggers.

As it turns out, neither the Duke nor the gentleman is quite the man he seems to be at first. Though he depicts himself as quite the courtly lover (suffering from passion so intense that he could not go on living if he were not allowed to enjoy the "favours" of the woman he loves), the Duke is feminized in several ways in this tale. Gary Ferguson observes that:

> The duke's . . . murder looks like a rape, not only because it substitutes for the intended rape of the murderer's sister, but also because a minion refuses to succumb, and a master finds himself "foulé," "suppedité," "subjugué," "abattu'"[24] (beaten, overpowered, subjugated, slaughtered).

The Duke is further feminized by striking parallels between his death and that of the *muletière* (mule driver's wife) of novella 2, who is raped and murdered by her husband's servant. Both the Duke and the *muletière* are surprised in bed by their attackers, each assailant clutching a bare sword, an "espée nue."[25] Both the Duke and the *muletière* are stabbed repeatedly, until the loss of blood prevents them from struggling. At this point, the *muletière*'s attacker rapes her and leaves her to die on the floor of her bedroom. Back in the Duke's bloody bedroom, once he is too weak to defend himself the gentleman and his servant finish him with their daggers. So, though the Duke's struggle is portrayed as valiant, it is no more so than that of a young woman protecting her honor—a brave and virtuous "martire de chasteté" ("martyr of chastity"),[26] but a woman nonetheless—and his demise closely resembles that of a female rape victim.

Nor is the Duke's gentleman quite as honorable and heroic as one might imagine. The narrator of the tale, a man, adds details to the story that cast the gentleman in a less-than-honorable light. Having slain the Duke, the gentleman decides that "[il] se pensa que son euvre seroit imparfaict, s'il n'en foisoit autant

---

22 Marguerite de Navarre, *L'Heptaméron*, 91; *The Heptameron*, 159 (see note 1).

23 Marguerite de Navarre, *L'Heptaméron*, 92; *The Heptameron*, 160 (see note 1).

24 Gary Ferguson, "History or Her Story? (Homo)sociality/sexuality in Marguerite de Navarre's *Heptaméron* 12," *Narrative Worlds: Essays on the* Nouvelle *in Fifteenth- and Sixteenth-century France*, ed. Gary Ferguson and David LaGuardia. Medieval and Renaissance Texts and Studies, 285 (Tempe, Arizona: Arizona Center for Medieval and Renaissance Studies, 2005), 97–122; here 121.

25 Marguerite de Navarre, *L'Heptaméron*, 19 (nouvelle 2) and 92 (nouvelle 12), (see note 1). My translation.

26 Marguerite de Navarre, *L'Heptaméron*, 21; *The Heptameron*, 81 (see note 1).

à cinq ou six de ceulx qui estoient les prochains du duc" ("his mission would be incomplete if he did not also dispatch the five or six men who had been close to the Duke").[27] Not only is this unnecessarily vicious, but, according to the manservant, the two of them would be unable to complete the brutal task before daylight, judging by the duration and intensity of their struggle to assassinate the Duke. Indeed, in that lethal battle, the Duke seems considerably more valiant than our gentleman.

The narrator points out that the Duke is unarmed, unlike the gentleman and his manservant, but he fights his attackers with great courage, and the gentleman is unable to defeat him without the help of his servant. The gentleman believes that by killing the Duke he has saved people from tyranny, but the narrator of the tale tells us that the gentleman suffers from a guilty conscience, "la mauvaise conscience,"[28] and describes the Duke's death as a "meudre" ("murder"),[29] rather than, for example, an execution, and tells us that the gentleman was "crainctif" ("nervous")[30] about what he had done—hardly the reaction of a true hero—so nervous that he flees to Turkey to avoid retribution. That is the last that we hear of him. And though the gentleman considered the Duke to be such a tyrant that he hoped his death would "mettre en liberté la chose publicque" ("set the state free"),[31] no one else within the tale seems to hold the same opinion. The only positive reaction to the Duke's death is that of the gentleman's sister: "combien qu'elle fust estonnée du cas advenu, si est-ce qu'elle en ayma davantaige son frere, qui n'avoit pas espargné le hazard de sa vie, pour la delivrer d'un si cruel prince ennemy" ("She was horrified by what had happened, but loved her brother the more for having delivered her from a prince who was so cruel a foe").[32]

Ultimately, though, the gentleman saves his sister from the Duke's assault on her honor. We are told that the story "engendra diverses oppinions" ("engendered diverse opinions")[33] among the *devisants*, but as Gary Ferguson observes,[34] the opinions fall along gender lines, typical of the *Heptaméron*: the men consider the gentleman a "traistre et meschant serviteur" ("traitor and a bad servant"),[35] his killing of the Duke represents, in their opinion, "trop grande ingratitude" ("the

---

27 Marguerite de Navarre, *L'Heptaméron*, 93; *The Heptameron*, 161 (see note 1).

28 Marguerite de Navarre, *L'Heptaméron*, 93 My translation (see note 1).

29 Marguerite de Navarre, *L'Heptaméron*, 94; *The Heptameron*, 163 (see note 1).

30 Marguerite de Navarre, *L'Heptaméron*, 93; *The Heptameron*, 162 (see note 1).

31 Marguerite de Navarre, *L'Heptaméron*, 93; *The Heptameron*, 161 (see note 1).

32 Marguerite de Navarre, *L'Heptaméron*, 94; *The Heptameron*, 163 (see note 1).

33 Marguerite de Navarre, *L'Heptaméron*, 95; *The Heptameron*, 163 (see note 1).

34 Gary Ferguson points out that "It is quickly revealed . . . that the opinions are not so much diverse, as clearly and deeply divided, split along the lines of gender . . . ." Ferguson, "History or Her Story," 200 (see note 24).

35 Marguerite de Navarre, *L'Heptaméron*, 95; *The Heptameron*, 163 (see note 1).

height of ingratitude"),[36] while the women insist that "il estoit bon frere et vertueux citoyen" ("he was a good brother and a virtuous citizen").[37] In the end, the author allows her *dames* the last word in this argument before the narrator cuts off debate on the topic; they claim that "le duc estoit si digne de mort, que bien heureux estoit celluy qui avoit faict le coup" ("the Duke was so deserving of death that the man who had slain him was blessed indeed").[38]

But not all men in the *Heptaméron* who punish others are described as "blessed." The friar in novella 46, for example, is decidedly wicked. He punishes a young girl for the "peché de paresse" ("the sin of sloth")[39] by raping her. Her alleged offense, according to the friar, is that "elle ne se levoit poinct au matin"[40] ("she did not get up in the morning") to listen to his sermons. Her true "crime," though, is being "fort belle" ("extremely beautiful")[41] and the object of the friar's lust. By the time the girl's mother discovers that the friar has in fact raped her daughter rather than dispensing the sort of punishment the mother had expected, the friar has already escaped the town and any punishment of his own.

One might expect betrayed women in these tales to punish their philandering husbands, for the reputations of married women would be less at risk than those of lively young widows pursued by charming and handsome gentlemen, like the widow we met in novella 4, but this does not happen in the *Heptaméron*. Margaret Harper maintains that "the wives of these tales opt for subversive, aggressive methods in order to discipline and cure their unfaithful husband. . . . Whereas men maintain their honor and control over their wives through completed acts of aggression, women seem to gain more dominance over their husbands through an aborted violent act, one which can be a further threat to the unfaithful spouse."[42] The wife in Novella 37, for example, is "tant saige et vertueuse qu'elle estoit aymée et estimée de tous ses voisins" ("so good and virtuous that she was loved and admired by all her neighbours").[43] But not, it seems, by her own husband, who is bored with their "honneste repos" ("quiet, respectable life")[44] and decides to look for excitement elsewhere. One day the wife discovers him in bed with a chambermaid; in anger she sets fire to some straw in the middle of the room where

36 Marguerite de Navarre, *L'Heptaméron*, 95; *The Heptameron*, 163 (see note 1).

37 Marguerite de Navarre, *L'Heptaméron*, 95; *The Heptameron*, 163 (see note 1).

38 Marguerite de Navarre, *L'Heptaméron*, 95; *The Heptameron*, 163 (see note 1).

39 Marguerite de Navarre, *L'Heptaméron*, 309; *The Heptameron*, 407 (see note 1).

40 Marguerite de Navarre, *L'Heptaméron*, 309; *The Heptameron*, 407 (see note 1). My translation.

41 Marguerite de Navarre, *L'Heptaméron*, 309; *The Heptameron*, 407 (see note 1).

42 Margaret Harper, "Violent Remedies: Feminine Aggression in the Heptaméron," *Violence et fiction jusqu'à la Révolution*, ed. Martine Debaisieux and Gabrielle Verdier. Travaux du colloque international de la Société d'Analyse de la Topique Romanesque (Sator), 9 Études littéraires françaises, 66 (Tübingen: Gunter Narr Verlag, 1998), 155–63; here 155–56.

43 Marguerite de Navarre, *L'Heptaméron*, 266; *The Heptameron*, 358 (see note 1).

44 Marguerite de Navarre, *L'Heptaméron*, 266; *The Heptameron*, 358 (see note 1).

the lovers are sleeping. Sylvie L. F. Richards observes that, in igniting hay in the room where her husband is asleep with a chambermaid, "The wife sets fire to the locus of transgression."[45] Nevertheless, this woman does not punish her spouse for that transgression. Before any harm can come to her faithless husband, she grabs him by the arm and shouts "'*Au feu! Au feu!*'" ("'Fire! Fire!'"),[46] waking him and saving him from injury or even death. During the conversation among the *devisants* following this tale, Longarine, a young widow, exclaims: "'de telz marys que ceulx-là, les cendres en seroient bonnes à faire la buée'" ("'Husbands like that ought to be burnt and their ashes used for the washing!'").[47] But her opinion that a woman ought to punish her cheating husband is undermined by another female *devisante*, Oisille, who reminds her: "'mais si n'avez-vous pas ainsy vescu avecq le vostre'" ("'but you did not live thus with your own husband'").[48] Oisille's comment suggests that Longarine's husband had not been entirely faithful, and despite Longarine's outrage at the behavior of the husband in the tale she had just heard, despite her indignant claim that he ought to be punished severely, she evidently had not punished her own husband for straying. Such men ought to be punished, perhaps, but in the *Heptaméron*, they are not.

Powerful women are not allowed to punish those who offend them, any more than working class women or betrayed *bourgeoises*. The queen in novella 21 is relentlessly angry with a young noblewoman, Rolandine: "la Royne, pour quelque inimitié qu'elle portoit à son pere, ne luy faisoit pas fort bonne chere"("since she bore some grudge against Rolandine's father, the Queen did not treat her at all kindly").[49] When Rolandine marries a bastard against the queen's wishes, the queen has her locked in a room to keep her from her husband. But it is a man, Rolandine's own father, who actually *punishes* the young woman. "Le pere . . . l'envoya à ung chasteau dedans une forest . . . et la tint là longuement en prison" (In a "castle in the forest, he kept her imprisoned for a long time").[50]

The women in the *Heptaméron* do not even punish their own misbehaving children. We recall the mother in tale 46 who encourages a Franciscan friar to punish her daughter for sleeping rather than attending the friar's sermons, (recognizing that it was the friar who initially observes the young girl's "sloth," and that he punishes her by raping her).

The mother in Novella 30 plans to punish her son for trying to seduce a young servant in the household; the mother waits in the servant's bed, ready to give her

45 Sylvie L. F. Richards, "The Burning Bed: Infidelity and the Virtuous Woman in *Heptameron* XXXVII," *Romance Notes* 34.3 (Spring 1994): 307–15; here 312.

46 Marguerite de Navarre, *L'Heptaméron*, 267; *The Heptameron*, 359 (see note 1).

47 Marguerite de Navarre, *L'Heptaméron*, 269; *The Heptameron*, 360–61 (see note 1).

48 Marguerite de Navarre, *L'Heptaméron*, 269; *The Heptameron*, 361 (see note 1).

49 Marguerite de Navarre, *L'Heptaméron*, 158; *The Heptameron*, 236 (see note 1).

50 Marguerite de Navarre, *L'Heptaméron*, 158; *The Heptameron*, 236 (see note 1).

son a scolding that he will never forget, but instead has sexual intercourse with him, without his realizing that he is in bed with his own mother. Certainly not the punishment that she had imagined dispensing.

Although women are rarely permitted to punish transgressors in the *Heptaméron*, their male counterparts are allowed free reign to do so. That philandering men in the *Heptaméron*'s tales should escape punishment while cheating wives generally do not should come as no surprise, for it reflects the reality of the era. Ian Morrison reminds us that: "Dans la réalité, l'époque était féroce pour les femmes adultères et indulgente pour les maris; au XVe siècle du moins, la loi admettait qu'un mari pût tuer, impunément, une épouse et un amant pris en flagrant délit adultère"[51] ("In reality, the era was brutal to adulterous women and indulgent toward their husbands; during the fifteenth century at least, the law permitted a man to kill with impunity both his wife and her lover if he caught them engaged in sexual relations"). Not surprisingly, men in the *Heptaméron* do punish women who betray them.[52] In Novella 36, for example, a president of Grenoble secretly poisons his wife for having been unfaithful to him. He waits two weeks after discovering his wife in bed with her lover, in order to avoid suspicion, then serves his wife a poisoned salad. She is dead within a day, victim of the ultimate punishment, but her murderous husband is never found out.

The narrator of this story, Ennasuite, seems to respect the betrayed and brutal husband. She ends her tale by concluding: "et par ce moien, se vangea de son ennemy et saulva l'honneur de sa maison" ("And so he avenged himself on his enemy and saved the honour of his house").[53] She adds, "'Je ne veulx pas, mes dames, par cela, louer la conscience du President, mais, oy bien, monstrer la legiereté d'une femme, et la grande patience et prudence d'un homme'" ("'It is not my wish, Ladies, to praise the President's conscience, but rather to portray a woman's laxity, and the great patience and prudence of a man'").[54] Ian Morrison remarks that "Le plus souvent, le mot de "patience" désigne dans le recueil, comme aujourd'hui, l'aptitude à supporter les désagréments, à persévérer. Parfois,

---

51 Ian Morrison, "Quelques remarques sur la patience et la prudence dans L'*Heptaméron* de Marguerite de Navarre (A propos des Nouvelles 35 et 36)," *Studia Neophilologica* 74 (2002): 113–20; here 118. For a discussion of the same sort of inequality in medieval Spain, see Connie L. Scarborough's contribution to this volume, "Women as Victims and Criminals in the *Siete Partidas*."

52 Some adulterous women in the *Heptaméron* avoid punishment, but most do not. Nancy Frelick points out that "While it is true that the women in these two tales [novellas 15 and 49] seem to suffer no grave consequences as a result of their illicit behaviour, other stories about female infidelity offer examples of cruel punishment inflicted on women who commit adultery." Nancy Frelick, "Female Infidelity: Ideology, Subversion, and Feminist Practice in Marguerite de Navarre's *Heptaméron*," *Dalhousie French Studies* 56 (2001): 17–26; here 21.

53 Marguerite de Navarre, *L'Heptaméron*, 263; *The Heptameron*, 355 (see note 1).

54 Marguerite de Navarre, *L'Heptaméron*, 263; *The Heptameron*, 355 (see note 1).

pourtant, le terme signifie plutôt maîtrise de soi."[55] ("Most often, the word 'patience,' as it is used in this collection, denotes the capacity to tolerate aggravation, to persevere, just as it does today. Sometimes, however, the term implies self-control.") This husband most certainly displays a great deal of self control with the goal of being able to murder his wife without arousing suspicion. He entertains friends and neighbors, once even insisting that his wife's (now former) young lover dance with her, and impresses upon everyone how greatly he loves his wife. All the while, he is preparing to assassinate her.

The husband in novella 35 is also remarkably patient; he waits through most of Lent for the opportunity to beat his wife for the offense of intending to be unfaithful to him. These two husbands exercise patience for a malevolent purpose—in order to impose a punishment on their wives that is arguably more severe than warranted. As Ian Morrison notes, in the *Heptaméron*, patience and prudence, both traditional Christian virtues, "sont très susceptibles de corruption par les hommes"[56] ("are very susceptible to being corrupted by men"). The vengeful husbands in novellas 35 and 36 are clear evidence of the corruption of that Christian virtue and the Duke in novella 51 is perhaps even more so.

The husband in novella 51, the Duke of Urbino, is yet another example of a man who distorts the virtue of patience for his despicable, vengeful purposes. He exercises impressive patience and self-control in order to punish a woman who had angered him. In this case, the guilty woman is not his wife, but rather his wife's lady-in-waiting. The young woman has been carrying messages from the Duke's son to the woman he loves. When the Duke discovers this, he is initially unable to control his rage. Afraid that his son will enter into an unworthy marriage, the Duke cannot hide his anger and the Duchess's lady-in-waiting hears that he is infuriated: "[L]a damoiselle . . . congnoissant la malice du duc, qu'elle esimoit aussi grande que sa conscience petite, eut une merveilleuse craincte" ("She was overcome with terror, for she knew the extent of the Duke's wickedness and that it was as great as his conscience was small").[57] The poor lady-in-waiting pleads with the Duchess to allow her to stay elsewhere, to hide from the Duke until his fury subsides. The Duchess hesitates, but relents and sends her off to a convent when she realizes the depth and danger of the Duke's wrath: "elle entendit bien tost le mauvais propos que le duc en tenoit" ("the Duchess very soon discovered how the Duke felt from the malevolent way he spoke of the affair").[58] The Duke's inability to mask his anger allows the lady-in-waiting to slip out of his vengeful clutches.

55 Morrison, "Quelques remarques," 113 (see note 51).
56 Morrison, "Quelques remarques," 119 (see note 51).
57 Marguerite de Navarre, *L'Heptaméron*, 329; *The Heptameron*, 429 (see note 1).
58 Marguerite de Navarre, *L'Heptaméron*, 330; *The Heptameron*, 429 (see note 1).

The Duke realizes that he will not be able to punish the young woman as long as she remains hidden away. He musters enough self-control to dupe his wife into believing that he will not harm her lady-in-waiting: "d'un visaige fainct et joyeux, [le duc] demanda à sa femme où estoit cette damoiselle" ("Putting on a good-humoured air, he approached his wife and asked her where the young woman had gone").[59] He convinces his wife to bring the girl back from the safety of the convent. The Duchess, in turn, assures the young woman that she will come to no harm, and persuades her to leave her safe refuge and return to court. His extreme self-control having served its purpose, the Duke abandons it and has the young woman arrested. In a definitive display of his ruthlessness and his immorality, "sans forme de justice, obliant Dieu et l'honneur de sa maison, feit cruellement pendre ceste pauvre damoiselle" ("ignoring all legal forms, God and the honour of his house, he had the girl cruelly put to death by hanging").[60] The dishonor of the Duke's actions is reiterated by the narrator of the novella: "Ainsy fut ceste damoiselle innocente mise à mort par ce cruel duc contre toute la loy d'honnesteté" ("this innocent young woman was put to death by this cruel Duke, against all laws of honour and justice").[61] There is nothing honorable about the Duke's actions. He has the poor lady-in-waiting executed not to defend his own honor, or that of his family, but rather because the "unworthy" marriage that might have resulted from her actions would have cost the Duke financially.[62] His opportunity for revenge at hand, the Duke throws all self-control to the wind, for his patience has served its decidedly un-Christian purpose and he no longer has any use for it.

The *Heptaméron* features patient women as well, but their patience serves a different purpose than that of the men in the novellas. The wife in novella 37, for example, the one who sets a fire in the room where her husband is in bed with a chambermaid, is also "patient," and exercises even more self control than do the murderous Président de Grenoble and the *gentilhomme* of novella 35. She says to her philandering husband:

> "Monsieur, j'ay essayé, ung an durant, à vous retirer de ceste malheurté, par doulceur et patience, et vous monstrer que, en lavant le dehors, vous deviez nectoier le dedans; mais quant j'ay veu que tout ce que je faisois estoit de nulle valleur, j'ay mis peyne de me ayder de l'element qui doibt mectre fin à toutes choses."

---

59 Marguerite de Navarre, *L'Heptaméron*, 330; *The Heptameron*, 430 (see note 1).

60 Marguerite de Navarre, *L'Heptaméron*, 331; *The Heptameron*, 430 (see note 1).

61 Marguerite de Navarre, *L'Heptaméron*, 331; *The Heptameron*, 431 (see note 1).

62 Gary Ferguson maintains that "l'avarice du duc d'Urbin l'entraîne à la cruauté" ("the duke's avarice drives him to cruelty"). Gary Ferguson, "Péchés capitaux et 'vices italiens': L'Avarice et ses complices dans l'*Heptaméron* de Marguerite de Navarre," *Seizième Siècle* 4 (2008): 73–87; here 79. Ferguson points out that in the discussion that follows novella 51, the *devisants* blame the Duke's cruel actions on his greed.

> ["Monsieur, I have been trying for the past year to save you from your wicked ways. I have tried to exercise patience and kindness, to show you that in washing the outside you should be also inwardly cleansed. But when I saw that it was all to no avail, I decided to employ that element which shall bring an end to all things."][63]

Sylvie L. F. Richards observes that "the wife, though she may have been long-suffering, did not effect change in her marriage through patience. In fact, the tale shows the failure of these virtues."[64] So, although women might share the characteristic of patience with men, ultimately they do not use that patience to inflict punishment on the guilty.

Many transgressors in the *Heptaméron* simply escape punishment. Ian Morrison observes that: "One must [. . .] underline that, though the *Heptaméron* does include some just endings, it also recognizes clearly the limitations of earthly justice, even in stories where royal justice may play some part."[65] Those who do manage to avoid retribution for their offenses are most often men, and they generally evade the punishment due them by fleeing. This reflects the actual state of affairs in sixteenth-century France. Natalie Zemon Davis reveals that:

> Often . . . the killer fled, perhaps directly from the scene of the crime . . . . Other times the guilty party waited for days or weeks while the victim nursed his wounds, probably compensating him and his angry family with a payment, and then when death occurred, "fearing the rigors of justice," fled out of the jurisdiction, the region, and sometimes even out of the kingdom of France. (The small number of royal sergeants and other police, the slowness of communication, and the absence of routine extradition made it quite possible to take refuge.)[66]

Women, however, seldom had the opportunity to escape. Claude Gauvard observes that "la femme n'a pas les moyens d'être 'fuitive' du royaume" ("women did not have the means to flee the kingdom").[67]

Marguerite de Navarre includes several tales of successful escapes in the *Heptaméron*. The wicked Franciscans in novellas 23 and 45 both escape, unpunished, after committing rape. The "malheureux" ("vicious brute")[68] in novella 2 stabs and rapes his victim, then, "quant il eut satisfaict à sa meschante concupiscence, s'en fouyt si hastivement, que jamais depuis, quelque poursuicte que on en ayt faicte, 'a peu estre retrouvé" ("When he had satisfied his lusts he

---

63 Marguerite de Navarre, *L'Heptaméron*, 267; *The Heptameron*, 359 (see note 1).

64 Richards, "The Burning Bed," 313 (see note 45).

65 Ian Morrison, "An Aspect of Justice in the *Heptaméron*," *French Studies Bulletin: A Quarterly Supplement* 76 (Autumn 2000): 13–15; here 15.

66 Natalie Zemon Davis, *Fiction in the Archives: Pardon Tales and Their Tellers in Sixteenth-Century France* (Stanford, CA: Stanford University Press, 1987), 7–8.

67 Claude Gauvard, *De Grace Especial*, 304 (see note 3).

68 Marguerite de Navarre, *L'Heptaméron*, 20; *The Heptameron*, 80 (see note 1).

made a speedy getaway, and in spite of all subsequent attempts to track him down, it has proved impossible to find him").[69] Even the gentleman in novella 12, who assassinated Duke in order to safeguard his sister's honor, escaped to Turkey, never to be apprehended.

Though men (unlike women) often avoid punishment in the *Heptaméron*,[70] and though women (unlike men) do not seem to be entitled to punish those who wrong them, Marguerite de Navarre nevertheless establishes a certain equality between the sexes where crime and punishment are concerned. In a number of her novellas, the author constructs a parallel between crimes committed by men and those committed by women, and she assigns them similar or even identical forms of punishment.

The first novella in this collection tells the story of a heinous couple, Saint-Aignan and his wife. The woman is unfaithful to her husband, and accuses one of her lovers (she did indeed have more than one) of shaming her, claiming that he "la pourchassoit incessamment de son honneur" ("pester[ed] her in a most dishonourable fashion").[71] The husband and wife conspire to have the young man assassinated. Thus we see from the beginning of the tale their shared guilt. The young man's body is burned and the bones that remain are mixed into mortar being used to build an extension onto the couple's house, a permanent physical representation of their malice. The story of the murder comes out, and the couple flees to England to avoid punishment. Equally guilty of this crime, the husband and wife are both tried: "le procès fut faict et parfaict en l'absence de Sainct-Aignan et de sa femme. Ils furent jugé par contumace et condemnez tous deux à la mort" ("The case was brought and tried in the absence of Saint-Aignan and his wife. Judgement was pronounced on the two defaulters, the sentence being death).[72]

Both are judged guilty, and they receive the same sentence. Eventually husband and wife turn against one another. He asks a sorcerer to bring about the death of his wife (along with that of her dead lover's father, and, for good measure, the death of the Duchess of Alençon); the wife, learning of his treachery, turns him in to the authorities. Though husband and wife are spared execution, they both spend the rest of their lives in misery: Saint-Aignan is sent to the galleys, and his wife "continua son peché plus que jamais et mourut miserablement" ("led a more

69 Marguerite de Navarre, *L'Heptaméron*, 20; *The Heptameron*, 80 (see note 1).

70 There are a few adulterous women who do seem to escape unscathed in the *Heptaméron*, but Nancy Frelick reminds us that "While it is true that the women in these two tales [novellas 15 and 49] seem to suffer no grave consequences as a result of their illicit behaviour, other stories about female infidelity offer examples of cruel punishment inflicted on women who commit adultery." Frelick, "Female Infidelity," 21 (see note 51).

71 Marguerite de Navarre, *L'Heptaméron*, 13; *The Heptameron*, 72 (see note 1).

72 Marguerite de Navarre, *L'Heptaméron*, 16; *The Heptameron*, 75 (see note 1).

immoral life than ever . . . and died a most miserable death").[73] Thus, Marguerite de Navarre establishes, at the very beginning of this collection of tales, a certain equivalence between men and women. Parallel crimes, equal guilt, and comparable punishment.

There are other instances of what we might call gender symmetry in the crimes and punishments of the *Heptaméron*. Novella 33 features a priest and his unmarried sister, both esteemed and beloved by the people of their village. The two have sexual relations and she becomes pregnant, a pregnancy they describe to the villagers as miraculous. According to the young woman:

> "Je n'en puis randre autre raison, sinon que ce soit la grace du Sainct Esperit, qui faict en moy ce qu'il lui plaist; mais si ne puis-je nyer la grace que Dieu m'a faicte, de me conserver vierge."
>
> ["I cannot explain it unless it be the grace of the Holy Spirit who performs in me what he pleases. But neither can I deny the grace which God has granted to me to keep myself a virgin."][74]

Together they devise a stratagem. He administers Holy Communion to her, or in fact he feigns doing so, for he uses a false host. His pregnant sister swears the following oath, to prove her innocence to the witnesses:

> "Je prendz le corps de Nosre Seigneur, icy present devant vous, à ma damnation, devant vous, Messieurs, et vous, mon frere, si jamais homme m'a toucha non plus que vous!"
>
> ["I take the body of Our Lord present here, before you, Messieurs, and before you my brother, to my damnation, if ever a man touched me any more than you.'"][75]

Brother and sister are equally guilty of lying, and they are equally guilty of religious hypocrisy. The Count of Angoulême sees through their clever word play, however, and turns the case over to the courts of law. The two are judged guilty by the courts, and once their son is born, "furent bruslez le frere et la seur ensemble" ("they burnt her and her brother together").[76] There was no real reason to wait for the baby's birth to execute the brother, except to treat the two guilty parties in exactly the same manner.

Novella 41 also features symmetrical crimes and symmetrical punishment. The story takes place in the home of the Countess of Egmont. The Countess had asked a Franciscan convent to send to her home "ung prescheur suffisant et homme de bien tant pour prescher que pour confesser elle et toute sa maison" ("a competent,

---

73 Marguerite de Navarre, *L'Heptaméron*, 17; *The Heptameron*, 77 (see note 1).

74 Marguerite de Navarre, *L'Heptaméron*, 248; *The Heptameron*, 338 (see note 1).

75 Marguerite de Navarre, *L'Heptaméron*, 248; *The Heptameron*, 338 (see note 1).

76 Marguerite de Navarre, *L'Heptaméron*, 249; *The Heptameron*, 339 (see note 1).

honest man who could preach, as well as hear confessions from herself and the whole household").[77] A young girl, the daughter of the Countess's lady-in-waiting, confesses her sins to the preacher; these sins are clearly of sexual nature, as her description of them "luy donna envie et hardiesse de luy bailler une penitence non accoustumée" ("made our good father think he would like to risk an unusual kind of penance").[78] The priest orders the girl to wear a cord against her bare flesh. She reluctantly accepts this penance, saying to him: "'Baillez-la-moy, mon pere, et je ne fauldray de la porter'" ("'Give it to me, father, and I will wear it'").[79] But the priest will not hear of this, insisting: "'Ma fille . . . il ne seroit pas bon de vostre main; il fault que les myennes propres, dont vous debvez avoir l'absolution, la vous aient premierement seincte'" ("'It is necessary that my own hands, these same hands which will give you absolution, should first fasten the cord around you'").[80] So as punishment for her sexual transgressions, the young lady is to be tied up by another, by the person who has, in effect, been asked by the lady of the house to inflict punishment on her.

The young girl refuses this highly inappropriate penance, and tells her mother about it; the mother subsequently reports the priest's attempt to sexually violate, at least to some degree, the young girl. The Countess takes matters into her own hands, figuratively speaking, as the priest had attempted to do, literally. She has the priest beaten until he confesses the truth. Like the young lady, this priest confesses his sexual transgressions, and the Countess has him tied up, "pieds et mains lyez" ("bound hand and foot"),[81] and sent back to his Superior. So, his punishment is to be tied up by a person who has been asked by the lady of the house to punish him, like the penance he had attempted to inflict on the daughter of the lady-in-waiting.

It appears at first glance that the "transgressors" in novella 70, one male and one female, are punished for precisely opposite crimes. A young nobleman, in the service of the Duke of Burgundy, secretly loves a young and beautiful widow. The Duke's wife, not at all a virtuous woman, lusts after the young nobleman. In a fit of jealously, she demands that her husband find out the identity of the nobleman's beloved, but the nobleman refuses to reveal her name, for "l'accord de luy et de s'amye estoit de telle sorte qu'il ne se povoit rompre, sinon par celluy qui premier le declareroit" ("there was a bond between them and an understanding that it would be broken if one of them were to make it known").[82] The Duke believes that

77 Marguerite de Navarre, *L'Heptaméron*, 283; *The Heptameron*, 377 (see note 1).
78 Marguerite de Navarre, *L'Heptaméron*, 284; *The Heptameron*, 377 (see note 1).
79 Marguerite de Navarre, *L'Heptaméron*, 284; *The Heptameron*, 377 (see note 1).
80 Marguerite de Navarre, *L'Heptaméron*, 284; *The Heptameron*, 377–78 (see note 1).
81 Marguerite de Navarre, *L'Heptaméron*, 285; *The Heptameron*, 378 (see note 1).
82 Marguerite de Navarre, *L'Heptaméron*, 407; *The Heptameron*, 520 (see note 1).

the nobleman is in love with his own wife, the Duchess, and is enraged at his refusal to answer. He tells the young nobleman:

> "Or, choisissez de deux cholses l'une: ou de me dire celle que vous aymez plus que toutes, ou de vous en aller banny des terres où j'ay auctorité, à la charge que, si vous y trouve huict jours passez, je vous feray morir de cruelle mort.'"
>
> ["Then make your choice. Either you tell me the name of this woman you love so much. Or you leave the lands under my jurisdiction forever, and on the understanding that if I find you here after eight days have elapsed I shall have you most cruelly put to death!'"][83]

The sentence for his "crime" of silence is death.

Ultimately the nobleman reveals to the Duke the identity of the woman he loves: not the Duchess, but *la Dame du Vergier*, who is the Duke's niece. The Duke in turn tells his wife that the nobleman loves *la Dame du Vergier*, but warns her: "si jamays elle le reveloit à creature du monde, elle ne mourroit d'autre main que de la sienne" ("if ever she should reveal it to any soul alive, it would be by his own hand that she would die").[84] So, the Duke threatens his gentleman with banishment and death for keeping a secret, and his wife with death if she does the opposite, that is, if she reveals that same secret.

However, the dénouement of this tale reveals another example of the parallel crime and punishment that Marguerite de Navarre had previously established in novellas 33 and 41. The Duchess cannot control her passions and cannot hold her tongue. She reveals to *la Dame du Vergier* that she knows of her secret lover, and the distraught *Dame* dies of grief. The young nobleman comes upon her lifeless body, and understands that he caused her death by betraying their love. He draws his dagger and stabs himself through the heart, thereby punishing himself for revealing their secret. The Duke discovers all that has come to pass, and carries out his threat: he stabs his wife to death for the very same "crime" that the nobleman had committed, revealing the identity of his beloved, using the very same weapon that killed the nobleman, his own dagger. The Duke has them buried in the same abbey, along with the first victim of the revealed secret, *la Dame du Vergier*. So even after death the symmetry persists. In the discussion following novella 70, the *devisants* do not object to the nobleman's suicide, nor do they comment upon the slaying of the Duchess. Both are accepted as merited and reasonable, confirming the symmetry established by Marguerite de Navarre in this tale.

Though, as we have observed, meting out punishment seems to be an exclusively male endeavor in the *Heptaméron*, Marguerite de Navarre sometimes feminizes men who punish women. For one such example, we return to novella

---

83 Marguerite de Navarre, *L'Heptaméron*, 408; *The Heptameron*, 521 (see note 1).

84 Marguerite de Navarre, *L'Heptaméron*, 411; *The Heptameron*, 525 (see note 1).

36, the story of the President of Grenoble, who saves the honor of his house by poisoning his unfaithful wife with a tainted salad. Being poisoned is not a particularly masculine fate, but it is quite feminine to prepare food, even a poisoned salad.[85] The *devisants*' primary preoccupation in the discussion following the tale is to find ways to absolve the murderous husband of guilt. There is much talk of passion and pardon. For the most part, the *devisants* agree on the wife's guilt. Not only did she deserve the punishment of execution, but many other women do, too. In this part of the discussion, the femininity of the husband's actions is emphasized. If unfaithful women were obliged to eat salads like this one, according to Parlamente, they would be less fond of "'*leurs* jardins'" ("'*their* gardens'");[86] *they* would rid the garden of herbs in order to avoid being poisoned.

The unfaithful wife in novella 32 is also punished in a manner that feminizes the punishing husband. Unlike the President of Grenoble, he does not murder his cheating wife, although he had killed his wife's lover in a jealous rage. This is yet another example in *L'Heptaméron* of a man allowed to punish a person who had wronged him. The husband's slaying of his rival is so thoroughly accepted by the *devisants* that the only mention of it in the discussion following the tale is the suggestion that the unfaithful wife had caused her lover's death and that *she* should feel guilty. Dagoucin announces: "'je m'esbahys comme elle ne mouroit de deuil, en regardant les oz de celluy, à qui, par son peché, elle avoit donné la mort'" ("'I am amazed she did not die of grief when she looked at the bones of the man whose death she had caused by her sin'").[87] In order to punish his wife, the husband forces her to drink from a cup made from the skull of her dead lover. He boasts:

> "Et, affin qu'elle n'en oblye la memoire, en beuvant et mangeant, luy faictz servir à table, au lieu de couppe, la teste de ce meschant; et là, tout devant moy, afin qu'elle voie vivant celluy qu'elle a faict son mortel ennemy par sa faulte, et mort pour l'amour d'elle celluy duquel elle avoit preferé l'amityé à la myenne."
>
> ["And so that she should never forget him even when eating and drinking, I made her sit [in front of me] at table and had her served from the man's skull instead of a cup, so that she would have before her both the living and the dead, both him whom

85 Nicole Castan describes the typical role of the wife in an early modern European family: "The wife was responsible for the family's material needs (cooking, health care, childrearing, burial of the dead). Her daily routine . . . at times led her to being suspected of witchcraft and poisoning." Nicole Castan, "Criminals," *A History of Women in the West*, ed. Natalie Zemon Davis and Arlette Farge. Vol. 3 (Cambridge, MA, and London: Harvard University Press, 1993), 475–88; here 476. Castan points out "how difficult it could be to get to bottom of family disputes . . . In such conflicts women were likely to get the blame owing to their 'perfidy and feebleness of nature,' which so often let do their being charged with poisoning." Nicole Castan, "Criminals," 479.

86 Marguerite de Navarre, *L'Heptaméron*, 264; *The Heptameron*, 355 (see note 1). My emphasis.

87 Marguerite de Navarre, *L'Heptaméron*, 246; *The Heptameron*, 335 (see note 1).

through her sin she had transformed into a mortal enemy and him whose love she had preferred to mine."][88]

Being forced to drink from a particular cup, no matter how gruesome, is not masculine. However, having a drink served to another is decidedly feminine; it is the role of the lady of the house to have others served, not the role of the husband. Furthermore, although this adulterous wife is "la plus belle qu'il estoit possible de regarder" ("the most beautiful woman it was possible ever to behold"),[89] her husband masculinizes her by having her head shorn. It is impossible not to see the resemblance, the symmetry, between the naked scalp of the shamed woman and the naked skull of her murdered lover.[90]

Although the husband's actions in novella 32 appear somewhat feminine, this is not a fundamentally subversive tale. Gruesome though his conduct seems, Parlamente, one of the *devisantes*, remarks that the wife's punishment is "'autant raisonnable qu'il est possible'" ("'extremely reasonable'").[91] She contends that "'l'offence est pire que la mort'" ("'the crime was worse than death'").[92] There is some disagreement among the women in the discussion following this tale: Ennasuite asserts that "'Il n'y a mesfaict qui ne se puisse amender; mais, après la mort, n'y a poinct d'amendement'" ("'there's no sin one can't make amends for while one is alive'"),[93] but Longarine declares: "'vous sçavez que, quelque chose que puisse faire une femme après ung tel mesfaict, ne sçauroit reparer son honneur'" ("'you know that nothing a woman can do after such a crime can ever restore her honour'").[94]

Despite their difference of opinion over whether an unfaithful wife can ever atone for such an offense, none of the *devisants* disagrees with the gravity of the crime nor with the severity of the punishment. Like the unfaithful wife in novella 36, the one poisoned by her husband, this woman is judged guilty, and deserving

---

88 Marguerite de Navarre, *L'Heptaméron*, 244; *The Heptameron*, 332–33 (see note 1).

89 Marguerite de Navarre, *L'Heptaméron*, 242; *The Heptameron*, 331 (see note 1).

90 There is no analogous story in *L'Heptaméron*, indeed anywhere in the literature of Marguerite de Navarre's era, where a man is forced to repeatedly confront the death of a lover for which he was responsible. François Rigolot points out that "Although equally cruel analogues could be found in Boccaccio's *Decameron*, Marguerite's strikingly macabre scene seems to be unique in Renaissance literature." François Rigolot, "Magdalen's Skull: Allegory and Iconography in *Heptameron* 32," *Renaissance Quarterly* 47.1 (Spring 1994): 57–73; here 57. Nevertheless, the masculine/feminine parallels in this story are evident. Rigolot observes that "the absence of hair [on the woman's head] implicitly suggests a strange analogy between the adulteress's head and her lover's skull." Rigolot, "Magdalen's Skull," 65.

91 Marguerite de Navarre, *L'Heptaméron*, 245; *The Heptameron*, 334 (see note 1).

92 Marguerite de Navarre, *L'Heptaméron*, 245; *The Heptameron*, 334 (see note 1).

93 Marguerite de Navarre, *L'Heptaméron*, 245; *The Heptameron*, 334 (see note 1).

94 Marguerite de Navarre, *L'Heptaméron*, 245–46; *The Heptameron*, 335 (see note 1).

of punishment, by all. The most valued feminine virtue in Renaissance France was chastity, as Weisner reminds us.

> Honor in this period was highly gender-specific, and, in the case of men, class-specific. For upper-class men, honor still revolved around notions of physical bravery and loyalty, a link that was also accepted by journeymen and marginal groups such as professional criminals. For bourgeois and most working men, honor was primarily related to honesty, good craftsmanship, and integrity. For all women, honor was a sexual matter . . . the worst thing a man could be called was "thief," while for women it was "whore." Because of ideas of female sinfulness, irrationality, and weakness drawn from tradition, religion, and science, however, women, particularly those in the middle and upper classes, were never regarded as able to defend their own honor completely without male assistance.[95]

The discussion following this tale, like many others in the *Heptaméron*, reinforces those traditional expectations of honorable behavior. Cathleen M. Bauschatz contends that "the difference between male and female moral codes is a central focus of the *Heptaméron*, and particularly of the discussions which take place after each tale."[96] Women are to behave like proper women, and men, like men.

Furthermore, casting the husbands in novellas 32 and 36 in a feminine role does not undermine them; rather, they remain in control, protect the honor of their name and their family, and prevail in the end. The feminization of men punishing women serves an entirely different purpose: it is a substitute for women being allowed to punish. It serves to support the opinion ventured by the *devisante* Oisille that men should punish men and *women should punish women*. Rather than weakening the men, Marguerite de Navarre's treatment of the husbands in these two novellas unexpectedly elevates the status of women. This is another way in which Marguerite de Navarre's treatment of crime and punishment in her *Heptaméron* mediates between patriarchal structures that sustain the social order and an increasingly significant subject position for women.

Men in the *Heptaméron*'s tales, in their traditional authoritative position, punish unfaithful wives. They also punish others who threaten their honor, including a Duke who has designs on one man's sister, and a lady-in-waiting whose actions threaten the marital prospects of another man's son. Women, though, punish neither their errant husbands, nor men who attack them, nor even their wayward children.

However, in some ways, Marguerite de Navarre challenges societal norms with her tales of crime and punishment. Within the tales, she creates situations where

95 Weisner, *Women and Gender in Early Modern Europe*, 34 (see note 3).

96 Cathleen M. Bauschatz, "To Choose Ink and Pen: French Renaissance Women's Writing," *A History of Women's Writing in France* (Cambridge: Cambridge University Press, 2000), 41–63; here 48.

a man and a woman are equally guilty of a crime, including a husband and wife who orchestrate a murder, and a priest and a nun (also brother and sister) who have incestuous relations and seem to desecrate a host. Moreover, the male and female villains in these tales of parallel crime are subject to equivalent punishment. There is no gentler treatment of a "fairer" sex in the *Heptaméron*, no harsher punishment of a sex considered stronger, more intelligent, more accountable. The frame story of the *Heptaméron*, too, contests standards of the era. In creating the *devisants* who recount and discuss her tales, Marguerite de Navarre fashions a society where women as well as men are permitted to judge. Throughout her *Heptaméron*, both in the novellas and in the frame story that weaves them together, Marguerite de Navarre suggests a society where women and men possess equal authority to determine what is right and what is wrong, and equal responsibility for their own conduct and misconduct. The imagined world of the *Heptaméron* is one that moves toward equal social responsibility.

Chapter 18

Nicolas Lombart
(Université d'Orléans, France)

Crimes et Châtiments d'Exception en France au Temps des Guerres de Religion: l'Utopie Judiciaire des *Commentaires* de Monluc (livres V à VII)

Vétéran des Guerres d'Italie jusqu'au controversé traité du Cateau-Cambrésis (1559) puis engagé de 1561 à 1570 dans les Guerres de Religion du côté catholique, le capitaine gascon Blaise de Monluc (v. 1500–1577) restitue minutieusement toute son expérience de soldat dans de substantiels *Commentaires* (édités en 1592 par Florimond de Raemond),[1] rédigés d'un seul jet de novembre 1570 à juin 1571, puis peu à peu enrichis de réflexions personnelles, de "remontrances" au pouvoir, et de conseils donnés aux jeunes capitaines. Si le regard de Monluc sur la réalité de la guerre est à la fois technique, tactique et politique, dominé par un évident sens pratique, il est aussi orienté, à partir du livre V, par une réflexion à la fois générale et dispersée sur l'exercice judiciaire, comme l'atteste l'insertion dans le livre VI

1 Et imprimés à Bordeaux chez Simon Millanges. Voir Blaise de Monluc, *Commentaires (1521–1576)*, éd. Paul Courteault (Paris: Gallimard, 1964). Toutes les références renvoient désormais à cette édition, les numéros de pages étant donnés directement entre parenthèses. Sur la vie de Monluc, voir Paul Courteault, *Un cadet de Gascogne au XVIe siècle: Blaise de Monluc* (Paris: Picard, 1909), et Jean-Charles Sournia, *Blaise de Monluc: soldat et écrivain. 1500–1577* (Paris: Fayard, 1981). Pour une analyse générale des *Commentaires*, voir Paul Courteault, *Blaise de Monluc historien. Étude critique sur le texte et la valeur historique des commentaires* (1908; Genève: Slatkine, 1970); Pierre Michel, *Blaise de Monluc. Travaux dirigés d'agrégation* (Paris: SEDES, 1971); Étienne Vaucheret, "Monluc (Blaise de)," *Dictionnaire des Lettres Françaises. Le XVIe siècle*, éd. Michel Simonin ([Paris]: Fayard et Librairie Générale Française – "La Pochotèque," 2001), 840–44. Sur le contexte historique de l'action de Monluc, voir notamment Arlette Jouanna, éd., *Histoire et dictionnaire des guerres de religion* (Paris: Robert Laffont, 1998), et Kevin Gould, *Catholic Activism in the South-West France, 1540–1570* (Aldershot, Hampshire, and Burlington, VT: Ashgate, 2006).

d'une digression sur la nécessaire réforme de la justice du royaume, décrite comme lente, coûteuse, et inefficace. De fait, Monluc est lui-même, en tant que capitaine et lieutenant du roi, sans cesse confronté à la nécessité de "rendre justice," et d'évaluer dans une relative urgence les crimes des huguenots ou des catholiques — tous également susceptibles en ces temps troublés d'enfreindre la loi (les *ordonnances* et *édits* royaux) et de s'élever ainsi contre l'autorité du monarque. La plupart du temps accompagné de deux bourreaux, Monluc procède à des jugements expéditifs et des exécutions sommaires, conscient d'incarner le "bras de justice" du roi et de représenter ce faisant en Guyenne le dernier rempart contre une possible sédition généralisée.

Loin de se limiter à une chronique militaire des Guerres d'Italie (Livres I à IV) puis des Guerres Civiles (Livres V à VII), les *Commentaires* peuvent donc être lus, dans leur deuxième partie du moins, comme une vaste "chronique judiciaire." La motivation même de l'ouvrage renforce cette dimension: Monluc, désormais éloigné des champs de bataille, entreprend d'écrire ses mémoires pour répondre à des accusations de concussion et de prévarication émanant de l'entourage du roi; comme tous les mémoires de l'époque, les siens constituent d'abord un long plaidoyer, lequel s'inscrit explicitement dans un "simulacre de procès."[2]

Laissant de côté les aspects strictement militaires du récit, il est en ce sens intéressant d'étudier comment, à travers l'écriture rétrospective des *Commentaires*, Monluc relate et comprend ces crimes et châtiments d'exception, et comment, le temps aidant, est analysée la nature précisément *exceptionnelle* de cette justice rendue. Dans cette perspective, les quelques scènes de châtiments dispersées dans les livres V à VII des *Commentaires* ne peuvent être réduites à de simples anecdotes émaillant le récit guerrier pour lui donner, par leur cruauté même, un degré supplémentaire de réalité; elles constituent bien au contraire les noyaux épars d'une méditation sur une nécessaire réforme de la justice du roi qui aboutit, au-delà de la chronique réaliste, à construire l'image fantasmatique, souterraine mais cohérente, d'une justice idéale où s'imposerait la figure quelque peu utopique d'un juge-soldat apte à mêler vertus guerrières et compétences judiciaires. L'objectif n'est pas de discuter la légitimité éthique des exécutions cruelles et expéditives assumées par Monluc (cette violence s'inscrit dans le contexte d'une

2 Voir Nadine Kuperty-Tsur, *Se dire à la Renaissance. Les mémoires au XVIe siècle* (Paris: Vrin, 1997), 19–43, et "Blaise de Monluc et Agrippa d'Aubigné: deux cas extrêmes d'écriture dissidente," *Monluc, d'Aubigné, deux épées, deux plumes*, éd. Jean Cubelier de Beynac et Claude-Gilbert Dubois (Agen: Centre Matteo Bandello, 1999), 247–66. Si la logique du plaidoyer appartient en propre au genre naissant des "mémoires aristocratiques" au XVIe siècle, les *Commentaires* s'inscrivent aussi dans la tradition plus ancienne des "mémoires militaires" (remontant aux *Commentaires sur la Guerre des Gaules* de César auxquels le titre de Monluc fait explicitement référence), étudiés par Yuval Noah Harari, *Renaissance Military Memoirs: War, History, and Identity, 1450–1600*. Warfare in History (Woodbridge, UK, and Rochester, VT: The Boydell Press, 2004).

guerre civile où les deux camps sont renvoyés dos à dos),[3] mais d'analyser les "micro-récits" de châtiment restitués dans les mémoires comme d'authentiques points d'articulation entre le récit de guerre et le discours sur la justice, entre le constat d'un héroïsme guerrier déclinant et la quête d'un héroïsme judiciaire inédit apte à revaloriser l'"estat" de la noblesse.

Soucieux de s'inscrire dans un courant renouvelé de l'écriture de l'Histoire (marqué par le réalisme, un refus d'idéalisation et un style brut),[4] Blaise de Monluc défend aussi une utopie judiciaire dont l'hypothétique efficacité ("essayée" par "nécessité" au cours de son intervention en Guyenne) viendrait finalement enrayer les vicissitudes de l'Histoire. Après avoir étudié comment les récits de châtiment s'inscrivent globalement dans la logique de la chronique militaire, on verra que leur mécanique narrative est analogique d'un authentique discours sur la justice à lire en filigrane de la relation héroïque. Pour Monluc, la justice d'exception peut alors jeter les bases d'une utopie judiciaire autour d'une figure inédite—mais déjà anachronique à la fin du siècle—de "capitaine-justicier."

Micro-récits de châtiments: désordres du monde versus ordre du récit

S'adressant au roi Charles IX dans une "remontrance" à la fin de ses *Commentaires*, Blaise de Monluc évoque rétrospectivement le sujet de son livre en prétendant ne s'être consacré qu'à la peinture de la guerre:

> Je laisse le tort que vous [= Charles IX] faictes de faire ces beaux edicts et donner tant d'advantage à voz ennemis; je laisse le desordre de vostre justice et de voz finances, et veux seulement, avec vostre permission, dire quelque chose qui concerne la charge des armes: car si je m'enfonçais plus avant dans ce qui a causé la ruyne de vostre royaume, je parlerois trop et non pas des petits (800).

---

3 Voir Paul Courteault, *Blaise de Monluc historien*, 614–18 (voir n. 1), et Jean-Charles Sournia, *Blaise de Monluc*, 376–94 (voir n. 1), qui montrent bien que la "légende noire" de Monluc s'est surtout constituée à partir du XVIIIe siècle chez certains auteurs protestants; certainement plus lucide quant à la violence, partagée par les deux camps, des guerres civiles, Aubigné ne condamne jamais Monluc dans son *Histoire universelle*, comme l'a souligné à juste titre André Thierry, "Monluc et d'Aubigné," *Bibliothèque d'Humanisme et Renaissance* 33.3 (1971): 505–24. Sur la difficulté à condamner tout à fait Monluc pour son action répressive, voir enfin l'intelligente mise au point de James J. Supple, "Monluc, La Boétie et la justification de la violence," *Monluc, d'Aubigné, deux épées, deux plumes*, 89–107 (voir n. 2).

4 Voir Claude-Gilbert Dubois, *La conception de l'Histoire en France au XVIe siècle. 1560–1610* (Paris: Nizet, 1977), 219–51. Ce style simple adopté par Monluc fut loué dès le XVIe siècle, par exemple par Brantôme.

Si l'auteur évoque sans surprise la "ruyne" de la France pendant les guerres civiles, c'est par prétérition qu'il faut comprendre la prétendue mise en retrait, dans le récit, du "désordre" de la "justice" et des "finances" royales: en réalité, actions militaires, activités judiciaires et menées financières ne cessent d'être articulées dans les *Commentaires*. Il y a bien ce qu'on pourrait appeler une mémoire judiciaire à l'œuvre au cœur des mémoires, lesquels s'efforcent de conter (et compter) par le menu les actes de justice auxquels a participé Blaise de Monluc en tant que représentant du roi.

C'est dans le cadre d'une justice désorganisée et fragilisée[5] qu'apparaissent donc les quelque douze récits de châtiment (exclusivement de protestants[6]), dont le capitaine gascon est à la fois acteur et narrateur:[7] [1] trois chefs huguenots sont décapités ou pendus, et un jeune diacre mortellement blessé, le 20 février 1562 à Saint-Mézard après avoir mené une sédition contre leur maître M. de Rouillac (483–85); [2] "cinq ou six huguenots," dont le capitaine Morellet, sont pendus à Villeneuve le 3 mars 1562 (486–87); [3] "trente ou quarante" huguenots (en réalité dix-neuf), sont condamnés pour sédition et pour l'assassinat de M. de Fumel, et "pendus ou mis sur la roue" à Fumel le 11 mars 1562 (487–88); [4] "quatre ou cinq des principaux seditieux" sont condamnés pour "rupture des eglises," "rapts" et "volemens," et pendus à Villefranche-de-Rouergue entre le 2 et le 11 avril 1562 (494–95); [5] des huguenots séditieux sont décapités en grand nombre à Toulouse, jugés par les capitouls, le 23 mai 1562 (505–06);[8] [6] "soixante ou quatre-vingts huguenots" sont pendus à Gironde, près de La Réole, pour sédition militaire en juillet 1562 (528–29); [7] "quinze ou seize" huguenots sont pendus le 31 juillet 1562 à Sauveterre pour sédition militaire (529); [8] "quinze ou vingt" huguenots, "entre autres tous les officiers du Roy et les consuls" et le capitaine Héraud, ancien compagnon d'armes de Monluc, sont pendus à Monségur le 13 juillet 1562 (532); [9] les prisonniers de Terraube sont tués et leur chef pendu, et les deux chefs de Lectoure sont pendus le 30 septembre 1562 (551–52); [10] les séditieux de La Roche-Chalais sont "accoustrez selon la vie qu'ils avoient menée" par les soldats de Monluc le 6 février 1569 (675–77); [11] les soldats de la garnison militaire huguenote de Mont-de-Marsan sont massacrés "par despêche" et "souz pretexte

5 Sur l'état de la justice à la fin du XVIe siècle en France, voir par exemple Arlette Lebigre, *La justice du roi. La vie judiciaire dans l'ancienne France* (Paris: Éditions Complexe, 1995), 35–57, et Benoît Garnot, *Justice et société en France. XVIe–XVIIe–XVIIIe siècles* (Paris: Ophrys, 2000), passim. La critique du fonctionnement de la justice est un lieu commun littéraire depuis le Moyen Âge, mais elle adopte un ton particulièrement virulent à la fin du XVIe siècle: voir *infra* n. 29.

6 Monluc peut cependant libérer des protestants retenus contre la loi royale ou exécuter des catholiques qui ne respectent pas la loi royale: sur ces cas particuliers, voir *infra* n. 17 et 18.

7 Pour signaler plus facilement ces événements dans la suite de l'article, chacun est ici numéroté entre crochets.

8 Mais un doute demeure quant à l'implication exacte de Monluc dans ces exécutions toulousaines : voir *Commentaires*, 1204 n. 3.

qu'ils estoient subjects de la royne de Navarre" le 20 septembre 1569 (724); [12] enfin, tous les habitants de Rabastens, y compris les femmes, sont passés au fil de l'épée ou jetés par dessus les murailles de leur ville pour l'avoir défendue le 23 juillet 1570 (783–84).

Quelques remarques s'imposent: ces micro-récits de châtiment sont dispersés dans la chronique militaire et, loin de la dominer, en paraissent à chaque fois une variante ou un prolongement ponctuels. Leur statut narratif n'est pas évident, et Monluc semble assurément plus à l'aise dans la relation d'un assaut ou d'une escarmouche que dans celle d'une pendaison ou d'une décapitation. Pour autant, la scène inaugurale de Saint-Mézard [1] ouvre une sorte de mécanique implacable de subversion/répression qui imprime au récit son rythme propre. En outre, et paradoxalement, chaque scène de châtiment se détache avec netteté sur la toile de fond d'une justice (notamment pénale) dont l'état de déshérence a déjà été évoqué plus haut. En ce sens, les mémoires constituent bien la reconstitution, par le récit rétrospectif et autour du *je* de l'énonciation, d'un ordre perdu. Le micro-récit de châtiment apparaît finalement comme un repère narratif important—à côté de la scène de bataille—dans la reconstitution de cet ordre.

Dans l'économie générale du récit de guerre, ces scènes de justice introduisent cependant une légère perturbation. Bien qu'insérées au récit principal des assauts, batailles rangées, accrochages, reconnaissances et mouvements tactiques, elles viennent rompre une possible héroïsation de la relation militaire; situées aux marges d'une narration virtuellement épique, les scènes de châtiment viennent rappeler que le code de la guerre a changé, que la violence qui s'y exprime ne relève plus de ce que Monluc appelle "le droict de la guerre" (655) ou "les règles ordinaires de la guerre" (666), c'est-à-dire le code intériorisé, non écrit, de la chevalerie et de la courtoisie.[9] Ainsi Monluc prend-il soin de rappeler la différence entre "guerres étrangères" et "guerres civiles," ces dernières n'étant plus menées selon des procédures et un code reconnaissables:

9 Sur cet ancien code martial qui nourrit évidemment la conception médiévale de la guerre, voir par exemple Philippe Contamine, *La Guerre au Moyen Âge* (1980; Paris: Presses Universitaires de France, 2007), notamment I, 8 ("Guerre et paix: droit, éthique et christianisme") et III, 10 ("La guerre: aspects juridiques, éthiques et religieux"), et les contributions du volume *Writing War: Medieval Literary Responses to Warfare*, éd. Corinne Saunders, Françoise Le Saulx et Neil Thomas (Woodbridge: D. S. Brewer, 2004). Parlant de la capture puis de la relaxe du capitaine catholique de Leberon par des capitaines huguenots, anciens compagnons de guerre de Monluc, ce dernier remarque: "Ce sont des honnestes courtoisies entre gens de guerre" (*Commentaires*, 747). Ce type de notation est fréquent, Monluc constatant (et acceptant parfois à contre cœur) l'évolution des techniques de combat et surtout de la mentalité du soldat ou du chef de guerre: voir Colette Demaizière, "Le vocabulaire de l'homme de guerre," *L'Homme de guerre au XVIe siècle*, éd. Gabriel-André Pérouse, André Thierry, et André Tournon. Actes du colloque de l'Association RHR [Renaissance, Humanisme, Réforme], Cannes, 1989 (Saint-Étienne: Publications de l'Université de Saint-Étienne, 1992), 349–63 (notamment 354–56), et Robert Knecht, "Monluc et l'art militaire," *Monluc, d'Aubigné, deux épées, deux plumes*, 111–20 (voir n. 2).

> Et si le Roy eust fait payer les compagnies, je n'eusse permis en ces guerres de introduire les rançons qui ont entretenu la guerre. Mais le gendarme ny le soldat n'estoit payé. Il est impossible d'y pourveoir, encores n'en y eust-il guères; c'est cela sans doute qui a entretenu la guerre. Ce n'est pas comme aux guerres estrangères, où on combat comme pour l'amour et l'honneur; mais aux civiles il faut estre ou maistre ou valet, veu qu'on demeure sous mesme toit. Et ainsi il faut venir à la rigueur et à la cruauté; autrement la friandise du gain est telle que on desire plustost la continuation de la guerre que la fin (519).[10]

Une étude rapide des douze micro-récits—et de leurs points communs—permet de comprendre ce passage des lois de l'"amour" et de l'"honneur" à celles, nécessaires, de la "rigueur" et de la "cruauté." Ces châtiments sont relatés très brièvement (d'où l'expression retenue de micro-récits), sans luxe de détails: Monluc y pousse à l'excès le principe du style simple et réaliste emblématique du renouvellement de l'écriture de l'Histoire à la fin du siècle.[11] Le narrateur prend cependant le temps d'indiquer la nature du crime, la forme du châtiment (pendaison ou décapitation majoritairement, mais aussi défenestration, supplice de la roue ou population passée au fil de l'épée) et une justification de la peine: Monluc tient systématiquement à placer son action sous l'autorité de la justice du roi, et elle s'inscrit de fait, dès que possible, dans le cadre des institutions judiciaires.[12]

Mais ce qui frappe dans la conduite du récit, c'est que la première exécution de Saint-Mézard [1] apparaît finalement comme le paradigme d'une même scène, répétée avec trois invariants: la vitesse d'exécution et le refus d'une procédure trop lourde d'abord (le châtiment est réalisé "sans sentence ny écriture" [1], "sans tant languir" [2], "sans procédure" [3], "sans autre cérémonie" [4], "dez le lendemain" [5], "sans despendre papier ni ancre" [7], "[avec] une très belle despêche" [9], "par

10 Dans une adresse au roi qui suit l'évocation de la bataille de Jarnac (13 mars 1569), victoire catholique qui vit la mort du prince de Condé, Monluc, qui déplore la mort de ce grand chef protestant, plaide l'utilité des "guerres estrangères," qui permettent de détourner l'ardeur militaire hors du royaume: voir *Commentaires*, 668–70. S'il s'agit d'un lieu commun des discours contre les guerres civiles, Monluc est cependant l'un des seuls à préférer aux "guerres de la Terre-Saincte [celles] des nouveaux mondes [. . .] comme faict le Roy d'Espagne" (*Commentaires*, 669).

11 Voir, outre Claude-Gilbert Dubois, *La conception de l'Histoire en France au XVIe siècle* (voir n. 4), les propres déclarations de Monluc à la fin des *Commentaires*, 829–30; plus loin, l'auteur oppose significativement son ouvrage aux romans, la réalité nue à la fiction: "Ne desdaignez, vous qui desirez suivre le train des armes, au lieu de lire des Amadis ou Lancellots, d'employer quelqu'heure à me congnoistre dans ce livre" (833).

12 À Fumel [3], les protestants séditieux sont jugés coupables par des conseillers du siège du sénéchal d'Agen et à Villefranche-de-Rouergue [4], par deux conseillers de la cour de Bordeaux (malgré la résistance de deux commissaires du roi, probablement réformés); les exécutions de Toulouse [5] sont organisées par les capitouls, sans que l'on sache exactement quelle part Monluc y a prise; Monluc doit aussi composer avec les deux commissaires du roi, Compain et Girard, soupçonnés d'être huguenots, et souvent réticents.

despêche" [11]); le rapport de force induit par cette vitesse ensuite: la "rage" (485) et la "rigueur" (784) d'un côté, la "peur et la frayeur" (486) de l'autre, dans la mesure où il faut, dit Monluc, "[tenir] les gens et le peuple en crainte" (488);[13] le rapport de force suggéré par cette pratique du châtiment enfin: du côté de Monluc, une forme de *révélation* et un souci de *sincérité*, du côté des huguenots, *dissimulation* et *mensonge*.[14] Les scènes de châtiment se distinguent donc des scènes de combat en ce qu'elles ne sont sujettes qu'à un faible travail de variation et surtout d'ornementation. Monluc répète une scène originelle de justice qu'il se refuse à transformer en spectacle, en "scène à faire." Il n'y a chez lui aucune complaisance pour la violence du châtiment, lequel est comme assumé par cette prise de distance qu'implique la relative sobriété stylistique,[15] moins évidente dans certaines scènes de combat où affleure parfois la tentation de l'épique.[16] C'est dans cette perspective qu'une typologie des crimes apparaît nettement d'une scène à l'autre.

Ne pas transformer la peine en spectacle, en scène pathétique donc attendue par le lecteur, c'est mettre en valeur le travail de la loi aux dépens du travail de l'écriture, c'est évoquer la capacité du chef de guerre gascon à *reconnaître* sans passion le crime—et la capacité du narrateur à rendre compte sans exaltation de cette reconnaissance. La sobriété stylistique a pour effet de suggérer la légalité de chaque punition et le légalisme du capitaine-narrateur, un légalisme qui apparaît plus clairement dans d'autres épisodes, en faveur des protestants[17] ou au

---

13 L'opposition apparaît explicitement dans les épisodes [1], [2], [3], [4], [6], [8], et [12], mais elle est suggérée partout par la description du climat dans lequel ont lieu les arrestations.

14 Voir surtout les épisodes [1], [2], [4], [6], [7], [9], et [10]. L'auteur suggère cette opposition éthique au-delà des scènes de châtiment, comme par exemple dans *Commentaires*, 589–90: Monluc décrit les nouvelles menées des huguenots dans le Sud-Ouest, signes avant-coureurs de troubles, mais aussi son impossibilité à agir dans le cadre légal des édits de paix dans la mesure où chez les ennemis tout est fait "en cachette."

15 Sur cette absence de complaisance ou d'idéalisation chez Monluc dans le rapport à la violence de la guerre, voir aussi Jean-Claude Arnould, "Pillage, profit, promotion: l'homme de guerre d'après les *Commentaires* de Monluc," *L'Homme de guerre au XVIe siècle*, 167–76 (voir n. 9), notamment 170: "Le discours de l'homme de guerre dément à chaque page les illusions que crée ce que j'appellerai par commodité la littérature idéalisante. Pillage et profit révèlent d'abord la vraie nature de la guerre: c'est un système économique, certes parasitaire et improductif pour la plupart, mais qui a ses propres lois."

16 L'auteur semble ainsi réserver son sens de l'héroïsation et de l'agrandissement au récit de sa propre mort symbolique à Rabastens, où il fut défiguré par une arquebusade: voir Jacques Pineaux, "Mort et transfiguration d'un héros: Blaise de Monluc à Rabastens," *Études seiziémistes offertes à V.-L. Saulnier* (Genève: Droz, 1980), 347–53. L'exploitation du *topos* du songe prémonitoire (*Commentaires*, 593–95) atteste également le goût de Monluc pour les procédés littéraires à la mode: voir Maurice F. Verdier, "Le songe de Monluc," *Bibliothèque d'Humanisme et Renaissance* 37.1 (1975): 7–14.

17 Voir *Commentaires*, 473. De manière habile, Monluc place au début du livre V le récit d'une libération qu'il fit de deux prisonniers protestants, détenus par les gens de justice à Plume, contre les ordonnances royales (qui interdisent alors la détention "pour faits de religion"). Il refuse aussi,

détriment des catholiques.[18] De manière significative, la seule occurrence du verbe "châtier" dans les livres V–VII des *Commentaires* apparaît dans un contexte où est soulignée l'impartialité de Monluc. Alors que le ministre protestant La Barelle lui rend visite pour se plaindre des destructions de temples "[lui] disant que les eglises avoient esté fort aises de [sa] venuë et de la charge que la Royne [lui] avoit baillé, et qu'ils s'assuroient d'avoir justice de ceux qui les avoient ainsi massacrez," Monluc "respondi[t] qu'il se pouvoit tenir pour certain que ceux qui auroient tort seroient chastiez" (476). Mais ensuite le ministre tente de corrompre Monluc, provoquant la "furie" de ce dernier, qui s'en prend physiquement au pasteur puis remarque ironiquement: "Cela me descria fort parmy ces ministres, car c'estoit crime de lèze-majesté d'en toucher un" (477). Cette autre scène inaugurale—Monluc rapporte pour la première fois un échange verbal avec un protestant—est elle aussi paradigmatique en ce qu'elle traduit le rapport constant que Monluc entretient au crime et à sa reconnaissance.

La colère n'y est pas systématiquement une passion négative, mais le symptôme affectif d'une identification presque instinctive d'un crime perçu dans sa dimension exclusivement politique: l'usage par antiphrase de l'expression "lèze-majesté" indique que l'autorité royale est le seul point de référence, l'unique pierre de touche dans l'évaluation d'une situation ambiguë. Monluc, qui n'évoque jamais des questions de théologie ou de dogme, identifie le roi, la loi et la justice, et considère que la sédition est exclusivement politique: "le masque est osté: il n'est plus question de messe ou de presche, c'est à la personne [du roi] que cela s'adresse" (609).[19] De fait, la "colère," la "furie" ou la "rage" sont récurrentes dans les scènes de châtiment.

Cette passion de la colère—propre à l'univers épique, où elle joue un rôle profondément structurel[20]—est l'expression extrême, et évidemment paradoxale, du "bon jugement," une vertu aussi bien judiciaire que guerrière, qui permet d'identifier le crime commun ou le crime de lèse-majesté avec une relative

---

en 1563, de sévir contre les Bordelais accusés d'être réformés: voir *Commentaires*, 472–73, 478 et 577–79.

18 Voir *Commentaires*, 581. Monluc raconte laconiquement comment il fit strictement appliquer l'édit d'Amboise de mars 1563 (lequel interdisait à tout soldat de porter les armes, sauf les gentilshommes), en faisant pendre deux soldats catholiques "ayant transgressé l'edict" puis deux huguenots (parité parfaite!), qui pensaient pourtant "eschapper à bon marché."

19 Sur ce thème, voir James J. Supple, "Monluc, La Boétie, et la justification de la violence," 99–101 (voir n. 3).

20 Voir par exemple Bruno Méniel, "La colère dans la poésie épique, de la fin du Moyen Âge à la fin du XVIe siècle: un envers de l'héroïsme?," *Cahiers de Recherches Médiévales et Humanistes* 11 (2004): 37–48.

netteté—comme elle permet d'évaluer la situation de l'ennemi sur le champ de bataille.[21]

Les crimes identifiés par Monluc peuvent ainsi être répartis en sept catégories, dont le classement hiérarchique ne peut qu'être difficilement établi dans la mesure où ils sont tous également punis de mort. Monluc ne punit que des crimes qui affectent directement la sûreté et l'autorité publiques ou, ce qui revient au même, la personne symbolique du roi: l'injure verbale à l'encontre du roi (cf. [1]: Charles IX est traité de "petit reyot de merde" (484)); l'assassinat de seigneurs (dans les faits, tous catholiques: cf. [2] et [3]); le prêche public et séditieux (cf. [2] et [3]: pour Monluc, par cette prédication, "ils [les huguenots] nous vouloient donner la loy" (487)); la destruction des biens, le pillage, et le massacre de catholiques (cf. [1], [4] et [10]); l'action dissimulée dans un but séditieux (cf. [5]); la sédition déclarée et le soulèvement militaire (cf. [6], [7], [8], [10], [11]); et enfin, le républicanisme et l'athéisme (cf. [10]: "c'estoient libertins et gens sans religion" (676) déclare-t-on à propos des insurgés).

Le respect de la volonté du roi, de sa parole à travers la loi, est véritablement obsessionnelle chez Monluc, pour qui la corruption généralisée du langage est déjà en soi une lèse-majesté ("[Je] me deliberay d'user de toutes les cruautez que je pourrois, et mesmement sur ceux qui parloient contre la majesté royale," 483) et explique la propension des protestants à la duplicité et au mensonge.[22] À l'inverse, lui-même cherche à faire entendre sa voix dans une atmosphère de tumultes, de dénonciations et de rumeurs, qui vient se greffer comme par malice sur le traditionnel paysage sonore de la guerre.[23] Placée par définition au cœur de la

---

21 Voir *Commentaires*, 571–72. Après le récit de la prise de Lectoure, Monluc conseille aux jeunes capitaines, dans une adresse digressive, de n'observer jamais que par eux-mêmes la position des ennemis ("Vos yeux voyent plus clair que ceux d'autrui à ce qui est nécessaire"), mettant en avant les capacités de "recognoissance" et de "bon jugement" du tacticien. Les jeux de mot sur la capacité à *juger* (d'une situation militaire, d'un crime) sont fréquents dans les *Commentaires*.

22 Le livre V s'ouvre sur ce constat d'un langage totalement corrompu chez les protestants; voir *Commentaires*, 472: "Quelques jours après mon retour, j'entendois de toutes parts de terribles langages et d'audacieuses parolles, que les ministres qui portoient une nouvelle foy tenoient, mesmement contre l'authorité royale." Construit autour d'une injure contre le roi, le récit de l'exécution de Saint-Mézard [1] aboutit à ce constat: "Ce n'estoit pas seulement là qu'ils tenoyent ce langage, car c'estoit partout;" un peu plus loin, le lien avec le goût du secret apparaît clairement: "Cela [*i. e.* l'exécution] ferma la bouche à plusieurs seditieux, qui n'osoyent parler du Roy qu'avec respect; mais en secret ils faisoyent leurs menées" (*Commentaires*, 484 et 485).

23 Voir par exemple *Commentaires*, 585 : "La France jouist cinq ans de ce repos avec les deux religions [après l'édit d'Amboise de mars 1563]. Toutesfois, je me doubtois tousjours qu'il y avoit quelque anguille sous roche; mais pour la Guienne je ne craignois pas beaucoup. J'avois tousjours l'œil au guet, donnant advis à la Royne de tout ce que j'entendois, avec toute la fidélité dont je me pouvois adviser. Pendant ce temps, le Roy visita son royaume. Estant arrivé à Thoulouse, je fuz baiser les mains à Sa Majesté, laquelle me fit plus honorable recueil que je ne meritois. Les huguenots ne faillirent à faire leurs praticques et menées, et me faisoient faux feu souz main, car à descouvert ils n'osoient le faire; mais je ne m'en donnois pas grand peine." L'auteur évoque aussi les bavardages de la cour (notamment des dames), qui peuvent causer d'infinis dommages: "Le Roy

pratique judiciaire, la parole est constamment menacée par les deux vices de la "chattemite[erie]" et de l'"opiniastreté," c'est-à-dire par la duplicité doucereuse[24] et par l'obstination aveugle.[25] Contre cette perversion généralisée du langage, la seule réponse possible est une forme de pragmatisme judiciaire que rend nécessaire la situation exceptionnelle de la guerre civile.

Une justice pragmatique: la "nécessité" du châtiment

Le thème du châtiment n'apparaît assurément pas de manière incidente au cœur de la chronique des guerres civiles. L'envers de ce récit militaire—et des scènes de justice qu'il fait ponctuellement apparaître—est bien une critique des pratiques judiciaires du temps qui finit par rendre visible chez Monluc un discours *sur* la justice, sinon légitime, du moins cohérent. Si les micro-récits de châtiment manifestent un rapport essentiellement pragmatique de Monluc à l'action de justice, cette action s'inscrit cependant assez clairement dans le cadre d'une critique de la justice du royaume fondée sur un argumentaire simple (voire simpliste) mais qui révèle paradoxalement une bonne connaissance de la juridiction française et de ses possibles dysfonctionnements.

Dès le début du livre V, Monluc constate amèrement que ce sont essentiellement des gens de justice qui passent à la Réforme, associant implicitement la faible

devroit clore la bouche aux dames qui se meslent de parler en sa cour; de là viennent tous les rapports, toutes les calomnies. Une babillarde causa la mort de monsieur de la Chastegneroye. S'il m'eust voulu croire, et cinq ou six de ses amis, il eust desmêlé sa fuzée contre monsieur de Jarnac d'autre sorte; car il combattist contre sa conscience et perdist l'honneur et la vie. Le Roy leur devroit commander de se mesler de leurs affaires. J'excepte celles que je dois. Leur langue a cousté beaucoup, et après il n'est pas temps, comme j'au dict" (*Commentaires*, 617).

24 Voir *Commentaires*, 735: "Le comte Mongommery [= chef protestant en Guyenne] vint à Euze, et, comme il fust là arrivé, les huguenots de Condom, qui estoient demeurez soubz l'edict du Roy [l'édit de Paix de Longjumeau, du 23 mars 1568], ayant faict tousjours la chattemite de ne vouloir prendre les armes, se couvrant souz la promesse du Roy, lesquels avoient esté traictez plus humainement que les catholiques mesmes, prindrent les armes et allarent trouver le comte de Mongommery à Euze." Monluc reproche sans cesse aux protestants de profiter des édits de paix pour préparer secrètement la guerre.

25 Voir *Commentaires*, 532: "Le capitaine qui commandait [la place forte de Monségur] s'appelloit le capitaine Heraud, qui avoit esté de ma compagnie à Moncallier et à Albe lance passade, un brave soldat s'il y en avoit en Guyenne, et fust prisonnier. Beaucoup de gens le vouloient sauver pour sa vaillance; mais je dis que, s'il eschappoit, il nous feroit teste à chasque village, et que je cognoissois bien sa valeur. Voilà pourquoi je le fis pendre. Il pensoit tousjours que je le sauvasse, pour ce que je sçavois bien qu'il estoit vaillant; mais cela le fist plustost mourir, car j'estois bien asseuré qu'il ne se retourneroit jamais de nostre costé, parce qu'il estoit fort opiniastre et coiffé de ceste religion. Sans cela je l'eusse sauvé." On notera l'importance du registre éthique, l'*opiniâtreté* religieuse étant perçue comme une scandaleuse inversion de la *vaillance* guerrière.

"nature" de cette profession au désir quasi maladif de "nouveautez."[26] De fait, "le peuple [est] abandonné de la justice [. . .], et n'y avoit sergent qui ozast entreprendre de faire executions pour les catholiques, sinon pour les huguenots seulement" (472); bien plus, les protestants—omniprésents, en Guyenne, dans les offices de justice—exploitent la complexité des procédures judiciaires à leur profit, contre toute forme d'impartialité.[27] Au fur et à mesure que le récit progresse, le discours critique s'étoffe; une courte digression du livre VI (déjà mentionnée en introduction) mérite ainsi d'autant plus l'attention du lecteur qu'elle fait plutôt exception, par les thèmes abordés, dans l'ensemble des mémoires de la fin du siècle:

> Et puisque la justice de France est regie et gouvernée par les loix des Romains, c'est bien raison que les roys de France se gouvernent par leurs coustumes. Que pleust à Dieu que le roi voulust faire parler de luy pourjamais, et laisser memoire de sa prudence, qui seroit à jamais louée! C'est qu'il fist brusler tous les livres des loix suivant lesquelles sa justice juge, et faire une justice toute nouvelle, juste et saincte car j'oserois dire qu'il n'y a monarque en chrestienté qui s'aide de ces loix que les roys de France; tous les autres ont des loix faictes par eux pour abréger tous procès, ouy mesmes Bearn et Lorraine (qui sont aux deux coings du royaume), et que les procès ne puissent durer plus de deux ans. Si le Roy faisoit cela, il se pourroit vanter d'avoir un monde de soldats qui seroient forcez de prendre les armes, puisqu'ils n'auroient que faire aux palais; car ostez ceste vacation, à quoy voulez-vous qu'un bon cœur noble et genereux s'adonne, sinon aux armes? [. . .] Je crois que les deux tiers

26 Voir *Commentaires*, 472: "Je voiois croistre de jour en jour le mal, et ne voiois personne qui se monstrat pour le Roi. J'oiois dire aussi que la pluspart de tous ceux qui se mesloyent des finances estoyent de ceste religion, car le naturel de l'homme est d'aimer les nouveautez; et le pis, d'où est procédé tout le mal-heur, que les gens de justice aux parlemens, seneschaucées et autres juges abandonnoient la religion ancienne et du Roy pour prendre la nouvelle." Une question reste (malicieusement?) en suspend: passent-ils à la Réforme en raison d'un "naturel" déjà faible, ou est-ce ce changement de religion qui les affaiblit ensuite? Le rôle important des gens de justice dans la diffusion de la Réforme avait été également très critiqué par Ronsard, qui reprochait aux "juges des cités" leur laxisme et, bien pire, leur "connivence" avec "le Huguenot mutin, l'heretique mechant": voir *Discours des Misères de ce Temps*, éd. Malcolm Smith (Genève: Droz, 1979), 127–28 (*Remonstrance au peuple de France*, v. 451–68). Ce rôle est bien attesté par les historiens, même si Monluc le surévalue sans doute à dessein: voir par exemple Arlette Jouanna, *La France du XVIe siècle* (Paris: Presses Universitaires de France, 1996), 331.

27 Remarquant en effet que les "judicature[s] grande[s] [ou] petite[s]" sont, en Guyenne, quasiment toutes entre les mains des protestants, Monluc insiste sur les faux témoignages, intimidations contre les catholiques, "piperies, ruses et finesses" diverses qui détournent la justice au profit de ceux de la nouvelle religion, qui ne cherchent qu'à gagner du temps pour échapper aux jugements : voir *Commentaires*, 486. La relation du procès de Cahors (mars 1562), dans lequel des catholiques sont jugés pour avoir attaqué des protestants, est pour Monluc l'exemple même de ce détournement de la justice par la Réforme; voir *Commentaires*, 488–89: "Ils avoient si bien fait qu'ils avoyent appellé neuf juges ou lieutenans des sièges, dont les six estoyent huguenots, et les trois ils les avoyent si fort intimidez de leur grand puissance et authorité qu'ils disoyent avoir en leur charge, que nul d'eux n'osoit dire sinon comme les autres."

> s'amusent en ces palais et plaidoyeries; et cependant, encor qu'ils ayent naturellement bon cœur, avec le temps s'apoltronisent. Ce royaume seroit formidable aux estrangers. Combien seroit-il riche et opulent! car toute la ruine de la noblesse ne vient que des mauvais conseils que les advocats donnent aux parties (620–21).

Ce passage est intéressant dans la mesure où il articule la pratique concrète du châtiment chez Monluc à une réflexion sur l'institution d'une "justice toute nouvelle, juste et saincte" fondée sur deux principes: le rejet du droit romain (celui des "livres," des lois écrites et de la longueur des procès) au profit de la coutume (du côté de l'oralité, de la tradition et de la brièveté); et la diminution des "vacations" judiciaires—il y a trop d'avocats dans les palais—pour libérer l'énergie guerrière de "cœur[s] noble[s] et genereux" aptes à prendre les armes au profit de la sauvegarde du royaume.

Le souhait de voir se développer un droit national (fondé sur la coutume et l'histoire) moins prisonnier de la complexité du droit savant est partagé par un certain nombre de juristes gallicans à la fin du siècle:[28] le discours de Monluc, quoique pauvre en arguments strictement juridiques, s'inscrit donc parfaitement dans un débat d'actualité. Surtout, ce discours prend tout son sens dans la composition d'ensemble des mémoires: si la critique de la "chicane" (la querelle judiciaire sans fin), un défaut typiquement français, est un lieu commun de la satire du monde judiciaire,[29] elle fait ici directement écho à la mécanique narrative mise en place par le narrateur dans ses scènes de châtiment.

Monluc traduit en effet le mécanisme idéal de ce que doit être pour lui la justice en termes de mécanique du récit: si "nécessité fait loi," elle commande aussi la narration.[30] Chaque micro-récit de châtiment constitue de fait une réponse à la fois

---

28 Voir par exemple Jean-Louis Thireau, "Droit national et histoire nationale: les recherches érudites des fondateurs du droit français," *Droits* 38 (2003): 37–51 et Jean-Louis Gazzaniga, "Rédaction des coutumes et codification," *Droits* 26 (1997): 71–80.

29 Voir notamment Michel de Montaigne, *Essais* [1595], II, 12, éd. Denis Bjaï, Bénédicte Boudou, Jean Céard et Isabelle Pantin (Paris: Librairie Générale Française – "La Pochotèque," 2001), 902: "Les avocats et les juges de notre temps, trouvent à toutes causes, assez de biais pour les accommoder où bon leur semble. A une science si infinie, dépendant de l'autorité de tant d'opinions, et d'un sujet si arbitraire, il ne peut être, qu'il n'en naisse une confusion extrême de jugements. Aussi n'est-il guère si clair procès, auquel les avis ne se trouvent divers: ce qu'une compagnie a jugé, l'autre le juge au contraire, et elle-même au contraire une autre fois. De quoi nous voyons des exemples ordinaires, par cette licence, qui tache merveilleusement la cérémonieuse autorité et lustre de notre justice, de ne s'arrêter aux arrêts, et courir des uns aux autres juges, pour décider d'une même cause." Si Montaigne ne cesse de critiquer l'abondance contradictoire des lois françaises, la vénalité des avocats, et le bavardage stérile des procès, on notera toutefois que, contrairement à Monluc, il plaide aussi pour une justice sans cruauté: voir Pierre Michel, "L'homme de colère et l'homme de paix! Monluc, Montaigne," *Bulletin de la Société des Amis de Montaigne* 2 (1972), 51–66, et dans le présent volume la contribution de Denis Bjaï.

30 Claude-Gilbert Dubois établit également une analogie entre l'habileté tactique de Monluc en termes militaires, et son habileté tactique en termes de composition narrative des scènes de guerre: voir "La rupture du pont de Port-Sainte-Marie (1569) d'après les *Commentaires* de Monluc,"

pragmatique et en quelque sorte contrainte, obligée, à l'incurie judiciaire. Si l'idée de "nécessité," maintes fois rappelée par Monluc au cours de sa chronique,[31] est un argument souvent utilisé par les criminels de guerre—adopter la solution la moins pire pour un résultat plus rapide et une plus grande efficacité—elle se traduit aussi dans l'ordre du récit par la mise en place d'une même scénographie du châtiment articulant une temporalité spécifique et la maîtrise d'un espace.

Dans l'ordre du temps, on l'a vu, Monluc insiste sur la rapidité d'exécution du châtiment qui n'est pas une précipitation (l'auteur insiste opportunément à d'autres endroits de ses mémoires sur le fait qu'il sait attendre) mais l'équivalent dans l'ordre judiciaire de la vertu guerrière de "diligence," mélange de vitesse et de précision, capacité d'anticipation de l'action ennemie.[32] Gagner du temps pour moins s'exposer, en revanche, est le propre du protestant duplice ou de l'hypocrite courtisan.[33] Dans l'ordre de l'espace, on notera la capacité de Monluc à adapter promptement la punition au lieu où il se trouve—improvisant une forme de décorum judiciaire aux détails parfois sinistres.

Le capitaine gascon rompt en effet avec une pratique ancienne: ce n'est plus le supplice qui est assujetti à un lieu prédéterminé (le centre de la cité, la place de grève, l'échafaud . . .), mais bien le lieu qui se soumet, dans l'urgence de la situation, à la nécessité du supplice. La plupart des scènes révèlent ainsi l'ajustement macabre du châtiment à la configuration spécifique du site: "[poussé] rudement en terre" par Monluc, le premier supplicié de Saint-Mézard [1] tombe de telle sorte que "son col alla justement sur le morceau de la croix de pierre [du cimetière catholique] [. . .] que [les huguenots] avoient rompue," et qu'il est aussitôt décapité, ironie du sort, sur le lieu même de l'exaction de ses coreligionnaires (484 et 485); à Villefranche-de-Rouergue [4], alors que les commissaires du roi—soupçonnés d'être eux-mêmes protestants—demandent la "relaxe" des "séditieux" jugés coupables de pillage d'église par deux conseillers

---

Monluc, d'Aubigné, deux épées, deux plumes, 123–31 (voir n. 2). Sur le lien entre l'"habile montage rhétorique" du récit de guerre et les notions de "compétence, mérite et reconnaissance," voir aussi Nadine Kuperty-Tsur, "Profil et fonctions du récit de guerre dans les *Commentaires* de Monluc," *La Lettre et le Récit de guerre dans les mémoires d'Ancien régime: Actes des journées d'étude de Nantes, 3–4 avril 2003*, éd. Jean Garapon (Tours: Université de Tours – UFR de Lettres, 2004), 43–59.

31 Voir par exemple *Commentaires*, 822: "La necessité de la guerre nous force, en despit de nous-memes, à faire mille maux, et faire non plus d'estat de la vie des hommes que d'un poulet." C'est significativement la dernière occurrence du mot *nécessité* dans le livre.

32 Voir par exemple *Commentaires*, 707: "Capitaines, encores que ce ne soit pas icy de grandes conquestes et batailles, si pouvez-vous apprendre, aussi bien qu'en autres endroits de mon livre, de quoy profite une grande diligence (je suis tousjours sur ceste leçon, on ne la vous sçauroit trop repeter), et comme il fait bon hazarder quand il est necessaire."

33 Sur la capacité des protestants à temporiser dans les procès, voir supra n. 27. Monluc ironise aussi sur les courtisans contrefaisant les empressés, alors qu'ils se perdent en bavardages et conseils creux; voir *Commentaires*, 591: "Ces messieurs les courtisans, qui ne manièrent jamais autre fer que leurs orloges et montres, parlent comme bon leur semblent; ils font des demy-dieux et font les empressez, comme si rien n'estoit bien faict s'il ne passoit par leur teste."

de la cour de Bordeaux, Monluc, passant outre, les "[fait] pendre aux fenestres de la maison de la ville" (495 et 496); à Gironde [6], les prisonniers sont pendus, lugubre commerce, "aux piliers de la halle" (528). De même que le bon chef de guerre sait s'adapter au terrain (être mobile et rapide), de même, l'homme de justice doit pouvoir s'adapter à la scène improvisée d'un supplice.

Ce que permet en fait au capitaine-justicier—et après lui, au narrateur—la maîtrise de l'espace-temps de la scène judiciaire, c'est bien de produire à travers son action répressive des marques ou empreintes directement perceptibles de la justice royale. Loin des "sentences" et "escritures" des procès ou des plaidoiries infinies des avocats (qui brouillent le message), le langage de la justice doit être immédiatement lisible et transparent. Ce qui idéalement doit caractériser la justice du roi, c'est sa simplicité: évoquant son entreprise de pacification de la Guyenne après la signature de la paix d'Amboise (15 mars 1563), Monluc conclut sur la réussite de cette action par une simple équivalence: "Bref, le Roy y estoit recongnu et la justice obéye" (581). Le châtiment relève alors d'une forme d'éloquence naturelle (celle que Monluc manifeste aussi bien dans ses discours auprès des cours souveraines que dans l'écriture des mémoires[34]), laquelle produit pour tous un *signe* évident: alors qu'il vient de faire prisonniers "soixante ou quatre-vingt huguenots" à Gironde [6], Monluc prend soin ensuite de préciser,

> Et m'en allay là, lesquelz feys tous pendre aux piliers de la halle, sans autre ceremonie, qui donna une peur si grande par tout le pays qu'ils abandonnarent tout le long de la rivière devers Marmande et Toneins [. . .]. On pouvoit cognoistre par là où j'estoie passé, car par les arbres, sur les chemins, on en trouvoit les enseignes. Un pendu estonnoit plus que cent tuez (529).

Au-delà du principe de la guerre psychologique et de l'effet de signature, Monluc utilise le corps du supplicié comme "enseigne"[35] tangible de la justice du roi: à Terraube [9], en représailles d'un piège tendu à Monluc par les assiégés de Lectoure sous couvert de vouloir parlementer, les prisonniers sont tués, le chef pendu, et tous les corps "[jetés] dans le puy de la ville, qui estoit fort profond, et s'en remplit tout, de sorte que l'on les pouvoit toucher avec la main" (552); puis

34 Monluc assume son style soldatesque, mais en constate aussi l'efficace; voir par exemple *Commentaires*, 654: "Et croy que c'est une très-belle partie à un capitaine que de bien dire. Je n'ay pas esté nourry pour cest effect; mais encor ay-je eu ce bonheur de pouvoir exprimer en terme de soldats ce que j'avois à dire avec assés de véhémence, qui sentoit le pays d'où je suis sorty. [. . .] Et croy qu'un homme qui a leu et retenu est plus capable d'executer de belles entreprinses qu'un autre. Si j'en eusse eu, j'en eusse fait mon proffit; encor avois-je assés de naturel pour persuader le soldat de venir au combat." Sur l'importance des discours dans les *Commentaires*, notamment devant la cour souveraine de Bordeaux et les notables agenais, voir *infra* n. 51 et 52.

35 Monluc joue sans doute volontairement des multiples sens du mot *enseigne* qui, dans la langue française du XVIe siècle, signifie entre autres "drapeau, étendard (dans le langage militaire)" et "signe, ce qui est manifesté, manifestation." L'analogie entre vertus guerrières et vertus judiciaires est présente au cœur même du lexique.

quatre huguenots de Lectoure sont "[pendus] en un noyer près de la ville, à la veuë des ennemis" (*id.*). Contre les huguenots cachés derrière leur "mine" (590) duplice, Monluc fait *toucher* et *voir* la justice royale. Ce faisant, il répond aussi aux "tristes marques" (535) laissées partout par les ennemis du royaume: églises pillées, villages dévastés, familles catholiques massacrées.

Pour autant, le récit ne mentionne aucun réel acharnement symbolique sur les corps traduisant ce que Denis Crouzet appelle "la portée sacrale des violences catholiques" dans le contexte des châtiments collectifs et populaires, orchestrés notamment par la Ligue à Paris.[36] Dans le récit proposé par Monluc, le corps de l'adversaire est à la fois présent et absent: il s'agit de montrer simplement un signe de la justice du roi, sans engagement dans une mystique du symbole qui renverrait à la colère de Dieu.[37] Les "enseignes" laissées par Monluc sont des "signes du roi" plus que des "signes de Dieu,"[38] même s'il invoque ici ou là l'autorité divine pour justifier son action;[39] de fait, malgré ses réticences à l'égard du fond même des édits royaux (qu'il juge trop tolérants), son action va bien dans le sens d'un renforcement de l'autorité judiciaire du roi à la fin du siècle, unique et exclusive, contre la dispersion de toutes les autorités locales ou régionales.[40] La justice est une affaire d'hommes, l'exercice du châtiment engage dans des situations concrètes dont il faut pouvoir assumer dans la pratique toutes les dimensions: c'est donc à partir de l'*ethos* renouvelé de l'homme de loi que Monluc

---

36 Denis Crouzet, "Imaginaire du corps et violence aux temps des troubles de religion," *Le Corps à la Renaissance. Actes du XXXe colloque de Tours [2–11 juillet 1987]*, éd. Jean Céard, Marie Madeleine Fontaine et Jean-Claude Margolin (Paris: Aux Amateurs, 1990), 115–27; ici 116. Sur la "violence mystique" et le "prophétisme panique" des catholiques durant les guerres de religion, voir surtout du même *Les Guerriers de Dieu: la violence au temps des guerres de religion (vers 1525-vers 1610)*. Les Classiques de Champ Vallon (1990; Seyssel: Champ Vallon, 2005).

37 Un rare exemple d'acharnement est celui des soldats de Monluc (non de Monluc lui-même) contre le corps du dénommé Brusquin, mais sans aucune référence à une dimension sacrale: voir *Commentaires*, 677.

38 Sur cette notion, outre les travaux de Denis Crouzet mentionnés n. 36, voir Myriam Yardeni, "Guerre de propagande et signes de Dieu à l'époque de la ligue," *Les signes de Dieu aux XVIe et XVIIe siècles. Actes du colloque de Clermont-Ferrand*, éd. Guy Demerson et Bernard Dompnier (Clermont-Ferrand: Association des Publications de la Faculté des lettres et sciences humaines de Clermont-Ferrand, 1993), 102–12.

39 Voir par exemple *Commentaires*, 521: "Par là on pouvoit juger que [les protestants] estoient maistres de la campagne, puisqu'ils osoient mener le canon; et si Dieu ne m'eust inspiré à m'opposer à eux et faire pendre ceux qui tomboient entre mes mains, je croy que tout le pays estoit perdu, car la douceur de Monsieur de Burie [= lieutenant général du roi en Guyenne] n'estoit pas de saison." Mais invoquer Dieu pour légitimer son action est un procédé plutôt banal à l'époque; Monluc n'en abuse pas, et associe rarement ces mentions d'un "Dieu partisan" à une véhémence mystique, comme chez beaucoup d'autres auteurs catholiques; en ce sens, nous ne souscrivons pas entièrement au jugement de Denis Crouzet analysant le songe prophétique de Monluc dans *Les Guerriers de Dieu*, 451–54 (voir n. 36).

40 Voir sur ce point la très suggestive étude de Penny Roberts, "Royal Authority and Justice during the French Religious Wars," *Past and Present* 184.1 (2004): 3–32.

va chercher à penser une nouvelle *praxis* de la justice—une forme d'utopie judiciaire?

Justice d'exception ou utopie judiciaire? L'*ethos* du capitaine-justicier

En plaçant son action de justice sous le signe de la nécessité, Monluc s'impose comme un acteur indispensable de la justice royale. Bien plus, en évitant soigneusement de développer ou d'embellir les micro-récits de châtiment, en suggérant que ceux-ci se rattachent de manière imprévue à la logique du récit de guerre traditionnel, il se présente lui-même comme une figure surprenante et originale du monde judiciaire—mais une figure toujours centrale grâce à l'omniprésence de l'énonciateur dans les *Commentaires*. Apte à prendre en charge, grâce à la dynamique de l'écriture autobiographique, une multiplicité de rôles qui sont autant d'inscriptions dans l'histoire des guerres civiles (chef de guerre, négociateur, diplomate, orateur, gestionnaire, maître ou pédagogue en art militaire, père de soldat, frère d'armes, etc.), il se compose aussi peu à peu une identité d'homme de loi. Loin d'être revendiquée explicitement, cette identité judiciaire se définit d'abord par défaut dans le contraste saisissant qui oppose Monluc aux avocats ou aux juges qui apparaissent aux détours des mémoires, et sont presque systématiquement l'objet de vives critiques. La digression sur la réforme de la justice, citée plus haut, s'achevait naturellement sur une satire générale des avocats "[s'amusant] en ces palais et plaidoyeries" et "[donnant] aux parties [de] mauvais conseils." À la fin du même livre VI, le portrait charge de l'avocat toulousain Charles du Sault insiste sur la "méchanceté" (c'est-à-dire la malveillance) propre à cette "vacation:"

> Et ce bon advocat du Sault estoit le premier qui publioit mes louanges par toute la court [i. e., de justice] et ville; et asteure, à son dire, je ne suys que ung pillart et ung larron. Car d'un meschant l'on n'en peult tirer que toute meschanceté, de là où la plupart des gens de son poil sont taichés (678).

Indépendamment du différend qui oppose Monluc à du Sault,[41] on notera ici la virulence d'une critique élargie à toute la profession—l'auteur jouant de l'image du col fourré emblématique de l'habit des hommes de loi ("des gens de son poil"),

41 Voir *Commentaires* 1321 n. 4: "Du Sault fut chargé, le 28 avril 1570, de porter au roi les doléances du Parlement de Bordeaux contre l'inaction de Monluc."

propice à des jeux de mots topiques sur l'engagement "fourré" (de pure forme) de cette profession.[42]

Les récits de châtiment s'inscrivent donc non seulement dans le cadre d'une crise judiciaire généralisée, mais aussi dans le cadre plus social de la concurrence entre gens de "robe courte" (la noblesse d'épée, à laquelle appartient évidemment Monluc) et gens de "robe longue" (la noblesse plus récente formée au droit[43]) dans la mainmise sur les "offices de judicature," autrement dit les offices de justice accordés par le roi. Cette concurrence apparaît explicitement dans une comparaison à travers laquelle l'auteur se défend, en tant que soldat et chef, de vouloir prolonger la guerre pour le plaisir:

> On dict que nous mesmes, qui portons les armes, entretenons la guerre et voulons alonger la couroye, comme on fait aux palais les procès. Le diable emportera tout. Si n'ay-je jamais eu ceste intention, pouvant dire avec la verité qu'il n'y a lieutenant de roy en France qui ait plus faict passer d'huguenots par le couteau ou par la corde que moy. Ce n'estoit pas vouloir entretenir la guerre (737).

Deux manières de faire justice s'opposent nettement ici, dont une seulement se veut efficace en ces temps exceptionnels de guerre civile. Mais c'est dans la remontrance finale au roi qu'apparaît l'argument central de la critique, Monluc rappelant fermement au monarque son devoir de vigilance et de jugement dans la distribution des offices de justice:

> Sire, quand Vostre Majesté baille un office de président ou conseiller, lieutenant general ou quelque autre office de judicature, vous vous reservez qu'ils ne pourront exercer la charge qu'ils ne soyent examinez par vos parlements, pleins d'hommes fort sçavans; et bien souvent vous ordonnez que vostre chancellier les examinera avant que les parlemens les voyent, afin qu'ils jugent s'ils sont capables et qu'ils ne puissent errer au jugement des procez de vos subjects, et que le droict soit rendu à qui il appartiendra. C'est une chose bonne et juste, Sire, car vous nous devez la justice droicte et au pois de la balance; c'est la première chose que vous nous devez (801).

On ne saurait faire plus bel éloge du roi garant de toute justice, par l'excellence de son choix, et par l'efficacité (théorique) des différentes instances de contrôle et de vérification de ce choix. Mais loin d'évoquer le problème endémique de la vénalité

---

42 Est-ce le cas lors de la prise de Monségur [8]? Voir *Commentaires*, 532: "La tuerie dura jusques à dix heures ou plus, pource qu'on les cherchoit dans les maisons ; et en fut prins quinze ou vingt seulement, lesquels nous fismes pendre, et entre autres tous les officiers du Roy et les consuls, avec les chapperons sur le col. Il ne se parloit point de rançon, sinon pour les bourreaux." Le *chaperon fourré* identifie en effet traditionnellement les docteurs en droit (et désigne par métonymie ces mêmes docteurs).

43 Peu après la critique de l'avocat Du Sault, Monluc conclut ainsi: "Ces gens de robe longue sont de fascheuse desserre, et nous batent tousjours de leurs privilèges" (*Commentaires*, 679).

des offices[44], Monluc suggère plutôt ici que la justice est menacée de dispersion entre les mains des gens de "robe courte," plus enclins à manifester leur science et leur éloquence dans les palais qu'à rendre bonne justice. Dans un pays où, selon Monluc, le droit est par essence coutumier, où se situe le vrai savoir juridique, qui peut le détenir, qui peut en faire bénéficier l'ensemble des justiciables? Monluc ne cesse de cibler le milieu robin, tout en mettant en garde la vieille noblesse d'épée: d'un côté, il reproche à celle-ci de ne pas suffisamment s'impliquer dans les charges de magistrat municipal[45], et de l'autre, il constate non sans crainte l'influence grandissante de celui-là à la cour, au détriment de la vraie sagesse des "vieux capitaines."[46] Son inquiétude est emblématique de cette période trouble de mutation sociale où, à la fin du siècle, dans le milieu de la noblesse, la "robe longue" prend peu à peu le pas sur la "courte," le livre sur l'épée, le cabinet d'étude sur le champ de bataille, la procédure judiciaire raisonnée sur l'antique instinct de justice[47].

Monluc cherche moins, pourtant, à maintenir l'opposition entre ces deux "estats" de noblesse qu'à les fondre en une seule figure de capitaine-justicier. La légitimité d'une telle figure repose nécessairement sur un retour aux sources d'une justice traditionnelle où l'éthique héroïque peut se confondre naturellement avec l'éthique judiciaire. Outre sa référence constante à la coutume, déjà relevée, Monluc ne cesse de défendre le serment et l'éloquence naturelle, deux formes emblématiques d'une justice traditionnelle et archaïque, marquées par l'oralité et opposées à toutes les "escritures" (607), en particulier les écritures savantes du droit moderne. Le serment—qui, dans le cas des *Commentaires*, mériterait à lui seul une étude à part—constitue la forme la plus ancienne de résolution des litiges (lorsqu'il est *assertoire*) et structure fortement les procédures judiciaires

44 Voir Arlette Lebigre, *La justice du roi*, 58–83. À ce problème de la vénalité des offices (instaurée par François Ier) s'ajoute surtout celui, plus épineux, de leur patrimonialité: en étant transmis de père en fils, l'office échappe totalement au contrôle de l'État.

45 Voir *Commentaires*, 685: "Il faut que j'escrive en passant une chose que j'ay tousjours dite et diray tant que je vivray: que la noblesse s'est faict grand tort et dommage de desdaigner ainsi les charges des villes, principalement des capitales comme Thoulouse et Bordeaus [. . .]. Car, refusant ces charges ou les laissant prendre, les gens de ville s'emparent de l'auctorité, et quand nous arrivons, il les faut boneter et leur faire la cour."

46 Voir *Commentaires*, 816: "Puis que vous [= le duc d'Anjou] tenez si grand lieu, d'où dépendent toutes charges qui procèdent des armes, et qu'il faut que nous tous mourions auprès de vous pour le service du Roy et vostre, il faut que vous mettés tout vostre soin et voz pensers en nous, qui suivons les armes, car tous les autres estats ne participent rien avec le vostre, de tant que tout le reste depend des gens de robbe longue; il y en a prou au conseil du Roy; vous n'avez rien à desmesler avec eux, car on dict: qui trop embrasse peu estraint."

47 Voir Arlette Jouanna, "La noblesse française et les valeurs guerrières au XVIe siècle," *L'Homme de guerre au XVIe siècle*, 205–17, en particulier 213–16 (voir n. 9).

traditionnelles (lorsqu'il est *promissoire*), au point d'être omniprésent dans la justice médiévale.[48]

De manière significative, Monluc place tout son récit des Guerres de Religion sous le signe d'un premier serment qui le lie indéfectiblement au roi. Alors que les églises réformées, par l'intermédiaire du capitaine Sendat, lui demandent de promettre de ne pas prendre les armes contre elles, il répond évidemment *en droit* ne pouvoir être lié par deux serments contradictoires: "Comment voulez-vous que la Royne ny le Roy, quand il sera grand, me tiennent en reputation d'homme de bien, veu que j'auray faict deux sermens l'un contre l'autre"? (480). Le risque n'est pas seulement celui du déshonneur, mais aussi celui d'une désorganisation complète d'un lien social pluriséculaire.[49] En ce sens, Monluc se distingue des princes et seigneurs calculateurs de l'entourage du roi, capables de produire de faux serments et de vains engagements.[50]

À l'opposé de l'espace courtisan marqué par la corruption du langage et de la promesse, la Guyenne devient un territoire idéalisé où les serments authentiques demeurent possibles: Monluc sait mettre en scène la solennité de ses interventions devant les cours souveraines (Toulouse et Bordeaux) ou les notables des villes (Agen), à travers lesquelles est censé apparaître nettement le lien étroit entre son éloquence naturelle (déjà évoquée) et un engagement véridique passé avec ces autorités urbaines. À Bordeaux, Monluc convainc les jurats de prendre les armes et de mobiliser la ville contre la menace du prince de Condé et des Provençaux, soulignant l'efficacité immédiate de sa "remonstrance,"[51] en dépit, ou plutôt grâce à la force de persuasion de son style soldatesque. Et c'est bien par serment solennel qu'il fait promettre aux Agenais de ne "rien espargner" pour combattre la Réforme:[52] "Alors, comme j'avoy levé la main, je leur fis lever la leur et faire le

48 Sur l'importance du serment au Moyen Âge, voir: *Le Serment. I, Signes et fonctions*, éd. Raymond Verdier (Paris: Éditions du Centre National de la Recherche Scientifique, 1991); *Serment, promesse et engagement: rituels et modalités au Moyen Âge*, éd. Françoise Laurent. Les Cahiers du CRISIMA, 6 (Montpellier: Presses Universitaires de la Méditerranée, 2008); et *Oralité et lien social au Moyen Âge (Occident, Byzance, Islam): parole donnée, foi jurée, serment*, éd. Marie-France Auzépy et Guillaume Saint-Guillain (Paris: Centre de Recherche d'Histoire et de Civilisation de Byzance, 2008).

49 Voir *Commentaires*, 480: "Que deviendray-je puis après que j'auray perdu mon honneur, moy qui n'ay jamais combattu que pour en acquerir? Je ne veux pas dire seulement que les gentilshommes ne me voudront veoir auprès d'eux, mais les vilains propres ne me voudroient veoir en leur compagnie."

50 Voir *Commentaires*, 587–89. Monluc évoque la signature de la déclaration royale du 18 mars 1565, par laquelle les princes, grands seigneurs, gouverneurs, et capitaines de compagnie jurent "estre liguez pour la deffence de la couronne" et promettent de ne s'associer en aucune autre ligue. Monluc, présent, souligne les attitudes duplices et les feintises, si bien que malgré les "serments," "on y peut veoir des gens en blanc et en noir, qui ont esté parjures à bon escient" (589). Sur la dégradation générale de la foi jurée, voir aussi *Commentaires*, 605–06.

51 Voir *Commentaires*, 652–53.

52 Voir *Commentaires*, 741–42.

mesme serment que j'avois faict" (742). Le sens du détail et de la gestuelle mérite d'être souligné.

Ces scènes sont essentielles dans la mesure où elles concourent à rendre visible l'intervention de l'homme de guerre dans un lieu où prévaut d'ordinaire le langage du droit. Reprenant l'image de l'homme de justice prêt à prendre les armes (déjà utilisée dans sa digression critique sur l'état de la justice du royaume, étudiée plus haut), Monluc invite les jurats bordelais à quitter les palais pour les champs de bataille, à l'exemple des "anciens Romains," à la fois "gens de lettres" et combattants:

> Messieurs, leur dis-je, je voy bien à voz visages que vous n'estes pas hommes pour vous laisser battre. Ceux qui ont la barbe et la teste blanche seront pour le conseil; mais un bon nombre que je voy icy sont propres à porter la picque. Combien pensez-vous que cela accouragera le peuple, quand il verra ceux qui ont puissance sur leur bien et sur leur vie prendre les armes pour leur deffence? Nul n'osera gronder; voz ennemis seront en peur, quand ils oyront que la cour de Parlement s'arme; ils verront que c'est à bon escient. Et puis tant de jeunesse que j'ay veu dans vostre salle, entrant céans, plus propre à porter un corcelet qu'une robbe longue (652–53).

La simplicité des oppositions encadrant le passage ("teste blanche" versus "picque" et "corcelet" versus "robbe longue") permet de mêler efficacement deux univers de valeurs, au point de ne plus les distinguer. L'image de l'avocat de parlement armé fonctionne en fait à la manière d'un miroir: elle impose comme incontournable, en son reflet, celle du capitaine-justicier avec laquelle veut s'identifier Monluc. Dans ses *Mémoires*, le capitaine gascon dépasse cependant la seule revendication d'une noblesse d'épée exigeant de ne pas être cantonnée uniquement dans les emplois militaires:[53] il suggère, bien au-delà, que vertus guerrières et vertus judiciaires sont les mêmes, que l'*ethos* du capitaine accomplit pleinement l'*ethos* du juge, ce qu'est bien sûr censée illustrer chaque micro-scène de châtiment. Les différents portraits éthiques du soldat généreux et vaillant—Monluc lui-même ou d'autres capitaines—dispersés dans les mémoires peuvent donc être systématiquement soumis à une double lecture: chaque "vertu" guerrière peut trouver son équivalent dans l'ordre de l'activité judiciaire—comme la "diligence," déjà étudiée plus haut. Un portrait synthétise d'autant mieux, vers la fin des *Commentaires*, cet idéal du capitaine-justicier, qu'il est dessiné à la lumière d'Alexandre le Grand et de César, subsumant de fait l'homme de guerre et l'homme de justice dans l'unique catégorie du "grand homme:"

53 Voir Arlette Jouanna, "La noblesse française et les valeurs guerrières au XVIe siècle," 206 (voir n. 47): "[Les nobles] estiment qu'il est de leur compétence de rendre la justice, et réclament que des charges leur soient réservées dans les tribunaux de baillage ou de sénéchaussée et dans les cours souveraines, en particulier les Parlements; ils protestent contre les inutiles complications du droit, que les gens de robe auraient introduites à dessein dans le but pervers de 'bannir la noblesse des judicatures', selon l'expression de Jean de Saulx-Tavanes."

> En vain ne portoit pas Alexandre le Grand la divise que j'ay dict cy-devant[54]. Regardez les Commentaires de Cesar et de tous ceux qui ont escrit de luy: vous trouverez qu'il donna en sa vie cinquante-deux batailles, sans en perdre jamais que celle de Dirache; et trente jours après il eust bien sa revenche contre Pompée, car il gaigna une grand bataille, où il le diffit. Vous ne trouverez point qu'en ces cinquante-deux batailles il aye combattu de ses mains trois fois; et par là vous cognoistrez doncques que toutes ses victoires luy sont advenues pour estre diligent, vigilant, et prompt executeur (779).

Certes, ni Alexandre ni César n'ont laissé de traces dans l'histoire comme grands hommes de justice ou comme modèles d'équité, et les trois qualités ci-dessus mentionnées de *diligence*, de *vigilance* et de *prompte exécution* relèvent d'abord de l'art de la guerre; pourtant, à la relecture des différentes scènes de châtiment, ce sont bien ces trois qualités qui sont, explicitement ou moins explicitement, largement mises en œuvre dans l'action de justice assumée alors par Monluc, laquelle requiert un soin et une application actives (la *diligence*), une disposition à repérer et identifier le crime (la *vigilance*), et enfin une capacité à le châtier dans l'urgence de la situation (la *prompte exécution*). De fait, dans chacun des micro-récits de châtiment l'auteur des mémoires réalise implicitement une synthèse entre l'idéal belliqueux, la compétence juridique et la performance judiciaire.

Si une telle synthèse peut d'abord être perçue comme le produit (artificiel) de l'écriture rétrospective, elle ne laissera pourtant pas indifférents, quelques années après la publication des *Commentaires*, Nicolas et Étienne Pasquier: est-ce vraiment un hasard si sous la plume de ces deux éminents juristes gallicans et robins, Monluc "n'est pas seulement le champion d'une littérature d'épée nationale, mais joue aussi pour le milieu de la robe gallicane le rôle du modèle social du parvenu honnête et méritant"?[55] Loin d'être simplement partisan, le jugement élogieux des deux frères reflète la personnalité complexe de Monluc, et invite à relire ses mémoires comme une œuvre capable d'être éthiquement exemplaire, et dépassant la dimension de la simple chronique militaire.

Monluc rêve-t-il simplement une utopie judiciaire? La figure du capitaine-justicier est-elle nécessairement chimérique? En un sens oui, dans la mesure où l'héroïsme justicier qu'il prône ne prend sens que dans le contexte difficile des Guerres de Religion, où seule une justice d'exception violente, généralisée et simplificatrice, peut réellement dominer le désordre civil pour faire entendre *quand même* la voix de la Loi et du Roi. La remarque qui conclut la dernière scène de châtiment, le

54 Voir *Commentaires*, 708: "ce que tu peux faire aujourd'huy, n'attens au lendemain." La même devise avait déjà été donnée dans deux autres "remontrances" aux capitaines (188 et 446).

55 Voir Denise Carabin, "La réception posthume des *Commentaires* de Blaise de Monluc chez Étienne et Nicolas Pasquier: naissance d'un symbole politique," *Revue d'Histoire Littéraire de la France* 102 (2002), 179–90; ici 190. Étienne Pasquier commente l'œuvre de Monluc dans une lettre (publiée dans l'édition posthume des *Lettres*, 1619), et Nicolas dans son traité *Le gentilhomme* (1611).

massacre de Rabastens [12], sonne à la fois comme une auto-justification un peu gênée, un quasi aveu d'impuissance, et le désir pressant d'un au-delà de la justice d'exception: "Ne pensez pas, vous qui lirez ce livre, que je fisse faire cette execution tant pour vanger ma blesseure que pour donner espouvente à tout le pays, afin qu'on n'eust le cœur de faire teste à nostre armée [. . .]. Et comme il faut de la rigueur (appellez-la cruauté, si vous voulez), aussi fait-il de l'autre costé de la douceur" (784).

On ne saurait mieux insister sur le caractère provisoire et contraint de la situation de guerre civile. Pourtant, Monluc fait preuve d'une réelle lucidité dans son désir de réforme de la justice du royaume, idéalement fondée sur une éthique renouvelée de l'homme de loi, la valorisation d'une éloquence naturelle et sincère, et la revendication d'un droit adapté au pays (à travers la coutume). Beaucoup des ajouts apportés par Monluc à la version initiale de son texte (dans les livres V à VII du moins) concernent le fonctionnement de la justice, parfois dans ses détails les plus concrets: au fur et à mesure que le temps passe, le cadre judiciaire prend de l'ampleur, devient presque aussi important que celui de la guerre, s'inscrit légitimement dans les débats du temps.

Mais c'est au cœur même de l'écriture des *Commentaires* que se cristallise cette refondation d'une image de la justice. L'intérêt majeur du texte de Monluc est en effet de présenter crimes et châtiments dans une matière et une manière brutes (sinon brutales), à l'opposé du style ampoulé et pathétique de l'historiographie officielle ou de la rhétorique juridique des traités théoriques sur la justice. Pour le mémorialiste, c'est au cœur de l'événement, puis au cœur du récit des mémoires que se joue concrètement l'avenir de l'action judiciaire. La scène de châtiment, pour violente qu'elle soit, n'est pas purement décorative: en elle se renégocie sans cesse (parce qu'elle s'inscrit dans l'urgence et le caractère exceptionnel de la situation de guerre civile) toute la logique de la justice, dont elle est le noyau à la fois nécessaire et redouté.

Chapter 19

Martha Moffitt Peacock
(Brigham Young University, Provo, Utah)

The Amsterdam *Spinhuis* and the "Art" of Correction

Since the 1980's when Foucault first discussed the prison as a theoretical model for social control in *Discipline and Punish,* various historians have similarly focused on the prison as a site for power and manipulation.[1] Using Foucault's model, scholars continued to discuss prisons as instruments of authoritarian control in which the inhabitants were constantly subjected to exploitative tyranny. Feminist historians of the prison expanded the use of this theoretical model by asserting that penal control also came in the form of patriarchal dominance over, and abuse of, women prisoners. Indeed many social histories of female inmates have demonstrated that prisons were horrifying institutions in which men not only had corrective control over women, but via this control they also seized power over women's bodies. For women, the atrocious consequences of this male domination and manipulation came in the form of being frequently raped or put into service as a prostitute.

The one early modern exception to this patriarchally-controlled penal nightmare for women was the *spinhuis,* literally house for spinning, established in Amsterdam in 1597. From the outset it was founded as a separate reform facility for women, with both female and male overseers, so that inmates did not face the same dangers of sexual abuse by male prisoners and guards. Visual imagery associated with the spinhouse emphasizes its unique character as an institution ruled by women. Indeed, the portraits of regentesses, or governesses, of the institution are significant indicators of this female authority and oversight. These visual tributes to the power and dignity of influential women were put on prominent public display within the regents' rooms of the spinhouse. In addition,

---

1 Michel Foucault, *Discipline and Punish: The Birth of the Prison* (Originally published in 1975 in France under the title *Surveiller et punir: Naissance de la Prison,* translated into English in 1977; New York: Pantheon Books, 1977).

these large and impressive paintings also contain meaningful and familiar signifiers that further referenced the power of women in the Dutch culture of correction. Some signifiers refer to traditional themes of strong women who usurp male authority, thus calling attention to female dominance at the spinhouse. Other visual signs invoke allusions to the serious, honorable, and ubiquitous images of female domestic skills produced in the Dutch Republic during the seventeenth century. Through these dual associations with female power and honorability, the spinhouse escaped the absolute control of patriarchy and its associated sexual abuse. Instead, the institution was able to focus on its original purpose—the reform of poor and indolent women into productive and skilled laborers within Dutch society.

It is crucial to consider this founding purpose of the Amsterdam spinhouse in order to understand its unique position in the history of women's prisons. Its origins were based on the assumption that women could be reformed. It was created as a charitable institution to take poor beggar women off the streets and make them into productive inhabitants by teaching them skills that would be useful in society. The name for the institution was given because women were indeed employed in spinning, weaving, sewing, and lace-making in the prison. In addition to poor women, some women were placed there because they were causing difficulties for their families. Some of the women were kept there day and night, while others were allowed to go home at night and still others were allowed out during the day time to work.[2] The institution was established in the former St. Ursula cloister, so from its very origins it was founded at a site that was historically and culturally oriented toward female power and control. Being established as a female charitable asylum, it carried historical connotations as an institution where women were brought back to God, brought back to honor, and brought back to chastity as they learned to work diligently in a sober and virtuous environment.

As previously stated, most feminist discussions of women's imprisonment indict patriarchy in its inappropriate treatment of female inmates. These abuses relate to the traditional categorization of women as weak and of a naturally evil nature that needed to be controlled by men. Moreover, these attitudes allowed men to have control over women's bodies. Lucia Zedner and Heidi Lee Cain have argued that such control led to constant instances of women being raped by male guards and fellow male prisoners, due to the fact that men and women were frequently

---

2 Pieter Spierenburg gives a very thorough archival history of the spinhouse and compares it to contemporary institutions in *The Prison Experience: Disciplinary Institutions and Their Inmates in Early Modern Europe* (Amsterdam: Amsterdam University Press, Amsterdam Academic Archive, 2007).

housed together.[3] The Bridewell prison of London, for example, became a veritable brothel with women being coerced by threats and beatings into prostituting themselves for the benefit of men at the prison. In the United States, prison conditions for women were not any better. As with most European institutions, men and women were housed together allowing for sexual abuse by inmates and guards alike. It was not until the nineteenth century that conditions for female prisoners improved in both Europe and America. Most of these early reforms were initiated by middle class women, usually Quakers and Unitarians, who were also actively engaged in promoting other social agendas such as temperance and anti-slavery. In the United States a group of these reformers established the Prison Association of New York in order to improve conditions for female prisoners in the city jails. In England Elizabeth Fry and her supporters established the Ladies Association for the Reformation of Female Prisoners in Newgate for a similar purpose. With the intervention of these powerful women's groups, officials soon acquiesced and began to establish separate women's prisons on both sides of the Atlantic. It is significant to note, therefore, that historical improvement for the conditions of female prisoners usually depended on the politically powerful voices of educated women.[4]

In order to better comprehend the attitudes that allowed for the type of sexual abuse found in almost all early modern prisons, it is important to be aware of the general social categorization of women as a segment of culture that could be appropriated by men. This allowed for the maltreatment of women that took place in the prison environment. In a society like the Dutch Republic, however, where women could not be so easily possessed by men, where they had more of a social voice, where they were constructors of society rather than merely being constructed by that society, a unique correctional institution was established that was quite enlightened for the early modern period.

The relative power of Dutch women in the seventeenth century has been attributed to a number of societal factors that center on the early development of an urban middle class culture, which in turn produced more independent women. Women publicly asserted themselves from the very establishment of the republic, as many of them attained heroine status in the war for independence from Spain.[5]

3 Lucia Zedner, "Wayward Sisters: The Prison for Women," *The Oxford History of the Prison: The Practice of Punishment in Western Society*, ed. Norval Morris and David J. Rothman (New York and Oxford: Oxford University Press, 1995), 329–61; Heidi Lee Cain, "Women Confined by Prison Bars and Male Images," *Texas Journal of Women and the Law* 18 (2008): 103–24.

4 Zedner, "Wayward Sisters," 331–37 (see note 3); Cain, "Women Confined," 106–09 (see note 3); Estelle B. Freedman, *Their Sisters' Keepers: Women's Prison Reform in America, 1830–1930* (Ann Arbor: The University of Michigan Press, 1981).

5 Alice Clare Carter, "Marriage Counseling in the Early Seventeenth Century: England and the Netherlands Compared," *Ten Studies in Anglo-Dutch Relations*, ed. Jan A. van Dorsten (Leiden:

Hajnal attributes a greater equality between men and women in the Dutch Republic to the fact that women often worked and put off marriage until a later age.[6] In addition, it has been noted that a comparatively large number of households were headed by single females in this society.[7] Other historians have discussed the evidence of women's greater power and independence in law, business, and Dutch culture generally.[8]

Clearly, when women as a social category were defined, at least in part, by women, the traditional pattern of men controlling women was disrupted, thus thwarting the opportunities for men to subjugate women. As Colette Guillaumin has argued, the natural fact of being a woman did not automatically result in the control of women; it was the social significance attached to women as beings who could be dominated that led to their appropriation by men.[9] In the instance of prisons, this was constituted by the prostituting of female prisoners. It is important to understand, however, that signifiers, such as the category "woman," are

---

Published for the Sir Thomas Browne Institute, at the University Press; London: Oxford University Press, 1974), 94–127; Martha Moffitt Peacock, "The Comedy of the Shrew: Theorizing Humor in Early Modern Netherlandish Art," *Laughter in the Middle Ages and Early Modern Times: Epistemology of a Fundamental Human Behavior, its Meaning, and Consequences,* ed. Albrecht Classen and Marilyn Sandidge. Fundamentals of Medieval and Early Modern Culture, 5 (Berlin and New York: Walter de Gruyter, 2010), 667–713; Martha Moffitt Peacock, "Proverbial Reframing—Rebuking and Revering Women in Trousers," *Journal of the Walters Art Gallery* 57 (1999): 13–34.

6 John Hajnal, "European Marriage Patterns in Perspective," *Population in History: Essays in Historical Demography,* ed. David Victor Glass and David Edward Charles Eversley (London: Edward Arnold Publishers, 1965), 101–41.

7 Ad M. van der Woude, "Variations in the Size and Structure of the Household in the United Provinces of the Netherlands in the Seventeenth and Eighteenth Centuries, "*Household and Family in Past Time: Comparative Studies in the Size and Structure of the Domestic Group over the Last Three Centuries in England, France, Serbia, Japan and Colonial North America, With Further Materials from Western Europe,* ed. Peter Laslett and Richard Wall (Cambridge: Cambridge University Press, 1972), 299–318.

8 For a discussion of the general cultural independence of women in the Dutch Republic see Simon Schama, "Wives and Wantons: Versions of Womanhood in Seventeenth-Century Dutch Art," *The Oxford Art Journal* 3.1 (1980): 5–13; Simon Schama, *The Embarrassment of Riches* (New York: Knopf, 1987), 384–91; Alice Clare Carter, "Marriage Counseling" (see note 5). See also the various essays in *Women of the Golden Age: An International Debate on Women in Seventeenth-Century Holland, England and Italy,* ed. Els Kloek, Nicole Teeuwen, and Marijke Huisman (Hilversum: Verloren, 1994). The absence of strong patriarchy in Dutch culture is discussed in Donald Haks, *Huwelijk en Gezin in Holland in de 17de en 18de Eeuw* (Assen: Van Gorcum's Historische Bibliotheek, 1982). The participation of Dutch women in business is discussed in Danielle van den Heuvel, *Women and Entrepreneurship: Female Traders in the Northern Netherlands, c. 1580–1815* (Amsterdam: Aksant, 2007); Martha Moffitt Peacock, "Early Modern Dutch Women in the City: The Imaging of Economic Agency and Power," *Urban Space in the Middle Ages and the Early Modern Age,* ed. Albrecht Classen and Marilyn Sandidge. Fundamentals of Medieval and Early Modern Culture, 4 (Berlin and New York: Walter de Gruyter, 2009), 667–711.

9 Colette Guillaumin, *Racism, Sexism, Power and Ideology* (London and New York: Routledge, 1995).

historically variable. Therefore, in a socio-cultural situation where the traditional patriarchal notions of women were not automatic and were instead constantly challenged, patriarchal ability to appropriate women's bodies was diminished. Indeed, the images associated with the Amsterdam spinhouse are compelling indicators of female subversion of traditional patriarchy. These images put women on more of an equal footing with men as governors, caretakers, and disciplinarians of the women inmates. They contain traditional assignations of female power and control. Furthermore, these images were associated with positive and traditional significations of women's economic value and socio-cultural contributions in terms of work and skill. As the discrete category "woman" and her traditional characteristics were deconstructed via such imagery, sexist ideologies and abilities to reduce "woman" to subjugated object also diminished.

Hence we come to a discussion of how and why the Amsterdam spinhouse was such a unique institution in the early modern period. Zedner who has studied the early modern prison from a feminist perspective called attention to the exceptionality of the spinhouse as the first, and for many years only, all female institution.[10] Even other spinhouses in The Dutch Republic and Germany combined male and female prisoners.[11] Many feminist writers on the prison have indicated the positive nature of separating male and female prisoners. For women such separation meant that they did not have to suffer the dangers of being regularly raped and prostituted by male prisoners and guards. Thus, in addition to being separated from male prisoners, the institution was overseen by both a *binnenmoeder,* indoor mother, and a *binnenvader,* indoor father.

As Pieter Spierenburg has discussed, the system therefore reflected the model of a family.[12] However, while he identifies this as a patriarchal model, I would suggest that female control within the domestic family environment in the Dutch Republic was, in practice, even greater than that of fathers. In Dutch society great import was given to mothers as caretakers and rulers of the household. Contemporary moralists like Jacob Cats encouraged women to supervise children and servants, and to control domestic expenses. Husbands were instructed to leave the household to the management of their wives. In fact, discussions of the household describe it as the *heerschappij* or dominion of women.[13]

This term of power was also applied to male rulers. Johann van Beverwijk goes even further in his praise and exaltation of housewives. He firmly asserts the importance of family and home, proclaims the family to be the fountain and origin of

---

10 Zedner, "Wayward Sisters," 329 (see note 3).

11 Spierenburg, *Prison Experience* (see note 2).

12 Spierenburg, *Prison Experience,* 105–34 (see note 2).

13 Jacob Cats, *Alle de Wercken, So ouden als nieuwe, van de Heer Iacob Cats, Ridder, oudt Raedtpensionaris van Hollandt, &c.* (Amsterdam: Ian Iacobsz Schipper, 1655), *Houwelick,* 79.

a republic, and states one must augment and preserve the family as one would govern and protect a city or state. He also declares that the housewife's reliable actions help lay the foundation for a well-ordered society, he considers the housewife's power great, and he compares her domain to a kingdom.[14]

A survey of domestic imagery produced during the seventeenth century underscores the prevalence of these attitudes. Images of the home rarely contain fathers, and when they are present, they are usually relegated to an insignificant position, often in the background, of the composition. Women dominate these scenes and they are frequently shown instructing children, servants, and vendors in their duties. A significant example of this type of authoritarian imagery is depicted in a painting of 1663 by Quirijn van Brekelenkam (Fig. 1). Here the mother is enthroned in the center of the composition with children and maidservant gathered around following her example and attending to her commands.

If, then, the spinhouse follows a familial model, it is important that the role of mother not be underestimated in Dutch society. Indeed, from the moment of entry into the Amsterdam spinhouse, one encounters a looming sense of female power. Over the doorway, a group of sculpted figures done by Hendrick de Keyser in 1607 displays the kind of female corrective power exercised within the prison (Fig. 2). On the left a young woman is seated dutifully spinning while a cat playfully interferes with her task. The young woman to the right appears to have been less diligent in her labor of producing the textile draped from her lap to the basket below. She is shrinking from the castigating blows of the whip wielded by the centrally placed indoor mother. Her disciplinary function has caused some scholars to identify this figure as *castigatio,* the allegorical representation of punishment or chastisement.[15] Such an allegorical sculpted figure with a whip can be found in Cornelis van der Voort's 1618 painting of the regents, or governors, of the male prison, the *rasphuis.* In addition, the inscription beneath the spinhouse portal sculpture written by Pieter Cornelisz Hooft stresses this punitive intent, "Do not be frightened; I am not avenging wrong but forcing to do good; my hand is severe but my mind is compassionate."[16] Thus the sculptural group undoubtedly served the function of warning inmates and informing the public as to the strict female power and discipline enforced at the institution.

The development of regent and regentess group portraits during the seventeenth century reveals an even more noteworthy and realistic example of the assignation of

---

14 Johan van Beverwijck, *Van de Wtnementheyt des Vrouwelicken Geslachts Verciert met Historyen, ende kopere Platen; als oock Latijnsche, ende Nederlansche Verssen van Mr. Corn. Boy,* vol. 2 (Dordrecht: Hendrick van Esch, 1643), 209–11.

15 Spierenburg, *Prison Experience,* 88 (see note 2); Norbert E. Middelkoop, Gusta Reichwein, and Judith van Gent, *De Oude Meesters van de stad Amsterdam: Schilderijen tot 1800* (Bussum: THOTH; Amsterdam: Amsterdams Historisch Museum, 2008), 105.

16 This translation was provided by Spierenburg, Prison Experience, 88 (see note 2).

female power to the spinhouse. The Dutch were unique among early modern European societies in granting women the right to serve as governesses in such prestigious public positions.[17] The regents and regentesses of the spinhouse formed the most powerful layer of oversight for the prison. They were the individuals that communicated with magistrates to discuss sentences and punishments for the prisoners.[18] They also oversaw the finances and management of the spinhouse. As was common with almost all Dutch group portraits of regents and regentesses of charitable institutions, the earliest portraits of the spinhouse governors separated them by sex. For example, a 1628 painting by Nicolaes Eliasz Pickenoy depicts the regents (Jan Jansz van Dorhout, Gerbrant Brouwer, Hendrick Boelisz, and Hendrick Dircksz Molenaer) in front of a table, with various managerial signifiers on display: the coins refer to both the monetary transactions and charity related to the spinhouse, the ledgers and writing materials also refer to their financial responsibilities, the bowl of food references the charitable duty of providing sustenance for the prisoners, and the indoor father bringing in a letter refers to their business communications with society outside of the spinhouse (Fig. 3).[19]

The painting within a painting hung on the back wall further situates the regents in their daily supervisory responsibilities. The four regents are again depicted seated behind a desk. In front of them mingle a crowd of respectable-looking citizenry, both men and women, who are presumably at the prison to survey the institution and its inhabitants.[20] For the payment of two *stuivers* (or one tenth of a *gulden*), the public could visit and observe the working women of the spinhouse. This was an important source of revenue for the prison.[21]

In parallel fashion, the regentesses (Lysbeth Hendricusdr Haeck and Styntje Thomas) were portrayed, along with the indoor mothers, in a separate painting with similar managerial signifiers by Dirck Dircksz van Santvoort in 1638 (Fig. 4).[22] To the

---

17 Spierenburg, *Prison Experience,* 107 (see note 2).

18 Spierenburg, *Prison Experience,* 106–09 (see note 2).

19 The regents are identified in the online catalog of the Amsterdams Historisch Museum, ahm.adlibsoft.com/ahmonline/advanced/detail.aspx# (last accessed on Dec. 10, 2010).

20 It has been suggested that the portrait was misidentified early on, and that these are actually regents of the orphanage. This argument is primarily based on the inclusion of a child in the painting on the back wall. Accordingly, the child has presumably lost its father and is now accompanied by family members to the orphanage. This, however, is a problematic suggestion in that the figures in the painting are grouped in pairs in conversation with their partners but paying no attention to the child. Moreover, they are all finely dressed, including the child and its presumed mother, which does not correspond to other depictions of orphans. These visitors are obviously not in need of the charity on display in the foreground, but are instead well-to-do citizenry who have come to the institution in order to discuss and observe. This identification debate is discussed in the online catalog of the Amsterdams Historisch Museum, see at: ahm.adlibsoft.com/ahmonline/advanced/detail.aspx# (last accessed on 12/9/2010).

21 Spierenburg, *Prison Experience,* 90–91 (see note 2).

22 The regentesses are identified in Middelkoop, *Oude Meesters,* 99 (see note 15).

right, one of the indoor mothers brings in a note to the seated regentess. The display of coins on the table and the ledger with a list of foodstuffs suggest that she is paying the bills of the spinhouse and providing sustenance for the inmates. These are similar to the signifiers represented in the regents's portrait. As with the regents, theirs was a society-related, as well as an intra-institutional, managerial function. There is, however, an important activity taking place in this painting that is not to be found in the regent portrait; this is the examination of textiles. The regentess seated at the far left of the painting takes out her spectacles to more carefully examine the textile work of the female laborers within the prison. A card of lace is being unwound for her perusal by another indoor mother. The textiles made at the spinhouse were sold to the public in order to help sustain the institution, but the proceeds were never great enough to support the inmates.[23] This portrait forcefully emphasizes the primary and original function of the spinhouse—the reform of poor women by teaching them a profitable skill in textile production. And it appears that this function mostly came under the control and jurisdiction of the regentesses and indoor mothers.

Female labor and female power are also emphasized in a later group portrait of spinhouse regents by Karel Dujardin from 1669 (Fig. 5). As with the previous regent portrait, the men are situated around a table in the manner of conducting a business meeting. The figures included are Michael Tielensz, Croock George, Henry Becker, John Commelin, and Muilman Willem de Jonge.[24] The indoor father once again hands them a communication. What is new, in contrast with most regent portraits, is the rather prominent female presence. In the right background, the indoor mother is predominantly situated so that she almost completely fills the doorway, thus blocking the figure of the indoor father behind her. She appears to be a rather sturdy looking figure capable of the necessary discipline in the prison.

There are three other females in the portrait but they are allegorical carvings on the back wall rather than live figures. The palatial décor of the setting corresponds to contemporary accounts of the grandeur of the new spinhouse. In actuality, several foreigners declared that the spinhouse did look more like a palace than a house of correction.[25] In this fashion, the Amsterdam spinhouse was once again a shining exception to the usual filth and disarray that characterized most early modern prisons. The three carved figures further ennoble the institution and the work done by the female inmates. The figure on the left uses a distaff; the woman in the center winds thread; the final figure holds the leaves of the flax plant that were used in the manufacture of linen. These lofty allegorizations dignify and assign value to women's

23 Spierenburg, *Prison Experience*, 115–34 (see note 2).

24 The regents are identified in the online catalog of the Rijksmuseum, Amsterdam www.rijksmuseum.nl/collectie/zoeken/asset.jsp?id=SK-C-4&lang=nl (last accessed on Dec. 10, 2010).

25 Spierenburg, *Prison Experience*, 88 (see note 2).

work, thus emphasizing the import of training the inmates. In spite of these references to the female prisoners and their work, however, the men are not represented as coming in direct or inappropriate contact with the prisoners. Indeed, the indoor mother stands as a guardian at the door of the inner institution. Thus the order, propriety, and honorability of the institution are maintained.

None of these group portraits, however, prepares us for the surprising and unique group portrait of combined regentesses (Catharina Brouwers and Pietertje de Vries) and regents (who cannot be specifically identified) that was painted by Bartholomeus van der Helst in 1650, soon after the rebuilding of the spinhouse due to a fire that took place in 1643 (Fig. 6).[26] This is only the second instance in Dutch group portraiture where regents and regentesses were combined in the same image.[27] And indeed, the regentesses are given equal footing in this portrait by portraying males and females in equal number, in spite of the fact that there were two regentesses and four regents at the time. Thus, the women are now truly given parallel power and prominence in signifying that they equally rule the spinhouse. Furthermore, the grouping of the figures gives significant prominence to the oldest regentess of the group, Catharina Brouwers. The other regentess and one of the regents both turn and listen with rapt attention to Brouwers who is depicted in a speaking attitude. She seems to be directing the meeting and is given "pride of place" in her throne-like chair at the head of the table.

Another aspect of this painting that similarly conveys a sense of female power is found in the adjoining view behind the portraits. The managerial duties of the indoor mother are portrayed as in the earlier regentess portrait, but now they are uniquely depicted as part of the daily activities in the prison's spinning room. It is a scene, like the portal sculpture, that emphasizes the strict discipline and control within the spinhouse. Once again, but in a more realistic mode, that discipline is in the hands of a woman. Behind the draped curtain the work of the inmates is put on display for the viewer and for the male and female prison visitors standing behind the wooden railing. Women and men both came as observers, but they were kept apart from the prisoners via a wall. Indeed, the spinhouse became a favorite tourist stop during the seventeenth century attracting visitors from both inside and outside the Republic.[28] While the first modern reaction to such observation might seem cruel and dehumanizing, there was certainly value to the inner workings of the prison system coming under constant public scrutiny. It obviously inhibited the kind of abuse found in other penal institutions.

In this image, the young females in need of reform are seated in a large room with their various textile tasks, lace-making and sewing, in their laps. The indoor mother's

---

26 The figures are identified and discussed in Middelkoop, *Oude Meesters,* 105 (see note 15).

27 Middelkoop, *Oude Meesters,* 104 (see note 15).

28 Spierenburg, *Prison Experience,* 90–92 (see note 2).

face displays her anger toward one of these young workers who evades the impending blow of her overseer. The indoor mother is obviously chastising the young girl, and the *pantoffel*, a woman's slipper, in her hand indicates the cause for the young worker's fear.

Images of women using their shoes as weapons were a common metaphorical *topos* in the seventeenth century. The *pantoffel*, or woman's slipper, was a signifier of powerful and overbearing women because it became a handy domestic weapon for the seventeenth-century Dutch woman. In art, this shoe-weapon was frequently wielded by shrewish housewives against their husbands. Indeed, "*pantoffelheld*" became the nickname for a henpecked husband, which gave rise to the expression "*Onder de pantoffel zitten*" or "to be under the slipper," implying that a man was ruled by his wife.[29]

The satirizing of this expression is to be found in a late seventeenth-century print by Jacob Gole after Cornelis Dusart (Fig. 7). It is one of five prints in which each of the senses is represented by a virago who rules over her husband. The print of *Tactus*, or the sense of touch, pictures a terrified husband who feels pain while being struck to the floor by his wife who brandishes a *pantoffel*. Another element frequently found in scenes of shrewish, overbearing wives is the bundle of birches hanging threateningly above the fireplace as a sign of who commands the household. Birches were used for the spanking of naughty children, and as this task usually fell to the wife, the birches became another handy weapon for the wife to use against her husband. The expression "onder de plak van zijne vrouw zitten" (to be under the stick or rod of his wife) meant that the husband was under the power of his wife.[30] Beneath the battling pair are inscriptions in Dutch and French that further emphasize the power of the woman and the total subjection of the henpecked husband:

> Doorluchte Vrouwen, al maakt uw bedryf veel spels,
> Uw degen, roept Quiryn wykt voor de muiyl van Els!
> Ha que l'Atouchement me blesse
> Destre daubbe d'une Diablesse.
>
> [Illustrious women, although you make your business very playful,
> Quiryn calls out, his sword gives way to the slipper of Els!
> Ah, how the touch hurts me to be struck by a she devil.]

Consequently, in van der Helst's group portrait of the regentesses and regents, the *pantoffel* as signifier of women's power, becomes an important allegorical, as well as

29 Frederik A. Stoett, *Nederlandsche Spreekwoorden, Spreekwijzen , Uitdrukkingen en Gezegden*, vol. 2 (Zutphen: W. J. Thieme, 1923), 138; Matthias de Vries and Lammert A. te Winkel, *Het Woordenboek der Nederlandsche taal*, vol. 12.1 (The Hague: M. Nijhoff, 1882–), 339

30 Stoett, *Spreekwoorden*, 2:138, 164; *Woordenboek* , 12.1:2186 (see note 28).

a realistic, indicator of female control within the spinhouse.[31] This scene recalls the depictions of women aggressively battling their helpless *pantoffelheld* husbands. And interestingly, like the typical weak *pantoffelheld*, the indoor father in this painting plays a similarly insignificant role. Isolated from the female prisoners, he is situated in a separate room to the far right of the painting as he passively consults a prison ledger that presumably lists the inmates of the spinhouse.[32] Thus, the paralleling of female power and control in the background with female authority in the foreground is a significant subversion of traditional patriarchy. More particularly, it asserts to the viewer the fact that men do not control the women of the spinhouse; men are separate and appropriate bystanders that do not come into direct contact with the women.

There is one final unusual detail in this painting and that is the noteworthy inclusion of a foot-warming stove under Catharina Brouwers's feet. This is an object not only absent in portraits of regents but also of regentesses. It is, however, a frequent motif in Dutch domestic imagery. The foot-warming stove was represented as a constant companion to women busy with the producing of textiles in the home. Through these associations, van der Helst evocatively links the nobility and honorability of all women's work within this portrait. The work of the inmates is recognized as important like the work of the mother in the Dutch home. The revered regentesses, the indoor mother, the prisoners (at least the obedient ones), and the female viewers are all linked in purpose via these important and honored skills of lace-making, weaving, and sewing.

The teaching of these skills within the prison by the indoor mother was metaphorically associated with the teaching of the same skills by the mother in the home, who also taught her charges in a disciplined manner. This societal import given to mothers in Dutch culture is exemplified by Jacob Cats's text *Houwelick* that was one of the most popular Dutch texts throughout the first half of the seventeenth century. This text was dedicated to a discussion of the various stages of a woman's life. In one of the illustrations to Cats's text, the example of the influential mother is clearly emulated by her daughters (Fig. 8). One daughter does lacework while the other spanks her "disobedient" doll. It is significant that these are also the very activities emphasized in the spinhouse and controlled by the regentesses and the indoor mothers. Thus, this revealing portrait meaningfully integrates a variety of visual signifiers in an attempt to create an original and compelling declaration of the import of female roles for the society at large.

---

31 The presumed preparatory drawing for this background scene in the painting also displays an indoor mother disciplining with her *pantoffel*. The drawing is attributed and discussed in the online catalog of the Amsterdams Historisch Museum at: ahm.adlibsoft.com/ahmonline/advanced/detail.aspx# (last accessed on Dec. 10, 2010). The drawing is in the Rijksprentenkabinet (inv. Nr. A 2789).

32 The inscription on the book reads, "Alphabet Anno 1650," and thus it is presumed to be a listing of incoming prisoners, as discussed in Middelkoop, *Oude Meesters*, 105 (see note 15).

Many scholars have discussed Dutch domestic imagery as an indication of patriarchal attitudes, rather than of female power. They use the popularity of Cats's moralizing text advocating domestic roles for women as an indicator that men mostly tried to confine women to low status tasks in the home.[33] However, the devotion of an entire text to the discussion of ordinary women's lives more importantly reveals attitudes regarding the significance of women and their activities for the culture at large. And while earlier seventeenth-century images and texts may have taken on a more moralizing tone, such examples soon gave way to more realistic and ennobling perspectives after mid-century. It was at this point in time that a profusion of domestic images were created starting with an influential series of prints on women's work by the female artist Geertruydt Roghman done about 1650.[34] Her depiction of two women sewing, for example, directly focuses the viewer's attention on the concentrated gaze of the woman on the left specifically (Fig. 9). Only the necessary details of the women's work have been included: cloth, needle and thread, spool, scissors, a lamp, and a footwarming stove with a poker for stirring the coals. The woman's averted gaze suggests a preoccupation with her own thoughts and activities, and creates a sense of discreetness in which the figure does not display herself for the moral edification or voyeuristic gaze of the viewer. Instead, the viewing position allows these women to go about their consequential daily tasks without becoming patriarchal symbols, objects, or allegories. Moreover, the depictions give visibility to, and thereby importance to, the domestic work performed. For those women familiar with the particular task, it also lent significance to that viewer's work.

This fascination with, and respect for, the work of women in Dutch society is indicated by the large number of domestic paintings produced after mid century. Some artists dedicated almost their entire oeuvre to these themes. In particular, the highly skilled and extremely intricate work of lace-making became a subject of fascination for artists, as in Johannes Vermeer's painting of about 1670 (Fig. 10). Like Roghman, Vermeer focuses our attention on this mesmerizing skill by directing the woman's gaze, and thus the viewer's gaze, to the elaborate display of threads and bobbins. The figure is brought close so that her work takes place directly in front of the viewer who inhabits the woman's same space and who almost participates in the

---

33 For a discussion of the historiography of this debate see Martha Moffitt Peacock, "Domesticity in the Public Sphere," *Saints, Sinners, and Sisters. Gender and Northern Art in Medieval and Early Modern Europe*, ed. Jane Carroll and Alison Stewart (Burlington, VT, and Aldershot, Hants, England: Ashgate, 2003), 44–68; Peacock, "Dutch Women in the City," 667–71 (see note 8). The most concentrated study on the patriarchal aspects of domestic imagery is Wayne Franits, *Paragons of Virtue: Women and Domesticity in Seventeenth-Century Dutch* Art (Cambridge and New York: Cambridge University Press, 1993).

34 For a more complete study of Roghman's print cycle see Martha Moffitt Peacock, "Geertruydt Roghman and the Female Perspective in Seventeenth-Century Dutch Genre Imagery," *Woman's Art Journal* 14.2 (1993–1994): 3–10; Peacock, "Domesticity" (see note 33).

intriguing task. Again, there is an absence of moralizing and symbolic devices. The painted illusion creates the effect of observing an actual woman at work and of recreating the experience of amazed admiration still felt by contemporary tourists gathered around Netherlandish lace-makers today.

The importance of teaching this valuable skill to young women is the subject of a painting by Quirijn van Breklenkam dated 1654 (Fig. 11). A woman is seated in the middle of the composition helping three young pupils to learn the highly admired art of lace-making. It clearly represents a workshop for the training of young lace-makers due to the numerous bolster cushions atop the shelf on the back wall. Consequently, there are clear connections between this mother and the indoor mother of the spinhouse who also instructs her young charges. Moreover, the *pantoffel* isolated in the central foreground may indicate more than the naturalistic removal of the woman's shoes in order to warm her feet on the wooden stove. Once again, it may have been a reference to female control, albeit in a less violent fashion. By association, then, it can be assumed that many women involved with the management and discipline of the spinhouse had goals similar to ordinary women—the training of young women to play useful roles in society through the respectable female work of textile production.

Other empowering discourses in association with women's textile production had a long history in Netherlandish visual tradition. Specifically, tools like the distaff used for spinning carried customary connotations of intimidating female power and subversion from a very early period. Already in the thirteenth and fourteenth centuries women are represented in the margins of manuscripts using distaffs as weapons in a "Battle of the Sexes." In depictions of wild folk, couples are often shown jousting with their characteristic and gendered tools—the male with a rake and the female with her distaff. Fear of the subversive power of women in connection with this female tool was further emphasized by images of distaff-carrying witches.[35] In one of Erasmus's Colloquia the connection between female insubordination and the distaff is made clear. Two friends, Eulalia and Xantippe, have a conversation regarding their husbands in which Xantippe describes how her husband comes home drunk and beats her. Eulalia exclaims, "A new sort of shield: You should have used your distaff for a lance."[36] Even in the later seventeenth century when the tool was becoming somewhat old fashioned, the distaff was still used as a metaphor for women generally and also more specifically for overbearing females. It is used as such in an expression found in

---

35 The use of the distaff in such images is discussed and illustrated, for example, in Timothy Husband, *The Wild Man: Medieval Myth and Symbolism* (New York: Metropolitan Museum of Art, 1980), 139–40.

36 *The Colloquies of Erasmus*, trans. Craig R. Thompson (Chicago: University of Chicago Press, 1965), 117.

Jacob Cats' *Regels voor de Huys-houdinge in Spreucken, Spreeck-worden, en Gedichten* (*Rules for Households in Sayings, Proverbs, and Poems*):

> Alwaer de spin-rock dwinght het sweert,
> Daer staet het qualick met den weert.
>
> [Wherever the distaff dominates the sword,
> There things are going badly for the head of the household.][37]

Distaffs were also frequently wielded in depictions of the proverbial "Battle for the Trousers." This theme more than any other, became a well-known metaphor for powerful, overbearing women. In such scenes, a wife struggles to win the pants, and therefore the power, from her husband. The expression "De broek aanhebben" ("to have the trousers on") or "De broek dragen" ("to wear the pants") referred to a person's being master in the house.[38] In relation to this theme, Israel van Meckenam put distaff weaponry in the hands of a fearsome wife who beats her husband to the ground in a print of ca. 1500 (Fig. 12). In addition, she holds the wrist of her struggling captive and even stands on his foot to make certain that he does not escape her violent blows. In front of the kneeling man lies a form of trousers—the object of dispute. The presence of a terrible demon reveals the fearsome nature of women who usurp traditional patriarchal power.

At other times the Battle for the Trousers took place among seven women all battling for the prized article of clothing. This metaphorical battle thus signified a desire to win the man and to then dominate him.[39] Such a combination of metaphors is found in an illustration to Adriaen van de Venne's *Tafereel van de Belacchende Werelt* (Painting of the Ridiculous World, 1635). The characters in the text are kermis guests and through their conversation, van de Venne moralizes about the foolish behavior of the world. One of the illustrations depicts a comical battle where women use both the distaff and the *pantoffel* as weapons to acquire the trousers (Fig. 13). The man to whom the trousers belong stands in the foreground showing great dismay over their conduct. In the text, van de Venne includes several relevant proverbs and expressions including "Laet Mannen by de Broeck en Wyve by de Doek" ("Let husbands wear the pants, and wives wear the apron").[40]

---

37 Cats, *Alle de Wercken. Spiegel van den Ouden en Nieuwen Tijdt: Regels voor de Huys-houdinge in Spreucken, Spreeck-woorden, en Gedichten. Rakende de onderlinge plichten tusschen man en wijf*, 119 (see note 13).

38 Stoett, *Spreekwoorden*, 1:140–41 (see note 17).

39 For a more complete discussion of these two types of battles, see Peacock, "Proverbial Reframing" (see note 5).

40 Adriaen van de Venne, *Tafereel van de Belacchende Werelt* (The Hague: published by the author, 1635), 240.

Significations of female power via the distaff are extended to the spinning room itself in other images of dominating females. This was a space ruled by women, and when men were present they usually suffered the brunt of female tyranny. A painting by Pieter de Bloot emphasizes the female dominance within the spinning room (Fig. 14). One powerful woman is depicted leading an army of women as she triumphantly waves a banner bearing the image of a hand. This motif indicates that it is now the women who have the power in direct contradiction to the natural order expressed in the saying, "*Manshand boven*" ("Man's hand above").[41] At the right, another fierce mob of women chase a terrified man with a stick. Central to the scene is a man on bended knee, respectfully removing his hat and giving the woman standing over him the "kiss of the thumb." This was a familiar metaphorical gesture signifying a man's submission to the power of his wife.[42] Further indications of the dominance of women are present in the forcing of men to do traditional female chores like spinning, indicated by the man with a winder evading the blows of his conqueror's stick to the left, or sweeping, indicated by the broom near the kneeling man in the foreground. Three women at the left join forces to remove the man's trousers and paddle him as he falls to his hands and knees. The tongs which the women use for punishing are a familiar reference to their shrewish natures as the Dutch word "*tang*" was a nickname for a shrewish woman.[43] Clearly, the spinning room was designated as a place of female power where men had to obediently submit to the control of women. It is not difficult to understand, then, why images of women in association with the spinhouse were represented in such surprisingly dominating ways. Representations of regentesses and indoor mothers must have similarly signified female power and control.

One final association given to the distaff was as a signifier of female economic power. While many modern feminist historians of the prison decry the employment of female inmates in textile work because they consider it a lowly and traditional feminine task, this ignores the value of such work in a preindustrial society.[44] Women's work, such as producing textiles, was not an insignificant contribution in Dutch society. This was true of women who worked in public mills like the Leiden Lakenhal or who worked in the home contributing to the family economy. Increasingly during the seventeenth century women began to participate very actively as guild members in the public textile industry. With such evidence, it has been argued that women's labor contributed significantly to the economic success

---

41 Alfons de Cock, *Spreekwoorden en zegswijzen over de vrouwen, de liefde, en het huwelijk* (Ghent: Boekdrukkers- en Uitgevershuis Ad. Hoste, 1911), 60.

42 Walter Gibson, "Some Flemish Popular Prints from Hieronymus Cock and His Contemporaries," *Art Bulletin* 60.4 (December, 1978): 673–81.

43 Stoett, *Spreekwoorden,* 2:345–46 (see note 17).

44 Cain, "Women Confined" (see note 3); Mary Bosworth, "Confining Femininity: A History of Gender, Power and Imprisonment," *Theoretical Criminology* 4.3 (2000): 265–84.

of the Dutch Golden Age.[45] A realization of female economic significance in this regard is witnessed in an anonymous Netherlandish allegorical painting from the first half of the seventeenth century entitled *The Struggle for Daily Bread*, (Fig. 15) where women with distaffs compete with men wielding the tools of blacksmiths, fishermen, soldiers, cobblers, tailors, bakers, etc. for their portion of economic prosperity from the large sack. Consequently, women's textile work was once again associated with the noble labor that so characterized the culture of the Dutch Republic. And it was also associated with the public power and influence of women in this society. Thus, textile production at the spinhouse must be understood to have had honorable, powerful, and valuable connotations in the Dutch cultural context.

Clearly, there were many significations of honorable female power to be found in the imagery both in front of and within the Amsterdam spinhouse. These references to female control, and therefore propriety, must have significantly inhibited male appropriation of women within the institution. It is why the spinhouse was such a unique institution for its time and why it was not imitated for many years to come. The founding of such an institution necessitated a cultural circumstance in which women, their skills, and their power, were given voice in the construction of social institutions. As a consequence, when women prisoners walked through the portal of the spinhouse they realized that they were now under female control. And while that discipline was strict, it was certainly more charitable for the long-term benefit of women prisoners than the patriarchal brothel/prisons found in other areas of early modern Europe.

45 I discussed the economic significance of women and textile production in Peacock, "Dutch Women in the City" (see note 8). Recent scholars who have researched Dutch women's economic contributions and freedoms include: Bibi Sara Panhuysen, *Maatwerk: Kleermakers, Naaisters, Oudkleerkopers en de gilden (1500–1800)* (Utrecht: University of Utrecht, 2000); Ariadne Schmidt, "Gilden en de toegang van vrouwen tot de arbeidsmarkt in Holland in de vroegmoderne tijd," *De Zeventiende Eeuw* 23.2 (2007): 160–78; Leo Noordegraff and Jan Luiten van Zanden. "Early Modern Economic Growth and the Standard of living: Did Labor Benefit from Holland's Golden Age?," *A Miracle Mirrored: The Dutch Republic in European Perspective*, ed. Karel Davids and Jan Lucassen (Cambridge: Cambridge University Press, 1995), 426; Elise van Nederveen Meerkerk, "Segmentation in the Pre-Industrial Labor Market: Women's Work in the Dutch Textile Industry, 1581–1810," *International Review of Social History* 51.2 (2006): 189–216.

Fig. 1: Quiringh van Brekelenkam, *Interior with Three Women and a Little Girl,* 1663, Kunsthaus, Zürich

Fig. 2: Hendrick de Keyser, *Spinhuis Portal Sculpture*, 1607, Amsterdam

Fig. 3: Nicolaes Eliasz Pickenoy, *Regents of the Spinhuis*, 1628, Amsterdam, Amsterdams Historisch Museum

Fig. 4: Dirck Dircksz van Santvoort, *Regentesses of the Spinhuis,* 1638, Amsterdam, Amsterdams Historisch Museum

Fig. 5: Karel Dujardin, *Regents of the Spinhuis,* 1669, Amsterdam, Rijksmuseum

Fig. 6: Bartholomeus van der Helst, *Two Regentesses and Two Regents of the Spinhuis,* 1650, Amsterdam, Amsterdams Historisch Museum

Fig. 7: Jacob Gole after Cornelis Dusart, *Tactus,* Atlas van Stolk, Rotterdam

Fig. 8: After Adriaen van de Venne, *Moeder*, From *Houwelick*, Koninklijke Bibliotheek, The Hague

Fig. 9: Geertruydt Roghman, *Two Women Sewing*, Rijksprentenkabinet, Rijksmuseum, Amsterdam

Fig. 10: Johannes Vermeer, *Lace-maker,* The Louvre, Paris

Fig. 11: Quiringh van Brekelenkam, *Lace-maker's School*, 1654, Present Location Unknown

Fig. 12: Israel van Meckenam, *Battle for the Trousers,*
Bibliotheque Royale Albert Ier, Brussels

Fig. 13: After Adriaen van de Venne, *Battle for the Trousers,* From *Tafereel van de Belacchende Werelt,* 1635, Atlas van Stolk, Rotterdam

Fig. 14: Pieter de Bloot, *Spinning Room,* Present Location Unknown

Fig. 15: Anonymous, *The Struggle for Daily Bread,* Amsterdam, Amsterdams Historisch Museum

Chapter 20

Thomas Willard
(University of Arizona, Tucson)

Pimping for the Fairy Queen: Some Cozeners in Shakespeare's England

In *Religion and the Decline of Magic*, the British historian Keith Thomas devotes a chapter to ghosts and fairies, and the last pages of that chapter to cases involving "frauds and tricksters, ready to exploit the credulity of their contemporaries."[1] Writing from an anthropological perspective, Thomas follows the general formula that Sir James George Frazer enunciated in the last chapter of *The Golden Bough:* "From Magic through Religion to Science."[2] At least he sees a continuum between medieval magic and reformed religion and "interconnections" with the New Science.[3] However, he sees no progress taking place. Human nature being what it is, people will always fall for something, whether it be from magic or religion or science. And the harder they fall, the more dramatic their stories, the better suited they are for dramatic presentation, whether tragic or, more often, comic. In Shakespeare's England, no one seemed more aware of the comic possibilities than the learned playwright Ben Jonson, to whom Thomas makes passing reference.

Thomas summarizes a half-dozen stories of people who were vulnerable to swindles because they believed in fairies. Such belief was widespread, he notes, and it had still wider recognition in the way of our Tooth Fairy today. In *A Midsummer Night's Dream*, first produced in 1594, the tough-minded Theseus dismisses the evening's entertainment and urges his guests to bed, saying: "tis almost Fairy time."[4] He has no belief in fairies; he does not think them responsible

---

1 Keith Thomas, *Religion and the Decline of Magic* (London: Weidenfeld & Nicolson, 1971), 732–34.

2 Sir James George Frazer, *The Golden Bough: A Study in Magic and Religion* (London and New York: Macmillan, 1922), 711.

3 Thomas, *Religion and the Decline of Magic*, 755–66 (see note 1).

4 William Shakespeare, *The Complete Works: Original Spelling Edition*, ed. Stanley Wells and Gary

for the love matches that were conveniently made the night before, and he hardly expects a fairy named Puck to appear on the scene after his guests retire for the night. But Shakespeare himself is not a believer, simply a user and shaper of popular myth.

In Shakespeare's England—by which I mean roughly the Elizabethan and Jacobean eras covering the last two decades of the sixteenth century and the first two decades of the seventeenth—the crime of preying on people's superstitions and gullibility in order to cheat them out of goods and money was known as cozenage. The verb 'to cozen' is first recorded in 1573, perhaps derived from the Italian *cozzonare* ('to cheat'). The noun 'cozenage' is recorded a decade later, in a tract on practices that the Puritan Philip Stubbes regarded as "abuses."[5] However, the words were never far removed from the older 'cousin' and 'cousinage,' the implication being that country cousins were exactly the sort of people on which street-wise cozeners liked to prey.[6] Cozenage was technically a type of fraud, and deliberate fraud at that, but the perpetrators often escaped with relatively light punishments compared to those given to people found guilty of simple theft.

Unlike many other crimes of fraud, where the unsuspecting victim did nothing to deserve the loss, cozenage of people who believed in fairies often shows greed all around: greed on the part of people hoping to earn the fairies' favor as well as those who preyed on them. Their twenty-first century counterparts are the people who want to believe the email from widows of Nigerian generals, not the ones whose identity is stolen while they sleep. We tend to say that such victims "had it coming." We may secretly admire the con artists.

For this reason, there was a steady demand for broadsides and pamphlets about notable cozeners and acts of cozenage.[7] The famous "conny-catching" pamphlets of Robert Greene, the "university wit" and playwright, purported to expose acts of "Coosenage . . . that hath brought many ignorant men into confusion." One title page announced a work offered as a public service, "Written for the general benefit of all Gentlemen, Citizens, Apprentices, Country Farmers, and yeomen, that may hap to fall into the company of such coosening companions" (see Fig. 1).[8]

Taylor (Oxford: Clarendon Press, 1986), 374; *Midsummer Night's Dream*, 5.1.353. See also Nicolas Tredell, *Shakespeare - A Midsummer Night's Dream*. Readers' Guides to Essential Criticism (Houndmills, Basingstoke, Hampshire, and New York: Palgrave Macmillan, 2010).

5 *The Oxford English Dictionary*, 2nd ed. (Oxford and New York: Oxford University Press, 1989), "cozen" v. and "cozenage" n. 1. Shakespeare used the verb "to cozen" in *The Merry Wives of Windsor*, 5.5.195; Shakespeare, *Complete Works*, 571 (see note 4).

6 See, e.g., the broadsheet ballad *The Countrey Cozen, Or: The Crafty City Dame* (London: P. Brooksby, 1685).

7 See, e.g., *The Elizabethan Underworld: A Collection of Tudor and Early Stuart Tracts and Ballads Telling of the Lives and Misdoings of Vagabonds, Thieves, Rogues and Cozeners, and Giving Some Account of the Operation of the Criminal Law*, ed. A. V. Judges (London: Routledge, 1930).

8 R[obert] Greene, *A Notable Discouery of Coosenage* (London: Thomas Nelson, 1592). Green released

Many later pamphlets by lesser, often anonymous writers took the same tack. Of course, the pamphlets were written and published to make money, and thus involved a certain amount of cozenage themselves. Like the swindlers they exposed, they depended on novelty: new terms, new tricks, new stories.

Take, for example, this pamphlet of 1595 (Fig.2). The title is very thorough, in the manner of the time:

> The brideling, sadling and ryding, of a rich churle in Hampshire, by the subtill practise of one Iudeth Philips, a professed cunning woman, or fortune teller VVith a true discourse of her vnwomanly vsing of a trype wife, a widow, lately dwelling on the back side of S. Nicholas shambles in London, whom she with her conferates, likewise cosoned: for which fact, shee was at the Sessions house without New-gate arraigned, where she confessed the same, and had iudgement for her offence, to be whipped through the citie, the 14. of February, 1594.[9]

The title establishes that Judith Philips confessed to having cozened the widow of a tripe merchant and was sentenced to be whipped through the streets of London. It makes for a good story, but it is not the main story. That story is about the cozening of a "rich Churle in Hampshire," for which she was neither tried in London nor convicted and punished, having been committed outside the court's jurisdiction. We might say the title is misleading, but there is no doubt that the pamphlet's author and publisher knew their market.

In both instances, Judith exploited the folk belief that some people have a talent for finding lost goods and hidden treasures. On each occasion, she pretended to see the marks of good fortune in the face of her victim. She then found a small sum of money that she had hidden and set certain conditions for finding the rest of the treasure. The Hampshire man had to let her saddle him up and ride him around a tree behind his house. He then had to wait, with the saddle still in place, while she met inside with the Queen of the Fairies. Needless to say, she disappeared, taking his best candlesticks and silverware.

One historian has likened the image of Judith Philips bridling the "rich Churle" to contemporary illustrations of the Whore of Babylon astride the beast with seven horns.[10] Pamela Brown notes that Philips carries a money bag where the great whore carries a cup of blood (Fig. 3). Surely, though, there is a closer resemblance to a famous illustration from the atelier of Albrecht Dürer, showing Phyllis, the mistress or queen of Alexander the Great, riding his tutor Aristotle (Fig. 4). In the medieval exemplum, Phyllis took offense at the moral precepts of Aristotle and

---

three further pamphlets on the subject in the same year, *A Disputation betweene a Hee Conny-catcher, and a Shee Conny-catcher*, *The Second and last part of Conny-Catching*, and *The Blacke Bookes Messenger*.

9 *The Brideling, Sadling, and Ryding of a Rich Churle* (London: William Barley, 1595).

10 Pamela Allen Brown, *Better a Shrew than a Sheep: Women, Drama, and the Culture of Jest in Early Modern England* (Ithaca and London: Cornell University Press, 2003), 165. See Revelation 17:1–6.

wanted to punish him. She therefore seduced him and, when he begged for sexual favors, told him he would have to come crawling like a horse before she would touch him.[11]

My guess is that the pamphlet's first readers took at least as much pleasure in the descriptions of the crime as in those of the punishment. They knew what it meant to be whipped through the streets—a punishment usually given to discourage vagrancy and begging, though sometimes leading up to the hanging tree at Tyburn—and they were eager to learn how this cunning woman fooled her victims. They may have been delighted to hear that she told the rich man in Hampshire, who was a suspected Roman Catholic, that she had come directly from the Pope and would swear on the Bible that she had, when in fact she had just deserted her husband in London, whose name was Mr. Pope. When she returned to London and married a gunsmith named John Philips, she did not tell him about her extra income. She worked with other confederates.

One couple teamed up as consorts of the fairies. John and Alice West wanted to steal money from a simple but wealthy man in the London suburb of Hammersmith, but knew the danger:

> because they knew common cousanages had for the most part common discovery, and so consequently a common and ordinary punishment denounced against offenders in that kinde, they therefore deuised a new forme, in which for the strangeness and varietie they could hardly be traced.[12]

They devised a plot to convince their victim that they were "familiarly acquainted with the King and Queen of Fairies" and that the fairies wanted "to bestew great summes of gold" on the man and his wife. Fairies were commonly considered to be the same size as humans; the tiny creatures of literature and art from Shakespeare to Pope to Disney had yet to enter the popular imagination. The Wests came to public notice after they fled with £4 that the man had entrusted to them—the equivalent of £600 in today's currency. At their trial in Newgate, it was revealed that they swore their victim to secrecy, then arranged "rites of sacrifice" in which he was relieved of his best linen and some gold. When no riches followed, they offered their victim a rare vision:

> they brought him into a vault, where they shewed him two attired like the King and Queene of Fayries, and by them little Elues and Goblings, and in the same place an

11 George Sarton, "Phyllis and Aristotle," *Isis* 14.1 (May 1930): 8–19. Sarton traces the story of Alexander and an eastern temptress to India and Persia, and suggests that Aristotle may have been added to the story on the influence of the *Secretum Secretorum*, as translated from Arabic by John of Seville (ca. 1120). He also mentions the eighteenth-century parlor game of "Le cheval d'Aristote," the loser of which had to crawl about the floor carrying a woman on his back.

12 *The Seuerall Notorious and levvd Cousnages of Iohn VVest, and Alice VVest* (London: Edward Marchant, 1613), sig, A4v.

> infinite company of bags, and upon them written, this is for *Thomas Moore*, this is for his wife, but would not let him touch any thing, which gave him some incouragement, to his almost dispairing hope . . . .[13]

Alice arranged a similar vision for the couple's maid:

> at length she drue the maid into a dark celler, & by some strong illusion shewed two in strange habits whom she termed the K. & Q. of Fayries, & them so much imaginaed trasure, that the maid insisted before the bench there could not be so little as seuenteen hundred thousand pound, al which this cheatresse affirmed was for her master . . . .[14]

The Wests demanded money for another ceremony, this one designed to appease Oberon, the Fairy King. When they had all they could hope to get from Moore, they left for London under the cover of darkness.

The sessions court convicted the Wests of cozenage, as charged, but the court recognized that Alice was the brains of the operation and sentenced her to a stiffer punishment:

> she was conuict with her husband, and iudged to bee whipt through London, & certain daies to stand on the pillory, which according to her iudgement, hath to the example of all such practisers beene performed, and she yet till further euidence can be brought against her, kept still a prisoner in Newgate.[15]

She had pleaded that she and her husband should be whipped and pilloried and then released, that being a common punishment for people who had done as they did. But the court suspected that the Moores were not their only victims, and then sentenced Alice to remain in prison and regularly on display outside the prison until further evidence could be gathered (see Fig. 5). By the time the pamphlet on their crimes was printed, eleven other cases had come to light, with victims ranging from a sailor's widow and a goldsmith's apprentice to a country gentleman. The pamphleteer had no final word on her sentence, only a parting message to readers: "Happy are they whom other mens harmes do make to beware."[16] The message remains a staple of "true crime" journalism.

No level of society seemed immune. In a lawsuit filed in the Court of Chancery, in 1610, a prominent family in Dorset brought charges against two neighbors who had cheated their son out of £6 (£900 in today's currency) by promising an introduction to the Queen of Fairyland and the assistance of a local wizard who would help win her hand in marriage. Although he had studied at Oxford and the Middle Temple and knew his way around the law courts, his family described the

---

13 *Seuerall Notorious and levvd Cousanages*, sig. B1v (see note 12).

14 *Seuerall Notorious and levvd Cousanages*, sig. B2r (see note 12).

15 *Seuerall Notorious and levvd Cousanages*, sigs. B2r–v (see note 12).

16 *Seuerall Notorious and levvd Cousanages*, sig. C4v (see note 12).

youth as "a very fantasticall and humerous fellowe by his behaviour." The imbalance of of bodily humors suggests some sort of handicap, physical or mental. One scholar infers that he was epileptic.[17] The young man's handicap, like the tripe wife's recent loss of her husband, made the court more sympathetic.

The case from Dorset was heard in February of 1610, a few weeks before the opening of the theater season. Lawyers and clerks who made their way from the Inns of Court to the new Blackfriars Theater would have heard echoes of the case in Ben Jonson's new play *The Alchemist*, one of the great English dramas of cozenage. In the Prologue, Jonson describes it as a play of "manners, now called humors,"[18] recalling that people with an excess of black bile were said to be melancholic and prone to superstition. Jonson's main character is a cozener not unlike the Dorset wizard to whom young Sir Thomas surrendered his gold. The similarities are close enough to make one wonder whether Jonson did not interpolate the story of an introduction to the fairy queen into *The Alchemist* at a relatively late stage, thus further extending the range of cheating, or cozening, that the play exposes.

The scene is set in a private house in the Blackfriars district when the nearby law courts are on vacation. It is summer, and there are rumors of plague in the city. In the owner's absence, the housekeeper has let in two confederates: a confidence man, unlicensed physician, and sometime alchemist called Dr. Subtle and a prostitute known as Doll Common. They are described in the printed text as "A cheater and his punk who / . . . were become / Coz'ners at large."[19] The housekeeper, or butler, is named Jeremy, but is called Face, perhaps to indicate his effrontery or cheek.[20] As the action begins, Subtle and Face are in the heat of an

---

17 C. J. Sisson, "A Topical Reference in *The Alchemist*," *John Quincy Adams Memorial Studies* (Washington, DC: Folger Shakespeare Library, 1948), 739–41. Also see Joseph T. McCullen, Jr., "Conference with the Queen of Fairies: A Study of Jonson's Workmanship in 'The Alchemist'," *Studia Neophilologica* 23.2 (1950): 87–95.

18 Ben Jonson, *The* Alchemist, ed. Alvin B. Kernan, The Yale Ben Jonson (New Haven and London: Yale University Press, 1974), 25; "Prologue," 9. All quotations from the play follow this edition. Unlike Shakespeare, Jonson carefully edited his own works—and he called them "works." Act and line numbers do not vary significantly from one edition to another. For the still-definitive old-spelling text, see *Ben Jonson*, ed. C. H. Herford and Percy Simpson, Vol. 5: *Volpone, or The Fox; Epicoene, or The Silent Woman; The Alchemist; Catiline* (Oxford: Clarendon Press, 1937), 273–407.In addition to studies cited in this essay, one may consult John S. Mebane, *Renaissance Magic and the Return of the Golden Age: The Occult Tradition and Marlowe, Jonson, and Shakespeare* (Lincoln, NE, and London: University of Nebraska Press, 1989), 137–55; Marion Gibson, *Witchcraft and Society in England and America, 1550–1750* (Ithaca, NY, and London: Cornell University Press, 2003), 199–205; and Ryan Curtis Friesen, *Supernatural Fiction in Early Modern Drama and Culture* (Brighton, England, and Portland, OR: Sussex Academic Press, 2010), 165–89.

19 Jonson, *The Alchemist*, 24; "The Argument," 4–6 (see note 18).

20 *Oxford English Dictionary*, "face" *n.* 3 *fig* (see note 5). Also see Jonson's dedication to Lady Mary Wroth, which concludes with a reference to "the ambitious faces of the time: who, the more they

argument, shouting threats and insults at each other, and Doll is clearly the only sane person in sight. She tries to silence the two lest neighbors get suspicious, and she succeeds only after the first victim has arrived.

Dapper is a young law clerk whom Face met the night before at the Dagger Tavern in Holborn, near the Inns of Court. He is addicted to gambling and hopes that he can turn his luck by persuading the doctor to give him a familiar spirit.[21] Subtle feigns horror at the prospect, telling Face that the youth will "win up all the money in the town."[22] When Face intervenes, passing along some of Dapper's money, Subtle explains that he is worried about Dapper's physiognomy. The youth has the kind of "complexion / The Queen of Faery loves."[23] Only after much persuading by Face, and much more money from Dapper, does Subtle agree to introduce him to the queen. This queen is Doll, who is a "quean" in the word's old sense of prostitute.[24] But first Dapper must go through elaborate rituals to purify himself, and separate himself from any taint of money.

It may seem odd that a play about an alchemist should include fairies. We must realize, however, that Jonson and his contemporaries lumped alchemy, astrology, witchcraft, and much more into the general category of magic. Alchemists dealt with nature spirits and astrologers with planetary spirits just as witches had commerce with incubi and conjurers with fairies. The difference between good and bad magicians was in the fruits of their labor, and so was that between true and false magicians. All possibilities were there for Jonson's audience; he simply exploited the dramatic possibilities. In the heat of the argument that opens the play, Face calls Subtle "Conjurer" and "Witch,"[25] but when Dapper arrives he is calling the same person a "noble Doctor."[26] As one recent editor has explained, the essential point of Jonson's "performative magic" is that "the audience desiring the entertainment believes, supports, participates in, and applauds the illusion."[27] Spectators came to the theater for exactly the same reason that Moore's maid was drawn into the "dark celler": to witness a "strong illusion." The only difference is

---

paint, are the less themselves"; Jonson, *The Alchemist*, 19 (see note 18). One editor has suggested that Jonson modeled Face on John Dee's sometime assistant Edward Kelly. See R. J. L. Kingsford, ed., *The Alchemist*, by Ben Jonson (Cambridge: University Press, 1928), xi. On Dee as the possible model for Subtle, see note 49.

21 Jonson, *The Alchemist*, 1.1.190–93 (see note 18).

22 Jonson, *The Alchemist*, 1.2.77 (see note 18).

23 Jonson, *The Alchemist*, 1.2.104–05 (see note 18).

24 See *Oxford English Dictionary*, "quean" *n.* 1; see "common" *a* 3 (see note 5).

25 Jonson, *The Alchemist*, 1.1.107 (see note 18).

26 Jonson, *The Alchemist*, 1.2.29 (see note 18).

27 Helen Ostovich, ed., *Jonson: Four Comedies: Volpone, or The Fox; Epicoene, or The Silent Woman; The Alchemist; Bartholomew Fair* (London and New York: Longman, 1997), 38. Also see David Bevington, "The Major Comedies," *The Cambridge Companion to Ben Jonson*, ed. Richard Harp and Stanley Stewart (Cambridge and New York: Cambridge University Press, 2000), 72–89; here 81–85.

that the theatergoers knew it to be an illusion, while characters like Dapper or victims like Moore did not. Indeed, the rites described in each court case are reminders that ritual is closely allied with drama, if not its very origin.[28]

While Dapper is preparing to meet the queen, other clients appear at the house. First, there is Drugger, an apothecary who wants to configure his new shop by the rules of geomancy, the western form of *feng shui*. Then there is Sir Epicure Mammon, who wants to learn the secret of making gold.[29] As his name suggests, he is an aristocrat and would have been well off did not his greed carry him to Jonson's "cheater." He is the one repeat customer in the play and already fancies himself an *adeptus minor*. Subtle supposes that he must be handing out chemical remedies to his syphilitic friends at the brothels and astrological charms to the women he hopes to seduce:

> Methinks I see him ent'ring ordinaries [inns],
> Dispensing for the pox [syphilis]; and plaguey [plague-stricken] houses,
> Reaching for his dose [chemical potion]; walking Moorfields for lepers,
> And off'ring citizens' wives pomander bracelets
> As his preservative, made of the elixir.[30]

Mammon is well intentioned, at least, and Subtle imagines him hoping to reform the world:

> I see no end of his labors. He will make
> Nature ashamed of her long sleep; shall do more than She
> In Her best love to mankind ever could.
> If his dream last, he'll turn the age to gold.[31]

He also dreams of having a harem as large as Solomon's with great works of erotic art on the walls.[32] In short, he is the perfect dupe, convinced that he can live a heroic life with the aid of his unworldly guide. When he first enters he expects to achieve the end of the alchemical work, and Subtle continues preying on this conviction. The learned doctor uses a barrage of alchemical terminology which, one critic suggests, serves as a kind of bewitching enchantment.[33]

---

28 The secondary literature on this connection is vast, going back at least to Cambridge Ritualists like Jane Harrison and Gilbert Murray, but extending to studies of dramatic works in England and in emerging nations. See, e.g., Robert Ackerman, *The Myth and Ritual School: J. G. Frazer and the Cambridge Ritualists*, Theorists of Myth (London and New York: Routledge, 2002).

29 There are many stories of duped aristocrats who dream of restoring their fortunes; for one of the strangest, see the contribution by Lia B. Ross in this volume.

30 Jonson, *The Alchemist*, 1.4.18–22 (see note 18).

31 Jonson, *The Alchemist*, 1.4.25–28 (see note 18).

32 Jonson, *The Alchemist*, 2.3.34–35 (see note 18).

33 Charles Nichol, *The Chemical Theatre* (London: Routledge, 1980), 97–100.

Other characters are less principled. There is Ananias, a Puritan with a similar wish to transmute base metals. He will thus enrich his congregation and, if he lives up to his biblical name, himself as well.[34] Later, there is Kastril, an "angry boy" who wants to marry off his widowed sister and turn her small dowry to a profit. Each person wants exactly what the three confederates want: riches. The scam works, in each instance, because Subtle poses as a simple doctor who knows nothing about such base desires. The four "humours" are all represented. Kastril is choleric, angry, as is the hot headed Ananias. Mammon is sanguine, hopeful; his friend Surly is phlegmatic, detached; and Dapper is somewhat melancholic about his losses, though with a sufficient streak of hope that his type would later be called enthusiastic.

The action reaches a crisis in act 3, when Subtle enters *"disguised like a Priest of Faery."*[35] He is wearing a robe which, he says, the queen herself gave to him.[36] After he has queried Dapper to make sure that the ritual has been followed, and after Face has checked to make sure Dapper's pockets are empty, Doll follows in the guise of an elf playing a cittern and threatening to bring more elves to pinch him if he has concealed any riches. Subtle tells Dapper that the queen herself is at supper and will not receive him until later in the day. That gives the confederates more time for their other victims before Dapper is brought in, blindfolded, in the penultimate scene. Doll now enters, dressed *"like the Queen of Faery."*[37] As Dapper kisses her skirts, she intones: "Much, nephew, shalt thou win; much shalt thou spend; / Much shalt thou give away; much shalt thou lend."[38] Dapper promises to share his future winnings, and the confederates demand earnest money. Before anything can be arranged, however, there is a great clamor as neighbors storm the door along with constables and the owner of the house.

So much for the crime, but what of the punishment? Unlike Judith Philips, Doll Common escapes whipping, and indeed escapes London with her lover Subtle. For Jonson and his urbane audience, it seems punishment enough that Subtle is forced out of London to a provincial setting like Chester or Yarmouth,[39] his schemes gone up in the smoke of his alchemical fire.[40] The owner could press charges, but he is a man of good humor, as his name Lovewit suggests.[41] He could dismiss his servant Jeremy, but is delighted by the man's inventiveness, especially when he takes the wealthy widow as his wife and gets the money that the cozeners had

---

34 See Acts 9: 1–20.

35 Jonson, *The Alchemist*, stage direction at 3.5.1 (see note 18).

36 Jonson, *The Alchemist*, stage direction at 3.5.7–8 (see note 18).

37 Jonson, *The Alchemist*, stage direction at 5.4.21 (see note 18).

38 Jonson, *The Alchemist*, 5.4.30–31 (see note 18).

39 Jonson, *The Alchemist*, 5.5.121–22 (see note 18).

40 Jonson, *The Alchemist*, 24; "The Argument," 12 (see note 18).

41 Jonson, *The Alchemist*, 5.5.144 (see note 18).

already taken from Kastril. Indeed, Lovewit is so delighted that he tells his servant, "I will be ruled by thee in anything."[42] This leaves Jeremy to deliver the final lines. Advancing to the front of the stage, he appeals to the audience and its sense of decorum. He has escaped from both his confederates and their dupes, but not from those who observed the acts of cozenage. He therefore tries to buy them off with promises of sharing his ill-gotten gains with them and their theater-going friends. "I put myself on you," he says in the play's concluding lines:

> and this pelf,
> Which I have got, if you do quit me, rests
> To feast you often, and invite new guests. [43]

Among the many sources of Jonson's learned satire is Erasmus's colloquy *De alcumista,* in which a swindled gentleman decides not to prosecute a pretend alchemist. The speaker who tells the tale considers this a wise move.

> Nay, he gave him [i.e., the alchemist] Money to bear his Charges, and conjur'd him by all that was sacred, not to speak a Word of what had happened between them. And in my Opinion, it was his Wisdom so to do, rather than to be the common Laughing-stock . . . .[44]

In Jonson's play, Lovewit serves as the judge of the cozeners and their victims. He seems content to keep any ill-gotten gains and to let the victims be punished for their greed, which made them vulnerable in the first place. The final lines serve as a reminder that the playgoers must form the "country"—that is, the jury—and pass judgment on the play and its characters. The characters represent a cross-section of London life, with types that Jonson's first audiences are expected to recognize. Indeed, *The Alchemist* was updated later in the seventeenth century, in John Wilson's Restoration comedy *The Cheats*.[45] The allusions remind us that there are more fools waiting to be swindled and more cozeners to swindle them. Members of the audience can both profit and protect themselves by knowing the tricks of the trade. Moreover, the most discerning members of his audience, who buy his published play, are advised to be on guard. "Thou were never more fair in the way to be cozened than in this age in poetry," he cautions, "especially in plays." One must use good judgment in attending plays, as in daily life. With

---

42 Jonson, *The Alchemist*, 5.5.142 (see note 18).

43 Jonson, *The Alchemist*, 5.5.163–65 (see note 18).

44 Erasmus, "The Alchymist," *All the Familiar Colloquies of Desiderius Erasmus*, trans. N. Bailey, 2nd ed. (London: P. Knapton et al., 1733), 270–79; here 279.

45 Thomas Willard, "John Wilson's Satire of Hermetic Medicine," *Literature and Medicine During the Eighteenth Century*, ed. Marie Mulvey Roberts and Roy Porter, Wellcome Institute Studies in the History of Medicine (London: Routledge, 1993), 136–50.

plays, says Jonson in the verse prologue, it is not so much a matter of crime and punishment as of "vices" and "remedies."[46]

Jonson's *Alchemist* is a *tour de force* of esoteric learning. Once entered on a course of esoteric study, a potential alchemist could turn to many subjects. Some alchemists were reputed to have made Faustian bargains to further their studies, and all aspiring adepts were advised to perform their chemical operations at the astrologically appropriate moment. The famous astrologer William Lilly (1602–1681) wrote that he had tried several times to contact the Queen of Fairies, convinced that she could teach him the secrets of his art.[47] Fairies and elves were said to be malevolent as often as they were benevolent, and Robin Goodfellow was a popular trickster figure in English folklore.[48]

Some literary historians have tried to identify the historical model of Jonson's alchemist Subtle. One popular candidate is Sir John Dee (1527–ca. 1608), who once served as astrologer and geographer for Elizabeth I.[49] However, his once elevated social status and subsequent distance from London make him seem a less likely choice than Simon Forman (1552–1611), who was a great frequenter of plays and a consulting astrologer to some members of Jonson's audiences.[50] His advice on matters of love and fortune was sought often enough that Jonson referred to him as "*Oracle-Forman*."[51] While Forman's business was clearly that of taking money from clients who consulted him, he claimed skill at various magical arts, including alchemy, astrology, necromancy, conjuring, and divination.[52] He was known to be a cunning man, much as Judith Philips was presented to the reading public as "a professed cunning woman, or fortune teller."[53] Unlike Philips, however, he was never charged with swindling. On those occasions when he was called upon to

---

46 Jonson, *The Alchemist*, 24; "The Prologue," 14–15 (see note 18).

47 William Lilly, *Autobiography*; cited in Thomas, *Religion and the Decline of Magic*, 727 (see note 1).

48 See *Oxford English Dictionary*, "Robin Goodfellow," n. Shakespeare's Puck is explicitly associated with Robin Goodfellow in *A Midsummer Night's Dream*, 2.1.34; Shakespeare, *Complete Works*, 357 (see note 4).

49 See, e.g., Frances A. Yates, *The Occult Philosophy in Elizabethan England* (London: Routledge, 1979), 161.

50 The claim is made without supporting evidence in A[lfred]. L[eslie]. Rowse, *Simon Forman: Sex and Society in Shakespeare's Age* (London: Weidenfeld & Nicolson, 1974), 150. The Shakespearean connection is pursued in Charles Nichol, *The Lodger Shakespeare: His Life on Silver Street* (New York: Viking, 2007), 112–27. Recent studies of Forman include Judith Cook, *Dr Simon Forman: A Most Notorious Physician* (London: Chatto & Windus, 2001, and Lauren Kassell, *Medicine and Magic in Elizabethan London: Simon Forman: Astrologer, Alchemist, and Physician*, Oxford Historical Monographs (Oxford: Clarendon Press, 2005).

51 Ben Jonson, *The Devil Is an* Ass, ed. William Savage Johnson. Yale Studies in English, 29 (New York: Holt, 1905), 53; 2.8.33. See the editor's note on 142.

52 Thomas, *Religion and the Decline of Magic*, 362–82 (see note 1); Cook, *Dr. Simon Forman*, 46–47 (see note 50).

53 *The Brideling, Sadling, and Ryding of a Rich Churle* (see note 9).

testify about his practice, he professed to follow the science of astrology, and to his credit he instructed the great mathematician Richard Napier in the principles of making of horoscopes.

Forman kept "casebooks" with meticulous records of his consultations, records which say more about the fears and desires of his clients than about any attempt to deceive them. He was said to be a pious man who spent long hours in prayer and meditation, and in that respect may have served as a model for the swindler who convinces Mammon that he "Has worn his knees bare and his slippers bald / With prayer."[54] Forman was a former schoolmaster, the author of a pamphlet on determining longitude.[55] Like Dee, he was a keen student of esoteric books and left a great many notes on his reading. It seems that he convinced himself first that he was skilled in the occult sciences, and only then decided he could be of service to others. However, the very nature of his services invited skepticism, and the stories of swindlers like Judith Philips and the Wests made him a potential model for Jonson's learned swindler.

Cozenage was a new word in Shakespeare's day, but the concepts of coveting and stealing were as old as the Decalogue. The cozeners of the era sought ever new schemes to cheat their victims, and they often did so in the hope of getting lighter punishments, if caught, than those given out for simple theft. The schemes hatched by Judith Philips in Hampshire, by John and Alice West in Hammersmith, and by still other confederates in Dorset appealed to the popular imagination precisely because they exploited popular, though moribund, faith in the existence and benevolence of fairies. The same schemes exposed the foibles of the victims, including their sense of self-importance and their desire for unearned riches. All of which made such tales of con artists pimping for the fairies an irresistible topic for stage satire. Shakespeare put the fairy king and queen on the stage, in the characters of Oberon and Titania in *A Midsummer Night's Dream*, as a kind of parallel to Theseus and Hippolyta, the human king and queen in the play. Shakespeare adapted the Robin Goodfellow of legend as his Puck, who in the epilogue provided a final comment on the whole stage illusion. Jonson showed how the illusion worked in the hands of a skilled cozener like Subtle.

In his alchemist, Jonson has created a brilliant but deeply flawed character, with an almost preternatural talent for discovering a victim's weakness and exploiting it. Meanwhile, he has educated his audience, first in "The Argument" spoken before the play is performed and then in the dedication and "The Prologue" prefixed to the printed play, so that its members can appreciate the trickery with

---

54 Jonson, *The Alchemist*, 2.2.103–104 (see note 18).

55 Simon Forman, *The Groundes of Longitude* (London: Thomas Dawson, 1591). Forman described himself on the title page as a "Student in Astronomie and Physique," i.e., astrology and medicine, and he promised to publish further books on astrology (sig. A7v).

the confidence that they would not fall for any of it. The amoral Face steps forward at the end, Jonson's mouthpiece and the character who has brought the others together in the play's action. A quick study, he has learned the lingo of alchemy and Subtle's other arts. He has aided and abetted Subtle and Doll, and is as guilty of cozenage as they; however, he has an understanding master, and he knows when to break his ties with the former confederates and their victims. Perhaps he has taken off his laboratory smock before he advances to the front of the stage in the play's final moment. Perhaps he substitutes a piece of his livery. Surely he speaks for the playwright as he invites the audience to pass judgment.

Notable Diſcouery of Cooſenage.

Now daily practiſed by ſundry lewd per-
ſons, called Connie-catchers, and
Croſſe-byters.

Plainely laying open thoſe pernitious ſleights that hath brought many igno-
rant men to conſuſion.

Written for the general benefit of all Gentlemen, Citizens, Aprentiſes, Countrey Farmers and yeomen, that may hap to fall into the company of ſuch cooſening companions.

With a delightfull diſcourſe of the cooſnage of Colliers.

Naſcimur pro patria. By R. Greene, Maiſter of Arts.

LONDON
Printed by Thomas Scarlet for Thomas Nelſon.
1592

Fig. 1. Robert Greene's exposé of cozenage

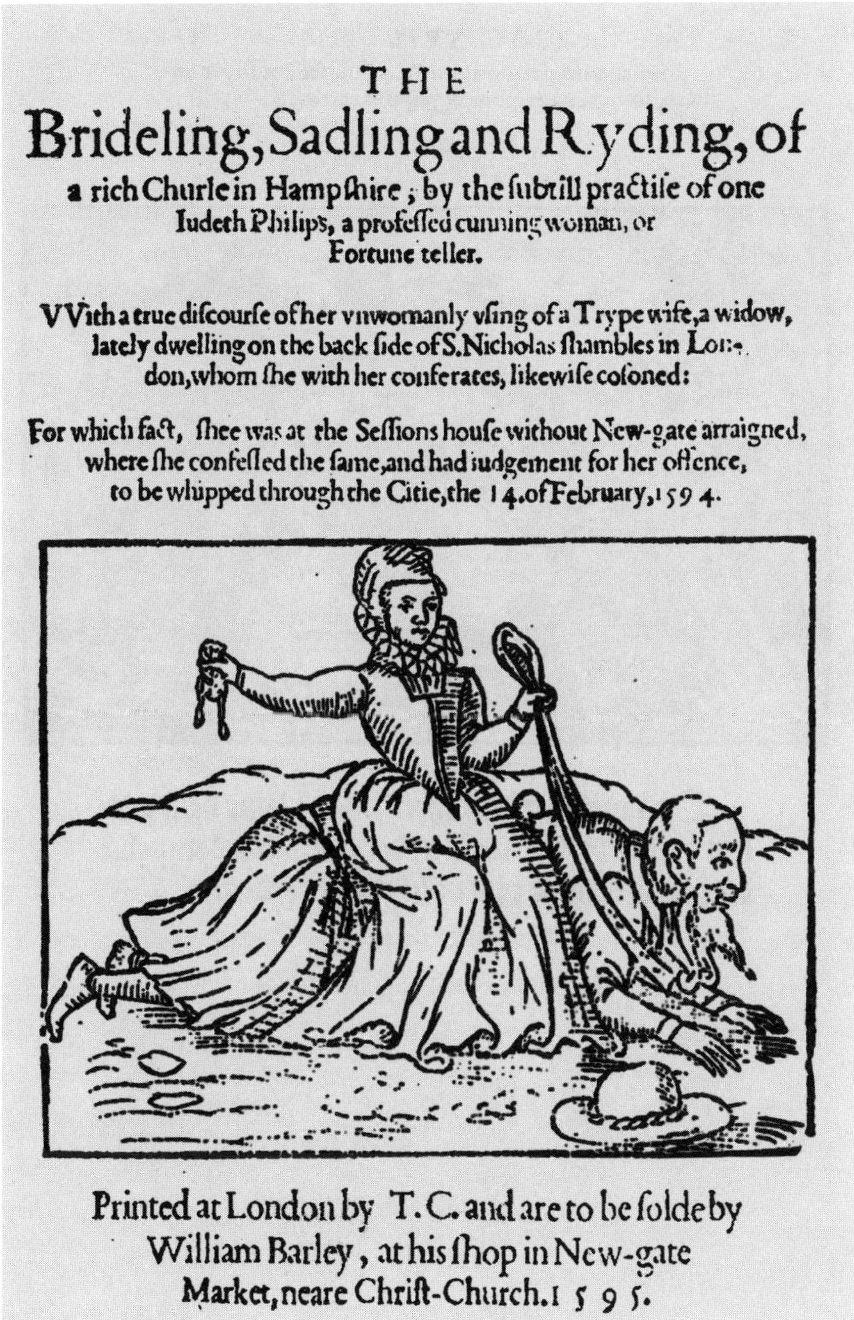

THE
Brideling, Sadling and Ryding, of
a rich Churle in Hampſhire; by the ſubtill practiſe of one
Iudeth Philips, a profeſſed cunning woman, or
Fortune teller.

VVith a true diſcourſe of her vnwomanly vſing of a Trype wife, a widow,
lately dwelling on the back ſide of S. Nicholas ſhambles in Lon-
don, whom ſhe with her conferates, likewiſe coſoned:

For which fact, ſhee was at the Seſſions houſe without New-gate arraigned,
where ſhe confeſſed the ſame, and had iudgement for her offence,
to be whipped through the Citie, the 14. of February, 1594.

Printed at London by T. C. and are to be ſolde by
William Barley, at his ſhop in New-gate
Market, neare Chriſt-Church. 1595.

Fig. 2. Judith Philips bridling a rich man

APOC. XVII.

Mulier cum poculo abominationis ſedens ſuper be-
ſtiam,adoratur à regibus & populis terræ.

Das weib vff dem thier ſitzend / mit dem gül-
den becher des grewels in der hand/wird angebä-
tet von Königen vnd völckern der erden.

Fig. 3. The Whore of Babylon by Albrecht Dürer

Fig. 4. Aristotle and Phyllis by Hans Baldung Grien in the atelier of Albrecht Dürer

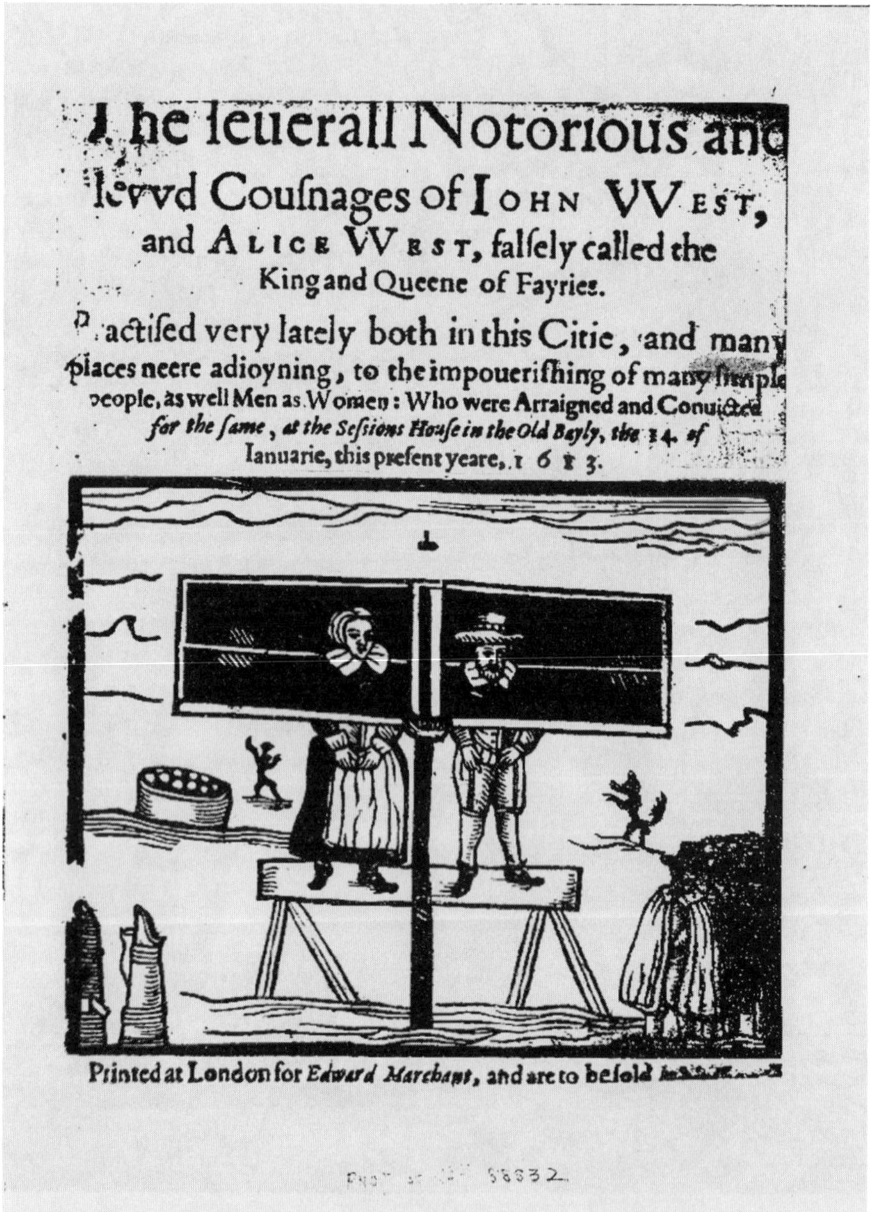

The ſeuerall Notorious and lewd Couſnages of IOHN VVEST, and ALICE VVEST, falſely called the King and Queene of Fayries.

Practiſed very lately both in this Citie, and many places neere adioyning, to the impoueriſhing of many ſimple people, as well Men as Women: Who were Arraigned and Conuicted *for the ſame, at the Seſsions Houſe in the Old Bayly, the* 14. *of* Ianuarie, this preſent yeare, 1613.

Printed at London for *Edward Marchant*, and are to be ſold

Fig. 5. Alice West and John West in the pillory

Chapter 21

Denis Bjaï
(Université d'Orléans/ ANR *JusLittera*)

Réflexions de Montaigne sur le châtiment des criminels

Les réflexions de Montaigne sur le châtiment des criminels lui sont inspirées par ses lectures, juridiques, historiques, philosophiques (qu'il serait trop long de recenser), et surtout par son expérience, quinze ans durant, de magistrat, de praticien du droit. Rappelons que Montaigne a d'abord été conseiller à la cour des Aides de Périgueux (compétente en matière de fiscalité), puis, à la suppression de celle-ci, réaffecté à la Chambre des Requêtes du Parlement de Bordeaux, devenue Chambre des Enquêtes, qui traitait essentiellement des litiges de droit civil.[1] Les causes criminelles étaient, elles, du ressort de la Grand'Chambre ou bien de la Tournelle, ainsi dénommée parce que l'on y siégeait à tour de rôle.[2] Si Montaigne n'y a peut-être pas été affecté, du moins a-t-il pu participer aux séances plénières du Parlement, "toutes chambres assemblées," où l'on statuait sur les affaires les plus graves, selon une procédure unilatérale privant l'accusé d'avocat et excluant tout appel.[3] Aussi les exécutions capitales ne sont-elles pas seulement prétexte,

---

1 Sur Montaigne au Parlement de Bordeaux et, plus précisément, à la Chambre des Enquêtes, voir André Tournon, *Montaigne en toutes lettres* (Paris: Bordas, 1989), 19–22; et *Montaigne: La glose et l'essai*, seconde édition revue et corrigée. Études montaignistes, 37 (1983; Paris: Champion, 2000), 185–202.

2 Article "Parlement de Bordeaux" de l'*Encyclopédie*. Cf. Jean Bodin, *La République*, IV, 6, cité par Littré, *Dictionnaire de la langue française, s.v.* Tournelle: "Nos pères ont très sagement ordonné que la chambre criminelle des parlements changera de trois en trois mois, qui pour ceste cause s'appelle tournelle, parce que tous les juges des autres chambres y jugent chacun en leur tour."

3 Suivant l'article 162 de l'ordonnance de Villers-Cotterêts (1539): "En matière criminelle, ne seront les parties aucunement ouïes, et par le conseil ne ministère d'aucunes personnes" (cité par Géralde Nakam, *Les* Essais *de Montaigne miroir et procès de leur temps: témoignage historique et création littéraire*. Publications de la Sorbonne / Série littérature / 2 ; 16 [Paris: Nizet, 1984], 138, n. 266). Voir

dans les *Essais*, à dévider — variante burlesque des *ultima verba* édifiants prononcés par les grands hommes — des bons mots prononcés sur l'échafaud (par exemple, "Un autre disoit au bourreau qu'il ne le touchast pas à la gorge, de peur de le faire tressaillir de rire, tant il estoit chatouilleux"[4]), ou bien des histoires singulières, comme celle de ce condamné à mort qui mourut subitement à l'annonce de sa grâce.[5] Au détour du texte, Montaigne laisse entendre combien il a pu lui coûter d'assister ès qualités à de tels supplices: "Les executions mesme de la justice, pour raisonnables qu'elles soient, je ne les puis voir d'une veue ferme."[6]

Mais ces arrêts sont-ils précisément *raisonnables*? Instruit par sa propre expérience, Montaigne porte un jugement lucide sur les tragiques erreurs commises par la justice de son temps. Dans le dernier chapitre des *Essais*, intitulé "De l'Experience," il pose deux questions incisives, dont la gradation constitue le plus terrible des réquisitoires: "Combien avons nous descouvert d'innocens avoir esté punis [. . .]; et combien y en a-il eu, que nous n'avons pas descouvert?"[7] Et Montaigne d'enchaîner sur une histoire survenue de son temps et peut-être dans le ressort même du Parlement de Bordeaux, sous les yeux du magistrat qu'il fut: des assassins présumés viennent d'être condamnés à mort par leurs juges quand ceux-ci apprennent que, dans une juridiction voisine, on détient des prisonniers qui sont passés aux aveux et qui ont, sans le moindre doute possible, accompli ce forfait.

Que faire? Justice a déjà été rendue, des juges ne sauraient se déjuger, les condamnés à mort sont donc pendus haut et court. "Somme, commente Montaigne, ces pauvres diables sont consacrez aux formules de la justice,"[8] c'est-à-dire qu'ils sont exécutés proprement pour la forme, sacrifiés à une raison judiciaire qui bat en brèche toute norme juridique. Le contre-exemple de Philippe de Macédoine, repris de Plutarque,[9] qui sut, dans un cas semblable, faire respecter

---

Gaston Zeller, *Les institutions de la France au XVIe siècle* (Paris: Presses Universitaires de France, 1948), 179.

4 Nous citons *Les Essais* dans l'édition Jean Balsamo *et al.* de la "Bibliothèque de la Pléiade" (Paris: Gallimard, 2007), ici livre I, chapitre 40, 259.

5 I, 20/21, 99 (voir n. 4).

6 II, 11, 452 (voir n. 4).

7 III, 13, 1117 (voir n. 4).

8 III, 13, 1117 (voir n. 4). Exemple de cas "perplexe" suivant St. Geonget, "Perplexité et scepticisme dans les *Essais* ou la souris ou le ver à soie (III, 1)," *L'écriture du scepticisme chez Montaigne*, ed. Marie-Luce Demonet et Alain Legros. Travaux d' Humanisme et Renaissance, 385 (Genève: Droz, 2004), 143–57; ici 151–52. (On rétablira, dans le titre de l'article, la référence correcte du chapitre: III, 13.)

9 Dans *Les dicts notables des anciens Roys*, trad. Jacques Amyot des *Œuvres morales et meslées* (Paris: Michel de Vascosan, 1572), 192B, où Plutarque met en scène le jugement par Philippe d'un certain Meletas. Mais Montaigne, toujours soucieux de ne pas passer pour un pédant, parle de "Philippus, ou quelque autre."

l'arrêt tout en dédommageant l'innocent condamné à tort, contrebalancer la justice par l'équité, ne saurait faire ici balance égale, car la vie de l'accusé n'était pas en jeu. Ce qui permet à Montaigne de pousser plus avant son réquisitoire contre les tribunaux du temps: "Mais il [Philippe] avoit affaire à un accident reparable; les miens furent pendus irreparablement. Combien ay-je veu de condemnations plus crimineuses que le crime?"[10] clausule ciselée autour d'un adjectif rare sous sa plume (*crimineux*, du latin *criminosus*, préféré ici à *criminel*)[11] et d'une paronomase cinglante introduite seulement dans le tout dernier état du texte.[12]

Confronté à une telle situation, comment le magistrat Montaigne s'est-il luimême comporté? Dans l'avant-dernier chapitre des *Essais*, "De la Physionomie," aux toutes dernières lignes, il laisse échapper cet aveu lourd de sens: "lors que l'occasion m'a convié aux condemnations criminelles, j'ay plustost manqué à la justice."[13] Le juge pénal, aussi allergique à la violence que l'homme privé, était donc naturellement porté à l'indulgence, sinon pour le crime, du moins pour le criminel. Et Montaigne s'autorise d'une sentence bien frappée de Tite-Live, qu'il réécrit à la première personne pour la faire pleinement sienne, sur la disproportion toujours à craindre entre le mal que les hommes sont capables de commettre et l'énergie nécessaire pour le réprimer: *Ut magis peccari nolim, quam satis animi, ad vindicanda peccata habeam*, "De sorte que je ne voudrais pas qu'il se commît plus de fautes que je n'ai de courage pour les punir."[14]

Les réflexions de Montaigne sur le châtiment des criminels s'ordonnent autour de trois questions-clés: un châtiment peut-il être juste? peut-il être proportionné? peut-il être utile? Première question: peut-il être juste? Il faut faire d'abord la part des passions humaines, comme la colère, la cruauté, la vengeance, qui viennent toujours influer sur la sentence. Colère du consul romain Piso, dans le chapitre consacré précisément à cette passion, lequel s'emporte contre un de ses soldats revenu seul du fourrage et suspecté d'avoir tué son compagnon; il le condamme à mort, jusqu'à ce que réapparaisse l'autre soldat, à la grande satisfaction du bourreau, qui peut ramener l'un et l'autre vivants, mais à la fureur redoublée du chef:

10 III, 13, 1117–1118 (voir n. 4).

11 Pas d'autre occurrence dans les *Essais*, d'après la *Concordance* de Roy Leake. 2 vol. Travaux d'Humanisme et Renaissance, 187 (Genève: Droz, 1981).

12 On lit dans les marges de l'Exemplaire de Bordeaux: "Combien ai-je veu de sentences [*préféré à* jugements] pires que le crime." Sur l'effort de Montaigne pour accentuer l'expression de sa réprobation, voir André Tournon, «Justice oblige», *Montaigne: la justice* [*Bulletin de la Société des Amis de Montaigne*, 8e série, nos 21–22 (janvier-juin 2001)], 71–79; ici 71, n. 3.

13 III, 12, 1110 (voir n. 4).

14 Le texte latin (*Histoire romaine*, XXIX, xxi, 11) porte *nolint* et *habeant*, par référence aux Locriens, portés à l'indulgence envers Scipion.

> il en fit trois coulpables, par ce qu'il en avoit trouvé un innocent: et les fit depescher tous trois: Le premier soldat, par ce qu'il y avoit arrest contre luy: le second qui s'estoit egaré, par ce qu'il estoit cause de la mort de son compagnon; et le bourreau pour n'avoir obey au commandement qu'on luy avoit faict.[15]

Cruauté des tyrans qui veulent ôter la vie à leurs ennemis en les faisant affreusement souffrir et qui recherchent tous les moyens imaginables "d'alonger la mort"[16]: Crésus, en faisant gratter et carder tout vif un gentilhomme;[17] Tibère, en "fais[ant] lier la verge à ses criminels, pour les faire mourir à faute de pisser "[18]; et le sultan Mehmet II, en faisant trancher les hommes en deux, au niveau du diaphragme, "d'où il arrivoit, qu'ils mourussent comme de deux morts à la fois: et voyoit-on [. . .] l'une et l'autre part pleine de vie, se demener long temps après pressée de tourment."[19]

Vengeance des commanditaires mêmes d'un meurtre sur ceux qu'ils ont employés à cette fin et qui leur apparaissent par la suite en être la vivante image, donc le vivant reproche, par exemple quand le même Mehmet II livre l'assassin de son demi-frère à la mère de celui-ci, qui "ouvrit à ce meurtrier l'estomach: et tout chaudement de ses mains, fouillant et arrachant son cœur, le jetta manger aux chiens."[20] Sans compter l'hypocrisie des juges, qui punissent volontiers chez autrui une inconduite qu'eux-mêmes s'autorisent, comme l'adultère,[21] ou qui, circonstance aggravante, châtient contre leur conscience: "tel condamne les hommes à mourir, pour des crimes, qu'il n'estime point fautes."[22]

Il faut faire aussi la part du hasard et de la chance, donc de l'arbitraire, qui permet quelquefois à un accusé de croiser sur son chemin un juge ce jour-là bien disposé, qui ne l'aurait peut-être pas été la veille ni ne le serait plus le lendemain. Montaigne y voit même l'origine d'une sorte d'adage judiciaire (qu'il semble être toutefois le seul à citer): "En la chicane de nos palais, ce mot est en usage, qui se dit des criminels qui rencontrent les juges en quelque bonne trampe, douce et debonnaire, *gaudeat de bona fortuna*,"[23] mot latin que les éditions parues du vivant de Montaigne font suivre de sa traduction, "qu'il jouisse de ce bonheur." Mais la médaille a naturellement son revers et l'adage, pour un accusé confronté à un tribunal moins bienveillant, pourrait aussi bien s'inverser en un *doleat de mala fortuna*!

---

15 II, 31, 754 (voir n. 4).
16 II, 27, 737 (voir n. 4).
17 P. 738 (voir n. 4).
18 III, 4, 879 (voir n. 4).
19 II, 27, 737 (voir n. 4).
20 III, 1, 839 (voir n. 4).
21 III, 9, 1035 (voir n. 4).
22 III, 9, 1035 (voir n. 4).
23 II, 12, 598 (voir n. 4).

Enfin un châtiment juste devrait résulter d'un procès équitable, lui-même fondé sur une instruction méthodique et sur le respect du contradictoire, non sur les simples suppositions ou conjectures d'un juge. Dans l'affaire Martin Guerre, rendue célèbre par les travaux de Natalie Zemon Davis, Montaigne prend ses distances avec les conclusions hasardeuses du conseiller toulousain Jean de Coras, alors enclin à expliquer par la magie[24] cette troublante usurpation d'identité entre Guerre et Arnaud du Tilh: "je trouvay beaucoup de hardiesse en l'arrest qui l'avoit condamné à estre pendu."[25] La *hardiesse*, c'est-à-dire le caractère aventuré, sinon erroné, du jugement d'appel[26] est ici d'autant moins recevable, admissible, que la vie d'un homme est en jeu. "À tuer les gens, ajoute Montaigne d'une plume cinglante, il faut une clairté lumineuse et nette,"[27] comme en convenait lui-même Coras, que le texte pourrait bien ici ironiquement démarquer.[28] Mais notre raison, infirme et déficiente, nous procure-t-elle jamais de telles clartés? Montaigne peut à bon compte renchérir: "c'est mettre ses conjectures à bien haut prix, que d'en faire cuire un homme tout vif."[29]

En matière criminelle, le moindre doute doit profiter à l'accusé et conduire la cour à surseoir son jugement, à reconnaître platement qu'elle ne comprend rien au cas qui lui est soumis, ou encore, comme le fit à Athènes l'Aréopage, à reconvoquer les parties à échéance de cent ans. Insérée dans le chapitre "Des boyteux," cette mise en garde contre les erreurs judiciaires n'a que l'apparence d'une digression. Elle entretient avec le thème-titre un certain rapport, sinon un rapport certain, que le diligent lecteur est invité à déceler. Pour Nicola Panichi, "les boiteux en question sont les juges, boiteux de l'âme, ou mieux, boiteux de la conscience et de ses tribunaux, boitant autant que leurs sentences."[30] Mais ce sont les *Essais* tout entiers qui répercutent la démarche claudicante de la justice.

Seconde question, un châtiment peut-il être proportionné? Montaigne fixe clairement la limite qui ne devrait jamais être outrepassée: "en la justice mesme,

---

24 Point de vue nuancé par Émile V. Telle: "Coras évoque vigoureusement, dans le texte imprimé [de l'*Arrest memorable du Parlement de Tolose*], la possibilité de sorcellerie mais n'en fait pas 'cas'. Il n'explique rien et ne tente pas de rien expliquer par la magie. Il se pose, ou plutôt, soulève la question" ("Montaigne et le procès Martin Guerre," *Bibliothèque d'Humanisme et Renaissance* 37 [1975]: 387–419; ici 394).

25 III, 11, 1077 (voir n. 4).

26 Sur le sens exact de ce terme, voir Katherine Almquist, "Montaigne et le plus sûr," *Montaigne: la justice*, 151–57; ici 151 (cité n. 12); et Nicola Panichi, "La boiterie de la raison," 171–83; ici 181.

27 P. 1078 (voir n. 4).

28 "Es causes criminelles, [. . .] il convient les preuves estre certaines, indubitables, et plus claires que le jour [. . .], les tesmoins, et preuves doyvent estre entieres et plus claires, et reluysantes que le soleil" (reproduit par Nicola Panichi, "La boiterie de la raison," article cité [n. 26], 179).

29 P. 1079 (voir n. 4).

30 Article cité, 173 (voir n. 26).

tout ce qui est au-delà de la mort simple, me semble pure cruauté."[31] La phrase sera reprise à l'identique dans le chapitre 27 du même livre, par un effet de symétrie soigneusement ménagé.[32] Présente, à cette double place, dès l'édition originale du livre, elle retint fin 1580–début 1581 l'attention de la censure romaine, comme le rapporte Montaigne lui-même dans son *Journal de voyage*: entre autres animadversions, il se vit reprocher "d'estimer cruauté ce qui est au-delà de mort simple."[33] L'exemplaire des *Essais* confisqué à l'auteur à son arrivée à Rome avait été soumis, en effet, à l'examen scrupuleux d'un et même de deux censeurs, dont les observations critiques, conservées dans les archives de l'Index, ont été récemment retrouvées.[34]

Tout ce passage de "De la cruauté" fut traduit en italien, pour en souligner l'hétérodoxie, parce que Montaigne avait cru bon d'ajouter: "Et notamment à nous, qui devrions avoir respect d'en envoyer les ames en bon estat; ce qui ne se peut, les ayant agitées et desesperées par tourmens insupportables." Il n'échappa pas au censeur romain que l'allusion pouvait viser les pratiques de la justice d'Église, en particulier de l'Inquisition, qui s'arrogeait le droit de tourmenter les corps pour sauver les âmes.[35] Finalement dédouané par le Maître du Sacré Palais, le dominicain Sisto Fabri, et même invité à son départ à ne tenir nulle compte des "sottises" consignées dans ce document,[36] Montaigne amplifiera, de réédition en réédition, sa condamnation des châtiments inhumains infligés aux condamnés.[37]

Qu'entend-il au juste par une "mort simple"? L'expression se rencontre à quatre reprises dans les *Essais*, toujours dans le texte primitif de 1580, la première fois à propos de ces gens du peuple "conduict[s] à la mort, et non à la mort simple, mais meslée de honte, et quelquefois de griefs tourmens."[38] *Griefs tourmens* ici, *tourmens insupportables* dans le chapitre "De la cruauté" précédemment cité, désignent ces

---

31 II, 11, 452 (voir n. 4).

32 Le livre II comptant en effet trente-sept chapitres, le 11e se lit après les dix premiers, le 27e avant les dix derniers. John McClelland voit en revanche dans cette répétition, que Montaigne aurait omis d'éliminer, l'indice d'une composition des *Essais* à partir de brouillons, ou "brouillars" ("La tradition de l'édition critique face au texte des *Essais*," *Éditer les* Essais *de Montaigne*, éd. Claude Blum et André Tournon. Études montaignistes, 28 (Paris: Champion, 1997), 203–26; ici 223).

33 Édition François Rigolot (Paris: Presses Universitaires de France, 1992), 119.

34 Pièce publiée par Peter Godman, *The Saint as Censor. Robert Bellarmin between Inquisition and Index*. Studies in Medieval and Reformation Thought, 80 (Leiden and Boston: Brill, 2000), Doc. no. 42, 339–42; puis par Philippe Desan, "Apologie de Sebond ou justification de Montaigne?," *Montaigne et la théologie*, Travaux d'Humanisme et Renaissance, 444 (Genève: Droz, 2008), 175–200; ici 197–200.

35 Voir Alain Legros, "Montaigne face à ses censeurs romains de 1581 (mise à jour)," *Bibliothèque d'Humanisme et Renaissance* 71.1 (2009): 7–33; ici 26.

36 *Journal de voyage*, 131 (voir n. 33).

37 Voir Malcolm Smith, *Montaigne and the Roman Censors*. Études de philologie et d'histoire, 37 (Genève: Droz, 1981), ch. VI, "Humane executions."

38 I, 14, 259 (voir n. 4).

raffinements sadiques dont la justice du temps croit bon d'accompagner ses châtiments, là où elle devrait se contenter de faire passer les criminels de vie à trépas, de les mettre "simplement" à mort. C'est la clémence de César qui est ici alléguée:

> ayant forcé les Pyrates de se rendre à luy, qui l'avoient auparavant pris prisonnier et mis à rançon; d'autant qu'il les avoit menassez de les faire mettre en croix, il les y condamna; mais ce fut après les avoir faict estrangler. Philomon son secretaire, qui l'avoit voulu empoisonner, il ne le punit pas plus aigrement que d'une mort simple.[39]

—exact décalque du latin de Suétone, *non grauius quam simplici morte puniit.*[40] Montaigne développe davantage, ajouté dans les marges de l'Exemplaire de Bordeaux, le contre-exemple du soldat prisonnier mis au désespoir par de macabres préparatifs[41] qu'il entend depuis sa cellule. Le malheureux tente par tous les moyens de se supprimer lui-même, jusqu'à se planter un vieux clou rouillé dans la gorge puis dans le ventre, avant d'apprendre, déjà à moitié inconscient, "qu'il n'estoit condamné qu'à avoir la teste tranchée."[42] Revirement complet d'attitude: il reprend courage, boit du vin, remercie ses juges, comme "delivré de la mort pour l'avoir changée." L'annonce d'une mort pure et simple l'a fait paradoxalement revenir à la vie.[43] Condamner un homme à la peine capitale ne donne pas en effet tous les droits sur lui, comme celui de le disséquer tout vif dans l'intérêt de la médecine ou bien de le livrer aux jeux du cirque, à l'exemple des anciens.[44]

Si raffinements de cruauté il doit y avoir, en vue de faire impression sur le peuple, ceux-ci doivent s'exercer, fait valoir Montaigne, sur le cadavre, non sur le corps vif. Il dit avoir assisté par hasard à Rome, en janvier 1581, à l'exécution d'un scélérat appelé Catena (de son vrai nom, Bartolomeo Vallante), pendu puis coupé en morceaux. À la "mort simple" du condamné succéda donc le traitement ignominieux et barbare réservé à sa dépouille, qui provoqua de vives réactions parmi l'assistance. "Car le peuple, rapporte dans le *Journal de voyage* le secrétaire de Montaigne, qui n'avoit pas senti de le voir estrangler, à chaque coup qu'on donnoit pour le hacher, s'escrioit d'une voix piteuse."[45] Non que les exécutions se

---

39 II, 11, 452 (voir n. 4).

40 Sur la réception de l'historien latin à la Renaissance, voir l'étude de Jessica Tvordi, "Constructing the Early Modern Criminal through Suetonius: The Cases of Buckingham and Castlehaven," dans notre volume.

41 De "roues, clous et croix, potences, estrapade peut-être ou écartèlement" (Géralde Nakam, *Les* Essais *de Montaigne,* 325 [voir n. 3]).

42 P. 453 (voir n. 4).

43 Voir G. Nakam (citée n. 3), 325–26.

44 II, 23, 721 et 723 (voir n. 4).

45 Éd. François Rigolot, 98 (citée n. 33).

déroulassent toujours ainsi à Rome: le même secrétaire dit avoir encore assisté, ce jour-là, à la mise à mort de deux frères assassins de leur maître, qui furent successivement tenaillés, amputés du poing, roués et égorgés. Mais c'est bien l'exemple de Catena qui est repris dans les *Essais*, à la faveur d'une addition introduite dans l'édition de 1582, au retour du grand voyage:

> Je me rencontray un jour à Rome, sur le point qu'on deffaisoit Catena, un voleur insigne: on l'estrangla sans aucune emotion de l'assistance, mais quand on vint à le mettre à quartiers, le bourreau ne donnoit coup, que le peuple ne suivist d'une voix pleintive, et d'une exclamation, comme si chacun eust presté son sentiment à cette charongne.[46]

Du *Journal de voyage* aux *Essais*, du compte rendu du secrétaire au témoignage de l'auteur réapparaissent les mêmes éléments narratifs, mais rendus plus signifiants par le travail de l'écriture: l'étroite connexion établie au moyen du tour consécutif entre l'action du bourreau et la réaction du public, l'hyperbate du second syntagme circonstanciel ménagée par la ponctuation et la comparaison finale qui fait revivre le cadavre à travers chacun des assistants. Ne saurions-nous, après tout, nous comporter aussi humainement que les cannibales du Nouveau Monde, qui ne font rôtir et ne mangent leurs victimes qu'une fois mortes? À deux reprises en effet Montaigne oppose ces pratiques anthropophagiques aux usages des peuples dits civilisés et la comparaison ne tourne pas à l'avantage de ces derniers:

> Je pense, déclare-t-il dans "Des Cannibales,"[47] qu'il y a plus de barbarie à manger un homme vivant, qu'à le manger mort, à deschirer par tourmens et par gehennes, un corps encore plein de sentiment, le faire rostir par le menu [. . .] que de le rostir et manger après qu'il est trespassé.[48]

Et il revient à la charge, pratiquement dans les mêmes termes, dans "De la cruauté": "Les Sauvages ne m'offensent pas tant, de rostir et manger les corps des trespassez, que ceux qui les tourmentent et persecutent vivans."[49]

Ne pourrait-on même se contenter d'un châtiment symbolique, qui réprimerait la faute commise sans attenter à la personne du coupable? Montaigne, grand lecteur des auteurs anciens traduits par Amyot, n'avait pas manqué de relever, dans Diodore de Sicile, la cuisante punition infligée aux lâches par le législateur grec Charondas: au lieu de les condamner à mort, suivant l'usage, "il ordonna

---

46 II, 11, 453 (voir n. 4).

47 Un des rares emplois du tour *je pense que* dans *Les Essais* (quatre occurrences, qui ne se rencontrent qu'aux livres I et II, dans le texte primitif de 1580 ensuite conservé). Sur le même sujet, voir l'étude d'Allison P. Coudert, "The Ultimate Crime: Cannibalism in Early Modern Minds and Imaginations," dans notre volume.

48 I, 30, 216 (voir n. 4).

49 II, 11, 452 (voir n. 4).

seulement qu'ils fussent par trois jours assis emmy la place publicque, vestus de robe de femme,"[50] c'est-à-dire soumis à une humiliation telle que le rouge au front ne manquerait pas de leur faire revenir le sang dans les veines. Et dans les *Moralia* de Plutarque, au traité des *Dicts notables des anciens Roys*, il avait noté cet apophtegme d'Artaxerxès, introduit dans "De la cruauté" à la faveur d'une addition de 1588: pour atténuer la rigueur des premières lois perses, le grand roi adapta le châtiment réservé aux mauvais ministres,

> ordonnant que les Seigneurs qui avoyent failly en leur estat, au lieu qu'on les souloit fouetter, fussent despouillés, et leurs vestemens fouettez pour eux; et au lieu qu'on leur souloit arracher les cheveux, qu'on leur ostast leur hault chappeau seulement.[51]

Le châtiment prend ici une forme spectaculaire, quasi théâtrale. Réduit à un simulacre, il se cantonne dans l'ordre du symbolique.[52] Est-il besoin à la justice d'une autre mise en scène?

Troisième et dernière question: un châtiment pénal peut-il être utile, et à qui? Le seuil du chapitre "De l'art de conferer," en trompe l'œil comme souvent dans *Les Essais*, aborde la question de biais. Montaigne s'y amuse en effet à opposer aux belles actions des grands hommes, hautement recommandables, ses propres insuffisances, qui indiquent du moins la voie à ne pas suivre. Mais il ne le fait qu'après un détour soigneusement calculé par les fautes autrement répréhensibles des criminels: "C'est un usage de notre justice, d'en condamner aucuns, pour le seul exemple des autres. On ne corrige pas celuy qu'on pend, on corrige les autres par luy."[53]

En se relisant la plume à la main, Montaigne remplace, dans l'Exemplaire de Bordeaux, "pour le seul exemple" par "pour l'advertissement" et intercale une nouvelle phrase (qui appelait la correction précédente): "De les condamner, par ce qu'ils ont failly, ce seroit bestise, comme dit Platon: Car ce qui est faict, ne se peut deffaire: mais c'est afin qu'ils ne faillent plus de mesmes, ou qu'on fuye l'exemple de leur faute." La référence à Platon, tirée du *Protagoras* ou des *Lois*,[54]

---

50 I, 15, 73 (voir n. 4).

51 II, 11, 453–54 (voir n. 4). *Haut chapeau* est repris d'Amyot, qui désigne ainsi la tiare, en forme de turban conique, portée par les dignitaires perses.

52 Sans que son efficacité soit moindre: reprenant l'anecdote dans *Sur les délais de la justice divine*, ch. 25, 565A, Plutarque précise que "eulx [les condamnés] aians les larmes aux yeux cryent et prient que l'on cesse" (*Les Œuvres morales et meslées*, trad. Amyot, 268C [citée n. 9]).

53 III, 8, 965 (voir n. 4).

54 *Protagoras*, 324AB, ou *Les Lois*, 11, 934A, suivant les divers éditeurs modernes des *Essais*. Les deux textes sont en fait assez proches, qui soulignent l'un et l'autre le caractère irréparable de la faute commise (le juge "ne saurait faire que ne se soit pas produit ce qui a été accompli," *Protagoras*, 324B, in *Œuvres complètes*, trad. Léon Robin, Bibliothèque de la Pléiade [Paris: Gallimard, 1950], t. 1, 93; "ce qui a eu lieu, on ne pourra jamais empêcher qu'il n'ait pas eu lieu," *Les Lois*, 11, 934A,

vient nuancer les assertions peut-être trop abruptes du texte de 1588. Le châtiment peut amender aussi le criminel, pour lui éviter de retomber à l'avenir dans les mêmes travers, si du moins un avenir lui est ménagé par une sentence autre que capitale!

Mais la première punition du coupable, c'est d'être tourmenté par le remords, poursuivi par ses propres "furies vengeresses," comme l'écrit Montaigne dans le chapitre "De la conscience," à propos, non d'Oreste, comme on l'attendrait, mais d'un parricide moins connu, le Péonien Bessus. Celui-ci, selon Plutarque, en abattant un nid au prétexte que les oisillons ne cessaient de l'accuser du meurtre de son père, aurait ainsi révélé un crime jusque là ignoré.[55] "Une Némèsis intérieure, commente Olivier Millet, se déchaîne dans la conscience du coupable, en attendant que vienne l'heure du châtiment extérieur."[56] Elle se déchaîne sitôt le forfait commis, d'après Platon (d'où le *motto* "La peine suyct le malfaiteur," attesté dans l'emblématique de la Renaissance),[57] voire concomitamment suivant Hésiode ("en l'instant et quant et quant le peché"[58]), et elle finit même par tourmenter, sur le tard il est vrai, le fameux "larron" rencontré par Montaigne en Armagnac et dont il résume plaisamment l'existence dans le chapitre "Du repentir": après avoir volé toute sa vie, ce paysan miséreux finalement enrichi consacre ses dernières années à réparer le mal qu'il a fait à ses victimes ou à leurs descendants, à charge pour ses propres héritiers de poursuivre la tâche![59] Montaigne sait bien ce que l'on se doit à soi-même, si l'on veut comparaître la tête haute devant le tribunal le plus rigoureux qui soit, celui de sa propre conscience:

> La condemnation que je fais de moy, est plus vifve et roide, que n'est celle des juges, qui ne me prennent que par le visage de l'obligation commune: l'estreinte de ma conscience plus serrée, et plus severe.[60]

Le châtiment pénal, qui fait trop souvent disparaître, avec le crime, le criminel lui-même, a-t-il du moins valeur exemplaire pour les autres hommes? L'ancien magistrat est loin d'en être persuadé. Dans le chapitre "Que notre desir s'accroist par la malaisance," il s'interroge même sur les possibles effets pervers de la sanction, faisant sienne "l'opinion d'un ancien, que les supplices aiguisent les vices

---

t. 2, 1078) et la double portée de la peine, à la fois pour le coupable dans l'avenir et pour les autres hommes dans l'immédiat.

55 II, 5, 385 (voir n. 4).

56 "Les emblèmes de la justice," *Montaigne: la justice*, 39–52; ici 44 (voir n. 12).

57 Aneau, *Imagination poetique* (Lyon: Macé Bonhomme, 1556), 40 (cité par Olivier Millet, 42 et 44 [voir n. 56]).

58 II, 5, 385 (voir n. 4). Montaigne continue ici de démarquer Plutarque, *Sur les délais de la justice divine*, VIII, 553F, dans la traduction d'Amyot.

59 III, 2, 852–53 (voir n. 4).

60 III, 9, 1012 (voir n. 4).

plustost qu'ils ne les amortissent: Qu'ils n'engendrent point le soing de bien faire [. . .]: mais seulement un soing de n'estre surpris en faisant mal."[61] L'auteur ancien allégué est Sénèque qui soutient dans le *De clementia*[62] que la répression encourage somme toute le délit, en avançant l'exemple du parricide, réprimé seulement à partir de Claude et dès lors multiplié sous son règne (*parricidæ cum lege cœperunt, et illis facinus pœna monstrauit*, les parricides ont commencé avec la loi et la sanction a donné l'idée du forfait). Mais sous le couvert de l'auteur ancien, c'est bien l'auteur moderne qui pousse plus avant l'argument: la menace du châtiment, loin de détourner du mal, n'en rend le contrevenant que plus ingénieux à éviter de se faire prendre. Ce que Montaigne craint surtout, c'est que le sang n'appelle le sang, avec le risque, en période de guerre civile, de lâcher la bride aux pulsions les plus sadiques.[63] À la fin de "De la Physionomie," après avoir laissé échappé l'aveu qu'en matière criminelle il avait pu lui arriver de manquer à la justice en prenant en considération l'homme davantage que la faute, il introduit cette ultime addition:

> Les jugements ordinaires, s'exasperent à la punition par l'horreur du meffaict. Cela mesme refroidit le mien. L'horreur du premier meurtre, m'en faict craindre un second. Et la laideur de la premiere cruauté m'en faict abhorrer toute imitation.[64]

Le magistrat et Montaigne ont toujours été deux, et il répugne à l'homme privé de voir la justice appliquer la loi du talion, tuer à son tour celui qui a tué, reproduire la cruauté qu'elle prétend précisément extirper. "Mise en cause radicale de la peine de mort," suivant Géralde Nakam, exceptionnelle chez un magistrat de la Renaissance.[65]

Ni justes ni proportionnés ni utiles, les châtiments infligés par la justice de son temps sont donc jugés sévèrement par l'ancien conseiller au Parlement de Bordeaux. Ne faudrait-il pas punir davantage les mauvais juges que leurs malheureuses victimes, à l'instar de ceux de Socrate, mis ensuite au ban de la cité et qui finirent par se pendre?[66] Montaigne lui-même, "encore vierge de procès,"[67] qui n'a encore comparu devant aucun tribunal, "pour quelque cause que ce soit,

61 II, 15, 653 (voir n. 4).
62 I, XXIII, 1.
63 II, 11, 454 (voir n. 4).
64 III, 12, 1110 (voir n. 4).
65 "'L'injuste tenu pour juste', ou la perversion des mentalités," *Montaigne: la justice*, 119–31; ici 120 (voir n. 12). Pour le (quasi-)consensus des hommes du temps sur la peine de mort, voir du même auteur, *Les* Essais *de Montaigne*, 138–39 (cité n. 3).
66 III, 12, 1101 (voir n. 4).
67 III, 10, 1063 (voir n. 4).

ou mienne, ou tierce, ou criminelle, ou civile,"[68] entend bien ne jamais encourir pareil risque.

Dans un système judiciaire fondé sur la suspicion générale, le mieux qu'on puisse attendre d'un juge, c'est de ressortir indemne d'entre ses griffes, sans même espérer voir son dommage réparé. "Nostre justice, résume Montaigne dans 'De l'Experience', ne nous presente que l'une de ses mains; et encore la gauche: Quiconque il soit, il en sort avecques perte."[69] Le gentilhomme périgourdin comprend et partage les appréhensions de ses paysans. Quand ceux-ci lui rapportent avoir, dans une forêt sienne, laissé agoniser un homme agressé sans lui porter secours, de crainte d'avoir maille à partir avec la justice, il n'y trouve rien à redire, parce qu'il sait, comme eux, que "cet office d'humanité, les eust mis en peine."[70]

Plus fondamentalement, les *Essais* posent la question de savoir si nous ne sommes pas tous des délinquants en puissance, susceptibles d'être sanctionnés un jour ou l'autre par la justice. À y regarder de près, dans une société aux normes juridiques de plus en plus complexes, qui peut se vanter de n'avoir jamais enfreint quelque règle que ce soit? "Il n'est si homme de bien, répond Montaigne en notre nom, qu'il mette à l'examen des loix toutes ses actions et pensées, qui ne soit pendable dix fois en sa vie."[71] Juges ou justiciables, nous ne sommes décidément tous que du gibier de potence!

---

68 III, 13, 1118 (voir n. 4).

69 III, 13, 1118 (voir n. 4). Cf., entre autres textes, la diatribe de Monluc contre les interminables procès du temps: "La ruyne vient aussi bien à celuy qui gaigne qu'à celuy qui pert; car ils [les avocats] tirent les procès en si grande longueur que, quand celuy qui a gaigné conte l'argent qu'il a despandu, il trouve avoir plus mis que gaigné, outre le temps qu'il a perdu" (*Commentaires*, éd. Paul Courteault. Bibliothèque de la Pléiade (Paris: Gallimard, 1964), 621).

70 P. 1117 (voir n. 4).

71 III, 9, 1036 (voir n. 4).

Chapter 22

Allison P. Coudert
(University of California, Davis)

The Ultimate Crime: Cannibalism in Early Modern Minds and Imaginations

From the tale of Saturn eating his children to the child-eating witch of nursery stories, from Pliny's dog-faced people feasting on human flesh to Christian depictions of the devil as a cannibalistic, defecating monster and Freud's conviction that civilization began when a band of brothers ate dear old dad, images of cannibalism have obsessed the western imagination. But new kinds of cannibals and new forms of cannibalism appeared in early modern Europe especially suited to the profound changes in mental and material life that accompanied the discovery of the New World, the religious conflicts generated by the Reformation and Counter-Reformation, and the emergence of a consumer society. Here the cannibal becomes a protean figure: on the one hand, he represents the primitive "other," a savage member of a regressive society, who stood in stark opposition to the progressive enterprise society of the Europeans; but on the other hand, and on a subconscious level that gradually emerged into the consciousness of at least some people, the new-world cannibals were mere pussycats, and sometimes noble pussycats, in comparison to a newer and more vicious kind of cannibal, those rapacious colonialists, imperialists, and capitalists, who literally devoured the peoples who stood in their way.

Christianity and Christian conflict further complicated the complex meaning of cannibalism in the early modern period. Religious fanatics on both sides of the religious divide were likened to cannibals as they tortured, mutilated, and murdered their religious enemies. The French Huguenot Jean de Léry (1536–1613) claimed that the livers and hearts of the Protestants slain on St. Bartholomew's Day were eaten by their Catholic killers, while the Catholic author of *Théatre des cruautez des Hereticques de nostre temps*[1] advised readers to "harden their hearts" before they looked at images of Protestants dismembering little Catholic babies and forcing a priest to eat his own roasted genitals. The parallel between Christian communion and cannibal feasts was relentlessly stressed by Protestants, who used the analogy to ridicule the Catholic doctrine of the transubstantiation of the Eucharist bread and wine into the body and blood of Christ.

But Protestant attacks on the Eucharist ignored the fact that in addition to everything else cannibalism was a powerful form of nostalgia appealing to those disaffected Europeans who felt themselves trapped in a Hobbesian world of unfettered individualism driven by will and appetite. For many people, and not just Catholics, the God who nourished his children from his own body and blood was a potent image of the magnitude of divine love, mercy, and forgiveness. And the children who partook of his body symbolized souls returning to the original state of unity between man and God shattered by the Fall.

In short, one might say that during the early modern period the issue of cannibalism was largely transformed from a story about non-European "others" to a story about Europeans themselves, although in reality stories about "others" are always in a profound sense about oneself.[2] But the cannibal did come home to roost in very tangible ways during the early modern period. The issue of cannibalism became involved in debates about what characterized human nature as well as the state of nature, not to mention the nature of the state. Were humans innately violent and the state of nature a generalized war of all against all as Robert Burton (1577–1640) maintained, when he described the outside world as a "Market" in which "we maul, persecute, and study how to sting, gall, and vex one another . . . preying upon and devouring, as so many ravenous birds?"[3] Or were humans basically good and their "fall" into society the cause of their moral turpitude, as Rousseau and others argued who deplored the dog-eat-dog world of an emerging consumer society? And what about governments? Did they save us from our own cannibalistic tendencies, as Hobbes believed, or were governments themselves cannibals par excellence, who devoured their citizens in their quest for power and dominion?

At the heart of these questions lay a more fundamental one about what exactly constituted the "self" both in this world and the next. Given the richness and

---

1 *Théatre des Cruautez des Hereticques de nostre temps*. Traduit du Latin [of R. V., i.e., R. Verstegan] (Anvers: A. Hubert, 1607 [1588]).

2 Hillerbrand, Hans J., "The 'Other' in the Age of the Reformation: Reflections on Social Control and Deviance in the Sixteenth Century. *Infinite Boundaries: Order, Disorder, and Reorder in Early Modern German Culture*, ed. Max Reinhart (Kirksville, MO: Sixteenth Century Journal Publishers, 1998), 245–69.

3 Robert Burton, *The Anatomy of Melancholy* (London: Printed and to be sold by Hen. Crips & Lodo: Lloyd, 1652), 407.

complexity of the idea of cannibalism, one can agree with Catalin Avramescu when he points out that the cannibal is "one of the great forgotten figures of philosophy."[4] The multifarious ways cannibals have been portrayed and the conundrums their existence have raised tells us a great deal about how we have arrived where we are today; and nowhere are cannibals more apparent and significant than in the early modern period, when their presence casts a long shadow over the birth of the modern world with its newly emerging ideas of the self, the nation, the nature of religion, and the effects of a capitalist economy.

* * *

Although the theme of cannibalism is an ancient one, the subject did not come into its own until the publication of William Arens's *The Man-Eating Myth* in 1979. Arguing that the idea of savage cannibalism had little basis in reality and was, in fact, simply a way for Westerners to demonize the "other" in order to justify colonialism, conquest, and even extermination, Arens's book caused a furor. While he conceded that some forms of "ritual anthropophagy" or actual cannibalism may have existed under extreme circumstances (like shipwrecks), he insisted that for the most part the myth of cannibalism was nothing short of a tool of empire, be it in the real world or the world of academia and the discipline of anthropology. Arens's thesis was excoriated by Marshall Sahlins, among others, who equated his denial of cannibalism with the postmodernist tendency to question the truth of anything, including the Holocaust.[5]

The stakes in the debate were obviously high, and since the publication of Arens's book much valuable work has been done to explain why the cannibal is the object of such "a veritable fixation" and why the fantasy of cannibalism has been "a psychic structure of long duration" in the West from both a psychological and historical point of view.[6] Obviously the historical part of the analysis is most germane to this essay, but before getting to that a word must be said about the undeniable fact that all of us start off as cannibals eating our mothers and trying to ingest the world as well. As we learn from Greek mythology, this is not a one-way street. Infanticide and cannibalism appear to be patriarchal prerogatives at the

---

4 Catalin Avramescu, *An Intellectual History of Cannibalism*, trans. Alistair Ian Blyth (2003; Princeton and Oxford: Princeton University Press, 2009), 2.

5 Marshall Sahlins, "Artificially Maintained Controversies: Global Warming and Fijian Cannibalism," *Anthropology Today* 19 (June 2003): 3–5 (part 1); (part 2) *Anthropology Today* 6.19 (2003): 21–23.The general consensus now is that cannibalism did and in some places still exists, but that it was also used as a way to demonize natives and justify colonialism. Cf. Katherine Biber, "Cannibalism and Colonialism," *Sydney Law Review* 27 (2005): 623–37.

6 Avramescu, *An Intellectual History of Cannibalism*, 10 (see note 4); Gananath Obeyesekere, *Cannibal Talk: The Man-Eating Myth and Human Sacrifice in the South Seas* (Berkeley: University of California Press, 2005), 28.

very heart of the establishment of the divine pantheon described in Hesiod's *Theogony* as Saturn eats his children and the Titans Dionysius. Freud took the argument many steps further in *Totem and Taboo* by arguing that the ritual murder of the father and the eating of his flesh by his sons created the guilt that sublimated the violence upon which civilization was built. For Freud individuals recapitulated this originary act of cannibalism in a figurative rather than a literal way as they progressed from the oral to the anal and finally to the genital stage of development. But no stage was ever completely left behind. Even a satisfactory attainment of the genital stage involves an unsuccessful attempt to recreate the absolute intimacy between mother and baby, a shadow of which is captured in the English language of love, which is replete with metaphors of eating and devouring the loved one, who among other things is a "sweetie pie" good enough to eat. In English consuming, consumption, and consummation are as applicable to sex as they are to eating. But even the most intense and passionate love fails to reestablish the complete unity that existed between mother and baby.

Consequently, in some cases the thwarted desire for unity manifests itself in an adult's aggressive attempt to consume the other. For Freud, human beings are pulled in two directions, the desire for autonomy that moves us forward and the desire for unity that involves regression or what Freud came to call "the death drive" (Todestrieb).[7] Moving to the present, we might well ask what is responsible for our contemporary fascination with vampire cannibals? What can Hannibal Lecter, a man of great refinement as well as taste, tell us about the consuming passions that consume us as well as those lambs, whose silence is deafening? The history of cannibalism in the early modern period can tell us a lot about both.

As many scholars have pointed out, during the seventeenth and eighteenth centuries curiosity is removed from the catalogue of vices and legitimated as a suitable response to the avalanche of news coming into Europe from the explosion of travel literature combined with the publication of new as well as old scientific and literary texts.[8] Unlike many of his more conservative contemporaries Francis

---

7 Freud first refers to the "death drive" in his *Beyond the Pleasure Principle. The Standard Edition of the Complete Psychological Works of Sigmund Freud*, vol. XVIII, ed. James Strachey (London: Hogarth Press, 1955 [first published in German in 1920]), 38–41, 49–57; Maggie Kilgour, *From Communion to Cannibalism: An Anatomy of Metaphors of Incorporation* (Princeton: Princeton University Press, 1990), 245; Leon Rappoport, "Champagne Slippers, the Twinkie Defense, and He-Man Diets," id., *How We Eat: Appetite, Culture, and the Psychology of Food* (Toronto: ECW Press, 2003), 161–82.

8 Paula Findlen, *Possessing Nature: Museums, Collecting, and Scientific Culture in Early Modern Italy* (Berkeley: University of California Press, 1994); Stephen Greenblatt, *Marvelous Possessions: The Wonder of the New World* (Chicago: University of Chicago Press, 1991); Barbara Benedict, *Curiosity: A Cultural History of Early Modern Inquiry* (Chicago and London: The University of Chicago Press, 2001); Neil Kenny, *The Uses of Curiosity in Early Modern France and Germany* (Oxford: Oxford University Press, 2004); Nicholas Dew, "Reading Travels in the Culture of Curiosity: Thévenot's Collection of Voyages," *Journal of Early Modern History* 10.1–2 (2006): 40–59.

Bacon (1561–1626) enthusiastically embraced the extension of intellectual boundaries that came with this new information:

> Nor should we ignore the fact that the distant voyages and overland travels which have become frequent in our day, have opened up and revealed to us many things in Nature which can throw new light on philosophy. And surely it would be disgraceful in a time when the regions of the material globe, that is of the earth, the seas and stars have been opened up far and wide for us to see, if the limits of our intellectual world were restricted to the narrow discoveries of the ancients.[9]

The verse from Daniel: "many shall run to and fro and knowledge shall be increased" (Dan. 12:4) appealed to Bacon and through him to Thomas Sprat (1635–1713). Sprat used it as a motto on the frontispiece of his history of England's Royal Society (1667), which he illustrated with a ship sailing suggestively through the pillars of Hercules and thus symbolically surpassing the ancients in the quest for knowledge. The widening of intellectual boundaries welcomed by Bacon and Sprat was not positively construed by everyone, however, and we can see this reluctance in the literature dealing with alleged cannibals.

Jonathan Z. Smith has emphasized the importance of place in both a culture's and an individual's self-perception. Since social change is inseparable from symbolic change, the question people ask and need to answer to ensure a stable existence is "where do I stand?" As Smith says: "At the heart of the issue of change are the symbolic-social questions: What is the place on which I stand? What are my horizons? What are my limits?"[10] These were precisely the questions that preoccupied and, in many cases, terrified individuals in the early modern world as they cleared away the debris of outmoded symbolic structures and struggled to build new ones suitable for a changing world. Smith emphasizes how difficult this is: "To change stance is to totally alter one's symbols and to inhabit a different world."[11] What caused individuals to change their stand on many key issues was the increasing incoherence in the symbolic systems governing contemporary culture, a disjunction revealing the lack of fit between the various elements within the prevailing systems of classification, be they social, intellectual, economic, political, or religious.

What thinking Europeans were forced to confront in the early modern period was the breakdown of previously established boundaries both in the heavens and on earth and between heaven and earth as the Aristotelian-Ptolemaic worldview gave way to the Copernican. Once the earth was recognized as a planet like every

---

9 Francis Bacon, *New Organum. With Other Parts of the Great Instauration*, trans. and ed. Peter Urbach and John Gibson (Chicago and La Salle: Open Court, 1994), Bk. 1, Ch. 84, 93.

10 Jonathan Z. Smith, "The Influence of Symbols on Social Change: A Place on Which to Stand," *Map is not Territory* (Chicago and London: The University of Chicago Press, 1978), 143.

11 Smith, "The Influence of Symbols on Social Change," 143 (see note 10).

other, where was heaven and how was it to be distinguished from earth? With the voyages of discovery and settlements in the Americas what had previously been considered the dangerous, unfathomable margins of the known world were absorbed into the cultural center, but not without considerable confusion and much opposition.

Establishing borders and boundaries, which is essentially to demarcate one thing from another, has been a fundamental aspect of human society from the beginning of recorded history and a necessary one; for as Structuralism made clear, without difference there can be no meaning. Poststructuralism has, however, muddied the waters by questioning the very dichotomies structuralists deemed basic aspects of human thought—dichotomies such as nature/culture, center/periphery/, voice/ writing, cooked/raw, public/private, spirit/flesh, high/low, male/female. In Jacques Derrida's view all these binary oppositions can be summed up in a single one, inside/outside, but this opposition itself is slippery and always in danger of collapsing because what appears to be outside any given system of thought is already fully inside.[12] For this very reason the most interesting binary opposition for this essay is inside/outside since cannibalism involves eating, and the act of eating is the most basic model for the dissolution of boundaries and the incorporation of foreign elements into an individual, group, or society.

Eating is therefore a potentially dangerous act and food a potent symbol for whatever is absorbed from outside, whether physically or mentally, literally or metaphorically. Food is more than a substance; it is an attitude, a circumstance, even a language.[13] One is reminded of certain English phrases such as, to "hunger" and "thirst" for God. We also "hunger" and "thirst" after knowledge and truth and in so doing may read "voraciously," "bite off more than we can chew," "swallow a story whole," "ruminate" over an issue, "digest an argument," "assimilate a source," and emerge with "half-baked" ideas or much "mental nourishment" and "food for thought." Something may look to you "good enough to eat," while others might dismiss it as "indigestible." Consequently, individuals have or do not have "good taste." We might go further and say that to eat or not to eat is the real existential question. Most societies are therefore careful to determine not only with whom one eats and how one eats but what one eats.

While maintaining the integrity and purity of individual bodies was an important aspect of medieval and early modern life, maintaining the boundaries of the body politic or the body of Christendom was equally important. Mary

---

12 Jacques Derrida, "Structure, Sign, and Play in the Discourse of the Human Science," *Writing and Difference*, trans. Alan Bass (Chicago: Chicago University Press, 1978), 278–95.

13 Claude Lévi-Strauss, "Le Triangle culinaire," *L'Arc* (Aix-en-Provence) 26 (1965): 19–29. For an English version, see "The Culinary Triangle," *Food and Culture: A Reader*, ed. Carole Counihan (London and New York: Routledge, 2008), 28–35.

Douglas has shown that the Jewish dietary laws did not affect individuals alone; the same substances that were prohibited entry into an individual's body were also prohibited from entering the precincts of the temple as well as the borders of Israel.[14] In the medieval and even more so in the early modern period Europeans were deeply concerned with establishing and maintaining borders. The fear that these borders had been penetrated and the body politic infiltrated and poisoned by sinister external forces provided the foundation for the attacks on Jews, heretics, and witches. From the thirteenth and well into the eighteenth centuries a key characteristic of these threatening external forces was their alleged cannibalism. In his *Chronica Majora* (1243) the Benedictine monk Matthew Paris (ca. 1200–1259) described the Mongolians in the following terms: "The Tartar chiefs, with the houndish cannibals, their followers, fed upon the flesh of their carcasses, as if they had been bread, and left nothing but bones for the vultures."[15] Pogroms against the Jews were launched on the grounds that they, too, practiced cannibalism.[16] The witch hunts of the sixteenth and seventeenth centuries were fueled by the conviction that witches were notorious eaters of human flesh, especially the flesh of innocent children.

The concern with purging heretics and pagans from within the body of Christendom occurred at the same time that the real meaning of the central Christian rite, the Eucharistic meal, was being debated. From the fourth Lateran Council (1215) on, the doctrine of transubstantiation, in which the wafer and wine were literally transformed into the body and blood of Christ at the exact moment the officiating priest pronounced the words "Hoc est enim corpus meum; hic est enim calix sanguinis mei," became central in the development of Catholic theology and the institution of the priesthood. Eucharist miracles began to proliferate, becoming the subject of visions, sermons, and paintings. Early in the fifteenth century Colette of Corbie, for example, had a vision of Jesus in a chaffing dish, carved up into fragments of bloodied meat. God informed her that human sin was responsible for Jesus's cruel dismemberment.[17] In his *Dialogus Miraculorum*, Caesar of Heisterbach (ca. 1180–ca. 1240) stresses the beneficial effect these miracles had in inculcating the reality of transubstantiation in the minds of the faithful: "[t]he Saviour condescends. . . to show the reality of His body in this sacrament to good priests in order than they may be comforted; to those who are wavering in their faith that they may be strengthened; to those who are living ill that they may be

14 Mary Douglas, "Deciphering a Meal," *Implicit Meanings: Selected Essays in Anthropology* (London and New York: Routledge, 1999), 231–51.

15 Merral Llwelyn Price, *Consuming Passions: The Uses of Cannibalism in Late Medieval and Early Modern Europe* (New York and London: Routledge, 2003), 7.

16 Norman Cohn, *Europe's Inner Demons: An Inquiry Inspired by the Great Witch-Hunt* (London: Heineman, 1975), 8.

17 Price, *Consuming Passions*, 27 (see note 15).

warned."[18] This was exactly what happened in Bolsena in 1263 to a priest who doubted transubstantiation but regained his faith when he saw that Jesus was really present in the communion wafer.[19] Price claims that the bloodier the miracle, the better:

> . . . among the holy, the especially gory and gruesome visions and miracles were received not with horror and disgust, but with joy and desire. The cannibalistic implications of feeding on the body of a sacrificed god are embraced and elaborated on . . . .[20]

The idea of transubstantiation did not sit well, however, with most Protestants. Zwingli drew a direct parallel between Catholics and Cannibals: transubstantiation was not "only impious but also foolish and monstrous, unless perhaps one is living amongst the Anthrophagi."[21] The Calvinist Léry drew the same connection: "They [Catholics] wanted not only to eat the flesh of Jesus Christ grossly rather than spiritually, but what was worse, like the savages named Ouetaca, of whom I have already spoken, they wanted to chew and swallow raw."[22] In his poem "The Holy Eucharist and the Papish Breaden God" (1625), Thomas Turke ridicules transubstantiation:

> As on the whale did Jonas, so they eat
> Him up alive, body and soul, as meat
> As men eat oysters, so on Him they feed;
> Whole and alive, and raw and yet not bleed.
> This cookery, void of humanity
> Is held in Rome for sound divinity.[23]

Milton took the idea of Catholic cannibalism to its logical conclusion:

> The Mass brings down Christ's body from its supreme exaltation at the right hand of God. It drags it back to earth, tho it has suffered every pain and hardship already, to a state of humiliation even more wretched and degrading than before: to be broken once more and crushed and ground, even by the fangs of brutes. Then, when it has been driven through all the stomach's filthy channels it shoots it out—one shudders even to mention it—into the latrine.[24]

---

18 Price, *Consuming Passions*, 28 (see note 15).
19 Raphael's fresco of this scene (1512) can be seen in the Vatican.
20 Price, *Consuming Passions*, 31 (see note 15), 31.
21 Price, *Consuming Passions*, 109 (see note 15).
22 Price, *Consuming Passions*, 109 (see note 15).
23 Kilgour, *From Communion to Cannibalism*, 83 (see note 7) .
24 Kilgour, From *Communion to Cannibalism*, 84 (see note 7).

Employing the Freudian notion of projection, Peter Hulme considers the growing concern with cannibalism on the part of Europeans a direct consequence of this insistence on the literal interpretation of transubstantiation:

> ... boundaries of community are often created by accusing those outside the boundary of the very practice on which the integrity of the community is founded. This is at one and the same time both a psychic process—involving repression and projection—and an ideological process whereby the success of the projection confirms the need for the community to defend itself against the projected threat, thereby closing the circle and perpetuating it.[25]

Maggie Kilgour takes a slightly different approach, attributing the fascination of Europeans with cannibalism to their own fierce desire to incorporate other cultures and the projection involved in this wish. The accusation of cannibalism against new world cultures was undoubtedly a useful form of projection, making the assimilation, even obliteration, of these cultures more palatable, one might say.

What both Hulme's and Kilgour's analysis leaves out is the fact that Europeans practiced real cannibalism on a routine basis. From earliest times fragments of the human body were routinely incorporated into medicines. Medical vampirism was a fact of life. The medicinal properties of blood were universally recognized. According to the Roman physician Celsus, warm blood from wounded gladiators or executed criminals cured epilepsy. Many Christians were convinced that Jews required the blood of young Christians to heal their innumerable infirmities.[26] The great Renaissance Platonist Marsilio Ficino was convinced that old men could be rejuvenated by sucking blood directly from the vein of a healthy youth. In Protestant areas of Germany the blood of those beheaded was sold and sometimes drunk on the spot by epileptics and other invalids. The last recorded example of this practice occurred in Marburg a. d. L. (north of Frankfurt) in 1865. The practice was less prevalent in Catholic areas, but at the execution of Louis XVI people dipped handkerchiefs, rags, and even a pair of dice in the royal blood to absorb its curative value.[27]

Right up to the nineteenth century cow's blood was considered a cure for anemia. In past ages medicines were also concocted from the bones of buried corpses. "Mummy" was another favorite medical ingredient. This came from the flesh of a mummified corpse, and it was applied both topically and ingested as a cure for bruising. Francis Bacon claimed that mummy has great force in

25 Peter Hulme, *Colonial Encounters: Europe and the Native Caribbean, 1492–1797* (London: Methuen, 1986), 85.

26 David Biale, *Blood and Belief: The Circulation of a Symbol between Jews and Christians* (Berkeley: University of California Press, 2008).

27 Avramescu, *An Intellectual History of Cannibalism*, 90–93 (see note 4). Cf. Richard J. Evans, *Rituals of Retribution: Capital Punishment in Germany, 1600–1987* (Oxford: Oxford University Press, 1996).

staunching blood. The great sixteenth century medical innovator Paracelsus (who called himself that to emphasize his superiority to the Roman physician Celsus) was a devotee of mummy: "If doctors were aware of the power of the substance, no body would be left on the gibbet for more than three days."

A special kind of fungus or "moss of the skull" called "usnea" was also highly regarded. It grew on the heads of dead or executed cadavers and was used to stop hemorrhaging. It was heartily endorsed by J. B. van Helmont, Richard Baxter, and Robert Boyle, among others. Boyle claimed he cured his nose bleeds with usnea. King Charles II was so devoted to the "spirit of the skull" that he paid the physician William Goddard six thousand pounds for the recipe and prepared it frequently in his private laboratory. It was the first thing he asked for when he woke up "feeling ghastly" four days before his death on February 2, 1685.[28]

Robert Boyle recognized how hypocritical it was for Europeans to condemn cannibals when they were cannibals themselves. As he says, we condemn cannibals, but we give infants mother's milk, which is "but blanched blood." We use mummy in medicines; we drink our own boys' urine "to prevent scurvey and the Gout." We use Albym Graecum, otherwise known as dog feces, for sore throats; sheep's dung is mixed with cheese in Holland "to give them a colour and a relish;" and we eat oysters whole and green dung out of lobsters.[29] None of these pertinent observations did much to lessen the dichotomy that the majority of Europeans saw between themselves and the New World's cannibal "others."

Greenblatt makes the cogent observation that however much Europeans may have wanted to discover what was real about the natives and cultures they encountered, access to such reality was inevitably mediated through preconceived notions. Columbus, for example was not a neutral observer but like every European had come to the Americas with a head full of ideas from Herodotus, Pliny, Marco Polo, and a host of other ancient and medieval commentators as to what lay beyond the known world. All this information was then filtered through the Christian story of the fall and redemption. While he initially viewed the Indians as modern inhabitants of the Garden of Eden because of their nakedness, generosity, and innocence, upon further reflection he concluded that what he had really discovered was a decadent civilization of naked, cannibalistic savages, whose generosity was a sign of their stupidity and who deserved to be enslaved because they were vicious and degenerate. As Hulme points out, this rapid reassessment was only possible because Columbus was able to give up his positive vision of the natives, the vision supplied by Marco Polo, and replace it with the a

28 Richard Sugg, "Corpse Medicine: Mummies, Cannibals, and Vampires," *The Lancet*, vol. 371, issue 9630 (June 2008): 2078–79; id. *Mummies, Cannibals and Vampires: the History of Corpse Medicine from the Renaissance to the Victorians* (London and New York: Routledge, 2011).

29 Avramescu, *An Intellectual History of Cannibalism*,174 (see note 4).

negative Herodotean vision. Consequently, he could move from comely native to dangerous cannibal with relative ease.[30] By the time Columbus wrote his famous letter to the Sovereigns Ferdinand and Isabella (15 February 1493) a further change in his view of the natives had occurred. All contradictions had been smoothed out. The natives were now bifurcated into docile, gentle ones, who will become good Christian subjects, and bad Caribs or cannibals, who will not:

> . . . the radical dualism of the European response to the native Caribbean—fierce cannibal and noble savage—had such obvious continuities with the classical Mediterranean paradigm that it is tempting to see the whole intricate web of colonial discourse as weaving itself in its own separate space entirely unaffected by any observation of or interchange with native Caribbean cultures.[31]

In truth, until the eighteenth century it was the rare European like Montaigne who could truly entertain the idea of the noble savage in anything more than a rhetorical sense, and even in the eighteenth century the noble savage was more of a straw figure or device to highlight the failings of European society than a reflection of reality. As in Columbus's case the superiority of the European "Us" versus the cannibal "Them" reasserted itself when challenged in any substantial way, leading to a reaffirmation of the superior beauty, intelligence, and morality of the Europeans in contrast to the mental inferiority, immorality, and ugliness of the natives.[32]

One powerful way in which European superiority was established was by stressing the inherent femininity of the new world inhabitants. In the last paragraph of his letter to the Sovereigns, Columbus asserts that "the island of the Indies, closest to Spain, is populated entirely by women, without a single man, and their comportment is not feminine, but rather they use weapons and other masculine practices." They were therefore just like the Amazons, whose defeat marked the rise of Greek civilization.[33] The author of "The Chronicle of the

---

30 Hulme, *Colonial Encounters*, 31–32 (see note 25). Price raises the question of how Columbus could have known there were cannibals since the interpreter accompanying him on his first voyage was a Converso with some knowledge of Arabic but none of native Caribbean language. Columbus admits the impossibility of communicating: "I do not know the language; the people do not understand me, nor I them, nor any of my company" (Journal, 27 November, cited in Price, *Consuming Passions*, 85 [see note 14]). At first Columbus was skeptical that the natives were cannibals, but what finally convinced him they were was their ugliness (Journal entry for January 13, cited in Prince, *Consuming Passions*, 39–40 [see note 14]). The connection between beauty, truth, reason, and virtue goes back to Plato and had obvious ramifications throughout western history for those deemed ugly like cannibals.

31 Hulme, *Colonial Encounters*, 47 (see note 25).

32 Albrecht Classen, "The Perception of America in Early Modern German Literature: From Sebastian Brant to Lohenstein," *Neuphilologische Mitteilungen* 95 (1994): 337–52.

33 Margaret Zamorra, "Columbus's 'Letter to the Sovereigns': Announcing the Discovery," *New World Encounters*, ed. Stephen Greenblatt (Berkeley: University of California Press, 1995), 8.

Anonymous Conquistador" claims that in the New World "the men have a custom of urinating sitting down, like our women, and the women standing up."

Patricia de Fuentes, who edited and translated this Chronicle, says the remark was intended as a witticism,[34] but as we know from Freud jokes reveal a great deal about the mental world of the jokester, in this case a European who naturally equated femininity with inferiority and considered a society in which women ruled or acted like men as utterly perverted and upside-down.[35] Non-Europeans occupied the same symbolic space as European women. They were part of nature and, like women, either passive and childlike or dangerous and aggressive.[36] In her important book *Gender and the Politics of History*, Joan Wallach Scott established the fact that gender is a primary way of signifying relationships of power.[37] It should come as no surprise then that the iconic image of Vespucci discovering America by Theodor Galle (after a sketch by Jan van de Straet) has a fully clothed and armored Vespucci encountering naked America, who rises from her hammock as if being awakened into reality from her primitive torpor (Fig. 1).

In this illustration America is surrounded by exotic flora and fauna, and among the fauna are cannibals, who appear in the background at the exact center of the picture. There one sees a group of cannibal women tending a barbecue of dismembered human limbs. The fact that the New World was named after the old world explorer Amerigo Vespucci (1454–1512) implies that prior to his arrival America had no past or future. This is indeed the "writing that conquers," as Michel de Certeau claims.[38] For to name something is to establish its identity, and Europeans were the ones who most successfully did this. They considered the New World virgin territory, and like any virgin she needed a man to make her fertile and useful. Ralegh's description of Guiana employs overtly sexual metaphors to whet the appetites of the Europeans he hoped would invest in colonial adventures:

> . . . Guiana is a country that hath got her maydenhed, never sact, turned, nor wrought, the face of the earth hath not bene torne, nor the virtue and salt of the soyle spent by

---

34 Patricia de Fuentes, ed. and trans, *The Conquistadores: First Person Accounts of the Conquest of Mexico* (New York: Orion, 1963), 180.

35 The theme of inversion is treated in Natalie Z. Davis, "Women on Top," *Society and Culture in Early Modern France* (Stanford: Stanford University Press, 1975), ch. 5; *The Reversible World: Symbolic Inversion in Art and Society*, ed. Barbara Babcock (Ithaca, NY: Cornell University Press, 1978).

36 Helen Carr, "Woman/Indian: 'The American' and his Others," *Europe and Its Others*, ed. Francis Barker (Colchester: University of Essex, 1985), 50.

37 Joan Wallach Scott, *Gender and the Politics of History* (New York: Columbia University Press, 1999).

38 Michel de Certeau, *The Writing of History*, trans. Tom Conley (New York: Columbia University Press, 1988), xxv: "This is *writing that conquers*. It will use the New World as if it were a blank, "savage" page on which Western desire will be written."

> manurance, the graves have not bene opened for golde, the mines not broken with sledges, nor their Images puld downe out of their temples. It hath never bene entred by any armie or strength, and never conquered or possessed by any Christian Prince.[39]

It was normal for European discoverers, colonists, and imperialists to identify land with female bodies and colonization with sexual mastery.[40]

Thus, when Europeans wrote about the New World and the people inhabiting it and when European artists illustrated these narratives, what both writers and artists were depicting had more to do and say about themselves than the people and places they encountered. This is especially apparent in the case of the multi-volume series of narratives and engravings published by Theodore de Bry (1528–1596) and members of his family between 1590 and 1634 and known under the rubric of the "Great Voyages." In her analysis of the de Bry illustrations Bernadette Bucher goes as far as to say that Europeans like the de Brys simply could not see what native Americans looked like: "One is immediately struck by the inability of the European draftsmen to grasp the physical differences that distinguish Amerindians from Europeans or other peoples."[41] Durer, for example, only recognized "two species of mankind, whites and negroes." Native Americans or people from the Orient were not on Durer's mental map.[42] Jean de Léry admits that he had great problems depicting native Americans:

> Although I diligently perused and marked those barbarian people, for a whole year together, wherein I lived amongst them, so I might conceive in my mind a certain proportion of them, yet I say, by reason of their diverse gestures and behaviors, utterly different from ours, it is a very difficult matter to express their true proportion.[43]

It was not just the physical nature of the Amerindians that escaped European perception, but the look of the land and culture as well.[44] The de Bry narratives and their accompanying illustrations do not show us the real nature of Indian life or the real look of the physical beings who lived that life but a European interpretation of both in the light of European interests and concerns. Cannibalism was one of the primary filters through which these concerns were mediated. The de Bry engravings left out the vibrant colors and frescos characteristic of

---

39 Cited in Louis Montrose, "The Work of Gender in the Discourse of Discovery," *New World Encounters*, 12 (see note 332).

40 Referring to Eric Partridge's *Shakespeare's Bawdy* (1948), Montrose points out that both "country" and "country matters" play off the word "cunt" (see note 39).

41 Bernadette Bucher, *Icon and Conquest: A Structural Analysis of the Illustrations of de Bry's Great Voyages* (Chicago: The University of Chicago Press, 1981), 32.

42 Bucher, *Icon and Conquest*, 32 (see note 41).

43 Michael Alexander, ed., *Discovering the New World. Based on the Works of Theodore de Bry* (New York: Harper & Row, 1976), 7–8.

44 Bucher, *Icon and Conquest*, 34 (see note 41).

Mesoamerican temples and cities, transforming them into a series of "poor huts or scaffoldings." The Mexican jewelry so admired by Dürer is replaced by "shoddy-looking objects." All in all, the engravings degrade "the image of the New World and dulls it from the outset, affecting it not only as a cultural whole but as a natural environment of tropical landscape."[45]

The de Bry's volumes further reflect the family's Protestant bias and the emotional, financial, and political interests of Dutch and English Protestants as they struggled with the Spanish for dominion in the Americas.[46] This bias explains the changing character of the depictions of the Amerindians as one moves from the first volumes to later ones, especially volume 9. In the first volumes, the relationship between the English settlers and Algonquian Indians of Virginia is idealized, as is the relationship between the French Huguenot colonists and the Timuscua Indians of Florida. Although the Timucua are described as doing cruel things such as sacrificing newborn infants, scalping enemies, and axing a Frenchman to death, they are romanticized and depicted in the Greek mode and shown welcoming the English and French with open arms as they establish amicable relations with them.[47]

The third volume is devoted to the cannibal tribes of Brazil, the famous Tupinambá, who captured and threatened to eat Hans Staden. The depiction of the Indians here is more aggressive, bloody, and savage, and this continues in volumes four through seven but with the mitigating factor that these parts of the "Great Voyage" deal with Spanish incursions into the Americas. What we find in these volumes is an indictment by Protestants of the tyranny of Spanish Catholicism and the devilish cruelty of the Spanish, which by implication makes fruitful cooperation with the natives impossible. By stressing the enslavement of the natives and the horrible tortures inflicted on them by their Catholic enslavers, de Bry's illustrations, even more than the texts themselves, contributed to the spread of the famous "black legend" excoriating the Spanish conquistadores. Here the Spanish are depicted as the real cannibals and whatever awful things the natives may have done is largely explained as a reaction against the unspeakable cruelty of their tormentors.

We know from Las Casas and other critics that the Spanish engaged in horrendous acts of violence against the natives, but what is so interesting about de Bry's illustrations is that the whole arsenal of tortures inflicted on Protestant "heretics" by the Inquisition in Europe appear in an American setting—

45 Bucher, *Icon and Conquest*, 34 (see note 41).

46 Bucher, *Icon and Conquest*, 9 (see note 41). Theodore de Bry, the patriarch of the family, was a Protestant and native of Liège. He had been exiled for his religion, settling first in Strasbourg and finally in Frankfurt, both centers of the Protestant book trade.

47 Bucher, *Icon and Conquest*, 14–15, 46 (see note 41).

flagellation, garroting, the strappado, burning at the stake, and the water torture, together with other acts of cruelty consistent with military conquest, the massacre of women and children, burning whole villages, throwing sodomites to the dogs, pillaging towns, rape, and forced labor (Fig. 2 & 3).[48] Not only are the Spanish depicted as being unnecessarily cruel but they are licentious as well. While they are shown trying to seduce Indian woman, the English in earlier volumes are models of propriety. For example, one illustration depicts the English settlers sending an emissary to ask for Pocahontas's hand in marriage.[49] The overall impression given by these illustrations is that the Spanish are infinitely more evil than the Indians. Even when the latter roasted their conquerors on grills and poured molten gold down their throats, the viewer concludes that some kind of justice is involved.

It is not that the Indians are given a completely free pass by de Bry. Even in the illustrations in volumes three through seven that so clearly condemn the Spanish, the Indians are presented as the dangerous, unpredictable "other." But once again, what is especially interesting is the way their "otherness" is communicated through motifs and themes that are already familiar to Europeans from their own history of violence and cruelty. One particular motif singled out by Bucher that will resonate with anyone who has studied the European witch hunts of the sixteenth and seventeenth centuries, is "the woman with sagging breasts" (Fig 4). She appears in the third volume of the Great Voyages for the first time, but reappears thereafter. Not only do her pendulous breasts connect her with the long-established iconography of the European witch but so, of course, does her age, her wrinkles, her wispy hair, her brutish look, and her cannibalistic instincts.

The European witch was the cannibal par excellence. She kidnapped, tortured, cooked, and ate dismembered infants, relished the grilled penises of bewitched or glamorized males, and found her stews and brews of simmered body parts just as finger-licking good as her Amerindian counterparts. Female cannibals in the Americas loved precisely the same things. Like witches they were said to love

48 Historians differ in their estimation of the effect the Inquisition had on the lives of the natives. J. Jorge Klor de Alva emphasizes the small number of Indians brought before the Inquisition before 1571, when a law was passed removing Indians from its jurisdiction. See "Colonizing Souls: The Failure of the Indian Inquisition and the Rise of Penitential discipline," *Cultural Encounters: The Impact of the Inquisition in Spain and the New World*, ed. Mary Elizabeth Perry and Anne J. Cruz (Berkeley: University of California Press, 1991), 3–22. Roberto Moreno de los Arcos argues that while the natives were not subject to the Inquisition, they were subject to a similar institution with various names: Office of Provisor of Natives, Tribunal of the Faith of the Indians, Secular Inquisition, Vicarage of the Indians, Natives' Courts, and that this institution generated an enormous number of trials, but very few have so far come to light. See his article in the same volume "New Spain's Inquisition for Indians from the Sixteenth to the Nineteenth Century," 23–36.

49 Bucher, *Icon and Conquest*, 10 (see note 41).

blood and fat, and, as one can see in Fig. 4, they licked their fingers greedily to get the very last drop of both, an indication perhaps of decayed or non-existent teeth.[50] The active and aggressive role that witches played in the Old World and cannibal women in the New represented the antithesis of European norms of political authority and gender relationships, another clear indication of a topsy-turvey world gone mad.

An even more frightening image of a woman with long pendulous breasts appears in the frontispiece to the thirteenth volume of the de Bry series as part of a monstrous couple with hypertrophied sexual organs (Fig. 5). The woman's long pendulous breasts hang below her waist, their length extended by long nipples like the teats of cows. Her male counterpart wears a penis sheath. Both have sharpened finger and toenails like animal claws. From their cheeks, ears, nostrils and chins hang mice and frogs, which further enhance their grotesque and brutish appearance.[51]

When it came to eating, it wasn't just cooked body parts that Amerindian cannibals ingested with such evident relish; they also loved what was raw, raw flesh to be exact, an additional sign that they were beyond the pale of civilization. In one engraving Dutchmen watch as a cannibal mother provides her offspring with a raw bird to assuage their hunger (Fig. 6):

> She tore the rest of the bird into pieces with her teeth, biting into it so that the blood ran down her breasts. The children did the same, and ate the bird raw. One of them was a four-year-old girl, the other was not more than six months old, but he already had a number of teeth and could walk by himself. They remained quite serious while they ate, and the woman showed not the slightest smile in spite of the sailors' outbursts of laughter.[52]

Another engraving provides evidence of how deeply European perceptions of the Amerindian cannibals was filtered through their own historical experiences and expectations. Here we see a naked cannibal Pandora. Nothing is said in the accompanying text about Pandora, but an incident is described by the Dutchman Sebald de Weert, during which he was accosted by a old women with sagging breasts, who carried a box. After circling around him three times, she knocked three times on the lid, creating a cloud of ashes that covered de Weert's clothing. What the precise meaning of her action was, no one knew, but by the time this incident was illustrated in the de Bry volumes, the woman had become a new world Pandora, as one learns from the caption (Fig. 7).

---

50 Bucher, Icon and Conquest, 49 (see note 41). The image of the female devourer is the negative side of the archetype of the good, nurturing mother. The voracious mouth is conflated with the *vagina dentata*, or "toothed vagina," that seduces as it devours. Cf. Erich Neumann, *The Great Mother*, trans. Ralph Manheim (Princeton: Princeton University Press, 1955), 168.

51 Bucher, *Icon and Conquest*, 136–37 (see note 41).

52 Bucher, *Icon and Conquest*, 90 (see note 41).

Dora and Erwin Panofsky have shown that there was a revival of iconographic and literary interest in the myth of Pandora in the sixteenth century.[53] The Panofskys attributed this to Erasmus's reference to the Pandora myth under the adage, "Gifts from enemies are not gifts," an adage accurately encapsulating European views of cannibal Amerindians.[54] A further indication of how profoundly European depictions of cannibals reflected their own psyches and cultural concerns comes in the depiction of pagan idols. An engraving of these idols is not hard to read in terms of the standard attributes of the Christian devil. They are all there: hoofs, horns, serpentine tail, and pitchfork.

What we see in the de Bry engravings is a reflection of European, in this case Protestant European, concerns and obsessions grafted onto information coming from the New World. This becomes especially clear by the ninth volume of the Great Voyages, when the illustrators become less kind to the cannibals. As Protestant involvement in the colonial/imperial enterprise became greater, the depiction of the natives grew more negative. Protestants needed a reason to demonize the "other" who refused to go gently into that dark night, and they found it in their justification of why such people deserved to be dominated and exterminated when necessary: they were cannibals.

The reluctance or inability of men like Columbus to fully appreciate the implications of their own experiences has led some historians to take a more cautious position on the destabilizing effects of the information explosion that hit Europe in the Renaissance and early modern period. In their view the power of tradition and authority was more durable than many scholars realize.[55] But while it is undoubtedly true that Europeans were reluctant to abandon inherited structures of knowledge or give up their own inflated sense of themselves, change did occur, and radical change at that, especially when it came to refashioning such basic concepts such as God, man, and nature. As the anxiety of the late medieval period gave way to the catastrophic religious and political warfare endemic in the sixteenth and seventeenth centuries, the debate about the nature of man and the state of nature became increasingly pessimistic and apocalyptic.

As the borders of the known world expanded, they included diabolical figures from the ancient world and the medieval imagination together with newly

---

53 Dora and Erwin Panofsky, *Pandora's Box: The Changing Aspects of a Mythical Symbol* (Princeton: Princeton University Press, 1962); Jorge Cañizares-Esguerra, *Puritan Conquistadors:Iberianizing the Atlantic, 1550-1700* (Stanford: Stanford University Press, 2006), claims Puritan and Spanish view of Amerindians were similar.

54 Bucher, *Icon and Conquest,* 94–95 (see note 41).

55 Anthony Grafton, with April Shelford and Nancy Siraisi, *New Worlds, Ancient Texts: The Power of Tradition and the Shock of Discovery* (Cambridge, MA, and London: The Belknap Press of Harvard University Press, 1992); *Cannibalism and the Colonial World,* ed. Francis Barker, Peter Hulme, and Margaret Iversen. Cultural Margins, 5 (Cambridge and New York : Cambridge University Press, 1998).

discovered groups that appeared equally threatening. It was among these that the cannibal emerged as the most potent symbol of the chaos caused by the breakdown of authority and hierarchical relationships. Commenting on the need for governmental authority Hugo Grotius declared, "If there were no Sovereign Power, we should swallow up one another alive."[56] With the value of hindsight and in the face of the continuing struggles over religion on the continent and in England, Robert Bolton warned his parishioners of the dangers of anarchy: "Take Sovereignty from the face of the earth, and you turn it into a cockpit. Men would become cut-throats and cannibals one unto another. We should have a very hell upon earth, and the face of it covered with blood, as it once was with water."[57]

Without sovereignty and the social hierarchy it entails men would be thrown into a state of nature of the kind made all too familiar by the wars of religion in sixteenth century France, the Thirty Years' War in Germany, and the Civil War in England. In the minds of many of his contemporaries, Thomas Hobbes's view of the state of nature as "nasty, brutish, and short" fit their own experiences, and in this context the idea of natural law made little sense, although most people continued to believe in the existence of a basic natural law, however much it was abrogated by the perversity of the human will.[58]

Even legitimate governmental authority, which many considered the only possible bulwark against the lawless anarchy of the state of nature, began to raise alarms. The motif of a raft of cannibals adrift on the sea becomes a stock theme in novels and travel diaries, leading to discussions about property law and the right of self-preservation at the expense of weaker individuals.[59] The idea that authority is predicated on natural or supernatural law gives way to the secular view that superior power and conquest legitimizes the subordination of one group or nation to another, which was essentially Hobbes's position.

But not everyone agreed, and in this regard the case of cannibals and cannibalism was crucial in setting the limits of any one group's or person's power. Jean Bodin, for example, excoriated the tyrant as one who "drinketh his subject's blood, gnaweth their bones, and out of them also sucketh even the marrow, so by all meanes seeking to weaken them."[60] Unlike the classical state predicated on

56 Grotius, *On the Rights of War and Peace* (London: printed for D. Brown; T. Ward; and W. Meares, 1715), vol. 1, 182. Cited in Avramescu, *An Intellectual History of Cannibalism*, 9 (see note 4).

57 Robert Bolton, "A Sermone Preached by Robert Bolton, 1621." Cited in Avramescu, *An Intellectual History of Cannibalism*, 9 (see note 4).

58 Avramescu points out that in the 16th and 17th centuries a number of works were published emphasizing the diversity and strangeness of different peoples and their customs (17). In his *Essays on the Law of Nature*, for example, Locke devoted a number of pages to strange customs, concluding that the law of nature is not "written in the hearts of men."

59 Pufendof, *On the Duty of Man and Citizen according to Natural Law*. Cited in Avramescu *An Intellectual History of Cannibalism*, 27 (see note 4).

60 Avramescu, *An Intellectual History of Cannibalism*, 202 (see note 4).

promoting the good life through justice, the rise of the modern bureaucratic state provoked profound anxieties, to such a point that the state itself begins to be imagined as a cannibal. The support governments gave to a nation's military ambitions led Baron d'Holbach (1723–1789) to describe the leaders as the "Caribs or true cannibals" because of the ease with which they sacrifice their citizens.[61] In his essay *Perpetual Peace: A Philosophical Sketch* (1795), Immanuel Kant compares the "savage Nations of Europe" to those in America, remarking on the former's greater inhumanity because instead of eating their enemies, they use them to fight further destructive wars:

> The main difference between the savage nations of Europe and those of America is that while some American tribes have been entirely eaten up by their enemies, the Europeans know how to make better use of those they have defeated than merely by making a meal of them. They would rather use them to increase the number of their own subjects, thereby augmenting their stock of instruments for conducting even more extensive wars.[62]

The commercial conquest that followed on the heels of exploration and colonization was no less cannibalistic in its effects, according to European critics of both. Reflecting on the catastrophic economic consequences of the enclosure movement, Thomas More (1478–1535) describes how sheep have turned into cannibals: the "sheep that were wont to be so meek and tame and so small eaters, now, as I hear say, be become so great devourers and so wild, that they eat up and swallow down the very men themselves."[63] It was the landowners, of course, who grazed their flocks on land appropriated from the commons who were the real cannibals, not the sheep. "Homo Economicus" was not such a pretty sight, nor was emerging cannibal capitalism. As Montaigne (1533–1592) wrote in his essay "Of Carriages" (1585–1588):

> Who ever set the utility of commerce and trading at such a price? So many cities razed, so many nations exterminated, so many millions of people put to the sword, and the richest and most beautiful part of the world turned upside down, for the traffic of pearls and pepper.[64]

In an earlier essay "Of Cannibals" (1578–1580) Montaigne was equally blunt about exactly who the real cannibals were:

> I think there is more barbarity in eating a man alive than in eating him dead; and tearing by tortures and the rack a body still full of feeling, in roasting a man bit by bit,

61 Avramescu, *An Intellectual History of Cannibalism*, 260 (see note 4).

62 Avramescu, *An Intellectual History of Cannibalism*, 261–62 (see note 4).

63 Avramescu, *An Intellectual History of Cannibalism*, 253 (see note 4).

64 Montaigne, *The Complete Works*, trans. Donald M. Frame. Everyman's Library (New York: Alfred A. Knopf, 2003), 844

> in having him bitten and mangled by dogs and swine (as we have not only read but seen within fresh memory, not among ancient civilizations, but among neighbors and fellow citizens, and what is worse, on the pretext of piety and religion), than in roasting and eating him after he is dead.[65]

The Spanish playwright Lope de Vega (1562–1635) accepted the widespread idea that the New World was the dwelling place of the devil and native religion idolatry, but in his play *The New World* (1614), both the figure of the Idolatry and the Devil show the Conquistadores for what they really are, and this does not include being emissaries of the true religion. As Idolatry implores:

> Do not allow, O Providence,
> This injustice to be done to me
> For they are impelled to undertake this feat
> By vilest greed. Under religion's cloak
> They go to seek silver, gold
> And treasure hidden deep.

The Devil concurs: "They are not bourne there by Christianity/ but by gold and greed."[66] The second act ends with the native leader Duncanquelin ordering an underling to kill four of his fattest servants and barbecue them for the Spaniards traveling with Columbus. Although many Europeans believed that eating flesh made cannibals stupid, this particular cannibal had no trouble recognizing the real motives of the European explorers: "These Spaniards, coveting the gold of your Indies, pretend to be saints, feign Christian decorum,/ While others come to take away your treasure."[67] Michael de Carvajal's fascinating play *Complaint of the Indians in the Court of Death* (1557) has the Chief of the Indians question Spanish justice:

> . . . But, Death, explain to us
> why when we worshipped other gods,
> bestial, false, and rude,
> not one of those who through our lands have passed
> did slaughter, plunder, or wage foul wars
> against us. But now, alas! That we are Christians
> it seems that lawless action, murders, flames,
> atrocities and burning coals rain down upon our hearths for this dark

65 Montaigne, *The Complete Works*, 189 (see note 64).

66 Susan Castillo, *Performing America: Colonial Encounters in New World Writing, 1500–1786* (London and New York: Routledge, 2006), 91–92.

67 Castillo, *Performing America*, 100 (see note 66). Many people believed that eating human flesh was unnatural and consequently produced nausea and illness, especially venereal disease. Marco Polo claimed that people who consumed raw flesh became coarse, stupid, and impotent (Avramescu, *An Intellectual History of Cannibalism*,163 [see note 4]).

lucre.[68]

A century and a half later Jonathan Swift (1667–1745) is even fiercer in his denunciation of the rapacity of European colonizers:

> A crew of Pirates are driven by a storm they know not whither; at length a boy discovers land from the top-mast; they go on shore to rob and Plunder; they see an harmless people, are entertained with kindness, they give the country a new name, take formal possession of it for their King, they set up a rotten plank or stone for a memorial, they murder two or three dozen of the Natives, bringing away a couple more by Force for a sample, return home, and get their Pardon. Here commences a new dominion acquired with a title by *Divine right*. Ships are sent with the first opportunity; the natives driven out or destroyed, their Princes tortured to discover their gold; a free license given to all Acts of inhumanity and lust; the Earth reeking with the blood of its inhabitants: and this execrable crew of butchers employed in so pious an Expedition, is a modern colony sent to convert and civilize an idolatrous and barbarous people.[69]

The critique of colonialism and imperialism found its most accomplished spokesperson in Joseph Conrad (1857–1924), who lays bare the cannibalistic nature of European colonialism in *Heart of Darkness*, a devastating picture of what Belgian imperialism did to the Congo, and in his penetrating portrait of Kurtz, for whom "my" had becoming the operating word as in "my ivory," "my station," "my river." Everything belonged to Kurtz, and anything that stood in the way of his imperial self deserved extermination. As Phillips comments: "The fantasy of total incorporation is wedded to the fantasy of absolute possession; thus 'oral' and 'anal' values meet on the plane of capitalist utopia."[70]

This analysis certainly fits the description of Kurtz given by Marlowe, the narrator in Conrad's story: "I saw him open his mouth wide—it gave him a weirdly voracious aspect, as though he wanted to swallow all the air, all the earth, all the men before him."[71]Europeans tended to see the historical antecedents of Kurtz and cannibalistic capitalists in the stereotype of the Jewish merchants and moneylenders, who appear in Marlowe and Shakespeare and antisemitic literature across Europe. As Salerio says in *The Merchant of Venice*, Shylock might appear to be "a creature that . . . bears the shape of man" but he "is so keen and greedy" in his devotion to man-eating that he is actually sub-human and beyond the bounds

---

68 Castillo, *Performing America*, 84 (see note 66).

69 Jonathan Swift, *Gulliver's Travel* (London: CRW publishing Limited, 2004), pt. 4, ch. 12, 363.

70 Jerry Phillips, "Cannibalism qua Capitalism: The Metaphorics of Accumulation in Marx, Conrad, Shakespeare, and Marlowe," *Cannibalism and the Colonial World*, ed. Francis Barker, Peter Hulme, and Margaret Iversen (Cambridge: Cambridge University Press, 1998), 190.

71 Joseph Conrad, *Heart of Darkness*, ed. Paul B. Armstrong. A Norton Critical Edition (New York and London: W. W. Norton & Company, 2006), 59.

of any human community. He is the "cutthroat dog," and "wolf," (iii.1.47) who is "starved" and "ravenous" (iv.1.137–38).

In *The Jew of Malta* Barnabas conforms to the stereotype, proudly admitting, "when we grin we bite" (ii.iii.20–22). Singling out the Jews was as unfair in the early modern period as it is today. For what really began the march toward cannibal capitalism was not Jewish moneylending, but the emergence of "possessive individualism" described by C.P. Macpherson in his book *The Political Theory of Possessive Individualism* (1962).

Historians disagree about exactly when possessive individualism emerged, but they agree that it was based on the idea that the individual was the proprietor of his own person, free from dependence on others and owing little or nothing to society. Bakhtin considers the Renaissance the period in which the individual broke away from the community, but dating the Renaissance is notoriously difficult since some people claim it began in Italy in the mid fourteenth century but only emerged in northern Europe and England in the time of Cervantes and Shakespeare. It is perhaps more helpful to see possessive individualism as emerging gradually during the early modern period, fostered by both the breakdown of the organic model of the universe characteristic of the Aristotelian worldview and the shattering of the ideal of Christian unity during the Reformation. Protestantism, especially in the Calvinist forms that had such influence on the two great economic powers of the seventeenth and eighteenth centuries, England and Holland, effectively placed religious authority in the individual, whose relationship with God was direct and unmediated by a religious institution or priest. The organic model of the body politic was replaced by a contractual one predicated on the idea that an individual had the duty and right to freely follow his own self-interest. This provided the foundation for the emerging capitalist and consumer society.

Ian Watt was the first to see Defoe's novel *Robinson Crusoe* as something of a capitalist manifesto. But he also claimed that the book was a deeply religious fable of Puritan spiritual life.[72] More recent commentators have been less kind to the book as well as to Crusoe's character. They have emphasized what Watt overlooked, namely the way the theme of cannibalism structures the story and reveals Crusoe's state of mind. From the moment Crusoe sees the footprint on the sand, he is convinced the cannibals will return, and he spends every night in expectation of "being murdered and devoured before morning" (ch. 14). When he returns to the beach and finds "skulls, hands, feet, and other bones of human bodies" (ch. 15)— the remnants of cannibal feast—he is completely overwhelmed, rushing to one of his hiding places and frantically building an enormous wall to

---

72 Hulme, *Colonial Encounters*, 179, 176 (see note 25).

protect himself, even though the place is so secluded that no one in all likelihood would ever find it.

Crusoe admits that "in the day great troubles overwhelmed my mind, and in the night I dreamed often of killing the savages, and of the reason why I might justify the doing of it" (ch. 16). This is very odd behavior indeed for a man described by earlier commentators as the prototype for "Homo Economicus," that model of healthy self-sufficiency and the rational calculator of his own self-interest. As Pearlman says in his fascinating psychoanalytic study of Crusoe, he had plenty of places to hide on the island, so both his fantasies about the dangers the cannibals presented and his eventual murder of them were completely unnecessary. Pearlman is astonished that no one before him investigated the cannibalistic fantasies upon which the novel is based or speculated about what they reveal about Crusoe's character.[73]

While cannibalism and violence are major themes in the novel, Pearlman points out the absence of sex, passion, and romance of any kind and sees this as a sign of Crusoe's immaturity and persistent childishness. Violence in conjunction with a sense of terrifying impotence is "the essence of his [Crusoe's] personality" and an indication that he has basically failed to grow up: ". . . the two characteristics of every infant, fantasied impotence and powerless rage, appear in the older Crusoe as the disposition towards the analogous polar attitudes of dominance and violence."[74] Like an infant, Crusoe fears that cannibals, who like mothers threaten to engulf, absorb, and devour him, but he also wants to do exactly the same thing to them and the world at large. The only solution he can come up with is to build a huge wall that essentially shores up his weak sense of self and self esteem. What, Pearlman asks, does it tell us that Robinson Crusoe is the most popular novel in English? It tells us something about ourselves that we should know but don't want to admit, namely that "Homo Economicus" has deep existential problems:

> The mystery is not that this is the most popular novel in English, but that so many readers have blinded themselves to the character of the hero. Crusoe is certainly a powerful and prophetic figure. He is a radical individualist and the prototype of a new economic man, but he is also an authoritarian of a dangerous kind and an unredeemed, uncivilized colonialist. For when the novel is stripped of its ethnocentric biases, what is left is the essence of the colonial encounter. A weak individual, unable to succeed in his own country, of restless and unstable character, moves to an exotic locale where the technological advantage of his civilization gives him immediate superiority over the indigenous population. There he exploits the land, slaughters the heathens and makes instruments (military and otherwise) of selected converts. He despises the natives, but is also terrified of them, and is prepared to justify massacre if he can fantasize a threat to himself. It is on this foundation that expansion and

73 Elihu Pearlman, "Robinson Crusoe and the Cannibals," *Mosaic* 10.1 (Fall 1976): 39–55.

74 Pearlman, "Robinson Crusoe and the Cannibals," 40 (see note 73).

> colonialism is reared, and it is for these reasons that Robinson Crusoe demands our continual attention.[75]

Pearlman's discussion of Crusoe's weak ego structure brings us to one of the most crucial issues that comes up in connection with cannibalism, and that is the issue of what exactly constitutes the "self" both while living and after death.[76] Since most Christians accepted the idea of bodily resurrection, how could the bodies of cannibalized individuals be resurrected? Augustine raises the case of a starving man who eats another. In what body will the man who has been eaten be resurrected? Will his flesh be restored? If it is, won't that leave holes in the body of the cannibal?[77]

Thomas Aquinas (d. 1273) took up the perplexing case of the identity of a child of cannibal parents. According to the reigning medical theory of the time, derived from the second century Roman physician Galen, both male and female parents produce seminal fluid, and this fluid is formed from every organ and limb in the body. Since the seminal fluid of the cannibal parents was produced from their physical bodies, at least some of it had to have been derived from the flesh of those they had eaten and incorporated into their own bodies. So, who exactly were the parents of the child?

In *A Voyage to the Moon* Cyrano de Bergerac proposes a thought experiment along these very lines: Suppose you eat a Muslim, he suggests. Once digested, the Muslim is transformed into flesh, blood, and sperm. If you then have a child, is it Christian or Muslim, and what will happen to the child on the Day of Judgment? Since it is both Muslim and Christian, will it be damned and saved at the same time? The complications cannibalism posed were innumerable. To give a further example: what if an animal ate a person, but then later another person ate that animal? Thomas Browne goes even further, taking literally the biblical phrase "all flesh is grass" (Isa. 40: 6) to argue that we are all cannibals and virtually eat ourselves:

> *All flesh is grasse,* is not onely metaphorically, but literally true, for all these creatures we behold are but the herbs of the field, digested into flesh in them, or more remotely carnified in our selves. Nay further, we are what we all abhorre, *Anthropophagi* and Cannibals, devourers not onely of men, but of our selves; and that not in an allegory, but a positive truth; for all the mass of flesh that wee behold, came in at our mouths;

75 Pearlman, "Robinson Crusoe and the Cannibals," 54–55 (see note 73).

76 The following section is deeply indebted to Avramescu, *An Intellectual History of Cannibalism*, ch. 5 "The Predicaments of Identity" (see note 4), where he lays out the problems cannibalism poses for the notion of bodily resurrection.

77 Augustine, *City of God*, book XXII, chapter 12.

> this frame we look upon, hath been upon our trenchers; in brief. We have devour'd our selves and yet doe live and remayne our selves (our selves is two words).[78]

Numerous attempts were made to solve the conundrums cannibalism posed for the idea of bodily resurrection. Some argued that cannibals cannot assimilate body parts or that they can only assimilate non-essential parts. Others claimed that whenever humans eat unnatural food, they would be struck by nausea, which leads to Avramescu's wry comment, "Nausea thus has an eschatological virtue."[79] Still others, like Augustine, believed that the flesh a cannibal absorbed would be returned to its rightful owner at the day of resurrection, and whatever gaps and holes were left in the body of the cannibal would be filled up by God.[80]

Such answers appeared less and less convincing in the early modern period, and the idea that the entire physical body would be resurrected declined accordingly. In the article on "Resurrection" in the French *Encylopédie*, the author turned to the philosopher Leibniz for help, arguing that all the essential parts of the body were found in its original single monad, from which everything developed. Thus this "seed" will be resurrected, a sort of prototype or blueprint or the body, but not the entire physical body itself. Interestingly enough Samuel Clarke, who sided with Newton and not Leibniz in the debate over who invented calculus, took the same position: "No man can say 'tis improbable, (and they who have been most and best versed in microscopical observations think it more than probable,) that the *original Stamina*, which contains all and every one of the solid parts and vessels of the body, not excepting even the minutest nerves and fibres are themselves the entire Body."[81]

This idea fit in with what was known at the time as the "preformation theory," according to which the body unfolds; it does not develop by adding matter as the rival theory of epigenesis would have it. In his *Physico-Theological Considerations about the Possibility of the Resurrection* (1675), Robert Boyle turned to his chemical expertise to provide examples of how bodily resurrection might occur even in the case of cannibalism or in the more widespread case of the bodily decomposition that naturally occurs after burial. While on numerous occasions he reiterates the idea that God is all-powerful and could therefore reunite the parts of an individual's body whatever the situation might be—he refers to Ezekiel's vision of the valley of dead men's bones resurrected by God (Ez. 37)—he also suggests that chemistry provides the useful example of the way gold dissolved in *acqua regis* can be recovered through the process of precipitation. Botany and alchemy

---

78 Thomas Browne, *Religio Medici*, ed. Jean-Jacques Deonain (Cambridge: Cambridge University Press, 1955), sec. xxxvii, 49.

79 Avramescu, *An Intellectual History of Cannibalism*, 132 (see note 4).

80 Augustine, *City of God*, ch. XXII, section 20.

81 Samuel Clarke, *The Works of Samuel Clarke*, 4 vols. (London: J. & P. Knapton, 1738), vol. 2, 690.

provide similar examples of how plant forms can be resurrected from their ashes.[82] He also offers cases in which milk tastes of a plant eaten by the cow and of pigs whose flesh tastes of the fish they have eaten to show that the particles of a body persist.

Libertines and skeptics like de Bergerac loved to exploit the kind of conundrums brought up so clearly by cannibalism in the case of resurrection. We have also seen how entwined the issue of cannibalism was with the Catholic doctrine of the Eucharist. The illustration of transubstantiation satirized by Hogarth (Fig. 8) provides a clear indication of what at least one English Protestant thought about this central Catholic doctrine. The Scottish Protestant David Hume also enjoyed tackling the problem of transubstantiation from the angle of cannibalism. In Hume's *Natural History of Religion*, a priest asks a Turk after he has converted to Christianity and received the sacrament, "How many gods are there?" The Turk replies: "None at all . . . . You have told me all along that there is but one God: And yesterday I ate him."[83] What better place to end an essay about the ultimate crime of cannibalism in the minds and imaginations of early modern Europeans.

---

82 François Secret, "Palingenesis, Alchemy and Metempsychosis in Renaissance Medicine," *Ambix* 26 (1979 July): 81–92.

83 Hume, *Dialogues and Natural History of Religion* (Oxford: Oxford University Press, 1993), 167–68. Cited in Avramescu, *An Intellectual History of Cannibalism*, 153 (see note 4).

Fig. 1: Amerigo Vespucci "discovering" America. Engraving by Theodor Galle, ca. 1580 (after a drawing by Jan van der Straet, c. 1575)

Fig. 2: The Cruelties of de Soto. Photo Courtesy of The Newberry Library, Chicago. Ayer 110 B 1590, vol. 5

Fig. 3: Sodomites savaged by dogs. Photo Courtesy of The Newberry Library, Chicago. Ayer 110 B 1590, vol. 4

Fig. 4: The woman with sagging breasts. Photo Courtesy of The Newberry Library, Chicago, Ayer 110 B 1590, vol. 3

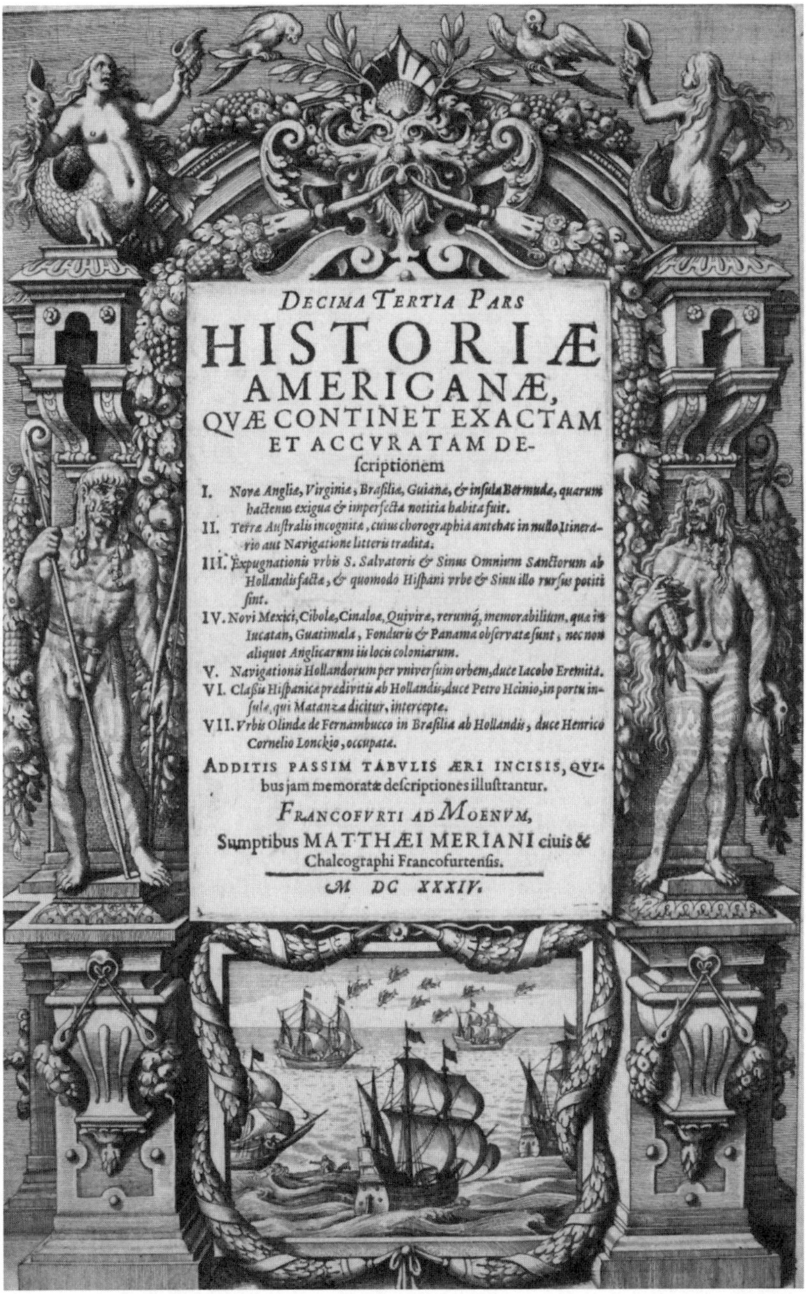

Fig. 5: Frontispiece. Photo Courtesy of The Newberry Library, Chicago. Ayer 110 B 1590, vol. 13

Fig. 6: Woman with raw bird. Photo Courtesy of The Newberry Library, Chicago. Ayer 110 B 1590, vol. 9

Fig. 7: Pandora. Photo Courtesy of The Newberry Library, Chicago. Ayer 110 B 1590, vol. 9

Fig. 8: William Hogarth, Transubstantiation Satirized (1794)

Chapter 23

Evelyne Luef
(University of Vienna, Austria)

Punishment Post Mortem – The Crime of Suicide in Early Modern Austria and Sweden

On February 21st 1710 the jury members of the lower court (*häradsting*) in Nordingrå, a village in today's Västernorrland county, Sweden, assembled for an extraordinary court (*extraordinarie* or *urtima ting*) to discuss the suicide of fifty-year-old unmarried maidservant Karin Mickelsdotter, who had hanged herself on February 7th.[1]

Like other offenses that were relevant under civil or criminal law, suicide left its marks in the records that document the work of premodern judicature. Of course, the suicide of Karin Mickelsdotter was not a singular case. Archives in Austria and Sweden conserve a vast range of source material which can be analyzed with regard to the question of how self-inflicted death was perceived and sanctioned in the seventeenth and eighteenth century. Criminal court records (e.g., court protocols, files, letters) produced by secular and ecclesiastical authorities are invaluable sources that inform us about the work that was conducted by early modern courts. Moreover, they indirectly—through witness accounts and statements given before the court—provide an insight into the lives of early modern women and men, their attitudes, conflicts, sorrows, and hopes. The German historian Gerd Schwerhoff characterizes criminal court records as multi-

---

1 Forskningsarkivet Umeå universitetsbibliotek, Södra Ång. A I a:10 Mk D52268 8/24, Nordingrå, February 21, 1710. Concerning the calendar dates given in this paper, it is important to consider that Austria followed the Gregorian calendar from 1582 and Sweden from 1753. From 1700 until 1712 Sweden followed its own Swedish calendar, which was one day ahead of the Julian calendar. See: Lemma "Kronologi," *Nordisk familjebok. Konversationslexikon och Realencyklopedi.* 2nd edition, Vol. 15 (Stockholm: Nordisk familjeboks förlags aktiebolag, 1911), 42, or online at: http://runeberg.org/nfbo/0037.html (last accessed on November 1, 2010).

perspective sources that allow us to examine the cultural values of premodern individuals.[2] However, the information provided in documents that were produced in a judicial context has to be interpreted with due diligence: It often contains testimonies logged and edited by third parties, usually representing the authority's perspective, and thus needs to be analyzed critically. When investigating judicial records one needs to keep in mind to what end and under which circumstances, intentions or even manipulations these documents were produced.[3] Bearing this in mind, the question is not to what degree testimonies, statements or other information contained in criminal court records are "true," authentic, right or wrong. Rather, insight can be gained into what was plausible, utterable, and thinkable for contemporaries, and how they explained and perceived suicide.

Though the act of self-killing may be timeless, the perception of and attitudes towards suicide changed notably during the course of the centuries and the phenomenon has proved to be a productive topic of historical research. In recent years, a range of historical and mental-historical studies on the subject, focusing on different regions, time frames and aspects, have significantly changed and broadened our knowledge of the handling and perception of suicide in the premodern world.[4] Taking up a comparative approach I will discuss suicide in early modern rural Austria and Sweden in the context of crime and punishment in this paper.[5] Based on normative texts and judicial records I will ask what constituted suicide as a crime and how individuals who committed suicide were punished. By doing so, I hope to draw attention to the challenging process of description, ascription and interpretation within the limits of early modern legal norm and practice.

In today's Western societies suicide and suicide attempt are in general exempt from judicial punishment. In early modern Europe, however, suicide primarily was perceived as a felony, a sinful deed and a crime against God, nature and

---

2 Gerd Schwerhoff, *Aktenkundig und gerichtsnotorisch: Einführung in die Historische Kriminalitätsforschung*. Historische Einführungen, 3 (Tübingen: Edition Diskord, 1999), 155.

3 See, for instance, Ulrike Gleixner, "Geschlechterdifferenzen und die Faktizität des Fiktionalen: Zur Dekonstruktion frühneuzeitlicher Verhörprotokolle," *WerkstattGeschichte* 11.4 (1995): 65–71.

4 See, for instance, the review papers by Róisín Healy, "Suicide in Early Modern and Modern Europe," *The Historical Journal* 49.3 (2006): 903–19, and David Lederer, "Suicide in Early Modern Central Europe: A Historiographical Review," *German Historical Institute London Bulletin* 38.2 (2006): 33–46. See also Albrecht Classen, "Desperate Lovers, Suicidal and Murderous: Early Modern Dawn Songs and Ballads," *Neuphilologische Mitteilungen* 100.2 (1999): 207–26.

5 More precisely, I study the Austrian archduchies above and below the river Enns and the Swedish Västernorrlands län.

society. Both suicide and suicide attempt were criminally prosecuted. They resulted not only in legal consequences but were also socially stigmatized.

The question if and under what circumstances it is legitimate to end one's own life has been discussed for hundreds of years. While in antiquity suicide was tolerated to a certain degree its perception increasingly narrowed in the Middle Ages.[6] The ban on suicide in the early modern period thus continued a long tradition of primarily negative attitude towards self-inflicted death. Especially Augustine's (354–430) conception of suicide remained powerful throughout the Middle Ages and the early modern times.[7] He clearly took the position against suicide under all circumstances in *The City of God*, invoking the commandment: "You shall not kill (murder)," thus equating suicide with murder.[8]

Suicide was sanctioned by canon law for the first time through decisions that were promulgated at the council of Orléans (533) and the council of Braga (561), where suicides were denied ceremonial rites.[9] However, according to Karsten Pfannkuchen this applied only to those who willfully and while of sound mind took their own lives, whereas suicide committed out of insanity or negligence was not sanctioned.[10] In the thirteenth century Thomas Aquinas (1224/1225–1274) outlined three main arguments against suicide, considering self-killing as a sin

6 Nicole Zeddies, "Verwirrte oder Verbrecher? Die Beurteilung des Selbstmordes von der Spätantike bis zum 9. Jahrhundert," *Trauer, Verzweiflung und Anfechtung: Selbstmord und Selbstmordversuche in mittelalterlichen und frühneuzeitlichen Gesellschaften*, ed. Gabriela Signori. Forum Psychohistorie, 3 (Tübingen: Edition Diskord, 1994), 55–90. See also Alexander Murray's comprehensive series *Suicide in the Middle Ages.* Volume I*: The Violent against Themselves* (Oxford: Oxford University Press, 1998), and *Suicide in the Middle Ages.* Volume II*: The Curse on Self-Murder* (Oxford: Oxford University Press, 2000).

7 See, for instance, Zeddies, "Verwirrte oder Verbrecher?," 67 (see note 6), and Vera Lind, *Selbstmord in der Frühen Neuzeit: Diskurs, Lebenswelt und kultureller Wandel.* Veröffentlichungen des Max-Planck-Instituts für Geschichte, 146 (Göttingen: Vandenhoeck & Ruprecht, 1999), 21–23.

8 Augustine argues: "It only remains for us to apply the commandment, 'Thou shalt not kill,' to man alone, oneself and others. And, of course, one who kills himself kills a man." Citation from Saint Augustine, *The City of God. Books I–VII*, trans. Demetrius B. Zema and Gerald G. Walsh with an introduction by Etienne Gilson. The Fathers of the Church. A New Translation, 8 (Washington, DC: The Catholic University of America Press, 1977), I, 20.

9 See Zeddies, "Verwirrte oder Verbrecher?," 67–69 (see note 6) and Karsten Pfannkuchen, *Selbstmord und Sanktionen: Eine rechtshistorische Betrachtung unter besonderer Berücksichtigung ostpreußischer Bestimmungen* (Berlin: Logos, 2008), 37–39.

10 See Pfannkuchen, *Selbstmord und Sanktionen*, 38–39 (see note 9).

against nature, society and God,[11] a view that prevailed as the almost exclusive position throughout the early modern period.

The perception and assessment of suicide in premodern Europe was—if not entirely—at least to a high degree coined by the prevailing Christian world view that penetrated almost every aspect of life. Like many other crimes, e.g. blasphemy, theft from a church, murder or adultery, suicide was a phenomenon positioned at the interface between religion and the state. Constituting both a crime and a sin, it concerned ecclesiastical as well as secular spheres, but was judged by worldly courts according to provisions in secular penal codes.[12] Of course, these "secular" penal codes also were based on Christian values and norms. This becomes particularly apparent, for instance, in an appendix containing extracts from the five books of Moses that the Swedish king Karl IX added to his ratification of the Swedish penal code in 1608.

However, self-inflicted death did not in any case constitute a criminal act. As mentioned above, the early sanctions by canon law applied only to those who willfully and when in one's right mind ended their lives voluntarily. In the criminalization of suicide both the Austrian and the Swedish penal codes followed this division of sanity/insanity.[13] In the archduchy Austria three penal codes were

---

11 *Summa Theologica,* Part II Question 64 article 5: "Suicide is completely wrong for three reasons. First, everything naturally loves itself, and it is for this reason that everything naturally seeks to keep itself in being and to resist hostile forces. So suicide runs counter to one's natural inclination, and also to that charity by which one ought to cherish oneself. Suicide is, therefore, always a mortal sin in so far as it stultifies the law of nature and charity. Second, every part belongs to the whole in virtue of what it is. But every man is part of the community, so that he belongs to the community in virtue of what he is. Suicide therefore involves damaging the community, as Aristotle makes clear (Ethics V, 11). Third, life is a gift made to man by God, and it is subject to him who is *master of death and life.* Therefore, a person who takes his own life sins against God, just as he who kills another's slave injures the slave's master, or just as he who usurps judgment in a matter outside his authority also commits a sin. And God alone has authority to decide about life and death, as he declares in *Deuteronomy, I kill and I make alive.*" (Deut. 32, 39). Cited from St. Thomas Aquinas, *Summa Theologiae.* Volume 38. "Injustice" (2a2ae. 63–79). Latin text and English translation, Introductions, Notes, Appendices and Glossaries (London and New York: Blackfriars in conjunction with McGraw-Hill and Eyre & Spottiswoode, London, 1975), 33.

12 See Susanne Hehenberger, "Entfremdung von Gott? Gotteslästerung und Kirchendiebstahl vor weltlichen Gerichten im 18. Jahrhundert," *Ermitteln, Fahnden und Strafen: Kriminalitätshistorische Studien vom 16. bis zum 19. Jahrhundert,* ed. Andrea Griesebner and Georg Tschannett (Vienna: Löcker, 2010), 141–63; here 141–43.

13 The criminal codes themselves, however, were of very different character for instance with regard to their extent and degree of detail. For a more detailed review of the provisions concerning suicide in Sweden confer Göran Inger, "Rätten över eget liv och över egen kropp," *Kungl[iga] Humanistiska Vetenskaps-Samfundet i Uppsala. Årsbok 1985* (Uppsala: Almqvist & Wiksell, 1986), 79–105, and Ann-Sofie Ohlander, "Suicide in Sweden: A Social History," *Death: the Public and Private Spheres,* ed. John Rogers. Meddelande från Familjehistoriska projektet, Historiska institutionen, Uppsala universitet, 6 (Uppsala: Uppsala universitet, 1986), 1–52. For Austria,see Stefan Schima, "Die rechtliche Entwicklung des Bestattungswesens im Spannungsfeld zwischen

effective from the mid seventeenth century to the late eighteenth century: the *Ferdinandea* (1656),[14] named after Holy Roman Emperor and Archduke of Austria Ferdinand III and applied to Austria below the river Enns; the so called *Leopoldina* (1675)[15] for Austria above the river Enns, which was named after Holy Roman Emperor and Archduke of Austria Leopold I. The provisions concerning suicide are almost identical in both penal codes.[16] In the eighteenth century both territorial penal codes were superseded by the code referred to as *Theresiana*[17] (1768), named after Holy Roman Empress consort and archduchess Maria Theresia, and in effect from 1770 until 1787.

The above mentioned distinction between premeditated suicide and suicide committed out of an infirmity of mind, melancholy, and illness was common to all three penal codes. Only those who killed themselves "auß bösem Willen/ und gottloser Verzweiflung" ("out of malice will and godless despair")[18] should receive severe and infamous punishment. Their bodies should be handled by the executioner like "unvernünftiges Vieh" ("unreasoning brutes"). Both the *Ferdinandea* and the *Leopoldina* also stipulated forfeiture in cases of premeditated suicide. However, suicide committed out of an infirmity of mind, melancholy and illness was not to be punished. These people should be granted a silent funeral in consecrated ground, i.e., without any ceremonial rites and in a secluded spot of the cemetery.

For Sweden the relevant penal code was *Kristofers landslag*, instituted by union King Christopher of Bavaria in 1442. Expanded by the above mentioned appendix this code was confirmed and re-published by the Swedish king Karl IX in 1608.[19]

Kirche und Staat. Das Tauziehen um das Suizidantenbegräbnis und der Konflikt um die Feuerbestattung," *Freund Hein? Tod und Ritual in der Geschichte*, ed. Wolfgang Hameter, Meta Niederkorn-Bruck, and Martin Scheutz (Innsbruck, Vienna, and Bozen: Studienverlag, 2007), 135–56, and Evelyne Luef, "… *boshaftig den entsetzlichen selbstmord angethann:* Selbsttötung als strafrechtliches Delikt im frühneuzeitlichen Österreich," *Ermitteln, Fahnden und Strafen:. Kriminalitätshistorische Studien vom 16. bis zum 19. Jahrhundert*, ed. Andrea Griesebner and Georg Tschannett (Vienna: Löcker, 2010), 165–90.

14 *Ferdinandea* (1656): "Land-Gerichts-Ordnung: Deß Erz-Herzogthumbs Oesterreich unter der Ennß," *Codex Austriacus* 1 (Vienna: Voigt, 1704), 659–729.

15 *Leopoldina* (1675): *Des Ihro Römisch=Kayserlich=und Königlich=Catholischen Majestät Leopoldi Ertzherzogens zu Österreich Unsers Allergnädigest gemachte Satzungen, Wie auch unterschiedliche in diesem Land eingeführte Ordnungen, Sammt einem ausführlichen Register über alle hierin vorkommende Materien zu gelegentlichem Gebrauch deren hierländigen Gerichts=Persohnen beygerucket worden* (Linz: Feichtinger, 1736).

16 *Ferdinandea* (1656), article 69 and *Leopoldina* (1675), part III, article 11.

17 *Theresiana* (1768): *Constitutio Criminalis Theresiana. Peinliche Gerichtsordnung.* Vollständiger Nachdruck der Trattnerschen Erstausgabe. Vienna 1769 (Graz: Akademische Druck- und Verlagsanstalt, 1993).

18 All translations given in round brackets are mine.

19 *Kristofers landslag* (1608): *Swerikes rijkes lands-lag, som af rijksens råd blef öfwersedd och förbättrat: och*

The subsequent *Sweriges Rikes Lag* (1734) was effective from September 1736 until the new criminal law of 1864 went into force.[20] Also the Swedish law distinguished between premeditated suicide and suicide committed out of an infirmity of mind. Those who took their own lives should—according to *Kristofers landslag*—be burnt at the stake in the woods.[21] Yet, people who committed suicide out of an infirmity of mind were to be buried outside the cemetery. In either case the heirs inherited the property of the deceased, i.e., unlike in Austria (until 1770) forfeiture was not part of Swedish law. However, even though this penal code was theoretically effective until 1736, several resolutions at the end of the seventeenth and the beginning of the eighteenth century altered these provisions: Resolutions from 1700 and 1701 prescribed that premeditated suicides should no longer be cremated but buried in the woods, resolutions from 1695, 1700 and 1701 declared that suicides due to insanity should be buried in the cemetery in silence and at a secluded spot.[22] In practice, however, these resolutions had already been implemented for quite some time before their formal announcement. Consequently, the new penal code of 1734, which stipulated that premeditated suicides no longer should be cremated but buried in the woods, merely stated what had been common practice for quite some time.[23]

The fact that a difference was made between premeditated suicides (*felo de se*) and suicides committed out of an infirmity of mind (*non compos mentis*) in all above mentioned criminal codes shows that suicide per se was not a felony according to the letter of the law, only suicides that were committed with intent and when of sound mind.[24] Or, in other words, one might say that suicide was a felony that, under certain circumstances, lost its criminal status, became excusable and was regarded rather as an indicator of a mental illness. Yet, it is safe to say, that some kind of stigma was attached also to "non-criminal suicides" as "silent burials,"

---

af k. Christofer, Swerikes, Danmarks, Norikes, Wendes och Götha konung, palatz-grefwe widh Reen, och hertigh af Beijeren, årom efter C. B. 1442. stadfäst: så ock af menige Swerikes rijkes ständer samtyckt, gillat och wedertagen, efter then stormächtige, höghborne furstes och herres, herr Carls then nijondes, Swerikes, Göthes, Wendes, finnars, carelers, lappars i norlanden, the caijaners, och esters i Lifland &c. konungs, nådige befalning, åhr 1608. af trycket vtgången, ed. Petter Abrahamsson (Stockholm: af directeuren Johan Henrich Werner med egen bekostnad, 1726).

20 *Sweriges Rikes Lag* (1734): *Sveriges Rikes Lag. Gillad och antagen på riksdagen år 1734. Till 250-årsdagen av lagens tillkomst efter den första i antikva tryckta upplagen av år 1780.* Med inledning av Stig Jägerskiöld. Utgiven i facsimile 1984. Skrifter utgivna av Institutet för rättshistorisk forskning grundat av Gustav och Carin Olin. Serien 1, Rättshistoriskt bibliotek (Stockholm: Institutet för rättshistorisk forskning, 1984).

21 *Kristofers landslag* (1608), Högmålsbalken, Section 4 (see note 19).

22 *Kristofers landslag* (1608), Högmålsbalken, Section 4 (see note 19).

23 *Sweriges Rikes Lag* (1734): Missgärningsbalken, Section 13 (see note 20).

24 Although not uncommon in other European countries, such differentiation, for instance, was not made in the duchies of Schleswig and Holstein. See Lind, *Selbstmord in der Frühen Neuzeit*, 340–45 (see note 7).

whether in or outside the cemetery, still must be regarded as milder forms of sanctioning.[25]

The distinction of "two kinds of suicide" in normative texts, whereof only one constituted a criminal offense, makes the matter rather complicated and raises questions about how these provisions should and could be followed in practice. For obvious reasons, individuals who had committed suicide could no longer be questioned with regard to their (criminal) offense and as to what motivated their self-destructive act—except in cases when they survived the suicide attempt. Nor was it possible to examine a suicide's state of mind at the time of the deed retrospectively. Apart from that, since there is no precise definition of what mode of behavior was classified as "normal" or "abnormal," "insane" and "melancholic," the determination was a matter of construction and interpretation. In his study on "spiritual physic" in early modern Bavaria, David Lederer points out the strikingly differentiated vocabulary that contemporaries used to describe a broad range of mental afflictions.[26] He also reminds us, that "[t]he culture of insanity manifests itself in a community relating through shared values of normal behavior."[27]

Without delving further into the realm of penal law, this short review of provisions concerning suicide in early modern Austrian and Swedish penal codes shows that suicide was ascribed to either a criminal mind or to a state of mental infirmity. The latter bore no legal consequences but was nevertheless stigmatized. The legal norms thus provided a wide scope for interpretation. In the following I will address how this room for construction was filled with meaning in legal practice. However, before turning to this question, I will give a brief outline of the administrative procedure which produced the unprinted sources I will draw upon in my further discussion.

In rural Sweden all suicides were investigated by the courts of first instance (lower courts), the so-called *häradsrätt* or *häradsting*, which also reached a (preliminary) verdict. Until 1720 this verdict had to be approved by the competent high court (*hovrätt*). For the case histories mentioned in this paper this was the Svea high

---

25 Alexander Kästner, "Tödliche Geschichte(n): Selbsttötungen und Suizidversuche in Kursachsen 1547–1815," Ph.D. diss., Technische Universität Dresden, 2009, 484.

26 David Lederer defines spiritual physic as a "specific form of mental health care [that] fell within the purview of the clergy." David Lederer, *Madness, Religion and the State in Early Modern Europe: A Bavarian Beacon*. New Studies in European History (Cambridge, New York, Melbourne, et al.: Cambridge University Press, 2006), 1. This spiritual art or practice of treating afflictions of the soul included remedies such as auricular confession, pilgrimage, and exorcism.

27 Lederer, *Madness, Religion and the State*, 3 (see note 26).

court in Stockholm, founded in 1614. Since 1720, the ruling of the *häradsrätt* served as a final judgment.[28]

Like other offenses that were relevant under civil or criminal law, suicides were documented in the *häradsrätt*'s protocol, the so called "judgment book" (*dombok*). Such judgment books were maintained by all lower courts in Sweden and contain information about where and when the court convened, the names of the usually twelve jury members (*nämndemän*) present, and provide a summary of the oral testimonies and statements that were presented before the court. The entry for each case heard usually closes with a resolution, i.e., the judgment that was pronounced by the lower court. A fair hand copy of these judgment books had to be submitted to the high court for scrutiny once a year. Besides these judgment books I draw upon letters sent from the Svea high court to the regional administrative unit (*Gävleborgs Läns Landskansli*), which until 1720 contained the final verdict.

In Austria the administrative organization was less well-structured than in Sweden. However, also in the Austrian archduchies a distinction was drawn between two levels of jurisdiction: low justice (*niedere Gerichtsbarkeit*) and high justice (*höhere Gerichtsbarkeit*). Low justice was held by the *Grundherrschaft*, noble or clerical manorial lords, who exercised jurisdiction over his or her subjects. It generally involved *causae minores*, e.g., petty theft or insults, i.e., affairs that were settled by limited fines, short-time incarceration and/or light corporal punishment. High justice, on the other hand, was exercised by the *Landgericht*. These "land courts" too were held by either noble or clerical proprietors—then called "freie Landgerichte" ("free land courts")—or, when the *Landgericht* directly was subordinated to the sovereign (*Landesfürst* or *Landesfürstin*), termed "landesfürstliches Landgericht."

In general, the *Landgerichte* were in charge of *causae maiores*, usually identical to the crimes listed in the territorial penal codes, and had the authority to impose aggravated corporal punishment and the death penalty. Depending on the kind of *Landgericht* ("freies" or "landesfürstliches Landgericht"), the province and the crime in question, they in turn were subordinated to higher ranking administrative and judicial authorities.[29] With regard to suicide the jurisdiction was split between the *Grundherrschaft* and the *Landgericht*. According to the above-made distinction,

---

28 *Kristofers landslag* (1608), Högmålsbalken, Section 4 (see note 19).

29 See, for instance, Andrea Griesebner and Susanne Hehenberger, "Entscheidung über Leib und Leben: Rechtsgutachter in frühneuzeitlichen Malefizprozessen im Erzherzogtum Österreich," *Experten und Expertenwissen in der Strafjustiz von der Frühen Neuzeit bis zur Moderne*, ed. Alexander Kästner and Sylvia Kesper-Biermann. Editionen + Dokumentationen, 1 (Leipzig: Meine Verlag, 2008), 17–31.

non-criminal suicides were a matter of the *Grundherrschaft*, the local authorities; premeditated suicides, however, were subjected to high justice, the *Landgericht*.

Not surprisingly, this arrangement created confusion in its practical implementation, and the source material contains several examples where *Grundherrschaft* and *Landgericht* disagreed about their respective rights and duties, and ultimately about the question of jurisdiction. Generally, local authorities had to report all cases of suicide to the responsible *Landgericht*. However, a thorough investigation by the *Landgericht* should only be conducted in cases when there was reasonable suspicion of a premeditated suicide. This suggests that the local authorities had important influence on how a suicide was presented when reported to the *Landgericht*, and thus whether an investigation was opened or a silent burial, maybe without further investigation, was authorized. We can also assume that this arrangement was reflected in the written documents that were produced in the course of an investigation. After all, the inspection of the corpse in an assumed non-criminal suicide was not necessarily followed by any further investigation, thus producing less "paperwork" found in today's archives. Consequently, concentrating on documents produced in the course of an investigation conducted by a *Landgericht* in my archival research, I assume that materials concerning suspected premeditated suicides primarily appear. The source material for Austria that I will draw upon in this paper ranges from protocol books and interrogation protocols to written communication between authorities.

While different administrative and judicial systems would make a quantitative comparison between the two study regions difficult, these differences benefit my qualitative analysis on how suicide was perceived and punished in early modern Austria and Sweden. The knowledge of the "other" produces multiple perspectives, which allow me to approach the respectively "other" material with fresh eyes.[30] Having concentrated on the normative and administrative aspects of suicide so far, we now turn to the practical level in the following section.

Sometimes the first step for the court was to establish if an individual had committed suicide in the first place or if s/he had died in an accident, of natural causes, or had become a homicide victim. This was not always an easy undertaking. The latter was relatively rare but was for instance the case in the investigation of the sudden death of 41-year old master carpenter Johann

30 Michael Werner and Bénédicte Zimmermann, "Beyond Comparison: Histoire croisée and the Challenge of Reflexivity," *History and Theory* 45 (2006): 30–50.

Pfundbauer from Austria above the river Enns.[31] Johann Pfundbauer died in 1792[32] after being sick for several days. According to the court records, before his death he had mentioned to several people that he suspected his wife of having poisoned his beer. After his death an autopsy was ordered and the suspicion of poisoning was confirmed when arsenic was found in his body. In the course of the investigation, witness statements confirmed an unhappy marriage between Johann Pfundberger and his wife, but also referred to suicide threats that he had uttered before his death and revealed that he had a drinking problem. Thus, the court was not sure if someone (his wife was the main suspect) had poisoned him, or if he himself was responsible for his death. Unfortunately the incomplete documentation of the case leaves us in the dark with regard to the outcome of the investigation.

Also interesting in this regard is the case of Jon Zachrisson from Ångermannland, Sweden.[33] In April 1711 he ended up with a mysteriously inflicted cut to his throat that caused his death some days later. Jon Zachrisson claimed that an unknown man had tried to steal hay from his hayrick and, in the course of fisticuffs, wounded him. On his deathbed he repeated his version of the events for the parish priest, but the story did not withstand closer scrutiny. The *häradsrätt* suspected Jon of suicide and ruled that he should be buried in the woods by the executioner. In its revision the high court acknowledged the *häradsrätt*'s reasoning, admitting that Jon might have made up the story in order to achieve a Christian burial. However, in the opinion of the high court the evidence did not satisfy a "högmålssak," meaning a matter of capital crime. Jon Zachrisson's case was not free of doubt and thus the high court extenuated the lower court's verdict and granted him a silent burial at a marginal spot in the cemetery.[34]

While homicide cases only rarely were disguised as suicides and vice versa, courts more often had to decide if they were dealing with suicide or accidental death. Sudden death especially by individuals who, for example, drowned, froze to death, or were killed by a fall from great height were always suspicious to a

---

31 *Oberösterreichisches Landesarchiv*, subsequently referred to as *OÖLA*, HA Puchheim, Schachtel 44 Bund 61 Nr. 42.

32 In 1792 the *Josephina* (1787) was the code in effect in the Austrian archduchies. *Josephina* (1787): "Allgemeines Gesetzbuch über Verbrechen und derselben Bestrafung (1787)," *Joseph des Zweyten Römischen Kaisers Gesetze und Verfassungen im Justiz=Fache. Für Böhmen, Mähren, Schlesien, Oesterreich ob und unter der Enns, Steyermark, Kärnthen, Krain, Görz, Gradisca, Triest, Tyrol und die Vorlande. In dem siebenten Jahre seiner Regierung. Jahrgang von 1786 bis 1787* (Vienna: Kaiserlich-Königliche Hof- und Staats-Aerarial-Druckerei, 1817), 7–60 ,or http://alex.onb.ac.at/ (last accessed on November 1, 2010).

33 Forskningsarkivet Umeå universitetsbibliotek, Södra Ång. A I a:10 Mk D52268 12/24, Sidensiö, May 3, 1711.

34 Forskningsarkivet Umeå universitetsbibliotek, Skrivelser från Svea hovrätt till Gävleborgs Läns Landskansli 1635–1736, DIIa:14 Mk S10553 1/10, May 25, 1711.

certain degree.[35] In September 1763, for example, the cottager and tailor Catharina Pührnsteinerin was found drowned in a weir.[36] A preserved letter that was presumably sent from the local authority (*Grundherrschaft*) to the *Landgericht* depicts and interprets the circumstances of her death. The writer of the letter provides three arguments that point towards a premeditated suicide and nine arguments in Catharina's defense, emphasizing mitigating circumstances and suggesting her innocence. The aggravating factors cited were that Catharina repeatedly lamented her poverty and the illnesses of her children. Moreover, she had not taken the usual way from her house to the weir on the night of her death, leading the writer to conclude that she must have had something "evil on her mind."

As for mitigating circumstances he mentioned her (1) Christian and edifying conduct, (2) the fact that she had lived peacefully and in harmony with her husband and the whole neighborhood as well as the (3) love and care she had shown for her constantly sick children. Moreover, though lamenting her poverty, (4) she had never uttered any words of desperation, and (5) according to the deceased's husband and the local "baderin" (the wife of the barber surgeon), Catharina had been sick before her death. The writer of the letter finally offered an alternative to the suicide scenario by suggesting (6) that Catharina might have fallen by accident into the weir on her way to see acquaintances, to whom she wanted to "pour her heart out" ("ihr herz auszuschitten"). He moreover argued, that (7) she could have drowned herself more easily in a river that she had to cross before she came to the weir.

Since she did not drown herself at the first opportunity the writer presumed that she did not have "evil in mind" ("nichts übles wird gedacht haben") when she passed the weir, and that she must have fallen into the water by accident. This theory was, in his opinion, also supported by the "fact" that (8) Catharina was found lying on her back, while in cases of "malicious" drowning a person was always found face down. Finally (9) an amulet, although no scapular, was found on her. For contemporaries this usually indicated hope and faith and thus made despair an unlikely motive for a suicide.

The writer of this letter clearly advocated leniency for Catharina Pührnsteinerin. Although Catharina's behavior shortly before her death pointed towards suicide with intent, the writer raised doubt by providing an alternative scenario and emphasized her Christian lifestyle, moral conduct and good integration into the

---

35 See, for instance, Bodil E. B. Persson, "Drunknad eller dränkt? Plötsliga oväntade dödsfall i Skåne 1704–1718," *Den frivilliga döden: Samhällets hantering av självmord i historiskt perspektiv*, ed. Birgitta Odén, Bodil E. B. Persson, and Yvonne Maria Werner (Stockholm: Bokförlaget Cura i samarbete med Forskningsrådsnämnden, 1998), 101–208.

36 OÖLA, HA Oberwallsee-Eschlberg, Schachtel 27.

local community. These personal characteristics were more important, it seems, than the actual event.

The examples presented demonstrate that the cause of death was not always clear and to a certain degree was determined by ascriptions and interpretations. Doubt was an important aspect in the investigation of sudden death and suicide and courts both in Austria and Sweden were urged to judge in favor of the defendant in doubtful cases.[37] However, reasonable doubt was a privilege that was not granted to everyone. A charge of premeditated suicide was often associated with sin and poor moral conduct. Thus, it was not unusual that one's lifestyle codetermined the judgment with regard to the cause of death. Good moral conduct and acknowledged conformist behavior increased the chances for lenience; yet, it was no guaranty.

The case of Catharina Pührnsteinerin also reminds us that it is impossible to gauge accurately the number of unrecognized suicides. In our analyses we depend on cases of self-inflicted death that were readily identifiable or at least suspect. Once established as a suicide, authorities then had to tackle the process of interpretation. In order to make the above described distinction between premeditated suicide and suicide due to an infirmity of mind it was crucial to determine why someone had taken his/her own life.

To reveal the reason or motivation that led to a suicide, the investigation sought to establish the circumstances of the suicide and the person's state of mind at the time of the deed. Authorities interrogated family members, neighbors and often inquired about the moral conduct of the deceased with the parish priest. Although the verdict, i.e., the burial decision, was reached by secular authorities, in the course of the investigation the opinion of the ecclesiastical authorities, such as the parish priest, was of great importance.[38]

Let us return to the case of Karin Mickelsdotter that was mentioned in the beginning of this paper in order to illustrate this decision making process in a case of apparent suicide.[39] According to the judgment book the extraordinary assembled court proceeded as follows: First, two jury members who had been sent for by the deceased's brother the day after the tragic occurrence reported on their

---

37 For Austria see, for instance, *Ferdinandea* (1656), article 69, § 9; *Leopoldina* (1675), part III, article 11, § 9 and *Theresiana* (1768), article 93, § 4. For Sweden see *Sweriges Rikes Lag* (1734), "domarregler" ("rules for judges"), number 31.

38 See, for instance, Alexander Kästner, "Experten für ein gutes Leben: Zur Rolle von lutherischen Pfarrern in Untersuchungsverfahren nach Selbsttötungen (Kursachsen 1700–1815)," *Experten und Expertenwissen in der Strafjustiz von der Frühen Neuzeit bis zur Moderne*, ed. Alexander Kästner and Sylvia Kesper-Biermann. Editionen + Dokumentationen, 1 (Leipzig: Meine Verlag, 2008), 85–98.

39 Forskningsarkivet Umeå universitetsbibliotek, Södra Ång. A I a:10 Mk D52268 8/24, Nordingrå, February 21, 1710 (see note 1).

external inspection of the dead body and the scene. Thereafter, Karin Mickelsdotters' mother, Märit Ersdotter, stated that she had noticed nothing out of the ordinary the day her daughter died. Allegedly Karin had devotionally read her morning prayers and had carried out some regular household chores before she went to a separate room to lie down for a while. When her mother came to look in on her about thirty minutes later, she found her daughter dead. On inquiry, the jury affirmed that Karin Mickelsdotter indeed not only had been able to read "in the book" (i.e., the catechism) but had also been diligent in singing. Moreover, none of the assembled people could recall any misconduct on her part; on the contrary, they all confirmed her "still" (i.e., good) lifestyle and agreed that she had never talked unreasonably.

However, the protocol also mentions that Karin already some thirty years ago had complained to her mother and brother about being anxious and saddened without any apparent reason. These recurring afflictions prompted her brother to ask the chaplain to talk to her and console her. But according to the protocol which presumably follows the statement of her brother, even after the spiritual help of the cleric the anxiety returned, leaving her fearful and feeling at a loss. On January sixth Karin had received Holy Communion at church for the last time. Chaplain Petrus Hernäus, who apparently was present at the examination, affirmed that Karin's brother had approached him five years ago with regard to his sister's condition. Indeed, he had tried to console her and confirmed that she suffered from anxiety and melancholy. If her condition had worsened or improved over the years, he did not know, but he reinforced that she knew her "christendoms stycke" ("Christendom's pieces") better than he had expected.

Two other men from the same village testified that she had been "opasslig" ("indisposed") for a couple of years, but they didn't know what exactly caused her to feel that way. They did assert, however, that Karin had always been of sound mind. Finally Karin's brother Olof requested that his sister's dead body be handled by her closest relatives and buried in silence at the northern side of the cemetery without the usual ceremony, arguing that she had taken her own life in a state of severe melancholy. However, the *häradsrätt* pronounced a different judgment: The court acknowledged the brother's request "äfter hon uthi ett starck melancolie tagit lyfwett af sig sielf, och sådan swårmodigheet iämbwähl för siukdom räcknas kan hos den som man ingen misgiärning wet med" ("because she took her own life in a state of severe melancholy and such melancholy can be regarded as an illness if the person has not been known for any misdeeds").

Nevertheless, the *häradsrätt* followed the Swedish penal code which prescribed that suicides should be buried in the woods unless it was obvious that they had been completely out of their minds. For the court this had not been the case with Karin who apparently had been melancholic, but still of sound mind. Therefore the *häradsrätt* saw no other choice than to determine that the executioner should bury her in the woods. Knowing that the verdict was sent to the high court for revision and confirmation the *häradsrätt* presumably anticipated a milder judgment by the superordinated instance. And indeed, in a writing by Gabriel Falkenberg, president of the Svea high court at the time, to the regional administration of the district court from March 3, 1710, the judgment was modified: Arguing that Karin Mickelsdotter had suffered from "hierteängslan" ("heart-anxiety") and melancholy so severe that a cleric had to visit her, and, considering that she otherwise had lived a still and god-fearing life, the high court ruled that her body should be handled by her relatives and granted her a burial at a remote place in the cemetery in silence.[40] In the end, the request of the deceased's brother was fulfilled.

In some regards the documentation of Karin's suicide in the judgment book is representative for many documented suicide cases in Sweden. Constitutive and recurring factors that are mentioned include an emphasis on the person's moral conduct, questions concerning church attendance, his/her knowledge of the scripture and when he/she last received Holy Communion. Also important was how well the deceased had been integrated in the local community and how he/she got along with family, neighbors and friends. The same aspects, as we have seen, were also of importance in assessing the Austrian Catharina Pührnsteinerin's drowning, mentioned above. It appears as if consideration of these factors was a common denominator throughout early modern Europe.[41] Of course, contemporaries were well informed of the possible consequences of a suicide, as Olof Mickelson's request for a funeral in silence indicates. Thus, we should assume that statements given before court were at least, to a certain degree, strategic—people knew what to emphasize and what to conceal in order to lead an investigation in a certain direction.

It is also interesting to note that the *häradsrätt,* although apparently well-disposed towards Karin, did not accept melancholy as a sufficient excuse but insisted on insanity—whatever that concept may have implied—as the only pardonable explanation for suicide. Interestingly, both the preliminary verdict by the *häradsrätt* and the final verdict by the *hovrätt* regarded melancholy only in conjunction with an otherwise "good" lifestyle as an argument for lenience.

Why, then, was the *häradsrätt* so strict in its judgment and insisted on the disposing of the body in the woods? In his contribution to this volume Christopher R. Clason distinguishes between "the letter of the law" and "the spirit of the law" as two analytical categories.[42] Applying this distinction to early modern Swedish

40 Forskningsarkivet Umeå universitetsbibliotek, Skrivelser från Svea hovrätt till Gävleborgs Läns Landskansli 1635–1736, DIIa:13 Mk S21057 12/14, March 3, 1710.

41 See, for instance, Kästner, *Tödliche Geschichte(n)*, 443–46 (see note 25), and Lind, *Selbstmord in der Frühen Neuzeit,* 360–62 (see note 7).

42 See Christopher R. Clason's contribution to this volume.

judicature suggests that the district courts had to stick close to the letter of the law while the interpretation of the spirit of the law was reserved for the high court, which also held the competence to show lenience.[43] Yet, the influence of the lower courts on the final judgment is not to be underestimated. After all, in Sweden the high court based its decision entirely on documents that were produced and transmitted by the lower courts. In Austria too, the *Landgerichte* to a high degree were reliant on the cooperation with the *Grundherrschaft*.

The examples highlighted here provide insights into the legal processes that constructed and labeled self-inflicted death as either a criminal or non-criminal act. In the following section we will turn towards the punitive aspects of suicide.

There is neither a simple nor a single answer to the question why it was considered to be so important to prosecute and punish suicides. Presumably, ecclesiastical and secular authorities were striving to stigmatize the deed as a felony and a sin in order to make clear that only God or the sovereign, in his place, had the power and control over a subject's life, death and body. In this regard the legal consequences of a suicide can be interpreted as display of power. At the same time the deterrent effect of the dishonorable and ignominious interment was intended to keep subjects from committing suicide.

However, focusing only on the interests of authorities does not suffice: Popular beliefs and superstitions associated suicide with disasters and misfortune. The fear that the burial of a suicide in the cemetery would cause bad weather or crop failures was widespread. Hence, sometimes individuals or communities supported or insisted upon excluding the body of a suicide from burial in the cemetery. To state that the dishonorable disposal of a suicide's body was solely driven by the ecclesiastical and secular authorities however would be overly simplistic because, in some cases, the community demanded that the bodies of suicides be handled disgracefully.

This was, for example, the case in 1754 when a female tailor committed suicide in a small village in Austria above the Enns.[44] According to the administrator of the *Landgericht*, who conducted the investigation, the woman had been melancholic for a while. She had been passive and unable to work for weeks despite being in good physical health. Moreover, she had actively tried to improve her condition by bloodletting and praying the rosary. Since no objection was raised

43 See Yvonne Maria Werner, "Självmord i det stora nordiska krigets skugga: En analys av självspillingsmålen vid Göta hovrätt 1695–1718," *Den frivilliga döden: Samhällets hantering av självmord i historiskt perspektiv*, ed. Birgitta Odén, Bodil E. B. Persson and Yvonne Maria Werner (Stockholm: Bokförlaget Cura i samarbete med Forskningsrådsnämnden, 1998), 31–99. Yvonne Maria Werner observes a tendency toward more lenience shown by the Göta high court during the period she investigates.

44 OÖLA, HA Puchheim, Schachtel 43 Bund 60 Nr. 29.

by the priest either, the woman was granted a Christian burial "without pomp" in exact accordance with territorial law.

However, the attempt to bury the woman failed when allegedly about hundred aroused parishioners restrained the pallbearers from entering the cemetery. The administrator first tried to negotiate with the enraged crowd and suggested burying the women outside the cemetery, in the place of burial reserved for "inculpable," i.e., unbaptized children, but even this concession did not suffice to appease the mob. According to the preserved documents the protesters did not challenge the ruling of the *Landgericht* identifying melancholy and insanity as causes for her suicide. Nevertheless they wanted to prevent the burial, fearing bad thunderstorms as its consequence, a belief that was referred to as "sträflicher aberglaube" ("criminal superstition") in the administrator's writing. Opposition against a suicide's burial in the cemetery did not necessarily culminate in a cemetery revolt but could take more subtle forms. In May 1769, for example, seven men appeared in person before the priest in the upper Austrian town of Gmunden, urging the cleric not to bury the body of the suicide Franz Kemptner in the cemetery.[45]

Cemetery revolts and other forms of influencing a suicide's burial were not uncommon in central Europe.[46] They demonstrate that parish communities were not always in agreement with the verdict reached by the authorities, and would under certain circumstances take matters into their own hands. Of course, as Alexander Kästner points out, revolts were rather rare occurrences compared to the number of burials without any incidents.[47] Yet, these tumults suggest that the criminalization and punishment of suicide was to a certain degree supported by the population.[48]

It seems as if similar protests were not un-heard of in Sweden either,[49] and the case of Anna Olofsdotter demonstrates the connection between suicide and

---

45 OÖLA, HA Ebenzweier, Schachtel 2.

46 See, for instance, Lind, *Selbstmord in der Frühen Neuzeit,* 457–62 (see note 7); David Lederer, "Aufruhr auf dem Friedhof: Pfarrer, Gemeinde und Selbstmord im frühneuzeitlichen Bayern," *Trauer, Verzweiflung und Anfechtung: Selbstmord und Selbstmordversuche in mittelalterlichen und frühneuzeitlichen Gesellschaften,* ed. Gabriela Signori. Forum Psychohistorie, 3 (Tübingen: Edition Diskord, 1994), 189–209 and Kästner, *Tödliche Geschichte(n),* 235–40 (see note 25).

47 Kästner, *Tödliche Geschichte(n),* 236 (see note 25).

48 Michael MacDonald and Terence R. Murphy, for instance, state for eighteenth-century England a growing divergency in the perception of suicide between "common people" and the educated upper classes. See Michael MacDonald and Terence R. Murphy, "Die Säkularisierung des Selbstmords: Literaten, Rechtsgelehrte und religiöse Fanatiker im frühneuzeitlichen England," *Trauer, Verzweiflung und Anfechtung: Selbstmord und Selbstmordversuche in mittelalterlichen und frühneuzeitlichen Gesellschaften,* ed. Gabriela Signori. Forum Psychohistorie, 3 (Tübingen: Edition Diskord, 1994), 233–81.

49 See, for instance, Werner, "Självmord i det stora nordiska krigets skugga," 49–50 (see note 43).

option was applied in practice in early modern Austria and Sweden urther scrutiny.[67]

the violent handling of the body was only one aspect of punishment. hen religion dominated life and the afterlife was considered more than the here and now by many people, the whereabouts of the soul kely deemed more important than the handling of the physical body. ng stance of the Catholic Church on suicide was outlined above with ns of Augustine and Thomas Aquinas—premeditated, intentional, uicide was considered a heinous sin with severe consequences for the soul. On the other hand, in her article on suicide in the Middle Ages, gnori emphasizes the growing influence of the concepts of purgatory As these concepts remained powerful in the early modern period one lude the possibility that contemporary Catholics drew hope for a ul from the grace of God or the Virgin Mary.

n Lutheranism was adopted in the first half of the sixteenth century r less completely enforced by the end of the century. Martin Luther's n suicide was somewhat inconclusive. He too emphasized the s obligation to conserve one's own life. At the same time he stressed the he devil over a suicide, suggesting that at the time of the deed the did not possess free will. However, even though Martin Luther often leniency should be shown by ecclesiastical authorities, he nevertheless he punishment imposed by secular authorities.[69]

y committing suicide both Catholics and Lutherans put their souls, the salvation, and eternal life at risk. In an atmosphere where salvation

---

ria, a regulation from 1742 stipulated that the *Landgerichte* had to deliver the bodies of criminals for anatomic studies, if requested by the university. However, it is yet unclear what degree this included premeditated suicides. See *Sammlung aller k. k. Verordnungen tze vom Jahre 1740 bis 1780, die unter der Regierung der Regierung des Kaisers Joseph des II. h ganz bestehen, theils zum Theile abgeändert sind, als eine Hilfs- und Ergänzungsbuch zu dem he aller unter der Regierung des Kaisers Josephs des II. für die k. k. Erbländer ergangenen ngen und Gesetze in einer chronologischen Ordnung*, ed. Joseph Kropatschek. Vol. 1 (Vienna: 786), 7, nr. 7 or http://alex.onb.ac.at (last accessed on Nov. 1, 2010). For Sweden, a royal m 1747 explicitly stipulated that the bodies of suicides and children born out of wedlock e delivered to the universities in Uppsala, Lund and Turku and the Collegium Medicum holm, if required. See Eva Åhrén, *Death, Modernity, and the Body: Sweden 1870–1940*, trans. V. Olson. Rochester Studies in Medical History, 15 (2002; Rochester, NY: University of er Press, 2009), 21.

Signori, "Rechtskonstruktionen und religiöse Fiktionen: Bemerkungen zur Selbstmordf- Mittelalter," *Trauer, Verzweiflung und Anfechtung: Selbstmord und Selbstmordversuche in erlichen und frühneuzeitlichen Gesellschaften*, ed. Gabriela Signori. Forum Psychohistorie, 3 en: Edition Diskord, 1994), 9–54.

tailed discussion of Martin Luther's position, see Kästner, *Tödliche Geschichte(n)*, 94–105 e 25).

misfortune in popular belief as expressed by the suicidal woman herself.[50] In May 1713 60-year-old Anna Olofsdotter went into the woods and stabbed herself in the throat. A little while later, the injured woman was found by her daughter-in-law and the neighbour Hans Pärsson. At first Anna did not want to accept their help and tried to send them away saying "rör intet med mig, ty det är giort, som giort är" ("don't touch me, what's done is done"). Hans Pärsson nevertheless reached out to her and asked if she wanted to come back with him to his home. According to the judgment book Anna Olofsdotter answered "att gården blir olyckelig, om hon kommer hem" ("that the farm would become unfortunate, if she came home"). Not until Hans Pärsson assured her that this would not be the case did she finally go with them. Nine days later she died as a result of her injuries.

These examples show that suicide concerned not only those who were close to the deceased or were somehow involved in the legal proceeding. To a certain degree self-inflicted death was a matter of public interest that concerned a wider circle of people who considered themselves to be affected by the incident, and thus also took interest in the outcome of the investigation.

However, generally the right to judge and punish a suicide was reserved for the secular authorities. Indeed, the idea of punishing a dead person appears strange from today's perspective. Nevertheless early modern justice found ways and means to chastise individuals who had ended their own lives. In the following I will briefly broach different aspects of punishment that affected the goods, the body, the soul, and the remembrance of the deceased.

As outlined above, Austrian (but not Swedish) law sanctioned premeditated suicide with forfeiture until the *Theresiana* came into effect in 1770.[51] Studies conducted by Vera Lind for Schleswig-Holstein,[52] David Lederer[53] for Bavaria, and Alexander Kästner for Kursachsen[54] show that confiscation was a rather rare occurrence in early modern central Europe. However, the Austrian source material contains evidence that this provision in fact was implemented in practice. Even though it is not yet clear to what extent forfeiture was executed, the materials indicate that it was not a rare phenomenon. In the case of Jacob Pauer, for example, who in 1762 "wickedly" drowned himself in Austria below the Enns, the *Landgericht* in a letter to the *Grundherrschaft* explicitly reserved its right to confiscate his bequest with reference to the respective paragraphs in the *Ferdinandea*.[55]

---

50 Forskningsarkivet Umeå universitetsbibliotek, Södra Ång. A I a:11 Mk D52269 4/19+5/19, Nora, May 18, 1713.

51 See also Pfannkuchen, *Selbstmord und Sanktionen*, 88–91 (see note 9).

52 Lind, *Selbstmord in der Frühen Neuzeit*, 340–47 (see note 7).

53 Lederer, *Madness, Religion and the State*, 251 (see note 26).

54 Kästner, *Tödliche Geschichte(n)*, 143 (see note 25).

55 Niederösterreichisches Landesarchiv, hence forward referred to as NÖLA, HA Raabs, Karton 44.

In 1687 the inheritance of the suicide Thomas Auer was confiscated by the *Landgericht*.[56] However, due to the poverty of his wife and two young children, the *Landgericht* did not insist on the two thirds of his bequest which it would have been entitled to by law. Instead an individual solution was negotiated with the widow. Also the son of the suicide Johann Mayr had to turn in two thirds of his inheritance to the *Landgericht* in 1723.[57] In the case of Stephan Pühringer[58] who killed himself in 1686, a conflict had arisen between the *Grundherrschaft* and the *Landgericht*. Against the opinion of the *Landgericht*, the *Grundherrschaft* was convinced that he had committed suicide out of an infirmity of mind and thus rejected the *Landgericht*'s claim for jurisdiction, which would have included the right to confiscate two thirds of his bequest if a case premeditated suicide was proven. These few examples show that forfeiture in the Austrian archduchies was an option until the *Theresiana* came into force.[59]

Generally the financial aspect of suicide was a point of contention between different authorities. Apart from forfeiture, where the *Grundherrschaft* had a strong interest to keep the money within their own *Herrschaft*, monetary questions played an important role in many respects. Like in other criminal cases conducted by the *Landgericht*, the delinquents themselves had to compensate all costs incurred during the trial and the investigation. In the case of suicide this money usually was taken from the deceased's bequest. However, impecunious suicides which did not have the means to pay these expenses incurred costs that the authority in charge had to pay. Thus, sometimes conflicts between different authorities would arise because neither of them wanted to be responsible for retrieving a dead body and the associated costs.[60]

Both in Austria and Sweden, the bodies of premeditated suicides should be handled by the executioner. Austrian laws explicitly state that they should be dragged through the streets or carried on the "Schindkarren" ("executioner's cart") to the place where the corpse should be "vertilgt" ("exterminated"). On the other hand, those to whom a silent burial had been granted should be taken care of by family members, neighbors or other "honest" people. Yet, once again, the information contained in archival records blurs the distinction between

56 NÖLA, KGA Krems, HS 173/102, fol. 31v–33v.

57 NÖLA, KGA Krems, HS 173/102, fol. 184–85.

58 OÖLA, HA Ebenzweier, Schachtel 2, Nr. 12.

59 The *Theresiana* stipulated confiscation only in cases when suicides prior to the self-killing had committed a crime that was punished with forfeiture. Hence, forfeiture as a punishment applied no longer to the act of self-killing but to the prior committed crime. See *Theresiana* (1768), article 93, section 7.

60 This concerned not only the bodies of suicides but, for instance, also unknown dead persons that were found on the roadside, especially in cases when the border between two *Landgericht* districts was unclear.

premeditated suicide and non-criminal su
wide scope of reactions, requests and indi
Generally, premeditated suicides were t
in most cases the executioner. However, d
skirt punishment while under arrest enc
corpses could be exposed to physical punis
one case is documented where a murderer
to the place of executions where his head w
executioner.[61] An anonymous script from 1
and thief who was carried to the place of e
wheel above which a gallows was erected.
Such aggravated measures were in acc
Austrian criminal codes until 1787,[63] and in
Swedish laws did not explicitly prescribe suc
some of my Swedish case histories show th
suicide while under arrest or after escap
treatment. The seventy-year old former sol
had been accused of theft but managed to
after his escape he was found dead with
wound in the throat. In the end the executi
under the gallows and not, as otherwise co
Another possible consequence of suicide t
for the sake of completeness was the p
premeditated suicide to the university's an

61 My thanks to Susanne Hehenberger for this refere
um Wien 1703–1803: Eine Datenbank, http://www.
2010).

62 Anonymous, *Der sträfliche Selbstmord, oder die u*
(Vienna: Jahnische Universitäts-Buchdruckerei, 17

63 The *Josephina* (1787) stipulated that in such cases th
a note with the name of the suicide and his/her
gallows and thus made public. See *Josephina* (1787)

64 See, for instance, Machiel Bosman, "The Judicial T
to Insanity: Suicide in Early Modern Europe, ed. Jeffrey
2004), 9–24.

65 Forskningsarkivet Umeå universitetsbibliotek, Skri
Landskansli 1635–1736, DIIa:13 Mk S10552 11/14,

66 For a more detailed discussion see, for instance, Kä
25) and Julia Schreiner, *Jenseits vom Glück: Suizid, Me*
Texten des späten 18. Jahrhunderts. Ancien Régime
Oldenbourg, 2003), 32–55.

degree this
still needs
Howeve
In times w
important
was most
The preva
the positi
desperate
deceased's
Gabriela S
and grace.
cannot ex
suicide's s
In Swed
and more
position
individua
power of
individua
argued th
agreed on
Hence,
prospect

67 For Au
execut
if and t
und Ge
theils n
Handb
Verord
Mößle,
letter f
had to
in Stoc
Daniel
Roche

68 Gabrie
rage i
mittela
(Tübi

69 For a
(see n

played a major role the whereabouts of the soul was an important issue; some suicidal people tried to arrange their death without actually harming themselves directly. The phenomenon, referred to as e.g. "indirect" or "concealed" suicide, "suicidal murder"[70] or "suicide by proxy,"[71] bears witness that individuals would not refrain from exceptional means in order to end their lives without dying at their own hands. Both Catholic and Lutheran believers occasionally committed or confessed to capital crimes, e.g. child murder, bestiality or blasphemy, with the purpose of being executed by the authority.[72] They thus avoided committing the sin of 'self-murder' and saved their soul by confessing their sins and receiving absolution before execution.[73]

Of course, we don't know how important the concept of salvation actually was to the men and women who took their own lives, or if they at all were concerned with that question. It can be assumed, though, that in a religiously charged atmosphere uncertainty regarding the whereabouts of the soul post-mortem was a concern for many people. This concern underlies the punitive character of a disgraceful burial outside the cemetery. For the fate of the soul a Christian funeral was of great importance. For Catholics the consecrated ground of the cemetery, prayers, songs and intercessions of the faithful were thought to provide support for the deceased. The deeds of the bereaved were thought to shorten the time in purgatory for the deceased and thus help the soul on its way to eternity. In this regard the ban on providing auxiliary spiritual means must have been a severe punishment both for the deceased, who knew about the consequences for his soul and for those who could not intervene for the repose of the soul of the deceased. To a certain extent the interdiction of auxiliary spiritual means affected not only premeditated suicides that were excluded from the cemeteries and handled by the executioner but also those who were granted a funeral in silence.

Unlike their Catholic counterparts Lutheran cemeteries in Sweden were not consecrated, which in theory made the ground in and outside the cemetery the same. Nonetheless the cemetery was also considered a special and honored place

---

70 See Arne Jansson, *From Swords to Sorrow: Homicide and Suicide in Early Modern Stockholm*. Stockholm Studies in Economic History, 30 (Stockholm: Almqvist & Wiksell, 1998), 49–69.

71 See Kathy Stuart, "Suicide by Proxy: The Unintended Consequences of Public Executions in Eighteenth-Century Germany," *Central European History* 41 (2008): 413–45.

72 With regard to false confession in the context of bestiality see, for instance, Jonas Liliequist, "Bekännelsen, döden och makten: En studie i social kontroll med utgångspunkt från tidelagsbrottet i 1600- och 1700-talets Sverige," *Historia Nu: 18 Umeåforskare om det förflutna. En vänbok till Kerstin Strömberg-Back.* Forskningsrapporter från Historiska Institutionen vid Umeå universitet, 4 (Umeå: Historiska institutionen Umeå universitet, 1988), 143–70.

73 For an excellent discourse analysis approach to this phenomenon, see Jürgen Martschukat, "Ein Freitod durch die Hand des Henkers: Erörterungen zur Komplementarität von Diskursen und Praktiken am Beispiel von 'Mord aus Lebens-Überdruß' und Todesstrafe im 18. Jahrhundert," *Zeitschrift für Historische Forschung* 27.1 (2000): 53–74.

by Lutherans.[74] It can be assumed that for suicides and their families it made an important difference whether they were buried in the cemetery or outside. After all, the spatial segregation of premeditated suicides from those who died a "good Christian death" symbolized also the exclusion from the Christian community in death. The cemetery was a community place to remember the dead whereas some remote, unidentified spot in the woods excluded the community from any further contact with the deceased. The same applies to the interdiction of burial rites. Even though Lutherans did not believe in the auxiliary effect of prayers, songs and intercessions because salvation could be achieved solely by God's grace, burial rites still played an important role for the family who derived comfort from them.

In this paper suicide in early modern Austria and Sweden has been approached from a broad perspective. Like in other countries, authorities both in Austria and Sweden had to deal with suicide as a societal phenomenon that was relevant under criminal law. In the first part of this paper, attention has been directed towards the legal norms that constructed suicide as a crime and the administrative procedures of a suicide investigation. Despite all distinctions in the details, the provisions concerning suicide in Austrian and Swedish judicial norms share the same general notion. By differentiating between premeditated suicides (*felo de se*) and suicides committed of unsound mind (*non compos mentis*) a wide scope for construction and interpretation was created. While judicial norms provide guidelines for the handling of suicide cases on a more abstract level, implementing these norms in practice was a complex process of interpretation.

The second part of the paper focused on the punitive components of suicide and its implementation in practice. Against the background of the two different study areas and religious denominations both similarities and differences have been revealed. Generally, the interpretation of self-inflicted death was closely connected to one's lifestyle, suggesting a high degree of flexibility with regard to the rules applicable. Thus, to a certain degree, a suicide's descriptions and ascriptions served as retrospective assessments of how well an individual had lived his or her life in conformity with the prevalent rules set by society. Studying suicide in early modern times makes it clear that crime and punishment not only concerned the here and now but also the fate of the soul in the afterlife. Dealing with suicide as a historical phenomenon reminds us that certain actions per se are not criminal, but that they are criminalized in a specific historical context and society, and that these assessments are subject to historical change.

---

74 See, for instance, Werner, "Självmord i det stora nordiska krigets skugga," 35 (see note 43). Yvonne Maria Werner suggests that some former, Catholic customs persisted until long after the reformation. Thus, cemeteries were continuously perceived as "consecrated" places by many people.

misfortune in popular belief as expressed by the suicidal woman herself.[50] In May 1713 60-year-old Anna Olofsdotter went into the woods and stabbed herself in the throat. A little while later, the injured woman was found by her daughter-in-law and the neighbour Hans Pärsson. At first Anna did not want to accept their help and tried to send them away saying "rör intet med mig, ty det är giort, som giort är" ("don't touch me, what's done is done"). Hans Pärsson nevertheless reached out to her and asked if she wanted to come back with him to his home. According to the judgment book Anna Olofsdotter answered "att gården blir olyckelig, om hon kommer hem" ("that the farm would become unfortunate, if she came home"). Not until Hans Pärsson assured her that this would not be the case did she finally go with them. Nine days later she died as a result of her injuries.

These examples show that suicide concerned not only those who were close to the deceased or were somehow involved in the legal proceeding. To a certain degree self-inflicted death was a matter of public interest that concerned a wider circle of people who considered themselves to be affected by the incident, and thus also took interest in the outcome of the investigation.

However, generally the right to judge and punish a suicide was reserved for the secular authorities. Indeed, the idea of punishing a dead person appears strange from today's perspective. Nevertheless early modern justice found ways and means to chastise individuals who had ended their own lives. In the following I will briefly broach different aspects of punishment that affected the goods, the body, the soul, and the remembrance of the deceased.

As outlined above, Austrian (but not Swedish) law sanctioned premeditated suicide with forfeiture until the *Theresiana* came into effect in 1770.[51] Studies conducted by Vera Lind for Schleswig-Holstein,[52] David Lederer[53] for Bavaria, and Alexander Kästner for Kursachsen[54] show that confiscation was a rather rare occurrence in early modern central Europe. However, the Austrian source material contains evidence that this provision in fact was implemented in practice. Even though it is not yet clear to what extent forfeiture was executed, the materials indicate that it was not a rare phenomenon. In the case of Jacob Pauer, for example, who in 1762 "wickedly" drowned himself in Austria below the Enns, the *Landgericht* in a letter to the *Grundherrschaft* explicitly reserved its right to confiscate his bequest with reference to the respective paragraphs in the *Ferdinandea*.[55]

---

50 Forskningsarkivet Umeå universitetsbibliotek, Södra Ång. A I a:11 Mk D52269 4/19+5/19, Nora, May 18, 1713.

51 See also Pfannkuchen, *Selbstmord und Sanktionen*, 88–91 (see note 9).

52 Lind, *Selbstmord in der Frühen Neuzeit*, 340–47 (see note 7).

53 Lederer, *Madness, Religion and the State*, 251 (see note 26).

54 Kästner, *Tödliche Geschichte(n)*, 143 (see note 25).

55 Niederösterreichisches Landesarchiv, hence forward referred to as NÖLA, HA Raabs, Karton 44.

In 1687 the inheritance of the suicide Thomas Auer was confiscated by the *Landgericht*.[56] However, due to the poverty of his wife and two young children, the *Landgericht* did not insist on the two thirds of his bequest which it would have been entitled to by law. Instead an individual solution was negotiated with the widow. Also the son of the suicide Johann Mayr had to turn in two thirds of his inheritance to the *Landgericht* in 1723.[57] In the case of Stephan Pühringer[58] who killed himself in 1686, a conflict had arisen between the *Grundherrschaft* and the *Landgericht*. Against the opinion of the *Landgericht*, the *Grundherrschaft* was convinced that he had committed suicide out of an infirmity of mind and thus rejected the *Landgericht*'s claim for jurisdiction, which would have included the right to confiscate two thirds of his bequest if a case premeditated suicide was proven. These few examples show that forfeiture in the Austrian archduchies was an option until the *Theresiana* came into force.[59]

Generally the financial aspect of suicide was a point of contention between different authorities. Apart from forfeiture, where the *Grundherrschaft* had a strong interest to keep the money within their own *Herrschaft*, monetary questions played an important role in many respects. Like in other criminal cases conducted by the *Landgericht*, the delinquents themselves had to compensate all costs incurred during the trial and the investigation. In the case of suicide this money usually was taken from the deceased's bequest. However, impecunious suicides which did not have the means to pay these expenses incurred costs that the authority in charge had to pay. Thus, sometimes conflicts between different authorities would arise because neither of them wanted to be responsible for retrieving a dead body and the associated costs.[60]

Both in Austria and Sweden, the bodies of premeditated suicides should be handled by the executioner. Austrian laws explicitly state that they should be dragged through the streets or carried on the "Schindkarren" ("executioner's cart") to the place where the corpse should be "vertilgt" ("exterminated"). On the other hand, those to whom a silent burial had been granted should be taken care of by family members, neighbors or other "honest" people. Yet, once again, the information contained in archival records blurs the distinction between

---

56 NÖLA, KGA Krems, HS 173/102, fol. 31v–33v.

57 NÖLA, KGA Krems, HS 173/102, fol. 184–85.

58 OÖLA, HA Ebenzweier, Schachtel 2, Nr. 12.

59 The *Theresiana* stipulated confiscation only in cases when suicides prior to the self-killing had committed a crime that was punished with forfeiture. Hence, forfeiture as a punishment applied no longer to the act of self-killing but to the prior committed crime. See *Theresiana* (1768), article 93, section 7.

60 This concerned not only the bodies of suicides but, for instance, also unknown dead persons that were found on the roadside, especially in cases when the border between two *Landgericht* districts was unclear.

premeditated suicide and non-criminal suicide to a certain degree. In practice, a wide scope of reactions, requests and individual solutions were applied.

Generally, premeditated suicides were to be handled by dishonorable people, in most cases the executioner. However, delinquents who committed suicide to skirt punishment while under arrest endured even harsher treatment. Their corpses could be exposed to physical punishment post mortem. In Vienna, in 1704 one case is documented where a murderer who committed suicide was dragged to the place of executions where his head was severed with a digging shovel by the executioner.[61] An anonymous script from 1781 reports on a presumed murderer and thief who was carried to the place of executions and lashed to the breaking wheel above which a gallows was erected.[62]

Such aggravated measures were in accordance with the above mentioned Austrian criminal codes until 1787,[63] and in use also in other European countries.[64] Swedish laws did not explicitly prescribe such aggravated punishments. However, some of my Swedish case histories show that in practice people who committed suicide while under arrest or after escaping from arrest had to fear harsher treatment. The seventy-year old former soldier Per Jönsson Lustig, for instance, had been accused of theft but managed to flee from arrest in 1709. Several days after his escape he was found dead with what appeared to be a self-inflicted wound in the throat. In the end the executioner was instructed to bury his body under the gallows and not, as otherwise common, in the woods.[65]

Another possible consequence of suicide that should be mentioned at this point for the sake of completeness was the possibility to transfer the body of a premeditated suicide to the university's anatomy department.[66] If and to what

---

61 My thanks to Susanne Hehenberger for this reference. See the online database *Kriminalität in und um Wien 1703–1803: Eine Datenbank,* http://www.univie.ac.at/iefn (last accessed on October 21, 2010).

62 Anonymous, *Der sträfliche Selbstmord, oder die unmenschliche Mordthat von Johann S. verübet,* (Vienna: Jahnische Universitäts-Buchdruckerei, 1781).

63 The *Josephina* (1787) stipulated that in such cases the actual body should not be violated, instead a note with the name of the suicide and his/her committed crimes should be attached to the gallows and thus made public. See *Josephina* (1787), part 1, section 124.

64 See, for instance, Machiel Bosman, "The Judicial Treatment of Suicide in Amsterdam," *From Sin to Insanity: Suicide in Early Modern Europe,* ed. Jeffrey R. Watt (Ithaca, NY: Cornell University Press, 2004), 9–24.

65 Forskningsarkivet Umeå universitetsbibliotek, Skrivelser från Svea hovrätt till Gävleborgs Läns Landskansli 1635–1736, DIIa:13 Mk S10552 11/14, November 25, 1709.

66 For a more detailed discussion see, for instance, Kästner, *Tödliche Geschichte(n),* 244–325 (see note 25) and Julia Schreiner, *Jenseits vom Glück: Suizid, Melancholie und Hypochondrie in deutschsprachigen Texten des späten 18. Jahrhunderts.* Ancien Régime, Aufklärung und Revolution, 34 (Munich: Oldenbourg, 2003), 32–55.

degree this option was applied in practice in early modern Austria and Sweden still needs further scrutiny.[67]

However, the violent handling of the body was only one aspect of punishment. In times when religion dominated life and the afterlife was considered more important than the here and now by many people, the whereabouts of the soul was most likely deemed more important than the handling of the physical body. The prevailing stance of the Catholic Church on suicide was outlined above with the positions of Augustine and Thomas Aquinas—premeditated, intentional, desperate suicide was considered a heinous sin with severe consequences for the deceased's soul. On the other hand, in her article on suicide in the Middle Ages, Gabriela Signori emphasizes the growing influence of the concepts of purgatory and grace.[68] As these concepts remained powerful in the early modern period one cannot exclude the possibility that contemporary Catholics drew hope for a suicide's soul from the grace of God or the Virgin Mary.

In Sweden Lutheranism was adopted in the first half of the sixteenth century and more or less completely enforced by the end of the century. Martin Luther's position on suicide was somewhat inconclusive. He too emphasized the individual's obligation to conserve one's own life. At the same time he stressed the power of the devil over a suicide, suggesting that at the time of the deed the individual did not possess free will. However, even though Martin Luther often argued that leniency should be shown by ecclesiastical authorities, he nevertheless agreed on the punishment imposed by secular authorities.[69]

Hence, by committing suicide both Catholics and Lutherans put their souls, the prospect of salvation, and eternal life at risk. In an atmosphere where salvation

---

67 For Austria, a regulation from 1742 stipulated that the *Landgerichte* had to deliver the bodies of executed criminals for anatomic studies, if requested by the university. However, it is yet unclear if and to what degree this included premeditated suicides. See *Sammlung aller k. k. Verordnungen und Gesetze vom Jahre 1740 bis 1780, die unter der Regierung der Regierung des Kaisers Joseph des II. theils noch ganz bestehen, theils zum Theile abgeändert sind, als eine Hilfs- und Ergänzungsbuch zu dem Handbuche aller unter der Regierung des Kaisers Josephs des II. für die k. k. Erbländer ergangenen Verordnungen und Gesetze in einer chronologischen Ordnung*, ed. Joseph Kropatschek. Vol. 1 (Vienna: Mößle, 1786), 7, nr. 7 or http://alex.onb.ac.at (last accessed on Nov. 1, 2010). For Sweden, a royal letter from 1747 explicitly stipulated that the bodies of suicides and children born out of wedlock had to be delivered to the universities in Uppsala, Lund and Turku and the Collegium Medicum in Stockholm, if required. See Eva Åhrén, *Death, Modernity, and the Body: Sweden 1870–1940*, trans. Daniel W. Olson. Rochester Studies in Medical History, 15 (2002; Rochester, NY: University of Rochester Press, 2009), 21.

68 Gabriela Signori, "Rechtskonstruktionen und religiöse Fiktionen: Bemerkungen zur Selbstmordfrage im Mittelalter," *Trauer, Verzweiflung und Anfechtung: Selbstmord und Selbstmordversuche in mittelalterlichen und frühneuzeitlichen Gesellschaften*, ed. Gabriela Signori. Forum Psychohistorie, 3 (Tübingen: Edition Diskord, 1994), 9–54.

69 For a detailed discussion of Martin Luther's position, see Kästner, *Tödliche Geschichte(n)*, 94–105 (see note 25).

List of Illustrations

Illustrations for Birgit Wiedl's article:

Fig. 1: Stiftsmuseum Klosterneuburg, Inge Kitlitschka, Klosterneuburg. Portable altar (around 1470) with four paintings (upper left: spontaneous ignition of candles, upper right: the Jew holding the host, bottom left: two blind regain their sight, bottom right: two crippled are cured)

Figs. 2 – 13: Stadtmuseum Korneuburg. Cycle of paintings, oil, 1660, eleven of the originally twelve paintings that were on display in the cloister of the monastery of Korneuburg, now kept at the Municipal Museum.

Fig. 2: "1301, the Jew Zerklin made a Christian sell a holy host wafer for money and a coat." Background, left: Zerkel offers a red coat and money to the Christian. [No donation]

Fig. 3: "Here, the Christian sells the host to Zerkel the Jew for money and a coat." Donated by Wenzeslaus Melzer, CRSA [= Canon Regular], parish priest of Korneuburg

Fig. 4: "Here, the Jew Zerkel throws the host into the well in the presence of the Jew Scholasticus."
Donated by Blasius Vitalis Seywald, imperial *Salzgegenschreiber* (official at the imperial salt authority)

Fig. 5: "Here, the Jew Scholasticus retrieves the host from the well, and the Jew Zerkel trods on it."
On the base of the well: "Johann Georg Rekinger, (member of) the local inner council who recovered the cloth which the most holy host had been wrapped in and which had been hidden in the local parish church for innumerable years, through divine direction."

Fig. 6: "Here, the Jew Zerkel shows it [= the host] to a Christian so that he should throw the host together with a white cloth into the Danube, but the Christian did not take the host." Donated by [inscription faded] Jacob Sn[. . .]hackner [. . .]

Fig. 7: "Here, the two Jews Zerkel and the Scholasticus cry and falsely complain, as if the Christian had carried the host into their house." Background: One of the Jews appears on the threshold with the host wrapped in cloth. Donated by Paulus Müller, senator of Korneuburg

Fig. 8: "Here, the two Jews Zerkel and Scholasticus again throw the host and the cloth to the floor and tread on it in anger." Donated by Wenzislaus Dyrnwald, notary public and syndic at Korneuburg

Fig. 9: "Here, an angel guides a backer called Luderich [!] from the bakery to the Jew Zerkel's house so that he should pick up the host; but as he was scared, the host miraculously appeared between his fingers [barely readable]." Background: The baker stoops down to pick up the host. [No donation]

Fig. 10: "Here, the baker puts the host with utmost reverence and obeisance on the stony doorstep, whereupon the host sweated blood and was thusly found." Background: Led by the angel, the baker carries the host. Donation: coat of arms and initials CFVS (according to Zeissl, *Das ehemalige Augustinerkloster*, 30 [see note 33], the coat of arms points at the family of Dachsenbeck)

Fig. 11: "Here, wax candles ignite upon being shown the host and the blood-stained cloth." Donated by Johann Nußdorfer, notary public at Korneuburg

Fig. 12: "Here, the blind are healed by being shown the host and by application of the cloth." [The bearded man appears to be handicapped.] Donated by Georgius Eberschwanger

Illustrations for Martha Peacock's article:

Figure 1: Quiringh van Brekelenkam, *Interior with Three Women and a Little Girl*, 1663, Kunsthaus, Zürich

Figure 2: Hendrick de Keyser, *Spinhuis Portal Sculpture*, 1607, Amsterdam

Figure 3: Nicolaes Eliasz Pickenoy, *Regents of the Spinhuis*, 1628, Amsterdam, Amsterdams Historisch Museum

Illustrations for Thomas Willard's article:

Illustrations for Allison P. Coudert's article:

Contributors

ROSA ALVAREZ PEREZ, Assistant professor of French at Southern Utah University. She has published the following entries, "The Biblical Judith"; "Jewish Tradition, Gender and Women"; "Rabelais"; "Judaism"; "Jewish Women's League" in the *Encyclopedia of Sex and Gender*, edited by Fedwa Malti Douglas (2007). She also has published several articles on aspects of the exchanges between Jewish woman and Christian society in medieval northern France (such as in *Urban Space*, ed. Albrecht Classen, 2009). She is presently working on several projects: a book project that recovers the final years of Jewish women moneylenders in Paris before the final expulsion of 1394; and an article that examines a peculiar cultural event in eighteenth-century London: an organized boxing match between a Jewish and a Christian woman (based on a newspaper clipping of the period). In parallel, she is also working on a translation of *Art profane et religion populaire au moyen âge* by Claude Gaignebet and J. Dominique Lajoux.

JOHN BEUSTERIEN is an Associate Professor of Spanish at Texas Tech University. Publications include *An Eye on Race: Perspectives from Theater in Imperial Spain* (Bucknell University Press, 2006) and an edited volume of essays entitled *Death and Afterlife in the Early Modern Hispanic World* (University of Minnesota Press, 2010). Beusterien is currently interested in the study of animals in different contexts in the medieval and early modern Spanish-speaking world. He is completing a manuscript entitled *Amor perro: Animal Studies and Early Modern Spain.* He is also beginning another project on the arrival of European animals to the North American Southwest.

DENIS BJAÏ, ancien élève de l'École Normale Supérieure, professeur de littérature française à l'Institut Universitaire de Formation des Maîtres de l'Université d'Orléans, a consacré sa thèse de doctorat à la poésie épique de la Renaissance (*La* Franciade *sur le métier: Ronsard et la pratique du poème héroïque*, 2001) et co-édité *Les Essais* de Montaigne, au Livre de Poche, sous la direction de Jean Céard. Il vient de terminer, en collaboration, une nouvelle édition critique de *La Sepmaine* de Guillaume du Bartas (3 vol., sous presse) et travaille également sur les rapports entre droit et littérature au sein de l'équipe *JusLittera*, pour l'Agence Nationale de la Recherche.

CHRISTOPHER R. CLASON is Professor of German at Oakland University in Rochester, Michigan. The focus of his research in Medieval Studies has been on Gottfried's *Tristan und Isolde* and Wolfram's *Parzival*. He has participated in two previous Arizona Colloquia, and he has contributed articles on the language of power, and on eroticism and the fulfillment of desire in *Tristan*. He has also published articles on Gottfried's continuators, on Romantic and modern reception of medieval epics, and on beds and material culture in German literature of the Middle Ages. He is a past President of the International Tristan Society and presently is serving as an Assistant Editor of German contributions to the journal *Tristania*. Clason has contributed several articles to the *Handbook of Medieval Studies* (ed. Albrecht Classen), and he is the collaborator with Albrecht Classen in the publication of *Rural Space in the Middle Ages and Early Modern Time*. His other research interests concentrate on German Romantic narrative, and he is currently engaged in a book project on complexity theory and ecocriticism in E. T. A. Hoffmann's *Die Lebens-Ansichten des Katers Murr* and *Die Elixiere des Teufels*.

ALBRECHT CLASSEN is University Distinguished Professor of German Studies at The University of Arizona. He has published more than fifty books, most recently *The Medieval Chastity Belt: A Myth-Making Process* (2007), *The Power of a Woman's Voice* (2007); the English translation of the poems by Oswald von Wolkenstein (1376/77-1445) (2008); a book on Sixteenth-Century German Jest Narratives (*Deutsche Schwankliteratur*, 2009); *Lied und Liederbuch in der Frühen Neuzeit*, together with Lukas Richter, 2009, and *Tiere als Freunde im Mittelalter*, together with Gabriela Kompatscher and Peter Dinzelbacher (2010). In 2011 he published his latest book, *Sex im Mittelalter*. Among the volumes that he has edited recently are *Words of Love and Love of Words in the Middle Ages and the Renaissance* (2008), *Sexuality in the Middle Ages and Early Modern Time* (2008), *Urban Space in the Middle Ages and Early Modern Time* (2009), *War and Peace* (2011), and *Rural Space in the Middle Ages and Early Modern Time* (2012). A three-volume *Handbook of Medieval Studies* (with Walter de Gruyter) appeared in 2010. In 2008 the University of Arizona bestowed upon him its highest award for research, the "Henry & Phyllis Koffler Award." In 2004 the German government awarded him with the *Bundesverdienstkreuz am Band* (Order of Merit), its highest civilian award. He has also received numerous teaching and service awards over the last two decades, most recently the "Five Star Faculty Award" (2009). He is serving as editor of *Tristania* and editor of *Mediaevistik*. For many years he has been the president of the Arizona chapter of the American Association of Teachers of German, and recently completed his function as President/Past President of the Rocky Mountain Modern Language Association.

ALLISON P. COUDERT received her Ph.D. from the Warburg Institute, University of London. She currently holds the Paul and Marie Castelfranco Chair in the History of Christianity at the University of California at Davis. Her focus of interest is on the interaction between religion and science in the West, with a special emphasis on Jewish contributions to science and on women and gender issues. Her most recent book, *Religion, Magic, and Science in Early Modern Europe and America,* was published by Praeger in 2011. Her other published work includes *Leibniz and the Kabbalah* (Dordrecht: Kluwer, 1995) and *The Impact of the Kabbalah in the 17th Century: The Life and Thought of Francis Mercury van Helmont, 1614-1698* (Leiden and Boston: Brill, 1999). Among her recent articles are, "Laughing at Credulity and Superstition in the Long Eighteenth Century," *Laughter in the Middle Ages and Early Modern Times* (2010); "Sewers, Cesspools, and Privies: Waste as Reality and Metaphor in Pre-modern European Cities," *Urban Space in the Middle Ages and the Early Modern Age* (2009); and "Probing Women and Penetrating Witchcraft in Early Modern Europe," *Hidden Intercourse: Eros and Sexuality in the History of Western Esotericism* (2008).

JOHN GOUGH, A native of Salt Lake City, Utah and a graduate in French Literature from the University of Utah, John Gough has just completed his first year's coursework at NYU in their French Literature Ph.D. Program. John's current areas of interest and research include French Revolutionary Theatre, spatial approaches and interpretations of the novels of Madame de Lafayette, as well as Pain and its function in Medieval and Contemporary French Literature.

STACEY L. HAHN is Associate Professor of French at Oakland University in Rochester, Michigan, where she teaches French language and literature. She received her doctorate from the University of Wisconsin-Madison in 1988. Her field of interest is medieval French prose romance, particularly the *Lancelot-Grail* Cycle and Jean d'Arras's *Roman de Mélusine*. Her most recent articles include "Feminine Sexuality in the *Lancelot-Grail* Cycle," *Sexuality in the Middle Ages and Early Modern Times: New Approaches to a Fundamental Cultural-Historical and Literary-Anthropological Theme,* ed. Albrecht Classen (Berlin and New York: Walter de Gruyter, 2008), 485-502; and "The Enigmatic Contours of the Bed in Yale 229," *Essays on the 'Lancelot' of Yale 229,* ed. Elizabeth M. Willingham (Turnhout, Belgium: Brepols, 2007), 69-88.

JEAN E. JOST is Professor of English at Bradley University where she teaches graduate and undergraduate courses on Chaucer, Arthurian Literature, Old and Middle English surveys, Medieval Drama, and Middle English romance. She has published *Ten Middle English Arthurian Romances; A Reference Guide* and edited a collection called *Chaucer's Humor: Critical Essays*. Currently she is editing the *Southern Recension of the Pricke of Conscience*. Her articles have considered Chaucer's Performative Criseyde, masculinities in the *Friar's* and *Summoner's Tales*, various Middle English romances (*Amis and Amiloun, Awntyrs off Arthur at the Terne Wathelyne, The Turke and Gowin, Tristan and Isolt*), the poetics of sexual desire in the *Merchants Tale, The Un-Chaucerian Tale of Beryn*, and lately The Gawain Poet. Her last NEH on the Old French Fabliaux has provided a new interest which she is pursuing.

JOLANTA N. KOMORNICKA is a Ph.D. candidate in History at Boston University (expected completion: 2011). Her dissertation field concerns crimes of *lèse-majesté* in France under the first three Valois kings (1328–1380). Her areas of research include judicial procedure in medieval France, particularly the relationship between theory and practice, the language of crime and its deployment, and the history of torture. She has published on the historiography of Jews in Poland, the role of the devil in the trial by ordeal, and the orc body in the work of J. R. R. Tolkien

NICOLAS LOMBART, ancien élève de l'École Normale Supérieure de Fontenay/Saint-Cloud, maître de conférences de littérature française du XVIe siècle à l'Université d'Orléans, a consacré sa thèse de doctorat au genre de l'hymne dans la poésie française de la Renaissance (2004) et participé à l'édition collective de *L'art poétique français* (1596) de Pierre Laudun d'Aigaliers (STFM, 2001). Ses articles portent principalement sur le lyrisme de célébration, les rapports entre littérature et politique, et la poétique de la poésie à la Renaissance. Il prépare actuellement, en collaboration, une édition critique du *Recueil de l'origine de la langue et poésie françoise, ryme et romans* de Claude Fauchet (1581) et de l'*Académie de l'art poétique* de Pierre de Deimier (1610). Il travaille aussi sur les rapports entre droit et littérature au sein de l'équipe *JusLittera* pour l'Agence Nationale de la Recherche.

EVELYNE LUEF is a PhD student at the Department of History, University of Vienna, Austria, currently working on suicide in early modern Austria and Sweden. She received her Magister degrees in History and Scandinavian Studies from the University of Vienna, focusing on domestic violence in historical and literary contexts. In the course of her studies she has conducted research at the Universities of Umeå and Gothenburg, Sweden. Her current research interests include the history of the body, gender studies, as well as early modern legal and criminal history with a special focus on historical suicide studies.

KATHLEEN M. LLEWELLYN is Associate Professor of French and International Studies at Saint Louis University. She has published articles on *L'Heptaméron* of Marguerite de Navarre (such as in *Approaches to teaching Marguerite de Navarre's Heptameron*, ed. Colette H. Winn, 2007), the poetry of Madeleine des Roches and Gabrielle de Coignard, and on the widow in early modern French literature (such as in *Aimer et Mourir: Love, Death, and Women's Lives in Texts of French Expression*, ed. Eilene Hoft-March and Judith Holland Sarnecki, 2009). She is currently working on a book on representations of the biblical figure of Judith in early modern French literature.

SUSANNA NIIRANEN studied history, Romance philology, and journalism at the University of Jyväskylä, Finland, where she received her Master's degree and Ph.D., focusing on the Occitan women troubadours, trobairitz: *"Miroir de mérite": valeurs sociales, rôles et image de la femme dans les textes médiévaux des trobairitz* (2009: http://urn.fi/URN:ISBN:978-951-39-3509-2). Since 2005, she has been a member of the project *Philosophical Psychology, Morality and Politics Research Unit*, the centre of excellence in research funded by the Academy of Finland. She has edited a wide-ranging *Handbook of Medieval Studies* (2009, with Marko Lamberg and Anu Lahtinen, first published medievalist's manual in the Finnish language). She has published articles dealing with various aspects of troubadours and medieval literature in various anthologies. Her most recent publications include an article dedicated to the troubadour Peire Vidal: "Peire Vidal – A Fool and a Troubadour" in *Behaving Like Fools: Voice, Gesture, and Laughter in Texts, Manuscripts, and Early Books*, ed. by Lucy Perry and Alexander Schwartz, 2010). Her current areas of interest and research include medieval and early modern medical recipe collections and their relation to the phenomenon of vernacularization as well as to human conception of well-being. She is currently working on a book project on Mental (Dis)orders in the Late Middle Ages.

MARTHA MOFFITT PEACOCK is Professor of Art History at Brigham Young University. She received her Ph.D. from The Ohio State University in 1989, specializing in the history of seventeenth-century Dutch art. Her research has particularly centered on the relationship of art to the lives of women—both as artists and subjects in art—in the Dutch Republic. She has published a number of articles and essays in both international and national art historical journals and books including: "Domesticity in the Public Sphere," *Saints, Sinners, and Sisters. Gender and Northern Art in Medieval and Early Modern Europe,* ed. Jane Carroll and Alison Stewart, 2003; "Hoorndragers and Hennetasters: The Old Impotent

Cuckold as Other in Netherlandish Art and Farce," *Old Age in the Middle Ages and Renaissance*, ed. Albrecht Classen, 2007; "Early Modern Dutch Women in the City," *Urban Space in the Middle Ages and the Early Modern Age*, ed. Albrecht Classen, 2009; and "Compatible Characters in Contrasting Cultures: Hieronymus Bosch and Jacopo Bellini," *Nord/Sud II*, University of Padua (2008). Currently, she is working on a book, *Heroines, Harpies and Housewives: Women of Consequence in the Dutch Golden Age*.

DANIEL F. PIGG is a Professor of English at The University of Tennessee at Martin where he teaches Chaucer, medieval British literature, and history of the English language. He has published widely in English Medieval Studies, ranging from *Beowulf* to Malory's *Works*. He has published articles dealing with various aspects of masculinity in historical contexts in Chaucer's *Canterbury Tales* and in the presentation of *Beowulf* in various anthologies available to high school students. His most recent publications include an article dedicated to Langland's *Piers Plowman* and Old Age that appeared in the collection of essays arising from the 2006 International Symposium on the Representation of Old Ages in the Middle Ages and Renaissance (ed. Albrecht Classen, 2007). He also published an essay on mercantile masculinity represented in Chaucer's *Cook's Tale* in a collection of essays arising from the 2008 International Symposium on Urban Space (ed. Albrecht Classen, 2009); then on issues of masculinity and sexual performance of Sir Gareth in Malory's *Tale of Sir Gareth* for *Sexuality in the Middle Ages and Early Modern Times* (ed. Albrecht Classen, 2008). He has also contributed to the *Handbook of Medieval Studies* (ed. Albrecht Classen, 2010) on scholarly studies of masculinity studies and social constructionism. Moreover, he is also working on a book on the cultural poetics of *Piers Plowman* and on articles on *The Dream of the Rood* and identity formation.

BERNARD RIBÉMONT est professeur de littérature médiévale à l'Université d'Orléans (France). Il est le fondateur et le directeur de publication des *Cahiers de Recherches Médiévales et Humanistes* et dirige plusieurs collections scientifiques sur la période médiévale (Honoré Champion, Klincksieck). Il est l'auteur de 130 articles sur le Moyen Âge, et a écrit et dirigé une trentaine d'ouvrages. Spécialiste des encyclopédies médiévales et de la littérature de la fin du Moyen Âge (Christine de Pizan en particulier), il travaille essentiellement sur les relations entre la littérature et les savoirs savants, la politique et l'histoire. Depuis peu, il s'intéresse particulièrement aux relations entre le droit et la littérature, en particulier dans la chanson de geste; il dirige le projet *Juslittera* de l'Agence Nationale pour la Recherche (http://bernard.ribemont.neuf.fr).

LIA B. ROSS holds a Ph.D. in European History (Medieval & Early Modern) from the University of New Mexico where she works full-time as computer analyst and (in the past) as part-time as history instructor. She specializes in cultural studies of fifteenth-century France, Burgundy, and England and is an active member of the *Centre européen d'études bourguignonnes. After* her book *Revisiting Decadence: a Behavioral Interpretation of Fifteenth-Century Historical Narrative* (2009) she has contributed to several volumes in the series "Fundamentals of Medieval and Early Modern Culture," edited by Albrecht Classen and Marilyn Sandidge, most recently to the volume on *Laughter* (2010).

MARIA CECILIA RUIZ teaches at University of San Diego. She has published a book on Don Juan Manuel, *Literatura y política: el Libro de los estados y el Libro de las armas de don Juan Manuel* (Scripta Humanística, 1990), and an article, "El humor en el *Libro del cauallero et del escudero*, el *Libro de los estados* y el *Libro enfenido* de don Juan Manuel" (*Estudios alfonsinos y otros escritos: en homenaje a John Esten Keller y a Anibal A. Biglieri*, National Endowment for the Humanities, 1991). Recent papers given on don Juan Manuel have been: "Nature, Man and Morality in don Juan Manuel's *Libro del cauallero et del escudero*" and "Religion in don Juan Manuel: Faith and Ambition." She is currently working on knighthood, readership and religion in don Juan Manuel.

CONNIE L. SCARBOROUGH (Ph.D. 1983 University of Kentucky) teaches at Texas Tech University. Most recently she published a book, *A Holy Alliance: Alfonso X's Political Use of Marian Poetry*. Among her previous books is a critical edition of the *Libro de los exenplos por a.b.c* and *Women in Thirteenth-Century Spain*. She has published articles in the volumes that resulted from previous symposia organized by Albrecht Classen on *Words of Love and Love of Words, Old Age*, and *Sexuality*. She has also published most recently an article in *Medievalia* entitled "Another Look at the Encounter with the *Serranas* in the *Libro de buen amor.*" She has also an article in *Alcanate* (Spain), "La voz personal de Alfonso X en una cantiga murciana." She has articles forthcoming in *Celestinesca, Hispanic Research Journal, Romance Notes,* and *Mediaevistik*. Her new research project is an application of ecocritical theories to works of Medieval Spanish literature.

SCOTT L. TAYLOR, Ph.D., J.D., is a retired attorney, currently teaching history and political science at Pima Community College, Tucson, Arizona. He has authored a number of papers and articles dealing with aspects of medieval law, including "Lawyers on the Margins: Gendered Images of the Legal Vocation in Medieval France," 75th annual meeting of the Medieval Academy of America, Austin, Texas, April 13–16, 2000, and "Reason, Rhetoric and Redemption: The teaching of law and the *Planctus Mariae* in the Late Middle Ages," 20th annual

Middle Ages Conference, Fordham University, March 24–25, 2000, published in *Medieval Education,* ed. Ronald B. Begley and Joseph W. Koterski, S.J. Fordham Series in Medieval Studies, 4 (New York: Fordham University Press, 2005), as well as his dissertation, "Mary between God and the Devil: Jurisprudence, Theology and Satire in Bartolo of Sassoferrato's *Processus Sathane*"(University of Arizona, 2005). His reviews have appeared in *Theological Studies,* and he has contributed to a number of other Walter de Gruyter publications, including *Old Age in the Middle Ages and the Renaissance,* ed. Albrecht Classen (2007), and *Laughter in the Middle Ages and Early Modern Times,* ed. Albrecht Classen (2010); several entries, including those on medieval law and political theory in the Middle Ages, in the *Handbook of Medieval Studies,* ed. Albrecht Classen (2010); and "The Conquest of Sodom: Symbiosis of Calumny and Canon in the *Jus Belli* from Ireland to the Indies," in *War and Peace: New Perspectives in European History and Literature, 700-1800,* ed. Nadia Margolis and Albrecht Classen (2011), as well as "*Usos rerum rusticarum: Malae consuetudines, male usos lege* and Peasant Rebellion as Resistance or Adaptation to Legal Change," in the forthcoming volume *Rural Space in the Middle Ages and Early Modern Age: The Spatial Turn in Premodern Studies,* ed. Albrecht Classen in collaboration with Christopher R. Clason.

JESSICA TVORDI earned her Ph.D. in English Literature at the University of Arizona in 2002. Her publications include articles on Shakespeare in *Maids and Mistresses, Cousins and Queens: Women's Alliances in Early Modern England,* edited by Susan Frye and Karen Robertson (Oxford University Press, 1999) and in *The Journal of the Wooden O* (2008), as well as a forthcoming article on Thomas Carew's *Coelum Britannicum* in *Quidditas.* Recently she also contributed an article on Robert Herrick to *Rural Space in the Middle Ages and the Early Modern Time* (ed. Albrecht Classen, 2012). She is currently working on a book-length project that examines how post-Reformation anxieties about institutional politics, civic morality, and national boundaries inform, and are informed by, early modern discourses on gender and sexual deviance. She holds the position of Assistant Professor of English at Southern Utah University, where she teaches courses on Shakespeare, Milton, and poetics, and also serves regularly as a guest lecturer for the Utah Shakespearean Festival's Camp Shakespeare series.

PATRICIA A. TURNING (Ph.D. 2007,The University of California, Davis) teaches medieval and early modern European history courses at Arizona State University. In 2009, she received The L. Christian Smith Teaching Excellence Award, Presented by Phi Alpha Theta. She published an article in the volume that resulted from previous symposia organized by Albrecht Classen on *Urban Space in the Middle Ages and the Early Modern Age.* She has also recently published an article in *French History* entitled, "The Right to Punish: Jurisdictional Disputes between Royal and Municipal Officials in Medieval Toulouse." She is currently finishing her manuscript, *"Fear Not the Madness of the Raging Mob:" Municipal Officials, Their Public and the Negotiation of Justice in Medieval Languedoc,* for the publication of research funded by the Birgit Baldwin Fellowship, presented by the Medieval Academy of America. Her next project is an examination of women in medieval prisons.

BIRGIT WIEDL is a research fellow at the Institute of Jewish History in Austria, St. Pölten, and a lecturer at the University of Salzburg. She studied History, German and Russian Philology at the University of Salzburg (Master and PhD), and History and Archivistics at the University of Vienna (Master). Her main field of research is the history of Jews in medieval Austria, urban history, and economic history. She is the author of *Alltag und Recht. Aspekte der Alltags- und Rechtsgeschichte im Handwerk* (2006), and has published a number of articles on the economic, urban, and social history of Jews in medieval Austria as well as edited anthologies on that topic. Together with Eveline Brugger, she conducts the research project "Documents on Jewish History in Medieval Austria," funded by the Austrian Science Fund (FWF), which aims at collecting charters, historiographic, and literary documents that bear reference to Austrian Jews. Volumes 1 and 2 of this collection have already been published (Eveline Brugger and Birgit Wiedl, *Regesten zur Geschichte der Juden in Österreich im Mittelalter*. Vol 1: *Von den Anfängen bis 1338.* Vol. 2: *1339–1365.* 2005, 2010; volume 3 is currently being completed. Online (for free download) at:
http://www.injoest.ac.at/projekte/laufend/mittelalterliche_judenurkunden/). She has been a regular contributor to the volumes in the book series "Fundamentals of Medieval and Early Modern Culture."

THOMAS WILLARD teaches English literature at The University of Arizona. He has edited the alchemical writings of Jean d'Espagne (2000). His occasional essays on aspects of Rosicrucianism have appeared in *Papers of the Bibliographical Society of America* (1984), *Theorien vom Ursprung der Sprache* (1989), *Secret Texts: The Literature of Secret Societies* (1995), and *Mystical Metal of Gold: Essays on Alchemy and Renaissance Culture* (2007). He has also edited a collection of writings by and about Northrop Frye (1991), and has published more than a dozen essays on Frye's criticism. Some of his articles appeared in French, such as in *Ésotérisme, gnoses & imaginaire symbolique* (2001). He has contributed repeatedly to the volumes dedicated to Theophrastus von Hohenheim, ed. by Albrecht Classen (*Religion und Gesundheit,* 2011; and *Wahres Leben und Tod vom 16. Jahrhundert bis zur Neuzeit,* 2012). He also contributed most recently to *Rural Space in the Middle Ages and Early Modern Time* (ed. Albrecht Classen, 2012).

Index

Acknowledgment and Gratitude

The current volume already makes up the eleventh volume in our series "Fundamentals of Medieval and Early Modern Culture." It is not even that long ago that Dr. Heiko Hartmann, then Editor-in-Chief at De Gruyter (now with Akademie Verlag), and Dr. Albrecht Classen, University Distinguished Professor at the University of Arizona, agreed on launching this series. Really the very first volume, *Childhood in the Middle Ages and the Renaissance* (2005) had not even yet been part of it, but if we include it in our calculation, the present volume would count as the twelfth (no. 1 was my monograph *The Power of a Woman's Voice in Medieval and Early Modern Literatures*, 2007). Moreover, several other volumes are already in preparation for publication, and others are currently in the planning stages. So it seems a very good time briefly to reflect backwards and to express my gratitude both to the many contributors and to De Gruyter and its wonderful staff both in Berlin and in Tübingen. The collaboration has been marvelous and unparalleled. We can all be very proud of the series, which has covered many fundamental aspects of medieval and early modern culture and will address many more in the future.

Although not part of our series, in 2010 appeared in print the three-volume *Handbook of Medieval Studies: Terms – Methods – Trends*, ed. by Albrecht Classen, and currently the new project, *Handbook of Medieval Culture*, also ed. by Albrecht Classen, is fully on its way. This clearly means that Medieval and Early Modern Studies are alive and well in terms of research, so we can only hope that this will also translate into renewed student interests and support by academic administrations worldwide, not to speak of the broader public. Our present is, as all these efforts and endeavors illuminate only too vividly, deeply determined by the premodern world, and we would all be well advised to heed carefully the messages from the past in order to forge ahead into the future. Human culture, philosophy, religion, literature, and the arts as developed in the Middle Ages and early modern times have always embraced the physical and the spiritual, so whether we look at the history of mentality or the history of everyday culture, fundamental aspects from that epoch continue to be of central relevance for us today and tomorrow.

I would like to express my particular gratitude to my steady and wonderful co-editor of this series, Prof. Marilyn Sandidge, whose calm and reliable support has been an incredible contribution throughout. My recent co-editors of individual volumes, Prof. Christopher R. Clason and Prof. Connie Scarborough, also deserve particular acknowledgment. Christine Haenschel, formerly at De Gruyter, and her successor, Daniel Gietz, have been as competent and supportive as Susanne Mang and Manuela Gerlof. I cannot give enough words of praise and thanks to all of them. But there are many other people in the background who also have contributed in many different ways, and I owe them all my gratitude. I would also like to acknowledge many of the regular contributors to our volumes, but that list would simply grow too long at this point. They all know how much I have appreciated and continue to appreciate their scholarly work, their patience with my constantly nagging questions, inquiries, requests, and (hopefully) constructive criticism, and how much I have felt honored to edit their subsequently impressive, polished, and thoroughly revised pieces. Dr. Hartmann, however, once again, as a kind of "spiritus rector" for our series and then also for the *Handbook of Medieval Studies*, deserves to be mentioned one more time. He has contributed in many ways to the well-being of Medieval Studies in Germany and on a global level.

We have always tried to achieve perfection, but nobody is perfect. Nevertheless, the goal remains to achieve the highest possible scholarly quality, and if we have failed, then we hope that our readers attribute this simply to the fact that we are human, after all.

But these words are not supposed to be an epitaph, on the contrary. We are in the midst now of a flourishing scholarly book series, and we all look forward to many more volumes to come forward since there are still so many other fundamental aspects of human existence in the Middle Ages and early modern time to be covered. It is a great honor to be published by De Gruyter.

I do not want to conclude these brief remarks without a quiet but deeply felt thank you to the central mainstay in my life without whom nothing would be really possible or matter for me, my beloved wife Carolyn, companion, friend, and mother of our son Stephan. What would we both be without him?